UNFINISHED REFORMS IN THE CHINESE ECONOMY

UNFINISHED REFORMS IN THE CHINESE ECONOMY

Editor

Jun ZHANG
Fudan University, China

World Scientific

NEW JERSEY • LONDON • SINGAPORE • BEIJING • SHANGHAI • HONG KONG • TAIPEI • CHENNAI

Published by

World Scientific Publishing Co. Pte. Ltd.
5 Toh Tuck Link, Singapore 596224
USA office: 27 Warren Street, Suite 401-402, Hackensack, NJ 07601
UK office: 57 Shelton Street, Covent Garden, London WC2H 9HE

Library of Congress Cataloging-in-Publication Data
Unfinished reforms in the Chinese economy / editor, Jun Zhang, Fudan University, China.
pages cm
Includes bibliographical references and index.
ISBN 978-9814434003
1. China--Economic conditions--21st century. 2. China--Social policy--21st century.
3. Income distribution--China. I. Zhang, Jun, editor
HC427.95.U545 2013
330.951--dc23

2012049838

British Library Cataloguing-in-Publication Data
A catalogue record for this book is available from the British Library.

In-house Editors: DONG Lixi/LU Shan

Typeset by Stallion Press
Email: enquiries@stallionpress.com

Printed in Singapore by World Scientific Printers.

PREFACE

Over the past 30 years, especially since the mid-1990s, China has achieved fabulous economic development and gone through fast process of social and political changes. However, its past performance in economic growth and social development has also created many unsolved problems. These problems have increasingly become the underlying factors that are hindering China's sustainable economic development and social stability. In recent years, the call for further reform has been rising in China and the Chinese leadership has been facing growing challenges.

To address these problems, China's policy makers should have a better understanding of them and a clear policy framework before creating and conducting further reform programs. Based on high-level empirical research on China's economic development and institutional transition by each contributor, this edited book provides an in-depth and clear analysis for many important issues facing China's new phase of economic development and institutional transformation, and it discusses the policy implications of future reforms.

Contributors of this book are mainly the faculty members of China Center for Economic Studies and School of Economics in Fudan University. Other co-authors are from the US, Japan, and other universities in China.

This book is the final product of the "Project 985" grant and the aim of this research grant is to advance the level of social sciences research of Fudan University. It aided the conducting of research for "Government and Market in China's Economic Transformation", which was sponsored by Fudan University in June 2011.

Fudan University, which sponsored the research project, is gratefully acknowledged. I am also grateful to the President Yuliang Yang, and the

Vice-President Shangli Lin of Fudan University for their support, and to Professor Yuan Ren at State-Building Research Center for his suggestion and help. Thanks also go to Ms. Rebecca Fu, the representative of the publisher, for her prompt acceptance of this product for publication, and to Ms. Lixi Dong for her excellent editing job. I also thank Professor Han Luo for his great job in translating and polishing the earlier version of some chapters. Finally, I am indebted to Dr. Yuan Zhang, without his commitments to administration and coordination, this volume may not have been brought out on time.

Jun Zhang

CONTENTS

NOTES ON CONTRIBUTORS

Chen, Jie

Associate Professor Jie Chen is working at the Department of Industrial Economics at the School of Management, Fudan University, where he also serves as the Executive Director of the Center for Housing Policy Studies (CHPS). He received his Ph.D. in economics in 2005 from Uppsala University, Sweden.

His research areas cover housing economics, housing finance, housing policy and urban development. He is a board member of Global Chinese Real Estate Congress (GCREC). He also frequently provides policy consulting for Chinese central and local government agencies on housing policy-making.

He has more than ten papers published in international peer-reviewed journals, including *Journal of Housing Economics*, *Urban Studies*, *Housing Studies*, *China and World Economy*, *International Real Estate Review*, *European Journal of Housing Policy* and *Chinese Economy.* He is also author of two books.

Chen, Lin

Lin Chen is an assistant professor at Business School, East China Normal University. Her research interests are China's trade policy, foreign direct investment in China, international trade and economics of transition. She has papers published in *China Management World*, *China World Economy*, etc.

Chen, Shiyi

Shiyi Chen is currently working as a research fellow at China Center for Economic Studies (CCES) of Fudan University. He holds a Ph.D. in econometrics from Kyungpook National University, Republic of Korea. His research interests are nonparametric econometric theory, time series forecasting and empirical studies on China's economic growth, financial market risk, and energy & emission.

His current works are published in English journals such as *Quantitative Finance*, *Journal of Forecasting*, *The World Economy*, *China Economic Review* and top Chinese journals. He serves as the editor for the *Journal of World Economic Papers* and as referee for English journals such as *The World Economy*, *Empirical Economics*, *Emerging Markets Finance and Trade Journal*, *Journal of the Asia Pacific Economy*, etc.

He has been awarded many academic honors. For instance, his book entitled *Energy-Save and Emission-Abate, Structural Adjustment and Transformation of Industrial Development Model in China* was selected as "National Achievements Library of Philosophy and Social Sciences" in 2010. One of his papers was awarded the first prize of the 10th "Shanghai Philosophy and Social Science Outstanding Research Achievement Award".

Chen, Zhao

Zhao Chen is the Deputy Director and Professor at the China Center for Economic Studies (CCES), Fudan University, Shanghai. He is interested in Chinese issues, especially entrepreneurs' political participation, economic development and the political system and urban and regional income inequality. He has published in publications such as the *Journal of Comparative Economics*, *Review of Income and Wealth*, *International Small Business Journal*, *Economic Modeling*, *China Economic Review*, *The Manchester School* and *Journal of the Asia Pacific Economy*. He also serves as referee for international journals such as *International Economic Review*, *European Economic Review*, *China Economic Review*, *World Economy*, *World Development*, *Economic Modelling* and *China Economic Journal*.

Du, Julan

Julan Du is currently an associate professor at the Department of Economics of the Chinese University of Hong Kong. He received his undergraduate and master's degrees from Fudan University and his Ph.D. in economics from Harvard University. His main research areas are economics of organization and institutions, finance, international economics, and development and transition.

Fan, Ziying

Ziying Fan is an associate professor of economics at Huazhong University of Science and Technology, Wuhan, Hubei province. His previous works focus on China's public finance and regional economics, the Chinese great famine of 1958–1961.

He has papers published in *The Economic Research Journal, China Economic Quarterly, Ecological Economics, Management World.* He was awarded the Annual Best Paper of *China Economic Quarterly* 2006/2007. He is a referee for *The Economic Research Journal, World Economy, World Economic Papers* and *China Economic Quarterly.*

Feng, Jin

Jin Feng is professor of Economics at Fudan University and the associated dean of faculty of economics. She is also a researcher in Employment and Social Security Research Center of Fudan University and Fudan Development Institute. She was a visiting scholar of University of Amsterdam and Tinbergen Institute, Bank of Finland (Bofit) and University of Paris. Her publications and research interests focus on health care and health insurance system in China, social security and social insurance reforms, labor supply in China.

She has papers published in *Journal of Comparative Economics, Frontiers of Economics in China, China and World Economy* and Chinese top journals. She has won grants for her research projects from National Science Foundation of China, Ministry of Agriculture of China and Ministry of Education of China, etc. She is serving on the boards of Gerontological Society of Shanghai, Chinese Women Economists Society, Committee of Undergraduate Study in Economics in Shanghai.

He, Lixin

Lixin He is currently an Associate Professor at the School of Economics, Fudan University (Shanghai, China), where she also serves as Vice Chair for the Department of Public Economics. She studied at the Graduate School of Economics, Hitotsubashi University (Tokyo, Japan) and was an Foreign Researcher of Japan Society for the Promotion of Science (JSPS) before joining the Fudan's faculty.

Her major publications are *The Public Pension System Reform in China: An Institutional and Empirical Analysis of the Economic System Transition Period* (University of Tokyo Press, 2008), "The distributional effects of public pension reform in urban China" (*Economic Research Journal* Vol. 3, 2007), "Public pension and household saving: evidence from urban China" (with Jin FENG and Hiroshi SATO, *Journal of Comparative Economics*, http://dx.doi.org/10.1016/j.jce.2011.01.002.) Her current fields of interests are social security, income redistribution and public finance.

Jefferson, Gary H.

Gary H. Jefferson is the Carl Marks Professor of Trade and Finance at Brandeis University. His research focuses on institutional reform, technological change, R & D, foreign direct investment, and energy in China. Jefferson's recent publications have appeared in the *Review of Economics and Statistics*, *Brookings Papers on Economic Activity*, and *Comparative Economic Studies*.

Jiang, Shiqing

Shiqing Jiang is a research associate at the Fudan Center for Industrial Development Studies. His research interests include labor market, migration, and economic development. He has published papers in top Chinese journals.

Lu, Ming

Ming Lu is Professor of Economics and Director of Fudan Center for Industrial Development Studies at Fudan University, China. He is also Research Fellow of Peking University-Lincoln Institute and Adjunct Professor of Zhejiang University. He has consulted for the World Bank and Asian Development Bank. He has a Ph.D. in economics from Fudan University. His papers have been published in *Journal of Comparative Economics*, *Review of Income and Wealth*, and top Chinese economics journals. His recent research covers labor economics (income distribution, and migration), development economics (urbanization, and regional development) and social economics (social network, trust and economic development).

Lu, Qianjin

Qianjin Lu received his Ph.D. in economics from Fudan University in 2000, and is currently an Associate Professor at the Department of International Finance at Fudan University. He was previously a visiting scholar at the Department of Economics at Columbia University. His research interests focus on international finance, monetary economics and policy. He publishes widely and is also a columnist for various newspapers in China.

Luo, Changyuan

Changyuan Luo is an Associate Professor of Economics at the School of Economics, Fudan University, where he is also a research fellow at the Center for European Studies and Institute of World Economy. From October 2010 till October 2011, he is a senior associate member of St Antony's College, Oxford University.

His research fields include factor income distribution, trade policy, foreign direct investment, China and the world economy. He has papers published in *The World Economy*, *Revue Internationale de Politique Compare*, *China & the World Economy*, *Social Sciences in China*, and *Frontiers of Economics in China*.

Sato, Hiroshi

Hiroshi Sato is Professor at the Graduate School of Economics, and Director of the Center for International Joint Research, Hitotsubashi University. He also works as an education coordinator and a group leader of Regional Studies and Market Analysis Group, Global Center of Excellence (G-COE) Program, Hitotsubashi University. He got his Ph.D. in economics from Hitotsubashi University. His research interests include development economics and labor economics. He is a well-known specialist on Chinese economy. His recent publications cover contemporary China studies on history, social and political development, labor market and inequality, social security, etc.

Wan, Guanghua

Guanghua Wan is Professor at Yunnan University of Economics and Finance. Previously, he was Senior Research Fellow, Project Director, and Program Director of the World Institute for Development Economics Research, United Nations University. He is honorary professor of more than 10 leading universities in China including Fudan University and Zhejiang University. Dr Wan worked as an consultant for UNDP, ActionAid, Winrock Foundation and a number of Chinese government Ministries.

Having authored hundreds of professional articles and a dozen of books including two by Oxford University Press, Professor Wan is an internationally recognized development economist and a leading scholar on Chinese economy. His books and research papers have won prizes in China and beyond. He has been invited to speak in some 30 countries.

In particular, Professor Wan is a pioneer in developing and applying regression-based decomposition frameworks for poverty and inequality analyses. His innovation is gaining popularity in China and globally.

Wang, Yong

Yong Wang is an Assistant Professor of Economics at the Hong Kong University of Science and Technology and also a research associate at the Federal Reserve Bank of Dallas. He obtained his Ph.D. in economics from the University of Chicago in 2009, his MA in CCER at Peking University (2003), and BA at Fudan University (2000). His research interests include economic growth, political economy, international trade, China and India economies. His most recent research mainly focuses on the macroeconomic analyses of structural change, industrial upgrading, industrial policies in developing countries, and China's state capitalism. Yong was a resident research fellow at the World Bank during the 2010–2011 academic year and also served as a consultant from 2008–2012. Yong won the Martin and Margaret Lee Prize for the best performance in the Ph.D. Core Exam at the University of Chicago in 2004. His academic website is ihome.ust.hk/~yongwang.

Wang, Yongqin

Yongqin Wang is currently an Associate Professor of the China Center for Economic Studies (CCES), Fudan University, and has held visiting position at Yale University (2008–2010). He got his Ph.D. in economics from Fudan University in 2004 and had also visited Queen's University (Kingston, Canada) and IDEI, University of Toulouse 1 (Toulouse, France) as visiting scholar. His main research interests include microeconomic theory, financial economics, development economics, political economics and public economics. He has published papers in both Chinese and international reviewed journals including *Journal of Chinese Political Science*, *The Studies in Regional Development*, *Economic Research Journal (Jingji Yanjiu)*, *China Economic Quarterly (Jingjixue Jikan)*, *World Economy (Shijie Jingji)*. He has published 4 books and two English books are forthcoming. He is also a referee for some journals.

Yuan, Tangjun

Tangjun Yuan is an Associate Professor at the School of Economics, Fudan University, China. He also holds a visiting research fellow position at the Institute of Economic Research, Hitotsubashi University, Japan. His primary research areas include development economics, productivity analysis, international comparison, and quantitative economic history with strong interests on Asian economies, particularly China. He has published articles in English, Japanese as well as Chinese. His major studies have appeared in international journals including *The Review of Income and Wealth, Explorations in Economic History* and *Journal of Chinese Economic and Business Studies*. His recent groundbreaking research book, *China's Economic Development — Initial Conditions, Policy Choices and Resource Allocation, 1860–2004,* (University of Tokyo Press, 2010) has received the 5th Junzo Kashiyama Prize in Japan.

Zhang, Jun

Jun Zhang is the Cheung Kong Professor of Economics at Fudan University, where he also serves as Director for the China Center for Economic Studies (CCES). He is an editorial member of *the Journal of the Pacific Economy, Economic Systems, East Asia Policy*, *China Social Sciences Review*, *China Economics Quarterly*, *China Economic Journal*, and editor-in-chief of *Fudan Economic Papers*.

He is one of the leading economists working on China's economic transition, economic development, property rights and institutional change, measurement of productivity, structural change and economic growth in China.

He has papers published in *The World Economy, China Economic review*, *Journal of Asian Economics*, *Journal of the Asia Pacific Economy*, *Journal of Chinese Economic and Business Studies*, and *East Asian Review*. He is the author or editor of many books including *Economic Transition with Chinese Characteristics: Thirty Years of Reform and Opening Up* (McGill-Queen University Press, 2008), *Transformation of the Chinese Enterprises* (Cengage Learning, 2009).

Zhang, Yuan

Yuan Zhang received his Ph.D. in economics from Fudan University, Shanghai China. He is an Associate Professor at the China Center for Economic Studies, Fudan University. His research interests include household financial activities, labor migration, poverty in rural China. He is an editor of *The World Economic Papers*, one of the core economics journal in China. He has papers published in *The Journal of the Asia Pacific Economy*, *Oxford Development Studies* and many top economics journals in China.

CHAPTER 1

REFORMING SOEs UNDER CHINA'S STATE CAPITALISM

*Julan Du and Yong Wang**

1.1. Introduction

The economic volatility in the developed world and the rise of state capitalism in emerging markets are the two prominent parallel developments in the world economy in the past decade. On the one hand, the advanced economies in Europe and North America have been hard hit by the global financial crisis and the Eurozone crisis. On the other hand, the emerging market economies represented by the BRICS have changed their development strategy from a Washington-consensus-based liberal capitalism model to a model of state capitalism. In Russia, the leadership in the past decade responded to the demand of the public for order and state control by reasserting direct state control over "strategic" industries and making private-sector oligarchs obedient to bureaucratic command. In China, the state advanced and the private sector retreated in the past decade. The state capitalism model has shown its extraordinary strength in the wake of the global financial crisis. China's fiscal stimulus package working primarily through state companies has rather quickly stabilized output growth and employment, helped the country weather the crisis, and even led the world

*We thank Weisen Li, Xi Li, Justin Yifu Lin, Xuewen Liu, Shang-Jin Wei, and Yang Yao for helpful comments and discussions at different stages. We are very grateful to Professor Jun Zhang, editor of this book, for inviting us and for providing very helpful suggestions and comments. Part of this research was conducted when Yong Wang visited the World Bank as a visiting research fellow and consultant in 2012.

out of recession. The dynamic economic growth in China as well as other major emerging markets has boosted the public and the leadership's confidence in state capitalism as a sustainable model rather than a transient one on the road to liberal capitalism. As the most important pillar of the state capitalism model, state-owned enterprises (SOEs) have been playing an instrumental role in the society. In China, state companies make up 80% of the stock market capitalization value (The Economist, 2012). The state typically holds a substantial proportion of shares in large companies, promotes state-controlled national champions through favorable industrial policies and generous financial support, and steers state-controlled companies to help the state to fulfill political and social objectives.

Besides the size of the SOE sector, the profitability of SOEs is also extremely impressive. If you take a look at the 57 Chinese firms on the list of Global Fortune 500 in 2011, you will find that almost all of them are SOEs (Li *et al.*, 2012). Moreover, among the top 500 firms in China, 81.88% of the total profits are made by SOEs. The ten most profitable firms in China are all state companies, among which the five state-owned commercial banks and the three state-owned oil companies earn profits twice as many as those of the 184 private companies in China's top 500 firms list (Du *et al.*, 2012). If you compare the average profitability of SOEs with that of non-SOEs, you will find that the SOEs have been outperforming the non-SOEs in the past decade, exactly opposite to what happened in the 1990s.

Figure 1.1 plots the average profit per worker for firms of different ownership in the industrial sector for 1998–2010. It shows clearly that the state-owned and the other state-controlled firms became more profitable than non-SOEs after 2002. Given the decade-long coexistence of high GDP growth and remarkable profitability of SOEs, which appears to contradict the public image of SOEs in the 1990s as the money-losing and growth-undermining entities, we must address three questions. First, what is the root of recent prosperity of SOEs in the macroeconomic and global context? Second, what will be the important possible consequences if SOEs stay in the status quo? Third, if it is imperative to transform the remaining SOEs, how to proceed?

The main focus of this chapter is to address the third question, but the prerequisite is a confident understanding of the first two questions. Why

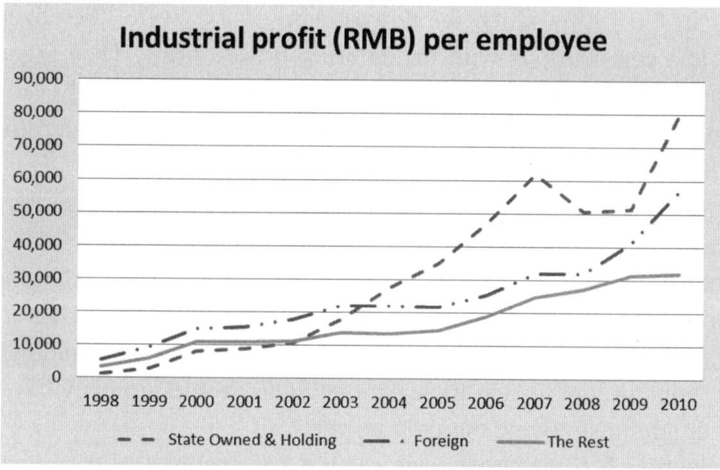

Fig. 1.1. Average profit per employee for 1998–2010.
Source: CEIC (taken from Li *et al.*, 2012).

after all should we worry about SOEs as they are making money now? Thus the chapter is structured as follows.

Section 1.1 briefly addresses the first two questions, which largely follows and summarizes the theoretical framework developed in Li *et al.* (2012). A simplified mathematical model is also developed here to show that the prosperity of China's SOEs is actually a symptom of the incompleteness of the market-oriented reforms. More specifically, we argue that the high profitability of the SOEs in the past decade is mainly due to that the remaining SOEs are monopolizing the upstream industries such as energy, raw materials, banks, and telecommunications while the downstream industries such as manufacturing and other tradable sectors are largely liberalized by year 2000. Therefore the expansion of the dynamic downstream sectors, which operate in fairly competitive markets and are facilitated by China's abundant labor endowment and its accession to WTO in 2001, leads to a huge increase in the demand for the upstream intermediate goods/services or production inputs, which are monopolized by the state via SOEs. Consequently, the upstream SOEs are able to extract monopoly rents from the downstream private sectors in this vertical structure. Li *et al.* (2012) also explain why SOEs were performing poorly in the 1990s, when the downstream sectors were liberalized and SOEs lost competitions with the entering private firms. They argue that the upstream SOE monopoly, if not reformed in time, would eventually strangle the growth of the downstream private sectors and undermine the growth sustainability of China.

Du *et al.* (2012) attempt to detect the existence and estimate the magnitude of SOE monopoly in the manufacturing sector from 1998–2005 and their finding is also summarized in this chapter. They show that the monopoly of SOEs hurts the productivity and the remaining SOEs are still enjoying quite non-negligible monopoly power even in the manufacturing sector, which suggests that the upstream SOEs would probably have even stronger administrative monopoly power.

In Section 1.2, we summarize several key features of the remaining SOEs. Section 1.3 to Section 1.5 is the core part of this chapter. In Section 1.3, we analyze the important economic, political, and social functions played by the remaining SOEs, which reveals the delicacy and complicatedness of potential SOE reforms at the current development stage of China. Section 1.4 explores more closely the possible economic and political causes of SOE monopoly in different sectors and discusses what possible prescriptions we could provide for the SOE reforms after the diagnosis. In particular, we highlight the importance of endowment-driven industrial upgrading and the related industrial policies when considering the reform of China's SOEs. We argue that government indeed should play an active and appropriate role in the structural transformation due to various market failures, but the current prevalence of SOEs in China is way beyond what is warranted by economic efficiency criterion. We argue that the SOE reforms have to be careful and case by case, not only should we underplay the positive contributions of SOEs in certain sectors and industrial policies, but also we should try to strictly confine the role of SOEs to the legitimate boundary where market failure is significant while the government failure (rent seeking) is limited. Instead of advocating overnight elimination of SOE monopoly in all sectors, we propose a strategy of case-by-case and sequential reforms of SOEs that is consistent with China's institutional reality and its endowment-driven industrial upgrading at the current development stage.

Successful SOE reforms cannot be isolated from other complementary institutional or policy support that is beyond the SOEs themselves, which is discussed in Section 1.5. We particularly emphasize the importance of political and legal reforms, which are crucial to preventing China from falling into a predatory state capitalism in which the special interest groups become strong enough to effectively block welfare-enhancing SOE reforms. Section 1.6 concludes.

1.2. Causes of High Profitability of SOEs

In analyzing the causes of high profitability of SOEs in China, the World Bank (2012) points out sharply that a large share of SOEs' profits comes from the monopoly power they enjoy. Governments at various levels typically impose limits on entry and competition to help SOEs maintain monopoly power; at the same time, governments typically offer public procurement contracts to SOEs and provide other favorable treatments to SOEs. In this sense, the high profitability of SOEs in China is a direct outcome of administrative monopoly.

The recent study of Li *et al.* (2012) examines the issue of administrative monopoly of SOEs in upstream industries and its impacts on the whole national economy in detail. In that chapter, they build a general-equilibrium model trying to explain why SOEs outperformed non-SOEs in the past decade while the opposite was true in the 1990s, although the GDP growth rates of China were stably high during the whole period.

Their key argument can be briefly summarized as follows. As a result of economic liberalization and SOE reforms in the 1990s, a vertical structure of state capitalism emerged around 2000. That is, SOEs have largely retreated from most of the downstream sectors (such as manufacturing and many services including hotel and restaurants) while SOEs continue to monopolize some key industries and markets in the upstream sectors (such as energy, finance, telecommunications), which provide intermediate goods or services that the downstream sectors need as necessary input for their business operations. The dynamism in the liberalized downstream sectors, especially after China's entry to WTO in 2001, is the main engine that drives the fast GDP growth. At the same time, the expansion of the downstream sectors enlarges the total demand for the upstream goods and services, which are monopolized by the upstream SOEs. Consequently, upstream SOEs are able to extract huge monopoly rents from the downstream, especially given low wages sustained by the large labor pool in China. This is why high GDP growth coexists with SOEs outperforming non-SOEs in the last decade.

To formalize this important idea, we will use a much simplified mathematical model adapted from Li *et al.* (2012) to illustrate the key mechanisms. Interested readers are strongly advised to read that chapter for a more complete and careful technical treatment.

Consider an open economy, where there are two sectors in the home country: one is the agriculture sector and the other is the industrial sector. There is a vertical structure of industries within the industrial sector, that is, there is an upstream industry and a downstream industry.[1] The upstream industry provides intermediate goods and services that the downstream one uses as inputs for its production. The upstream industry can be imagined as energy or raw materials. The downstream industry can be imagined as manufacturing. Suppose there is a continuum of households with measure equal to unity. Each household is endowed with L units of labor (time). All these households share the same utility function as follows:

$$u = c_0 + c_d^{\theta}, \quad \theta \in (0,1), \tag{1.1}$$

where c_0 denotes the consumption of the agriculture product and c_d denotes the consumption of the downstream good. θ is a parameter that determines the price elasticity of demand for the downstream good.

Suppose labor is the only production factor and all the technologies are constant returns to scale.[2] More precisely, one unit of labor produces one unit of agriculture good, which is produced by perfectly competitive farms. So the price of the agriculture good is equal to wage w, which is normalized to unity. The agriculture good is also called the numeraire good in this paper.

[1] In Li *et al.* (2012), there are a continuum of horizontally differentiated downstream industries and partial liberalization of the downstream industries is also explicitly studied under non-competitive market structure.

[2] Both capital and labor are needed in the model of Li *et al.* (2002), which also addresses the question why China's labor income share is declining in the past two decades. Also see Brandt *et al.* (2008, 2010).

Suppose one unit of labor produces η units of the upstream good, denoted by x_u, where the subscript denotes "upstream". So the unit cost of upstream good is $\frac{w}{\eta}$. The upstream industry has only one firm, which monopolizes the supply of the upstream good. This upstream monopolist firm is State-owned but actually controlled by an elite group in this society. No private firms are allowed to enter the upstream industry. Good x_u cannot be used for consumption.

The downstream industry is perfectly competitive with free entry, and each firm has the following Cobb-Douglas production function:

$$x_d = Ax_u^{\alpha} l^{1-\alpha},$$

where parameter A is the TFP of the downstream industry, x_u and l are the upstream intermediate good and the labor used in the production. Let p_d and p_u denote the prices of the downstream good and the upstream good, respectively.

Therefore, we must have equilibrium price of downstream good given by

$$p_d = \frac{p_u^{\alpha} w^{1-\alpha}}{A\alpha^{\alpha}(1-\alpha)^{\alpha}}. \tag{1.2}$$

A household maximizes his utility function (1) subject to the following budget constraint:

$$c_0 + p_d c_d = I, \tag{1.3}$$

where I denotes the total income of this household. This household optimization problem yields the following equilibrium demand for the downstream and numeraire goods:

$$c_d = \left(\frac{p_d}{\theta}\right)^{\frac{1}{\theta-1}} \tag{1.4}$$

and

$$c_0 = I - p_d\left(\frac{p_d}{\theta}\right)^{\frac{1}{\theta-1}}. \tag{1.5}$$

Observe that the household demand for the downstream good is independent of his total income, which captures the reality that domestic private Consumption-GDP ratio is sustainably low in China,[3] therefore Equation (1.4) is also the aggregate domestic demand for the downstream consumption good (recall there is a unity measure of households).

By Shepard's Lemma, to produce one unit of downstream good, it requires $\frac{\partial p_d}{\partial p_u}$ units of upstream good and $\frac{\partial p_d}{\partial w}$ units of labor. Therefore, by revoking (1.2), we obtain the aggregate domestic demand for upstream goods that are used to produce domestic consumption good as given by

$$D_u = \left(\frac{p_d}{\theta}\right)^{\frac{1}{\theta-1}} \frac{\partial p_d}{\partial p_u} = \alpha \left(\frac{1}{\theta}\right)^{\frac{1}{\theta-1}} \left[\frac{w^{1-\alpha}}{A\alpha^{\alpha}(1-\alpha)^{\alpha}}\right]^{\frac{\theta}{\theta-1}} p_u^{\alpha\frac{\theta}{\theta-1}-1} \quad (1.6)$$

Remember this is an open economy model and suppose the rest of the world has the following demand function for the downstream goods produced in the home country[4]:

$$D_d^f = B \cdot p_d^{-\gamma}, \quad \text{where } \gamma > 1.$$

Therefore the total upstream goods needed to produce for this external demand of downstream good is given by

$$D_u^f = B \cdot \alpha \left[\frac{w^{1-\alpha}}{A\alpha^{\alpha}(1-\alpha)^{\alpha}}\right]^{-\gamma+1} p_u^{\alpha(1-\gamma)-1}. \quad (1.7)$$

The upstream monopolist SOE tries to maximize its profit by solving the following problem:

$$\Pi \equiv \max_{p_u} \left(p_u - \frac{w}{\eta}\right) \cdot \left[\alpha \left(\frac{1}{\theta}\right)^{\frac{1}{\theta-1}} \left[\frac{w^{1-\alpha}}{A\alpha^{\alpha}(1-\alpha)^{\alpha}}\right]^{\frac{\theta}{\theta-1}} p_u^{\alpha\frac{\theta}{\theta-1}-1} + B \cdot \alpha \left[\frac{w^{1-\alpha}}{A\alpha^{\alpha}(1-\alpha)^{\alpha}}\right]^{-\gamma+1} p_u^{\alpha(1-\gamma)-1}\right], \quad (1.8)$$

[3] This ratio is only 35% in China and far lower than the international average, which is above 55%. This is partly due to the income inequality, which is discussed in Li *et al.* (2012).

[4] The foreign demand function is endogenously derived together with the endogenous trade pattern in a general-equilibrium two country model in Li *et al.* (2012).

where the first parenthesis is the net return for each unit of output and the second parenthesis is (1.6) + (1.7), i.e. the total sum of the domestic and external demand for the upstream good.

Obviously, if $B = 0$, then the home country is a closed economy. In that case, the solution to the above monopolist problem is

$$p_u = m \cdot \frac{w}{\eta},$$

where the markup m is defined as $m \equiv \frac{\alpha\theta - (\theta - 1)}{\alpha\theta}$.

On the other hand, if all the downstream output is only to serve the foreign demand, then

$$p_u^* = m^* \cdot \frac{w}{\eta},$$

where the markup m^* is defined as $m^* \equiv \frac{\alpha(1-\gamma)-1}{\alpha(1-\gamma)}$.

The solution to the original problem (1.8) cannot be obtained in a closed-form way, but it exists and is unique. The equilibrium markup $\hat{m}$ is a weighted average of m and m^*. The larger the external demand shifter B, the closer $\hat{m}$ is to m^*, which would imply an endogenous and time-varying SOE price markup when extended to a dynamic model.

Proposition 1.1. $\frac{\partial \Pi}{\partial A} > 0; \frac{\partial \Pi}{\partial B} > 0$.

The proof is straightforward. The first inequality in the above proposition says that the upstream SOE profit will increase when the downstream private firms have a higher productivity. This is because a more productive downstream industry will imply a lower price of the final consumption good and hence a larger consumer demand, which raises the total demand for the upstream good as the downstream production scale expands. This induced increase in the demand for the monopolized upstream intermediate good will then lead to a larger SOE profit. Notice that this is diametrically opposite to the case when the SOE and private firms are competing in the same or horizontally differentiated industries, as what was happening during the SOE reforms in the 1990s. At that time, SOEs and private firms were rivals, so a higher productivity of the opponent private firms would imply a lower profit of SOEs.

The second inequality in the above proposition says that a larger foreign demand for the downstream goods will imply a higher profit of the upstream SOE in the home country. The intuition is also straightforward because more exports of the downstream good will imply more expansion of the production scale of the downstream (private) industry in the home country, therefore the upstream SOE can sell more of their intermediate good/service to the downstream private firms and hence extract more monopoly rents. This is consistent to the fact that China's export expanded rapidly after its entry to the WTO in 2001. In fact, the timing is also consistent to the fact that the profit of SOEs accelerated and first exceeded that of the private firms around 2002 (see Figure 1.1). If China were a closed economy, then the total demand for the downstream sector would be limited by domestic consumption demand, therefore the total profit of upstream SOE would not be that impressive. Notice that, in our model, upstream SOE benefits more from trade liberalization in the downstream industry although the upstream SOE is not directly involved in export. In reality, SOEs indeed only accounts for less than 15% of the total export in China in recent years, but they are much more sensitive to the external market conditions.

Proposition 1.2. *When L is sufficiently large, we have* $\frac{\partial w}{\partial L} = 0; \frac{\partial \Pi}{\partial L} = 0$. *When L is sufficiently small, we have* $\frac{\partial w}{\partial L} < 0; \frac{\partial \Pi}{\partial L} > 0$.

The proof is straightforward and hence skipped. The intuition is the following. When labor supply is abundant, the industrial sector cannot absorb all the labor, so the agricultural (numeraire good) output is still positive. Therefore the wage is sustained at a constant level (equal to one) despite the expansion of the industrial sector, for example, due to increased foreign demand or rising domestic productivity. And because of this constant wage level and the fact that the total demand for the downstream and hence the upstream good is independent of income I, as reflected by (1.4) and (1.7), the labor endowment does not affect the upstream SOE profit either. However, when L becomes sufficiently small, then eventually all the labor will be absorbed by the industrial sector in home country, therefore the wage will no longer be constant after all the labor has moved out of agriculture. More labor supply leads to a lower wage. In that scenario wage will increase as the industrial sector expands and hence the upstream SOE will have a smaller profit due to the rising labor cost.

This proposition highlights the importance of labor abundance in contributing to China's upstream SOE profitability. If China were a small country, then the wage would rise immediately after the downstream private industry expanded, which would squeeze the room for markup pricing charged by the upstream SOE for its monopolized intermediate good. To put it more precisely, this model shows how the upstream SOE achieves its prosperity by extracting monopoly rents from the competitive downstream private sector via domestic and foreign consumers by taking advantage of China's abundant labor endowment.

Now when wage rate rises as the economy develops, how to make this development model of state capitalism sustainable, especially when the foreign demand is weak (when B is small, due to, for example, world financial crisis)?

The above model suggests that there are only two prescriptions, that is, to reduce the price markup of the upstream SOE and raise the productivity of upstream SOE (η). Otherwise, the final downstream good would no longer remain competitive in the international market, especially when another country such as Vietnam is competing with China for the downstream good. This indicates that the upstream SOE monopoly has to be reformed in order to relax the growth bottleneck for the downstream sector and for the whole economy.

In Li *et al.* (2012), they also use the same framework to explain why SOEs were performing poorly in the 1990s. At that time, the downstream sectors started to be liberalized on a massive scale, so the entry of private firms and other types of non-SOEs enhanced the market competition. Not surprisingly, the SOEs were unable to compete with those new entrants and thus incurred more financial losses than before. At the same time, upstream SOEs such as state-owned banks were required to extend various subsidies to those dying SOEs, which resulted in pervasive non-performing loans and worsened the aggregate performance of SOEs even further. Thus SOEs on average performed poorly during this period when compared with private firms and other types of non-SOEs. Nevertheless, the aggregate economy still grew rapidly thanks to the improved resource allocation from the low-efficiency SOEs to high-productivity non-SOEs, in addition to the technological progress and so on. The impact of capital market frictions in this process is carefully explored in Song *et al.* (2011).

Thus, we can conclude that the transition of the SOE sector from financial plight in the 1990s to high profitability in the 2000s primarily stems from the fact that SOEs largely withdrew from market competition with non-SOEs in downstream industries and enjoyed administrative monopoly rents in the upstream industries. Various forces such as government protection, abundant supply of low-wage labor, strong export demand, etc. work together to contribute to the prosperity of the SOE sector. By exploring the experience of SOE restructuring and privatization from 1998–2005 as a quasi-natural experiment, Du *et al.* (2012), attempts to detect the existence and changes of administrative monopoly power for SOEs in China's manufacturing sector. This is a challenging task because monopoly power is typically covert and hard to measure. They investigate the changes in firm-level markup, i.e., the wedge between product price and marginal cost and then combine this analysis of markup with that of total factor productivity (TFP) following the SOE restructurings. By examining a comprehensive dataset of Chinese enterprises, i.e., Chinese Industrial Enterprise Survey compiled by the National Bureau of Statistics in China, they recover the firm-level markup estimates and TFP estimates. Then, they investigate the changes in markup and TFP for privatized SOEs before and after restructuring, and compare them with the changes in markup and TFP for the control group firms that remained as SOEs throughout the sample period. An implicit assumption is that the privatized SOEs would have followed the same trend in markup and TFP changes if they had not been restructured. The differences in the changes of markup and TFP between privatized SOEs and the firms in the control group capture the effects of state ownership on markup, that is, the administrative monopoly power.

Their study finds that privatized SOEs experienced a statistically significant decline in markup and a significant rise in TFP in the post-restructuring years. These changes occurred primarily in the year of privatization and the immediate following year, which gives support to the claim that the changes in markup and TFP stem from the change in the ownership nature of the firms. Theoretically speaking, a reduction in firm-level markup could be an outcome of a decrease in product price, an increase in production costs, or both. Given that TFP has increased following privatization, the decline in markup is unlikely to be driven by an increase in marginal costs. On the contrary, a reduction in market prices of products and hence administrative monopoly power should be the primary reason for the drop in markup for privatized SOEs. This in turn demonstrates that SOEs had overcharged for their products and obtained substantial monopoly rents before they were restructured.

In Du *et al.* (2012), they focus on mostly downstream manufacturing industries where non-state enterprises and foreign enterprises have kept entering for decades in the reform period and the state ownership has gradually reduced its presence. Even in these industries, they still detect the existence and very significant impacts of administrative monopoly power. It is imaginable that in some more strategically important upstream industries where the state has strictly prevented the entry of non-state enterprises and foreign investment, the administrative monopoly power could be even more prevalent and severe.

To summarize, the above researches both show that administrative monopoly is a crucially important feature of the remaining SOEs, no matter in the SOE-dominant upstream industries or the gradually-liberalized downstream industries. Furthermore, Li *et al.* (2012) argue that the root of recent prosperity of SOEs in China is the incompleteness of the market-oriented reforms in China: the downstream sectors are largely liberalized as the SOEs were "let go", either becoming bankrupt or privatized, and trade liberalization is also deepened by China's entry to WTO, but the upstream SOEs still maintain the monopoly position, which enables them to extract monopoly rents from the non-SOEs in the liberalized downstream sectors.

Naturally, we will have to ask the following question: what will happen if SOEs continue to monopolize the upstream sectors? Or put differently, is this development model of state capitalism sustainable?

To understand the possible causes of existing SOE monopoly in different sectors, it is crucial to first briefly re-examine the key characteristics of existing SOE and the economic, political, and social roles they are playing, which we now turn to in Section 1.2.

1.3. Key Characteristics of Existing SOEs

First of all, SOEs have largely retreated from the downstream industries such as manufacturing and the remaining SOEs are largely concentrated in the upstream and high-profit margin industries such as energy, raw materials, telecommunications, banks, etc. This vertical structure has been documented in details in Li *et al.* (2012).

Second, the remaining SOEs are typically large. In 2007, the total number of SOEs in China stands at approximately 112,000. The government has cultivated a host of national champions such as Petro China, China Petrochemical Corporation, State Grid Corporation of China, etc. Tables 1.1 and 1.2 show the characteristics of the large firms in China in year 2007. At present, SOEs account for 63.2% of China's top 500 enterprises in terms of number, 82.82% in terms of operational income, and 90.40% in terms of total assets. China's largest SOE, China Petrochemical,

Table 1.1. Structure and performance of top-500 Chinese enterprises in 2007, by ownership (%).

Ownership	No. SOEs	Assets	Profit	Employees	Taxes	ROA
State	69.8	93.6	87.9	89.3	92.7	1.4
Collective	5.8	4.2	2.2	2.4	1.7	0.8
Private	17.8	1.7	7.1	7.0	3.9	6.1
Foreign	6.6	0.5	2.8	1.3	1.7	8.5

ROA = return on assets.
Source: From Xiao *et al.* (2009).

Table 1.2. Structure and performance of top-500 Chinese enterprises in the service industry 2007, by ownership (%).

Ownership	No. SOEs	Assets	Profit	ROA
State	61.4	93.6	92.4	0.8
Collective	11.4	5.4	1.1	0.2
Private	23.2	0.8	5.3	5.3
Foreign	4.0	0.1	1.2	8.3

Source: From Xiao *et al.* (2009).

has an operational income ten times as large as Huawei, the largest private enterprise in China (Du *et al.*, 2012).

The dominance of SOEs among large firms is more pronounced in the service sector.

Third, most of the largest SOEs, especially those in the upstream industries, are supervised and directly controlled by the central government via SASAC while the local governments are mainly in charge of the relatively small SOEs via local SASAC branches. Szamosszegi and Kyle (2011) provide a detailed documentation on this feature.

Fourth, the SOE sector incurred tremendous inefficiency due to administrative monopoly. It is likely that the social costs the sector has imposed on the national economy are larger than the social benefits it has created. SOEs provide social safety net for a small group of stakeholders at the expense of low production efficiency. SOEs extract substantial monopoly rents by overcharging their products and services, which undermine seriously the interests of the general public. SOEs lag far behind private enterprises in technological innovation. SOEs account for only 35%, 25%, and 20% of the total number of patent applications, the total number of technological innovations, and the total number of new products developed, respectively, in China (Du *et al.*, 2012). Hence, it is doubtful whether the positive effects produced by SOEs could outweigh the negative effects incurred (Also see Sun *et al.*, 2003).

Fifth, the SOE sector has formed a vested interest group that actively seeks rents through administrative monopoly. The administrative monopoly power allows bureaucrats overseeing SOEs, SOE management and employees, and other stakeholders to reap substantial rents to benefit themselves. One striking indicator is that the SOE sector's high profitability does not lead to sizeable profit contributions of SOEs to the state. Theoretically speaking, SOEs are obliged to not only pay taxes to the state as do non-SOEs but also contribute profits to the State because the State, representing all the people, are the owner of the SOEs and are thus entitled to receive the profits generated from state-owned assets. In reality, the SOE sector has made a surprisingly small amount of profit contributions to the state. In 2011, only 7.4% of SOE profits were contributed to the state. A big chunk of profits were used to raise SOE management and employee salaries, fringe benefits, benefit governments and bureaucrats at various levels, etc. In view of these patterns, we can largely claim that the SOE sector has become a vested interest group, which would strongly oppose the deepening of market-oriented reforms.

1.4. Roles of SOEs in China's Macroeconomic Policies

1.4.1. *Roles of SOEs in China's fiscal and monetary policies*

SOEs play a key role when China's government implements counter-cyclical fiscal and monetary policies. For instance, to cope with the recent world-wide economic recession, China government released a stimulus package worth four trillion RMB mainly through capital injection into the state-owned banks and provision of cheap loan and large investment into large SOEs.

Expanding fiscal policies, roughly speaking, refers to tax cut and increases in government expenditure. However in reality government spending seems more often used than tax policies in China. This is partly because the effect of increasing government spending is more speedy and significant. Fiscal policies working through government expenditure could more efficiently and accurately translate the government's intensions to investments into certain target areas and projects. SOEs are the best party to execute government expenditure plans as they are administered by the government. More importantly, China is a fast-growing and populous developing country, where industrialization and urbanization are taking place at an enormous scale. Therefore, a lot of public infrastructures are needed to not only support the manufacturing sector to serve the international market, but also to facilitate the process of massive urbanization and real estate market. In other words, the expanding fiscal policy in China is not merely a short-term Keynesian prescription, but rather a long-term investment as well. This is certainly different from the old-fashioned "dig-hole-and-fill-hole" Keynesian therapy for developed countries (see Lin, 2010).

Since upstream industries such as electricity, telecommunications, petroleum and petroleum chemicals, coal and gases, oversea transportation, steel and metal production, railways and railway construction, shipbuilding, civil aviation are almost all monopolized by SOEs, it is natural that expanding fiscal policy will be carried out mainly via those upstream

SOEs, which in turn are expected to provide relatively cheaper inputs and intermediate services, public and private, that are needed by the downstream private sectors.

There is another political economy reason for why China's government tends to favor expanding government expenditure as a means to implement expanding fiscal policy. Local government leaders, partly for their own promotion purposes in the political tournament, are more inclined to invest in physically visible projects such as public infrastructure and real estate markets rather than reducing individual or corporate taxes. This is because the spending helps attract FDI and facilitate the growth of the manufacturing sector, public investment and foreign export.[5] Besides, the major source of tax revenue for the local governments is the earnings from leasing the publicly-owned land to the businessmen. Since the amount of total tax revenues collected is an important criterion of judging the performance of local government leaders by their superiors and part of the tax revenues needs to be used to finance the public spending, thus local government leaders have less incentives to cut taxes when implementing fiscal policies.

The monetary policy in China also mainly relies on the state-owned banks and SOEs. The debt market and stock market are underdeveloped in China, and thus banks are the dominating form of financial intermediaries and the major avenue for firms to mobilize external finance. Most banks are however state-owned and the interest rate is not entirely determined by the market. Thus the central bank controls the money and credit supply by mainly setting the quota for the total amount of loans to be lent to firms. Compared with private firms, SOEs are more closely and politically connected to those State-owned banks and therefore, holding everything else equal, SOEs receive a disproportionally large fraction of loans. Sometimes, due to the hold-up problem, SOEs can continue to obtain more generous loans in the future from the banks even if they cannot pay back their debt in time.

Another important reason why SOEs tend to get loans from the banks more easily is because of the mismatch between the current financial

---

[5] Wang (2010) develops a political-economy macroeconomic model to explain why China has attracted twelve times more FDI than India due to the endogenous policies chosen by the central and local governments in the presence of vest interest groups.

institutions and the industrial structure in China. Namely, there exist insufficient amounts of small and medium-sized banks, which can better serve most of the small and medium-sized (often labor-intensive) firms. Since remaining SOEs are generally large firms while private firms are largely of small and medium sizes, SOEs are much better served by the existing large banks (mostly state-owned banks) and therefore less budget-constrained than the private firms. Not surprisingly, SOEs, despite their shrinking numbers as compared with private firms, are still the major players for China's monetary policy as well.

1.4.2. *Roles of SOEs in the industrial policy and external capital market*

In 2006, China government identified seven "strategic" sectors — defense, electric generation and distribution, petroleum and petrochemicals, telecoms, coal, civil aviation and waterway transport. It was explicitly articulated that the state would keep "absolute control" in these sectors. Consequently, new entry is highly restricted even though several state firms might compete with one another. Moreover, China government also designated the following industries as "basic or pillar" industries — machinery, automobiles, information technology, construction, steel, base metals, and chemicals — the state would retain "somewhat strong influence" (Owen *et al.*, 2007). In such sectors, private participants could face a range of entry barriers or other constraints.

As the world's largest manufacturer, China consumes a huge amount of energies and raw materials every year. It is therefore crucial for China to seek new energies and new materials to eventually substitute for the exhaustible resources. This is also important for the purpose of environmental protection. These upstream industries exhibit enormous positive externality and also require large investment, and pollution-intensive technologies tend to persist due to the path-dependence in technological progress (Acemoglu *et al.*, 2012). Therefore it makes sense that the government should adopt industrial policies to support the R&D for these industries (Also see Rodrik 2008 and Wang 2012b).

However, in China this ownership-neutral and justifiable industrial policy is actually equivalent to ownership-discriminating policy in favor of SOEs because only SOEs are allowed to enter and operate in these industries. Clearly, limited competition and high risks associated with R&D are likely to result in low efficiency and over subsidy. Then why are SOEs more favored by the government to implement industrial policies?

First of all, some SOEs are for national defense and military purpose, so it is understandable that they are subsidized by the government. For a large country like China, the demand for the weapons and other military equipment is huge, but they are sometimes too expensive to import or sometimes even not purchasable in the international market for political reasons. Government procurement is another important way to support such SOEs.

Second, some upstream civil industries such as energy and telecommunications are related to national security and these industries typically also exhibit the characteristic of natural monopoly. Government regulation has to be introduced in order to restore social efficiency. Given the large fixed investment and entry cost, new private firms can hardly enter and compete with the incumbent SOEs even if they are allowed to enter. At the same time, these industries have strong positive externality and may be undersupplied by profit-seeking private firms.

Third, China government is trying hard to develop some "national champions" in the international market. Despite the large export, China still has few, if any, internationally renowned high-quality brands. The general image of China's exports in the world is cheap and of low quality. To change this bad image and to facilitate the switch from "made in China" to "created in China", China government is eagerly trying to help develop or strengthen some national brands. Large SOEs seem too big to fail, namely, less likely to be defeated at the domestic and international market, especially given that they are backed up by the government. And precisely because of this previous government support, many large SOEs are already enlisted in foreign stock markets. The presence of those firms in the international stock market by itself serves as an important and free advertisement on their brand names. Consequently, China's government finds it less risky to continue to support these incumbent large SOEs, which the government is very familiar with, rather than to identify and support new private firms to develop national champions. Besides, SOEs are more likely to follow the instructions from the government to achieve certain non-profit-seeking objectives.

Fourth, China's SOEs are also undertaking the majority of outward FDI, especially in the energy and raw materials industries. China has accumulated a large stock of foreign reserve, which is largely composed of low-return US Treasury bills. One way to raise the return rate is for SOEs to make outward FDI, especially in those upstream industries such as natural resources in those resource abundant countries. This is also to ensure a more secure and stable supply of those exhaustible inputs to support China as the world's largest exporter of manufacturing goods. Chinese private companies make much less outward FDI, either due to the lack of capital or personnel support from the government, or simply because they are not allowed due to capital control. Moreover, outward FDI is sometimes made for China to achieve certain political and diplomatic goals, which make China's government favor SOEs to non-SOEs.

1.4.3. *Roles of SOEs in maintaining social stability*

In the process of China's economic reforms, SOEs have been serving as social stabilizers. In the absence of an adequate social safety net, the oversized labor employment and the provision of various social services by SOEs have contributed tremendously to the maintenance of social stability and the formation of a stable business environment for the development of non-SOEs. Many existing large SOEs are much more than business companies. They also provide schools, hospitals, housing, entertainment facilities and other benefits to the employees, retirees, and their family members (Lin *et al.*, 1998). One common feature of SOEs is overemployment because those SOEs have to accept the new people assigned by the superior government. Moreover, when hit by negative shocks, SOEs are less likely to fire workers than non-SOEs for the sake of protecting job security and maintaining social stability. For example, Daqing city is a new city where almost all the citizens are related to the Daqing Petroleum field, which is state-owned. Suppose those large SOEs are privatized, we would naturally expect to see massive layoff and the termination of many other non-profitable social functions that are served by these SOEs. This can easily cause social instability in those regions, especially because most people work in the same large SOEs and also live in the same region. By the logic of collective actions, those who are hurt by the SOE privatization can be better coordinated to voice out their oppositions.

1.5. How to Reform SOEs

Our discussions in this chapter as well as in our related chapters show clearly that the high profitability, low productivity, and slow technological innovations in the SOE sector are the symptoms of the collusion between SOEs and bureaucrats to seek rents at the expense of the establishment of competitive markets.

This collusion in rent seeking could stem from several factors. First, bureaucrats like to see the presence of a sizeable SOE sector, which facilitates them to steer production to achieve their political objectives including maintaining employment and achieving social stability. One widely recognized reason why SOE reforms are often ineffective is the political control of managerial appointment (Qian, 2002). Under this circumstance, SOEs are ensured to be instruments of bureaucrats to fulfill their political objectives. Second, bureaucrats like to grant SOEs monopoly rents in order to relieve the burden of subsidizing SOEs so that fiscal budget could be released for bureaucrats to pursue other political objectives. Third, bureaucrats also have strong motivations to improve SOE performance as a showcase of their administrative performance. SOEs have been regarded as the leading force of a "socialist market economy", and numerous efforts were made to improve SOE performance. A natural way for bureaucrats to support SOEs is to help maintain SOE monopoly through means such as reducing the competition pressures from non-SOE entrants and offering government procurement contracts to SOEs. Hence, administrative monopoly is an effective means of seeking rents for government officials and SOE managers. Once enjoying administrative monopoly rents, the SOE sector and bureaucrats form a vested interest group that vehemently oppose market liberalization. This has become a critical issue in current socioeconomic reforms. No doubt to continue with SOE reform we need to further emancipate our mindset and overcome the resistance forces of the various interest groups.

From the methodological point of view, discussion of SOE reforms inevitably involves how to draw a borderline between market and government, which is under debate all the time even within the academia, not to speak of the policy circle. However, the guiding economic principle is clear: government should intervene only when market fails sizably and when the government failure is sufficiently limited in the sense that intervention can be well implemented and monitored to avoid large efficiency loss and rent seeking. When it comes to policy implementation in reality, political feasibility must be considered.

Both the progress of economic theory and policy practice in China's reform history convey the following message compellingly: Reforms should be pragmatic and the policy recommendations should be formulated case by case in the realistic, concrete, and specific context rather than provided ideologically even before appropriate diagnosis is conducted. It is naïve to peddle the panacea of privatizing all the SOEs overnight as proposed in the so-called "Washington Consensus". Instead, the useful experiences from the successful experimental and pragmatic approach of China's reform should all be kept in mind. Examples include installing the household responsibility system in the rural reform, establishing special economic zones and facilitating regional industry agglomeration, and nurturing township and village enterprises. They also point to the importance of entrusting and making best use of the innovativeness of ordinary people and local government in the whole market-oriented reform in an imperfect environment.

On the other hand, we must emphasize that the scope of SOEs, or government intervention at large, should be kept as limited as possible in order to cultivate a business-friendly and fair-competition environment. This becomes increasingly important because China has already achieved the status of a mid-income country and therefore it has to switch from the current investment-based mode of growth to the innovation-based mode of growth (Acemoglu *et al.*, 2006). So far, no economic system is known to perform better than a free private enterprise system in terms of inducing innovation.

Due to the limit of knowledge and space, we will only focus on several specific aspects of SOE reforms, which we view as of first order importance. No attempt is made to provide a comprehensive discussion or conclusive prescription about how to reform all the different kinds of SOEs optimally.

As argued in Section 1.1, monopoly of SOEs in the upstream sectors may ultimately strangle the dynamic growth of the downstream private sectors if price markup is charged continuously. Theoretically, the causes of monopoly in different sectors can be mainly divided into two different categories. One is natural monopoly, which is purely due to technological characteristics such as economy of scale and economy of scope. Textbook examples include sectors such as electricity and telecommunications. The other is administrative monopoly, which is granted by government via regulations on entry and operations. A classic example is the national defense industry.

We can see that most of the "strategic industries" and "pillar industries" mentioned in Section 1.2 are the mixture of these two types, and they are also often entangled with industrial policies and political factors discussed in Section 1.3. This tremendously complicates the policy analysis.

1.5.1. *Natural monopoly and SOE reforms*

It must be emphasized up front that natural monopoly itself is not a legitimate excuse for SOEs to exist in such sectors. The necessity of exercising certain government regulation in such sectors does not mean that the firms have to be state-owned or state-controlled, especially when sufficient regulatory power is established. In addition, the large market size of China often makes it possible to accommodate multiple firms that can all reach the efficiency scale.

The reform of the telecommunication industry is a case in point. From 1999–2000, with the rapid increase in the market demand, the former China Telecom was first divided into four independent groups based on the business lines: fixed network, mobile network, satellite communications, and radio paging. In addition, several competitive carriers such as China Unicom and China Netcom were also gradually emerging and consolidated. As a result, economic performance of this industry as a whole has been improved rapidly as more competition has been introduced. In 2011, two Chinese firms in the telecommunication industry entered the list of Fortune Global 500: China Mobile Communications (ranked 87th) and China Telecommunications (ranked 211th).

In spite of all the achievements of the previous reforms in the telecommunication sector, however, there is still big room for further reform. Many types of operations and services are still not as cost efficient as many other countries after quality adjustment, while at the same time private investment is still *de facto* virtually restricted in this industry. Given the current oligopoly market structure, the coexistence of high sales revenues but relatively high quality-adjusted cost indicates the plausibility of further enhancing the market competition and industry efficiency by privatizing some big firms and encouraging more entry. Similar argument can be also made for the Petroleum industry in China.

1.5.2. *Infrastructure investment and SOE reforms*

Public infrastructure such as transportation facilities, electricity supply and telecommunication service is crucial for economic development. China's manufacturing sector would not be so successful without sufficient provision of public infrastructure, as evidenced by international comparison. Due to the huge positive externality and large fixed investment, these sectors cannot fully develop without government support. Given China's institutional environment (such as land being publicly owned and banks also being largely state-owned), SOEs can effectively utilize public resources and circumvent much coordination and transaction cost in the building process of such infrastructure. In reality, SOEs indeed have played an important and positive role in the infrastructure provision from the social efficiency point of view.

However, once the public infrastructure is built, there seems to be no sufficient reasons why the daily operation has to be still conducted by SOEs. More private competition could be introduced in different forms such as by running a public auction and/or sub-contracting to private firms. Aviation in China is state-owned, and their profitability is low and often negative. The large market size of China should have allowed for more than one firm to stay profitable in the business. In fact, there are already quite a few airlines in China competing for customers, and it seems possible to consider privatizing some of those regional airlines to see how the gradual reform works. Major airlines such as the United Airline or the American Airline in the United States are all private firms, so it seems justifiable to allow for such gradual reform experiment in China's Aviation industry.

1.5.3. *Industrial policies and SOE reforms*

As discussed in Section 1.3, some industries such as national defense are for non-civil purposes so it seems justified to keep those firms as state-owned. However, in some other industries including the aviation industry or telecommunication industry, national security seems largely used by the incumbent as an excuse to maintain the administrative monopoly and government protection. In the United States, AT&T and T-Mobile are both private firms in the telecommunication industry. Many large oil companies, banks, insurance companies are all private as well. This contrast indicates that national security is not a sufficient reason to justify state-ownership and administrative monopoly in these industries.

We should make it clear that we are not arguing that those aforementioned industries should be allowed to operate in the laissez faire manner. They do need some appropriate government regulations. But we only want to emphasize that the entry of private investment should be also carefully considered before it is blindly excluded without sufficient and objective justifications. If, for some strong and plausible reason (such as national security), no private firms are allowed to enter, then the possibility of having more than one SOE should be still seriously considered in order to induce more competition. At the same time, the non-crucial part of the production should be outsourced to the private sectors as much as possible.

Moreover, justifiable industrial policies such as R&D support, especially for civil purposes, are often ownership-neutral and therefore, from the social efficiency point of view, government should not discriminate against private firms in the implementation process. In reality, it is clear that the most successful and most innovative firms in the world, such as Apple, Google, Microsoft, GE, are all private. Although government subsidy on R&D is still justifiable for those companies and the related industries, the profit-maximizing motive of those individual firms is already very strong for them to voluntarily invest huge amounts of expenditure on R&D (Aghion and Howitt, 1992).

In order to understand the nature of industrial policies in China and the related SOE reforms more deeply, we should first well recognize that the main driving forces of industrial upgrading are different between developed countries like the United States and the developing countries like China. The former is already at the world technological frontier so industrial upgrading can be achieved mainly by new inventions and innovations via R&D. By contrast, the latter is still at the lower end of the technological ladder and their industrial upgrading is mainly achieved by the adoption and adaptation of foreign existing technologies without being able to enjoy the legal monopoly rent via patent protection.

The major incentives for firms in those developing countries to upgrade technologies and enter a new industry are to seek production opportunities that can best utilize the most abundant and hence the cheapest production factors in the economy. Only by doing so can these firms fully take advantage of the endowment comparative advantage and become cost competitive in the world market. More specifically, socially optimal industrial upgrading in China and other developing countries are endowment-driven, that is, industries are moving from labor-intensive and low value-added industries to more and more capital-intensive and high value-added industries. This endowment-driven structural change is formalized in a tractable closed-economy growth model with infinite industries in Ju *et al.* (2011). Later, Wang (2012a) also explores theoretically how international trade and international trade policies affect the endowment-driven industrial upgrading.

Then the natural question arises: What is the role of industrial policies and SOEs in the socially optimal process of the endowment-driven industrial upgrading in China, or developing countries in general? In a recent research by Ju *et al.* (2011), they develop a theoretical model of optimal industrial policies, which features the "market-led-and-government-facilitated" approach instead of government "picking the winner". They show that, in the presence of Marshallian externality, laissez faire market equilibrium is no longer efficient and government should use industrial policies to rectify the market failure by coordinating the firms to the right and time-varying target industry which follows the endogenously evolving comparative advantage of the economy. This is actually what the government of the East Asian miracle economies followed after World War II.

By contrast, the government of China in the pre-reform era failed in its industrial policies because the government tried to prematurely push the overly capital-intensive industries such as steel as the target industry, which violated the principle of Heckscher–Ohlin comparative advantage. Similarly, former Soviet Union, India, and many Latin American countries also failed to grow fast in the same periods as their industrial policies were also to promote prematurely the overly capital-intensive industries that prevailed in the most developed countries at that time. And precisely because the "winner industry" picked by the government could not be supported by the market itself as it significantly defied the comparative advantage, SOEs and resource rationing had to be established to pursue the wrong industrial goals of the government. The larger the deviation of the target industry from the economy's endowment structure, the more badly SOEs are needed and the more perverse the rent-seeking becomes as it requires more central planning and non-market resource allocation. That can at least partly why SOEs were pervasive (and also performing badly) not only in China and former Soviet Union, but also even in capitalist countries such as India and many Latin American countries (Also see Lin, 2009).

An implication of these analyses is that, fewer SOEs will be needed and the scope of rent seeking will be also more limited if China follows its comparative advantage and upgrades its industrial structures sufficiently in response to the market signals of the factor prices. As the relative wage increases along the economic growth path, China should gradually leave those labor-intensive sunset industries and upgrade toward more capital-intensive industries with high value added. This may help us not only understand the path dependence of China's SOE reforms but also give hints on how to avoid too much SOE dependence in the future industrial development.

1.5.4. *Tax revenues and SOE reforms*

Some downstream industry such as tobacco and wine is still highly monopolized by state-owned enterprises in China. Stable tax revenues from these industries with low price-demand elasticity are presumably the main reason why the government does not give up the SOE monopoly. Notice that the monopoly rent is sizable also because the tariff rates on these consumption goods are high.

So, as long as the government can have stable fiscal revenues from the private sectors, it is socially optimal to privatize such industries, which exhibit no obvious market failure that justifies government intervention or state ownership. Recall that Du *et al.* (2012) show that there is still room to eliminate administrative monopoly of SOEs in China's manufacturing sector, although the sector itself becomes more and more dominated by non-SOEs.

Then a natural question is why not privatize all these SOEs and just levy taxes. Gordon and Li (2009) argue that, in many developing countries, the taxation ability is limited especially when the informal sectors are large and a substantial part of transactions are not traceable in the formal financial institutions, so the effective tax base is limited to that easy to implement (such as tariff). Thus it can be argued that enforcement constraint faced by government is smaller when taxing SOEs than non-SOEs. This issue involves financial institutions and the system of public finance, which we will revisit briefly.

Besley and Persson (2009) highlight the weak "state capacity" of many developing countries that government power is too weak to ensure that fiscal revenues can be effectively collected. However, the argument of state capacity does not seem particularly applicable in China's case as the government is strong and it has much higher taxation ability than other developing countries like those in Africa.

Acemoglu and Robinson (2006) argue that the incumbent refuses to give up monopoly in exchange for pure taxation because they fear that their political power will be undermined when losing monopoly. In terms of China's remaining SOEs, they are typically large firms supervised by SASAC. The managers have high official ranks and are powerful, often also have strong ties with central government leaders. The management levels can directly benefit from high profitability of the SOEs in their charge, for example, by having high on-job consumption, or diverting some SOE resources into their own pockets, or even simply enjoying the sense of achievement in managing a large firm. They will lose all of these benefits if SOEs are privatized. Consequently, these powerful people (together with their allies) are most likely to oppose the privatization of the SOEs even if the total tax revenues can increase after privatizing all the SOEs, as the general tax revenues are much harder to tap directly for this special interest group.

1.5.5. *Speed and sequence of SOE reforms*

Given the perverse consequences if SOEs continue to enjoy administrative monopoly power, should the administrative monopoly power be completely and immediately deprived of the SOEs or be phased out only gradually? If the gradualist approach is adopted, how fast and at what sequence should the SOE reform take place? Should these SOEs be privatized as well and if so how to proceed?

One useful lesson that can be drawn from China's reform history in the past few decades is that gradual reform is more likely to mobilize enough political support and succeed at the right sequence and speed. Shock therapy that advocates once-and-for-all complete reform overnight is often both politically infeasible and economically too costly. These are well received wisdom now (see Roland, 2000). But at what sequence should the reform proceed?

Wang (2011) formalizes the mechanisms behind the observations that successful and sequential reforms often work as follows: As an economy develops, some institutions or policies become the most binding growth bottleneck, and so these binding constraints are relaxed by reform and the economic growth resumes until a new growth bottleneck is reached, triggering another around of reform to relax this new constraint, so on and so forth. That chapter also analytically shows that the magnitude of the reform is monotonically changing over time, depending on the power of the government and the redistributive effects of the reforms. A more powerful government tends to have a smaller fixed cost for each reform as the policy making process is easier and quicker. The more pronounced distributive impact of a reform, the larger the opposition force and hence the higher the variable cost associated with a reform. So the optimal reform is more piece-meal and gradual when the fixed cost of reform is less important relative to the variable cost of reform. This applies for authoritative countries like China. By contrast, the optimal reform should be less frequent but with more dramatic change for each reform if the opposite cost structure is true. This seems to be more likely to happen in countries where the central government is relatively weak and legislation process to initiate a reform is difficult.

More specifically, for the SOE reforms, the above analysis suggests that we need to first identify the most binding constraint for sustainable growth caused by SOEs at each development level. When the labor cost is still cheap, the monopoly of the upstream SOEs is not fatal enough to strangle the dynamic growth of the private downstream sectors as the overall export price of the downstream sector is still internationally competitive. However, once the labor cost rises sufficiently with the deepening of industrialization and urbanization, or when China's external demand falls due to world financial crisis, or when another country can effectively compete against China in the world market, then the monopolistic price markup charged by the upstream SOEs on energy, raw materials, telecommunication services, and financial services will become the most binding force that undermines the development of downstream sectors as well as the whole economy.

If the national leadership of China really wants to maintain high growth and avoid the "mid-income trap", then the upstream SOEs will have to be reformed. In other words, we expect that the deteriorating external markets and the increasing pressure from other competitors may serve as a useful catalyzer for further SOE reforms. The upstream SOEs may first have to reduce their price markup to lower the production cost and enhance the competitiveness of the downstream sectors in the international markets. Then to survive the increasingly fierce international competition, upstream SOEs would have to improve their productivities sufficiently fast, which would require that more competition is introduced into the monopolized upstream sectors or even induce privatization eventually.[6]

Different from the small and medium-sized SOE reform in the downstream sectors in the 1990s, now the remaining SOEs are much larger and less of them are directly controlled by local government. So the central government will have to take more initiatives and play a more active role in this new round of SOE reform. In addition, now the SOEs to be reformed are mostly rich and making money, different from the money-losing SOEs in the downstream sectors in the 1990s. These new features naturally make further SOE reforms much harder than before.

From the political feasibility point of view, it seems plausible to start from the easiest reforms. First, the existing money-losing SOEs with no strong positive externality, especially those remaining in the downstream liberalized sectors, should receive no more preferential public subsidy and let go. Second, for those rich SOEs, preferential policies such as

[6] Li *et al.* (2012) discuss the sustainability of the model of China's state capitalism.

low-interest loans or low tax rates should be gradually canceled to reveal the true profitability of those SOEs. Third, more competition should be introduced into those "strategic industries" even without privatization, for example, by dividing the incumbent giant into several competing entities or developing new state-owned competitors. Fourth, for industries such as tobacco and wine, it simply makes no economic sense why they have to be monopolized by SOEs. Instead, central government should immediately level the field and allow private firms to enter and compete, including paying the same tax rates. At the same time, those SOEs can be fully privatized. Fifth, the antitrust law should be enforced more effectively. At least the illegal part of the monopoly power enjoyed by some SOEs should be eliminated. Sixth, for those SOEs hard to privatize at present, the governance structure can be at least improved by making the selection of CEOs more transparent and more based on entrepreneurial capability. The remuneration and punishment schemes should be reformulated to be more consistent to the market rule.

1.6. Associated Policy and Institutional Changes Needed for SOE Reforms

Our analyses and arguments have shown that the current presence of state ownership in the Chinese economy has been far more than what is warranted by the legitimate role assigned to SOEs in economic theory, and SOEs in China have displayed various symptoms that impede improvements in economic efficiency such as administrative monopoly and low production efficiency. In Section 1.4, we provide prescriptions for SOE reforms. The general principle of these recipes is to keep SOEs confined to the areas that state ownership can truly help overcome market failures and enhance economic efficiency, and prevent SOEs from becoming rent-seekers in the national economy. In other words, we are attempting to make China's model of state capitalism a benevolent one rather than a predatory one.

Nevertheless, the reform of the state sector cannot be successful without the support of a host of associated policy and institutional changes. Among many supporting reforms required (such as the financial reform and pension reforms), the SOE reform particularly calls for the modernization of the political and legal institutions and culture.

There is no doubt that appropriate industrial policies and legitimate government intervention could benefit China's economic development tremendously. Generally speaking, state capitalism can potentially play a positive role in the catch-up process of economic development. In the history of the currently developed countries, quite a few of them, e.g. Germany, had adopted the state capitalism model or incorporated central elements of state capitalism.[7] Theoretically speaking, state capitalism can effectively overcome market failures and kick-start economic development when private capital lacks incentives and capability to do so. The state can invest in infrastructure projects whose investment costs typically need a way too long period to recover for private capitalists. The state can launch and invest in technological innovations whose costs are too large and whose returns are too risky for private capital to undertake. The state can support the development of infant industries that private capital typically shuns because of daunting business risks involved. In these areas, among many others, state capitalism is expected to be able to overcome market failures and guide economic development. In this kind of intervention to facilitate the catch-up process for developing countries, the likelihood of the state making big mistakes in choosing wrong targets and making flawed strategies is relatively small. In economic catch-up, developing countries can typically learn from and follow the model of advanced economies to identify the key areas for state support so as to speed up the process of growth and development. Technically speaking, it is not too difficult for the state to make correct strategies to launch state initiatives in developing countries. Unlike mature economies where the state has no information advantage over development strategy, it is not essential in the catch-up stage to rely on private initiatives to explore areas of great potentials for development. In this sense, state capitalism can play a very constructive part.

Nonetheless, the technical feasibility for benevolent state capitalism does not necessarily mean that an efficient state capitalism model can be realized in practice. In developing countries, the primary obstacle to a beneficial state capitalism model comes from weak public institutions

[7] Among others, Wade (1990), Chang (2003), Evans (2005) are all comprehensive monographs highlighting the positive and active role of government in the economic development.

where corrupt bureaucrats collude with various interest groups to take advantage of state intervention to seek rents. Under weak institutions, the rent-seeking and office-seeking bureaucrats excessively expand the scope and scale of SOEs to turn them into powerful means of controlling the economy, realizing various social and political objectives that violate the criteria of economic efficiency, and seeking private benefits. Under weak institutions, the corrupt bureaucrats and the interest groups form alliances to establish administrative monopoly for SOEs, to overcharge for SOEs' products and services, and to give privileged treatment to SOEs in public procurement contracts, which in turn produce high profitability for SOEs at the expense of the public interests. In other words, the negative features of SOEs are largely the outcomes of unfettered state power that infringe upon the rights of the citizenry.

The problems faced by China's state capitalism are no exception. In the past decade, in the face of the rising state capitalism in China, the public has expressed deep concerns over the SOE sector, especially the mounting worries over administrative monopoly and the vested interest groups in the state sector. At the same time, economists are concerned with the emergence of bureaucratic capitalism, where bureaucrats and their families come to dominate the business sector by wielding their political power and political connections. In fact, a big chunk of bureaucratic capitalism is related to the predatory state capitalism, where bureaucrats and their family members control large SOEs so as to turn SOEs into instruments of rent-seeking with the backing of their political power. The arrival of bureaucratic capitalism and predatory state capitalism poses serious threats to economic and political reforms and the realization of a harmonious and fair society. In this sense, any serious reform must address the issue of SOE reform. As pointed out by the World Bank (2012), one key issue in China's reform agenda is to break administrative monopoly and further deepen SOE reforms.

The most important policy and institutional change essential to SOE reforms is a fundamental reshuffle of the political and legal institutions and culture, the core of which is to establish a civil society based on rule of law where the citizenry can impose effective constraints on the government. This is particularly necessary and urgent for a country like China that lacks cultural and institutional tradition for a civil society. Examining the tradition and current status of political and legal institutions and culture, we admit that China has a long way to go to build a modern civil society. In the traditional feudalist society of China, laws are simply the wills of the emperor or the political ruling class to constrain the behavior of the ordinary people. In the Chinese legal tradition, civil codes are almost non-existent and no attempt was made to extend laws to civil disputes. Laws are primarily confined to criminal offenses, and are treated as equivalent to penalties for criminals. Unfortunately, China has no tradition and awareness of using laws to uphold the interests and rights of individuals. Since 1949, China has introduced the Soviet Union version of Marxist legal doctrines in which laws are regarded as the instruments of proletariat to crack down enemies. This is not surprising at all as the Communist regime emerged from fierce class struggles and internal wars. This practice, however, has strengthened the Chinese political and legal culture tradition of ignoring individuals' rights and treating laws as instruments to rule the people, which clearly deviate from the ideals of the Western legal tradition to use laws to constrain the executive and uphold the rights of individuals (Liang, 2002; Ji, 2002). This is one of the fundamental institutional and cultural reasons for the prevalence of the mentality and practices of a bureaucrat-oriented society and unchecked state power in China. This also enables the unconstrained executive power to nurture a predatory state capitalism model that has aroused widespread concerns and worries.

To our pleasure, we see remarkable progress has been made toward political and legal institution reforms. As analyzed in depth in Jefferson and Zhang (2012), various positive developments including the rise of the middle class, local elections, frequent public protests, the increasingly independent legislature and judiciary, and the rise of non-government organizations have pushed China to move toward a modern civil society. It is also noteworthy that various developments such as the expansion of the internet access, the accompanied relaxation of government control on public expressions of opinions and the increasing responsiveness of the government to public concerns have all contributed to the democratization of the society and the increasing constraints on the executive power. These positive movements toward a modern civil society could provide the best support to the prevention of a predatory state capitalism.

1.7. Conclusion

In this article, we explore the role of SOEs and also study their ongoing reform in China's development model of state capitalism. Based on our previous research findings, we first explain why the SOEs have recently become more profitable than non-SOEs in the past decade. We argue that SOEs maintain monopoly power in the upstream industries such as energy, finance, and telecommunications and therefore these SOEs can extract monopoly rents from the liberalized and expanding downstream industries such as manufacturing, especially after China's entry to WTO in 2001. In addition, the remaining SOEs in some downstream industries, albeit shrinking, are shown to still have significant administrative monopoly power. We argue that a deeper SOE reform is urgent and imperative in spite of their seemingly high profits because the monopoly power of SOEs will eventually strangle the development of the private downstream industries, which is the true engine of China's growth, especially when the labour cost rises due to the deepening of industrialization and when the external demand declines due to world financial crisis and intensified competitions from other developing countries.

As an analytical preparation for the discussion on how to reform SOEs, we then briefly document several salient features of the existing SOEs and also examine the instrumental and delicate roles played by SOEs in China's fiscal, monetary, industrial, and social policies. In terms of how to reform SOEs, we argue that, although SOEs may be justified to continue their existence and operations in certain industry (such as national defense), it is important to stick to the principle that their roles should be confined only to those areas where the market fails significantly and the government failures are limited.

More specifically, we argue that the reform of SOEs has to be consistent with the structural change and the endowment-driven industrial upgrading in China. Government and SOEs could play a positive and active role in the provision of public infrastructure and industrial upgrading at the current development stage, but the abusive administrative monopoly power of SOEs are undermining economic efficiency and are inclined to cultivate vested interest groups to oppose to the reform at the expense of the public interest and long-term national development. If the industrial development is against China's comparative advantage, the scope of rent seeking will be much wider and SOE reforms will be also more difficult. Taking both political feasibility and economic cost into account, we propose that China's remaining SOE reforms should be undertaken sequentially by the order of declining urgency. That is, the most binding constraint that SOEs impose on economic growth at each development stage has to be correctly identified and reformed afterwards with high priority. This strategy could be also complemented by and consist with the successive reform in an increasing order of difficulty.

Certainly, SOE reform in China cannot be isolated from other ongoing reforms. A successful and thorough SOE reform must require supporting reforms in other associated institutions and policies. Eventually and most fundamentally, political reform and establishment of a rule-of-law-based society are keys to prevent China's society from becoming a predatory state capitalism. China is at the critical moment of history to deepen its reforms of the remaining SOEs and other inefficient institutions, not only to just avoid falling into the mid-income trap, but also to ensure a sustainable and inclusive long run growth and prosperity.

References

Acemoglu, D., Aghion, P., Bursztyn, L. and Hemous, D. (2012). "The Environment and Directed Technical Change." *American Economic Review*, 102(1), 131–66.

Acemoglu, D. and Robinson, J. (2006). *Economic Origins of Dictatorship and Democracy.* Cambridge University Press.

Acemoglu, D., Aghion, P. and Zilibotti, F. (2006). "Distance to Frontier, Selection and Economic Growth", *Journal of European Economic Association*, 4(1), 37–74.

Aghion, P. and Howitt, P. (1992). "A Model of Growth Through Creative Destruction." *Econometrica*, 60(2), 323–351.

Besley, T. and Persson, T. (2009). "The Origins of State Capacity: Property Rights, Taxation, and Politics." *American Economic Review*, 99(4), 1218–1244.

Brandt, L., Hsieh, C-T. and Zhu, X. (2008). Growth and Structural Transformation in China. *In China's Great Economic Transformation*, ed. L. Brandt, and T. G. Rawski. New York: Cambridge University Press, 683–728.

Brandt, L., Tombe, T. and Zhu, X. (2010). "Factor Market Distortions Across Time, Space and Sectors in China," Working Paper.

Canda, V. (2006). *Technology, Adaptation, and Exports: How Some Developing Countries Got It Right*. World Bank.

Chang, H.-J. (2003). *Kicking Away the Ladder: Development Strategy in Historical Perspective*, London: Anthem Press.

Du, J., Lu, Y., Tao, Z. and Yu, L. (2012). "The Twin Costs of State Ownership in China." Work in Progress.

Evans, P. (2005). *Embedded Autonomy: States and Industrial Transformation.* Princeton University Press.

Gordon, R. and Li, W. (2009). "Tax Structures in Developing Countries: Many Puzzles and a Possible Explanation." *Journal of Public Economics*, 93(7–8), 855–866.

Groves, T., Hong, Y., McMillan, J. and Naughton, B. (1994). "Autonomy and Incentives in Chinese State Enterprises." *Quarterly Journal of Economics*, 109(1), 183–209.

Jefferson, G. and Zhang, J. (2012). " The Trajectory of China's Political Reform: A Property Rights Interpretation." In *Unfinished Reforms in Chinese Economy*, ed. J. Zhang. Singapore: World Scientific.

Ji, W. (2002). "The Transformation of China's Legal Culture and its Internal Contradiction." In *The Selected Papers of Comparative Law*, ed. J. Mi. Law Publishing House: Beijing, pp. 54–65.

Ju, J., Lin, J.Y. and Wang, Y. (2010). "Endowment Structure, Industrial Dynamics, and Economic Growth." HKUST Working Paper.

Ju, J., Lin, J.Y. and Wang, Y. (2011). "Marshallian Externality, Industrial Upgrading, and Industrial Policies." HKUST Working Paper.

Li, W. (1997). "The Impact of Economic Reform on the Performance of Chinese State Enterprises, 1980–1989." *Journal of Political Economy*, 105(5), 1080–1106.

Li, X., Liu, X. and Wang, Y. (2012). "A Model of China's State Capitalism." HKUST Working Paper.

Liang, Z. (2002). "The Past, Present and Future of the Chinese Law: A Cultural Assessment." In *The Selected Papers of Comparative Law*, ed. J. Mi, Law Publishing House: China: Beijing, pp. 29–46.

Lin, J.Y. (2009). *Marshall Lectures: Economic Development and Transition: Thought, Strategy, and Viability*. London: Cambridge University Press.

Lin, J.Y. and Monge, C. (2010). "Growth Identification and Facilitation: The Role of the State in the Dynamics of Structural Change." Policy Research Working Paper #5313, World Bank.

Lin, J.Y., Cai, F. and Li, Z. (1998). "Competition, Policy Burdens, and State-owned Enterprise Reform." *American Economic Review*, 88(2), 422–427.

Qian, Y. (2012). "How Reform Worked in China." William Davidson Working Paper #473.

Owen, B.M., Sun, S. and Zheng, W. (2007). "China's Competition Policy Reforms: The Antimonopoly Law and Beyond." SIEPR Discussion Paper No. 0632.

Rodrik, D. (2008). *Normalizing Industrial Policies*. Washington, DC: World Bank Press.

Roland, G. (2000). *Transition and Economics: Politics, Markets, and Firms*. The MIT Press.

Sun, Q. and Ton, W.H.S. (2003). "China Share Issue Privatization: The Extent of its Success." *Journal of Financial Economics*, 70(2), 183–222.

Song, Z., Storesletten, K. and Zilibotti, F. (2011). "Growing Like China." *American Economic Review*, 101(1), 196–233.

Szamosszegi, A. and Kyle, C. (2011). "An Analysis of State-owned Enterprises and State Capitalism in China." Prepared for the US and China Economic and Security Review Commission.

The Economist. (2012). "The Rise of State Capitalism: Emerging Market Multinationals." January 21.

Wade, R. (1990). *Governing the Market: Economic Theory and the Role of Government in East Asian Industrialization*. Princeton University Press.

Wang, Y. (2011). "A Model of Sequential Reforms and Economic Convergence." HKUST Working Paper.

———. (2012a). "Industrial Dynamics, International Trade, and Economic Growth." HKUST Working Paper.

———. (2012b). "Market Structure, Factor Endowment, and Industrial Upgrading." HKUST Working Paper.

———. (2010). "Fiscal Decentralization, Endogenous Policies and Foreign Direct Investment: Theory and Evidence from China and India." HKUST Working Paper.

World Bank and China Development Research Center of State Council (2012). "China 2030: Building a Modern, Harmonious, and Creative High-Income Society".

Xiao, G., Yang, X. and Janus, A. (2009). "State-owned Enterprises in China: Reform Dynamics and Impacts." In *China's New Place in a World in Crisis: Economic, Geopolitical and Environmental Dimensions*, ed. R. Garnaut, L. Song, W.T. Woo. Asia Pacific Press, 155–178.

CHAPTER 2

REBALANCING CHINA'S ECONOMY: INCREASING THE ROLE OF INTEREST RATES AND RMB EXCHANGE RATES REFORM

*Qianjin Lu**

2.1. Introduction

China's financial industry witnesses its gradual transition and development in the process of China's economy shifting from planned economy to market economy. During the planned economy, Chinese government conducted strict regulation on both exchange rates and interest rates. Since China's reform and opening up in 1978, the market began to play an important role in the distribution of resources. As two crucial macroeconomic indicators, interest rates and exchange rates have greater influence on economy with the construction of the socialism market economy system. China's interest rates and exchange rates are transiting from governmental regulation to market adjustment.

China is opening wider to the outside world and pushing forward financial reform steadily. In the long run, China's market-oriented reform of interest rates and exchange rates is based on the principle of gradual progress so that some potential financial risks can be initiatively controlled. Firstly, gradual reform may prevent possible chaos caused by over-liberalization and

*I would like to express my sincere gratitude to professor Zhang Jun for his advice and useful suggestions and also gratefully acknowledge his help in the completion of this Chapter. Special thanks should go to Li Ming, Ma Yan, Shao Fei, and Zhang Qingyun, who offer help.

over-flowing of speculative capital into financial market. Secondly, it can help to achieve a smooth transition from governmental planning to market-oriented management. Market participants can be guided and the gap can be narrowed between regulated and market-implied interest rates and exchange rates. Thirdly, it is conducive to the implement of monetary policy because the central bank's money control may be weakened if the exchange rates and interest rates are deregulated rapidly when the mature market foundation is not yet built. From China's practice, gradual process seems to be successful when we see in retrospect the past experience of market-oriented reform of exchange rates and interest rates. China had successfully gone through the Asian financial crisis during 1997–1998 and the global financial crisis in 2008. Moreover, the pricing mechanism of domestic financial assets has been greatly improved and the financial market has also been steadily developed. China's financial reform has attached great importance on both the market-oriented system establishment and the prevention of potential financial risks; and the government tries to seek a balance between these two and select a path of gradual reform.

In the process of liberalization of interest rates and exchange rates, perfecting the formation mechanism of interest rates and exchange rates and increasing the flexibility have been the main part of the market-oriented reform. Theoretically, interest rates and exchange rates affect each other; however China's interest rates and exchange rates are almost mutually independent and play its own different functions separately on the economy. So the construction of market-oriented pricing system of interest rates and exchange rates will be beneficial to the development of the finance market and the transition of regulation mechanisms of the central bank's monetary policy.

2.2. Evolution of China's Interest Rates and Exchange Rates Reform

2.2.1. *Historical review of the market-oriented reform of interest rates in China*

In the period of China's centralized planned economy (1949–1978), interest rates were strictly regulated by the government and financial institutions had no autonomy to set interest rates.

Firstly, the management system on interest rates was highly centralized. In the planned economy, the allocation of money and credit was determined by the state. As a result, the economic function of money was greatly reduced. As the accessory of the economy, money had to accommodate the real economy in a passive and static way. Therefore, the government did not need to regulate money supply and demand through interest rates which were kept very low in order to serve the large scale of economic construction then.

Secondly, interest rates policies were designed to adapt to the socialist transformation and socialist construction. At that time, as the economic levers, interest rates faced functional degeneration. The aim of interest rates policies was not to promote the growth of social productivity but to serve the socialist transformation and socialist construction.

Since 1978, the strict interest rates regulation has been relaxing gradually. The interest rates were adjusted frequently and financial institutions were given certain privileges of floating interest rates. In 2003, the Third Plenary Session of the 16th CPC Central Committee passed "*Decisions to Improve the Socialist Market Economic System*", indicating "Pushing forward the liberalization of interest rates steadily, establishing and improving market-oriented interest rates formation mechanism and guiding market interest rates through monetary policy tools by the central bank." The liberalization of interest rates continued to move forward, but there still existed a certain rigidity of the interest rates, the changes of interest rates were still not able to affect the price adequately (Mehrotra, 2007).

2.2.1.1. *Liberalization of money market interest rates*

The liberalization of interest rates in China started in 1996. On June 1, 1996, interbank interest rates were loosened by the People's Bank. In 1996, through the Stock Exchange platform of the bond market, the Ministry of Finance accomplished the issuing of treasure bonds in the market-based way. In June 1997, referring to the experience of the interbank interest rates, the interbank repo rate and the price of cash bond transaction were liberalized at the same time and negotiated to set by both parties involved. In September 1998, the National Development Bank also issued the bonds in the market-based way for the first time. In October 1999, the treasure bonds were issued by means of market bidding mechanism. Those measures meant that China realized the liberalization of interbank interest rates, issuing interest rates of the treasure bonds and policy financial bonds.

2.2.1.2. *Expanding the floating range of deposit and lending interest rate*

In January 1987, the People's Bank of China (PBOC) first attempted to liberalize loan interest rates, which required that the loan interest rates of the commercial bank could float upward based on state-set lending rate of working capital and the maximum floating range was 20%. From 1998 to 1999, the People's Bank expanded the floating range of loan interest rates of financial institutions three successive times. To encourage financial institutions to support the development of SMEs, the floating ceiling of loan interest rates for small- and medium-sized enterprises (SMEs) was expanded from 10% to 30%, and for Rural Credit Cooperatives (RCCs) it was expanded from 40% to 50%, the ceiling of loan interest rates remained at 10% and the floating floor was at 10% for large enterprises.

Since 2003, the People's Bank has taken important steps towards the liberalization of loan interest rates. In August 2003, loan interest rates of RCCs could float upward no more than twice as much as the benchmark level in the allowed experimental areas.

On January 1, 2004, the People's Bank decided that the floating interval of loan interest rates of commercial banks and urban credit cooperatives was expanded to [0.9,1.7] and that of RCCs was expanded to [0.9,2]. The floating interval of loan interest rates was set no longer based on enterprise ownership and scale, but on reputation, risk and some other factors of the companies.

On October 29, 2004, the People's Bank raised the deposit and lending interest rates of commercial banks and then announced that the loan interest rates ceiling of financial institutions (excluding urban and rural credit cooperatives) was completely relaxed and that the loan interest rates ceiling of urban credit cooperatives were expanded to 2.3 times as much as the benchmark and the floor remained at 0.9 times. These measures demonstrated that the central bank's control on the interest rates would gradually loosen, and commercial banks would have more autonomy to set their interest rates.

In addition to the loan interest rates, the liberalization of RMB deposit interest rates has also made significant progress. In October, 1999, the People's Bank authorized that Chinese-funded commercial bank could do CDs business (minimum deposit of 30 million yuan and over five years (excluding 5 years)) for Chinese-funded insurance company and negotiate to determine the interest rates with them, which was an initial attempt to liberalize the deposit interest rates. In February and December of 2002, depositors of this business were extended to the National Council for Social Security Fund and the provincial social insurance agencies that had completed the experimental reform of the pension insurance individual accounts fund. In November 2003, rural credit cooperatives and commercial banks were allowed to offer postal contracted deposits (minimum deposit of 30 million yuan and the period was reduced to three years (excluding three years)). On October 29, 2004, the People's Bank allowed RMB deposit interest rates of financial institutions to reduce the deposit rates below their own benchmark, which meant the successful accomplishment of the periodic target of the deposit interest rates liberalization — "relaxing the floor and controlling the ceiling." And economic behavior was increasingly sensitive to interest rates (Koivu, 2009).

On June 8, 2012, the Central Bank announced that the floating ceiling of financial institutions deposit interest rates was expanded up to 1.1 times the benchmark interest rate and the floor of loan interest rate could reach 0.8 times, which was a substantive step of interest rate liberalization since October 2004. In fact, prior to this, the deposit interest rates of financial institutions were not allowed to float in accordance with the relevant regulations of the central bank, and then the floating floor for the loan interest rate was 0.9 times. People's Bank of China, on July 6, 2012, lowered the RMB benchmark deposit and lending rates once again. In addition, the loan rate floating floor of financial institutions was adjusted to 0.7 times the benchmark interest rate. Loan interest rate floating interval of individual housing kept unchanged, financial institutions were required to continue to strictly enforce the policies differentiation of housing credit, and inhibit speculative investment purchases.

2.2.1.3. *Liberalization of foreign currency interest rate*

In addition to the domestic currency interest rates, the liberalization of foreign currency interest rates was also further pushed forward. In September 2000, the interest rates of the foreign currency loan and large foreign currency deposit over three million U.S. dollars (including 300 million) were relaxed; the interest rates of foreign currency deposit less than 3 million U.S. dollars remained under the control of the People's Bank. In March 2002, the PBOC unified foreign currency interest rates management of both Chinese and foreign financial institutions in order to achieve fair treatment. In July 2003, the central bank relaxed the interest rates of small savings denominated by the British pound, Swiss franc and Canadian dollar, which would be determined by commercial banks independently. In November 2003, the central bank only controlled interest rates ceiling of small savings denominated by the U.S. dollar, Japanese yen, Hong Kong dollar and euro. Commercial banks could independently determine these interest rates below the ceiling. On November 18, 2004, the central bank raised the interest rates ceiling of one-year small dollar savings to 0.875%; the People's Bank no longer announced the interest rates ceiling of the biennial dollar, euro, Japanese yen and Hong Kong dollar savings. Commercial banks were allowed to determine and publish them later.

From above, it can be seen that the liberalization reform of interest rates obeys the principle: from foreign currency to domestic currency, from loan to deposit, from large amount to small savings, from rural area to urban area, and from money market to credit market. During this process, regulated and marketable interest rates, and limited floating and freely flexible co-exist. So China's interest rates are still influenced by both the market and governmental regulation (Hong *et al.*, 2010) and some outstanding problems still remain to be resolved in future reforms.

2.2.2. *Review of China's RMB exchange rate regime*

2.2.2.1. *RMB exchange rates controlled by the state in the period of planned economy (1949–1978)*

RMB exchange rates against the U.S. dollar were initially listed in Tianjin Exchange on January18, 1949. From 1949 to the end of 1952, which is the recovery period of the national economy, RMB exchange rates were basically linked with the prices. During this period, foreign trade was mainly conducted by private merchants. In order to make private merchants profitable as well as be conducive to overseas Chinese remittances, the movements of RMB exchange rates served for and played a positive regulatory role on exports and overseas remittances (Wu and Chen, 2002).

During the period of socialist construction (from 1953 to the end of 1967), RMB exchange rates kept relatively stable, which were in accordance with fixed price and planned price management system. During this period, RMB exchange rate was basically fixed, and especially since 1955, had been maintained at the level of 2.46 yuan/dollar. RMB exchange rate was departing from the prices gradually, mainly as an accounting tool for making internal accounting planning then.

Due to the large depreciation of the British pound in November 1967, floating exchange rates were adopted by major western countries in 1972. China entered the RMB pricing settlement period for foreign businesses from 1968 to the end of 1978. To avoid exchange rate risks, RMB exchange rates were calculated based on currencies weighted method and the fluctuation situation of these currencies in the international market.

2.2.2.2. *Implementing the double-track exchange rate system (1978–1993)*

From 1981 to the end of 1984, RMB internal settlement price and official exchange rates co-existed in China. In August 1979, the State Council decided to reform the current RMB exchange rates regime. In addition to retaining the announced exchange rates which continued to apply to non-trade settlement, the State Council decided to set the internal settlement price for foreign trade. During this period, the announced non-trade exchange rates were mainly used to deal with external businesses and the trade settlement price was applied to handle domestic relations. The aim of internal trade settlement price was to encourage export and restrict import, and strengthen economic accounting of enterprises in order to earn more foreign exchange for the state (Wu and Chen, 2002).

In 1985, China abolished the internal settlement price, which marked the beginning of the coexistence (from 1985 to the end of 1993) of official exchange rates and exchange rates of foreign exchange swap market. In order to meet the foreign trade system reform, implement contract system and gradually cancel fiscal subsidies, since 1988, the proportion of foreign exchange retention had been increased, and the foreign exchange swap centers had been established and exchange rates in the foreign exchange swap market had been loosened,[1] which formed the coexistence of official exchange rates and swap market exchange rates.

2.2.2.3. *Managed floating exchange rates system since 1994*

Since January 1, 1994, double-track RMB exchange rates were merged and managed floating exchange rates system based on market supply and demand was set up, which basically eliminated the black market of foreign exchange. This regime was characterized by integrating double-track RMB exchange rates and replacing foreign exchange quota system with foreign exchange buying and selling system and nationwide internet-linked interbank foreign exchange market replacing previous official exchange rates and decentralizing swap foreign exchange market, as well as managed floating exchange rates replacing previous dual exchange rate regime. All these measures increased the competitiveness of the foreign trade (Zhang, 2001). In this period, RMB exchange rates were basically pegged to the U.S. dollar and kept stable.

To establish and improve managed floating exchange rates system based on the market supply and demand, on July 21, 2005, China began to implement managed floating exchange rates system based on market supply and demand with reference to a basket of currencies. RMB exchange rates were no longer pegged to the U.S. dollar, but referred to a basket of currencies (Williamson, 2006; Ma and McCauley, 2011), which formed a more flexible RMB exchange rates system. RMB exchange rates

[1] In the early 1979, the State Council decided to implement the foreign exchange retention system. This system allowed exports units to use part of foreign exchange which would be turned over to the country. In October 1980, Bank of China began the foreign exchange swap operations in 12 cities. Since August 1981, foreign exchange quota had been traded in the swap market. But in the early development of the swap market, the swap price did not play a significant role in China's foreign trade, because retention ratio was low and price ceiling was regulated in the swap market at that time.

against the U.S. dollar basically kept up a continuous appreciation in this period (2005–2010).

On June 19, 2010, a new round of reform of exchange rate system was carried out in order to enhance the flexibility of RMB exchange rates. The objective of the reform was to further perfect managed floating exchange rates system based on market supply and demand with reference to a basket of currencies.[2] The target of the currency basket exchange rate, replacing the U.S. Dollar, would be the important part in this reform,[3] but the outstanding feature of this reform was to further increase the flexibility of RMB exchange rate against the U.S. Dollar.

In China, the reform of RMB exchange rate formation mechanism is gradual; so the flexibility of RMB exchange rate against the U.S. Dollar is also increased step by step. At the same time, RMB exchange rates are maintained at an administratively controllable level (Lu, 2004), so that relevant risks might be prevented (Huang and Wang, 2004).

2.3. Problems Facing China's Interest Rates and Exchange Rates

2.3.1. *Problems of China's interest rates*

2.3.1.1. *Benchmark interest rates*

The situation of interest rates hanging upside down were very obvious. For example, before July 11, 1993, the loan interest rate was equal to or slightly higher than deposit rates in commercial banks, sometimes even lower than deposit rates, making commercial bank deposit and lending business at a

[2] On February 13, 2011, the deputy governor of the People's Bank of China and the Secretary of the State Administration of Foreign Exchange, Yi Gang pointed out that China implemented the managed floating exchange rate regime based on market demand and supply with reference to a basket of currencies, which should always be insisted and is the best choice at present for China's socialist market economic system. Hu Xiaolian (the deputy governor of PBOC): "Three Points of the Managed Floating Exchange Rates System." http://www.pbc.gov.cn/detail.asp?col=4200&id=320. Hu Xiaolian: "Implementing the Managed Floating Exchange Rates System is China's Declared Policy." http://www.pbc.gov.cn/detail.asp?col=4200&id=325.

[3] For example, RMB exchange rate target may turn from the U.S. Dollar to RMB effective exchange rate.

loss. Meanwhile, commercial banks had relatively high reserve interest rates from the central bank. From August 23, 1996 to March 25, 1998, reserve interest rates were higher than the deposit interest rates, and relending interest rates were higher than lending rates, thus interest rates hanging upside down were very wide-spread. When reserve interest rates were higher than deposit interest rates, state-owned banks were more willing to put the funds in the central bank to earn interest and weakened commercial banks' motive to lend, which hindered the funds flowing into the real economy and the transformation of specialized banks into commercial banks. Relending rates were higher than lending rate and failed to fulfill the function of the base interest rate, which was also not conducive for the central bank to the shift from direct control to indirect regulation.

Before March 25, 1998, China's reserve ratio was 13%, and the excess reserve ratio was 5%–7%, the total reaching 18%–21%. With the development of the financial system and the changes in the financial environment, in 1998, the central bank launched reforms on the reserve system, combining reserve and excess reserve accounts, and allowed reserve account to directly associate with liquidation. On March 25, 1998, the central bank further adjusted these interest rates and rationalized the reserve interest rates, the relending rate and the rediscount rate. And the deposit and loan interest rates were reduced with the decrease of the reserve ratio which was beneficial for reducing the operating costs of commercial banks. Meanwhile the decrease of reserve interest rate could reduce central bank's payment of interests, it was beneficial for the central bank to lower relending and rediscount rate. The relending interest rate should be slightly lower than the one-year lending rate, but higher than the rediscount rate.

In general the central bank did not pay interest for reserve deposit, the establishment of which was to resist the possible risks of bank runs and to maintain certain liquidity for commercial banks. In the 1990s, the PBOC paid interest for reserve deposit, which was almost equal to the deposit interest rates and greatly reduced the opportunity cost of commercial banks' reserves, and it was not conducive for commercial banks to strengthen liquidity management. The gap between reserve interest rates and the one-year deposit interest rates was zero on March 25, 1998. The gap between the one-year lending and relending interest rate was also zero. In fact, the reserve interest rate should be lower than the deposit rate; otherwise the commercial banks would rather deposit the funds in the Central Bank than lend to earn interest. On July 1, 1998, the central bank again lowered its deposit, lending interest rates and required reserve interest rates and relending interest rates. On December 21, 2003, the People's Bank reformed the reserve interest rate system, setting two different interest rates for required reserve and excess reserve in the same account of financial institutions. And required reserve interest rates maintained at 1.89% while the interest rate for excess reserves fell from 1.89% to 1.62% (see Table 2.1).

Since 2006, the People's Bank had adjusted deposit and lending interest rates and central bank base interest rates several times. With interest rates adjustment, the central bank gradually rationalized deposit and lending interest rates, reserve rate, relending rate and rediscount rate, which made interest rates play a better role in the allocation of resources.

2.3.1.2. *Coordination between domestic currency and foreign currency interest rates*

With the deepening of market-oriented interest rates reform and the further opening up of capital account, the coordination of the domestic currency interest rates and foreign currency interest rates would become a prominent issue. The linkage of interest rates between domestic financial markets and international financial markets would be further strengthened. The changes of foreign currency interest rates and RMB exchange rates would affect the adjustment of domestic RMB interest rates. In highly integrated market economy, there would be some conflicts among domestic and foreign interest rates, the exchange rate due to currency arbitrage and interest arbitrage.

How to coordinate local currency interest rates, foreign currency interest rates and interest rates of foreign currency was the key problem (see Figure 2.1). From January 1994 to July 21, 2005, RMB was basically fixed against the U.S. dollar. Theoretically, the domestic and foreign interest rates should be in the same trend if RMB was freely convertible.

As China's capital account was not fully liberalized, the domestic U.S. dollar interest rates and RMB interest rates were relatively independent. Comparing one-year domestic deposit rate of U.S. dollars with that of

Table 2.1. Evolution of reserve interest rates, deposit interest rates, lending rates, the relending rate and the rediscount rate.

	Date	One-year deposit rate	One-year lending rate	Required reserve rate	Excess reserve rate	One-year relending rate	Rediscount rate
1	1990.3.21	11.34	10.08	7.92	7.92	9.00	(*)
2	1990.4.15	10.08	10.08	7.92	7.92	9.00	(*)
3	1990.8.21	8.64	9.36	6.84	6.84	7.92	(*)
4	1991.4.21	7.56	8.64	6.12	6.12	7.20	(*)
5	1993.5.15	9.18	9.36	7.56	7.56	9.00	(*)
6	1993.7.11	10.98	10.98	9.18	9.18	10.62	(*)
7	1996.5.1	9.18	10.98	8.82	8.82	10.98	*
8	1996.8.23	7.47	10.08	8.28	7.92	10.62	*
9	1997.10.23	5.67	8.64	7.56	7.02	9.36	*
10	1998.3.25	5.22	7.92	5.22		7.92	6.03
11	1998.7.1	4.77	6.93	3.51		5.67	4.32
12	1998.12.7	3.78	6.39	3.24		5.13	3.96
13	1999.6.10	2.25	5.85	2.07		3.78	2.16
14	2002.2.21	1.98	5.31	1.89		3.24	2.97
15	2004.10.29	2.25	5.58	1.89	1.62**	3.87***	3.24***
16	2006.4.28		5.85		0.99****		
17	2006.8.19	2.52	6.12				
18	2007.03.18	2.79	6.39				
19	2007.05.19	3.06	6.57				
20	2007.07.21	3.33	6.84				

(*Continued*)

Table 2.1. (*Continued*)

	Date	One-year deposit rate	One-year lending rate	Required reserve rate	Excess reserve rate	One-year relending rate	Rediscount rate
21	2007.08.22	3.60	7.02				
22	2007.09.15	3.87	7.29				
23	2007.12.21	4.14	7.47				
24	2008.09.16		7.20			4.68*****	4.32*****
25	2008.10.09	3.87	6.93				
26	2008.10.30	3.60	6.66				
27	2008.11.27	2.52	5.58	1.62	0.72	3.6	2.97
28	2008.12.23	2.25	5.31			3.33	1.8
29	2010.10.20	2.50	5.56				
30	2010.12.26	2.75	5.81			3.85	2.25
31	2011.02.09	3.00	6.06				
32	2011.04.06	3.25	6.31				
33	2011.07.07	3.50	6.56				
34	2012.06.08	3.25	6.31				
35	2012.07.06	3.00	6.00				

Source: Kong (1994); *China Financial Yearbook* (2009); www.pbc.gov.cn.

Note: (*) — 5%–10% lower than the lending interest rates of the same period; * — 5%–10% lower than the relending rate of the same period; ** — On December 21, 2003, the excess reserves interest rates fell from 1.89% to 1.62%; interest rate of the required deposit reserves remained at 1.89%; *** — On March 25, 2003, **** — On March 17, 2005; ***** — On January 1, 2008.

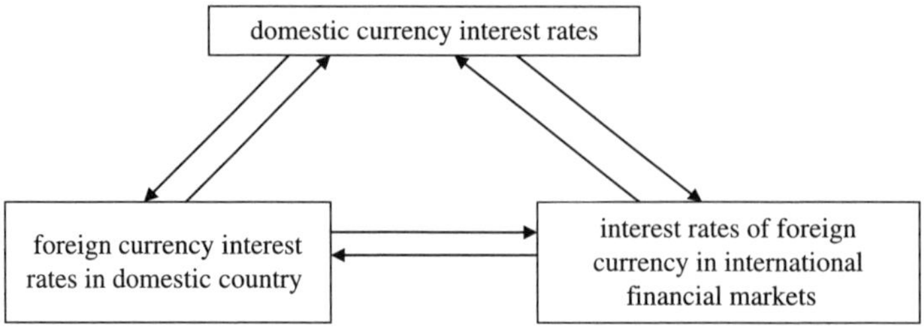

Fig. 2.1. The relation between domestic currency interest rates and foreign currency interest rates.

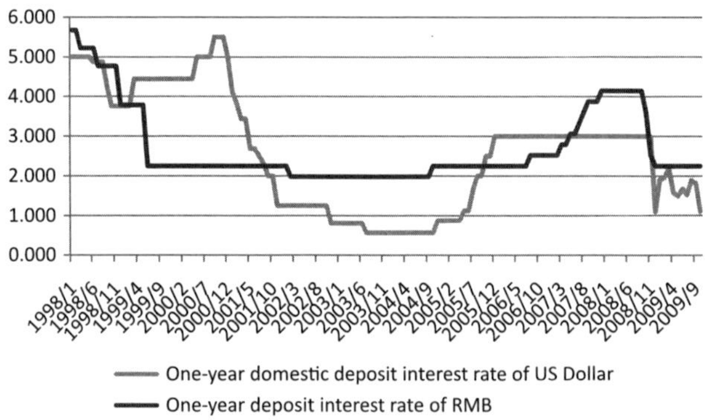

Fig. 2.2. The one-year domestic deposit interest rates of the U.S. dollar and the one-year deposit rate of the RMB.

Source: CEIC database.

RMB, both had different trend (see Figure 2.2). The interest rates adjustments of domestic currency and foreign currency were not strongly correlative and consistent. The reason such kind of independence exists is that RMB could not be converted freely.

Likewise, there was not a strong correlation between local currency interest rates and foreign currency interest rates of the international financial market. The adjustment of domestic interest rates was also independent from the international financial markets. With the deepening of market-oriented reform, the link between domestic financial markets and international financial markets would be further strengthened. In fact, in a highly integrated market economy, changes in foreign interest rates would inevitably induce changes in exchange rates or domestic interest

Table 2.2. Interest arbitrage and currency arbitrage cases of foreign capitals.

Condition	$E(\dot{S}) > i^* - i$		
Case	1) $i^* = i$	2) $i^* > i$	3) $i^* < i$
Result	The earning can be obtained by currency arbitrage but no interest arbitrage.	The earnings of currency arbitrage is larger than the loss of interest arbitrage.	The earning can be obtained by both currency arbitrage and interest arbitrage at the same time.

rates, otherwise one-way arbitrage capital flows must happen. With the expectation of RMB appreciation, domestic interest rates should be lower than foreign U.S. dollar interest rates in order to prevent speculative capital arbitrage. On the contrary, "hot money" inflows would appear if domestic interest rate was higher than foreign U.S. dollar interest rate.

Supposing the rate of return of foreign capital investment in the domestic market would be: $E(\dot{S}) + i$ (the appreciation rate of RMB exchange rate against the U.S. dollar + RMB interest rates), which includes interest incomes and capital gains due to the appreciation of RMB; the rate of return when investing in the American market is assumed to be i^*. So when (the appreciation rate of RMB against the U.S. dollar + the RMB interest rates) = (rate of investment return in America),[4] the speculative capital in the domestic rate of investment return equals foreign rate of investment return, and speculative capital could not get profit. When (the appreciation rate of RMB exchange rate against the U.S. dollar + RMB interest rates) < (rate of investment return in America), the return of investment speculative capital in the domestic market is lower than that in the foreign market. The speculative capital will not flow into domestic market.[5] When (the appreciation rate of RMB exchange rate against the U.S. dollar + RMB interest rates) > (rate of investment return in America), investment return of speculative capital in the domestic market is higher, the inflow of speculative capital will get more profit (see Table 2.2).

[4] The result comes from the interest rate parity theory.

[5] In this case, the arbitrage capital flows out.

In reality, according to the benchmark interest rates of RMB, U.S. dollar and the appreciation rate of RMB (without considering transaction costs), the driving force of hot money flowing into China was strong from 2008 to 2010. Speculative capitals had both interest arbitrage and currency arbitrage opportunities in China, because both the RMB interest rates and the appreciation rate of RMB exchange rate against the U.S. dollar were greater than the interest rate of the U.S. dollar. At the time when U.S. dollar interest rates continued to fall in 2008, the rising of RMB interest rates in 2010 would expand the profit margins, attracting more speculative capital inflows.

RMB had been fully convertible under the current account in December 1996. Compulsive buying and selling foreign exchange was abolished by the Foreign Exchange Control Regulation which was announced by the State Council in 2007. Enterprises could retain the foreign exchanges from their current account voluntarily and individual's demand for foreign exchange had also been basically satisfied. At the same time, China continued to promote RMB convertibility under the capital account, thus propelling the pace of the foreign exchange market internationalization. So the flows between domestic and foreign capital would become more frequent in the future (Shen, 2001). The further reform of foreign exchange system would expand the breadth and depth of the foreign exchange market. The linkage between the RMB exchange rates and interest rates would be much closer, and so the liberalization of the exchange rates and interest rates would also become more important.

2.3.1.3. *Negative real interest rates*

In 1973, the American economists Shaw and McKinnon made a profound research on financial repression and financial deepening of developing countries in their two published books, *Financial Deepening in Economic Development* and *Currency and Capital in Economic Development*. They thought that in the developing countries, due to artificially suppressing interest rates, the real interest rates were often negative, the demand of investment was excessively expanding and credit rationing had to be adopted, which caused many problems such as low capital efficiency, financial disintermediation, etc. Over the years, China had experienced

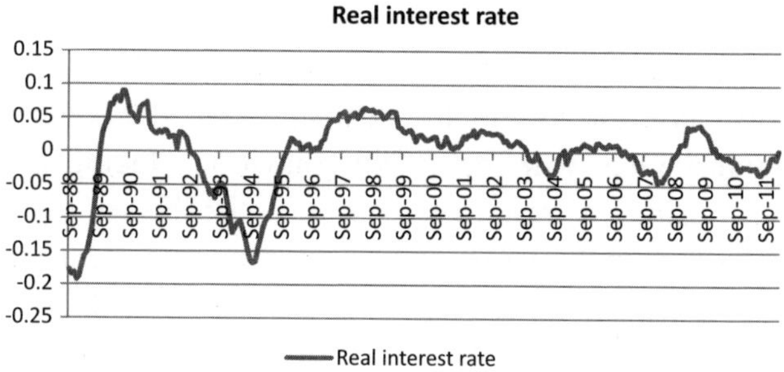

Fig. 2.3. China's real interest rates (Sep. 1988–Feb. 2012).
Source: CEIC database (nominal interest rate-inflation rate).

the situation that the inflation rate was in excess of the deposit interest rate many times. Due to high inflation, the real interest rates were negative in 1987–1988 and 1993–1994 (see Figure 2.3). And in recent years China again faced the dilemma of negative real interest rates, such as 2007–2008 and 2010–2011. The negative real interest rates lead to inefficiency of resources allocation, while the positive interest rates can attract funds and promote investment effectively. The positive interest rates are also in favor of narrowing the gap between the bank interest rates and the black-market interest rates and give the central bank more space to regulate the interest rates.

From the point of view of savers and borrowers, when the deposit and loan rates keep unchanged, inflation is a key element and affects differently on savers and borrowers. The higher the inflation rate is, the greater savers will lose and the more borrowers will benefit. Therefore, in general, with higher inflation rate, savers do not want to save but borrowers are more willing to borrow. Savers prefer current consumption than savings because the quantities of the purchased goods will decrease in the future by the savings. Borrowers are willing to borrow currently because the amount of money for purchasing the same goods now is less than that in the future. Similarly, if increasing of the interest rates cannot keep up with inflation, savers do not want to save and borrowers would like to borrow more.

In 2011, the price rose rapidly and the real interest rates was negative in China. The central bank hoped to obtain the positive level by raising nominal interest rates. If the nominal interest rates were raised and exceeded the rate of inflation, the real interest rates would be positive. The inflation will cause the loss of the depositors but the increasing of the nominal interest rates will rectify this situation. Taking into account the PBOC's raising interest rates, we turn the Fisher equation "real interest rates = nominal interest rates − inflation rate "into" real interest rates = previous nominal interest rates + increase of interest rates − the rate of inflation". Even if the real interest rates are positive, the real purchasing power of principal and interest at the end of deposit will depend on the increase of interest rates and inflation. There are two cases to be considered (see Table 2.3).

It can be seen from Table 2.3 that if the real interest rate is negative, the current real purchasing power of principal and interest is lower than the purchasing power of the principal, which leads to an absolute loss in current deposit. If the real interest rate is positive, the current real purchasing power of principal and interest is higher than the purchasing power of the previous principal, depositors will benefit from the savings. However, due to inflation, if the interest rates increase is equal to the rate of inflation, the purchasing power of the current principal and interest equals that of the previous one, and the depositors have the same return of the previous period; if the increase interest rates increase is greater than the inflation rate, then the purchasing power of the principal and interest is higher than that of the previous period, and the incomes of current deposits are larger than that of previous deposits; if the interest rates increase is less than the rate of inflation, the purchasing power of the current principal and interest is less.

One example could be found in 2007. At that time, the nominal interest rates plus the increasing of interest rates was less than the inflation rate, leading to absolute losses in deposits. As the result, more deposit funds flew into the stock market and real estate market, pushing up the asset prices.

2.3.1.4. *Private lending and interest rate*

Over the years, the financing of SMEs have been problematic in China's economic development. According to a survey conducted by the National Association of Industry and Commerce, 90% of SMEs had no borrowing

Table 2.3. The impact of inflation on the depositors in China.

Real interest rates = previous nominal interest rates + interest rates increasement – the rate of inflation	Comparison of current and previous deposits' purchasing power
1. Previous nominal interest rates + interest rates increasing < inflation rate, so real interest rates is negative	Purchasing power of principal and interest < purchasing power of previous principal, so depositors still face losses.
2. Previous nominal interest rates + interest rates increasing > inflation rate, so real interest rates is positive	Purchasing power of principal and interest > purchasing power of previous principal, so depositors will benefit.
i) Interest rates increasing = inflation rate	Purchasing power of principal and interest = purchasing power of previous principal and interest, so the incomes of current deposits is the same with that of previous deposits.
ii) Interest rates increasing > inflation rate	Purchasing power of principal and interest < purchasing power of previous principal and interest, so the incomes of current deposits is larger than that of previous deposits.
iii) Interest rates increasing < inflation rate	Purchasing power of principal and interest < purchasing power of previous principal and interest, so the incomes of current deposits is smaller than that of previous deposits.

relationship with financial institutions; so were 95% of micro and small enterprises. According to official data, the scale of Wenzhou private capital was more than 600 billion yuan; 80% of small and medium enterprises in Jiangsu and Zhejiang provinces relied on private lending with annual interest rates up to 180%, while the gross profit margin rate of most SMEs was only between 3%–5%. Ordos official research data also revealed that since the real estate bubble and the boom of mining investment, Ordos had become the hot spot of private lending in northern China. The size of Ordos private lending funds might be more than 200 billion yuan. Some officials and staffs of the banks were continuously involved in usurious loans and illegal fund-raising cases. The wife of the manager of the Inner Mongolia branch of Bank of China was kidnapped with a ransom of up to 200 million yuan, which was originated from illegal financing and private lending. In Wenzhou's private lending, it was estimated that more than 80% of the creditors were civil servants. Private lending's bubble breaking also occurred in Zhejiang, Guangdong, Inner Mongolia, Jiangsu, Henan, and Fujian. According to an incomplete statistics, in one year or more, there were 10 private lending suicide cases, 200 people were running away, 284 people were detained due to criminal charges in Wenzhou, Zhejiang Province alone.[6]

"*The Announcement of the People's Bank of China On Banning Underground Banks and Hitting Usurious Loan*" was issued by the central bank in 2002, which indicated that private lending rate should be consulted by both lenders and borrowers, but the negotiated interest rate should not exceed four times that of the benchmark lending interest rates of the same period of financial institutions announced by People's Bank of China. Those that exceeded the above criteria were defined as usurious loan and not protected by the law. But some scholars questioned the provision about four times of the interest rates (Mao, 2011). The central bank regulated that the lending rates of financial institutions were no longer set

[6]See: "The Wenzhou Dispute of Private Loan Blew Out and Grew More Than 4 Times in 5 Years", March 07, 2012, *Jurisprudence Daily*. "Because Several Billions Loans Are Unable to Repay, a Running-off Female Boss in Changshu is Arrested", March 30, 2012, *Beijing Times*. "Involving Dispute of Private Loan, the Chairman of a Education Group in Wenzhou is Arrested", February 06, 2012, *Qianjiang Evening News*.

a ceiling in principle in 2004, which was not inconsistent with the provisions of not exceeing four times the benchmark lending rates.

SMEs' financing in China is mainly dependent on private lending. However, private financing is lacking of a legal basis, and has relatively high interest rates risks; the chain of funds is vulnerable to the changes of the macroeconomic situation and policy. Therefore, the private lending market needs to be regulated urgently and should be "sunshine" to achieve orderly and healthy development.

2.3.2. *Problems of the RMB exchange rate*

2.3.2.1. *RMB exchange rate is rigid and less flexible against the U.S. dollar*

The foreign exchange system reform in China started in 1994. After January 1, 1994, RMB exchange ratc experienced a slow appreciation. By the end of June 1995, RMB exchange rate against the U.S. dollar had appreciated to 8.3011, increasing by 4.8%. Then RMB exchange rates entered a period of relative stability. In 1997, notwithstanding the shock of the Asian financial crisis, Chinese government still insisted on not depreciating RMB and maintained the basic stability of RMB exchange rate against the U.S. dollar between 8.27 and 8.28.

On July 21, 2005, China carried out the foreign exchange system reform, and RMB exchange rate against the U.S. dollar fell about 2% all at once,[7] reaching 8.11 yuan/dollar. In fact, due to the twin surplus of the balance of payments, RMB exchange rate against the U.S. dollar kept appreciating after the exchange rates reform. By the end of August 2008, RMB against the U.S. dollar had appreciated by 18.58% and during this period RMB was basically a crawling peg to the dollar. The U.S. subprime mortgage crisis broke out in 2007, the Fed adopted expansionary macroeconomic policies to stabilize and stimulate the economy; the U.S. federal

---

[7]Tung and Baker (2004) argued that the optimal currency adjustment was a one-time maxi revaluation of roughly 15% versus the U.S. dollar to a new fixed rate but to a modified anchor, that was, a trade-weighted currency basket. Goldstein and Lardy (2003) proposed a two-stage reform of the RMB exchange rates and that the RMB should shift from the dollar peg to peg the currency basket containing the U.S. dollar, the euro and the Japanese yen.

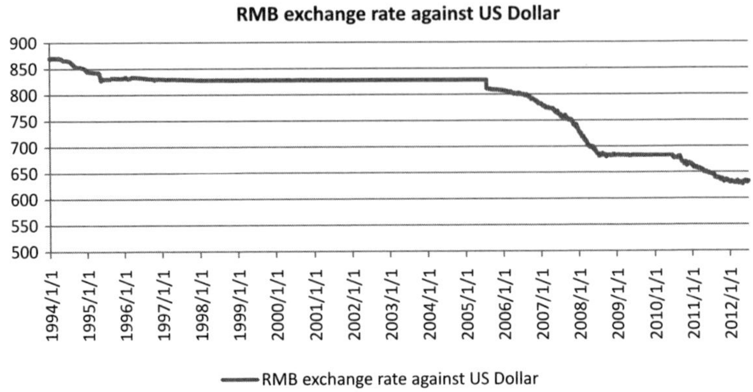

Fig. 2.4. RMB exchange rate against the U.S. dollar (Jan. 1, 1994–Jun. 29, 2012).
Source: www.safe.gov.cn.

fund rates went down continuously. On the contrary, RMB exchange rate against the U.S. dollar kept appreciating. However, with the spread and aggravation of the U.S. subprime mortgage crisis, the global economic situation further deteriorated and China faced risks of economic downturn and foreign capital outflow. Therefore, after August 2008, China stopped consistent appreciation of RMB and kept its exchange rate basically stable against the U.S. dollar around 6.83 under the shock of the international financial crisis (see Figure 2.4).

The recent new exchange rate reform took place on June 19, 2010. RMB began to appreciate against the U.S. dollar again. Consequently, the RMB exchange rate against the U.S. dollar experienced continuing appreciation but the flexibility remained to be further expanded.

2.3.2.2. *RMB exchange rates against non-U.S. dollar currencies*

RMB exchange rate against the U.S. dollar is the dominant exchange rate of China's exchange rates system. Although RMB continued to appreciate against the U.S. dollar, RMB exchange rates against non-U.S. dollar currencies and the effective exchange rate of RMB fluctuated wildly. On January 4, 2006, according to the central bank's regulations, the middle price of RMB exchange rates against the euro, Japanese yen and HK dollar were set by China Foreign Exchange Trading Center based on the cross exchange rates of the middle prices of RMB exchange rate against the U.S. dollar as well as euro, Japanese yen and Hong Kong dollar exchange rates against U.S. dollar at 9:00 in the international foreign exchange market.

Under the current RMB exchange rates regime, to prevent speculative arbitrage between RMB against the U.S. dollar and RMB against non-U.S. dollar currencies to maintain the stability of the foreign exchange market, the PBOC needs to set RMB exchange rates against non-U.S. dollar currencies through the cross exchange rates so that it is difficult for speculators to take advantage of the exchange rates difference. Assuming RMB exchange rate against the U.S. dollar is $S1$ yuan/dollar, U.S. dollar exchange rate against the euro is $S2$ dollar/euro, and euro exchange rate against RMB is $S3$ euro/yuan, only when ($S1$ yuan/dollar)*($S2$ dollar/euro)* $S3$(euro/dollar) = 1, the speculators just cannot get the arbitrage profits. Taking logarithm and differential on both sides: $\frac{dS_1}{S_1}+\frac{dS_2}{S_2}+\frac{dS_3}{S_3}=0$, that is to say, the sum of changes of U.S. dollar exchange rate against RMB, euro exchange rate against U.S. dollar and RMB exchange rate against euro is zero, so that speculators will not be able to earn profits. The above equation can be is turned into: $\frac{dS_3}{S_3}=-\frac{dS_1}{S_1}-\frac{dS_2}{S_2}$. If RMB exchange rate against the U.S. dollar keeps stable, that is $\frac{dS_1}{S_1}=0$, so $\frac{dS_3}{S_3}=-\frac{dS_2}{S_2}$. It implies when RMB exchange rate against the U.S. dollar is stable, the trend of RMB exchange rate against euro and the U.S. dollar against euro is basically the same (see Figure 2.5). During the European sovereign debt crisis, U.S. dollar became stronger. At that time, if RMB exchange rate against the U.S. dollar remained stable, with the appreciation of the U.S. dollar against the euro, RMB against euro would follow the appreciation, so RMB exchange rate against euro will reflect the changes of the U.S. dollar exchange rate against euro. For example, from December 1, 2009 to June 18, 2010, both RMB and the U.S. dollar against euro appreciated substantially (see Figure 2.5).

Since the exchange rates reform on June 19, 2010, RMB against the U.S. dollar continued to appreciate from 6.8275 yuan/dollar on June 21, 2010 to 6.2951 yuan/dollar on February 17, 2012, appreciating by 8.5%. And during this period, the U.S. dollar against euro depreciated from 1.2391 U.S. dollars/euro on June 21, 2010 to 1.3158 U.S. dollars/euro on February 17, 2011, depreciating by 5.83%. However, because of the larger

Fig. 2.5. Euro exchange rate against RMB and Euro against U.S. dollar (Sep. 1, 2008–Jun. 18, 2010).

Source: CEIC database.

appreciation of RMB against the U.S. dollar, although there were some depreciation of U.S. dollar against the euro, RMB still strengthened against the euro. In fact, RMB exchange rate against the euro appreciated from 8.4825 yuan/euro on June 21, 2010 to 8.2658 yuan/euro on the February 17, 2011, appreciating by 2.62%, mainly because RMB appreciation against the U.S. dollar was greater than U.S. dollar depreciation against the euro.

2.3.2.3. *RMB effective exchange rates*

In order to fully understand RMB exchange rates changes, we must still look into RMB effective exchange rates. Compared with the bilateral exchange rates, the effective exchange rates of RMB, as an important macroeconomic indicator, better reflects the competitiveness of the whole foreign trade. The effective exchange rate of RMB is the comprehensive measure of RMB exchange rates against currencies of all trading partners by trade-weighted average. According to the definition of the effective exchange rate, we choose the geometric weighted effective exchange rates index as RMB effective exchange rates formula.

$NEER_t = NEER_{t-1}\Pi_{i=1}^{n}(S_{i,t}/S_{i,t-1})^{W_{i,t}}$: $NEER_t$ is the nominal effective exchange rates of RMB in the period of t; $NEER_{t-1}$ is the nominal effective exchange rates of RMB in the period of $t-1$; $S_{i,t}$ is the RMB exchange rates against the currency of country i in the period of t; $S_{i,t-1}$ is the RMB exchange rates against the currency of country i in the period of $t - 1$; $W_{i,t}$ is the trade weight of the RMB against the currency of country i in the period of t.

According to the principle of triangular arbitrage, $S_{i,t} = S_{1,t} \times X_{i,t}$, where $S_{1,t}$ is the RMB exchange rates against the U.S. dollar in the period of t; $X_{i,t}$ is the U.S. dollar against non-U.S. currencies in the period of t.

From the definition:

$$NEER_t = NEER_{t-1}\prod_{i=1}^{n}(S_{i,t}/S_{i,t-1})^{w_{i,t}} = 100\prod_{i=1}^{n}(S_{i,t}/S_{i,0})^{w_{i,t}}$$

$$= 100\left[\frac{S_{1,t}{}^{w_{1,t}} \times (S_{1,t} \times X_{2,t})^{w_{2,t}} \times (S_{1,t} \times X_{3,t})^{w_{3,t}} \cdots \times (S_{1,t} \times X_{n,t})^{w_{n,t}}}{S_{1,0}{}^{w_{1,t}} \times (S_{1,0} \times X_{2,0})^{w_{2,t}} \times (S_{1,0} \times X_{3,0})^{w_{3,t}} \cdots \times (S_{1,0} \times X_{n,0})^{w_{n,t}}}\right]$$

$$= 100\left(\frac{S_{1,t}}{S_{1,0}}\right)^{w_{1,t}+w_{2,t}+w_{3,t}+\cdots w_{n,t}}\left[\frac{X_{2,t}{}^{w_{2,t}} \times X_{3,t}{}^{w_{3,t}} \cdots X_{n,t}{}^{w_{n,t}}}{X_{2,0}{}^{w_{1,t}} \times X_{3,0}{}^{w_{3,t}} \cdots X_{n,0}{}^{w_{n,t}}}\right]$$

$$= 100\left(\frac{S_{1,t}}{S_{1,0}}\right) \times M_t$$

where

$$\left[\frac{X_{2,t}{}^{w_{2,t}} \times X_{3,t}{}^{w_{3,t}} \cdots X_{n,t}{}^{w_{n,t}}}{X_{2,0}{}^{w_{1,t}} \times X_{3,0}{}^{w_{3,t}} \cdots X_{n,0}{}^{w_{n,t}}}\right] = M_t$$

M_t stands for the appreciation or depreciation of the U.S. dollar against $n - 1$ non-USD currencies, and is also regarded as an index. Although the weights of the index M_t and the U.S. dollar effective exchange rate index are different, but as both indexes include a variety of the same currencies and the weights are very disperse, even some are much closer, so M_t is also close to the U.S. dollar effective exchange rate index.[8] Assuming $S_{1,0}$ is fixed, then $S_{1,t}$ and M_t will affect RMB effective exchange rate. So the effective exchange rate of RMB can be basically determined by the

[8] It implies that $M_t \approx$ the effective exchange rate of the U.S. Dollar.

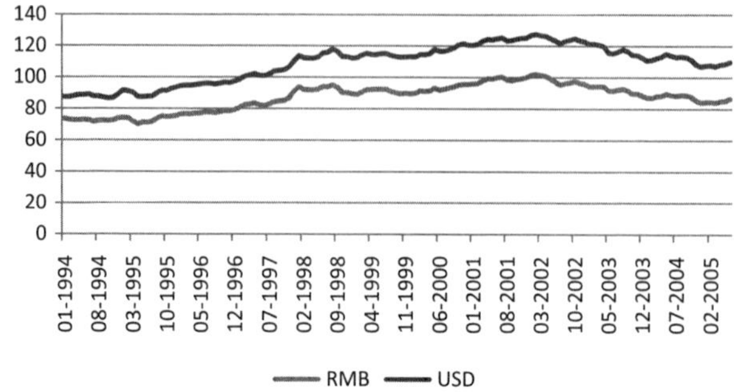

Fig. 2.6. RMB and U.S. dollar nominal effective exchange rates (Jan. 1994–Jun. 2005).
Source: www.bis.org (2010 = 100).

U.S. dollar effective exchange rates and the RMB against the U.S. dollar exchange rate.

With the movements of M_t and the RMB exchange rates against the U.S. dollar, the RMB effective exchange rate will change accordingly. If the RMB exchange rate against the U.S. dollar keeps stable, the effective exchange rate of RMB and the U.S. dollar effective exchange rate will be close to each other or in the same direction. For example, from 1994 to 2005, the RMB exchange rate against the U.S. dollar remained relatively stable ,[9] the RMB and the dollar's effective exchange rates were similar in the direction (see Figure 2.6).

If the RMB exchange rate against the U.S. dollar is appreciated, the RMB effective exchange rate will get closer and closer to the U.S. dollar effective exchange rate. From July 2005 to August 2008, the RMB exchange rate appreciated against the U.S. dollar continuously. With the appreciation of RMB, the RMB and the dollar effective exchange rates tended to close (see Figure 2.7).

During the period of the global financial crisis, the RMB against the U.S. dollar remained relatively stable. So the effective exchange rates of the RMB and the U.S. dollar remained in the same trend until the recent

[9]Between 1996 and 2005, the RMB against the U.S. dollar had a slow appreciation and then tended to keep stabilizing.

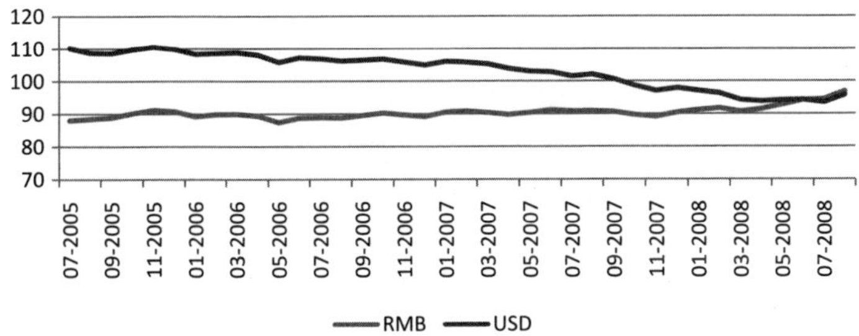

Fig. 2.7. RMB and U.S. dollar nominal effective exchange rates (Jul. 2005–Aug. 2008).
Source: www.bis.org (2010 = 100).

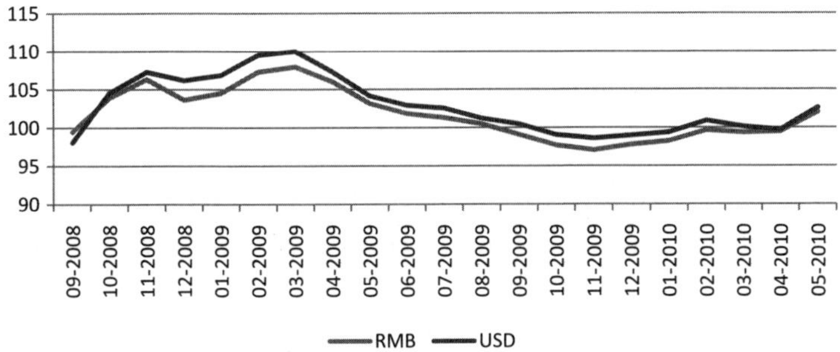

Fig. 2.8. RMB and U.S. dollar nominal effective exchange rates (Sep. 2008–May 2010).
Source: www.bis.org (2010 = 100).

round of exchange rates reform (from September 2008 to May 2010) (see Figure 2.8). Therefore, if the RMB pegs to the U.S. dollar, the effective exchange rates of the RMB will follow the U.S. dollar effective exchange rate's path.

After the exchange rate reform in 2010, the RMB exchange rate against the U.S. dollar continued to appreciate. The gap between the effective exchange rates of the RMB and the U.S. dollar was growing (see Figure 2.9). With the appreciation of the U.S. dollar, the appreciation of the RMB became larger.

Based on the above analysis, we can conclude that if the RMB pegs to the U.S. dollar, the effective exchange rate of the RMB will also basically follow the effective exchange rate of the U.S. dollar.

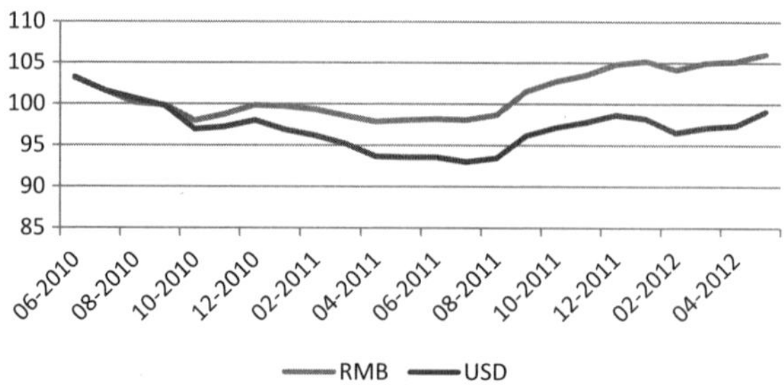

Fig. 2.9. RMB and U.S. dollar nominal effective exchange rates (Jun. 2010–May 2012). *Source*: www.bis.org (2010 = 100).

2.3.3. *The fluctuation interval of RMB exchange rates*

2.3.3.1. *The fluctuation interval of RMB exchange rates in the interbank foreign exchange market*

In the exchange rate system reform on July 21, 2005, the central bank announced that the daily closing price of the dollar exchange rate and other currencies against the RMB at the end of each working day would be regarded as the middle price of the currencies exchange rates against the RMB in the next working day. The U.S. dollar exchange rate against RMB in interbank foreign exchange market was allowed to float up and down within 3% of the middle price of the U.S. dollar. Meanwhile, the central bank also ruled that non-U.S. dollar currencies exchange rates against RMB floated up and down within 1.5% interval of central parity which was the closing price of non-U.S. dollar against RMB in the previous working day. In fact, from the perspective of triangular arbitrage, within each working day the changes of the RMB against non-U.S. dollar currencies can hardly reflect the movements of the U.S. dollar against non-U.S. dollar currency exchange rates in the international financial markets. The stable triangle relationship among the RMB against the U.S. dollar, the RMB against the non-U.S. dollar currencies and the dollar against non-U.S. dollar of the international financial markets may be difficult to maintain, so there may often exist stable foreign exchange arbitrage profits. So on January 4, 2006, the central bank announced that the middle price of the RMB exchange rates against the non-U.S. dollar currency was obtained by calculating the cross exchange rate (see Table 2.4).

Table 2.4. The floating range of inter-bank RMB exchange rates.

Date	The adjustment of middle price and floating interval of RMB exchange rates
July 21, 2005	The central bank ruled that the daily closing price of the dollar and other currencies against the RMB exchange rates at the end of each working day would be regarded as the middle price of the currencies against the RMB in the next working day in the interbank foreign exchange market. RMB exchange rate against U.S. dollar floated within 0.3% interval of the middle price announced by the central bank. Meanwhile, non-U.S. dollar currencies against RMB floated within 1.5% interval of the middle price announced by the central bank.
September 23, 2005	The floating interval of middle price of non-U.S. dollar currencies against RMB was expanded from 1.5% to 3%.
January 4, 2006	The central bank introduced inquiry transactions and the market maker system in the interbank foreign exchange market to determine the middle price of the daily RMB against the dollar; the middle prices of RMB against the euro, yen and HK dollar were determined by the China Foreign Exchange Trade Center to calculate the cross exchange rates based on the daily RMB against the U.S. dollar and the euro, yen, HK dollar exchange rates against the U.S. dollar at 9:00 a.m. in the international foreign exchange markets.
May 21, 2007	The floating interval of RMB exchange rate against the U.S. dollar expanded from 0.3% to 0.5%.
April 16, 2012	Since April 16, 2012, in the inter-bank foreign exchange market, the floating interval of RMB exchange rate against the U.S. dollar expanded from 0.5% to 1%. That is to say, the daily RMB exchange rate against the dollar in the inter-bank spot foreign exchange market could float within 1% interval of the daily middle price of the RMB against the dollar which was announced by the China Foreign Exchange Trade Center.

Source: ww.pbc.gov.cn.

The exchange rates of RMB against non-U.S. dollar currencies rely on RMB exchange rates against U.S. dollar. Hence, the floating interval of non-U.S. dollar currencies against RMB in the interbank foreign exchange market, the fluctuations interval of RMB against the U.S. dollar currency as well as the fluctuation range of U.S. dollar against non-dollar currencies all affect and restrict each other.

From the above, $S_1 \times S_2 \times S_3 = 1$, so $S_2 = \frac{1}{S_1 \times S_3}$. (Exchange rates S_1, S_2, S_3 are the middle prices), assuming the ceiling of the S_2 volatility is x. In order to prevent speculators' arbitrage, the following holds: $S_2(1+x) = \frac{(1+0.03)}{S_1(1-0.01) \times S_3}$, so we get $x = 0.0404$. If the floor of the S_2 is y, so $S_2(1-y) = \frac{(1-0.03)}{S_1(1+0.01) \times S_3}$, to obtain $y = 0.0396$.

Therefore, the fluctuation interval of S_1 is $[S_1(1-0.01), S_1(1+0.01)]$ and $1/S_3$ is $[1/S_3(1-0.03), 1/S_3(1+0.03)]$ (i.e. the fluctuation interval of S_3 is $[S_3/(1+0.03), S_3/(1-0.03)]$), and S_2 is $[S_2(1-0.0404), S_2(1+0.0396)]$.[10] In other words, if the central bank restricts the fluctuation intervals of the RMB exchange rates against the U.S. dollar and non-U.S. dollar currencies, it also restricts the fluctuation interval of the U.S. dollar exchange rates against non-U.S. dollar currencies indirectly, which, however, is determined by the international financial markets but not by the central bank. Therefore, once the volatility of S_2 is beyond $[S_2(1-0.0404), S_2(1+0.0396)]$ in the international financial markets, the fluctuation interval of the RMB exchange rates against the U.S. dollar and non-U.S. dollar currencies will not be able to meet with this change, implying there exists an arbitrage opportunity which can only be eliminated by adjusting the next day's middle price of the RMB exchange rates.

2.3.3.2. *The fluctuation interval of listed exchange rate of the commercial banks in the counter market*

In fact, after 21 July 2005, the central bank required that the buying and selling prices of the U.S. dollar against RMB listed for customers was not allowed to exceed 0.2% interval of the middle price of U.S. dollar which was announced by the central bank (see Table 2.5). The fluctuation interval in the counter market was smaller than that in the inter-bank market, which might cause commercial banks' losses since the selling price of U.S. dollar in the counter market might be lower than the selling price in the interbank market. Therefore, the banks had to fix the buying and

[10] Prior to April 14, 2012, the fluctuation interval of exchange rates was much smaller.

Table 2.5. The floating interval of commercial banks' listed exchange rate.

Date	Floating interval of commercial banks' listed rate
July 21, 2005	The buying and selling prices of RMB against the U.S. dollar listed for customers was not allowed to exceed up and down 0.2% interval of the middle price of U.S. dollar which was announced by the central bank. The buying and selling prices of foreign exchange cash should not exceed 1% interval of the middle price. The middle price of non-U.S. dollar currencies against the RMB in spot foreign exchange transaction listed by designated foreign exchange banks for customers was set by calculation and adjustment of cross exchange rates with reference to the middle price of U.S. dollar in the interbank foreign exchange market. The spread of buying price and selling price of non-U.S. dollar currencies against the RMB should not exceed 0.8% interval of the middle price of the spot foreign exchange buying and selling ([spot buying price – spot selling price]/the middle price of spot foreign exchange transaction $\times$ 100% $\leq$ 0.8%). The spread between cash selling price and cash buying price should not exceed 4% of the middle price in spot cash transaction ([cash selling price – cash buying price]/the middle price of spot cash transaction $\times$ 100% $\leq$ 4%).
September 23, 2005	The U.S. dollar exchange rates listed by the banks for customers were under spread margin management. The spread between the spot U.S. dollar selling price and buying price was not allowed to exceed 1% of the transaction middle price; the spread between cash selling price and buying price was not allowed to exceed 4%. The banks could adjust the daily listed U.S. dollar price within the stipulated spread independently. In addition, the spread limit of non-U.S. dollar currencies listed by the banks for the customers was cancelled. Banks could set the non-U.S. dollar currencies exchange rates against the RMB freely and the cash buying price and the spot foreign exchange buying price of all listed currencies could be negotiated with customers.
April 14, 2012	The spread between the highest U.S. dollar cash selling price and the lowest buying price listed by the designated foreign exchange banks for the customers daily was expanded from 1% to 2%, and other provisions were still enforced in compliance with Notification of the People's Bank of China on Relevant Issues Concerning Managements of the Exchange Rates in the Interbank Foreign Exchange Market and the Listed Exchange Rates by Designated Foreign Exchange Banks.

Source: www.pbc.gov.cn.

selling price of the listed rate at both ends of the floating intervals, which led to the banks' U.S. dollar listed exchange rate unchanged every day.

On September 23, 2005, the U.S. dollar exchange rate listed by the banks for customers was implemented under the spread margin management. The spread between the U.S. dollar selling price and buying price was not allowed to exceed 1% of the middle price. While in the interbank foreign exchange market, the U.S. dollar exchange rate against the RMB floated up and down within 0.5% interval of the middle price of the U.S. dollar announced by the central bank. The interval in the counter market was basically equal to that of the interbank market, but it was asymmetric and more flexible. On April 24, 2012, the central bank expanded the fluctuation intervals of the exchange rates of the interbank and the counter foreign exchange markets. If the central bank further liberalizes the floating interval of the U.S. dollar exchange rate against the RMB listed for customers by the banks, the floating interval of RMB against the U.S. dollar should be adjusted in the interbank foreign exchange market at the same time. If only the floating interval of RMB against the U.S. dollar is relaxed in the counter market, there may appear exchange rate arbitrage. If the price of buying U.S. dollar in the counter market is low, the banks will sell the U.S. dollars in the interbank market to obtain the profit and meanwhile the banks try to press down U.S. dollar price in the counter market. Therefore, if the fluctuation interval in the counter market is less than that in the interbank market, the banks may face losses; similarly, if the counter market interval is larger than that in the interbank market, banks can have exchange arbitrage opportunities. So the central bank needs to determine and coordinate the fluctuation interval of RMB exchange rate against the U.S. dollar in the counter market and the interbank market before RMB exchange rates are relaxed completely.

2.4. Exchange Rates, Interest Rates and the Openness of Capital Account in China

The stable exchange rates of RMB against the U.S. dollar may also somewhat weaken the independence of monetary policy in China. In order to maintain the stability of exchange rates, the central bank must intervene in the foreign exchange market, and monetary policy must serve for the stability of exchange rates and will lose the independence, so it is necessary to strengthen the coordination between monetary policy and exchange rates policies (Xie and Zhang, 2003). Based on China's situation, not only the RMB against the U.S. dollar remains relatively stable, but Hong Kong SAR does not have an independent monetary policy because Hong Kong dollar against U.S. dollar is fixed under the linked exchange rates system. Hong Kong is a small highly-open economy and the capital moves freely, according to the "impossible trinity" (Obstfeld *et al.*, 2004), when the HK dollar is pegged to the dollar with the free capital flows, independent monetary policy cannot exist, that is to say, in the case of free capital flows, Hong Kong should either choose the fixed exchange rates and give up independent monetary policy, or choose an independent monetary policy and abandon the fixed exchange rates. At last Hong Kong chooses the fixed exchange rates and gives up independent monetary policy. In order to maintain a fixed exchange rate, Hong Kong's interest rates must follow that of the United States. If the U.S. cuts the federal funds rate, Hong Kong must also lower its benchmark interest rates to maintain a high degree of consistency of the interest rates policy.

The Chinese mainland is slightly different. Though RMB against the U.S. dollar is stable, the independence of the monetary policy of the mainland is still relatively high because of RMB inconvertibility and capital control. However, as China continues to promote financial liberalization and capital control to be relaxed, independence of monetary policy will be declined. In order to maintain the fixed exchange rates, the central bank has to intervene in the foreign exchange market, which means passively buying dollars and selling RMB. Therefore, under a stable RMB exchange rate against the U.S. dollar, the mainland is facing the situation that is similar to Hong Kong. If the appreciating expectation of RMB increases, the capital will flow in and the central bank has to buy dollars and sell RMB. At the same time, the central bank must issue central bank bills to sterilize monetary base, so independence monetary policy will be affected to a certain extent.

In China under interest rates and exchange rates control, the adjustments of interest rates and exchange rates often face the conflict. Assuming i_t, i_t^* are interest rates of the domestic currency and foreign currency from the period t to $t + 1$. S_t is the spot exchange rate in the

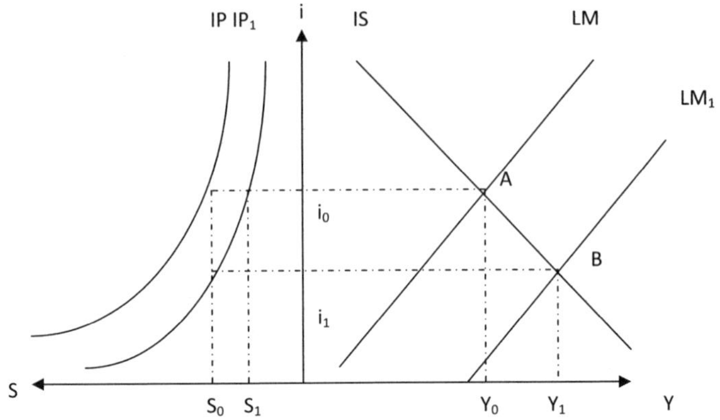

Fig. 2.10. Contradiction between interest rate and exchange rate stability.

foreign exchange market (the exchange rate is in a direct quotation). E_tS_{t+1} is the expected spot exchange rate of $t + 1$. The interest rates parity is:

$$E_tS_{t+1}(1+i_t*)=S_t(1+i_t)$$

or

$$(E_tS_{t+1}-S_t)/S_t=(i_t-i_t*)/(1+i_t*)$$

In Figure 2.10, IP is the interest rates parity relationship in the left, and the right is the IS-LM curve. The initial equilibrium is at point A, and the interest rate is i_0, the exchange rate is S_0.

If RMB is expected to appreciate, that is to say, E_tS_{t+1} will decline, and IP will move rightward to IP_1; if we maintain the exchange rate at S_0, arbitrage capital will flow in to increase foreign exchange, money supply will also increase at the fixed rate, and the LM curve moves rightward to LM_1. Equilibrium point will be at B and the interest rate declines to i_1.[11] If the economy is on the way of expanding, in order to control the over-heated economy, the central bank will tighten money supply and issue the central bank bills for sterilization which make LM_1 back to LM and the

[11] If the currency is expected to depreciate, the result is exactly the opposite.

interest rate will return to i_0. At this moment, arbitrage capital will continue to flow into the domestic market.[12] Thus, if there exists the expectation of appreciation, money will expand and the interest rates will decline under stabilizing the exchange rate, which will lead to domestic inflation. Meanwhile the central bank tightens money with rising interest rate may cause speculative arbitrage capital inflows.

In fact, it is the dilemma that the central bank is facing. For instance, during the global financial crisis, the loose monetary policy in America led to the devaluation of the U.S. dollar and the appreciation pressure on RMB. In order to stabilize the exchange rate, the central bank had to buy foreign exchange and put in RMB, the central bank had no autonomy of monetary policy. That is to say, the monetary policy is mainly used to maintain the stable exchange rate, thus the independence of the monetary policy is lost.

In short, Hong Kong is the currency board system which features the fixed exchange rate, complete capital flows but no independent monetary policy. In the Chinese mainland, even if the RMB against the U.S. dollar exchange rate remains relatively stable, the capital does not completely flow, and the monetary policy is to some extent independent. Meanwhile, the American monetary policy is completely independent. So Hong Kong's interest rates have to go along with the Fed and the American monetary policy has a great spillover effect on Chinese mainland and Hong Kong.

Along with the increase of the flexibility of the RMB exchange rate and gradual opening of the capital account, RMB exchange rate can better reflect the changes of market demand and supply in the future. The independence of monetary policy will also be further enhanced. In the open economy, monetary authorities can realize macroeconomic goals through a mix of the monetary policy and fiscal policy (Mundell, 1963). In the liberalization reform of interest rate and exchange rate, the rhythm, the sequence and the intensity of relaxing the fluctuated intervals in the exchange rate and interest rate should be arranged and coordinated (McKinnon, 1993) in order to keep financial market relatively stable.

---

[12]From 2007 to 2008, the RMB appreciated continuously and the central bank raised interest rates several times, which led to the increase of short-term capital inflows.

2.5. The Future Liberalization of Interest Rates and Exchange Rates

2.5.1. *Policy recommendations for China's market-oriented interest rates reform*

Compared with the quantitative instruments of monetary policy, price instruments (mainly interest rates) may be more effective (Zhang, 2009). In general, people often suspect whether there are some necessary connections between financial liberalization and financial crisis. The economist, M.J. Fry, thought that lack of adequate management and supervision was the main reason of failure in the financial reform (Fry, 1995). In China, market-oriented reforms of interest rates mainly focused on lessening controls on interest rates and increasing the floating interval of the interest rates. However, due to a high degree of the monopoly of state-owned banks, the competitiveness of the credit market was very weak. So market-oriented reforms of interest rates should break up high concentration in the banking industry and encourage market entry. Currently, a fully competitive credit market have not been set up, and private loans need to be further standardized. The difficulties of SMEs loans have become increasingly prominent and it is hard to form a competitive market interest rate. Therefore, the market-oriented reforms of interest rates in China should not only focus on interest rates themselves but improve market basis in breadth and depth.

1. Breaking up monopoly of state-owned banks and encouraging private capital into the financial sector are the next important steps of China's financial reform. The pricing of financial products will become more reasonable when monopoly is broken up, which will benefit market-oriented reforms of deposit and lending rates.[13]

[13]On March 28, 2012, the central government decided to set up the comprehensive experimental zone of financial reform in Wenzhou in order to standardize the development of private financing. New policies included: Encourage and support private capital to participate in the reform of the local financial institutions; establish or share the equity in new financial organizations such as village banks, small-loan companies, and rural fund cooperatives in accordance with the law. Comprehensive experimental zone of financial reform in Wenzhou would promote the liberalization of interest rates as well as the

2. Developing small-loan companies and village banks. The CBRC (China Banking Regulatory Commission) promulgated "*Guidance Suggestions on Small-loan Company Experiment*" in 2008, in which the investors of great fortune were encouraged to finance SMEs and the interest rates could be adjusted freely based on current market funds conditions. Small-loan companies and village banks are beneficial to relieving the financing problems of SMEs and increase the sources of funds.[14]
3. Establishing a deposit insurance system. Over the years, although the deposit insurance system has not been implemented in China, the public believes that the government must intervene once severe problems appeared in the banks, which actually is an implicit guarantee by the government. Compared with the implicit insurance, explicit deposit insurance are more effective, banks will have to bear the part of the cost and can operate cautiously. However, under implicit deposit insurance system, as there is no clear responsibilities and obligations, rent-seeking behavior of banks will take place, which is not conducive to the improvement of operational efficiency, regulation and information transparency. Recently, China has been determined to break up banking monopoly and encouraged private capital to enter into the financial sector. Therefore, the establishment of deposit insurance system will be accelerated, which will create a favorable external environment for the financial reform.
4. Gradually relaxing the floating interval of lending and deposit rates. As Chinese enterprises' financing mainly comes from bank loan, with the progress of the interest rate liberalization, the banks should take initiative of funds pricing. Commercial banks should have the courage and the capacity to bear the responsibility of the risk-based pricing; the central bank will gradually loosen the floating interval of RMB interest rates, and the RMB interest rates will be determined more by commercial banks themselves.

---

standardization and the legalization of private lending. Wenzhou would go ahead in the liberalization of interest rates and its successful experience would be the reform model for the whole country.

[14]In fact, eligible small-loan companies in Wenzhou were still able to be transformed into a village bank.

5. Controlling the inflation. On the one hand, inflation leads to the decline of real interest rates which is not conducive to the efficient allocation of resources; on the other hand, it seriously interferes with the expectation of the residents and enterprises, which leads to the unstable and unreasonable pricing of financial products.
6. Establishing a perfect credit rating system. China should set up authoritative credit rating agencies, including assessment for commercial banks and enterprises according to business and credit conditions, which plays an important role in the determination of the interest rates level. Different credit ratings of the banks and the enterprises will have different interest rates. For example, both the central bank to different financial institutions and the commercial banks to different enterprises should choose the different interest rates by different credit ratings.
7. Perfecting laws, regulations and the supervision system. In the process of carrying out the financial institution reform, it is important to accelerate the reform of financial institutions (Lardy, 1998), improve management and operational efficiency, reduce non-performing loans, and strengthen its supervision, improving the funds efficiency, which will make interest rates truly reflect the financing situation.

2.5.2. *Reform on the middle price of the RMB exchange rates*

With the gradual opening up of China's capital account, the flexibility of RMB exchange rate should be enhanced further, the pace of the RMB market-oriented reforms should adapt to the transformation of China's economic structure. In the past, external demand was an important engine of China's economic growth, economic growth and trade surplus had been the goals of macroeconomic policy and the RMB pegged or crawlingly pegged to the dollar, which was the first phase and it came to end. On July 21, 2005, although the RMB exchange reform was implemented to establish the RMB exchange rate regime with reference to a basket of currencies, however, in fact the RMB exchange rate was still pegged to the dollar. If the central bank sets the daily middle price of the RMB against the U.S. dollar based on target of the RMB effective exchange rate,[15] the flexibility of the RMB against the U.S. dollar exchange rate will increase significantly. RMB effective exchange rate is the good representative of a basket of currencies. Actually, the establishment of the RMB exchange rate with reference to a basket of currencies is just the second and transitory stage. In the third phase, RMB exchange rate should be determined by market supply and demand freely. RMB exchange rate movements will reflect the optimization of consumers and producers, and the exchange rate will converge to the equilibrium level of real exchange rate. At this stage the main driving power of economic growth should be domestic demand, the contribution of external demand to economic growth will gradually decline, and the RMB exchange rate will play the role in resources allocation and market regulation.

In sum, the reform of the exchange rate system in China will be improved step by step, following the initiative, progressive and controllable principles and gradually increasing the flexibility. With the transformation of the style of China's economic growth, domestic demand, especially household consumption, will increase substantially, foreign demand is no longer the important engine of economic growth, the liberalization of RMB exchange rate system reform will adapt to the adjustment of the economic structure and the change of the goals of monetary policy.

2.5.3. *Enlarging the fluctuation interval of the RMB exchange rate*

With the opening up of the financial market, the supply and demand of the foreign exchange will change more frequently. The central bank should continue to expand the fluctuation interval of the RMB against the U.S. dollar exchange rate, which is conductive to determining a reasonable RMB exchange rate. At the same time, the RMB exchange rates against the non-U.S. dollar currencies are mainly affected by the RMB exchange rate against the U.S. dollar and the U.S. dollar against other

[15] Of course, the target of the effective exchange rate can be changed according to specific economic situation.

non-U.S. dollar currencies exchange rates in the international financial markets. So the interval of RMB exchange rates against non-U.S. dollar currencies also needs to be expanded.

If the RMB exchange rate refers to the target of effective exchange rate, assuming the daily movements of the basket of currencies is up and down within α% interval of middle price of effective exchange rate [$NEER_t(1 + \alpha\%)$, $NEER_t\ (1 - \alpha\%)$], then the daily fluctuation interval of the RMB against the U.S. dollar or non-U.S. dollar currency rates can be determined at the same time.

In this process, firstly, the fluctuations of the RMB against the non-U.S. dollar currencies should be liberalized. Next the fluctuations of the RMB against the U.S. dollar exchange rate should be expanded until the market-oriented exchange rate of the RMB against the U.S. dollar is determined. China will realize the ultimate goal that RMB exchange rates move on the basis of self-adjustment of the market supply and demand.

In fact, the liberalization of the RMB exchange rate is also a comprehensive process which needs to be accompanied by multiple measures.

Firstly, reform the administration system of the foreign exchange. At present, the deregulation of foreign exchange control is more reflected in buying and selling foreign exchanges. There is still a need to further improve the investment of foreign exchange. Therefore, China should continue to deepen the foreign exchange administration system reform, loosen restrictions on foreign exchange investment overseas, and encourage domestic residents to make full use of the international financial market to optimize asset investment, disperse investment risk, and increase capital return. These foreign exchange administration reforms will be conducive to promote the liberalization of RMB exchange rates.

Secondly, reduce the intervention of the central bank in the foreign exchange market. The intervention of the central bank is also an important factor which influences the movement of the RMB exchange rates. Besides the buyers and sellers in the foreign exchange market, the central bank is one of the biggest foreign exchange market participants. Usually the intervention of the central bank is to keep the foreign exchange markets healthy and orderly, prevent the large fluctuation of the exchange rate, and eliminate the shock of the short-term capital. However, if the central bank keeps long-term consistent intervention, it will be hard to find the real market exchange rate and the public also tend to get the wrong expectations of exchange rates, which mean the exchange rate will not be able to accurately reflect the supply and demand of the market. So it is important to gradually reduce the central bank intervention in the foreign exchange market and make the RMB exchange rate regulated by the market mechanism.

Thirdly, develop the foreign exchange derivatives market. The liberalization of the exchange rates means that the fluctuations of the RMB exchange rates will be more frequent and the uncertainty of the RMB exchange rates will increase, so the foreign exchange risks that enterprises and residents face will be greater. It is necessary to actively promote the development of foreign exchange derivatives market, and introduce more financial instruments of the foreign exchange market to avoid risks such as forwards, futures and options products, etc. The liberalization of exchange rates and the development of foreign exchange derivatives market interact with each other and help each other.

In addition, the coordination between the RMB exchange rate and interest rate is really necessary. In China, the movements of the RMB exchange rates and the interest rates are basically isolated and the linkage is quite weak. In the developed financial markets, the exchange rates are quite sensitive to movements of interest rates. At present, the central bank can control them to a certain degree. In order to perfect the pricing mechanism and give full play to the function of market mechanism, the central bank should also gradually shift to rely on the adjustments of the base interest rates to affect the RMB exchange rates. Thus the movements of the RMB exchange rates and interest rates are largely depending on the supply and demand in the local currency market and foreign currency market.

To sum up, along with the development of the financial market in China, China should further perfect the forming mechanism of interest rates to establish a reasonable structure and levels of the interest rates, which is beneficial to the macro-regulation of the central bank. At the same time, China should introduce private capital to participate in the competition, gradually promote the liberalization of the interest rates, which is determined by the market mechanism and adjusted by the central bank. Similarly, the free floating of the RMB exchange rate and market-oriented system reform will be closely associated. The market-oriented reform of the RMB exchange rate is a systematic project (Lin and Schramm, 2003), which needs a wide range of coordinated measures so as to form the market-oriented RMB exchange rate determined by supply and demand of the market.

References

China Financial Yearbook (2009). China Financial Publishing House.

Fry, M.J. (1995). *Money, Interest and Banking in Economic Development*, Second Edition. Baltimore: The Johns Hopkins University Press.

Goldstein, M. and Lardy, N. (2003). "Two-Stage Currency Reform for China." *Wall Street Journal*, September 12.

Hong, Y.M., Lin, H. and Wang, S.Y. (2010). Modeling the Dynamics of Chinese Spot Interest Rates." *Journal of Banking & Finance*, 34(5), 1047–1061.

Huang, H.Z. and Wang, S.L. (2004). "Exchange Rates Regimes: China's Experience and Choices." *China Economic Review*, 15(3), 336–342.

Koivu, T. (2009). "Has the Chinese Economy Become More Sensitive to Interest Rates? Studying Credit Demand in China." *China Economic Review*, 20(3), 455–470.

Kong, X.Y. (1994). *Practical Interest Rates Management*. China Financial Publishing House (Chinese).

Lardy, N.R. (1998). *China's Unfinished Economic Revolution*. Brookings Institution Press.

Lin, G.J. and Schramm, R.M. (2003). "China's Foreign Exchange Policies Since 1979: A Review of Developments and an Assessment." *China Economic Review*, 14(3), 246–280.

Lu, D. (2004). China's Capability to Control its Exchange Rates. *China Economic Review*, 15(3), 343–347.

Ma, G.N. and McCauley, R.N. (2011). The Evolving Renminbi Regime and Implications for Asian Currency Stability." *Journal of the Japanese and International Economies*, 25(1), 23–38.

Mao, Y.S. (2011). "How Does Planned Economy Succeed?" Available from http://blog.sina.com.cn/s/blog_49a3971d0102dtxo.html.

McKinnon, R. (1993). *The Order of Economic Liberalization: Financial Control in the Transition to a Market Economy*, Johns Hopkins Studies in Development. Baltimore: John Hopkins University Press.

McKinnon, R. (1973). *Money and Capital in Economic Development*. Washington: The Brookings Institution.

Mehrotra, A.N. (2007). "Exchange and Interest Rates Channels During A Deflationary Era — Evidence from Japan, Hong Kong and China." *Journal of Comparative Economics*, 35(1), 188–210.

Mundell, R.A. (1963). "Capital Mobility and Stabilization Policy Under Fixed and Flexible Exchange Rates." *Canadian Journal of Economics and Political Science*, 29(November), 475–485.

Obstfeld, M., Shambaugh, J. and Taylor, A. (2004). "Monetary Sovereignty, Exchange Rates, and Capital Controls: The Trilemma in the Interwar Period." National Bureau of Economic Research, Working Paper No. 10393.

Shaw, E.S. (1973). *Financial Deepening in Economic Development*. Oxford University Press.

Shen, J.G. (2001). "China's Exchange Rates System after WTO Accession: Some Consideration." Working Paper, Bank of Finland Institute for Economies in Transition.

Tung, C.Y. and Baker, S. (2004). "RMB Revaluation will Serve China's Self-Interest." *China Economic Review*, 15(3), 331–335.

Williamson, J. (2006) "How Does the Basket Peg Work?" *International Economic Review*, 1, 39–40 (Chinese).

Wu, N.L. and Chen, Q.G. (2002). *Research on the RMB Exchange Rates*. China Financial Publishing House (Chinese).

Xie, P. and Zhang, X.P. (2003). "The Coordination Between Monetary Policy and Exchange Rates Policy in an Open Economy in Transition: A Case Study on China from 1994 to 2000." *Journal of Asian Economics*, 14(2), 327–336.

Zhang, W.L. (2009). "China's Monetary Policy: Quantity Versus Price Rules." *Journal of Macroeconomics*, 31(3), 473–484.

Zhang, Z.C. (2001). "Choosing an Exchange Rates Regime During Economic Transition: The Case of China." *China Economic Review*, 12(2–3), 203–226.

CHAPTER 3

CHINA'S LABOUR MARKET, RURAL-URBAN MIGRATION AND GROWTH PATTERN: FUTURE PROSPECT

*Zhao Chen, Shiqing Jiang, Ming Lu and Hiroshi Sato**

3.1. Introduction

Rural-to-urban migration and hence urbanization are key symbols of economic development. Especially for developing countries, policies promoting migration from the countryside to cities are structural forces for sustainable growth. However, in post-reform China, large-scale rural-to-urban migration is accompanied by fast industrialization, but low level of urbanization. China has become a world-wide manufacturing center. In contrast, as a consequence of migration-constraining institutions like

*We thank Jack W. Hou, Hubert Jayet, Mark Rosenzweig, Yves Zenou, Yaohui Zhao and seminar/conference participants at K. U. Leuven, Fudan University, University of Lille 1, Xiamen University, and Zhejiang University for their useful comments. We gratefully acknowledge financial support for the CHIP 2002 survey provided mainly by the Ford Foundation, the Swedish International Development Cooperation Agency (SIDA) and partly by the Japan Society for the Promotion of Science (JSPS) and Hitotsubashi University. Financial support from the Chinese Ministry of education, the Shanghai Leading Academic Discipline Project (B101), JSPS Grants-in-Aid for Scientific Research (No. 18203018), the Heiwa Nakajima Foundation, and the Global COE Program "Research Unit for Statistical and Empirical Analysis in Social Sciences," Hitotsubashi University, and the Fukino Project, Hitotsubashi University, is also gratefully acknowledged.

hukou (a residential permit system) and land system, the urbanization process has not fully promoted consumption growth. So migration and urbanization are a fundamental issue in the understanding of China's growth pattern. Apparently, any analysis on China's migration and urbanization should be able to explain its current situation.

Many empirical studies have explored migration determination. In migration studies for China, the classical framework is also applicable. Using cross-sectional data in the Sichuan rural areas, Zhao (1999a, 1999b) finds evidence consistent with findings in other countries: male workers have a higher probability of outward migration, while aging and more household land area will significantly decrease the probability of migration. Zhu (2002) finds that the income gap between farming and nonfarm activities will affect the migration decision, which is consistent with the Harris–Todaro model. Cai *et al.* (2003) discover that although the income gap between west and east China is greater than that between middle and east China, migration is more prevalent from middle to east than from west to east, which seems to contradict the Harris–Todaro prediction but still can be explained by distance effects.

Recent studies add the role of social networks to the analysis of the migration decision. Using Chinese data, Zhang and Li (2003) find that rural residents have higher probability in nonfarm employment if their family has social ties outside the village. Bao *et al.* (2007) find that province-to-province migration rates rise with the size of the migrant community in the destination province. Zhao (2003) shows that larger numbers of local experienced migrants will significantly increase the migration probability of villagers in the same village, and she argues that this is the result of job information sharing among villagers.

However, the existing empirical studies cannot well explain why urbanization seriously lags behind industrialization in China. This encourages us to further explore the determination of labour migration. In this chapter, we attempt to answer two questions. First, how does the neighborhood effect — interdependence in decision making — affect the migration decisions of rural residents in China? Second, how do heterogeneous social distances affect the neighborhood effect in migration?[1] As Bauer *et al.*

[1]Before we go further to focus on the heterogeneity of neighborhood effect, we first explain why we use the term "neighborhood effect", instead of "network effect", in this

(2002) point out, peers in the community also contribute to herd effect, another name of neighborhood effect, and within-community interdependence of behavior, even in the presence of migration networks. In fact, in rural China, villagers form strong social and economic ties in their daily lives, so the behavior of a person would be affected by his or her village neighbors. Bauer *et al.* (2002) and Araujo *et al.* (2004) find strong evidence that neighborhood effects exist in labour migration from rural Mexico to urban areas and from Mexico to the USA, respectively. In our study, using data from rural China, we further confirm the existence of the neighborhood effect in labour migration. The existing literature of neighborhood effect in labour migration has not told us how the magnitude of neighborhood effect and the corresponding social multiplier are determined. Using CHIPS 2002 (2002 Chinese Household Income Project Survey) data, we find strong evidence that the neighborhood effect exists in the outward migration decision in rural China. In the presence of the neighborhood effect, other policies, such as increasing the education of rural residents, have larger effects than previous estimates because of the spillover of the neighborhood effect or the so-called social multiplier (Glaeser *et al.*, 2003).

The presence of the neighborhood effect implies multiple equilibria in labour migration, either a low-level equilibrium, which may be the current situation in China's rural-to-urban migration as our model shows, or a high-level one. If social interactions of different types and frequencies affect the neighborhood effect in migration, new social policy tools can be utilized to push ahead rural-to-urban migration and urbanization. Policy makers seeking to encourage outward migration can either promote information sharing among villagers or substitute within-village mutual help in farm work by providing more efficient services to rural residents. When migration is trapped in the low equilibrium with neighborhood effect, those social multiplier enhancing policy tools, together with direct migration promoting

---

chapter. Network can be distinguished as within-community (bonding) and cross-community (bridging) network. Relatives and friends outside the community constitute bridging network, while within-community network is the social network that provides information to reduce migration costs. Focusing on within-village social interaction and network, we prefer to use the terminology, neighborhood effect, while we also control out-of-village network in the empirical model.

policies, may not be enough to help rural people escape the low equilibrium of migration ratio. Therefore, the policy makers should eliminate urban-rural divide and urban-biased policies and accelerate social integration between rural and urban areas. This is another policy implication in our chapter: the institutional "big-push" in China.

The rest of this chapter is organized as follows. Section 3.2 reviews the institutional background and stylized facts of labour migration and urbanization in China. Section 3.3 establishes a simple model to demonstrate how the neighborhood effect is affected by heterogeneous social distances. Section 3.4 describes the data and Section 3.5 presents the econometric model and empirical findings. In Section 3.6 we do some robustness checks. Section 3.7 contains the policy simulation of how rural-to-urban migration can be enhanced based on our empirical model, and the final section concludes with policy implications.

3.2. Migration, Urbanization and Growth Pattern: Institutions and Facts

3.2.1. *Institutional backgrounds*

In China, rural-to-urban migration and urbanization is constrained by several urban-biased policies, as well as an obstacle of the current land system. Particularly, discrimination against migrant workers is represented in three aspects, which are employment, social security and public service, respectively.

First, migrants are facing discriminatory employment policies. In early times, city governments used to restrict enterprises from recruiting migrant workers through direct regulations, by levying extra fees on those enterprises using migrant workers as a major means. Meanwhile, migrant workers were kept out of certain industries and job positions. Today, although most discriminatory policies are abolished, it is almost impossible for migrant workers without local urban *hukou* to enter either government agencies or high-income monopolistic industries. Using recent survey data from China Health and Nutrition Survey (CHNS) in 2006, Qiao *et al.* (2009) find that higher income jobs are almost all occupied by those with urban *hukou*. Even in inferior labour market, urban residents are in more favorable positions. Zhou and He (2009) found that since the 1990s, most of rural workers have found jobs in private sectors (so-called *tizhi wai* — literally "without the system", i.e., not taken care of by the governments), few of whom are able to enter public sectors (*tizhi nei* — "within the system").

Second, discrimination in social security system. Present social security system in China is maintained by the local fiscal resources and operated at city level independently. Thus, social security system is mainly open for local residents. Even if some cities provide social security services for migrants in particular, the welfare secured is lower and participation rate of migrants is quite low. It is worth mentioning that, although Chinese government has put much effort to make personal pension account transferable across regions, it is hitherto not realized. Under present rules, in general, a migrant cannot receive pension until he has contributed to the system for 15 years in the place where he works. If having paid less than 15 years, he has to quit the system. Thus, only the funds contributed by himself in the personal account can be withdrawn, while the contribution paid by the employer should be left to the system, which is quite a large loss to the migrants.

Third, discrimination in public services, especially in education. Some services provided by local governments such as landscaping and public transportation, are not discriminative. However, there are still public services that are linked to *hukou* identity, among which children's education is particularly important. Beginning from kindergarten, without a local urban *hukou*, a child cannot be enrolled at a public kindergarten by paying the standard fee for local residents. As for compulsory education, local public school did not receive migrants' children in the past. Even if some migrants' children were admitted to public schools, fees paid were higher, which leads to the emergence of many schools for migrants' children. Obviously, education quality of such schools is much more inferior to that of the public ones, for they are not supported by local public finance. Now public primary and secondary schools open their doors to migrants, while those best schools have not yet admitted migrants' children equally as local urban students. Moreover, cities with concentrated resources of higher education tend to allocate more university admission quotas to local students. Migrants' children have to return to their hometown to take college entrance exams, where competition is much more intense. Apparently, this will result in inequality in higher education opportunities. Besides, it will hinder inter-generational income and social mobility. A related discriminative policy is that senior high school education in cities, especially big cities, is actually not equally accessible for migrants.[2]

Rural-to-urban and cross-regional migration is facing another obstacle from the current land system. To maintain "national food security", Chinese government has to keep certain amount of agricultural land, which leads to the "construction land quota system". Every year the central government determines the total quota. Although in distributing the quotas to every province, the central government has considered the different demand for economic development of different areas, yet the allocation of land quota is more biased to equalitarianism. The consequence is: the coastal areas which are in deadly need of construction land are in lack of quotas, while inland areas are given quotas more than what they need. The land use efficiency in inland is much lower than that in coastal areas. Suppose there is a trading mechanism that those areas which need more quotas than allocated could buy quotas from those who need less quotas than allocated, so that buying areas could turn more agricultural land into land for non-agricultural use, while selling areas need to increase agricultural land reservation equivalently. However, until the writing of this chapter, trading quota of construction land across provinces is still prohibited. Every migrant family from countryside to city owns a piece of residential land. By nature, a piece of residential land is corresponding to a construction land quota, which is banned from being traded as assets. Consequently, migrants tend to go back to their hometown since their residential land use rights are not tradable.

3.2.2. *Stylized facts of migration and urbanization*

Although all kinds of institutional rural-to-urban and cross-regional segmentations have made the mobility of Chinese labour far from free and

[2]See Wang and Zuo (1999) for an early comment on social segmentation between groups of people with different kinds of *hukou*.

sufficient, labour migration has still developed into a large scale in the process of industrialization, urbanization and globalization. If we have to summarize the most important characteristics of Chinese labour migration, we think that there are two main points.

First, in time dimension, the scale of Chinese labour migration increased fast over time. Until the beginning of the 1990s, the scale of cross-regional and rural-to-urban labour migration was still small. However, nowadays, the scale of Chinese labour migration is very large. According to the second National Agriculture Census, the number of migrants employed outside their villages reached 132 million in 2006, accounting for 25% of the total labour resources in rural areas. If adding 80–90 million rural workers employed in local non-agricultural activities, then the amount of rural labour force transferred to non-agricultural sector is approximately 210–220 million, more than 40% of the total rural labour resources.[3] Based on the survey of National Bureau of Statistics, Sheng (2008) provided the time series estimation of the scale of labour migrations, from which the growing trend of migration is quite clear. See Table 3.1.

Second, in the pattern of labour migration, labour migration from rural areas to cities in China has shown the short-term features, but not the whole household migration. In cities, migrants from rural areas cannot share equal rights as urban citizens have in employment, social security and children's education, which largely increase the uncertainty of income from working outside hometown, thus reduce the real income. Meanwhile, living expenses in cities such as housing are very high, preventing the whole family migration. Besides, for migrants who do not live with their family in the city, nor can they take care of the family members, they are facing extremely high psychological costs in the cities. If they move the whole family to city and leave their lands deserted, it is possible to lose the land use rights. So leaving the elderly and women in the countryside is also a rational choice. According to Sheng's (2008) estimation, the percentage of workers migrating with the whole family in total rural labour force was about 5% in 2005, while the percentage of all

---

[3]Source: Second National Agriculture Census, main data announcement (No. 5). http://www.stats.gov.cn/tjgb/nypcgb/qgnypcgb/t20080227_402464718.htm.

Table 3.1. The scale of rural labour force migration (1985–2005).

	Total amount of rural workers (in 10000)	Local rural workers in non-agricultural industries	Proportion of non-agricultural workers in rural areas (%)	Workers employed outside rural areas (in 10000)	Proportion of workers employed outside rural areas (%)	Migration from rural to urban areas (in 10000)#	Urbanization ratio calculated by population with urban *hukou* (%)
1985	37065	6233	16.8	800	2.2	260	20.2
1986	37990	6682	17.6	900	2.4	248	20.9
1987	39000	7050	18.1	1050	2.7	235	21.6
1988	40076	7361	18.4	1250	3.1	290	21.9
1989	40939	7558	18.5	1500	3.7	212	22.1
1990	42010	7694	18.3	1800	4.3	198	21.6
1991	43093	7916	18.4	2140	5	228	21.8
1992	43802	8380	19.1	2592	5.9	221	22.2
1993	44256	9209	20.8	2752	6.2	222	22.9
1994	44654	9798	21.9	2888	6.5	223	23.6
1995	45042	10257	22.8	3000	6.7	254	24.3
1996	45288	10378	22.9	3400	7.5	257	24.9
1997	45962	10610	23.1	3890	8.5	299	26
1998	46432	10804	23.3	4936	10.6	339	26.3
1999	46897	10955	23.4	5240	11.1	377	26.7
2000	47962	11224	23.4	7600	15.8	507	26.8
2001	48229	11532	23.9	9050	18.8	258	26.8
2002	48472	11873	24.5	10470	21.6	780	27.2
2003	48884	12080	24.7	11390	23.3	694	27.5
2004	49676	12753	25.6	11823	23.8	520	27.5
2005	50387	13480	26.7	12578	24.2	600	27.7

Source: Sheng (2008) Page 9, Table 1-4 and Page 72, Table 5-1.

Note: # "Migration from rural to urban area" means those migrants who have received urban *hukou*. For this amount of people is much less than the total population of migrant labour force, the urbanization ratio calculated by population with urban *hukou* is far less than the real ratio by using permanent residents.

worker employed outside was nearly 20%. However, evidence also shows that migration is becoming long-term. The trend is that whole family migration and women migration seem to be more popular recently (Robert, 2005; Duan *et al.*, 2008; Hou, 2009).

3.2.3. *Lagged urbanization and growth pattern*

In post-reform China, large-scale rural-to-urban migration is accompanied by fast industrialization, but low level of urbanization. With the sufficient labour supply from the agricultural sector, China has become a worldwide manufacturing center. In contrast, as a consequence of migration-constraining institutions, the urbanization process has seriously lagged behind industrialization. Figure 3.1 shows the trend of industrialization and urbanization since the late 1970s. The share of secondary industry in GDP has kept at around 50%. Because of the faster growth of tertiary sector, the share of secondary plus tertiary sectors has kept rising to around 90%. The proportion of non-agricultural population is also going up, but it is still lower than 50%. We should notice that non-agricultural population includes those migrants, as long as they live in a city for more than 6 months per year, although they do not have a local urban *hukou*. As Table 3.2 presents, if only people with urban *hukou* are counted as urban, the urbanization ratio was even lower than 30% in 2005.

The urbanization process should have promoted faster consumption growth, which does not take place in China. Compared with urban residents, migrants have higher mobility, lower social safety net coverage and face stronger credit constraints. Thus, the *hukou* system has seriously constrained migrants' consumption. According to the estimation by Chen *et al.* (2010),

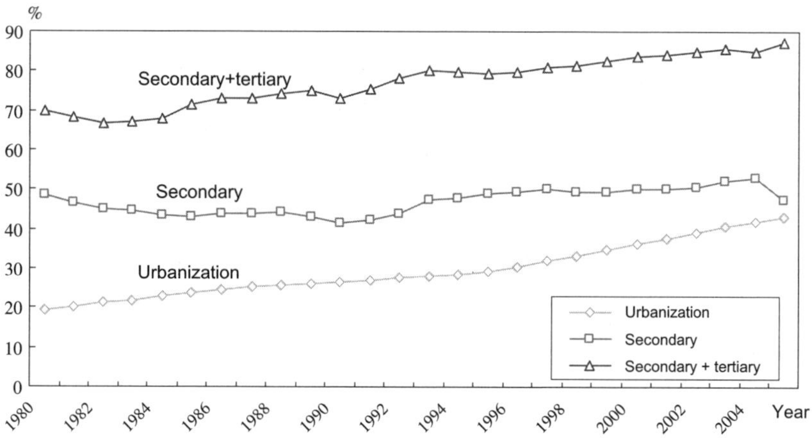

Fig. 3.1. Industrialization and urbanization (1980–2005).

Table 3.2. The variable definition.

Neighborhood effect	**Village migration ratio (NE) village mig ratio 1998**	**Village migration ratio (excluding one's own family) in 2002 village migration ratio in 1998**
Individual characteristics	female	dummy variable, female = 1
	age	age
	married	dummy, married = 1
	primary school	dummy, if education is primary school, primary school = 1
	junior high school	dummy, if education is junior high school, junior high school = 1
	senior high school	dummy, if education is senior high school, senior high school = 1
	tech school or more	dummy, if education is technical school or college education, tech school or more = 1
	communist	dummy, if respondent is communist party member, communist = 1
	health good	dummy, if health is very good or good, health good = 1
	health bad	dummy, if health is very bad or bad, health bad = 1
Family characteristics	household labour force	the number of labour force of a family
	family per capita land	family per capita land
	kids no. under 6	the number of children under age six of a family
	kids no. between 6 and 12	the number of children aging between six and twelve of a family
	elder no. over 65	the number of elders over age 65 of a family
	friends or relatives outside	dummy, if a family has friends and relatives outside village, friends or relatives outside = 1
	friends or relatives village cadre	dummy, if a family has friends and relatives as village cadre, friends or relatives village cadre = 1

(*Continued*)

Table 3.2. (*Continued*)

Neighborhood effect	Village migration ratio (NE) village mig ratio 1998	Village migration ratio (excluding one's own family) in 2002 village migration ratio in 1998
Village characteristics	distance to nearest transportation terminal	the distance from village to a nearest transportation terminal, unit: kilometers
	distance to the country seat	the distance from village to the county seat, unit: kilometers
	village per capita income	village per capita income, unit: hundred Yuan
	mountain area	dummy, if a village locates in the mountain area, mountain area = 1
	hill area	dummy, if a village locates in the hill area, hill area = 1
Social interaction with other villagers	info exchange	Cardinal order variable, with "exchange information of employment" "very frequently", "often", "just so so", "sometimes" and "none/few" as 5, 4, 3, 2, 1, respectively.
	mutual help	Cardinal order variable, with "mutual-help during busy season" "very frequently", "often", "just so so", "sometimes" and "none/few" as 5, 4, 3, 2, 1, respectively.
	info very frequently	dummy, if "exchange information of employment" is "very frequently", information very frequently = 1
	info often	dummy, if "exchange information of employment" is "often", information often = 1
	info just so so	dummy, if "exchange information of employment" is "just so so", information just so so = 1
	info sometimes	dummy, if "exchange information of employment" is "sometimes", information sometimes = 1
	help very frequently	dummy, if "mutual-help during busy season" is "very frequently", help very frequently = 1
	help often	dummy, if "mutual-help during busy season" is "often", help often = 1
	help just so so	dummy, if "mutual-help during busy season" is "just so so", help just so so = 1
	help sometimes	dummy, if "mutual-help during busy season" is "sometimes", help sometimes = 1

the marginal consumption rate of migrants is lower than that of urban residents by about 14.6 percentage points. Without considering the general equilibrium effects of the policy change, they estimate that, if restriction of *hukou* were removed in 2002, average consumption of migrants would rise by 20.8%, and aggregate consumption would grow by 2.2%, which could compensate for about 47.1% in the decline in household consumption during 2002–2003. Using the estimates of their model, the migrants' consumption constrained by the *hukou* system can explain about 40.8%–64.2% of the decline in household consumption during 2000–2005.

Since urbanization has not fully promoted consumption growth, China relies heavily on investment and export to fully engage its production capacity. High savings ratio and investment-GDP ratio have led to fast growth of production capacity, which again enhances China's dependency on investment and export to absorb its production. So the key to understanding Chinese economy and its structural problems is the constrained migration and lagged urbanization. This is also why the remaining job of this chapter is to model the determinants of migration and how migration and urbanization can be accelerated.

3.3. A Model of Migration Decision: Social Distance and Neighborhood Effect

Our model is mainly based on network models such as Ballester *et al.* (2006) and simplifies some of their assumptions. In our model, we explicitly assume that social distance is a function of the type and frequency of social interactions.

There are N individuals in a village. Here, we simply assume each individual is friends with everybody else in network. Every person in our model has heterogeneous attitudes toward the behavior of peers, thus is a different social distance from the network. That is to say, $g_{ik} \neq g_{jk}$ if $i \neq j$. It also implies that friendship is not a reciprocal relationship.

Group influence/neighborhood effects are expressed as:

$$\frac{\sum_{i=1} g_{ij} m_j}{\sum_{i=1} g_{ij}} = \frac{g_i}{n-1} \sum_{i=1} m_j = g_i \bar{m}. \tag{3.1}$$

g_i measures the social distance to the network. The standard neighborhood effect model implies g_i equals a constant; thus, g_i cannot be estimated. Here we write $g_i = J + \lambda_i s_i$, with J, $\lambda_i > 0$ to capture the heterogeneous social distances of different individuals to other villagers. J is a constant, while s_i is the individual interaction frequency with other villagers, λ_i is the parameter linking social interaction frequency to social distance. It is natural to assume that if one person is more involved in the local interaction, the social distance is shorter, so that the neighborhood effect will be greater.

Because more local interactions s_i will squeeze out the time that can be allocated to outward migration, we standardize s_i and m_i to be continuous and m_i, $s_i \in [0,1]$, and simply assume:

$$s_i + m_i \leq 1, \tag{3.2}$$

where the total time available is standardized as 1. Social interactions with neighbors make Equation (3.2) binding or loose depending on the type and frequency of interactions. Usually, when people exchange labour market information, it is not time consuming. The utility that individual i obtains from outward migration is:

$$U(m_i) = a + b_i m_i - cm_i^2 + g_i \cdot m_i \cdot \bar{m}, \tag{3.3}$$

where $a>0$ is a constant, $b_i > 0$ is the linear marginal benefit of migration. The cost of migration is simplified as a squared term of migration time, with $c>0$. The last term on the right-hand-side is the social utility that depends on the average migration time of the peer villagers. g_i captures the heterogeneous social distance of villager i.

If Equation (3.2) is not binding, we may insert equation $g_i = J + \lambda_i s_i$ into (3.3) and we obtain:

$$U(m_i) = a + b_i m_i - cm_i^2 + [J + \lambda_i s_i] \cdot m_i \cdot \bar{m} \tag{3.4}$$

An individual optimizes the time allocated to outward migration work (First order condition):

$$dU(m_i)/dm_i = b_i - 2cm_i + \bar{m}(J + \lambda_i s_i) = 0 \tag{3.5}$$

So,

$$m_i = \frac{b_i + \bar{m}(J + \lambda_i s_i)}{2c} \tag{3.6}$$

where m_i is positively correlated with $\bar{m}$ and s_i amplifies the interdependence between m_i and $\bar{m}$.

However, for some people who mutually help in the busy season, social interactions are time-consuming, so Equation (3.2) is binding. Thus, we may insert equations $g_i = J + \lambda_i s_i$ and $m_i = 1 - s_i$ into (3.3), and we obtain:

$$U(m_i) = a + b_i m_i - c m_i^2 + [J + \lambda_i (1 - m_i)] \cdot m_i \cdot \bar{m} \tag{3.7}$$

An individual optimizes the time allocated to outward migration work (First order condition):

$$dU(m_i)/dm_i = b_i - 2cm_i + \bar{m}[J + \lambda_i - 2\lambda_i m_i] = 0 = G(m_i, \bar{m}) \tag{3.8}$$

The following second-order condition guarantees an interior solution:

$$\partial G(m_i, \bar{m}) / \partial m_i = -2c - 2\lambda_i \bar{m} < 0, \tag{3.9}$$

$$\partial G(m_i, \bar{m}) / \partial \bar{m} = J + \lambda_i - 2\lambda_i m_i \tag{3.10}$$

From the derivation calculus of implicit functions, we obtain:

$$\frac{dm_i}{d\bar{m}} = -\frac{G_{\bar{m}}'}{G_{m_i}'} = \frac{J}{-G_{m_i}'} + \frac{\lambda_i}{-G_{m_i}'} + \frac{2\lambda_i m_i}{G_{m_i}'} \tag{3.11}$$

$\frac{dm_i}{d\bar{m}}$ is the core concept in our chapter: the neighborhood effect. Here, it can be decomposed into three parts. $\frac{dJ}{-G_{m_i}'} > 0$, where $G_{m_i}' < 0$ is guaranteed by (3.9), corresponds to the standard linear neighborhood effect, and we can see that when the village migration ratio increases, the individual allocates more time to migration work. $\frac{\lambda_i}{-G_{m_i}'} > 0$ represents the positive effect of social interaction on the neighborhood effect. When an individual increases his or her social interaction strength λ_i, the social distance is shortened and the neighborhood effect rises. $\frac{2\lambda_i m_i}{G_{m_i}'} < 0$ is the third part and it shows that when individual i spends more time on outward migration, the time for social interaction will be squeezed out due to time constraint, and thus the effect of peer behavior decreases. In summary, Equation (3.11) can lead to two hypotheses: (1) individual migration time is positively related to group mean migration time; and (2) combining terms 2 and 3, social interaction can have either positive or negative effects on the neighborhood effect, depending on whether social interaction greatly reduces outward migration time.

3.4. Data Description

The data used in our research are from the 2002 Chinese Household Income Project Survey (CHIP 2002) collected by the Chinese Academy of Social Sciences. Survey data are from 121 counties, 961 administrative villages, 9200 households and 37,969 individuals. The sampling frame for the survey is a subsample of the official rural household survey conducted by the National Bureau of Statistics (NBS).[4] The questionnaires were collected in February 2003, the Chinese Lunar New Year when almost all the Chinese including rural migrants returned home and celebrated the Spring Festival (*chunjie* in Chinese) together. Therefore, the survey captures information of all members of rural households including outward migrants. The data contain individual information, such as sex, age, education, job status, family information such as family structure, family economic condition and village geography, village population and economic conditions. More importantly, it also includes information on family social interactions with other villagers.

The explained variable "migrant or not" is a 0–1 dummy variable. Defining the migration variable as discrete makes identification possible in the presence of the reflection problem. The reflection problem coined by Manski (1993) is a difficulty in estimating the neighborhood effect.

[4]The stratified sampling of the NBS rural household survey followed two steps. First, sample administrative villages were directly selected in each province according to income level, and second, sample households (generally 10) were chosen from each sample village. For details of the sampling framework and sampling method of the CHIP 2002 survey, see Gustafsson, Li, and Sicular (2008).

Simply speaking, in a linear model, individual characteristics affect one's decision linearly. The average characteristics and average choice (measurement of the neighborhood effect) are perfectly collinear so that parameters cannot be identified if we control them simultaneously in the regression model. However, Brock and Durlauf (2001) prove that the reflection problem can be avoided in the nonlinear model. Personal characteristics influence the choice nonlinearly in a nonlinear model such as probit or logit, so that they are not linearly correlated if we put them together in the regression model.

In CHIPS 2002, individuals reported the days away from their family in a year. Because of the data limitation, we consider the urban areas in China as the only migration destination in our chapter and do not differentiate between migration locations. We follow Zhao (2003) and define an individual as a migrant if he or she lives away from home more than 180 days in a year. Obviously, leaving family for more than six months in a year does not necessarily mean a person is a migrant. Therefore, with personal job status information in the questionnaire, we dropped all long-term out-of-village students, as well as the nonfarm employees who work in the township enterprise outside the village. The largest change in our sample is that we only include the working-age population, i.e., observations of male individuals aged 16–60 and females aged 16–55 according to the official definition in China. We also drop observations whose important variables are missing. Finally, 16,401 observations remain for the analysis.

From the CHIPS 2002 questionnaire data, we obtain information on the village population and village migrant numbers. We calculate the village migration ratio using the following equation:

$$\text{village migration ratio} = \frac{\text{no. of village migrants - no. of family migrants}}{\text{village population - family population}}. \quad (3.12)$$

This is the measure of village peer behavior in our chapter. For a certain household, the village migration ratio is calculated as the ratio for other villagers to exclude the effects from one's own family. Another advantage of this is that we can have variances in "village migration ratio" among different households. This definition is close to the one used in Zhao (2003), who used the absolute number of migrants in a village to measure the network effects of migration. While using the migration ratio of village peers to capture neighborhood effects, we also control the number of friends and relatives outside the village as the household's bridging network.

Social interactions between one's family and other villagers are assumed to affect social distance and then the magnitude of neighborhood effects in our study. Here, we categorize the social interactions into two types: interactions in information sharing, and those in labour markets. In Chinese rural areas, the widening rural–urban income gap makes outward migration an effective way of earning income. Since urban and rural labour markets are segmented, and many migrants seek urban jobs across provinces, rural residents exchange information for better job destination and higher income. The market for labour services is still so unfledged that rural residents cooperate a lot in labour-sharing activities. In the CHIPS 2002 data, a series of questions record the social interaction strengths of a family with their relatives and neighbors in "exchange information on employment", and "mutual help during busy seasons". The answers to these questions are discrete: (1) very frequently, (2) often, (3) just so-so, (4) sometimes, and (5) none/few. We construct two variables with cardinal order of information sharing and mutual help strength. On that basis, we interact the two social interaction variables with the village migration ratio (neighborhood effect), and use the interaction terms to capture the heterogeneous neighborhood effect. We use the continuous measurement of social interaction as our baseline model. The discrete measurements of social interactions will be used for the robust checks.

All the explanatory variables are listed in Table 3.2, and the basic statistical descriptions are in Table 3.3. We can see from Table 3.3 that among the 16,401 rural workers, 2,675 individuals participated in outward migration in 2002, which indicates an overall migration ratio of 16.31%. Even in the basic statistics, we can see some differences between migrants and non-migrants. Fewer women are employed in outward migration, and in the migrants sample, 50.24% individuals are unmarried, compared with 25.21% in the non-migrants sample. The outward migrants are much younger with an average age of 27.1, lower than the 36.1 years in the non-migrants' sample. All these explanatory variables are controlled in our regression model. However, in the regression analysis, we focus on the

Table 3.3. Statistical description of variables.

	Full sample 16401		Migrants 2675		Non-migrants 13726	
Variable	**Mean**	**s.d.**	**Mean**	**s.d.**	**Mean**	**s.d.**
Individual Characteristics:						
female	0.4459	0.4971	0.3727	0.4836	0.4602	0.4984
age	34.6344	12.4495	27.1166	8.34829	36.09952	12.5880
married	0.6993	0.4586	0.4501	0.4976	0.7479	0.4343
primary school	0.2649	0.4413	0.1806	0.3847	0.2813	0.4496
junior high school	0.5033	0.5000	0.6191	0.4857	0.4807	0.4996
senior high school	0.1321	0.3386	0.1140	0.3179	0.1356	0.3424
tech school or more	0.0659	0.2481	0.0789	0.2696	0.0634	0.2437
communist	0.0710	0.2568	0.0303	0.1714	0.0789	0.2696
health good	0.8688	0.3376	0.9458	0.2265	0.8539	0.3533
health bad	0.0328	0.1781	0.0120	0.1087	0.0368	0.1884
Family Characteristics:						
household labour force	2.7678	1.2718	3.3544	1.2583	2.6534	1.2427
family per capita land	2.0937	2.3302	1.6258	1.7300	2.1849	2.4196
kids no. under 6	0.1818	0.4285	0.2011	0.4534	0.1780	0.4234
kids no. between 6 and 12	0.3354	0.6014	0.2819	0.5630	0.3458	0.6081
elder people no. over 65	0.1806	0.4535	0.1966	0.4794	0.1775	0.4482
friends or relatives outside	0.5726	0.4947	0.5922	0.4915	0.5688	0.4953
friends or members village cadre	0.2240	0.4169	0.2456	0.4305	0.2198	0.4141
Village Characteristics:						
distance to the country seat	25.2382	21.6849	27.1437	20.3367	24.8668	21.9194
distance to nearest transportation terminal	5.4653	8.3177	5.3916	7.9651	5.4797	8.3849
village per capita income	2.3886	1.3957	2.1802	1.1521	2.4292	1.4349
mountain area	0.2187	0.4134	0.2426	0.4287	0.2140	0.4102
hill area	0.3436	0.4749	0.4426	0.4968	0.3243	0.4681
Neighborhood effect:						
village migration ratio (NE)	0.1703	0.1474	0.2297	0.1533	0.1588	0.1434
village mig ratio 1998	0.0882	0.0786	0.1204	0.0814	0.0819	0.0764

(*Continued*)

Table 3.3. (*Continued*)

	Full sample 16401		Migrants 2675		Non-migrants 13726	
Variable	**Mean**	**s.d.**	**Mean**	**s.d.**	**Mean**	**s.d.**
Social Interaction Strength:						
info exchange	2.4816	1.2039	2.6860	1.2080	2.4418	1.1991
mutual help	2.9152	1.2424	2.8277	1.2639	2.9322	1.2375
info very frequently	0.0465	0.2106	0.0587	0.2351	0.0442	0.2054
info often	0.1722	0.3776	0.2213	0.4152	0.1627	0.3691
info just so so	0.2855	0.4517	0.2916	0.4546	0.2844	0.4511
info sometimes	0.2077	0.4057	0.2041	0.4031	0.2084	0.4062
help very frequently	0.1138	0.3176	0.0983	0.2978	0.1169	0.3213
help often	0.2198	0.4141	0.2329	0.4228	0.2173	0.4124
help just so so	0.3057	0.4607	0.2662	0.4420	0.3134	0.4639
help sometimes	0.1890	0.3915	0.2034	0.4026	0.1862	0.3893

magnitude and direction of the neighborhood effect and the interaction term between social interaction strength and the neighborhood effect.

3.5. Regression Model and Result

Based on the theoretical model, we define a latent variable Y^*, thus the latent utility function is:

$$Y_i^* = X_i\beta + g_i\bar{M}_i + \varepsilon_i, \tag{3.13}$$

with:

$$\begin{aligned} M_i &= 1 \ if \ Y_i^* \geq \alpha_i \\ &= 0 \ otherwise \end{aligned} \tag{3.14}$$

Here M_i represents the migration decision of household i, and equals one if the utility from migration is greater than some subjective threshold, which we denote as α_i. Thus we can write a probit model as follows:

$$\begin{aligned} \Pr(M_i = 1) &= \Pr(Y_i^* \geq \alpha_i) = \Pr(X_i\beta + g_i\bar{M}_i + \varepsilon_i \geq \alpha_i) \\ &= \Pr(\varepsilon_i \geq \alpha_i - X_i\beta - g_i\bar{M}_i) = \Phi(-\alpha_i + X_i\beta + g_i\bar{M}_i) \end{aligned} \tag{3.15}$$

The marginal effect of the neighborhood effect is $\partial \Pr(M_i = 1)/\partial \bar{M}_i = \Phi' \cdot g_i$, where Φ is the cumulative distribution function (CDF) of a standard normal distribution, since ε_i is assumed to follow a standard normal distribution, and $g_i = J + \lambda_r s_i$ as explained before.

To fit our data to the model, we establish the following probit model to explore the determinants of outward migration:

$$P(Y_{ijk} = 1) = \Phi(X_{ijk}\beta + J\bar{M}_{jk} + \bar{M}_{jk} \times \Sigma\, \lambda_s s_{jks}) \tag{3.16}$$

Equation (3.16) is the determination function of outward migration probability. i, j and k represent the individual, family and village, respectively. X_{ijk} is a vector of individual, family and village characteristics variables. $\bar{M}_{jk}$ is the village migration ratio and it is the measurement of the neighborhood effect that we are mostly concerned with in our chapter. Notice that each household j within the same village k may have a different "village migration ratio" since one's own family is excluded from his household's "village migration ratio". s_{jks} are the social interactions of a family with their relatives and neighbors, where subscript s denotes either "exchange information on employment" or "mutual help during busy seasons" interactions.

The regression results are reported in Table 3.4. Equation (3.1) is the baseline regression, where only individual and household variables are included as explanatory variables. Equation (3.2) adds the village migration ratio (neighborhood effect) and its interaction terms with social interactions in information exchange and labour market. R-squared increases from 0.1828 to 0.2136, indicating a not negligible neighborhood effect in migration. Worrying about the potential missing-variable-bias in the estimation of the neighborhood effect, we put the village migration ratio in 1998, a variable based on retrospective information in our survey, in Equation (3.3). Equation (3.4) controls for village-level characteristics. Equation (3.5) adds the county dummies to avoid remaining missing-variable-bias in the estimation.

In Equations (3.2) to (3.5), three results have positive signs for the coefficients of current neighborhood effects. Compared with Equation (3.2), the coefficients of current neighborhood effects drop substantially from 1.503 to 0.650 in Equation (3.3), while the coefficient of migration ratio

Table 3.4. Probit regression result (continuous social interactions). Dependent variable: migrant or not (Migrant = 1, Non-migrant = 0).

Migrant (yes or no)	**(1)**	**(2)**	**(3)**	**(4)**	**Marginal effect based on (4)**	**(5)**
NE		1.503***	0.650***	0.656***	11.21%***	0.002
		(0.163)	(0.194)	(0.195)		(0.228)
village mig ratio 1998			2.024***	1.903***	32.56%***	1.111***
			(0.250)	(0.252)		(0.317)
info exchange* NE		0.262***	0.260***	0.241***	4.13%***	0.187***
		(0.046)	(0.046)	(0.046)		(0.053)
mutual help* NE		−0.176***	−0.164***	−0.184***	−3.15%***	−0.138***
		(0.044)	(0.044)	(0.044)		(0.050)
female	−0.286***	−0.275***	−0.274***	−0.264***	−4.45%***	−0.258***
	(0.027)	(0.028)	(0.028)	(0.028)		(0.030)
married	−0.574***	−0.592***	−0.603***	−0.591***	−11.76%***	−0.649***
	(0.048)	(0.049)	(0.049)	(0.049)		(0.054)
age	0.198***	0.201***	0.200***	0.199***	3.40%***	0.209***
	(0.011)	(0.011)	(0.011)	(0.011)		(0.012)
age squared	−0.003***	−0.003***	−0.003***	−0.003***		−0.003***
	(0.000)	(0.000)	(0.000)	(0.000)		(0.000)
communist	−0.170***	−0.160**	−0.163**	−0.163**	−2.54%***	−0.062
	(0.065)	(0.066)	(0.067)	(0.067)		(0.072)
health good	0.168***	0.186***	0.209***	0.229***	3.51%***	0.230***
	(0.055)	(0.057)	(0.057)	(0.058)		(0.063)
health bad	−0.053	−0.001	0.020	0.021	0.36%	0.001
	(0.112)	(0.114)	(0.115)	(0.115)		(0.123)
primary school	0.287**	0.291**	0.303***	0.282**	5.25%**	0.293**
	(0.115)	(0.118)	(0.118)	(0.118)		(0.126)
junior high school	0.358***	0.383***	0.397***	0.415***	7.13%***	0.416***
	(0.114)	(0.117)	(0.117)	(0.118)		(0.127)
senior high school	0.183	0.220*	0.227*	0.254**	4.90%**	0.223*
	(0.119)	(0.122)	(0.122)	(0.123)		(0.132)
tech school or more	0.118	0.194	0.196	0.243*	4.75%*	0.180
	(0.124)	(0.126)	(0.127)	(0.127)		(0.138)
household labour force	0.240***	0.242***	0.242***	0.234***	4.01%***	0.248***
	(0.011)	(0.011)	(0.011)	(0.011)		(0.013)
family per capita land	−0.084***	−0.070***	−0.066***	−0.073***	−1.25%***	−0.035***
	(0.007)	(0.007)	(0.007)	(0.008)		(0.010)

(Continued)

Table 3.4. (*Continued*)

Migrant (yes or no)	(1)	(2)	(3)	(4)	Marginal effect based on (4)	(5)
kids no. under 6	–0.040 (0.032)	–0.033 (0.033)	–0.030 (0.033)	–0.047 (0.034)	–0.81%	0.011 (0.037)
kids no. between 6 and 12	–0.056** (0.024)	–0.047* (0.024)	–0.045* (0.025)	–0.057** (0.025)	–0.98%**	–0.033 (0.028)
elder people no. over 65	0.051* (0.027)	0.050* (0.028)	0.049* (0.028)	0.040 (0.028)	0.69%	0.051* (0.031)
friends or relatives outside	0.030 (0.029)	0.047 (0.030)	0.051* (0.030)	0.071** (0.030)	1.20%**	0.095*** (0.034)
friends or members village cadre	0.065* (0.034)	0.062* (0.034)	0.070** (0.035)	0.059* (0.035)	1.03%*	0.047 (0.038)
distance to the country seat				0.001 (0.002)	0.01%	–0.002 (0.002)
distance to nearest transportation terminal				0.000 (0.001)	0.01%	0.002** (0.001)
village per capita income				–0.054* (0.031)	–0.92%*	–0.041 (0.058)
village per capita income squared				0.001 (0.004)		–0.005 (0.006)
mountain area				0.163*** (0.039)	2.97%***	–0.027 (0.081)
hill area				0.189*** (0.032)	3.35%***	0.017 (0.058)
constant	–4.180*** (0.215)	–4.632*** (0.221)	–4.706*** (0.222)	–4.667*** (0.228)		–10.784*** (0.572)
County Dummy						Y
Number of obs	16401	16401	16401	16401		15730
Pseudo R2	0.1828	0.2136	0.2181	0.2232		0.3030

Note: NE = neighborhood effect. *, **, ***: Coefficient different from zero at 10, 5, 1 percent significance levels respectively. Standard errors are in parentheses.

in 1998 is highly significant and three times that of neighborhood effect in 2002 in Equations (3.3) and (3.4). This is consistent with the finding of Munshi (2003): past network is more significant than current network. Intuitively, more information is accumulated in network as time passes. In Equation (3.5), when county dummies are controlled, current neighborhood effect becomes insignificant and negligible in magnitude, but the past neighborhood effect is still highly significant and much stronger compared with current neighborhood effect.

We are more interested in the interaction terms of social interactions and neighborhood effect. In Equations (3.2) to (3.5), all the interaction terms are highly significant. Observing the significance level and the size of the coefficients of the interaction terms, we may get the following conclusions: (1) for information exchange, the more frequently people interact, the stronger the neighborhood effect is in migration decision, (2) for mutual help in the labour market, the more frequently people interact, the weaker the neighborhood effect is in migration decision. The difference in the signs of the two interaction terms can be explained as follows: Information sharing enhances neighborhood effects. However, labour exchange is time consuming, squeezes the time for migration, and mitigates neighborhood effects in migration, although labour exchange reduces social distance.[5] However, the negative sign of the interaction term between labour exchange and neighborhood effect is because many people face time constraint for outward migration when they have helped their neighbors in the busy season. If this is the case, we need to seriously consider how outward migration and mutual help in the labour market are simultaneously determined. Fortunately, with the discrete measurement of mutual help in the busy season, we find that not everybody frequently interacts with his neighbors in the labour market. We will show that modest mutual help in the labour market enhances neighborhood effect in migration decision in the next section.

---

[5]In the questionnaire, we also know the number of days that a household is involved in within-village labour exchange. If we substitute the labour exchange frequency measurement by the days of labour exchange, the results will not change. However, the number of observations is reduced to about 10,000, due to missing of information.

Nevertheless, the fact that within-community social interaction may play a negative role in labour migration has previously been neglected in the literature except for those studies by Narayan (1999) and Alesina and Giuliano (2007). Narayan (1999) separates social capital into within-community "bonding" social capital and between-community "bridging" social capital. He argues that if a community has higher bonding social capital, it will have higher internal welfare, but they will also lose many outside job opportunities. Alesina and Giuliano (2007) find that stronger family ties can decrease the geographical mobility of individuals. However, social interactions in the labour market are perhaps the spontaneous substitutes of an unfledged labour service market in the rural areas. Therefore, we can expect that with the economic development, more and more emerging labour market services will make more efficient the interactions of rural residents in the labour exchange, thus promoting neighborhood effect in outward migration.

Based on Equation (3.4), for a representative person who has a medium-level social interaction and all the other characteristics at the mean level, the marginal neighborhood effect is calculated as 0.1413. Not surprisingly, we can see that a one percentage increase in the village migration ratio increases the individual probability of outward migration by 0.1413%. This is termed a "social multiplier" in the literature (Glaeser *et al.*, 2003).

This result has confirmed the existence of the neighborhood effect in the outward migration decision in rural China. However, the positive relationship between the village migration ratio and individual migration probability also indicates the potential danger of low equilibrium in outward migration: if village peers are less inclined to migrate because of institutional obstacles such as urban–rural segmentation in China, the negative effects will also be amplified by the social multiplier.

All the other coefficients are consistent with the findings in previous studies. We interpret the estimation based on Equation (3.4).

(1) Individual characteristics will significantly affect the migration decision. Women are less inclined to migrate, with a probability that is 4.45% lower than males. Being married will greatly decrease the probability of outward migration by 11.76%. Age has an inverse U-shaped relationship with the migration probability. A worker has a maximum migration probability at the age of 33, and beyond this age the marginal

effect of age is decreasing. All these findings are consistent with existing empirical results. Zhao (2003) finds that all levels of education are insignificant in migration determination, which is in contrast to our result that education levels are all significantly positive with illiteracy as the reference point. However, the influence of education is nonlinear; villagers who receive a junior high school education have the highest probability of migration, 7.13% higher than the illiterate group, while villagers with a primary education have the second-highest probability of migration, 5.25% higher than the illiterate group. If a person has a higher education level, the probability of outward migration is moderately higher than the illiterate group. The probability of migration for villagers with a technical school education or higher is 4.75% higher and for senior high school education is 4.9% higher. Our findings seemingly imply that higher education for the rural residents may be at the expense of a lower outward migration probability. For the policy makers, there may be some "optimal" education level for the purpose of rural–urban migration. However, we need to be cautious about this conclusion: one possible explanation for the nonlinear "education return" is that the higher education receivers have permanently stayed in the city areas after gaining their urban *hukou* (residence registration), so that they are not included as "migrants" in the rural sample. Another explanation is that better-educated workers are more likely to participate in local nonfarm employment (Zhao, 1999a, 1999b; Liang and White, 1997), which is included as non-migration in our regression.

(2) Family characteristics also significantly affect the migration decision. For an additional worker in a family, the individual probability of migration increases by 4.01%. Meanwhile, if a family has more arable land, the probability of outward migration declines because of the labour substitution between local farming and migration work. The family structure can also influence the individual migration decision. Families that have one additional child aged between 6 and 12 have a 0.98% lower migration probability. One additional older person does not significantly influence the migration decision because they can be either an effective worker in the household or a person to be taken care of in rural China. Being aware of the existence of household-specific network besides the village-level network of migration, we also control other measurement of the household social network that can also promote labour

migration. If one's family has social ties outside the village or has kin as village cadre, the probability of outward migration increases by 1.2% and 1.03%, respectively.

(3) Village characteristics also matter. An increase of village income by RMB 1000 yuan increases the opportunity costs of migration and decreases the individual migration probability by 0.92%. People living in the mountainous and hilly areas have a higher probability of migration. These two dummies may have captured unobserved poor living conditions regardless of village income. The distance from a village to the county seat and to the nearest transportation terminal does not significantly influence the migration decision.

3.6. Robustness Check

In the previous section, we use continuous measurement for the frequency of social interactions in information exchange and labour market mutual help. To check the robustness of whether labour market interactions always diminish the neighborhood effects, we utilize the discrete frequency of mutual help in labour market form. Correspondingly, the discrete frequency of information exchange is also used. The hypothesis is that only those people who have frequent mutual help with their neighbors in the labour market have lower neighborhood effects in migration decision, because they face time constraint. However, for those people who only interact a little with their neighbors in the labour market, they may have shorter social distances with their neighbors, and the neighborhood effect in migration decision is amplified through labour market interaction.

Table 3.5 reports the results where the interaction terms of social interaction and neighborhood effect are constructed using the discrete measurement of social interaction. Table 3.5 shows that adding neighborhood effect and its interaction terms with social interaction frequency increased R-squared from 0.1828 in Equation (3.1) to 0.2149 in Equation (3.6). In Equations (3.7) to (3.10), we find: (1) for information exchange, the more frequently people interact, the stronger the neighborhood effect is in migration decision. When information exchange is few, the neighborhood effect is not significantly increased, if village-level variables are controlled for; (2) for mutual help in the labour market, the more frequently

Table 3.5. Robustness check (discrete social interactions). Dependent variable: migrant or not (Migrant = 1, Non-migrant = 0).

Migrant (yes or no)	**(6)**	**(7)**	**(8)**	**(9)**
NE	1.422***	0.584***	0.584***	0.138
	(0.148)	(0.181)	(0.182)	(0.213)
village mig ratio 1998		2.032***	1.907***	1.089***
		(0.251)	(0.253)	(0.318)
info very frequently *NE	0.976***	0.984***	0.930***	0.646**
	(0.244)	(0.245)	(0.246)	(0.283)
info often *NE	0.920***	0.931***	0.832***	0.512***
	(0.170)	(0.170)	(0.171)	(0.190)
info just so so *NE	0.424***	0.414***	0.368**	0.144
	(0.156)	(0.156)	(0.157)	(0.174)
info sometimes *NE	0.271*	0.339**	0.259	−0.154
	(0.165)	(0.165)	(0.166)	(0.181)
help very frequently *NE	−0.705***	−0.598***	−0.696***	−0.496**
	(0.218)	(0.219)	(0.220)	(0.246)
help often *NE	−0.226	−0.240	−0.305*	−0.224
	(0.166)	(0.166)	(0.167)	(0.187)
help just so so *NE	−0.300*	−0.330**	−0.373**	−0.306*
	(0.157)	(0.157)	(0.158)	(0.175)
help sometimes *NE	0.371**	0.349**	0.291*	0.155
	(0.169)	(0.170)	(0.170)	(0.183)
female	−0.275***	−0.273***	−0.264***	−0.258***
	(0.028)	(0.028)	(0.028)	(0.031)
married	−0.593***	−0.604***	−0.592***	−0.650***
	(0.049)	(0.049)	(0.049)	(0.054)
age	0.201***	0.200***	0.199***	0.209***
	(0.011)	(0.011)	(0.011)	(0.012)
age squared	−0.003***	−0.003***	−0.003***	−0.003***
	(0.000)	(0.000)	(0.000)	(0.000)
communist	−0.159**	−0.162**	−0.161**	−0.060
	(0.067)	(0.067)	(0.067)	(0.072)
health good	0.188***	0.210***	0.230***	0.231***
	(0.057)	(0.057)	(0.058)	(0.063)
health bad	−0.006	0.014	0.015	−0.003
	(0.115)	(0.115)	(0.115)	(0.123)
primary school	0.298**	0.310***	0.288**	0.303**
	(0.118)	(0.118)	(0.119)	(0.127)
junior high school	0.389***	0.403***	0.420***	0.426***
	(0.117)	(0.118)	(0.118)	(0.127)

(*Continued*)

Table 3.5. (*Continued*)

Migrant (yes or no)	**(6)**	**(7)**	**(8)**	**(9)**
senior high school	0.223*	0.231*	0.256**	0.231*
	(0.122)	(0.123)	(0.123)	(0.133)
tech school or more	0.202	0.204	0.248*	0.189
	(0.127)	(0.127)	(0.128)	(0.138)
household labour force	0.243***	0.242***	0.235***	0.249***
	(0.011)	(0.011)	(0.011)	(0.013)
family per capita land	−0.070***	−0.066***	−0.073***	−0.034***
	(0.007)	(0.007)	(0.008)	(0.010)
kids no. under 6	−0.037	−0.034	−0.051	0.009
	(0.033)	(0.033)	(0.034)	(0.037)
kids no. between 6 and 12	−0.045*	−0.044*	−0.055**	−0.030
	(0.024)	(0.025)	(0.025)	(0.028)
elder people no. over 65				
friends or relatives outside	0.050*	0.049*	0.040	0.049
	(0.028)	(0.028)	(0.028)	(0.031)
friends or members village cadre	0.045	0.050*	0.069**	0.095***
	(0.030)	(0.030)	(0.030)	(0.034)
have_relative/ friend_as_cadre	0.066*	0.074**	0.062*	0.048
	(0.035)	(0.035)	(0.035)	(0.038)
distance to the country seat			0.001	−0.002
			(0.002)	(0.002)
distance to nearest transportation terminal			0.000	0.002**
			(0.001)	(0.001)
village per capita income			−0.050	−0.046
			(0.032)	(0.058)
village per capita income squared			0.000	−0.005
			(0.004)	(0.006)
mountain area			0.162***	−0.022
			(0.039)	(0.081)
hill area			0.186***	0.019
			(0.033)	(0.058)
constant	−4.640***	−4.718***	−4.684***	−10.784***
	(0.222)	(0.223)	(0.229)	(0.546)
County Dummy				**Y**
Number of obs	16401	16401	16401	15730
Pseudo R2	0.2149	0.2193	0.2242	0.3037

Note: NE = neighborhood effect. *, **, ***: Coefficient different from zero at 10, 5, 1 percent significance levels respectively. Standard errors are in parentheses.

people interact, the weaker the neighborhood effect is in migration decision. Interestingly, when mutual help is at the lowest level, the neighborhood effect may even be increased. The intuition is: when people help mutually, but not frequently, they do not face time constraint to migrate, and social distances among people are closer, so that neighborhood effects are enhanced. Here, since time constraint is not binding for those people who interact with their neighbors in the labour market, but not much, the simultaneity problem is not a major concern.

In both Tables 3.4 and 3.5, when village migration ratio in 1998 is controlled, the significance level and magnitude of the current migration ratio are reduced. Therefore, we want to see whether village migration ratio in 1998 is a better measurement to test heterogeneous neighborhood effect. To do so, we interact village migration ratio in 1998 with social interaction frequency measurements to repeat the estimation. The results are reported in Table 3.6.

Compared with the results in Table 3.4, where we measure neighborhood effect using current village migration ratio, most of the results are robust in Table 3.6. The only difference is that the interaction terms are less significant. In Equation (3.11), where we control interaction terms using discrete social interaction frequency and county dummies, most interaction terms are insignificant, but the signs of the coefficients are the same as those in Table 3.4. In summary, we have robust evidences of neighborhood effect regardless of using current or historical migration ratio. However, the heterogeneity of neighborhood effect is more significant when using current migration ratio as the measurement of neighborhood effect.

3.7. Neighborhood Effect and Public Policy

Our empirical results show that the neighborhood effect exists in rural China's labour migration. Furthermore, the neighborhood effect is nonlinear. Information sharing and modest labour market interaction enhances the neighborhood effect, while too frequent interaction in the labour market reduces the strength of the neighborhood effect. The existence of a nonlinear neighborhood effect has rich implication for policy makers. Theoretically, the neighborhood effect will lead to multiple equilibria in the economic process. When the mean group behavior outcome is at a low

Table 3.6. Robustness check (using village migration ratio in 1998 as NE). Dependent variable: migrant or not (Migrant = 1, Non-migrant = 0).

Migrant (yes or no)	**(10)**	**(11)**	**(12)**	**(13)**
NE	0.749***	0.109	0.777***	0.107
	(0.136)	(0.163)	(0.135)	(0.162)
village mig ratio 1998	1.694***	1.211***	1.729***	1.013**
	(0.349)	(0.415)	(0.377)	(0.449)
info very frequently	1.636***	1.012*		
*village mig ratio 1998	(0.468)	(0.532)		
info often	1.389***	0.712**		
*village mig ratio 1998	(0.321)	(0.356)		
info just so so	0.795***	0.327		
*village mig ratio 1998	(0.295)	(0.327)		
info sometimes	0.678**	–0.173		
*village mig ratio 1998	(0.323)	(0.351)		
help very frequently	–0.990**	–0.625		
*village mig ratio 1998	(0.442)	(0.488)		
help often	–0.800**	–0.531		
*village mig ratio 1998	(0.323)	(0.366)		
help just so so	–0.937***	–0.749**		
*village mig ratio 1998	(0.303)	(0.338)		
help sometimes	0.336	0.203		
*village mig ratio 1998	(0.329)	(0.354)		
info. exchange			0.415***	0.278***
*village mig ratio 1998			(0.088)	(0.099)
mutual help			–0.332***	–0.231**
*village mig ratio 1998			(0.087)	(0.099)
female	–0.264***	–0.259***	–0.264***	–0.259***
	(0.028)	(0.030)	(0.028)	(0.030)
married	–0.595***	–0.652***	–0.594***	–0.651***
	(0.049)	(0.054)	(0.049)	(0.054)
age	0.199***	0.209***	0.199***	0.209***
	(0.011)	(0.012)	(0.011)	(0.012)
age squared	–0.003***	–0.003***	–0.003***	–0.003***
	(0.000)	(0.000)	(0.000)	(0.000)
communist	–0.158**	–0.059	–0.160**	–0.059
	(0.067)	(0.072)	(0.067)	(0.072)
health good	0.228***	0.229***	0.227***	0.230***
	(0.058)	(0.063)	(0.057)	(0.063)

(Continued)

Table 3.6. (*Continued*)

Migrant (yes or no)	(10)	(11)	(12)	(13)
health bad	0.009	−0.006	0.015	−0.001
	(0.115)	(0.123)	(0.115)	(0.123)
primary school	0.284**	0.298**	0.280**	0.291**
	(0.118)	(0.127)	(0.118)	(0.126)
junior high school	0.417***	0.421***	0.414***	0.414***
	(0.118)	(0.127)	(0.117)	(0.127)
senior high school	0.253**	0.225*	0.251**	0.220*
	(0.123)	(0.133)	(0.122)	(0.132)
tech school or more	0.244*	0.183	0.241*	0.177
	(0.127)	(0.138)	(0.127)	(0.137)
household labour force	0.234***	0.249***	0.234***	0.248***
	(0.011)	(0.013)	(0.011)	(0.013)
family per capita land	−0.073***	−0.034***	−0.073***	−0.034***
	(0.008)	(0.010)	(0.008)	(0.010)
kids no. under 6	−0.051	0.009	−0.047	0.011
	(0.034)	(0.037)	(0.033)	(0.037)
kids no. between 6 and 12	−0.054**	−0.030	−0.056**	−0.032
	(0.025)	(0.028)	(0.025)	(0.028)
elder people no. over 65	0.041	0.048	0.040	0.051*
	(0.028)	(0.031)	(0.028)	(0.031)
friends or relatives outside	0.070**	0.095***	0.070**	0.096***
	(0.030)	(0.034)	(0.030)	(0.034)
friends or members village cadre	0.063*	0.050	0.061*	0.049
	(0.035)	(0.038)	(0.035)	(0.038)
distance to the country seat	0.001	−0.002	0.001	−0.002
	(0.002)	(0.002)	(0.002)	(0.002)
distance to nearest transportation terminal	0.000	0.002**	0.000	0.002**
	(0.001)	(0.001)	(0.001)	(0.001)
village per capita income	−0.051	−0.049	−0.053*	−0.041
	(0.032)	(0.058)	(0.031)	(0.058)
village per capita income squared	0.001	−0.005	0.001	−0.005
	(0.004)	(0.006)	(0.004)	(0.006)
mountain area	0.164***	−0.013	0.167***	−0.022
	(0.039)	(0.081)	(0.039)	(0.081)
hill area	0.188***	0.021	0.190***	0.016
	(0.033)	(0.058)	(0.032)	(0.058)

(*Continued*)

Table 3.6. (*Continued*)

Migrant (yes or no)	(10)	(11)	(12)	(13)
constant	−4.686***	−10.786***	−4.669***	−10.787***
	(0.228)	(0.572)	(0.228)	(0.546)
County Dummy		Y		Y
Number of obs	16401	15730	16401	15730
Pseudo R2	0.2237	0.3032	0.2228	0.3027

Note: NE = neighborhood effect. *, **, ***: Coefficient different from zero at 10, 5, 1 percent significance levels respectively. Standard errors are in parentheses.

level, the economic process may converge to a low-level equilibrium because of interdependences in decision making; however, when the mean group behavior outcome surpasses some threshold, the economic process will converge to a high-level equilibrium with social interaction (Zanella, 2004).

In the context of our chapter, China's urbanization would be dampened if there was a low-level equilibrium in rural–urban labour migration. We use the regression parameters in Table 3.4, Column 4 to simulate the equilibrium condition in the labour migration decision. Figure 3.2 reflects the relationship between the village migration ratio and the mean individual migration probability. The horizontal axis represents the village migration ratio and the vertical axis stands for the individual migration probability. The solid line is the 45 degree line. The dash-dot line, the individual response curve, shows the relationship between individual migration probability and village migration ratio. Here we have only one point of intersection between the individual migration probability curve and the 45 degree line, with a slope less than one that guarantees a stable equilibrium with an average village migration ratio of 8.56%. As the pdf (probability density function) of the probit model is a standard normal distribution and its cumulative distribution function is assumed to be S-shaped, the low-level and high-level equilibriums can be differentiated according to the intersection point between the 45 degree line and the response curve. If the intersection point lies below 50% of the village migration ratio, the equilibrium is a low-level one. In contrast, if it is above 50%, the equilibrium is high level and stable, meaning that any departure within a limited

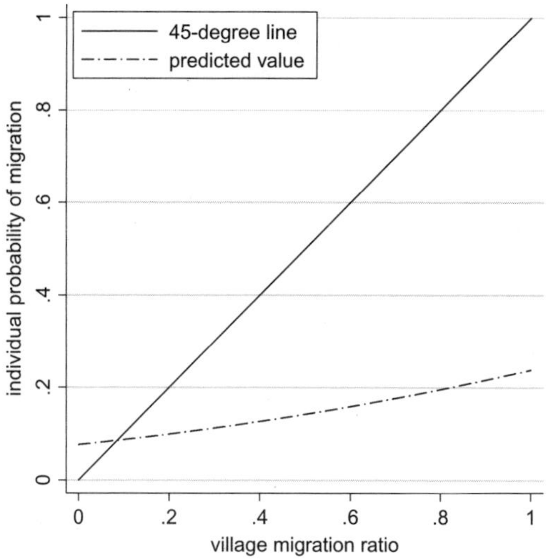

Fig. 3.2. Simulation of labour migration equilibrium.

Note: Figure 3.2 shows the relationship between village migration ratio and mean individual out migration probability (simulation parameters are from Table 3.4). When the two values equal (cut the 45 degree line), it is the equilibrium migration ratio. As shown in the graph, the equilibrium migration ratio is 8.56%.

range from the equilibrium will converge to the high equilibrium during dynamic adjustment. From Figure 3.2, we see that the intersection of the response curve and 45 degree line lies in the lower half of the S curve. That is to say, with the coefficients of the model unchanged, even if an exogenous shock increases the village migration ratio along the response curve, the labour migration ratio still converges to the low-level equilibrium trap under the influence of the neighborhood effect.

Promoting rural-to-urban labour migration is not only beneficial to rural residents, but also to China's economic growth. Thus, our policy design aims to promote labour migration from rural to urban areas. In the following policy scenario analysis, we distinguish policies of three types and simulate their effects.

The first kind of policy is to move the response curve by changing individual characteristics such as education level. This policy can increase the migration probability but has no impact on social interaction among villagers, and thus does not change the slope of the response curve.

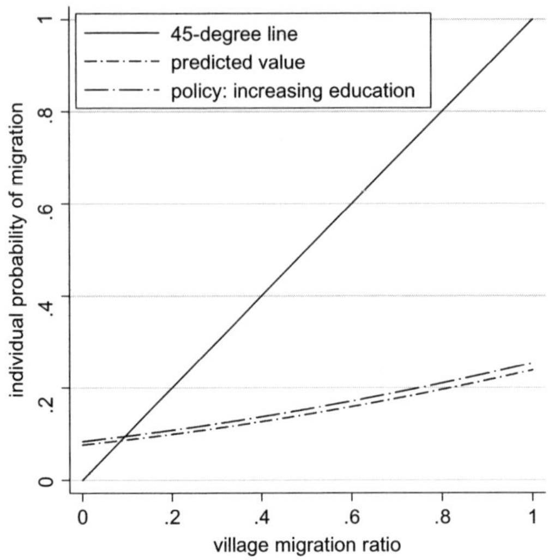

Fig. 3.3. Policy effect: increasing educational level.

Note: Figure 3.3 shows the policy effect of increasing education investment on out migration decision. We assume every sample individual receives at least nine year compulsory education (junior high school level). The equilibrium migration ratio increases to 9.47%.

Among the variables controlled, only the education level can be largely improved through economic policy. In Figure 3.3, we assume that policies are to improve the education of the villagers so that all villagers that are illiterate or have a primary school education can have the compulsory junior high school education. From the regression, we have already learned that the enhancement of rural residents' education will increase the probability of outward migration. Figure 3.3 again shows this result. We find that the individual migration probability curve moves upwards and intersects with the 45 degree line at a higher point where the village migration ratio equals 9.47%. However, it should be noted that the effect of the policy is still limited and the point of intersection resumes the characteristics of a low-level equilibrium.

The second policy is to increase the social interaction that contributes to the neighborhood effect, and decrease the social interaction that reduces the neighborhood effect. Graphically, this means rotating the curve anti-clockwise while holding the intercept of the response curve constant. Figure 3.4 shows clearly this case. If we create policies to encourage more

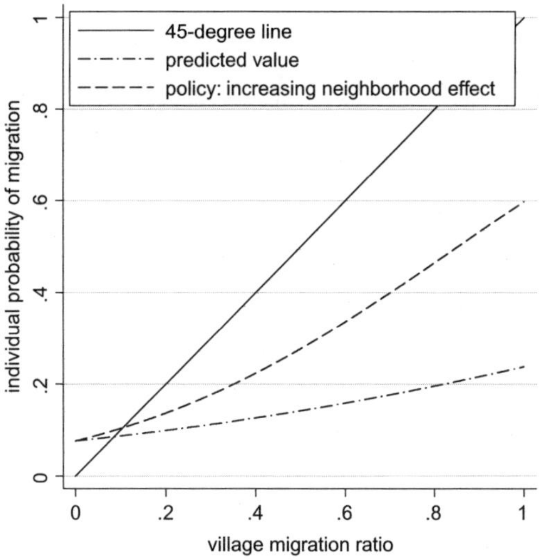

Fig. 3.4. Policy effect: increasing pro-peer effect social interaction.

Note: Figure 3.4 demonstrates the policy effect of increasing pro-peer effect social interaction on migration decision. In here, we control the information sharing interaction at "very frequently" while set the labour market interaction at "none/few". The intuitive policy measures are establishing formal job information broadcasting institution and labour service enterprises in rural areas. For such policies, the equilibrium migration ratio reaches 10.51%.

extensive interactions among villagers about job information sharing (we define the state of "exchange information on employment" as "very frequently") and at the same time establish a rural labour service market to decrease the interactions on the labour market (we define the state of "mutual help during busy season" as "none/few"), we may find a significant counter-clockwise twist of the migration curve and a higher point of intersection on the 45 degree curve with a corresponding village migration ratio of 10.51%. In addition, we observe from Figure 3.4 that the individual migration probability curve becomes S-shaped; however, the equilibrium is still at a low level.

What if we combine the above two policies? Figure 3.5 shows that by altering simultaneously the villagers' education and their social interactions strength, the combined policy will increase the migration ratio in equilibrium with a corresponding village migration ratio of 11.89%. However, the labour migration equilibrium is still at a low level even if the

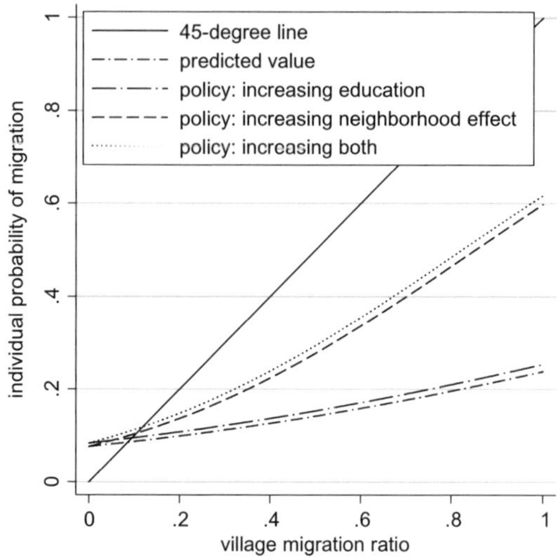

Fig. 3.5. Policy effects: increasing educational level and pro-peer effect social interaction.

Note: Figure 3.5 combines Figure 3.3, and additionally shows the overall policy effect of increasing both education level and pro-peer effect social interaction. The combining policy will lift up equilibrium migration ratio to 11.89%.

two policies are implemented together. In other words, new policies should be found to escape the low-level equilibrium of labour migration.

To facilitate the transition from a low-level equilibrium of migration to a high-level one, an important approach is the integration of the urban and rural labour markets through institutional reform, which is also the third kind of policy we could propose to increase labour migration within our analytical framework. Graphically, the policy will further heighten the intercept of the response curve. Although the current migration decision from rural to urban areas is in fact basically a free decision process, the existence of urban–rural segmentation and urban-biased economic policy still exerts extensive discrimination against rural migrants and labour migration is thus constrained. If we could eliminate this kind of urban-biased economic policy and promote rural–urban social integration, then the expected return of outward migration and thus the probability of outward migration increase. In Figure 3.6, we conduct a simulation and increase the intercept from –4.6672 to –4.1255, that is, an increase of

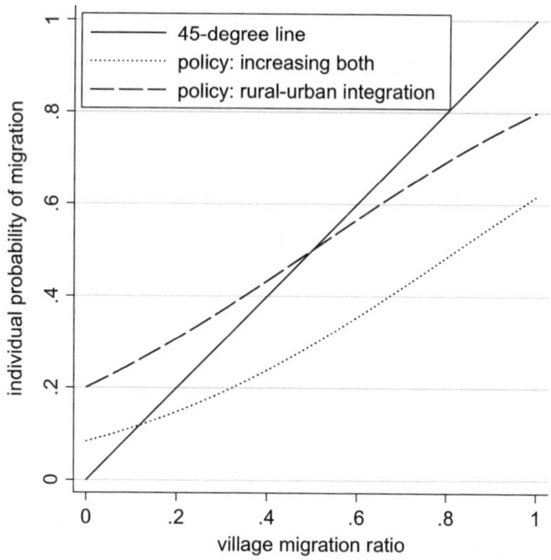

Fig. 3.6. Policy effect: institutional "big push" in rural-to-urban integration.

Note: Figure 3.6 shows the effect of rural-to-urban labour market integration on out migration decision (long dash line). Though in our framework we do not have explicit parameters to measure the extent of labour market discrimination against rural migrants, we increase the intercept term, which is exogenous and homogenous to every sample individual and thus can represent the "institutional change", to demonstrate the effect of market integration. We increase intercept from –4.6672 to –4.1255 and the equilibrium migration ratio reaches 50%.

0.5417 in absolute value. Combined with the improvement in the rural education level and social interaction, this leads to an equilibrium migration ratio of 50%, which is obviously the threshold point of having a high-level equilibrium of labour migration. If the high-level equilibrium appears in the figure, by relying on the neighborhood effect and social multiplier, a small-scale positive impact to increase the labour mobility can result in the migration ratio converging to an even higher equilibrium. For the transition from a low-level equilibrium to a high-level one, a "big push" in the institutional environment is needed.

An institutional "big push" that enhances migration and urbanization should be a package composed of the following policies: First, *hukou* system ought to be gradually reformed as only a residence registration. The threshold for migrants to get urban *hukou* should be gradually lowered. The difference between those migrants who do not have local *hukou* and local residents should be narrowed in terms of labour market treatment, social security, health care, access to education and public housing, etc. Second, fiscal polices are needed. Fiscal transfer from the central government should be directed to support the cities that attract more migrants and to subsidize the sending regions in public services. Absorbing cities need to provide more public services to their new residents based on their marginal growth in fiscal expenditures. Third, land reform is also necessary. Although land cannot move by nature, land use rights can be transferred. The migrant-absorbing cities should be allowed to buy "non-agricultural land quotas" from migrant-sending regions. Migrants should be able to sell their "non-agricultural land use rights" corresponding to their housing land in their hometown to the cities that provide them with *hukou*, social security and public services. Then, their housing land should be converted into agricultural land to keep the amount of agricultural land unchanged at the national level. Finally, social integration policies are required to help migrants. To reduce the social costs because of social segmentation between migrants and local residents, policies should be carried out to remove discrimination against migrants in their working places and daily life.

3.8. Conclusion

It is already a consensus that China's sustainable growth depends on whether the urbanization level could be successfully raised in the next three decades. So what are the policy constraints and what policy-makers can do need careful and detailed study. In this chapter, we try to understand the lagged urbanization based on a migration decision model with neighborhood effects. With this empirical model we can compare the relative effects of different policy tools that can push ahead urbanization. Our empirical results suggest the following conclusions: (1) the neighborhood effect exists in migration decision making, after past network and current bridging social network are controlled; and (2) the magnitude of the neighborhood effect is heterogeneous. Families who are more frequently involved in information sharing or modestly have mutual help in the labour market can enhance the neighborhood effect, while more frequent interactions in the labour market will reduce the positive neighborhood effect.

These findings have important policy implications. First, apart from the traditional development policies like education and training, rural-to-urban migration can be enhanced through neighborhood effect if a policy can raise village-level migration ratio. Second, social multiplier can be utilized to promote rural-to-urban migration. If information sharing is promoted, or if within-village labour exchange can be substituted by more efficient services, the social multiplier can be greater in amplifying the neighborhood effect in rural-to-urban migration. Third, a society could be trapped in a low equilibrium of rural-to-urban migration if there is neighborhood effect in migration decision. It is possible that even if the policies like increasing education and enhancing the neighborhood effect can increase the labour migration ratio, however, neither of these policies can shift the low-level equilibrium to a high-level one as our simulation result shows. Thus, only measures of institutional reform, constituting a "big push", can change the low-level labour migration equilibrium to a high-level one. In the China case, these measures include the elimination of rural–urban labour market segregation policy and the promotion of social integration between migrants and urban residents.

References

Alesina, A. and Giuliano, P. (2007). "The Power of the Family." NBER Working Paper 13051.

Araujo, C., de Janvry, A. and Sadoulet, E. (2004). "Peer Effects in Employment: Results from Mexico's Poor Rural Communities." Working Paper, University of California at Berkeley.

Bao, S., Bodvarsson, O.B., Hou, J.W. and Zhao, Y. (2007). "Interprovincial Migration in China: The Effects of Investment and Migrant Networks." IZA Discussion Paper No. 2924.

Bauer, T., Epstein, G. and Gang, I.N. (2002). "Herd Effects or Migration Networks? The Location Choice of Mexican Immigrants in the U.S." IZA Discussion Paper No. 551.

Brock, W.A. and Durlauf, S.N. (2001). "Discrete Choice with Social Interactions." *Review of Economic Studies*, 68(2), 235–260.

Cai, F., Wang, M. and Du, Y. (2003). *The Political Economy of Labour Migration* (in Chinese). Shanghai: Shanghai Sanlian and Shanghai People's Publishing House.

Chen, B., Lu, M. and Zhong, N. (2010). "Institution, Identity and Consumption Heterogeneity: Migrants' Expenditure Constrained by Hukou in Urban China." Working Paper, Fudan University.

Duan, C., Yang, G., Zhang, F. and Lu, X. (2008). "Nine Trends of Chinese Floating Population Since the Opening and Reform." (in Chinese). *Population Study* (Renkou Yanjiu), 32(6), 30–43.

Glaeser, E., Sacerdote, B. and Scheinkman, J. (2003). "The Social Multiplier." *Journal of the European Economic Association*, 1(2–3), 345–353.

Gustafsson, B., Li, S. and Sicular, T. (eds.) (2008). *Inequality and Public Policy in China*. New York: Cambridge University Press.

Hou, J. (2009). "The Trend of Whole-Family Migration and the Effects of Individual Factors." (in Chinese). *Population Study*, 33, 55–61.

Liang, Z. and White, M.J. (1997). "Market Transition, Government Policies, and Interprovincial Migration in China: 1983–1988." *Economic Development and Cultural Change*, 45(2), 321–339.

Manski, C.F. (1993). "Identification of Endogenous Social Effects: The Reflection Problem." *Review of Economic Studies*, 60(3), 531–542.

Munshi, K. (2003). "Networks in the Modern Economy: Mexican Migrants in the U.S. Labour Market." *Quarterly Journal of Economics*, 118(2), 549–599.

Narayan, D. (1999). "Bonds and Bridges: Social Capital and Poverty." World Bank Policy Research Working Paper.

Qiao, M., Qian, X. and Yao, X. (2009). "Labour Market Segmentation, Hukou and Urban-Rural Employment Differentials." (in Chinese). *Chinese Population Science*, 1, 32–41.

Roberts, K. (2005). "The Trend and Change of Chinese Labour Migration: The Implications of the Longest-Lasting Migration." (in Chinese). *Chinese Population Science*, 6, 17–29.

Sheng, L. (2008). *Mobility or Migration: An Economic Analysis on Chinese Rural Labour Migration*. Shanghai: Shanghai Fareast Press.

Wang, F. and Zuo, X. (1999). "Inside China's Cities: Institutional Barriers and Opportunities for Urban Migrants." *American Economic Review, Papers and Proceedings*, 89(2), 276–280.

Zanella, G. (2004). "Social Interactions and Economic Behavior." Working Paper, University of Siena.

Zhang, X. and Guo, L. (2003). "Does *Guanxi* Matter to Nonfarm Employment?" *Journal of Comparative Economics*, 31, 315–331.

Zhao, Y. (1999a). "Leaving the Countryside: Rural-to-Urban Migration Decisions in China." *American Economic Association Papers and Proceedings*, 89(2), 281–286.

Zhao, Y. (1999b). "Labour Migration and Earnings Differences: The Case of Rural China." *Economic Development and Cultural Change*, 47(4), 767–782.

Zhao, Y. (2003). "The Role of Migrant Networks in Labour Migration: The Case of China." *Contemporary Economic Policy*, 21(4), 500–511.

Zhou, J. and He, Y. (2009). "An Empirical Study on the Absorption of Rural-to-Urban Migrant Workers and Regional Economic Growth." (in Chinese). *World Economc Papers*, 1, 33–49, 93.

Zhu, N. (2002). "The Impact of Income Gaps on Migration Decisions in China." *China Economic Review*, 13(2–3), 213–230.

CHAPTER 4

CHINA'S POVERTY REDUCTION VIA ECONOMIC GROWTH: LOOKING BACK AND FORWARD

Yuan Zhang

4.1. Introduction

The reform and opening-up policy ushered in an era of sustained and rapid economic growth for China, a developing country with a still predominantly agricultural population; hence a "Chinese miracle" is being unfolded. Therefore, when it comes to the achievements of China's economic development, some scholars have even suggested an emergence of a "Beijing Concensus" to represent China's own paradigm of social and economic change. As a matter of fact, China stands out not only in terms of the rate and duration of the economic growth, but also in terms of rural poverty reduction, which is confirmed by China's official statistics indicating that the headcount ratio of rural poverty has dropped from 30.7% in 1978 to 1.6% in 2007 (cf. Table 4.1). There are, of course, many critics from academia claiming that China's official poverty threshold is set too low to reflect the actual rural poverty. Nevertheless, even the World Bank admitted that even if the standard international poverty line had been adopted to measure China's poverty, the impoverished population in rural China would still have been declining (World Bank, 2001); the UNDP also pointed out in its *Human Development Report 2005* that China had already achieved the MDG target ahead of schedule by halving the incidence of poverty since 1990 to $1 a day. These observations duly recognize China's achievements in reducing rural poverty and inevitably

Table 4.1. Economic growth and rural poverty reduction in China (1978–2008).

	GDP growth rate (%)	GDP growth rate of primary industries (%)	Number of absolute poverty (million)	Poverty indices (%)
1978	11.7	4.1	250	30.7
1980	7.8	−1.5	220	26.8
1981	5.2	7.0	152	18.5
1982	9.1	11.5	145	17.5
1983	10.9	8.3	135	16.2
1984	15.2	12.9	128	15.1
1985	13.5	1.8	125	14.8
1986	8.8	3.3	131	15.5
1987	11.6	4.7	122	14.3
1988	11.3	2.5	96	11.1
1989	4.10	3.1	102	11.6
1990	3.84	7.3	85	9.4
1991	9.18	2.4	94	10.4
1992	14.24	4.7	80	8.8
1993	13.96	4.7	75	8.2
1994	13.08	4.0	70	7.7
1995	10.92	5.0	65.4	7.1
1996	10.01	5.1	50	6.3
1997	9.30	3.5	49.62	5.4
1998	7.83	3.5	42.1	4.6
1999	7.62	2.8	34.12	3.7
2000	8.43	2.4	32.09	3.4
2001	8.30	2.8	29.27	3.2
2002	9.08	2.9	28.20	3.0
2003	10.03	2.5	29.00	3.1
2004	10.09	6.3	26.10	2.8
2005	10.43	5.2	23.65	2.5
2006	11.60	5.0	21.48	2.3
2007	13.00	3.7	14.79	1.6
2008	9.00	5.5	—	—

Sources: Data of 1993 and 1996 come from "Attacking Poverty", *World Development Report 2000/2001*; others with respect to the absolute poverty and poverty incidence originate from *China Yearbook of Rural Household Survey 2005*, while the GDP growth rates are from *China Statistical Yearbook 2009*.

add a new dimension to the "Chinese miracle". Paul Wolfowitz, former president of the World Bank, once neatly summarized China's large-scale poverty reduction during his visit to China in 2005 in the following passage: "China, as we all know, has been the fastest growing economy in Asia for the past 20 years and has lifted more than 400 million people above US$1 a day poverty levels in that time … Since 1980, China accounted for 75% of poverty reduction in the developing world … a remarkable achievement."

Against a backdrop of an enormous agricultural population, China's historical accomplishment in reducing rural poverty is of great significance to the world economic development as a whole. A question that naturally comes to mind is then: has China's economic growth already become pro-poor? To answer this question entails an inquiry into a series of relevant themes: Have China's rural poverty-relief policies fulfilled their objectives? Does China's agricultural growth contribute to the decline of rural poverty? Is China's industrialization itself pro-poor? And what lessons can be drawn from China's campaign against rural poverty? The answers to these questions will have profound implications for other developing countries, as well as for China's strategic decision-making with respect to the choice of path for future development. Just as one of China's prominent economists, Cai (2008), once put it: "China has by far created unprecedented reform, opening-up and drastic changes to the surprise of the world, and its successful experiences accumulated during this process have tremendously enriched the body of knowledge in the field of development economics." However, there is little effort at present to give the lessons learned a thorough review. Actually, a handful of economists and scholars have once reflected on the success stories from other emerging economies. For instance, John Williamson coined the term "Washington Consensus" to reflect the policy advices for the economic recovery of Latin America; later Joseph Stiglitz generalized a "Post-Washington Consensus" after critically examining the basic assumptions and deficiencies of its predecessor; and at the 2nd Summit of Americas held in Santiago, Chile in April 1998, a new consensus was contemplated with respect to the role that governments should play in economic development, which was named by former president of the World Bank James D. Wolfensohn as "Santiago Consensus". Leading scholars have provided some early reviews on China's experience of economic development. For instance, Lin *et al.* (1994) expatiated on how China's catching-up and overtaking strategies catapulted its then backward economy into a trajectory of high growth; Naughton (1994) and Che and Qian (1998) and others explored the significance of rural industries in China's successful economic transition; Xu (2010) analyzed, from the institutional perspective, the causes underlying the success of China's economic reforms; and Swinnen and Rozelle (2006), in light of the comparison of the outcomes of agricultural transition between China and other economies, contended that China's success in this respect lied in a hybrid approach of bottom-up initiatives and top-down sanction. The most recent effort to reflect on the legacy of China's economic development is a paper titled "The Beijing Consensus" by the former senior editor of *Time* magazine Joshua Cooper Ramo in 2004, and ever since then the term "Beijing Consensus" has gained popularity worldwide. To Ramo, the new consensus was an attractive formula of development that can be a source of inspiration for other developing countries.

Apart from the literature mentioned above, there are only a few studies trying to directly summarize China's experience of reducing rural poor. For instance, the World Bank (2001) held that because agricultural income constituted the principal part of rural population's earning, the imbalance of agricultural development influenced China's poverty rate straightway, and in the regions where agricultural growth was slow poverty reduction accordingly suffered a rather prolonged progress, while in regions where agricultural growth enjoyed an accelerated tempo, poverty reduction rate will be boosted as a result. Similarly, Ravallion and Chen (2004) and Montalvo and Ravallion (2009) pointed out that with respect to rural poverty reduction, the increase in the agricultural sector is far more important than that in the industrial sector and the service sector; and in another study, Ravallion (2008), after comparing China's success in reducing poverty with Africa's failure of doing so, came up with the conclusion that improving the productivity of smalltime farmers was vitally important and could only be realized through market incentives and government support, and what played an equally pivotal role were strong central and regional governments along with a whole pack of effective public administration systems.

The above literature, however, only focuses on the direct impact of agricultural growth on rural poverty reduction, leaving the indirect effect of other industries largely unattended. Therefore, based on the existing documents and the analyses on rural household panel data in the 1990s, this chapter aims to re-examine the relationship between China's economic growth and rural poverty reduction, and to further discuss briefly on some questions that China's future economic development might face.

4.2. Have China's Rural Poverty-Relief Policies Fulfilled their Objectives?

It is not an easy task to measure the effect of China's policies for poverty alleviation since many thus challenged researchers often lack two sets of essential statistic data, i.e. the impoverished population and the input of various relief funds. An early study on the impact of the "Work for Food Program" interconnected poverty relief, growth and development and submitted that this policy in favor of labour-intensive technologies gave full play to the rich labour resources in poverty-stricken rural areas, thus contributing to the improvement of the infrastructure and social services of poor areas as well as the increase of employment opportunities and the income of the poor (Zhu and Jiang, 1994). Special attention was given to China's rural poverty in the *Country Reports 2001* of the World Bank in which reference was made to a study done by Jalan and Ravallion (2001). Based on a set of rural household data from 1985 to 1990 covering those counties on the list of China's official poverty alleviation projects, they found that the increase rate of household consumption in the poverty-stricken counties high on the state poverty relief agenda was higher than what had been expected. On close inspection on a county-level data set spanning from 1981 to 1995, Park and Wang (2001) concluded that the poverty alleviation input raised the per capita income by 2.28% annually from 1985–1992, and 0.91% from 1992 to 1995 respectively. Jalan and Ravallion, however, pointed out that Park *et al.* possibly overestimated the effect of the relief projects since they did not take into account all the public expenditures for poverty reduction (World Bank, 2001).

In addition, researches based on the rural household data collected from Sichuan and Shaanxi provinces revealed that the change in poverty rate in most cases could be explained by economic growth, the foremost force in mitigating poverty, and therefore China's poverty relief policies yielded little, if any, effect on poverty alleviation (Rozelle *et al.*, 2000). Another empirical study found that among the many government sponsored anti-poverty projects, poverty relief loans were of little avail in tackling poverty, which was mainly attributable to the inefficient target mechanism of these projects and the misemployment of the funds (Fan, 2003). Moreover, another study also argued that the development-oriented anti-poverty measures militated in favor of reducing chronic poverty whereas did not work on transient poverty (Jalan and Ravallion, 1998, 2000). One important cause rendering China's poverty relief policies less effective is that the government investment is mainly channeled to those regions listed in the official poverty alleviation projects. However, the rural poor in these areas only represent part of a larger whole if the picture is zoomed out; thus naturally, no direct causal link can be readily drawn between the government-led poverty alleviation and the decline of the poor in the rural areas that unfortunately fell out of the focus of the anti-poverty campaign.

4.3. Economic Growth as Principal Driving Force in China's Rural Poverty Reduction

In spite of the above findings, there are still many recent studies suggesting that the decline of rural poverty in China could be put down to the drastic economic growth powered by a series of market-oriented reforms and opening-up. For instance, many scholars shared the understanding that China's increase in prosperity and wealth had played a significant role in fighting rural poverty (Rozelle *et al.*, 2000; Feng Lu, 2001; Yuan Zhang *et al.*, 2009; Yuan Zhang and Guanghua Wan, 2010). Tao and Xu (2005) believed that China's fast economic growth spawned by its transition to a market economy greatly improved the status quo of its poverty problem. Likewise, CSLS (2003) attributed China's fast economic growth with a synchronized slump in poverty incidence to the increase in productivity. Meanwhile, some other studies expounded on the impact of public investment in agriculture and rural areas on rural poverty. One of them indicated that the government expenditure on education had the foremost important effect on poverty reduction and the second most on production growth, while the one on R & D and technology dissemination had the paramount importance to agricultural growth and the third most to poverty reduction, and the one on rural telecommunication was the second most important to poverty reduction and the third most to agricultural growth (Fan *et al.*, 2000). Another research dedicated to the comparison between China and India found that the investing more in the less developed regions would not only decrease poverty to the greatest extent but also generate the maximum economic return; and while the global poverty reduction was losing its momentum during the last two decades, China, thanks to a series of reforms in policies and government organizations which provided rural residents equal access to social services and productive assets, had achieved great success in fighting poverty (Fan, 2003).

Basically, the belief that economic growth is conducive to the poverty reduction enjoys a long history. In the early sixties of the 20th century, Bhagwati brought forward the "Bhagwati hypothesis" that assigned economic growth as the fundamental driving force for reducing poverty and has been sustained by many subsequent empirical tests (Rozelle *et al.*, 2000; Besley and Burgess, 2003). Some scholars believed that free trade best promoted economic growth over absolute poverty because: it created new markets where the poor might get more benefit; motivated the poor to react, in a positive manner, to the changes in relative prices and new market opportunities; availed the poor of an indirect spill-over effect, and improved the government's public spending, etc. (Anderson, 2004). Dollar and Kraay (2002), after investigating the impact of the economic growth on the income of poor populations using the macro data covering 92 countries, recognized that the fluctuation pattern of the income of the 20% population with the lowest income was in tune with that of the per capita income in these countries, and thus they emphasized that economic growth was as favorable to the poor as to the others and the policies for high economic growth should be the core of any effective anti-poverty regime. By the same token, countries like China, Vietnam, Indonesia and India have provided many successful cases in which the reforms to promote free market and trade have shrunk their respective poor populations. Studies identifying marketization and trade liberalization as the mainspring of poverty reduction are abundant. For instance, in their study on the impact of the change of prices for agricultural products on the level of household welfare through a set of Vietnamese household data, Minot and Goletti (1998) found that the liberalization of rice price increased farmers' average real income. Liu (2001) also used a set of Vietnamese microdata to explore the impact of the market-oriented reform on income inequity and poverty, which led to the conclusion that the reform significantly decreased poverty but the reduction rate in rural areas was slower than that in urban areas.

4.4. Did Agricultural Growth Play a "More Significant" Role in Reducing Rural Poverty?

A brief review on the relevant literature reveals that a widely accepted opinion represented by the World Bank emphasizes the "more important" implications of the growth in China's agricultural sector for the decline of rural poverty (World Bank, 2001; Ravallion and Chen, 2004; Montalvo and Ravallion, 2009). However, there are still some studies arguing otherwise. For instance, CSLS (2003) found that with respect to poverty reduction, the rise in productivity in China's industrial sector mattered more than that in its agricultural sector; once the productivity levels of different sectors were controlled, labour productivity in the industrial sector was the chief influencing factor in lowering poverty while only a weak positive correlation could be noticed in the agricultural sector; therefore a conclusion was arrived at that, since the prices for agricultural products were lower than those for industrial products, agricultural population was unable to get the benefit from the increase in agricultural productivity. It is thus believed that there exist many reasons for us to rethink whether agricultural growth indeed looms larger in the alleviation of rural poverty.

Apparently, a direct review on the relationship between agricultural growth and the population of rural poor will easily educe a misleading conclusion because agricultural growth is very likely accompanied by an increase in output, input and prices for agricultural products. For instance, if agricultural production cost rises quickly, even though gross agricultural output value goes up, farmers' net income will not necessarily increase nor will rural poverty decrease accordingly. China's early economy adopted urban-biased policies including the tight control over agricultural production, the suppression of the prices for agricultural products and the restriction of rural-urban migration via the resident registration system. These policies caused the relative profit of agricultural production to fall, and even many micro-data indicated that the net profit from the agricultural production of those rural households thus engaged was negative (Wan, 2004). To further investigate farmers' agricultural income, the following research based on the panel data of farm households in the 1990s is carried out.

The panel data used in this chapter are from *CERC/MoA database on Chinese rural households* which was established by a set of questionnaires on the grain production of China rural residents over 5 years (1993–1995 and 1999–2000) which was co-conducted by the Chinese Economy Research Centre of the University of Adelaide and the Policy and Regulation Department of the Ministry of Agriculture of China under the auspices of Australian Centre for International Agricultural Research. This survey covered six provinces including Henan, Jilin, Shandong, Guangxi, Sichuan and Guangdong, and the sampling in each province consisted of about 200 households scattering in 4 to 5 counties and a set of panel data was thus established. The statistics describe in detail various agricultural inputs, outputs, distributions, consumption, land policies, prices for agricultural products and the like, which provides us a bonanza of information to investigate farmers' production activity. Moreover, being panel data, they better capture the changes in farmers' activity for agricultural production in the 1990s.

Table 4.2 records the per acre yields of five major crops grown by the farmers. It can be seen that from 1993 to 2000, the average yield for corns fluctuated slightly around its initial level while those for winter wheat and rice climbed up. Generally speaking, the increase of yields for all the five crops was not sharp; therefore it can be envisaged that if the prices rise by a small margin, farmers' per acre income generated by crop growing will not take a sudden surge.

The increase in per acre yield of agricultural products implies the rise of agricultural productivity; however whether it further promises reduction in rural poverty depends on whether it can step up farmers' net income, which in turn depends on the prices for agricultural products and agricultural means of production. In cases where agricultural production

Table 4.2. Crop yields per acre (unit: half a kilogram).

	Corn	Winter wheat	Early long-grained nonglutinous rice	Intermediate-late long-grained nonglutinous rice	Japonica rice
1993	765.47	610.40	799.32	793.56	930.29
1994	778.68	628.03	846.97	858.33	943.19
1995	833.14	665.41	717.25	871.27	1013.78
1999	821.61	674.24	709.27	875.57	997.49
2000	725.35	695.66	771.44	875.53	1016.98

Sources: All the data used have been processed by the authors based on the *CERC/MoA database*.

Table 4.3. Input costs per acre of major crops (unit: yuan).

Year	Corns	Winter wheat	Early long-grain nonglutinous rice	Medium-late long-grain nonglutinous rice	Japonica rice
1993	77.58	81.44	57.69	47.86	63.90
1994	53.06	84.92	87.40	80.34	104.46
1995	77.78	108.87	106.37	97.57	138.22
1999	67.42	127.77	108.46	104.89	153.26
2000	75.10	132.83	100.00	92.03	173.59

produces low or even negative profits, the increase of gross agricultural output value will not necessarily bring about the drop in rural poverty. Since when the grain is cheap, the farmers suffer, the increase of gross agricultural output even bears the risk of exacerbating rather than alleviating rural poverty. Table 4.3 displays the income costs per acre of 5 major crops from which a trend can be recognized, i.e. the income costs for all the other crops except corns experienced a marked rise, with that for winter wheat having going up by more than 50% and that for rice having almost doubled.

In relation to the net income of agricultural production, apart from direct input cost, agricultural tax and various charges levied on farmers by local communities and governments (such as fees collected for the revenue reserve for overall planning, add-ons for rural education) also need to

Table 4.4. Per acre and per capita income taxes (unit: yuan).

	1993	1994	1995	1999	2000
Per acre agricultural income tax	—	25.35	28.91	16.23	20.10
Per acre revenue reserve for overall planning	—	9.13	4.94	70.20	82.64
Per capita agricultural income tax	22.12	33.86	37.02	32.86	31.04
Per capita revenue reserve for overall planning	8.26	11.96	6.46	127.41	125.31

Note: The per acre agricultural income tax and per acre revenue reserve for overall planning in 1993 are not available.

Table 4.5. Gross income per acre of major crops (unit: yuan).

Year	Corns	Winter wheat	Early long-grain nonglutinous rice	Medium-late Long-grain nonglutinous rice	Japonica rice
1993	197.65	177.91	203.26	310.20	283.91
2000	246.56	184.07	310.20	359.24	352.99

be taken into consideration because handing over these charges will immediately decrease farmers' disposable income. Table 4.4 shows the average taxation of the panel households calculated by the area of cultivated land and by population. It is obvious that per acre taxes fell, while per capita taxes rose. However, both per acre and per capita various fees displayed a noticeable ascending trend — a tenfold rise in 2000 over 1994.

Table 4.5 reveals the gross income per acre of 5 major crops which was calculated by multiplying the per acre yields by the levels of market price and then deducting the costs for various direct input factors but preserving the paid taxes and charges as well as depreciation of the fixed assets for agricultural purposes. From Table 4.5 it can be seen that from 1993 to 2000, the highest increase rate of the gross incomes per acre of the above crops registered at 50%. If all the taxes per acre of cultivated land and other uncounted costs are taken out, farmers' per acre net income from crop cultivation will increase at an even lower rate.

Thus it can been said with certainty that there is little room of margin for the augmentation of farmers' net income generated from crop cultivation, which also proves the fact that the crop planting industry exerts limited effect on increasing farmers' income and reducing rural poverty. And because crop planting industry constitutes the principal part of agricultural production, it is sensible to conclude that agricultural growth has little influence on the increase of farmers' net income and the reduction of rural poverty.

4.5. The Increase of Non-Agricultural Income as Pivotal Role in Reducing Rural Poverty

In the previous analysis of the direct impact of agricultural growth on the reduction of rural poverty based on the household survey data, it is believed that the impact is not as significant as what the World Bank has asserted. In this chapter, it is suggested that it is the non-agricultural income that plays the pivotal role in reducing China's rural poverty through a mechanism that works on farmers' employment opportunities, working time and level of income via a trickle-down effect.

As we all know, China used to adopt an economic strategy that prioritized the development of heavy industry and impropriated agricultural profits as subsidies to industry under a series of urban-biased policies. Therefore, the relative profits or incomes from non-agricultural production were higher than those from agricultural production, which was attested by plenty of micro researches. For instance, according to the survey data of rural residents from National Bureau of Statistics of China, the net income of the work force engaged in the secondary industry in the early 1990 was 2.6 times as much as that of rural labour, and the per capita net income of concurrent households was around 50% higher than that of pure peasant households; and the indicator that measured the success of China's rural economic development was the progress of the non-agricultural industries (Li, 2003). In addition, Yao (2000) noticed in his study that the development of township enterprises was conducive to the reduction of rural poverty. These findings make it clear that as China's economy booms, the improvement of non-agricultural sectors provides more and more employment opportunities, resulting in an upsurge in the demands for agricultural surplus labour which enables the rural low-income households to be employed by non-agricultural sectors and to eventually benefit from the faster growth in these sectors as well.

To explain this mechanism, Table 4.6 displays the net income sources of the panel households used in this chapter and their respective increase rates in the 1990s. Apparently, from 1993 to 2000, farmers' per capita net income grew from 1 269.87 yuan to 2 534.88 yuan, completely doubling itself. Once the income sources are broken down, the two basic facts will be easily identified: farmers' agricultural net income increased by 102%, which exactly synchronized with the growth rate of their gross net income; and the net income from non-agricultural sectors such as industry, construction industry, transportation industry and commercial industry and the money sent back to hometowns by migrant workers were quite high and hence had a far greater contribution to the increase of farmers' net income than agriculture. (It is worth noting that a small amount of migrant workers were still engaged in agricultural production, but survey data show that they only take up a small proportion of the sampling.)

In this chapter it is believed that the main dynamic that propels the decline of rural poverty relies on the trickle-down effect on poverty-stricken households created by the economic growth. This effect is realized by providing them with the opportunity of entering the labour force in non-agricultural sectors and thus earning higher income than in the agricultural sector. For instance, Table 4.7 provides the statistic description of the working time of poverty-stricken households, from which it can be seen that the overall annual working time of these households fluctuated from 1993 to 2000, but generally maintained steady. However, when this working time is broken down to agricultural and non-agricultural working time, it will be highlighted that the former experienced a marked downtrend whereas the latter an ascending trend. This means that China's economic development does provide poor households with increasing number of opportunities to be employed by non-agricultural sectors.

To further explore the implications of non-agricultural employment on the reduction of poverty, only those households that were trapped in poverty in 1993 and pulled out of poverty by 2000 were sampled from the overall panel households. In this way, the effects of various income sources on their escape from poverty can be revealed through examining how their income increased. Table 4.8 reports the statistic results from which it can be seen that the increase rate of the per capita income of poor

Table 4.6. Farmers' net income sources and their increase rates (1993–2000) (unit: yuan).

	Overall net income	**Net income from agriculture**	**Net income from forestry**	**Net income from livestock husbandry**	**Net income from fishery**	**Net income from industry**	**Net income from construction industry**	**Net income from transportation industry**
1993	1269.87	599.29	15.34	251.54	13.56	15.63	31.62	17.17
2000	2534.88	1213.23	7.95	393.27	22.93	59.93	75.53	67.13
Increase rate	2.00	2.02	0.52	1.56	1.69	3.83	2.39	3.91
	Net income from commercial industry	Net income from other businesses in service industry	Salary of township enterprises	Collective distribution	Collective subsidies to loss of working-time	Money sent back to hometowns by migrant workers	Dividends	Other net incomes
1993	15.14	88.31	38.49	19.66	51.91	59.15	9.91	43.19
2000	52.29	183.73	40.08	29.13	96.89	202.64	11.22	78.94
Increase rate	3.45	2.08	1.04	1.48	1.87	3.43	1.13	1.83

Table 4.7. The allocation of working-time of poverty-stricken households (unit: day).

	1993	**1994**	**1995**	**1999**	**2000**
Overall working-time	529.16	514.77	355.08	417.42	531.39
Agricultural working-time	434.43	343.39	249.37	333.94	358.56
Non-agricultural Working-time	94.73	171.38	105.72	83.48	172.84

households from 1993 to 2000 registered at 345%, faster than that of all the households. Among the various income sources, the agricultural income indeed went up more rapidly. During these years, the agricultural income of those households that had shaken off poverty rose to 402% of its original level, which however was not the fastest-growing one. Apparently, the income gained from fishery, construction industry, transportation industry, commercial industry and the money sent back home by migrant workers increased by a larger margin than agricultural and overall incomes. Moreover, it was highly likely that the money sent back home only constituted part of the overall earning of the migrant workers (those income that was not sent home by the migrant workers' was missed by the survey), and therefore the statistic data in Table 4.8 have the inherent risk of underestimating the contribution of the rural out-migration for employment to the increase of the income of rural or poor households.

4.6. China's Pro-Poor Industrialization

The previous analysis of this chapter actually reveals an "enigma" of China's reduction of rural poverty — why having adopted a set of urban-biased policies that are hostile to rural areas and agriculture, China still has managed to significantly decrease rural poverty? Ravallion (2001) pointed out that although the present evidence indicated that the poor population in developing countries could indeed share the benefit of the increase in gross output, the extent of the sharing in different countries varied greatly, so was the impact on the poor population; and multinational researches were often troubled with data, and failed to truly answer

Table 4.8. The income sources of farmers who have already shaken off poverty and their increase (unit: yuan).

Net income and sources	1993	2000	Increase rate from 1993 to 2000
Overall income	682.20	2355.02	3.45
Overall income from agriculture	217.14	873.12	4.02
Overall income from forestry	5.87	20.18	3.44
Overall income from livestock husbandry	215.50	498.67	2.31
Overall income from fishery	9.26	48.30	5.22
Net income from industry	13.21	24.51	1.86
Net income from the construction industry	14.39	125.33	8.71
Net income from transportation industry	3.02	28.95	9.59
Net income from commercial industry	3.37	29.31	8.70
Net income from other businesses in service industry	57.96	156.72	2.70
Salary of township enterprises	4.26	4.44	1.04
Collective distribution	3.58	12.26	3.42
Collective subsidies to loss of working-time	27.51	46.28	1.68
Money sent back to hometowns by migrant workers	74.94	423.27	5.65
Dividends	3.64	1.23	0.34

the question about the impact on welfare, which could mislead development policies. Therefore, he thought that it was necessary to further the micro empirical analysis on the changes of the increase and allocation of income, and only via such analysis, a solid foundation could be established for measuring the effect of a specific policy or programme, which preconditioned the implementation of development-oriented policies. As for the Chinese miracle of reducing rural poverty, it is believed by the authors that the key driving force rests with industrialization that creates the vast employment opportunities out of and absorbs a mass of surplus rural labour, which eventually leads to a trickle-down effect on the rural poor households.

The migration of surplus rural labour to cities has profound significance to their welfare because it shows that farmers can enter the urban labour market to access to more opportunities of non-agricultural employment of better earning potentials. Therefore, the above panel data are utilized again to test whether there exist any determinants of migration among farmers. Table 4.9 shows the regression analysis based on the data spanning from 1994 to 1995, 1999 to 2000, and 1999 to 2000 respectively. The dependent variable in the model used in the analysis is whether there are farmers who migrated outside hometown to find jobs, the independent

Table 4.9. Determinants of emigration among family members (Probit Model).

Variants	1994–2000		1999–2000	
	Model 1	Model 2	Model 3	Model 4
pvt93	0.319***		0.357***	
	(0.069)		(0.096)	
ptv		−0.191***		−0.288***
		(0.074)		(0.102)
hhage	−0.000	0.000	−0.003	−0.002
	(0.004)	(0.004)	(0.006)	(0.006)
hhedu	0.001	−0.003	−0.015	−0.019
	(0.014)	(0.014)	(0.020)	(0.020)
hhlabour	0.021	0.050	0.066	0.102**
	(0.030)	(0.031)	(0.043)	(0.045)
landsize	−0.008	−0.019**	0.012	0.001
	(0.007)	(0.007)	(0.009)	(0.010)
logfixasset	0.020**	0.020**	0.009	0.009
	(0.010)	(0.010)	(0.014)	(0.014)
timetrend	0.092	0.080	−399.908**	−399.980**
	(0.060)	(0.059)	(177.093)	(176.689)
constant	−185.057	−161.352	0.357***	−0.288***
	(118.853)	(117.111)	(0.096)	(0.102)
observation	2432	2432	1226	1226
Pseudo R^2	0.1251	0.1191	0.1240	0.1194
Log likelihood	−1039.51	−1046.70	−523.53	−526.29

Note: The values in the parentheses are standard error; *, ** and *** denote the values are significant at 10%, 5% and 1% respectively; and the regression coefficients of provincial dummy variables are not present.

variable that is concerned by this chapter is "pvt93", i.e. whether farmers were trapped in poverty in 1993, and "pvt" denotes whether farmers were poverty-stricken in the following years. Table 4.9 produces some interesting results: the coefficient of "pvt93" is significantly positive, which indicates that more farmers who were once trapped in poverty in 1993 migrated to cities in the following years; however that of "pvt" is significantly negative, which means that less poor households chose to migrate to cities in the very year. The regression results signify that it was not necessarily that more poor households were able to migrate in the very year (of course, there is also the possibility of a bi-directional causality), however, the poverty in the past years remarkably increased the rate of rural-to-town migration in the subsequent years. Since the migrants in cities mainly engaged in industrial production, they were gradually assimilated into the China's industrialization process. This finding is consistent with the study of Li and Zhong (1999) who found that migrants in prosperous areas were mainly from rural low-income rather than high-income households.

In view of the above, China's industrialization is pro-poor. It helps lift rural households out of poverty whose mechanism lies in the fact that poverty can significantly boost the rate of migration in the following years since the non-agricultural employment enabled by the migration can greatly improve the level of income

4.7. China's Experiences in Reducing Rural Poverty

Only from the perspective of reducing rural poverty, the present studies universally criticize China's early economic strategies and the parallel urban-biased policies. For instance, Carter (1997) thought that the sluggish agricultural growth was the major negative effect that the urban-biased policies exerted on agricultural production, and meanwhile the rural factor markets were also distorted. Yang (1999) believed that China's urban policies would affect human resource input and further widen the rural-urban divide, which is detrimental to China's future economic development. Yang and Cai (2000) also held that urban-biased policies could distort the whole economy and ultimately slow down the increase rate of agricultural growth and economic growth at large. A great number of studies criticize the widening rural-urban gap brought about by the policies biased again rural regions (Knight and Song, 1993; Brandt and Zhu, 1998; Yang and Zhou, 1999; Yang, 1999; Tian, 2001; Zhang, 2003; Kanbur and Zhang, 2004). Nevertheless, from the viewpoint of economic growth, the industrialization bolstered by urban-biased policies constitutes the primary motivating force of China's economic boom. Since the foundation of the People's Republic of China, its strategy of prioritizing the development of heavy industry and the corresponding planned economy system indeed successfully elevated the rate of capital accumulation almost from scratch to 15% or even higher, and built up a relatively complete industrial economic system in a short period (Lin *et al.*, 1994). It is logically sound to say that China's early economic strategies bear profound significance on the industrialization and economic take-off of a developing country with an overwhelming agricultural population; and these strategies, in particular, paved the way for the reform and opening-up launched in 1978 and the subsequent sustained economic growth. Thus, even though there are plenty of critiques with respect to these policies, it is worth noting the following issues.

First, under certain historical circumstances, urban-biased policies no doubt held some disadvantages to the reduction of rural poverty, the steady decline of the rural-urban divide, and agricultural growth. Nevertheless, without them, it would have been impossible for China to accumulate the prerequisite capital for the economic boom without which China in turn would not have recorded a continual decline of rural poverty.

Second, with a huge rural population, to build industrialization upon a shabby foundation China needed to accumulate an astronomical sum of capital. In cases where this could not be achieved from external sources, China had no choice but to rely on a "growth first, then distribution" strategy to mobilize the internal resources because otherwise the general economy would have suffered an inadequate accumulation. In short, judged against historical settings, these urban-biased policies at least successfully launched China in a fast lane of economic development.

Third, the issue of "vast population, limited arable lands" looms large as a bottleneck of development in China, the most populous country in the world. Against such a backdrop, it would not necessarily be good policy choice to fuel the whole economic growth, decrease rural poverty and actively participate in international trade via expanding agricultural economy that has a relatively low added value of development. Moreover, agricultural growth does not necessarily imply the alleviation of rural poverty because it is also subject to the influence of other factors such as the fluctuation of the prices for agricultural products and agricultural input factors, which are in turn closely related to marketization and trade liberalization.

Fourth, upon the accomplishment of the historical objective of accumulating capital to propel the economic boom through a set of urban-biased policies, Chinese government began to redress the resource allocation that was once distorted by these policies in an attempt to advance the reform and opening-up in a more measured fashion and has succeeded in the transition from a planned economy to a market economy.

Fifth, Lin *et al.* (1994) put forward the following acute observations on China's early economic policies. Running counter to the comparative advantages of resources, China's economic structure was seriously distorted by the artificially imposed development strategies that prioritized the growth in heavy industry. As a result, China missed the opportunity of achieving a "faster growth rate" that could have otherwise achieved. The overly dense constitution of capital restrained the comparative advantage of rich labour resources from being brought into full play, blundering away the otherwise obtainable level of employment and urbanization in a dual-economy in which the conventional and modern departments were separated from each other. The economic growth sustained only by accumulation distorted the distribution of national income, leading to a sluggish improvement in living standards. This distorted industrial structure also created an economic shutoff that eliminated the possibilities of giving full play to China's advantages and offsetting its comparative disadvantages at the same time through international trade. Then a question emerges from the previous discussion — China has already created a miracle of economic growth; however if the economic strategies had been better designed it would have achieved an even faster growth rate to the point of creating "a miracle of miracles", then what is the driving force behind this miracle? Neither neo-classical economics nor endogenous growth theory provides us with a complete answer to this question. Nevertheless, some important clues can be found in the development economics. First of all, since the foundation of P. R. China, the threshold of the economic growth was extremely low, which allowed the growth rate to be maintained at a relatively high level. Second, the path China has covered during the past 60 years of development is after all a road to industrialization that is the very core impetus to societal betterment and economic development (Zhang, 1992). China, actually, is on a structuralism course of development to achieve industrialization. That is, industrialization has created a mass of nonagricultural positions to absorb the vast rural surplus labour. And once it migrates outside rural areas, the agricultural output does not fall, while the industrial output grows, which eventually promotes the whole economic growth. Third, China is home to the biggest population of labour force in the world. Although macro statistic data indicate a steep growth in Chinese labour force, one piece of truth is concealed — the rural surplus labour has been migrating to industry and the tertiary industry during the process of industrialization and the absorption of recessive unemployment. The microdata in the previous part show that an increasing number of migrants enter cities and their nonagricultural working time is on an absolute increase.

Last, it must be borne in mind that China's economy so far has only fulfilled industrialization in its most early phase. The urban-biased policies apparently can hardly further fuel the sustained growth of China's economy. It remains as a big question mark that whether the next phase of industrialization will continue to produce phenomenal achievements. If China's economy can maintain the present robust growth in the following 20 to 30 years, then it is indeed worthy of the name of "a miracle of miracles".

In view of the above analysis, it is believed in this chapter that the miracle of China's economic growth is closely related to the counterbalance of the distorted resource allocation by marketization and the driving force of industrialization to the economic boom. And the reduction of China's rural poverty is mainly caused by more chances for the rural poor to share the spoils of this development as the economic structure is undergoing a transition. The most important way of this sharing then is the employment in nonagricultural sectors enabled by the rural-urban migration. In this model of development, the reduction of China's rural poverty is not achieved mainly through promoting agricultural growth, but rather through the preferential distribution of the limited capital or resources to the industrial sector since, once they have become stronger, rural surplus labour can be absorbed and agricultural technologies be promoted accordingly. In a final analysis of the above discussion, the following are the experiences of China's success in reducing rural poor.

China, as developing country with a huge agricultural population, is facing a bottleneck of "vast population, limited arable lands". In this context, it is not necessarily a wise strategy to promote economic growth and reduce rural poverty through prioritizing the development in agriculture that has a relative low added value. The miracle of China's economic growth cannot be properly interpreted without the context of marketization and industrialization. During the very process, China adopted a lopsided stratagem, i.e. to accumulate a vast sum of capital for industrialization and to create economic growth poles (that is, the development and rapid growth of the industrial sector) through urban-biased policies. Then as the full-fledged industrial sector began to absorb plenty of rural surplus labour, the rural poor, like the others, have been able to benefit from the industrialization. Employment in cities or the industrial sector is no doubt the prerequisite for the rural poor to have their fair share of the "economic growth cake". Meanwhile, a considerable portion of China's industrial sector is labour-intensive. In the circumstances, even though the rural poor are normally poorly educated and badly qualified, they still have the opportunities to participate in the process of industrialization and hence to gain from the whole economic growth as well. China's marketization changes the efficiency of resource allocation, which benefits the overall economic growth. However, it does not necessarily follow that the rural poor will for sure also be beneficiaries of this change as well. Therefore, marketization is a necessary condition for the decline of rural poverty, whereas industrialization the sufficient condition.

A recurring emphasis in the previous parts is the significance of the rural population's entering into cities and being employed by the industrial sector — the two factors that allow the poor to enjoy some of the fruits of the economic growth. Likewise, Bardhan and Udry (1999) also assigned the increase in employment opportunities that enabled the poor to acquire productivity as the most crucial way of helping the poor through economic growth, such as the self-employment opportunities on farms and in informal urban sectors. Therefore, including the poor into the trajectory of economic growth assumes paramount importance to the alleviation of poverty. However, for many reasons, there are still some poor people being excluded from the course of the growth. A case in point is that an immature capital market makes poverty an inescapable fate for the poor who have low skill level and little property. Additionally, problems can still ensue from the process of the economic growth itself. For instance, under economy of scale, the convergent force inherent in the process of economic growth may let the resources flow outside the backward regions so that the disparity between regions is reinforced. Thus, having created economic growth poles through lopsided stratagems, whether the poor will then enjoy the opportunities to benefit from the growth becomes the crux of the possibilities of further reducing poverty. In this chapter, it is held that for China it is crucial to gradually reform two key channels of sharing the fruits of economic growth — the present residence registration system and the employment policies prejudiced against migrant workers. If no policies that enable the rural and poor households to equally benefit from the growth are guaranteed to replace the previous biased ones once the growth poles have created, a serious polarization may ensue or economic growth may come to a halt.

It is worth mentioning that China's experiences in its path choice for economic development and the reduction of rural poverty may be more suitable for densely populated countries with a relative low threshold of development. In particular, it is vital to make sure whether there exists a political system that ensures low-income groups the equal opportunities of sharing in the fruits of economic growth. Meanwhile, the land reform in rural areas has complex impacts. The success of the household responsibility system in China does not necessarily imply that the same results can be expected if land reform is transplanted in other nations.

4.8. What to do Next?

The urban-biased policies have profound implications for the capital accumulation for industrialization and the realization of the economic take-off, as discussed in the previous parts, however, it does not necessarily follow that the economic growth propelled by these policies is sustainable. The stratagem of prioritizing the development of heavy industry, along with the urban-biased policies, is the crux of many prominent issues that are pertinent to most of the observed disparity in economic development in China, such as the ever-yawning income gap between rural and urban areas, the phenomenon that the poor are mainly populated in rural areas, the unequal access to the public goods and services, the imbalance within the national economy between different regions, rural and urban areas and industries, etc. In view of all these issues, an overwhelming challenge with which China will be faced on its way to future economic development is whether it can avoid the pitfall known as the "Middle Income Trap".

For a developing economy, there are multiple factors that may lead to the "Middle Income Trap", such as the stagnation of industrial structure, laggard technologies, overly wide income divide and the like. With respect to China, it has entered the list of lower-middle-income countries in terms of per capita GNI or GDP, and its next goal is then to upgrade into the list of high-income countries. Whether a country with a large population like China can manage to avoid the trap is of great significance to the future economic development of the whole world, and therefore it also arouses a worldwide concern. In 2007 the World Bank warned East Asian economy of the "Middle Income Trap" in one of its reports. One challenge particularly pointed out was how to deal with the ubiquitous issue of a widening income gap (Gill and Kharas, 2007). The concern of the World Bank is not groundless because the income distributions are generally quite fair in Japan, a country that is acknowledged as a successful case of jumping from middle-income to high-income economy, and the Four Asian Tigers, whereas in those Latin American countries, which are caught in the "Middle Income Trap", income distribution is highly unequal. According to the World Bank, income distribution that is deteriorated to the point of jeopardizing the economic incentives and social stability will engender resistance to economic growth, making per capita income incapable of continual growth. China's widening income gap has brought similar anxiety. According to the annual report of the World Bank in 2006, out of the 127 countries of unequal income distribution, 94 countries had a Gini Coefficient that was lower than that of China's; and only

29 were higher than China — among which 27 were from Latin America and Africa; and in Asia, only Malaysia and the Philippines had a Gini Coefficient that was higher than China (World Bank, 2006). Whether China can avoid the "Middle Income Trap" is closely related to whether China can change fundamentally the unbalanced development policies in due time. If it fails to provide the poor or the low-income group with more chances to share the fruits of the economic growth, China is likely to face an embarrassing situation where the same cause may lead to both the success and the failure of the development.

In addition, it can be concluded from the previous analysis that re-allocating the rural surplus labour in the fast growing industrial sector is of great significance to the reduction of rural poverty. This teaching bears important implications for a sustained and healthy development of national economy in the future for the following reasons. First of all, in light of the development economics theory developed by Zhang (1949), whether a nation has realized industrialization is determined not only by the proportion of the industrial output to the whole national economy but also by that of the industrial employment to the overall employment in all sectors. At present, the GDP by industry has already exceeded 50%, however the labour employed in the industrial sector is much lower than 50%. In this sense, China still has a long way to go to fulfill industrialization. Accordingly, how to create more jobs to absorb rural labour is arguably a major challenge for China's economy in the future, and also a pivotal way to further reducing the rural poor and narrowing the rural-urban income gap. Second, China's rural labour generally has poor education and low level of work skills. The improvement in agricultural technologies will produce more such labour and the capital deepening in the process of industrialization will also accelerate the replacement of human labour by machines. However, since 2000 China's urban registered unemployment rate has been kept high, and 20 million migrant workers were deprived of their jobs and sent back home in the global financial crisis in 2008. If there had been 130 million migrant workers very year, the unemployment rate would have hit 15.3%. Therefore, it is worth bearing in mind that advancing industrialization or promoting the development of labour-intensive industries at some stage or in certain areas to create more employment opportunities should still be the foremost important objective of policy making for China's future economic development. At the same time, the necessary conditions for healthy development of China's economy in the future will remain as there is a continual relaxation on the employment policies that are prejudiced against migrant workers, a unified health care system, pension policies and a minimum living security system that covers both the urban and the rural residents.

However, the above policy discussions are mainly aimed at how to further reduce the rural poverty rather than how to help China avoid the middle income trap. Apart from narrowing the disparities between urban and rural areas, different regions and various groups by way of the primary and secondary distribution of national income, other policy choices are equally worth considering. The first issue to be thought about is how to upgrade industries against the backdrop of a structural reform. Although there is no universal answer in the existing literature on the effectiveness of developing countries' industry portfolios, nevertheless Chinese central and regional governments are no doubt striving for sound policies in this respect. These efforts are best characterized by "thirst for investments" as well as "thirst for technologies" so that upgrading industrial technologies is put high on the agenda of various governments. Even though Chinese governments at various levels are increasingly aware of the growing challenge of sustaining the economic growth merely through the export of labour-intensive products and services, they have so far given few mature considerations as to how to achieve the much-longed-for technology upgrade. Importing advanced technologies of course provides one solution, and that is why during his US visit in January 2011, President Jintao Hu urged the United States to ease restrictions on high-tech exports to China. However, for a country as populous as China, it is not realistic to expect its technologies upgraded simply through technology imports. Under China's M-shaped governmental organization, the governments at all levels are dedicated to finding themselves a set of optimal industrial policies. Then the problem is whether an optimal policy at a regional level is still the best for the whole nation? And what is even alarming is that the industrial policy in one region runs the risk of shifting its own troubles to other regions. Controversial as it is, policy making or reforms to tackle the issue will not lead to an overall failure;

nevertheless, it is by no means a sufficient condition for a country to make a successful industrial stratagem. Next, as the second largest economy, China is facing many enormous challenges — how to enjoy a sustained technological advancement, how to participate in the fierce international competition with more ease, and how to achieve a peaceful rise, just to name a few. So far China has not found satisfactory solutions to them. Nevertheless, the most crucial challenge of all, instead of whether China will tackle the above issues, is how to juggle economic and policy reforms while maintaining a stable environment for cultivating and implementing sound policies to promote technological development and industrial upgrade. One thing for sure is that China's future reforms will not work on its economic growth exactly the same way as three decades ago when a sectoral reform or a local reform in one line of business (for instance, the agricultural reform, the privatization of state-owned enterprises in cities, the reform of state-owned banks, the reform of the revenue system, etc.) could promote the national economy as a whole. Any future reform will undoubtedly be a whole set of policy choices that integrates considerations with respect to many aspects of social life. And of course such reform must be the focal point of China's policy makers.

References

Anderson, K. (2004). "Agricultural Trade Reform and Poverty Reduction in Developing Countries." World Bank Policy Research Working Paper 3396, Washington DC.

Bardhan, P. and Udry C. (1999). *Development Microeconomics.* Oxford: Oxford University Press.

Besley, T. and Burgess R. (2003). "Halving Global Poverty." *Journal of Economic Perspectives*, 17(3), 3–22.

Brandt, L. and Zhu X. (1998). "Soft Budget Constraints and Inflation Cycles: A Positive Model of The Macro Dynamics in China During Transition." Mimeo, University of Toronto.

Cai, F. (2008). "Can Chinese Economy Escape from Middle-Income Trap?" *Transaction of Graduate School, Social Science of Chinese Academy*, 1, 13–18.

Carter, A.C. (1997). "The Urban-Rural Income Gap in China: Implications for Global Food Markets." *American Journal of Agricultural Economics*, 79, 1410–1418.

Che, J. and Qian, Y. (1998). "Insecure Property Rights and Government Ownership of Firms." *Quarterly Journal of Economics*, 113(2), 467–496.

CSLS (2003). "China's Productivity Performance and Its Impact on Poverty in the Transition Period." Centre for the Study of Living Standards Research Report 2003–07, Ottawa.

Dollar, D. and Kraay, A. (2002). "Growth is Good for the Poor." *Journal of Economic Growth*, 7, 195–225.

Fan, S. (2003). "Public Investment and Poverty Reduction, What Have We Learnt from India and China?" Paper prepared for the ADBI conference, "Infrastructure Investment for Poverty Reduction: What Do We Know?" Tokyo, June 12–13, 2003.

Fan, S., Zhang, L. and Zhang, X. (2000). "Growth and Poverty in Rural China: the Role of Public Investments." EPTD Discussion Paper, No. 66, International Food Policy Research Institute, Environment and Production Technology Division.

Gill, I. and Kharasm, H. (2007). *An East Asian Renaissance: Ideas for Economic Growth*. Washington DC: The World Bank.

Jalan, J. and Ravallion, M. (1998). "Transient Poverty in Post-Reform China." *Journal of Comparative Economics*, 26, 338–357.

Jalan, J. and Ravallion, M. (2000). "Is Transient Poverty Different? Evidence for Rural China." *Journal of Development Studies*, 36(6), 82–99.

Kanbur, R. and Zhang, X. (2004). "Fifty Years of Regional Inequality in China: a Journey Through Central Planning, Reform, and Openness." United Nations University WIDER working paper, No. 2004/50.

Knight, J. and Song, L. (1993) "The Spatial Contribution to Income Inequality in Rural China." *Cambridge Journal of Economics*, 17, 195–213.

Li, S. (2003). "Review and Outlook of Individual Income Distribution in China." (in Chinese). *Economic Quarterly*, 2(2), 379–403.

Li, S. and Zhong, W. (1999). "Labour Migration and Income Distribution in Rural China." In Zhao, R. *et al.* (eds), *A Restudy on Income Re-distribution of Chinese Citizens* (in Chinese). Beijing: Publishing House of Chinese Fiscal and Economy.

Lin, J.Y., Cai, F. and Li, Z. (1994). *China Miracle: Economic Strategy and Economic Reform* (in Chinese). Shanghai: Sanlian Bookstore and Shanghai People's Publishing House.

Liu, A.Y.C. (2001). "Markets, Inequality and Poverty in Vietnam." *Asian Economic Journal*, 15, 217–235.

Lu, F. (2001). "China Searching for Another Anti-Poverty Strategy," Working Paper, no. C200104, China Center for Economic Research, Peking University.

Minot, N. and Goletti, F. (1998). "Export "Liberalization and Household Welfare: the Case of Rice in Vietnam." *American Journal of Agricultural Economics*, 80(4), 738–749.

Montalvo, J.G. and Ravallion, M. (2009). "The Pattern of Growth and Poverty Reduction in China." World Bank Policy Research Working Paper 5069, World Bank.

Naughton, B. (1994). "Chinese Institutional Innovation and Privatization from Below." *American Economic Review*, Papers and Proceedings of the Hundred and Sixth Annual Meeting of the American Economic Association, 84(2), 266–270.

Ravallion, M. (2001). "Growth, Inequality and Poverty: Looking Beyond Averages." *World Development*, 29(11), 1803–1815.

Ravallion, M. (2008). "Are There Lessons for Africa from China's Success Against Poverty?" World Bank Policy Research Paper 4463, World Bank.

Ravallion, M. and Shaohua, C. (2004). "China's (Uneven) Progress Against Poverty." World Bank Policy Research Working Paper 3408, World Bank.

Rozelle, S., Zhang, L. and Huang, J. (2000). "China's War on Poverty." Working Paper No. 60, Center for Economic Research on Economic Development and Policy Reform, Stanford Institute for Economic Policy research, Stanford University.

Swinnen, J. and Rozelle, S. (2006). *From Marx and Mao to the Market: The Economics and Politics of Agricultural Transition*. USA: Oxford University Press.

Tao, R. and Xu, Z. (2005). "Urbanization, Land Tenure and the Social Protection of Migrants: A Perspective of a Big Transitional Country and its Policy Option" (in Chinese). *Economic Research Journal*, 12, 45–56.

Tian, Q. (2001). "China's New Urban-Rural Divide and Pitfalls for the Chinese Economy." *Canadian Journal of Development Studies*, 22(1), 165–190.

UNDP (2005). *Human Development Report 2005*. USA: Oxford University Press.

Wan, G. (2004). "Accounting for Income Inequality in Rural China." *Journal of Comparative Economics*, 32(2), 348–363.

Wan, G., Lu, M. and Chen, Z. (2006). "The Inequality-Growth Nexus in the Short and Long Runs: Empirical Evidence from China." *Journal of Comparative Economics,* 34(4), 654–667.

World Bank (2001). *World Development Report 2000/2001, Attacking Poverty.* New York: Oxford University Press.

World Bank (2006). *World Development Report 2006: Equity and Development.* Washington DC: World Bank.

Xu, C. (2010). "The Institutional Foundations of China's Reforms and Development." CEPR Discussion Paper No. DP7654.

Yang, D.T. (1999). "Urban-Biased Policies and Rising Income Inequality in China." *American Economic Review*, Papers and Proceedings of the One Hundred Eleventh Annual Meeting of the American Economic Association (May 1999), 89(2), 306–310.

Yang, D.T. and Fang, C. (2000). "The Political Economy of China's Rural-Urban Divide." Working Paper No. 62 of Center for Research on Economic Development and Policy Reform, Stanford University.

Yang, D.T. and Hao, Z. (1999). "Rural-Urban Disparity and Sectoral Labour Allocation in China." *Journal of Development Studies*, 35(3), 105–133.

Yao, S. (2000). "Economic Development and Poverty Reduction in China Over 20 Years of Reforms." *Economic Development and Cultural Change*, 48(3), 447–474.

Yuan, Z., Wan, G., Xu, Q. and Liu, X. (2009). "Market Transaction and Rural Poverty: An Empiric Study from a Micro Perspective." *The Journal of World Economy* (in Chinese), 32(9), 3–14.

Yuan, Z. and Wan, G. (2010). "Market Formation and Share of Economic Growth Fruit: the Micro Evidence from China and Indonesia." *Journal of Agrotechnical Economics* (in Chinese), 1, 18–26.

Zhang, P. (1949). "*Agriculture and Industrialization.*" PhD. Thesis, Harvard University, Harvard.

Zhang, P. (1992). *Neo-Development Economics* (in Chinese). Zheng Zhou: Henan People's Publishing House.

Zhang, X. (2003). "Inequality of Education and Medical and Health" (in Chinese). *Economic Quarterly*, 2(2), 405–416.

Zhu, L. and Jiang, Z. (1994). *Work-for-Food and Poverty Reduction* (in Chinese). Shanghai: Sanlian Bookstore and Shanghai People's Publishing House.

CHAPTER 5

POVERTY OF CHINESE FARMERS: WHAT SHOULD THE CHINESE GOVERNMENT DO?

Tangjun Yuan

5.1. Introduction

On the relationship between economic development and income distribution, Kuznets holds that, in the early stage of economic development, a country's standard of living is on the edge of subsistence and people's income remains relatively equal; with economic development, inter-industry productivity differentials lead to a rising income gap across industries; and when the economy sustains its growth and realizes full employment of resources, income distribution will be once again near equal — the Kuznets inverted U-shaped hypothesis (Kuznets, 1955). China's economic development was slow during the planned economy, policy-makers tried to find a balance between overcoming the lack of capital for industrialization and providing adequate food and clothing, and the rural and urban residents were very poor. In the early stages of the economic reform, the collective mode of agricultural production — the people's communes — was abandoned and the household responsibility system was introduced, which improved agricultural productivity. Meanwhile a substantial increase in state procurement prices of agricultural products significantly uplifted the rural household income in 1978–1984. In the late 1980s with the sudden emergence of rural township and village enterprises, the income of rural residents soared and hence narrowing down the urban-rural income gap. However the 1990s witnessed an

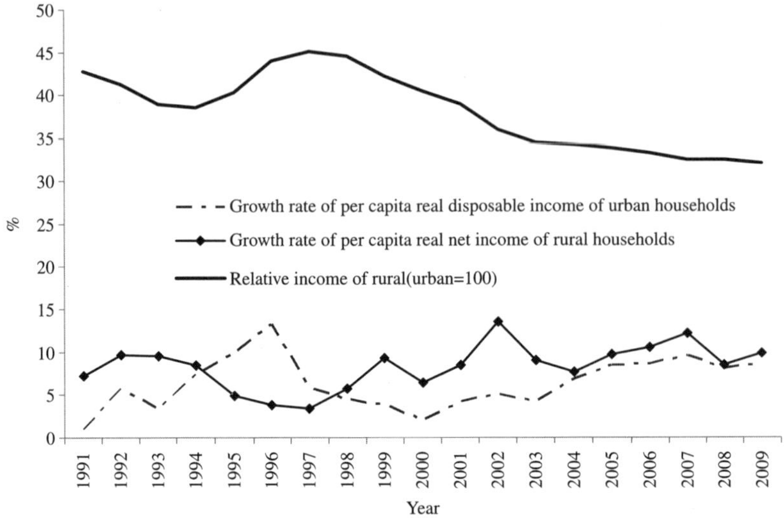

Fig. 5.1. Increasing urban-rural income gap.

Source: *China Statistics Yearbook* (various years).

ever-increasing regional and urban-rural income gap. With a population of over 1.3 billion, of which 70% still live in rural areas, China's per capita disposable income of urban residents reached 3.3 times that of farmers in 2009 compared with 2.2 in 1990 (Figure 5.1). With the rapid progress of life in urban areas, the issue of relative poverty in rural areas becomes more prominent, for such issues will not only cause a lot of social unrest but also hinder China's economy from transforming from one relying on external demand into a one relying on domestic demand.

There is numerous literature on rural poverty in China, many of them insightful, e.g., on various system factors, "price scissors" problem, unreasonable expenditure, employment and inequality in education and social security system, and other issues. Especially for the reform and opening-up period, there is an increase in urban and rural income disparities. Lu and Chen (2004) hold that urbanization, economic openness, denationalization, etc. significantly increase the urban-rural income gap, and the government expenditure structure significantly affects the urban-rural income gap. Wang (2006) clearly points out that along with the reform and opening up, while marketization has tended to reduce the urban-rural income gap, weak financial support and the "price scissors" of industrial and agricultural products have tended to widen the urban-rural income gap. Hu *et al.* (2007) think that economic growth does not automatically improve the distribution of income — such growth is a necessary condition for poverty reduction but not a sufficient one. The provision of laws, regulations and policies of the government serves to establish links between fairness and efficiency and is a prerequisite for turning a necessary condition into a sufficient condition. He (2004) points out that the cause of China's absolute poverty in rural areas lies in the following facts: dwindling rural land resources and declining land quality (lack of agricultural investment); deterioration of the agro-ecological environment; large rural population base; large number of rural women of reproductive age with high fertility; etc. Meanwhile, agriculture-related policy and institutional problems exacerbates the rural poverty. For example, incomplete agricultural land property rights system, underdeveloped and deficient financial and taxation systems, as well as national grain procurement policies all result in an excessive hidden drain on rural physical capital. As for the measures in to eradicate rural poverty, Ning (2009) also points out that, from an educational point of view, simply increasing funds for education without related reforms of the education system and labour market is of little help in reducing income inequality. He proposes to reform the examination system and improve the quality of education; to adjust through market mechanisms the return to education so as to reflect labour productivity; and to develop the labour market in order to reduce inter-sectoral and inter-industry income gap. Zhang and Zhan (2006) consider that the financial development may affect the urban-rural income gap via three effects in different directions: first of all, the threshold effect — under the conditions of financial constraints, due to their own restrictions on capital accumulation of wealth, the poor fail to reach the threshold level (such as the threshold for financial services) and miss the high-yield returns, while the rich, due to their advantages in capital accumulation, can enjoy high-yield returns and, therefore, the financial development affects the income gap of a society; second, the effect of unbalanced financial development — in developing countries the overall financial resources are limited, which may result in an unbalanced allocation of financial resources across regions and departments and between urban and rural areas, that is to say, an unbalanced financial development helps exert the income gap between sectors and areas; and third, the poverty-reduction effect of financial development — financial development promotes economic growth, in which the poor can enjoy more financial services and reduce their poverty, hence financial development affects social income gap.

However, most studies are limited to the description, analyzing the poverty of Chinese farmers from the perspective of a very particular cause. The issues of agriculture, rural areas and farmers are a long-term and common phenomenon of economic development. Agricultural economics defines them as "three-stage agricultural issues", namely (1) the food problems when income is low (food and clothing), (2) the urban-rural income gap when middle income is realized, and (3) the structural adjustment problems when income level is high (Hayami and Godo, 2002). In China, the issues are called the "three rural issues". In the long-term economic development, rural issues are not completely independent in time sequence and different development patterns and policy options make these issues become inextricably inter-woven and mutually affected. In general, against the background of the dual structure in the economy, it is the relatively backward agricultural productivity that generates these issues. Hence the key to solving these issues depends on the increase of agricultural productivity and the efficient allocation of labour and capital and other resources so as to fundamentally eliminate the dual structure and achieve the policy objective of common prosperity in urban and rural areas.

China's economic development is a transition from a planned economy to a market economy. One of the main features of both the planned economy period and the reform and opening-up period is that industrial sector has been expanding very rapidly. But considering the early days of the very weak industrial base of China, and when the industrial sector itself had not enough surplus, where did the capital accumulation come from? Was there a squeeze on agriculture? After reform and opening-up, the share of market economy has grown, and per capita income has increased rapidly, has China's agricultural issue been shifted to the so-called middle-income relative poverty? Government has abolished the agricultural tax, and reduced the burden by the implementation of a series of policies, but did not achieve significant results, why? Have policy and institutional problems affected the allocation of resources so as to create an invisible channel to squeeze agriculture? In this chapter, to explore the causes of poverty in the countryside and of farmers and propose relevant solutions, we try to comprehend China's current agricultural problems in the background of China's long-run economic development. This may help find out why the long-term agricultural productivity is so low and why rural migrant workers cannot successfully settle down in urban sectors. In Section 5.1, based on international comparisons the characteristics of China's economic growth, we show China's amazing speed of capital accumulation. Section 5.2 is a brief account of the studies of scholars on agriculture in China — the debate of squeezing, and the discussion on the inconsistencies between existing theoretical researches and empirical results. In Section 5.3, we take international prices as a benchmark for a long period of time from 1950 till present to measure the difference between the domestic and international prices of agriculture and industry products. We therefore define the term of *relative price* as "indirect taxation" on agriculture, which helps understand the causes of China's backward agricultural productivity. Lastly, Section 5.4 will further discuss the impact of China's current model of economic development on income distribution, and its policy implications for reducing the urban-rural income gap.

5.2. The Characteristic of China's Economic Growth — High Ratio of Capital Formation

5.2.1. *Amazing speed of industrialization*

Development economics emphasizes the "Petty-Clark Law" on the relationship between economic development and structural change, i.e., in the course of economic development, the proportion of primary industry decreases, followed by the increase of that of secondary and then tertiary industries. This law has been utterly embodied by the long-term economic development of China after the war. The most remarkable feature is the rapid expansion of the industrial sector. Either in the planned economy

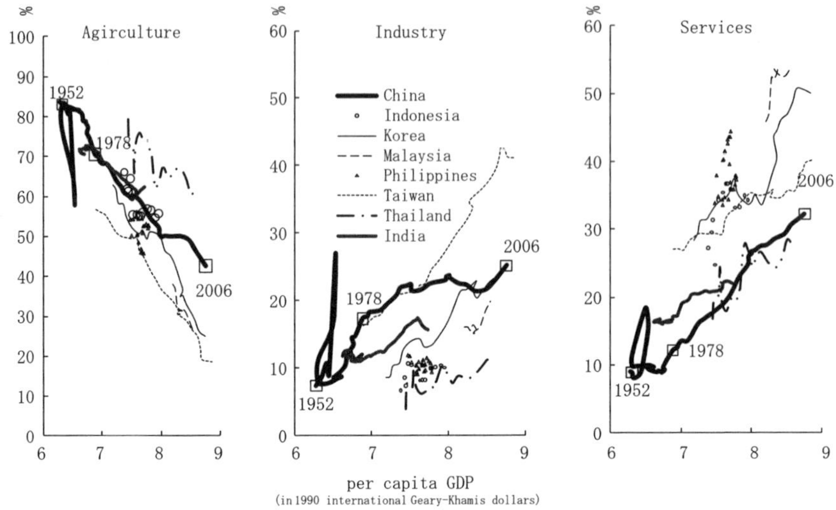

Fig. 5.2. International comparison of employment structure.

Source: The Conference Board and Groningen Growth and Development Centre, Total Economy Database (http://www.conference-board.org/economic), World Bank WDI (2007).
Note: Per capita GDP as logarithmic measured.

period or after the reform and opening-up, compared with other countries at the same stage of development, China's industrialization has been on a much faster track (Figure 5.2). In terms of the share of output of the last two decades, from 1990 to 2009, the proportion of primary industry of GDP decreased from 27.1% to 10.3%, and that of secondary industry increased from 41.3% to 46.3% (*China Statistical Yearbook*, 2010), similar to the structure of Japan in the early 1960s and that of Taiwan in the mid 1970s. The overall trend of the employment structure also satisfies the rule. In comparison with Asian major countries, we can confirm the fact that at the same stage of development (in Figure 5.2, the same position on horizontal axis implies the same per capita GDP), the percentage of China's industrial sector is greater. However, in contrast with the output structure of agriculture, employment rate of agriculture is somewhat higher and that of service sector appears relatively low. Such changes in industrial structure are related to the development strategy of heavy industry in the planning economy and are the inevitable results of the development model after reform.

5.2.2. *Patterns of economic development after the 1990s*

Upon entering the 1990s, China's economic growth mainly has the following features. The first is the export-led growth. The total imports and exports assume over 40% of GDP, with exports accounting for less than 7% of GDP in the 1980s up to 26% — a high foreign dependence, whereas the share of exported manufactured goods increased from less than 50% in the 1980s to 90%. It can be said that China's rapid economic growth is driven by the foreign expansion of industrial production. The second is investment-led growth. Since the 1990s, the tendency of such growth has become more and more significant. Investment took up an average 30% of GDP before 1992 and now surpasses 40%, far greater than that achieved by Japan in the period of its rapid growth. But it is worth noting that this increase in investment includes a variety of non-efficiency factors, so such economic growth can be defined as an extensive growth (i.e., factor-inputs-increase type). Especially in the latter half of the 1990s, the policy orientation of supporting state-owned enterprises led to the excessive investment by public sectors and, consequently, a decrease in the annual returns of the industrial capital (Zhang, 2001). For example, local governments, local enterprises, local branches of state-owned banks, all strive for the expanded production of state-owned industrial enterprises and the repeated investments become a very serious problem (Yuan, 2010). Growth featured by the increase of factor inputs does not contribute much to the technological progress. For example, the average economic growth rate of the 1990s was as high as 9.5%, of which the contribution of capital was 63% — an absolute proportion — while the total factor productivity (TFP) contributed only 21%, leaving 16% attributed to labour. It is rather low compared with about 40% in Japan in its fast growing period (with an annual growth rate of 9.2%). A recent study by Wu and Yuan (2010) also shows that after joining the WTO, China has witnessed a rapid decline of its industrial TFP growth. Related to this, the third characteristic is that, in the first ten years after the reform and opening-up, the development of rural and township enterprises attracted a large number of rural surplus labour, and since the 1990s, with the coastal development depending on foreign capital and the policy-orientation favoring the state-owned enterprises, the labour absorption capacity of industrial sector has plunged (Yuan, 2002). China's economy is still at the stage of the dual structure, and the above development model has an overwhelming impact on income distribution.

5.2.3. *Relatively backward development of agriculture*

By contrast, the development of agriculture is undesirable. Before the reform, the rural economic development went through three stages. The first stage is the early ten years (1949–1958). The success of land reform allowed farmers to have their own land, which greatly stimulated the enthusiasm of farmers in the production — an increase in yield for nine years running and a general improvement of farmers' lives. The second stage was after 1958. Along with the rapid expansion of people's commune system, improper promotion of agricultural technology and the leap-forward of industrial sectors seriously dampened the enthusiasm of farmers and agricultural production plunged down. Coupled with natural disasters in 1960, the Chinese economy experienced three years of economic difficulties known as the "Big famine". After 1961, the policy focused on agriculture, the people's communes were divided into production brigades, investment increased in agricultural fertilizers, and adjustments were made in crop cultivation to improve agricultural production, hence by 1966, we restored the production to 1957 levels. The third stage is the Cultural Revolution (1967–1976), when the interference of political movements rendered a long-term stagnation of agricultural production. In the early days of reform and opening-up, policy focused on accelerating rural economic development, by adjusting the relationship between industry and agriculture, increasing agricultural investment, upgrading agricultural and sideline products purchasing price, and ending the implementation of collective management by executing the household responsibility system — all these greatly enhanced production enthusiasm of farmers, which in turn greatly improved rural living standards. Reforms after 1984 shifted the focus to the industry. After joining the WTO in 2001, the government paid much attention to ensuring the safety and self-sufficiency of food and the international competitiveness of agricultural products. But not until 2005 did the three rural issues become one of the government concerns about its agricultural development and increase in farmers' income. The above development

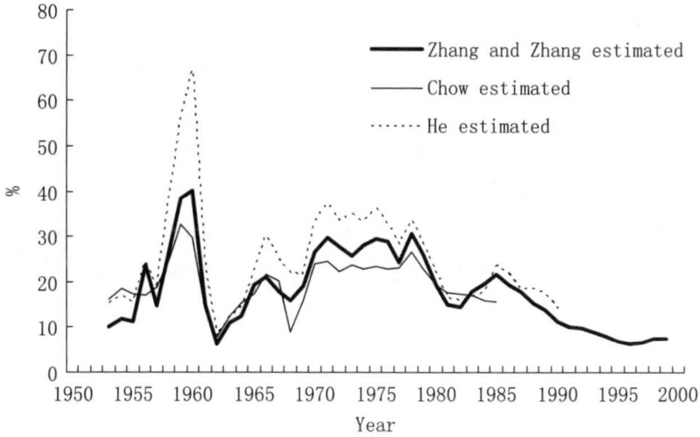

Fig. 5.3. The ratio of industrial equipment investment to GDP (%).
Source: Zhang and Zhang (2003), Chow (1993) and He (1992).
Note: The net value after the deduction of capital depreciation.

model, which emphasizes heavy industry rather than agriculture, fully reflects the impact of the structural ideology of development economics, namely, industry in China is the focus of economic development, and thus more resources are being used to promote the development of the industrial sector. As shown in Figure 5.3, the share of industrial sector equipment investment in GDP remains high for a long period.

5.2.4. *The mystery of low initial conditions and high capital accumulation*

The early stages of economic development saw a lack of capital, which was relatively expensive. So if we want to speed up the pace of industrialization, the primary problem would be how to ensure the capital formation of industrial sector. In China, from the beginning of the late Qing's Self-Strengthening movement to the eve of the World War II, the overall level of economic development lagged behind.[1] Although it experienced a few

[1]According to Fukao *et al.* (2006) and Yuan *et al.* (2010), their studies show that in 1930 China's per capita real consumption level is only 33% of Japan, 42% of Taiwan and 73% of Korea. And the labour productivity (per capita production) of modern factories is only equivalent to 1/3 of Japan and 1/10 of the United States.

brief periods of rapid growth, the modern industrial sector production took a share of less than 10%. Nearly 90% of national income originated from agriculture and traditional handicrafts, while nearly 90% of the population lived in rural areas. It is worth emphasizing that the traditional handicraft production was of small scale, almost without any remaining surplus to finance the modernization of the industrial sector. Generally speaking, under such conditions of the early stages, without the financing through international financial markets, to achieve capital accumulation must depend on improving agricultural productivity in order to overcome the pressures of population growth to ensure the basic living standards. This continues till the agricultural sector is able to provide sufficient surplus to fund industrialization. In the case of insufficient agricultural development in some countries, policy-makers will strictly control population growth and consumption so as to generate surplus as much as possible. And then they impose taxes on agriculture. And the expenditures are biased toward the investment in industrial sector investment. This is a direct policy-related transfer of resources. There are also some countries that have adopted price intervention or restriction on the labour movement and other indirect means, so that agricultural and industrial relative price deviate from the market equilibrium price (scissors difference) to indirectly promote the transfer of resources from the agricultural sector to the industrial sector to achieve the target of capital accumulation (Teranishi, 1997). The latter is also known as the first hypothesis of Preobrazhensky (hereinafter referred to as P1) — this socialist way of capital accumulation was adopted by the former Soviet Union and other socialist countries.

Looking back on the history of China's economic growth, after the World War II and the Civil War until the 1978 economic reforms, the increase in agricultural productivity was not obvious,[2] while the population growth rate was relatively high.[3] Therefore, the first condition is clearly insufficient, that is, China's per capita output of the agricultural sector was at a relatively low level, failing to provide adequate funding for capital

[2] Yamamoto (1999).

[3] The annual population growth rates were 2.1%, 2.4% and 1.4% for 1962–1978, 1949–1958 and 1979–1995, respectively. This growth rate is relatively high prior to the reform and opening-up.

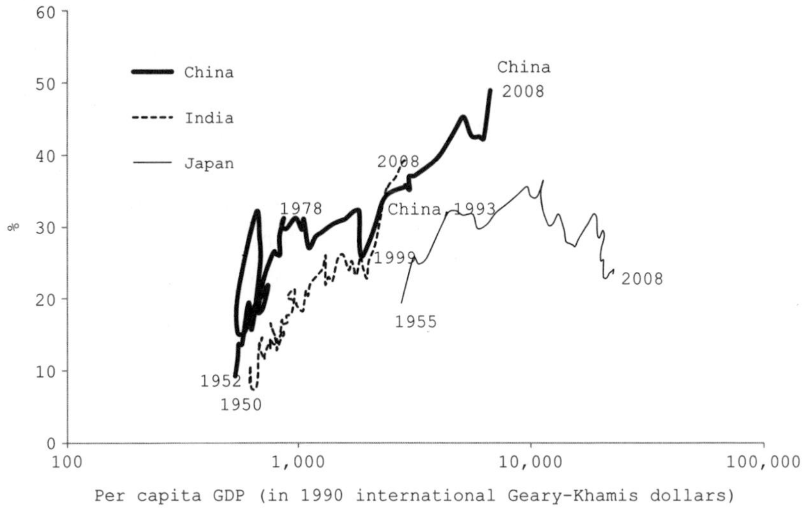

Fig. 5.4. International comparison of capital formation.

Source: Per capita GDP from Maddison *Statistics on World Population, GDP and Per Capita GDP, 1-2008 AD*. For gross capital formation rates: those for Japan from *Economic and Social Research Institute*, Cabinet Office, Government of Japan, those for India from the Reserve Bank of India (RBI), and those for China from National Bureau of Statistics of China.
Note: Per capita GDP as logarithmic measured.

formation in the industrial sector. At the same time, given the worsened Sino-Soviet relations during the Cold War coupled with other reasons, the capital accumulation necessary for China's industrial development could not be dependent on foreign capital. But in fact the growth and expansion of China's industrial sector were significant, even showing a greater rate of capital formation than that of Japan who created a miracle of economic growth after World War II (Figure 5.4). Many studies have considered that this is achieved through the "price scissors" via the policy-related transfer of resources. But scholars have for years — from the planned economy era to the present — argued over this issue of China's transfer of resources between agriculture and industry. In the 1960s, scholars in Japan and China did many empirical analyses on the transfer of resources between agriculture and industry. And after 1980, scholars represented mainly by the United States researchers carried out theoretical analysis employing the model of neoclassical economic theory. Unfortunately, though the majority view holds that there exists agricultural squeeze in China, it is rarely supported by the related empirical results. Thus, Barry (2010) also emphasizes the failure of five major functions of agriculture to industrial development in China. In official documents, we find more papers on how to support agriculture through fiscal spending and on the efforts in tax relief to improve the lives of farmers. If we say that foreign investment is one of the major sources of industrial capital after China's reform and opening-up, then the origin of China's huge capital formation, at least in the period of planned economy, remains a mystery.

5.3. Debate on Agricultural Squeeze

5.3.1. *Perplexed academia*

In the empirical field on the transfer of resources between China's agriculture and industry, the first study was done by Yishikawa (1966), one of the pioneers of development economics in Japan. His calculation method ISRF (Inter-sectoral Resource Flow) that was applied to the research on the transfer of resources in China's First Five-Year Plan period has been widely adopted and used afterwards, such as by Yishikawa (1990), Nakagane (1982 and 1992), Yamamoto (1999) and others. Based on this method, a series of empirical results show that, long since the new China was founded, there was no large-scale transfer of resources from agriculture to industrial sector; on the contrary, many times there was in fact transfer of more resources from the industrial sector to the agricultural sector.[4] Yimaoka (1976) focuses on the net savings of the agricultural sector assuming that savings are equal to the outflow of resources. His study on the First Five-Year Plan period also confirms the conclusion that agriculture did not significantly contribute to the capital accumulation of the industrial sector. We will label the above studies as negation of agricultural squeezing thesis. The corresponding study is by Hayashi (1976) who uses the fund circulation method and finds that in the First Five-Year Plan period, with the exception of 1956, agriculture was indeed

[4]This conclusion is consistent not only with the idea of supporting agriculture advocated by the Chinese government, but also with view of Barry (2010) that agriculture does not contribute much to China's economic development.

a sector with production surplus, and the government, by employing "price scissors" and fiscal and monetary policies, transferred the agricultural surplus to industrial and commercial sectors. Lardy (1983) is the first scholar who points out the problem of China's statistical system and holds that the studies of the negation camp used unreliable data. By utilizing the data collected by himself, Lardy proves that agriculture is the main provider of funds for China's industrialization. Related studies include the one by Feng and Li (1993), which from the perspectives of agricultural tax, the savings rate and the "price scissors", finds empirical support to P1, that is, agriculture has made tremendous sacrifices to China's industrialization. All in all, the view that there is agricultural squeezing is mainly based on a direct approach to measure agricultural surplus. But it fails to quantitatively analyze, in a correct way, the full contribution of agriculture to capital formation. However, Nakagane (1992) points out that, in the socialist countries, political factors are often implicit in the agricultural/rural issues and that the concepts of "unequal transfer between agriculture and industry" and "price scissors" upon which the argument of agricultural sacrifices is based are of great significance in political/sociological areas rather than in the field of economics.

Since 1980, there have mainly been the European and American economists who engage in this field and actively analyze the effect of "price scissors" under socialism. Sah and Stiglitz (1984) use general equilibrium model to prove that the artificial change of the relative price of agriculture and industry in the socialist economic system is an effective means of capital formation. Sah and Stiglitz (1986, 1987), in view of the unbalanced foreign trade and other factors suggested by Blomqvist (1986), Carter (1986) and others, improve their model to further prove the effectiveness of P1. Unfortunately, Li and Tsui (1990) have employed the above model in their empirical study but failed to achieve the relevant results. With the premise of stressing that there is policy intervention, validity of P1 may not be apparent. Recently Lin and Yu (2009), by modifying the Sah and Stiglitz model, demonstrate that, from 1949 to 1992, in the target functions of Chinese government's economic policy, the weight of farmers is less than that of workers and the weight of farmers' welfare is also less than that of the capital accumulated. Another study by Knight (1995), using the Offer-curve analysis of the international trade theory, also supports theoretically the validity of P1. Unfortunately, the above theoretical analyses only provide the qualitative analysis and do not correctly measure the extent to which the interest of Chinese agriculture and farmers were sacrificed during China's industrialization.

5.3.2. *The issues of the previous empirical analyses*

One reason for the fact that theoretical analyses represented by Sah and Stiglitz are not supported by the results of empirical analyses may go to the lack of credible data. But more importantly, there is the ignorance of the characteristics of the socialist economy, which distributes resources according to the plan rather than through a free market system, that is the assumption of free factors mobility among sectors does not hold. Therefore the prices include various non-market factors, deviating greatly from those under the market equilibrium. In the following part, we will focus on three main empirical results — (1) the ISRF method based on the relative price of agriculture and industry, (2) the fund circulation method which emphasized rural consumption and savings, and (3) the "price scissors" approach method that embodies Preobrazhensky's thesis of socialist primitive accumulation. And their respective problems will be dealt with along the discussion.

(1) ISRF method

The formula of ISRF method[5] might be written as:

$$B' = \frac{E}{P_E} - \frac{M}{P_M}$$

$$= \frac{E-M}{P_M} + \frac{E}{P_E}\left(1 - \frac{P_E}{P_M}\right)$$

[5] $E = C_{AN} + X_{AN}$, $M = C_{NA} + X_{NA} + I_{NA}$
We use AN and NA for the flow directions of resources from A to N and from N to the A, respectively, then export E is equivalent to the commercialized surplus of agricultural sector, and $E - C_{AN}$ is the net surplus of agriculture.

In which, P_E and P_M, respectively, are the agricultural sector and non-agricultural sector price index. The first to the right is the visible resource transfer (Visible flows), and the second is the invisible transfer of resources (Invisible flows). If these two sectors of agriculture and industry are considered as equivalent to a country, then the first one is real outflow from the agricultural sector to the non-agricultural sector, while the second one is the amount of transferred resources incurred by the change in relative price. Using the above method, Yishikawa, Nakagane and Yamamoto have estimated that except for a few years during the period in question, there was no observable resource transfer from agriculture to industry but the opposite and the results are similar to what shown in Figure 5.5.

The method is somewhat effective in the analysis of the increase or decrease in the amount of resource transfer and of the change in the direction of transfer of resources in the long-term. But it cannot correctly grasp the direction and absolute amount of transfer of resources arising from the policy interventions. The reasons are as follows. First, part of the calculated results of the invisible flows is closely related to the selection of the starting point. Since the relative price of the starting point is

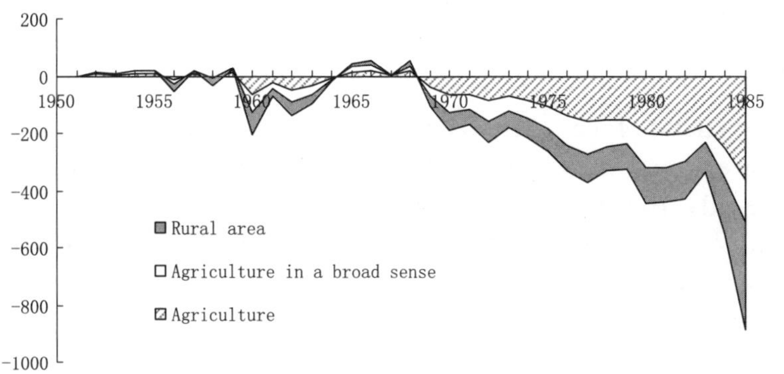

Fig. 5.5. The transfer of resources between agriculture and industry based on ISRF method (Unit: 100 million yuan).

Source: Nakagane (1992, p. 55, Table 2–1).
Note: Negatives denote the transfer from industry to agriculture.

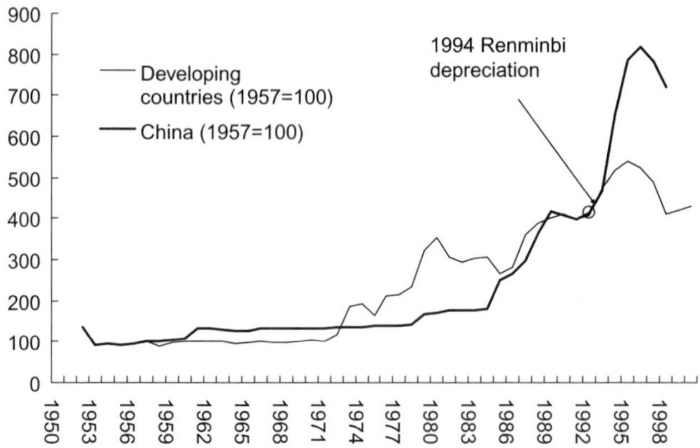

Fig. 5.6. Price indices of domestic and international agricultural products (1957 = 100). *Source*: The price indices of China's agricultural products are from Cheng (1998) and those of other developing countries are from IMF.

assumed to be 100, it implies that, in accordance with the international economics, the market equilibrium price should be chosen. Second, price interference will have an impact on the visible flows. Sometimes it produces results just in the opposite to the direction of the actual transfer of resources.[6] Typically, relative to agriculture, the industry is capital-intensive and witnesses more rapid technological progress. Meanwhile, with the expansion of the industrial sector and the increase demand of agricultural products, the prices of the former will relatively decline whereas those of the latter go up.

However, as shown in Figure 5.6, compared with the international market, the rise in prices of agricultural products in China is not fast, and it is a bit slow from 1972 to 1984. In the 1994 Renminbi (RMB) depreciation, agricultural prices somewhat rose, but later they again had a downward trend.

[6]For example, when agricultural prices rise closer to international prices and industrial prices fall closer to international prices, the second item, the Invisible flows, on the right side of the formula will very likely become negative, resulting in the misunderstanding that the transfer of resources is from industry to agriculture.

(2) Fund circulation method[7]

Fund circulation method takes into account the net surplus of agricultural sector and defines the net outflow of funds as the difference between the rural revenues and the agricultural self-consumption and capital formation. Ohkawa *et al.* (1978) and Teranishi (1982) make a very precise estimate for Japan before the World War II. It is noteworthy that the same way yields quite different estimates. The former analysis shows that at the early stage of Japanese industrialization, agriculture had a great contribution to the industry and the latter shows that the initial capital for Japan's industrialization mainly came from commerce and that the contribution of agriculture was not obvious. The results of the fund circulation method are subject to the data of propensity to consume in the agricultural sector, as shown in Table 5.1, and the different results are determined by the adoption of different propensities to consume.

Which of the two propensities to consume is more accurate? If the domestic market is not exactly a free market, it is hard to accurately judge. In a totally competitive and open economy, different industries and the domestic and international markets can reach an equilibrium and the internal and external price differences can be eliminated through the movement of production factors. Therefore, only in such a case can one make use of the propensity to consume calculated on the domestic prices. However, in a closed economy or in a developing country with a less developed market system, the factor markets are immature, so the domestic prices are different from international prices. Hence the propensity to consume calculated based on these domestic prices may produce errors.

The neo-classical economic theory argues that only under the perfectly competitive market can the allocation of resources efficiently enable the flow of production factors to industrial sectors of higher productivity, maximizing social benefits. Government intervention or imperfect market imposes a direct effect on commodity prices and production, and therefore

[7] Yishikawa (1990) and Nakagane (1992) call it the "savings surplus". Nakagane (1992) and others include the industrial sector in rural areas when referring to the agricultural sector in applying this method. The agricultural sector in this chapter is limited to a narrow sense of agricultural sector.

Table 5.1. Different estimates of agricultural surplus due to different propensities to consume.

	Teranishi estimate		Ohkawa takamatsu estimate	
	A%	**S-I (mil yen)**	**A%**	**S-I (mil yen)**
1899–1902	97.9	1	83.5	44
1903–1907	90.4	13	82.1	86
1908–1912	95.6	4	80.5	144
1913–1917	88.0	43	77.0	266
1918–1922	92.0	207	85.8	243
1923–1927	96.6	24	90.7	–65
1928–1932	93.4	–12	93.7	–189
1933–1937	87.9	222	87.5	82

Source: Teranishi (1982, Chapter 4, Table 4–19).
Note: A = Estimated propensity to consume.

the transfer of resources occurs, subject to different marginal propensity to consume (save) across sectors.

(3) Socialist theory of value

The argument that China's economic development relies on agricultural squeezing is mainly based on the concept of "price scissors". Han and Feng (1992) point out that the effect of "price scissors" differs when using different prices. Generally speaking, the "price scissors" argument concerns with the following issues — (1) the rise and fall of the prices of agricultural product relative to those of industrial goods and (2) the gap (increase or decrease) between the purchase price and the retail price of agricultural products.

Obviously the first point, i.e., the domestic agricultural and industrial relative price contain incomplete information about policies and market, needs to consider the deviation of such prices from those under the market equilibrium. Second, the deduction of the charges of flow is equivalent to consumption tax. However the problem is: in the socialist planned economy, this consumption tax is not just for agricultural products, but also for industrial products. As Figure 5.7 shows that, in the planning period the

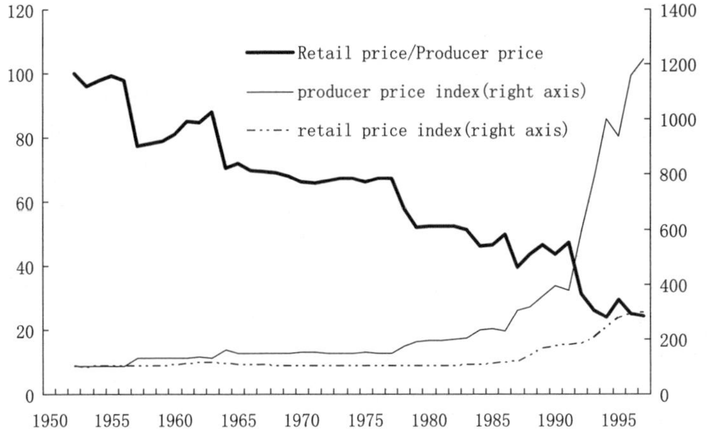

Fig. 5.7. Indices of Chinese producer prices and retail prices of industrial products (1952 = 100).

Source: Index of producer price of industrial products is from Yuan (2010) and index of retail price is from Cheng (1998).
Note: The index of retail price refers to that of rural industrial products.

producer prices for industrial goods were low and the consumer prices are relatively high. In addition, the theory of value of socialism also stresses that, in the planned economy, the government purchases at lower and unified prices and provides goods to the employees of the industrial sector so as to ensure that the industrial development is achieved with lower labour costs. However, a quantitative analysis of farmers' contribution to industrialization relies on proper prices. Obviously, these prices should be the equilibrium prices in the free market, not the arbitrary prices that contain political implications.

5.3.3. *What price can be taken as a benchmark?*

Through the above discussion, we have seen that the greatest problem of the previous empirical researches lies in their adoption of a certain price system — a price system without any clear and credible price deemed as a benchmark for relative price. Neo-classical economic theory suggests that only when the market is complete can the allocation of resources become efficient. If it is a small and open economy, then by the free flow of domestic production factors among sectors, it can achieve its inter-sectoral equality in the marginal productivity. Meanwhile, the relative prices (Relative price) of exports and imports will also be equalized between domestic and foreign industries because they are price takers. When the government interferes in factor markets or there is a market failure, the efficiency of resource allocation will decrease and the internal prices will deviate from the external ones. From the perspective of national income, this will incur the transfer of resources among sectors. According to this logic, when the domestic relative price of a product deviate from its international relative price measured in international prices, the production will be shifted from the industry whose production price is relatively undervalued to another industry, which is equivalent to imposing an indirect taxation on the former. Clearly, that theoretical researches have not been supported by existing empirical studies is because the former neglect the deviation of the domestic inter-sectoral relative price from international prices.

Lardy (1983) once examined the differences of the domestic and international prices of China's agricultural and industrial products. Unfortunately, since the information is limited, he considered only rice and chemical fertilizers. In addition, his international comparisons are also limited to a few countries, such as India and Thailand (Nakagane, 1992). Yuan (2010) applies more detailed types of commodities and his industry-specific estimates cover the long-term trend of internal and external price differences from 1949 till recently (Figure 5.8). We can see that, in the various industries and economic development in China in different periods, the internal and external price differences of tradable goods show the following characteristics:

1. The domestic prices of agricultural products, coal, minerals and other primary products are far below the international prices;
2. The domestic prices of chemical and mechanical products were well above international prices;
3. For textiles and miscellaneous for daily use, domestic and international prices were basically the same;

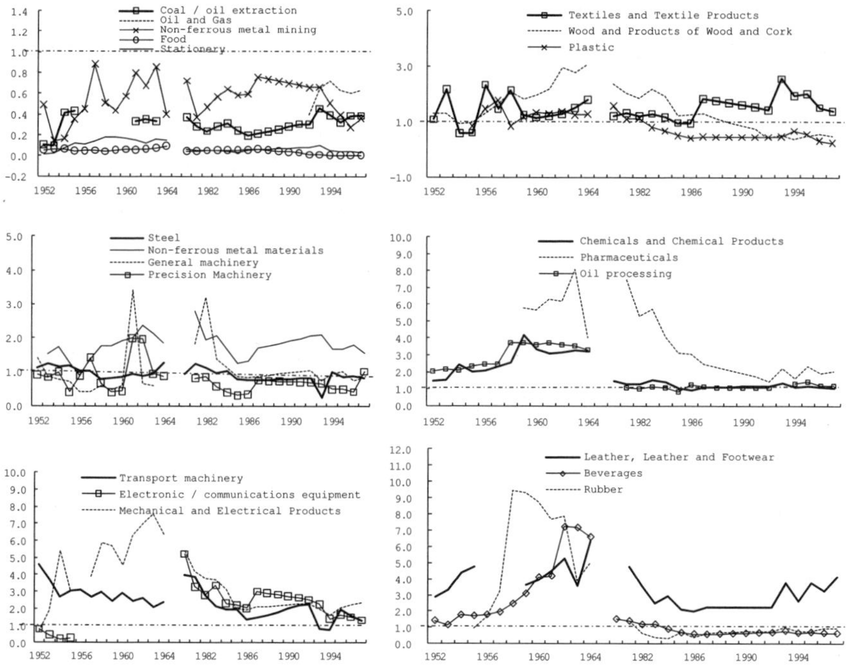

Fig. 5.8. Internal and external price difference by industrial (international price = 1).
Source: Yuan (2010).

4. The price gap was relatively small in the first few years since the founding of the new China;
5. The biggest difference between internal and external prices was observed from the full swing of planned economy in 1957 till 1984 when the price liberalization began with a dual-track system; and
6. Along with the reform and opening-up up to 1994 during which the RMB depreciated, the internal and external price differences tended to go down, but rose again afterward.

The existence of internal and external price difference was the result of the following causes. The planned economy emphasized the development of heavy industry and, to earn the foreign exchange for imported equipment, exported agricultural and primary products, and set a high level for the RMB exchange rate. In the early stages of development, the wages of urban sector were mainly used for food consumption, so in order to reduce the cost of industrialization and to ensure the supply and demand balance of grain, a unified purchase and sale of agricultural products was practiced — purchasing at a low price and rationing to city residents at a low price. Hence the price of agricultural products was cheaper than the international market. During this period, industrial capital accumulation was relatively insufficient and the limited capital was devoted to the development of capital-intensive heavy industry, so the overall industrial production costs were high and of poor quality. At the same time, the domestic prices of the majority of industrial production were higher than those on the international market.

1994 saw a poor harvest of grain production. The government raised, in a great measure, the domestic purchase price of grain. Although this initiative improved the production of farmers by stimulating their enthusiasm, it increased the financial burden on the government. So when the reform of grain circulation started in 1998, the surplus of reserve grain coupled by other factors led to a decline again in agricultural prices. After joining the WTO in 2001, the government's agricultural price policies have been inclined to protect agricultural products that have international competitiveness. Agricultural prices, on the whole, tend to be increasingly market-oriented, narrowing the gap with the international market prices. But it is worth emphasizing that, in the years after 2001, China's exports have been changed from mainly agricultural and primary products have to the industrial products. The 1994 devaluation of the RMB exchange rate is no doubt aimed at promoting exports, so the domestic prices of industrial products show again an upward trend in comparison with international prices. From the 1997 Asian financial crisis to 2006, the RMB exchange rate is actually fixed. With the rapid development of the domestic economy, a substantial increase took place in the export of industrial products. Since the underpriced RMB exchange rate is equivalent to subsidies to the export of industrial products, the international prices of industrial products are also lower than the domestic prices in China, hence China's agriculture has long been in an unfavorable position (Figure 5.9).

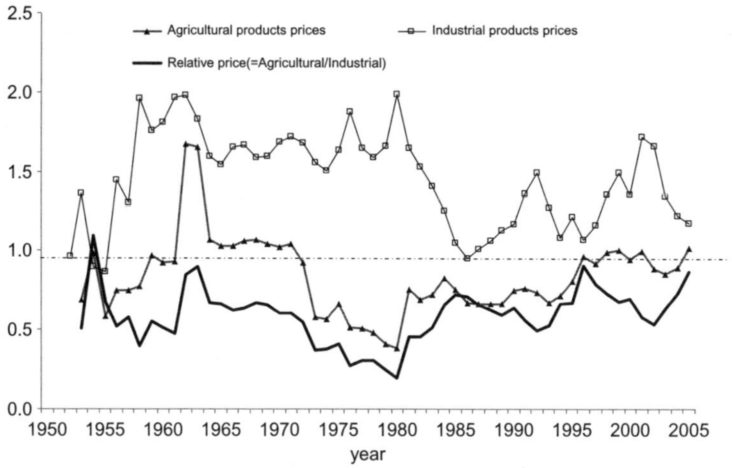

Fig. 5.9. The ratio of internal to external relative price of agricultural and industrial products (international relative price = 1).

Source: Computation based on Yuan (2010).

5.3.4. *The invisible transfer of resources between agriculture and industry*

Bellerby, early in the 1960s, pointed out that the incomplete market of production factors and the institutional deficiencies will affect the product prices of different sectors, hence resulting in transfer of resources that leads to low productivity and poverty of the unprotected industries. He explained the relative poverty of agriculture by measuring the price difference between agricultural and industrial products in the early stages of economic development of European and other developed countries (Bellerby, 1966). Schiff and Valdes (1992), using international prices as a benchmark, further analyzed the indirect taxation on agriculture in developing countries. Unfortunately, due to the limited data, his study did not include China. Yuan (2010), through collecting the prices of China's agricultural products, industrial products and imports and exports, estimates industry-specific difference between internal and external prices from 1952 to 2000 and thus calculates China's indirect tax on agriculture.

According to Schiff and Valdes (1992), the indirect taxation rate on agriculture is measured by a ratio of international-domestic price difference to international price, which is also expressed as the sum of domestic and international nominal protection rates, NPR_D and NPR_I, respectively:[8]

$$t = NPR_D + NPR_I = \frac{\frac{P_A^*}{P_M^*} - \frac{P_A}{P_M}}{\frac{P_A^*}{P_M^*}} = \frac{p^* - p}{p^*}$$

where P = domestic producer price, P^* = border prices (international prices). The subscript A and M denote the agricultural sector and industrial sector, respectively. And NPR termed as nominal protection rate, and the subscript D and I respectively denote the direct effect and the indirect effect.

As shown in Table 5.2, compared to the indirect agricultural taxes of 13 countries calculated by Schiff and Valdes (1992), tax rate of China is higher. Judging from the long-term trend in Figure 5.6, from the early days of the founding of China to 1994 when RMB devaluation took place,

[8]The total indirect tax rate, in light of the policy intervention, can be directly targeted at either the prices of agricultural products or other production means apart from the agricultural products, hence the effect is divided into direct one and indirect one.

Direct effect

$$NPR_D = \left(\frac{P_A}{P_M} - \frac{P_A^*}{P_M}\right) \Big/ \frac{P_A^*}{P_M^*}$$

Indirect effect

$$NPR_I = \left(\frac{P_A^*}{P_M} - \frac{P_A^*}{P_M^*}\right) \Big/ \frac{P_A^*}{P_M^*}$$

That is, direct tax rate NPR_D reflects the direct effect of international trade, export tax, import quota, policies on non-agricultural sectors on the domestic prices of agricultural products. Indirect tax rate NPR_I reflects the indirect effect of subsidies for agricultural products, policies, finance and the protection of goods that compete with imports on the prices of agricultural products (invisible). Sazanami *et al.* (1995) and others define direct effect as nominal protection rate.

Table 5.2. Agricultural indirect tax rate based on the relative price for agriculture and industry (%).

	1960–72	**1976–84**
Korea	–0.8	–77.5
Malaysia	17.4	17.6
Philippines	15.5	37.6
Thailand	47.3	35.4
Pakistan	22.3	57.7
Sri Lanka	37.0	37.4
Argentina	41.8	44.7
Brazil	62.6	18.7
Chile	29.3	4.0
Columbia	26.6	32.3
Dominican Rep.	50.1	29.7
Côte d'Ivoire	49.7	74.1
Ghana	70.6	32.9
	1957–84	1985–97
China	48.2	33.7

Source: Data of other countries are from Schiff and Valdes (1992).

Note: Positives denote the tax on agriculture and negatives the subsidy for agriculture.

there was an inverted U-shape in the period of analysis, that is, in the 1950s and after the reform and opening-up, the internal and external price difference was demonstrating an obvious narrowing tendency. In the whole period of planned economy, this difference remained wide and reached its maximum in the late 1970s, which implies that, at the eve of reform and opening-up, the intensity of policy interventions, such as import substitution and so on, was enormous. This result is consistent with our theoretical conjecture. In line with the strategy of heavy industry development, the extent to which the various sectors of national economy were intervened by the Chinese government policies was greater than that of any other developing countries, and hence great is the difference between internal and external prices.

It should be noted that in the latter 1990s the internal and external difference of relative price of agriculture and industry shows again a widening trend. During this period, though the prices of agricultural products and the vast majority of industrial products except oil and other energy products are marketized, the internal and external difference of relative price for agriculture and industry was not narrowed. The reason can be attributed to factors other than price, such as the aforementioned subsidies for industrial exports incurred by exchange rate policies, resulting in the phenomenon that the prices of industrial products are higher within than without. In addition, the residential permit system (*hukou* in Chinese) has an inhibiting effect on the free movement of labour. And social security, unequal opportunities in education and other treatments all hinder the smooth flow of rural surplus labour into the urban sectors. In the latter half of the 1990, the allocation of resources in favor of state-owned enterprises rather than the private ones also impedes the healthy development of the latter, which leads to the distortions of factor and product markets. All these practices, while raising labour productivity of the industrial sector, strengthened the barrier to the transfer of rural surplus labour to the industrial sector (Yuan, 2009). This inevitably forced more surplus labour to stay in agriculture and rural areas, hence further depressing agricultural labour productivity and lowering the prices of agricultural products against those of industrial products.

5.4. Over Squeeze and Inadequate Input — A Comparison of the Redistribution of Fiscal Policy

Since the founding of the new China, the government has taxed as well as subsidized agriculture through fiscal expenditures. We need to understand is that with the agricultural indirect tax, which is invisible, what is the net effect upon agriculture.

5.4.1. *Fiscal revenue and direct tax*

According to the expenditure approach, national income is mainly used for consumption, investment and government expenditures. The direction of investment is chiefly reflected by: 1) investment in infrastructure aimed at expanding the production and increase in the liquidity of business; 2) non-production infrastructure, such as national defense, culture, education and other related programmes; and 3) national reserves (savings). And consumption includes the government and private consumptions. The socialist capital accumulation is realized through the redistribution of national income, that is, via the ways of fiscal revenue and fiscal expenditure.

Figure 5.10 shows the changes in the structure of fiscal revenue. The different taxes account for the largest proportion in the entire period of the analysis. Among these taxes, the industrial and commercial tax, before reform and opening-up, assumed around 40% and always retained its dominant position. The business income rose from about 10% of the total tax revenue in the early days to over the average of 50% after the completion of socialist transformation in 1956. After 1985, the business income tax, through the reform of "tax for profit", has been gradually incorporated into industrial and commercial tax as well as the newly established corporate income tax. The agricultural tax that we are concerned constituted the major revenue in the "liberated areas" before the founding of the new China and afterwards, especially after 1953, its levied amount was fixed at 3–3.5 billion yuan, gradually losing its share in the total.

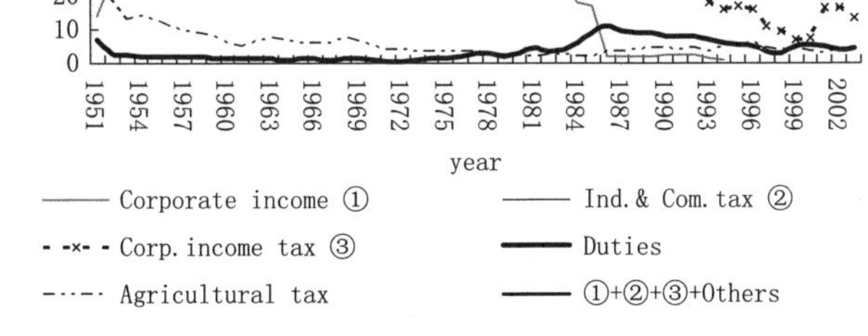

Fig. 5.10. Main items of fiscal revenue.

Source: *China Statistics of Fixed Asset Investment.*

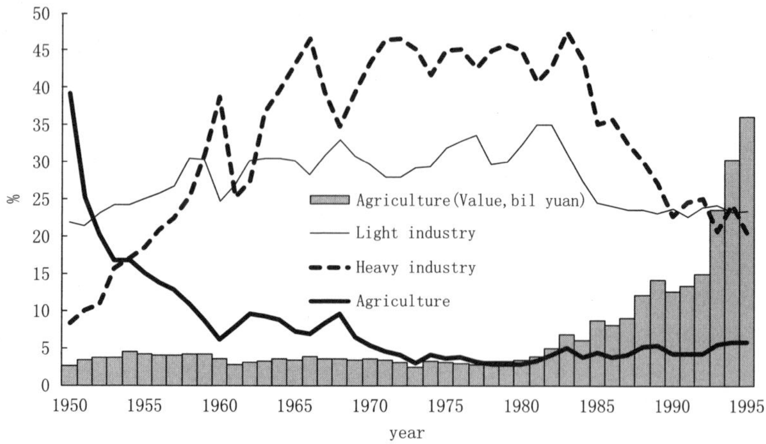

Fig. 5.11. The contributions of agriculture, light industry and heavy industry to fiscal revenue (%).

Source: *China Statistics of Fixed Asset Investment.*

If one compares the contributions of agriculture, light industry and heavy industry to the revenue (Figure 5.11), one can see that light industry always maintained around 20–30%. The heavy industry, before the reform and opening-up, always shows an upward trend, the greatest once more than 45%. But with the advancement of economic liberalization, it witnesses a significant decline to about 20% in 1995. The contribution of agricultural tax is great in the early years of new China, but gradually decreases after 1970s, maintaining a level of about 5%.

5.4.2. *Government expenditure and redistribution*

China's fiscal expenditure mainly covers the costs in economic construction, social cultural and educational programmes, defense, administration and other items. Shown in Figure 5.12, in the period of planned economy, the Chinese government spent most revenue on economic development. In terms of the sectors, the investment on industry, especially heavy industry, always takes an absolutely high proportion since the founding of new China, reaching, before the reform and opening-up, as high as over 50%. In terms of fiscal revenue and expenditure, the heavy industry receives more than it contributes. Investment in the light industry sector remained

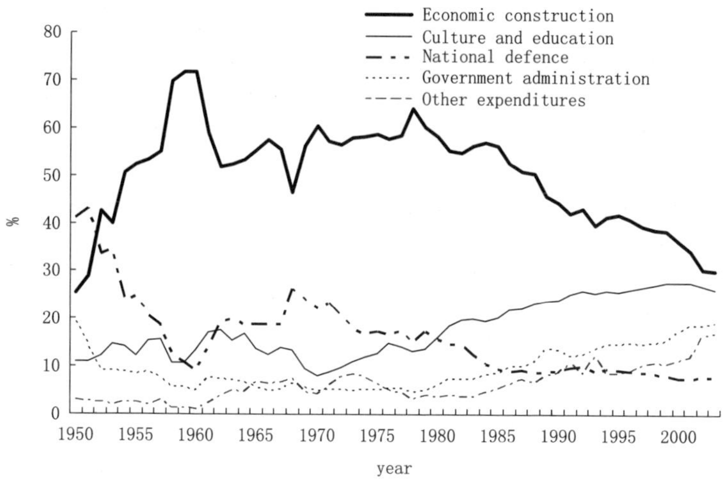

Fig. 5.12. Composition of fiscal expenditures.

Source: *China Statistics of Fixed Asset Investment.*

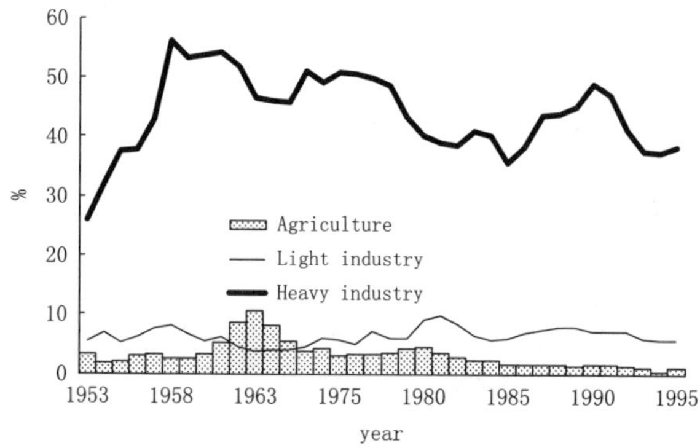

Fig. 5.13. The proportions of different sectors in the total investment (%).

Source: *China Statistics of Fixed Asset Investment.*

at 5–10% for a long time — it contributed more than it received and bore, *de facto*, a heavier indirect tax. This is also the reason for the long-term underdevelopment of China's light industry, which ultimately affects the economic development. The main momentum for China's economic development from the reform and opening-up to the first half of the 1990s comes from the development of the rural township and village enterprises and other non-state-owned labour-intensive industries. It is worth emphasizing that the heavy industry has always been the focus of the government's financial support. In the latter half of the 1990s the government supported the state-owned enterprises rather than the private ones. And the energy, transportation and other monopoly industries enjoy the preferential financing by the government. All these have resulted in the deteriorating returns on the overall investment in industry (Figure 5.14). By a comparison with heavy industry, investment in agriculture, excluding the three years of natural disaster, has been at a low level. From the perspective of redistribution, before the reform and opening-up, it turned over more than it received in return, and after the reform and opening-up, it paid less but also received less.

In summary, the Government redistributes through fiscal revenues and expenditures. Different sectors hand over to the government part of their output in the form of taxes or business income. At the same time, they receive subsidies from the government in the form of investment and support. The difference between these two practices can be defined as the net

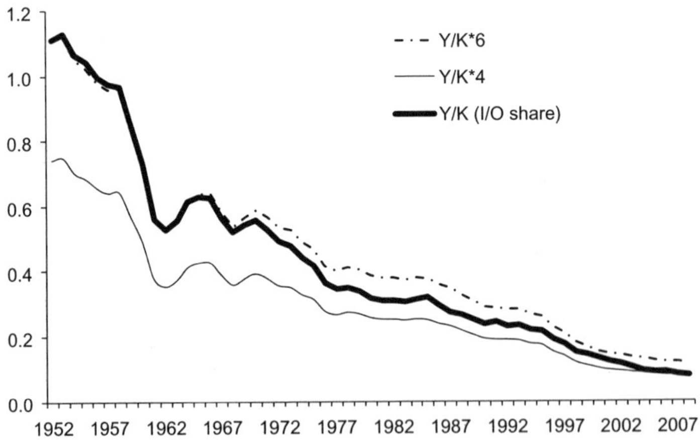

Fig. 5.14. The ratios of return on capital (marginal output coefficient) of industrial sectors.

Source: Wu (2011).
Note: *Y/K*6* and *Y/K*4*, capital income share is assumed as 60% and 40%, separately. Y/K(I/O share) means capital income share as given by Chinese I/O table & estimated.

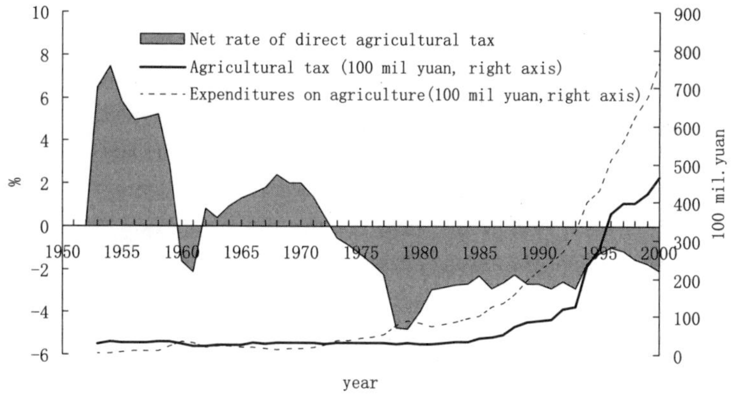

Fig. 5.15. Net rate of agricultural tax (%).

Source: *50-Year Fiscal Statistics of New China.*
Note: Net rate of agricultural tax = (agricultural tax- fiscal expenditures on agriculture)/agricultural output value.

rate of agricultural tax and then we can calculate the agriculture direct net rate (Figure 5.15). It can be seen that, apart from the early days of new China, the net rate of agricultural tax reached 7–8%. However since the late 1970s, for a long period of time till now, the net rate of agricultural tax has been negative, showing that at least the visible fiscal spending subsidizes agriculture. Also in recent years, the government increases the income of farmers by taking a series of measures, such as the abolition of agricultural tax, to relieve the burdens on farmers. But the empirical results suggest that the main burden on farmers came from policies that caused resource distortions favoring non-agricultural industries rather than the direct agricultural tax. And the government direct subsidies also fell far short of the burdens imposed on farmers by the distortions (i.e. indirect taxation).

5.4.3. *Excessive squeeze and low agricultural productivity*

According to the above results, we can roughly calculate the annual amount of invisible transfer of resources from agriculture to industry (Figure 5.16). This can be really astonishing. It is clear that the long-term invisible way of plundering agriculture results in the immature development of rural areas without sufficient resources. The fiscal expenditures,

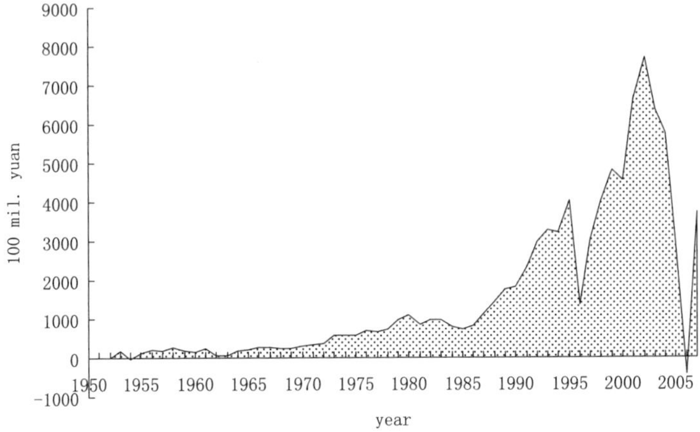

Fig. 5.16. The amount of indirect tax on agriculture (100 million yuan).

Source: *60-Year Economic Statistics of China's Agricultural Production.*

Note: Calculated according to $T = Y_A \times t$, where T, Y_A and t represent, respectively, the indirect tax, agricultural output value, and indirect tax rate.

constrained by the development strategies that emphasize industry rather than agriculture, were spent less than required in agriculture, thus making agriculture lag far behind the pace of the reform and opening-up and industrialization. This can be confirmed once again in Figure 5.13. From the share of Chinese investment in agriculture in the entire investment in national economy, it remained generally at more than 9.5% in 1980 and before, rapidly declined to 2.4% in 1994, and rebounded somewhat afterwards — though the increase is quite limited. However, after China's joining WTO, the share of the investment in fixed assets of agriculture in the national total steadily dropped from 2.38% in 2002 to 1.67% in 2005 and further down to 1.42% in 2007.

The insufficient investment leads to the stagnation of China's agricultural labour productivity. Compared with Asian countries, agricultural labour productivity of China is not only lower than those of Japan, South Korea and other middle-income countries, but also lower than those of other low-income countries. In the 1960s, it was the lowest of the sample countries and remained unimproved till after 2000 (Table 5.3). By contrast, the enhancement of land productivity is very rapid — almost equivalent to those of Japan and South Korea — which relies on heavy

Table 5.3. International comparison of agricultural productivity.

	Per capita GDP (in USD2000)		Labor Productivity (based on value added, in USD2000)		Land productivity (rice, t/ha)	
	1961–63	2001–2003	1961–63	2001–2003	1961–63	2001–2003
Nepal	138	242	171	208	1.9	2.8
Cambodia		303		292	1.1	2
Laos		343		459	0.9	3.1
Bangladesh	259	383	220	309	1.7	3.5
Burma					1.6	3.5
Vietnam		444		290	2	4.5
India	182	485	253	399	1.5	2.9
Pakistan	197	535	323	690	1.4	2.9
Indonesia	183	762	263	538	1.8	4.5
Sri Lanka	286	886	556	737	1.9	3.5
China	71	988	118	357	2.4	6.1
Philippines	641	1022	673	1013	1.2	3.3
Thailand	356	2156	248	583	1.8	2.6
Malaysia	844	3900	1814	4571	2.1	3.2
Korea	1155	11799	1745	9888	4	6.4
Japan	8500	37665	6620	25340	5	6.4

Source: Tsubota (2007).

inputs in seed improvement and chemical fertilizers. It is noteworthy that, the rise in the prices of agricultural production means, particularly chemical fertilizers, leads to the increase in the costs of grain-based agricultural production, and the rising costs in turn lead to price increases that eventually will make Chinese agricultural products less competitive on the international market.

Meanwhile, the low labour productivity also implies the existence of a large number of rural surplus labour. Since, at this stage in China, there still exist barriers, such as the residential permit system, social security system, and unequal educational opportunities, so how to successfully lower the proportion of agricultural employment is still one of the major problems of China's economic development. If in the period of planned economy such low productivity is mainly due to the harsh price intervention, the nowaday agriculture-related and non-agriculture-related policies that distort the efficient allocation of resources foster the internal and external price differences, resulting in a serious invisible agricultural squeeze. The failure to alter this phenomenon will probably offset the effect of fiscal investment. Without the effective increased investment in agriculture, agricultural labour productivity could hardly be raised.

5.5. Policy Implications for China's Agricultural Development in Future

5.5.1. *A review of China's agricultural policy*

Upon China's accession to WTO, international trade exerts a huge impact on our industry. The same is true for agriculture, especially when food production has been emphasized in China's agricultural production structure. Food production is land-intensive, yet it concentrates in the Eastern region, densely populated with a very high labour-land ratio. With the long-standing development strategy biased towards heavy industry, investment in agriculture has been insufficient, making the latter less competitive in the world market. Since the reform and opening-up, the Chinese government, in order to promote agricultural and rural development, has adjusted the structure of agricultural production. For example, against the surplus food production in 1984, it encourages the production of edible oil, hemp plant, livestock, etc. In 1992, it takes measures to promote high productivity, high yield, high quality and high profits, and expands fruit and vegetables production. In response to the influence of international trade upon China's entry into WTO, the structural adjustment after 1998 has been shifted to cultivating a competitive agricultural production, constructing production base of green food, and improving storage and preservation technology. It promotes the agricultural industrialization by setting up rural and township enterprises and developing processing industry for agricultural products to increase their added value. The green food is featured by organic cultivation, reduced use of artificial pesticide and chemical fertilizer in pursuit of "safety, quality, and healthy food" (including raw materials and processed products). The main production of green food is concentrated in the eastern region and is labour-intensive, showing a comparative advantage in the world market. It can be expected that, in the international trade environment in the future, the lack of competitiveness of the grain production of China's inner regions would deal a heavy blow to the agriculture of concerned regions, resulting in the decreased price of grain and increased surplus of rural labour, which will exacerbate urban-rural income gap.

In order to increase rural incomes and agricultural productivity so as to solve three key rural problems, the government holds every year since 2004, the CPC (Central Committee Rural Work Conference) and declares major policies and issues to be solved via the CPC Central Committee Document No. 1. Although the key words may be slightly adjusted, the general idea is to: (1) increase investment in agriculture and rural areas; (2) enhance the support for agriculture; (3) to stabilize the prices of agricultural products; and (4) strengthen the rural financial services. For instance, the theme of 2004 was to increase the income of farmers. In 2005, it was to achieve stability, improve and strengthen the agricultural policies. In 2006, it was to consolidate infrastructure construction, promote comprehensive rural reform, and increase rural incomes. In 2007, the theme was to develop modern agriculture and construct new socialist countryside. In 2008, it was to strengthen the agricultural infrastructure and promote agricultural development and raise farmer's income. In 2009, the policies were mainly reflected on the promotion of a stable agricultural development and sustained growth of farmers' income, including the further increase in inputs in agriculture and rural areas, the greater increase in agricultural subsidies, the maintenance of a reasonable price level of agricultural products, and the enhancement of the capacity of rural financial services. The agricultural subsidies cover direct subsidies to crop-growing farmers, comprehensive subsidies for agricultural production means, quality seed subsidies, and farm machinery purchase subsidy — all of the above are referred to as "four kinds of subsidies". In 2010, the government further increases, substantially, the investment in agriculture and rural areas, improves the agricultural subsidy system, raises the minimum grain purchase prices, makes efforts to promote the allocation of resources to the rural areas, changes the mode of agricultural development, tries to narrow the development gap between rural and urban public utilities, and strengthen agriculture and rural areas development drive. In response to the financial crisis, as part of the efforts of expanding domestic demand, the government promotes the sale of household appliances in rural areas. This year (2011), the policy focuses on the use and protection of water resources, including the development of Huaihe River basin. Special emphasis is laid on the improvement and protection of agricultural water infrastructure.

In general, the agricultural policies in recent years have been oriented from maintaining social stability via protecting the interests of farmers to fully revitalizing rural areas and agriculture and to expanding domestic demand. And agricultural protection is also growing in importance as one of the key measures. Especially after 2001, measures have been adopted in price protection, direct subsidies to farmers to increase their income and ensure food supply. However, judging from the experience of Japan and other countries, this is not a very appropriate choice, because, to some extent, direct subsidies do increase the income of farmers in the short term, however they may in turn affect the positive transformation of rural labour into the industrial sector. More importantly, these policies may not directly and effectively increase agricultural productivity. The empirical analysis of Cao *et al.* (2009) shows that the growth rate of the rural economy and the rate of the return on capital in agriculture demonstrate a stable relationship of co-integration and the price level of agricultural products and the rate of capital profits have significant positive relations. Therefore it is better to emphasize the formation mechanism of the prices of agricultural products than resort to price protection so that, via the regulation of international market, the output structure of agriculture will be transformed from land-intensive production of crops into labour-intensive production of cash crops that boast the comparative advantage, and the safety and added value of crops will be increased.

Of course, it is a long-term process to achieve the effect of the implementation of agricultural policies. Although the effects of policies in recent years are not yet clear, the next 10 years, with the popularization of agricultural mechanization, the expansion of international trade of agricultural products and the changes in consumption structure of agricultural products, are expected to witness the makeover of China's agriculture from land-intensive grain farming to labour-intensive cash crops production. To ensure food security (supply and price stability) in the international competition, the mechanized mass production of food crops will be a trend, releasing, however, more surplus agricultural labour force. If this portion of the labour force continues to stay in the rural areas and cannot be smoothly transferred, it will inevitably affect the increase of labour productivity of the overall agriculture and, consequently, retard the fundamental solution to the three agricultural issues.

5.5.2. *Labour mobility and income distribution under the dual structure*

As mentioned earlier, another way to raise agricultural labour productivity is to promote the departure of rural labour force from agriculture (soil). Relevant policies still need to be placed, at the starting point, within the framework of the dual structure. Dual structure can be divided into two kinds: Lewis model and Harris-Todaro model (Lewis, 1954; Harris and Todaro, 1970), showing different performances in the equality (income gap) of distribution. Lewis stresses that the capital savings through the industrial sector guide the movement of the rural surplus labour force to the industrial sector and when, the surplus labour have all been absorbed by the urban sector (the so-called *turning point*), urban-rural income distribution will tend to be equal. This model emphasizes the positive effects of farmers' departure from agriculture. According to the Harris-Todaro model, if the urban job opportunities are not sufficient enough, the blind departure from the agriculture (soil) will not generate sufficient employment in the city, forming the so-called hidden unemployed urban population in the informal sector, substantively affecting the narrowing efforts in the income gap.

Before the arrival of the Lewis turning point, the accumulation of industrial capital has limited effect on the improvement of relative incomes in rural areas. Therefore, if the industrial development centres on capital-intensive industries, urban-rural income gap will widen. In Harris-Todaro model, the urban-rural income gap will be relatively narrowed only when the influx of rural labour force renders the wages of the urban sector rigid, while the income of rural areas rises due to population outflows. However, if, affected by institutional factors or the quality of labour, the surplus labour or the urban hidden unemployed people cannot successfully move into the modern sectors, the rural population would then either return to the countryside or stay in the urban informal sectors. On the surface the Gini coefficient between urban and rural areas may be reduced, but not to the substantial effect of eliminating the income gap between urban and rural areas. Therefore, under the dual structure, the prerequisite for narrowing income gap between urban and rural areas is that capital accumulation of urban sectors effectively reduces the proportion of population in primary industry so as to increase the relative income of rural areas.

5.5.3. *The key lies in the correction of distortions in resource allocation*

According to the analysis of this chapter, the existence of China's three key rural problems is related to both historical factors and direct impact of unreasonable agriculture-related policies and the indirect impact of non-agricultural policies. Such a rural-urban income gap, also a common phenomenon in developing countries, embodies the aftermath of socialist primitive accumulation and the structural factors of reform and opening-up, of which the distorted allocation of resources has brought about the greatest indirect impact. Different economic development strategies result in different allocations of resources. Generally speaking, the development strategies and their corresponding growth strategies that go against the comparative advantage, lead not only to the distroted and inefficient allocation of resources, but more importantly, to the invisible transfer of resources, which squeezes non-protected industries. This is the root cause of China's absolute and relative poverty of rural areas.

The situation of China's resource endowment remains unchanged: that is, the labour is abundant and the capital is relatively short, therefore, to continue the development of capital-intensive industries focusing on state-owned enterprises will reduce the demand for industrial labour and hence obstructing labour moving from the agriculture to non-agricultural sectors and from the rural areas to urban areas, and increasing the difficulty of tackling the dual structure of labour distribution. Conversely, if the formation of development strategy is to follow the principle of comparative advantage, according to the characteristics of China's current resource endowments, labour-intensive industries will continue to be greatly developed and provide opportunities for the transfer of surplus rural labour. The key to increasing farmers' income and bridging the income gap between agriculture and industry under the dual structure lies in the smooth departure of farmers from agriculture (soil). Therefore, the elimination of rural poverty depends not on rural areas and farmers but on the macro- level corrections of institutional and policy factors that have distorted the allocation of resources.

Also worth emphasizing is that, in the consumption structure of a high Engel coefficient, the blind urbanization without increasing agricultural productivity will not only result in a worsened Harris-Todaro dual structure, but also lead to a serious problem of inadequate supply of food. The experience of the model of development of rural and township enterprises — encouraging farmers to leave soil (agriculture) not to leave home — in China's reform and opening-up in the first half of 1980s and the Japanese model of creating opportunities for farmers to engage in different industries in the post-war period of rapid growth shed light on the positive policies in ensuring food supply and increasing rural incomes.

References

Barry, N. (2010). *The Chinese Economy: Transition and Growth.* Shanghai: Shanghai People's Publishing House.

Bellerby, J.R. (1966). *Agriculture and Industry Relative Income*. London: Macmillan & Co., Ltd.

Blomqvist, A.G. (1986). "The Economics of Price Scissors: Comment." *The American Economic Review*, 76(5), 1188–1191.

Cao, Y., Ye, C. and Lin, C. (2009). "Empirical Study on the Trend and Causes of Changes in the Profit Margins of Agricultural Capital." FED Working Papers Series, No. FC20090165.

Carter, M.R. (1986). "The Economics of Price Scissors: Comment." *The American Economic Review*, 76(5), 1192–1194.

Cheng, Z. ed. (1998). *China Price in 50 Years*. Beijing: China Price Press.

Chow, G.C. (1993). "Capital Formation and Economic Growth in China." *The Quarterly Journal of Economics*, 108(3) (Aug.), 809–842.

Feng, H. and Cheng, L. (1993). "The Quantative Research on Capital Accumulation of Agriculture for Industrialization." *Economic Research*, 9.

Fukao, K., Ma, D. and Yuan, T. (2007). "Real GDP in pre-war East Asia: A 1934–36 Benchmark Purchasing Power Parity Comparison with the U.S." *Review of Income and Wealth*, 53(3), 503–537.

Han, Z. and Feng, Y. (1992). *New China 40 Years of Agricultural Prices*. Beijing: China Water Power Press.

Harris, J.R. and Todaro, M.P. (1970). "Migration, Unemployment and Development." *American Economic Review*, 126–142.

Hayami, Y. and Goda, Y. (2002). *Agricultural Economics* (New edition). Tokyo: Iwanami Shoten.

He, D. (2004). "China's Labour Migration from the Perspective of Poverty." *Market Economy Research*, 6, 28–30.

He, J. (1992). "Estimation of the Assets." *Quantitative and Technical Economic Studies*, 8, 24–27.

Hu, B., Lai, J. and Hu B. (2007). "Economic Growth, Income Distribution and Poverty Alleviation — Evidence From Rural China: 1985–2003." *Technical and Econometric Research*, 24(5), 33–42.

Hayashi, N. (1976). "Structural Adjustment of China's Capital." In Institute of China's Capital and Savings (ed.), *The Development and Institution of China's Economy*. Chiba: Institute of Developing Economies, 112–113.

Ikegami, A. and Hoken, H. (2008). "The Structural Change of Agricultural Production Due to China's Rural Reform Policy and Agricultural Industrialization." Report of Asian Institute of Economic Research.

Imaoka, H. (1976). "Mechanism of Capital Accumulation in China." *In Chinese Economic Development and Institution* (in Japanese).

Jiang, Y. and Ren, R. (2004). "Estimated Return on Capital of China's Industry." *Economics* (quarterly), 3(4), 877–888.

Knight, J. (1995). "Price Scissors and Intersectional Resource Transfers: Who Paid for Industrialization in China?" *Oxford Economic Papers* (New Series), 47(1), 117–135.

Kuznets, S. (1955). "Economic Growth and Income Inequality." *American Economic Review*, 45, 1–28.

Lardy, N. (1983). *Agriculture in China's Modern Economic Development*. Cambridge: Cambridge University Press.

Lewis, A.W. (1954). "Economic Development with Unlimited Supplies of Labour." *Manchester School of Economic and Social Studies*, 22, 139–191.

Li, D. and Tsui, K. Y. (1990). "The Generalized Efficiency Wage Hypothesis and the Scissors Problem." *The Canadian Journal of Economics*, 23(1), 144–158.

Lin, J. Y. and Yu, M. (2009). "The Political Economy of Price Scissors in China: Theoretical Model and Empirical Evidence." *Economic Research*, 1, 42–56.

Lu, Ming and Chen, Z. (2004). "Urbanization, Rural and Urban Economic Policy and Tendency of Urban-Rural Income Gap." *Economic Research*, 6, 50–58.

Nakagane, K. (1982). "Structure Change of Chinese Agriculture: A Quantitative Approach" (In Japanese). *Asian Economies*, 23(8), 2–17.

Nakagane, K. (1992). *The Political Economy of Agro-industrial Relationships in Contemporary China*. Tokyo: University of Tokyo Press.

Ning, G. (2009). "Can Education Expansion Improve the Income Distribution Gap? — Evidence From CHNS 2006 Data." *World Economic Forum*, 1, 1–14.

Ohkawa, K., Shimizu and Takamatsu, N. (1978). "Agricultural Surplus in an Overall Performance of Saving-Investment." *Papers of Proceedings of the Conference on Japan's Historical Development Experience and the Contemporary Development Countries: Issues for Comparative Analysis*, Tokyo: International Development Center of Japan.

Sah, R.K and Stiglitz, J.E. (1984). "The Economics of Price Scissor." *The American Economic Review*, 74(1), 125–138.

Sah, R.K and Stiglitz, J.E. (1986). "The Economics of Price Scissors: Reply." *The American Economic Review*, 76(5), 1195–1199.

Sah, R.K and Stiglitz, J.E. (1987). "Price Scissors and the Structure of the Economy." *The Quarterly Journal of Economics*, 102(1), 109–134.

Sazanami, Y., Shujiro, U. and Hiroki, K. (1995). *Economics of Internal and External Price Difference*. Tokyo: Toyo Keizai Shinposha.

Schiff, M. and Valdes, A. (1992). "The Political Economy of Agricultural Pricing Policy." in *A Synthesis of the Economics in Developing Countries*. A World Bank Comparative Study.

Teranishi, J. (1982). *Japan's Economic Development and Finance* (2004 Reprint). Tokyo: Iwanami Shoten.

Teranishi, J. (1997). "The Resource Transfer, Opposition and Macroeconomic Stability Among Sectors in Economic Development." A. Masahiko *et al.* (eds.), *East Asian Economic Development and the Role of Government*, Chapter 10. Tokyo: Nihon Keizai Shimbun.

Tsubota, K. (2007). "An Observation on the Long-Term Changes in Agricultural Productivity Gaps in Asia." *Proceedings of Asian Integrated Policy Center*, Kyushu University, No. 2.

Wang, R. (2006). "Analysis on the Changes of China's Urban-Rural Income Gap: Also on the Applicability of "Inverted U" Hypothesis." *Statistical Research*, 4, 14–19.

Wu, H.X. (2011). "Accounting for China's Growth in 1952–2008: China's Growth Performance Debate Revisited with a Newly Constructed Data Set." RIETI Discussion Paper Series 11-E-003.

Wu, H.X. and Yuan, T. (2010). "Has Resource Allocation in China Been in Line with the Productivity Performance of Industries? — Implications for the Role of the Government." In JCER (ed.), *Chinese Economic Growth and the Role of the Government*, Chapter. 1, Japan Center for Economic Research, 1–22.

Yamamoto, H. (1999). *China's Agricultural Policy in the Reform and Opening-up — Economic Analysis of Institutions and Organizations*. Kyoto: Kyoto University Academic Press.

Yishikawa, S. (1966). "Transfer of Resources Between Agriculture and Industry in the Process of Development." *Economic Research* (Institute of Economic Research, Hitotsubashi University), 17(3), 202–208.

Yishikawa, S. (1990). *Basic Issues of Development Economics*. Tokyo: Iwanami Shoten.

Yuan, T. (2002). "The Effect of the Redistribution of Resources and Economic Growth in Economic Transition — an Empirical Study on China's Manufacturing Industry." *Asian Economies*, January, 2–24.

Yuan, T. (2009). "Research on the Level of Total Factor Productivity of Chinese Enterprises." *Economic Research* (CASS), 6, 52–64.

Yuan, T. (2010). *China's Economic Development: Initial Conditions, Policy Choices, and Resource Allocation, 1860–2004*. Tokyo: University of Tokyo Press.

Zhang, J. (2001). "Model of Changes in the Profitability of China's State-Owned Sector: 1978–1997." *Economic Research*, 3, 19–28.

Zhang, J. and Zhang, Y. (2003). "Again on the Estimation of China's Capital Stock." *Economic Research*, 7, 35–43.

Zhang, L. and Zhan, Y. (2006). "Impact of China's Rural Financial Development on the Urban-Rural Income Gap." *Financial Sciences*, 4, 53–60.

CHAPTER 6

RISING INTER-INDUSTRIAL INCOME INEQUALITY IN CHINA: CAN IT BE NARROWED AND HOW?

Zhao Chen, Ming Lu and Guanghua Wan[*]

6.1. Introduction

As one of the fastest-growing countries in the world, China needs to face the challenge of widening income inequality. Although many researchers have focused on interregional and urban-rural income inequality, as well as individual-level inequality, few have studied the rising inter-industrial wage differential. In this chapter, we use regression-based inequality decomposition to sort various factors that influence income inequality according to their importance. Our results suggest priorities for policies that reduce income inequality. We find that inter-industry wage differentials have increasingly contributed to Chinese urban inequality during 1988, 1995, and 2002, mainly due to the high rapid income growth in

[*]Zhao Chen: China Center for Economic Studies, and Center for Industry Development, Fudan University, Shanghai, China, Email: zhaochen@fudan.edu.cn; Ming Lu: School of Economics, Fudan University and Zhejiang University, Email: lm@fudan.edu.cn. Guanghua Wan: Asian Development Bank, Email: gwan@adb.org. Financial support from the National Social Science Foundation (08BJL008), MOE Project of Key Research Institute of Humanities and Social Sciences at Universities, National Science Foundation (71063022) and "100 Plan in Yunan" are greatly appreciated. We thank seminar participants at WIDER in January 2008 for their useful comments. The content of this article is the sole responsibility of the authors.

monopolistic industries. This finding is particularly important for understanding the direction of the Chinese market economy. Combating monopoly power is essential for China's next step in reforms to build a competitive and efficient market, as well as to narrow income inequality and achieve social justice.

Worldwide research into inter-industry wage differentials has continued for more than 20 years. Research in China indicates that higher salaries in monopolistic industries are regarded as "unfair" rather than "an inequality" justified by factors such as workers' higher education or job skills. Although many argue that China should pay greater attention to rising inequality among industries, there has been no measure of the magnitude of the industry factor's contribution to income inequality or to the trend of this magnitude. Therefore, we do not know to what extent the competition-inducing policies to combat a monopoly can narrow income inequality and whether China's current marketization reform can reduce inter-industry wage differentials.

In a well-developed market system, full competition in the labour market guarantees equalization of income among different industries. In other words, as long as specific industries impose no entry barriers on the labour market, inter-industry income differentials would be determined only by the individual characteristics rather than by the industries where people work. Therefore, in the process of marketization toward full competition, inter-industry factors should have decreasing contribution to income inequality, which would indicate that China is becoming a market economy with fair competition. However, we have obtained the opposite finding. Although competition has been intensifying in the market, the extent of competition varies across industries. The state-owned monopolistic industries have been minimally affected by reform. The legal system for antitrust activities is by no means effective, and it was especially ineffective before August 2008, when China's first Antitrust Law came into effect. In the financial sector the four major state-owned banks were commercialized according to the Law of Commercial Banks in 1995, but it is hard to say that the banking sector has become highly competitive. For instance, in the late 1990s urban credit cooperatives in cities were merged into some urban commercial banks, thus increasing market power of the existing banks. The effect of competition policy in the telecommunications sector is also unsatisfactory. In 2002, China Netcom[1] was separated from China Telecom and was supposed to compete with the new China Telecom. At that time, China Netcom seized the market share of Northern China and China Telecom captured the South. However, in February 2007 China Netcom and China Telecom agreed not to enter each other's market. These instances imply that China's gradual reform is not necessarily leading to a market economy with full competition. Without narrowing inter-industry wage differentials, the current marketization reform in China may result in an unfair market economy. The finding also indicates that controlling inter-industry wage differentials would be a conducive and important policy to reduce Chinese urban inequality.

The remainder of this chapter is organized as follows. Section 6.2 briefly reviews literature related to inter-industrial inequality. Section 6.3 describes the background and facts of the Chinese labour market reform and inter-industry inequality. Section 6.4 reports data and income equations. Section 6.5 presents results of the regression-based income inequality decomposition. The final section concludes and discusses policies based on previous analyses.

6.2. What Do We Know About Inter-Industry Inequality? A Literature Review

Since the mid-1980s, it has generally been accepted that inter-industry wage differentials are widely evident. The following research has inquired mainly into the causes of inter-industry wage differentials. The basic conclusion is that in the income equation using OLS estimation the omitted variables (such as ability) might be correlated with an industry variable, thereby leading to an over-estimated inter-industry wage differential. In recent research using siblings' data to control unobserved fixed effects, 11% to 24% of inter-industry wage differentials are correlated to unobserved factors jointly owned by brothers in North Europe, while in the U.S., this percentage is up to 50%. After controlling those fixed effects by differencing siblings' data, the range of inter-industry wage differentials for the U.S. and North Europe are close (Björklund *et al.*, 2004).

[1]In 2008, China Netcom was merged into China Unicom.

Haisken-DeNew and Schmidt (1999) used panel data in Germany and the U.S. to control fixed effects. They found that personal heterogeneity can explain almost a half of inter-industry wage differentials. Even by controlling the standard human capital, job characteristic, job identity, and geographical factors, inter-industry wage differentials in Germany and the U.S. are still large and similar. Pinheiro and Ramos's (1994) research in Brazil discovered a huge inter-industry wage differential in the labour market. Even after controlling the differences in workers' productivity and occupation characteristics, the inter-industry wage differential remains and cannot be explained by quality of work, worker's heterogeneity, discrimination, short-term excess demand in specific sectors, or fluctuations in macroeconomic status and policies.

What other factors influence the inter-industry wage differential? Theoretically, reduced competition in goods and labour markets are important factors explaining the inter-industry wage differential. Monopoly power enables enterprises to obtain monopoly profits that allow employers to pay higher wages. Non-competitiveness of labour markets is another condition contributing to inter-industry wage differentials. If there are no entry barriers in the labour market, employers need not pay wages above the market-clearing equilibrium. Krueger and Summers (1988) found that inter-industry wage differentials exist even after controlling measurable and immeasurable labour quality, working conditions, excess welfare, short-term demand shock, unionization threats, bargaining power of labour union, an enterprise's scale, etc. They also found that higher wages were related to lower labour-turnover in an industry, which demonstrates that high-wage industries obtain some rent from non-competitiveness. Katz and Summers (1989) also believed that workers receive rents in high-wage industries. These rents might appear because some industries are willing to pay above-market wages to achieve higher productivity. This mechanism is called "an efficiency wage". Evidence provided by Chen and Edin (2006) supports the efficiency wage hypothesis. Similarly, Gittleman and Wolff (1993) found that inter-industry wage differentials are positively correlated to an industry's productivity growth rate, output growth rate, capital intensity, and export orientation. Arbache (2001) used comparable and measurable productivity characteristics to explain wage differentials. He finds no evidence to support the compensatory wage, but he does find the existence of an efficient wage mechanism in manufacturing industries.

The inter-industry wage differential is widening in transitional economies like China and Russia and remains stable in developed economies. In China, Shi (2007) reported the trend of widening inter-industry wage differentials. The ranking of industry wages changed dramatically in the 1980s and stabilized after the mid-1990s. In Russia, the relative change of the inter-industry average wage was the main reason for the widening income gap (Lukyanova, 2006). In other countries, empirical research shows that inter-industry wage differentials in the U.S. widen after the 1970s, mainly because of the widening wage differential between the primary and secondary sectors (Davidson and Reich, 1988). Using panel data from the 14 OECD countries for the period 1970–1985, Gittleman and Wolff (1993) found that rankings of inter-industry wages were stable. They found that inter-industry wage differentials in the U.S. were generally widening, but the trend in other countries is unclear. Haisken-DeNew and Schmidt (1999) found that inter-industry wage differentials for Germany and the U.S. were stable during the 13 years they studied. Between 1984 and 1998, a period of dramatic structural change in Brazil, its wage structure was relatively stable (Arbache, 2001; Arbache *et al.*, 2004). Using historical data for the U.S., Krueger and Summers (1987) found that the correlation coefficient of relative wages for nine main industries was 0.62 during the period 1900–1984, while correlation for the years between 1970 and 1984 was 0.91.

Of all the literature that we have surveyed there seem to be few researches using decomposition methods to determine various factors' contribution (including an industry factor) to income inequality and the trend of the contribution. Pinheiro and Ramos (1994) used the decomposition method to study Brazil's data. After controlling other variables, they found that the contribution of labour market segmentation to income inequality is between 7% and 11%. In this chapter, we use Chinese data to show the contribution of inter-industry wage differentials to income inequality and to document how the contribution changes over time. We will provide new empirical evidence of inter-industry wage differentials in China as it undergoes economic transition. Knight and Song (2003) decomposed Chinese urban residents' income inequality, but they did not consider the contribution of inter-industry inequality. Gustafsson and Li (2001) decomposed income inequality according to income sources, but their method cannot identify the contribution of basic determinants of income to income inequality. To our knowledge, only the recent paper by Deng and Li (2009) decomposed urban inequality and derived the contributions of each factor over time. Their decomposition results indicate that the effects of gender and membership in the Communist Party of China on earnings inequality have changed little. While work experience had a reduced effect on earnings inequality, the effects of education and occupation have increased. The contributions of ownership status and industry to earnings inequality have increased. Regional effects have been the largest recent contributor to earnings inequality. Unlike the work of Deng and Li (2009), where the industry factor is a minor result in their study, our focus is how inter-industry wage differentials contribute to income inequality and how the contribution changes over time in China. We also will provide evidence indicating that relatively rising earnings in several industries dominated by state-owned-enterprises mainly explain why the contribution of industry to inequality increases over time. In model specification, our income-generating function also differs slightly from Deng and Li (2009). Our approach includes more explanatory variables, such as dummies for holding a second job and employment status during the whole year, to capture the structural change of the labour market and to alleviate potential missing-variable-bias.

6.3. Chinese Labour Market Reform and Inter-Industry Inequality: Background and Fact

Among components of overall income inequality in China, urban residents' income inequality is becoming increasingly significant. Income inequality of rural and urban residents and overall income disparity are widening. Urban residents' inequality is smaller than rural residents', but the difference between these two inequalities is decreasing. In 2001, the rural Gini coefficient was 36.48, the urban Gini coefficient was 32.32, and the national overall Gini coefficient was 44.73 (Ravallion and Chen, 2007). Figure 6.1 shows the basic pattern of rising of China's income inequality in different dimensions. Other researches that analyzed data of

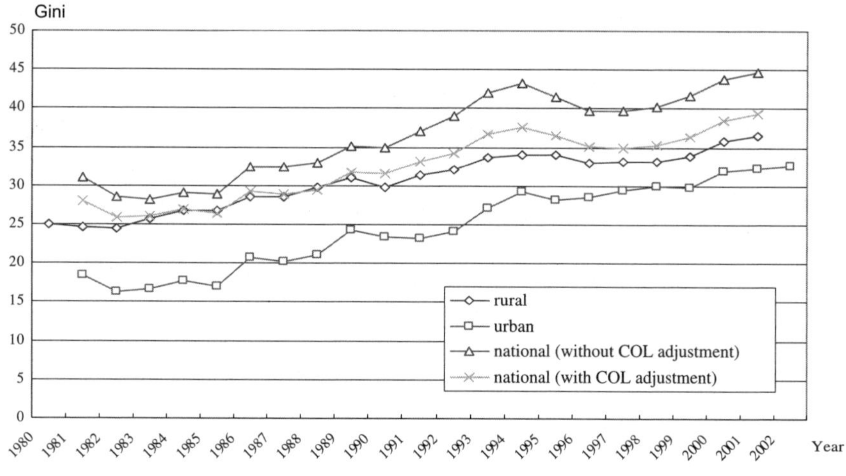

Fig. 6.1. China's rising income inequality.

Source: Based on the data from Ravallion and Chen (2007).

1988, 1995 and 2002 found that income inequality widened rapidly between 1988 and 1995, but it changed little from 1995 to 2002. The overall Gini coefficient changed from 46.9 to 46.8, while the urban Gini coefficient declined from 33.9 to 32.2. In fact, the stable trend of overall income inequality is mainly due to income convergence in the eastern provinces (Gustafsson *et al.*, 2008).

Some factors in the process of urban reform increase income inequality. Before reform and opening-up, all urban Chinese workers were employed by state-owned or collective-owned enterprises; and all their income came from wages, which were solely decided by the planning system. Except for factors such as position and age, the value system of "equal pay for equal work" controlled returns on other factors, such as education and gender, at a low level. For the determination of wages, working age was more important than productivity (education) (Gustafsson *et al.*, 2001). Since wage levels were set by the labour administration department, generally speaking, the profit differential across industries and enterprises did not produce a difference in wages for employees.

Since the reform and opening-up, the greatest change in the determination of wage and income is the increase of education returns and the widening inter-industry wage differential. Marketization reform raised the return on human capital, which was previously distorted under the planning system. Many empirical researches have found that along with China's reform and opening-up, the returns to education rose continuously (to name a few: Zhang *et al.*, 2005; Li and Heckman, 2004; Li and Ding, 2003). Education has an increasing influence on income inequality (Gustafsson *et al.*, 2008). For example, according to empirical evidence from Shanghai, the commercial center of China, education has the greatest contribution to income inequality (Tian and Lu, 2007).

Let us look at the widening inter-industry wage differentials. Figure 6.2 shows wage inequality among more than 10 industries since 1978 according to two indexes. The simplest index is the ratio of the highest to the lowest industry average wage. From 1978 to 1997, this index rose from 1.66 to 2.26, and then rapidly rose to 4.75 until 2006. The other index is the Gini coefficient of all industries' wages. We take all employees from the same industry as a group earning the same wage and use the number of employees from this industry as the size of the group to calculate the Gini coefficient. The result calculated in this way also shows a rising trend. The Gini coefficient was 0.05 in 1978, 0.1 in 1997, and rose rapidly to 0.19 until 2006.[2]

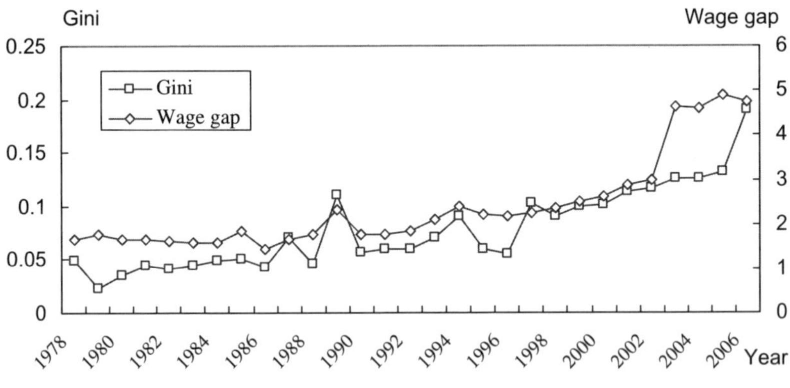

Fig. 6.2. China's inter-industry wage differential (1978–2006).

Sources: The authors' calculation based on *China Statistical Yearbook* (various years), *Chinese Statistics Press*.

[2]Because of neglecting wage differential within the same industry, the Gini coefficient calculated here is smaller than the real value of Gini coefficient for all employees.

We mark 1997 as the dividing line to compare the change of inter-industry wage differentials because 1996 was the watershed year for labour market reform. Before 1996, reform in the labour market was relatively moderate. The obvious adjustment at that time was that wages had dropped continuously as a share of total income (Lu and Jiang, 2008). The decentralization reform in the 1980s gave enterprises more power in deciding wages and bonuses. Enterprise revenue differentials were reflected in the income inequality. Incentive scheme reform significantly promoted enterprise efficiency (Groves *et al.*, 1994). However, at the same time, it rendered the revenue differential among industries and enterprises a great contribution to the differential in employees' wages. Using survey data of state-owned enterprise (SOE) in 1981 and 1987, Meng and Kidd (1997) found that the inter-industry wage differentials among Chinese SOEs had become more remarkable since 1987. The main reason, as they believe, is that, after the reform of the employment system, enterprises implemented profit-linked bonuses (Meng and Kidd, 1997). In 1996, with the re-employment service center as an intermediary, Shanghai began to lay off redundant workers in SOEs. After that, labour market reform accelerated, employment structure adjusted rapidly, and the labour force participation rate decreased sharply (Lu and Jiang, 2008). The widening of urban income inequality after 1996 resulted from labour market restructuring (Meng *et al.*, 2005). It is noteworthy that labour market reform after 1996 began in money-losing enterprises, which were mostly in the competitive sector. Policies at that time allowed SOEs with two years of losses to cut redundant employment through lay-offs and repositioning. However, competition in the labour market existed marginally. Monopoly sectors such as public utilities, post and telecommunications, and finance were less influenced by the labour market competition. During the 1980s, although the labour market became more flexible, the labour flow both between urban and rural areas and among cities was not remarkable (Davis, 1992). After the mid-1990s, numerous rural-to-urban migrants intensified competition in the urban labour market, but this marginal increase in competition was concentrated only in industries with fewer labour market entry barriers. The influence of increasing competition is different for various industries; that is the main reason for the widening inter-industry wage differentials.

In the following two sections, we will see the contribution of the inter-industry wage differential to income inequality and its changes over time. In addition, we will see that the increasing contribution of the inter-industry wage differential to inequality results primarily from several state-owned monopolistic industries.

6.4. Data and Income Equation

Data used in our research are from the Chinese Household Income Project Survey (CHIPS) which was conducted by the Chinese Academy of Social Sciences and the National Bureau of Statistics. CHIPS data, collected randomly following a strict sampling process, are nationally representative and widely employed in research. In our data, the 1988 urban survey covers 10 provinces including Beijing, Shanxi, Liaoning, Jiangsu, Anhui, Henan, Hubei, Guangdong, Yunnan, and Gansu. The 1995 data include one additional province, Sichuan. The 2002 data cover the same provinces as 1995 plus the new municipality, Chongqing.

Our research has two steps. First, we need to estimate a semi-log income-generating equation, and then we decompose income inequality based on this equation. The income-generating equation we estimate can be written as:

$$\ln W_{it} = \beta_t' X_{it} + \varepsilon_{it}$$

where W is the individual's annual earnings (including wage, bonus, price subsidy, income in kind, and secondary job income), i denotes the individual, t denotes year (t = 1988, 1995, and 2002), and X is a vector of the explanatory variables. Following existing literature, explanatory variables for income include age and its square, years of schooling, dummies for holding a second job, being employed the whole year, gender, party membership, minority groups, ownership types, and occupation classifications. We also controlled the city dummy. β_t is a vector of parameters to be estimated. In order to make the income data comparable across region and time, we need to deflate income data. Brandt and Holz (2006) provided the interregional price index in 1990, which indicates the purchasing power of the Renminbi (RMB) among different regions. Using this

Table 6.1. Gini coefficients of China urban income inequality.

	1988	1995	2002
Deflated income	0.232	0.291	0.343
Original data	0.246	0.310	0.362
Difference (%)	6.034	6.529	5.539

interregional price index in 1990 and the provincial level urban consumer price index, we obtain the price deflator for 1988, 1995, and 2002. By doing so, the deflated income becomes comparable not only across time but across regions. Table 6.1 reports the Gini coefficients of income inequality. We can conclude that: first, income inequality is widening; and second, income inequality is relatively small when measured via deflated income data.[3] The urban income inequality estimation in our report is different from those of Gustafsson *et al.* (2008) because our income definition does not include unearned income, and it is deflated by the interregional deflation indexes. Moreover, when we compute income inequality, we only use the effective samples to estimate the income-generating function.

Table 6.2 reports the result of wage equation estimation. In each equation for 1988, 1995 and 2002, we controlled regular variables including dummies for party membership, education level, ownership type, occupation type, city dummies, which are not reported in the table to save space. The model explains the yearly earnings quite well with relatively high adjusted R squares. It is worthy to mention that the coefficients of having a second job increased in 1995 and then decreased in 2002. Nevertheless, our decomposition results will show later that the contribution of this factor to total income inequality is always increasing. That is to say, only the coefficients of the variable are not enough for us to understand the driving force of income inequality, and regression-based decomposition is also important.

[3]This is because of the higher purchasing power in lower income area. Ravallion and Chen (2007) found that income inequality is reduced when interregional purchasing power parity is taken into consideration.

Table 6.2. Income-generating functions of different years.

	1988	1995	2002
Socio-economic characteristics			
Second job (yes = 1)	0.058**	0.362***	0.150***
Being employed the whole year (yes = 1)	0.643***	0.455***	0.444***
Gender (male = 1)	0.079***	0.152***	0.122***
Age	0.084***	0.160***	0.055***
Age square	−0.001***	−0.002***	−0.0006***
Minority group (yes = 1)	0.024	−0.013	−0.036
Industry			
Farm, forest, husbandry and fishery	0.014	0.039	0.011
Mining and exploration industry	0.065***	0.020	−0.0007
Geological prospecting, irrigation administration	−0.028		0.116
Electricity, gas and water supply facilities			0.317***
Construction	0.001	−0.051	0.070
Transportation, storage, post office and telecommunications	0.001	0.047*	0.163
Wholesale, retail and food services	−0.004	−0.028	−0.027
Real estate	−0.069***	−0.022	0.203
Social services	−0.186***		−0.091
Health, sports and social welfare	0.016	0.036	0.050
Education, culture and arts, mass media and entertainment	0.0001	0.068***	0.067
Scientific research and professional services	−0.017	0.064	0.110
Finance and insurance	0.003	0.196***	0.210***
Government agents, party organisations and social groups	−0.038***	0.014	0.084
Other industries	−0.018	−0.259***	0.047
City dummy	yes	yes	yes
Constant	6.529***	4.861***	7.088***
Number of Observation	17568	10933	6121
Adj-R^2	0.473	0.336	0.383

Notes: (1) The classification of industries is consistent with CHIPS questionnaire, which is a little different from the classification of *China Statistical Yearbook*. (2) Control variables include dummies for party membership, education level, ownership type, occupation type, city dummies, etc. Because of space limitations, we do not report coefficients of party membership and education level. (3) *, **, and *** denote significance at 1%, 5% and 10% level respectively. To save space, standard errors are not reported.

According to Table 6.2, the wage difference among industries does exist after controlling for other variables. More specifically, taking the manufacturing sector as reference group, four different industrials have significantly different wage level compared with manufacturing industries in 1988 and 1995.[4] In 2002, wages in six industries are significantly different from manufacturing industry. That is to say, the relative wage among industries has changed significantly. Particularly, the coefficients of "transportation, storage, post office and communication" and "finance and insurance" industries both changed from insignificant in 1988 to significantly positive in 1995. The coefficients kept significant and increased in 2002. Or, in 2002 workers in "transportation, storage, post office and communication" and "finance and insurance" industries are overpaid 16.3% and 21.0% respectively.

6.5. Regression-Based Decomposition of Income Inequality

In this section, using a regression-based decomposition framework developed by Shorrocks (1999), we analyze how different variables contribute to income inequality, focusing on the contribution of industry variables and its change across time. The idea of this method is to calculate a sample average value of an argument (such as X) in the income determination function, then substitute X by its average, predict income data, and compute the inequality index of this predicted income. This new inequality index does not include the influence of "X." X's contribution to income inequality is measured by the difference between this new index, and the income inequality computed before X is replaced by its average. Above is a brief introduction to the decomposition method in this chapter. A more detailed introduction can be found in Wan (2004) or Wan and Zhou (2005).

Because we choose a semi-log model in the income-generating function, we will get erroneous results if we use the logarithm of income as the dependent variable to do decomposition; therefore, we take the exponent while writing the income-generating equation for decomposition.

$$y = \exp(\hat{a}_0) \bullet \exp(\hat{a}_1 X_1 + \hat{a}_2 X_2 + \cdots + \hat{a}_k X_k) \bullet \exp(\hat{u})$$

[4]We take manufacturing industries as reference group because it is the industry with a largest sample size and has a medium-wage level.

In the above equation $\exp(\hat{a}_0)$ is a scalar. When we compute indices of income inequality, the scalar can be omitted from the equation without affecting the results (Wan, 2002). Considering the influence of residual $\hat{u}$, we employ a popular method that can be used by any index to measure inequality. We take the difference between the inequality index of original income y and the inequality index when assuming $\hat{u} = 0$ as residual $\hat{u}$'s contribution to the actual income inequality. In the ideal status, the residual is 0, and total income inequality can be explained 100% by variables in the income-generating function that perfectly fits the data. Generally, however, the residual is seldom 0, so the analysis of residual influence is necessary. In Table 6.3, we adopt the ratio of the residual's contribution to total income inequality as the proportion explained by the residual. The rest reflects the income inequality contributed by the explanatory variables in the model (Wan, 2002). According to this principle, our model can explain approximately 81%, 78%, and 67%, respectively, of total income inequality.

Because there is some difference in industrial classification in these three years, we cannot directly compare income inequality decomposition results of different years. So we first focus on the decomposition results for 2002. Because the regression-based decomposition method that we use can be applied to different inequality indices, we use data in 2002 to decompose four different indices of income inequality. Table 6.4 reveals an issue that arises when using different indexes: although the factors employed in each index are the same, their contributions to income inequality differ in each index. This is because each index applies a different weighting to income groups from the poorest to the richest. Notwithstanding this variation among indexes, however, each factor's rank in contributing to income inequality does not change.

Table 6.3. Gini coefficients of urban income and the proportions explained.

	1988	**1995**	**2002**
Gini coefficient computed by original income data	0.232	0.291	0.343
Gini coefficient computed by predicted income data	0.189	0.227	0.228
Proportion explained by residual (%)	18.534	22.129	33.448
Proportion explained by model (%)	81.466	77.871	66.552

Table 6.4. Decomposition of income inequality for 2002 (industry is of original category).

	Gini	%	GE(0)	%	GE(1)	%	CV	%
Second job	0.009	3.982	0.002	2.749	0.002	2.787	0.005	2.811
Being employed the whole year	0.015	6.613	0.008	9.253	0.007	7.926	0.012	6.828
Gender	0.011	5.004	0.004	4.287	0.004	4.203	0.007	4.112
Age and its square	0.016	6.803	0.005	6.151	0.005	5.595	0.009	5.034
Party membership	0.008	3.321	0.003	3.060	0.003	3.104	0.006	3.176
Minority group	0.000	0.074	0.000	−0.019	0.000	−0.016	0.000	−0.017
Education	0.024	10.373	0.009	10.118	0.009	10.656	0.020	11.296
Ownership	0.024	10.630	0.008	9.753	0.008	9.665	0.017	9.547
Occupation	0.025	11.148	0.009	10.910	0.009	10.799	0.019	10.771
Industry	0.023	10.067	0.008	9.186	0.008	9.332	0.017	9.422
City dummy	0.073	31.984	0.029	34.551	0.030	35.948	0.067	37.020
Total	0.228	100.000	0.085	100.000	0.084	100.000	0.180	100.000

The most important contributor to income inequality is the city dummy variable, which represents different regional factors such as geography, institution and culture, etc. This variable's contribution to income inequality ranges from 31.984% to 37.02%. The great contribution of region dummies to urban residents' income inequality reflects the persistent barriers to Chinese labour mobility that are noted by Davis (1992). Based on Gini decomposition results, the second level contains four factors: occupation, ownership, education, and industry, each contributing approximately 10% to income inequality. Contribution factors at the third level are age, being employed the whole year, and gender, which have contributed between 5% and 6.8%. Contributions of holding a second job and party membership are 3.321% and 3.982%, respectively. The contribution of the minority group dummy is trivial. In fact, in our income-generating function, membership in a minority group is also an insignificant factor, which means that China does not have discrimination against minority groups.

What importance does the variable "Industry" have in contributing to income inequality? If we decompose income inequality and estimate the income equation entirely according to industrial categories based on original data, this factor contributes increasingly to income inequality, from 1.03% in 1988 to 3.02% in 1995, and then to 10.07% in 2002. Its rising contribution from 1995 to 2002 is dramatic. To accommodate for the official re-classification of industries in three different years, we combine some industries to make industry dummies comparable across time. For instance, we combined the exploration and mining industries for 1988 and 2002. Also for these two years, we combined the category "Social services" with "Public health, sports, and social welfare", which also merges the category "Electric, gas, and water suppliers" for 2002. After doing so, we establish 13 industries, including "Others", which falls into categories that are comparable across several years.

In Table 6.5, we report 11 factors contributing to income inequality in all three years. It shows the following trends: (1) The industry factor's contribution to income inequality grows. For 2002, we combine the category "Electricity, gas, and water production and supply" that has higher income, with "Social services" that has lower income, and with "Public health, sports, and social welfare", which has insignificantly higher income compared to manufacturing. Therefore, the contribution of industrial category to income inequality is lower, but it still produces a greater contribution to income inequality than in 1995. (2) The location factor, represented by the urban dummy, has a growing contribution to income inequality. In 1988, the location factor contributed 14% to income inequality, ranking in first place, but its contribution had increased to 30% in 1995, becoming the most important contributor to income inequality. It could explain one-third of total income inequality in 2002. The regional variable's rising contribution to income inequality can be explained by barriers to labour flow for low-skilled workers among cities, but relatively free mobility for high-skilled workers. (3) Education has an apparently increasing contribution to income inequality. Now that reform permits higher wages for education and training, its increasing contribution is not

Table 6.5. Income inequality (Gini) decomposition (industries combined).

	1988		1995		2002	
	Gini	**%**	**Gini**	**%**	**Gini**	**%**
Second job	0.000	0.147	0.001	0.558	0.009	4.178
Being employed the whole year	0.061	32.501	0.017	7.422	0.015	6.733
Gender	0.009	4.603	0.014	6.245	0.012	5.363
Age (and its square)	0.053	27.868	0.051	22.378	0.016	7.116
Party membership	0.006	3.252	0.010	4.383	0.007	3.219
Minority group	0.000	0.114	0.000	0.049	0.000	0.081
Education	0.004	1.939	0.019	8.410	0.025	11.122
Ownership	0.018	9.475	0.023	9.967	0.028	12.250
Occupation	0.011	5.641	0.018	7.735	0.028	12.623
Industry	0.001	0.406	0.007	3.019	0.011	5.086
City dummy	0.027	14.055	0.068	29.834	0.072	32.229
Total	0.189	100.000	0.227	100.000	0.225	100.000

surprising. (4) Ownership and occupation also contribute increasingly to income inequality, although occupation's contribution increases faster. This may be explained by intense restructuring in forms of ownership and occupation. (5) Being employed the whole year has an apparently decreasing contribution to income inequality. For 1998, this factor explains up to one-third of income inequality, which was caused by a large number of surplus workers in enterprises. In our 1988 sample, 9.47% of people were not employed the whole year. But in 1995, this factor's contribution had decreased dramatically to 7.4%. In that year, only 7.86% of people were not employed the whole year. In 2002, this factor's contribution dropped to 6.7%. (6) Age also has an understandably decreasing contribution. Older workers were paid more under traditional working system, so it had a great contribution from 1988 to 1995. But in 2002, along with the rapid labour market reform that started 1996, age's importance has dropped, while other factors of productivity have influenced income more. And (7) Holding a second job has an apparently increasing contribution to income inequality. In 1995 its contribution to income inequality was more than three times that of 1988, and in 2002 its contribution was 7.5 times that of 1995.

According to regression results of Table 6.2, the coefficients of two industries — "Transportation, storage, post office and telecommunications" and "Finance and insurance" — change from insignificant to increasingly significant. Coefficients of these two industry categories also increase. We suspect that these two industries rapidly enhance the industry variable's contribution to income inequality. Galbraith *et al.* (2004) note that in Russian and Chinese industries having the strongest monopoly power gained relatively during economic restructuring. In both countries, the financial sector gained the most, while the agricultural sector lost the most. Therefore, in the following step we exclude these two industries, which have the highest income. In conclusions presented in Table 6.6, the contribution of factors other than industry changes little, but industry

Table 6.6. Income inequality (Gini) decomposition (industries combined, and two highest income industries excluded).

	1988		**1995**		**2002**	
	Gini	%	**Gini**	%	**Gini**	%
Second job	0.000	0.137	0.001	0.627	0.010	4.430
Being employed the whole year	0.060	31.892	0.017	7.511	0.016	7.177
Gender	0.009	4.656	0.015	6.457	0.013	5.621
Age (and its square)	0.052	27.634	0.048	21.367	0.015	6.868
Party membership	0.006	3.383	0.010	4.382	0.008	3.526
Minority group	0.000	0.136	0.000	0.091	0.000	0.173
Education	0.004	2.090	0.018	8.149	0.023	10.194
Ownership	0.018	9.570	0.023	10.230	0.028	12.695
Occupation	0.010	5.547	0.018	8.073	0.031	13.712
Industry	0.001	0.424	0.005	2.421	0.005	2.292
City dummy	0.027	14.529	0.070	30.691	0.074	33.313
Total	0.188	100.000	0.227	100.000	0.223	100.000

contribution has greatly decreased. For 2002, industry leaves the second layer of factors in terms of their contribution. Its contribution to income inequality ranks 9th of 11 factors and dropped by 0.13% from 1995 to 2002. Therefore, we can conclude that two industries — "Transportation, storage, post office and telecommunications" and "Finance and insurance" — have become the important elements in widening urban residents' income inequality, while the income of these two industries is relatively rising. Due to data limitation, we lack more detailed categories of industries. However, the two industries excluded from the analysis include state-owned sub-industries with monopoly powers.

6.6. Rising Inter-Industrial Income Inequality in China: Can It Be Narrowed and How?

How will urban income inequality change in the future? To answer this question, we need to see the trend. Table 6.5 shows the contribution of different factors to income inequality. It seems that the contribution of inter-industrial wage differential is not so important as compared with that of regional, education, ownership and occupation factors. However, the increasing rate of the contribution of inter-industrial wage differential to urban income inequality is much larger than those of other factors as listed in Table 6.7. That is to say, decreasing inter-industrial wage differential is very important for narrowing rising income inequality in urban China.

Can it be narrowed and how? According to our analysis, to decrease inter-industrial wage differential, we need to implement effective competition policies. For instance, entry barriers against private enterprises at

Table 6.7. Increasing rate of contribution for selected factors.

	1995	**2002**
Education	333.73	32.25
Ownership	5.19	22.91
Occupation	37.12	63.19
Industry	**643.60**	**68.47**
City dummy	112.27	8.03

Note: Calculated according to Table 6.5.

industrial level should be broken down. Besides, breaking down labour market entry barriers at industrial level is also important for equalizing wages among industries, which calls for reform on the current *hukou* system according to Chen *et al.* (2009).

However, could inter-industrial wage differential easily be narrowed? It is hard to give an exact answer. Nevertheless, we would better not be optimistic about it. Why? Let us look at the changing patterns of average wage for different industries since reform. Before that, we need to make it clear that the difference of average wage for different industries might not necessarily reflect what we call wage differentials, because the higher average wage could be the result of higher human capital accumulation. This again emphasizes the importance of regression-based decomposition of income inequality, focusing on the role of inter-industrial wage differentials.

To show the changing patterns of average wage for different industries, we use the Spearman rank correlation coefficient. Suppose there are n industries and we have the average wages of each industry for two years. The average wage of industry i ranks the X_ith highest in year one and Y_ith in year two. Then we use $D_i = X_i - Y_i$ to measure change of the rank for industry i. And the Spearman rank correlation coefficient (R_s) is given by:

$$R_s = 1 - \frac{6\sum_{i=1}^{n} D_i^2}{n^3 - n}$$

The value of R_s varies between −1 and 1. The larger R_s is, the greater the ranking of wages of all the industries has changed. If R_s equals 1, then there is no change for the ranking of wages. If R_s equals −1, then ranking of wages in year one changes totally, which means the ranking in year two is just the opposite.

Figure 6.3 shows that during the mid-1980 and the early 1990s the Spearman rank correlation coefficient decreased substantially because of the labour market reform and enterprise reform. In the mid-1980s, the labour market reform began and SOEs have more freedom to hire worker in the labour market. In the early 1990s, SOEs began to lay off surplus workers. However, since the late 1990s, the Spearman rank correlation coefficient converges to 1, which implies that it is very difficult to decrease the

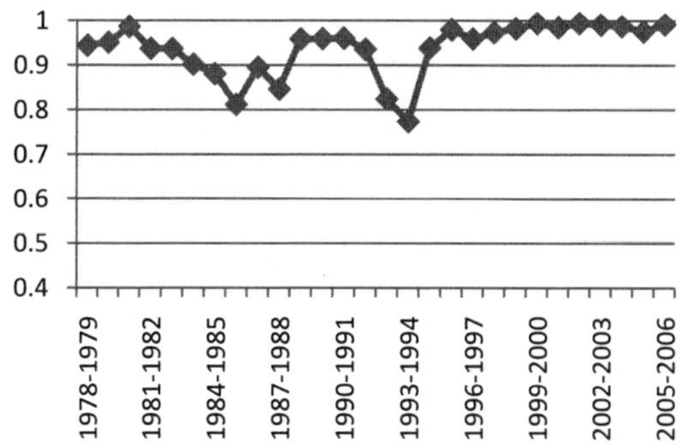

Fig. 6.3. Spearman rank correlation coefficient for average wage of industries in China (1978–2006).

Sources: Authors' calculation based on *China Statistical Yearbook* (various years), *Chinese Statistics Press*.

average wage of those industries with monopolistic power. The following two tables show the ranking of average wages in four selected industries since 1990 to 2006. They are separated into two tables because the categories of industries are different for years before and after 2002.

Table 6.8. Rank of average wage for selected industries (1990–2002).

Selected industries among 15	Rank in 1990	Rank in 2002	Variance of the rank
Finance & insurance	12	1	18.17
Transportation, storage, post office and telecommunications	4	4	0.44
Farm, forest and fishery	15	15	0.00
Electricity & gas supply	2	3	0.86

Table 6.8 indicates that the average wage in finance & insurance industry has increased substantially, which makes the wage in this industry rank 1st among all 15 industries, while it ranked 12th in 1990. That is to say, finance & insurance is a typical industry that gains a lot during transition. From 2003, ranking of the average wage of this industry does not change. Two industries, namely "Transportation, storage, post office and telecommunications" and "Electricity & gas supply" always have high average

Table 6.9. Rank of average wage for selected industries (2003–2006).

Selected industries among 19	Rank in 2003	Rank in 2006	Variance of the rank
Finance & insurance	2	2	0.00
Transportation, storage, post office and telecommunications	9	6	2.25
Farm, forest and fishery	19	19	0.00
Electricity & gas supply	4	4	0.00

wage. All these industries with monopolistic power stay among the top few. The implication behind is that such industries with monopolistic power become large interest groups, which is not easy to fight against. So, we should never be optimistic about narrowing inter-industrial income inequality in China.

Therefore, we might further infer that the key to effectively narrowing the inter-industrial income inequality lies the breaking down of the monopolistic power of some industries. And this solution depends equally on the conquest over the resistance of these monopolistic interest groups and the resolution of the government to reign over these groups.

First the resistance of the monopolistic interest groups. With the deregulaton of pricing in the market reform, the ability by which the monopolistic industries gain profits has been increasingly strengthened. Accordingly their power has been increased and their status has been consolidated. The industry of mobile telecommunications is one of such numerous cases. In this market, the whole China is under two giant operation businesses: China Mobile and China Unicom. In order to enter this lucrative market, China Telecom introduced in 1998 a new business called "PHS" (personal handy-phone system) — the business circumvented the policy restraint and gained the access, via pretext of the extension of fixed-line telephone and under the acquiesce of the regulators, to the mobile telecommunications market.

Compared with the mobile businesses of China Mobile and China Unicom, China Telecom "PHS" boasted its price advantages of low fees and one-way toll collection and its performance advantages of long stand-by time and low radiation. This made the business widely recognized and quickly won the popularity particularly among the urban middle- and low-income groups. However, PHS met resistance from other mobile phone businesses and was criticized for being technically backward. In February 2009, the Ministry of Industry and Information issued a notice requiring that the band of PHS give way to 3G, that the relevant business stop recruiting new users, and that by the end of 2011 the net be shut down to the PHS users. This is an administrative order *de facto* requiring the withdrawal of PHS from the mobile telecommunications market and signifies a further strengthening of the monopolistic position of China Mobile and China Unicom, two largest businesses, in the market of mobile telecommunications. Although it is difficult to provide palpable evidence that the two monopolistic businesses persuaded the government regulators to maintain their monopoly position, at least we can see that the current status of the monopolistic firms is really difficult to be weakened.

Then let us take a look at the government's determination to fight against interest groups of monopolistic industries. As we have discussed, in China industrial monopoly chiefly originates from administrative monopoly resulting from government regulation, just as the case, mentioned above, with the industrial monopoly in the telecommunications market. It is a pity that, while China has introduced the Antitrust Law, the Law itself has evaded the administrative monopoly. Therefore, this long-awaited birth of Antitrust Law has dwarfed its great significance.

In addition to breaking up the industrial monopoly *per se*, there exit other measures to bridge the income gap — for example, let the general public to share on an equal basis the profits of listed companies of monopolistic industries. But such measure still seems difficult to be implemented. Generally speaking, the listed companies in China rarely pay dividends, and the government does not have a valid constraint in this regard over the listed companies — with the result that on the one hand the listed companies do not pay dividends to public investors, and on the one hand they pay excessively high salaries to their own staff, especially those senior executives.

In short, because of the ever-growing power of the monopolistic interest groups and the feeble determination of the government to break down the monopoly and to narrow the industry wage differential, we are not so optimistic as to predict that the trend would emerge soon in alleviating the inter-industrial income inequality in China.

6.7. Conclusions and Policy Implications

This chapter primarily explores inter-industry wage differentials by examining the contribution that industry variables make to urban residents' income inequality and how the contribution changes over time. We find that, concerning the process of widening urban residents' income inequality, inter-industry wage differentials also expand. Among all factors that widen inequality in our model, the importance of inter-industry wage differential is increasing. During the period of 1995–2002, the increasing contribution of inter-industry wage differential was mainly attributable to the monopolistic industries of "Transportation, storage, post office and telecommunications" and "Finance and insurance". This suggests that in the marketization process, some industries benefit more, and more intense competition in the labour market does not equally affect every industry. In addition, we found that region, education, ownership, occupation, and holding a second job also increasingly contribute to income inequality, while the factors like age and being employed the whole year have a decreasing contribution.

The main policy implication of this chapter is clear: if China wants to control urban income inequality, removing entry barriers in the labour market and breaking monopoly power in the goods market are essential. China needs to build a fairly competitive market economy to control income inequality. According to the results of 2002, urban residents' income inequality would decease 5%–10% if China could remove inter-industrial wage differentials. In fact, just removing several industries' unreasonably high wage can make the industrial factor much less important in urban income inequality. However, with the ever-growing power of the monopolist interest groups, their status is becoming more and more consolidated. Meanwhile, the government has not set up a resolute mind to break up (especially, administrative) monopoly. Hence the narrowing trend in the industrial wage differential might not be warranted in the near future.

Of course, in order to reduce urban income inequality, the policy for regional and educational equality is also important. The high inter-regional income inequality reflects the situation that workers cannot freely move across regions because of institutional barriers induced by the household registration (*hukou*) system. Therefore, the main policy for reducing regional income inequality should be to eliminate barriers to labour mobility, not relying on the present policy of inter-regional financial transfers. Higher income through higher education is an inevitable result of marketization reform. Therefore, reducing income inequality can better be achieved by equalizing educational opportunity than by artificially suppressing wages of the educated. When inter-regional labour migration becomes much freer in the future, income inequality will be greater, despite increased returns on education, if rural residents receive insufficient education before they enter the cities.

The empirical results of this chapter suggest that many current market reforms are not producing a more fair and competitive economy. Widening inter-industrial inequality reflects injustice in the labour market, which induces increasingly greater dissatisfaction in the population. Having provided evidence of inter-industrial inequality, we now need to provide evidence explaining its causes. In Chen *et al.* (2009) evidence indicating who receives the opportunity to enter overpaid industries is presented.

References

Arbache, J.S. (2001). "Wage Differentials in Brazil: Theory and Evidence." *The Journal of Development Studies*, 38(2), 109–130.

Arbache, J.S., Dickerson, A. and Green, F. (2004). "Assessing the Stability of the Inter-Industry Wage Structure in the Face of Radical Economic Reforms." *Economics Letters*, 83(2), 149–155.

Björklund, A., Bratsberg, B., Eriksson, T., Jäntti, M. and Raaum, O. (2004). "Inter-Industry Wage Differentials and Unobserved Ability: Siblings Evidence from Five Countries." IZA Discussion Paper Series, No. 1080.

Brandt, L. and Holz, C.A. (2006). "Spatial Price Differences in China: Estimates and Implications." *Economic Development and Cultural Change*, 55(1), 43–86.

Chen, P. and Edin, P.-A. (2006). "Efficiency Wages and Industry Wage Differentials: A Comparison Across Methods of Pay." *The Review of Economics and Statistics*, 84(4), 617–631.

Chen, Y., Démurger, S. and Fournier, M. (2005). "Earnings Differentials and Ownership Structure in Chinese Enterprises." *Economic Development and Cultural Change*, 53(4), 933–958.

Chen, Z., Lu, M. and Hiroshin, S. (2009). "Social Networks and Labour Market Entry Barriers: Why Inter-Industrial Wage Differentials in Urban China?" Working Paper.

Davidson, C. and Reich, M. (1988). "Income Inequality: An Inter-Industry Analysis." *Industrial Relations*, 27(3), 263–286.

Davis, D. (1992). "Job Mobility in Post-Mao Cities: Increases on the Margins." *China Quarterly*, 132, 1062–1085.

Deng, Q. and Li, S. (2009). "What Lies Behind Rising Earnings Inequality in Urban China? Regression-Based Decompositions." *CESifo Economic Studies*, 55(3–4), 598–623.

Dong, X. (2005). "Wage Inequality and Between-Firm Wage Dispersion in the 1990s: A Comparison of Rural and Urban Enterprises in China." *Journal of Comparative Economics*, 33(4), 664–687.

Galbraith, J.K., Krytynskaia, L. and Wang, Q. (2004). "The Experience of Rising Inequality in Russia and China During the Transition." *The European Journal of Comparative Economics*, 1(1), 87–106.

Gittleman, M. and Wolff, E.N. (1993). "International Comparisons of Inter-Industry Wage Differentials." *Review of Income and Wealth*, 39(3), 295–312.

Groves, T., Hong, Y., McMillan, J. and Naughton, B. (1994). "Autonomy and Incentives in Chinese State Enterprises." *Quarterly Journal of Economics*, 109(1), 183–209.

Gustafsson, B. and Li, S. (2001). "The Anatomy of Rising Earnings Inequality in Urban China." *Journal of Comparative Economics*, 29(1), 118–135.

Gustafsson, B., Li, S. and Sicular, T. (2008). *Inequality and Public Policy in China.* New York: Cambridge University Press.

Gustafsson, B., Li, S., Nivorozhkina, L. and Katz, K. (2001). "Rubles and Yuan: Wage Functions for Urban Russia and China at the End of the 1980s." *Economic Development and Cultural Change*, 50(1), 1–17.

Haisken-DeNew, J.P. and Schmidt, C.M. (1999). "Industry Wage Differentials Revisited: A Longitudinal Comparison of Germany and USA (1984–1996)." IZA Discussion Paper Series No. 98.

Katz, L.F. and Summers, L.H. (1989). "Can Inter-Industry Wage Differentials Justify Strategic Trade Policy." In R. Feenstra (ed.), *Trade Policies for International Competitiveness.* Chicago: University of Chicago Press, 85–124.

Knight, J. and Song, L. (2003). "Increasing Urban Wage Inequality in China: Extent, Elements and Evaluation." *Economics of Transition*, 11(4), 597–619.

Krueger, A. and Summers, L. (1988). "Efficiency Wages and the Inter-Industry Wage Structure." *Econometrica*, 56(2), 259–293.

Li, S. and Sai, D. (2003). "Long-Term Change in Private Returns to Education in Urban China" (in Chinese). *Social Sciences in China*, 6, 58–72.

Li, X. and Heckman, J.J. (2004). "Heterogeneity, Selection Bias and the Return to Education: An Empirical Analysis Based on Chinese Micro-Data" (in Chinese). *Economic Research Journal*, 4, 91–99.

Lu, M. and Jiang, S. (2008). "Labour Market Reform, Income Inequality and Economic Growth in China." *China & World Economy*, 16(6), 63–80.

Lukyanova, A. (2006). "Wage Inequality in Russia (1994–2003)." Moscow: Economics Education and Research Consortium, Working Paper Series, No. 06/03.

Meng, X. and Kidd, M.P. (1997). "Labour Market Reform and the Changing Structure of Wage Determination in China's State Sector During the 1980s." *Journal of Comparative Economics*, 25(3), 403–421.

Meng, X., Gregory, R. and Wang, Y. (2005). "Poverty, Inequality, and Growth in Urban China, 1986–2000." *Journal of Comparative Economics*, 33(4), 710–729.

Pinheiro, A.C. and Ramos, L. (1994). "Inter-Industry Wage Differentials and Earnings Inequality in Brazil." *Estudios de Economia*, 21, November, 79–111.

Ravallion, M. and Chen, S. (2007). "China's (uneven) Progress Against Poverty." *Journal of Development Economics*, 82(1), 1–42.

Shi, X. (2007). "Monopoly Causes Inter-Industry Wage Differentials." *China Economist*, November, 53–61.

Shorrocks, A. (1999). "Decomposition Procedures for Distributional Analysis: A Unified Framework Based on the Shapley Value" (unpublished manuscript). Department of Economics, University of Essex.

Tian, S. and Lu, M. (2007). "Contribution of Education to Within-City Income Inequality: Evidence from Shanghai Household Data" (in Chinese). *South China Journal of Economics*, 5, 12–21.

Wan, G. (2002). "Regression-Based Inequality Decomposition: Pitfalls and a Solution Procedure." World Institute for Development Economics Research Discussion Paper 2002/101, Helsinki.

Wan, G. (2004). "Accounting for Income Inequality in Rural China: A Regression-Based Approach." *Journal of Comparative Economics*, 32(2), 348–363.

Wan, G. and Zhou, Z. (2005). "Income Inequality in Rural China: Regression-Based Decomposition Using Household Data." *Review of Development Economics*, 9(1), 107–120.

Zhang, J., Zhao, Y., Park, A. and Song, X. (2005). "Economic Returns to Schooling in Urban China, 1988 to 2001." *Journal of Comparative Economics*, 33(4), 730–752.

Appendix 1. Descriptive Statistics

Scale and binary variables.

	1988				1995				2002			
	Mean	**S.D.**	**Min**	**Max**	**Mean**	**S.D.**	**Min**	**Max**	**Mean**	**S.D.**	**Min**	**Max**
Yearly income	2197	1146	4.66	34186	2964	1673	0.53	26032	4889	3719	21.78	70778
Age	37.23	10.63	1	75	39	9.85	5	77	40.37	9.16	1	77
Fully employed	0.91	0.29	0	1	0.92	0.27	0	1	0.93	0.25	0	1
Male	0.52	0.50	0	1	0.53	0.50	0	1	0.56	0.50	0	1
Have second job	0.01	0.11	0	1	0.01	0.10	0	1	0.04	0.19	0	1
Communist party member	0.24	0.43	0	1	0.25	0.43	0	1	0.22	0.42	0	1
Minority	0.04	0.19	0	1	0.04	0.20	0	1	0.04	0.19	0	1
Number of observations	17568				10933				6121			

Education level (%).

	1988	1995	2002
College or above	6.23	7.62	5.65
Professional school	6.69	15.08	17.15
Middle level professional school	11.08	16.79	12.12
Upper middle school	24.82	24.15	32.51
Lower middle school	38.6	30.53	29.13
Elementary school (completed)	10.41	5.24	3.19
Elementary school (3 years or more)	1.08	0.59	0.24
Less than 3-year elementary school	1.08		
Total	17568	10933	6121

Industries (%)

	1988	1995	2002
Farm, forest, husbandry and fishery	0.99	1.69	0.67
Mining and exploration industry	3.15	1.06	2.3
Manufacturing	42.9	42.08	37.02
Geological prospecting, irrigation Administration	0.87		0.47
Electricity, gas and water supply facilities			4.41
Construction	3.44	2.98	4.64
Transportation, storage, post office and telecommunications	6.77	5.18	10.52
Wholesale, retail and food services	14.59	14.74	17.01
Real estate	1.41	3.99	1.19
Social services	1.09		10.86
Health, sports and social welfare	4.62	4.56	1.42
Education, culture and arts, mass media and entertainment	7.28	7.09	1.55
Scientific research and professional services	2.07	2.29	0.98
Finance and insurance	1.57	1.98	3.1
Government agents, party organisations and social groups	8.58	11.61	1.06
Other industries	0.67	0.76	2.78
Total	17568	10933	6121

Appendix 2. The Highest Income and Lowest Income Industry (1978–2006)

Year	Highest Income (*yuan*)	Highest Income Industry	Lowest Income (*yuan*)	Lowest Income Industry	Ratio
1978	809	Geological	486	Agriculture	1.66
1979	885	Geological	503	Health etc.	1.76
1980	1029	Geological	626	Agriculture	1.64
1981	1058	Geological	645	Agriculture	1.64
1982	1088	Geological	668	Agriculture	1.63
1983	1110	Geological	701	Agriculture	1.58
1984	1237	Geological	786	Agriculture	1.57
1985	1690	Geological	911	Agriculture	1.86
1986	1543	Transport	1075	Agriculture	1.44
1987	1942	Transport	1162	Agriculture	1.67
1988	2298	Geological	1311	Agriculture	1.75
1989	3288	Construction	1417	Agriculture	2.32
1990	2718	Mining	1541	Agriculture	1.76
1991	2942	Mining	1652	Agriculture	1.78
1992	3392	Electricity etc.	1828	Agriculture	1.86
1993	4320	Real estate	2042	Agriculture	2.12
1994	6712	Finance	2819	Agriculture	2.38
1995	7843	Electricity etc.	3522	Agriculture	2.23
1996	8816	Electricity etc.	4050	Agriculture	2.18
1997	9734	Finance	4311	Agriculture	2.26

(*Continued*)

Appendix 2. (*Continued*)

Year	Highest Income (*yuan*)	Highest Income Industry	Lowest Income (*yuan*)	Lowest Income Industry	Ratio
1998	10633	Finance	4528	Agriculture	2.35
1999	12046	Finance	4832	Agriculture	2.49
2000	13620	Science	5184	Agriculture	2.63
2001	16437	Science	5741	Agriculture	2.86
2002	19135	Finance	6398	Agriculture	2.99
2003	32244	Information	6969	Agriculture	4.63
2004	34988	Information	7611	Agriculture	4.60
2005	40558	Information	8309	Agriculture	4.88
2006	44763	Information	9430	Agriculture	4.75

Notes: The classification of industry is from *China Statistical Yearbook*, various years. For abbreviation, Geological = Geological prospecting and exploration; Agriculture = Agriculture, forestry, animal husbandry and fishery; Transport = Transport, storage, and post; Health = Health care, sports & social welfare; Electricity, etc. = Production and distribution of electricity, gas and water; Information = Information transmission, transportation, computer service and software; Science = Scientific research and technical services.

CHAPTER 7

CHINA'S HEALTH TRANSITION AND FUTURE HEALTH CARE FINANCING

*Jin Feng**

7.1. Introduction

With remarkable transition in economic development, China is facing challenges from social changes including health transition and increasing demand for health care. We can state that there have been significant gains in life expectancy and some other health indicators over the past several decades, but the pace of improvement in general health indicators (life expectancy, infant mortality rate) is slower in contrast to the strong economic performance and structural changes. A study, using cross-country regression linking under-five mortality to per capita income, finds that although China was a well-performing example in the 1960s and 1970s, it was an under-performer in the 1980s and 1990s (its rate of mortality reduction lagged its "expected rate") (Wagstaff *et al.*, 2009c). Besides, the incidences of some chronic diseases have increased during economic transition and demographic transition. According to WHO (2005), China's overall disease profile now resembles that of a developed country, with more than 90% of deaths due to non-communicable diseases.

The evolving burden of disease in China has been reflected in a picture of rising health care expenditure. There is limited literature on estimating the

*The author is grateful to financial support from the National Science Foundation of China. (71273056, 70573024, 70973027)

determinants of health care spending in China, though the majority opinion holds that fiscal decentralization in health care and negative incentives in public hospitals are all responsible for rising cost. Studies using micro data show that income elasticity of medical care in both urban and rural areas is lower than 0.5 (Mocan *et al.*, 2004; Feng *et al.*, 2010). In this chapter, we use provincial-level data for the period of 2002–2008 to examine the determinants of heath expenditure. The results suggest that increasing per capita income and aging population significantly drive up health expenditure. Moreover, the impact of time dummy explains approximately one-third of the increase of health expenditure, which implies that technological and institutional changes are also very important drivers in China. Under some possible assumptions for future economic growth, population aging and medical inflation, we simulate the future health care expenditure in China.

China's health care sector failed to meet the demand during the economic transition (Ministry of Health, 2005). China is likely to face even greater health policy challenges related to financial risk protection and affordable access to health care in future years. However, health care reform is in process. In April 2009, China finally unveiled its health care reform to assure that every citizen has equal access to affordable basic health care by 2012. The announced policy explicitly states the government's role of ensuring equity and providing public goods, which at the same time encourages the introduction of market mechanisms. RMB 850 billion yuan (USD 125 billion) over the next three years to invest in five specific areas — expanding insurance coverage, increasing government spending on public health services, establishing community health centers in urban areas and township health centers in rural areas, reforming the pharmaceutical market, and reforming public hospitals.

In this chapter, we put emphasis on health care financing and explain that the prospects for future improvement depend on increasing government investment, reforming health insurance arrangement and encouraging non-government input. Section 7.2 describes health transition during economic transition and relates health transition to economic growth, population aging and regional imbalance. In Section 7.3, we estimate the main drivers of health care in China and project the future trend. Section 7.4 discusses health care financing and government initiatives. Section 7.5 discusses our conclusions.

7.2. Health Transition During Economic Transition

Economic transition since the late 1970s and 1980s has led to dramatic changes in the lives of billions of people. Economic development has improved living standards, offered more qualified medical care, equipped people with more knowledge, which have all contributed to the longer average life expectancy and lower infant and child mortality rates. For instance, infant mortality rate declined from 195 per mill during 1950–1955 to 39.9 per mill during 1980–1985 and further to 22.9 per mill recently, and life expectancy increased by nearly 8 years in the last 30 years and reached to 73 years currently (Table 7.1). It is worth noting that economic reform does not lead to an improvement in health status for certainty. Experience in Russia and other Central Eastern European countries suggests that economic transition may have an adverse impact on health status (Liu *et al.*, 1998). Life expectancy in Russia decreased after economic reform (Table 7.2) and mental and social health problems increased, where the leading causes of deaths are accidents, suicides and homicides (Liu *et al.*, 1998).[1] In contrast, thanks to the gradual reform without too many economic and social disruptions, China's strategy of economic reform has fewer negative effects on health.

However, if compared to many other countries except Russia and some Central Eastern European countries, the dramatic improvement in general health outcomes became less. Life expectancy improved at a slower rate than those of some medium- and high-income countries or regions in the same period. For example, China, Malaysia and Mexico have the same level of life expectancy at the initial stage, but after 30 years, Malaysia outpaces China by 1 year and Mexico by 3 years. The absolute decline of infant mortality rate has been dramatic, but compared to most of other economies, current infant mortality rate in China is still much higher, about 6 times Japan's and Hong Kong's, about twice Malaysia's (Table 7.2).

---

[1]One of the major reasons for the worsening mental and social health problems in Russia seems to be embedded in the manner in which radical economic reforms have been conducted (so called "shock therapy"). Dramatic changes including price liberalization, privatization, and rapid political transformation occurred too quickly and too dramatically, and caused too many social disruptions for most of the population to cope with. Social protection system was not given adequate time to develop, and many vulnerable populations simply fell through the safety net (Liu *et al.*, 1998).

Table 7.1. Changes of health indicators in China.

Indicator	1950–55	1960–65	1970–75	1980–85	1990–95	2000–05	2005–10
Crude birth rate (births per 1,000 population)	43.8	38	28.6	21.5	18.9	14	13.5
Crude death rate (deaths per 1,000 population)	25.1	17.1	6.3	7.3	7.1	6.6	7.0
Infant mortality rate (infant deaths per 1,000 live births)	195	120.7	61.1	39.9	29.9	25.6	22.9
Life expectancy at birth, both sexes combined (years)	40.8	49.5	63.2	66.4	68.8	72.0	73.0
Life expectancy at birth, males (years)	39.3	48.7	62.5	65.3	67.4	70.5	71.3
Life expectancy at birth, females (years)	42.3	50.4	63.9	67.6	70.3	73.7	74.8

Source: Population Division of the Department of Economic and Social Affairs of the United Nations Secretariat, *World Population Prospects: The 2008 Revision*.

When evaluating the health status and health transition in recent China, it is worth noting that behind these general health indicators, multi-dimension measurements of health status will provide more sophisticated information, and have more implications for health improvement and future health care reform. These include the morbidity rate for various diseases, incidence of chronic diseases, obesity, etc. We will show that economic development and population aging are major forces driving health transition in the past several decades.

7.2.1. *The epidemiologic and disease transition*

The profile of the incidence of major disease is being transformed. Preventable communicable diseases are common in low-income

Table 7.2. Comparing China to other economies.

	Life expectancy (year)			Infant mortality rate (infant deaths per 1,000 live births)		
	1975–1980	**2005–2010**	**change**	**1975–1980**	**2005–2010**	**change**
China	65.3	73	7.7	52	22.9	–29.1
Malaysia	65.3	74.2	8.9	33.8	8.9	–24.9
Mexico	65.3	76.1	10.8	56.8	16.7	–40.1
Korea	64.6	79.4	14.8	34	4.4	–29.6
Hong kong	73.6	82.2	8.6	12.9	3.7	–9.2
Japan	75.3	82.7	7.4	12	3.2	–8.8
US	73.3	79.2	5.9	14.1	5.9	–8.2
Russia	68	66.5	–1.5	29.5	11.9	–17.6

Source: Population Division of the Department of Economic and Social Affairs of the United Nations Secretariat, *World Population Prospects: The 2008 Revision*.

countries, but the incidence of infectious diseases declined rapidly in China. According to National Health Service Survey, between 1993 and 2008, the morbidity rate of infectious diseases declined by 56% in urban area and 62% in rural area. At the same time, the incidence of non-communicable diseases increased dramatically. Diseases whose incidence increased faster are hypertension, diabetes, cerebrovascular disease and heart disease. The results in Table 7.3 were based on the self-report illness which had been diagnosed by doctors. The morbidity rate of infectious diseases in urban is lower, and morbidity rates for most diseases are significantly higher than those in rural area in each period of time. Although there are biases or errors in reported data, there is an obvious tendency in either urban or rural area that the incidence of infectious is declining while the incidence of diseases related to economic development and population aging is increasing.

Chronic non-communicable diseases which are common in high-income countries have become increasingly prevalent in China. China's overall disease profile now resembles that of a developed country, with more than 90% of deaths due to non-communicable diseases and injuries (WHO, 2005). The major causes of death in China are cardiovascular disease, cancer, and chronic respiratory disease (Wang *et al.*, 2005). The

Table 7.3. Changes in morbidity rate (%).

	Urban			Rural		
Disease	**1993**	**2008**	**Change (%)**	**1993**	**2008**	**Change (%)**
Infectious	4.85	2.1	–56.3	6.04	2.3	–62.3
Respiratory disease	72.04	40.5	–43.7	62.42	50.4	–19.3
Digestive disease	27.72	20.6	–25.8	21.85	28.5	30.3
Hypertension	9.51	60.8	539.4	1.95	20.9	971.9
Cardiovascular disease	3.28	7.7	134.0	0.89	5.2	484.1
Heart disease	11.48	20.4	77.4	2.36	7.2	207.0
Diabetes	2.54	15.5	510.3	0.15	2.6	1635.5
Cancer	1.05	2.2	106.8	0.35	0.7	89.8
Injury	4.7	4.4	–6.2	4.2	6.0	43.8
Mental disorder	0.81	1.7	109.7	0.68	1.2	74.0

Sources: *National Health Service Survey* (1993, 2008).

Notes: *National Health Service Survey* (1993, 1998, 2003 and 2008) adopts multi-level random sampling. 54 thousands households, 215163 individuals were chosen from 92 counties or cities (27 cities, 65 counties) in 1993. 57 thousands households, 216101 individuals were chosen from 95 counties or cities (28 cities, 67 counties) in 1998. 56 thousands households, 180 thousands individuals were chosen from 94 counties or cities (28 cities, 66 counties) in 2008. Urban and rural areas are classified into several categories. According to population size, there are three kinds of cities, big city (more than 1 million population), medium and small city (less than 300 thousands population). According to economic development, there are four kinds of county — richer, second richer, poorer and poverty county. Illness was reported if it was diagnosed by doctors 6 months before the survey.

probability of dying between the age of 15 and 60 has fallen markedly to 130 per mill and only slightly above that in the United States (WHO, 2010). WHO calculated Healthy Life Expectancy at birth (HALE) of 2007 for the member states.[2] Japan ranked first with a HALE of 76 years, US is 70 years, India is 56 years and China is 66, which is much higher than the average of total 191 member states, 59 years (WHO, 2010). The relatively longer HALE of China highlights the emergence of non-communicable diseases and injuries as the predominant health condition.

[2]HALE represents the average number of years that a person could expect to live in "good health" by taking into account years lived in less than full health due to disease and injury.

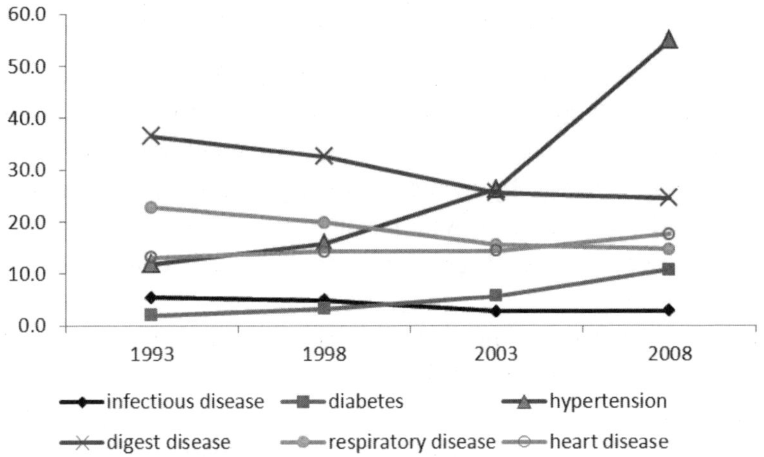

Fig. 7.1. Incidence of chronic diseases.

Source: *National Health Service Survey*.

Chronic, non-communicable diseases account for 70% of total HALE loss in China.

The increasing incidence of several chronic diseases has been shown in all related surveys. China's comprehensive surveys in the fields of nutrition and health were done in 1992 and 2002.[3] According to the survey, hypertension increased from 14.4% in 1991 to 18.8% in 2002 in adults. In 2002, among those who have hypertension, 30% were aware of their situation, 25% had treatment and in 1991 these numbers were 26.6% and 12.2% respectively. And between 1993 and 2003, the prevalence of cardiovascular disease increased from 31.4% to 50.0%; diabetes increased from 1.9% to 5.6% (Wang *et al.*, 2007). The results from National Health Survey are lower, but the increasing tendency of incidence of hypertension and diabetes is consistent with other surveys (Figure 7.1).

[3] In 2002 survey, 91,971 households were chosen from 132 counties of 31 provinces, autonomous regions and the municipalities, suing the central government household census, and 243,479 people were included in the survey. The health status was based on the medical examination.

7.2.2. *Economic development and health transition*

Since spectacular economic development after 1978, health gains in China have begun to take place and have been assisted not only by transfer of knowledge about sanitation, and the vaccination and treatment of infectious diseases, but also by increased literacy, family spacing, improved nutrition and vector control. As a result, some chronic diseases, such as infectious, digestive disease and respiratory disease, become less and less prevalent over time.

On the other hand, Chinese people have experienced many dramatic changes in their lifestyles thanks to a boost in family income and an increasing availability of food owing to advances in agriculture and expanded global trade. The increase in intake of animal-source foods and edible oils, along with increase of fast food and soft drink consumption, has led to large increases in the energy density of the diet (Popkin, 2008). Recent surveys and studies suggest that the prevalence of overweight and obesity has increased in China. Obesity increases the risk of a number of other chronic diseases such as cardiovascular disease, hypertension, diabetes, and some cancers.[4] According to 1992 and 2002 surveys, the general prevalence of overweight and obesity increased by 49.3% from 14.6% in 1992 to 22% in 2002, about 200 million people.[5] Between 1992 and 2002, the prevalence of obesity and overweight had increased in both men and women, in all age groups, and in rural and urban areas. In light of the WHO's BMI standard, 2.9% of Chinese adults aged 18 years or over were obese. The prevalence of overweight was high and had reached a level similar to that in many European countries and the increasing rate was higher in China (Figure 7.2). China's increasing tendency in overweight population will continue to increase the incidence of major chronic diseases.

---

[4] Increasing evidence suggests that obesity has become a global epidemic. Both industrialized countries and developing countries have been affected. In recent years, obesity has been recognized as a primary public health concern in many countries. In the US, obesity is a leading cause of preventable death, second only to smoking (Wang *et al.*, 2007).

[5] BMI greater than 30 is considered obese, and BMI of 25–29.9 is considered overweight.

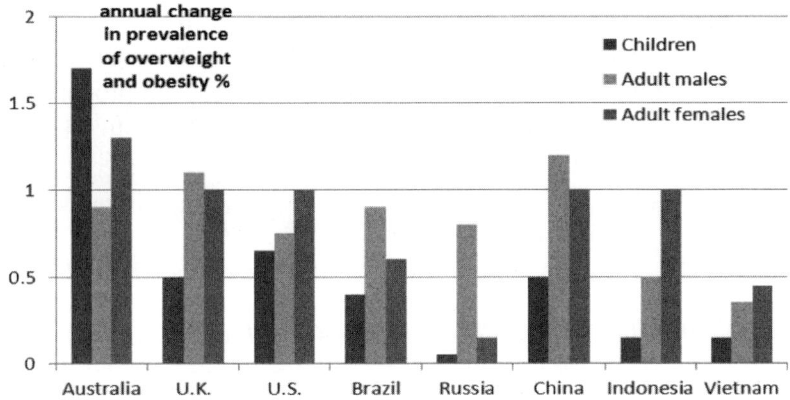

Fig. 7.2. Annual percentage change in prevalence of overweight and obesity in eight countries, from 1985–1995 to 1995–2004.

Source: Popkin, 2008.

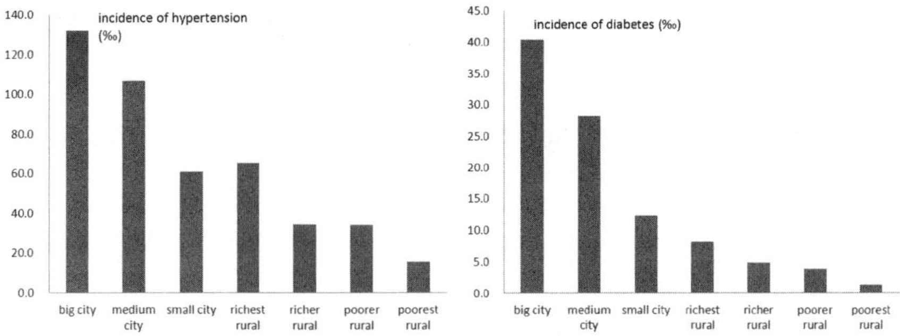

Fig. 7.3. Incidence of hypertension and diabetes (2008).

Source: *National Health Service Survey*.

In urban areas, people's standard of living is far higher. Although it is true that urban residents are more aware of their health condition, there are obvious different levels of incidence of chronic diseases in cities and rural areas with various development stages (Figure 7.3).[6] Large cities have

[6] Hou (2008) find urban hypertensive adults are less likely to be undiagnosed and untreated, even after controlling for socioeconomic and lifestyle variables, suggesting that there are other reasons for the urban-rural disparity of undiagnosed and untreated hypertension. Liu *et al.* (2008) report the survey result that 42% and 27% of people living in urban and rural areas respectively with hypertension knew about their condition.

much higher incidence than medium-sized and small cities and rural areas and the higher incidence is in rural areas with higher income. During these years, the rapidly expanding urban areas in China led the proportion of people living in urban settings increase from 18% in 1978 to 46% in 2008, and the number of cities increased to nearly 700. It is expected that with more urbanization in future, the incidence of chronic diseases keeps increasing.

7.2.3. *Population aging and health transition*

Besides economic transition, demographic transition is another major force driving the health transition. Due to the declining fertility rate and mortality rate, share of population aged 65 years or older increased from 4.4% in 1950 to 4.7% in 1980 and to 8.2% in 2010. According to the projection of United Nations, this figure will increase to 16% in 2030 and to 23% in 2050 (Figure 7.4). A rising share of older age groups in the population will put pressure on the incidence of diseases. Morbidity rate by age groups shows that morbidity rate of people older than 65 is much higher than other age groups. The lower morbidity

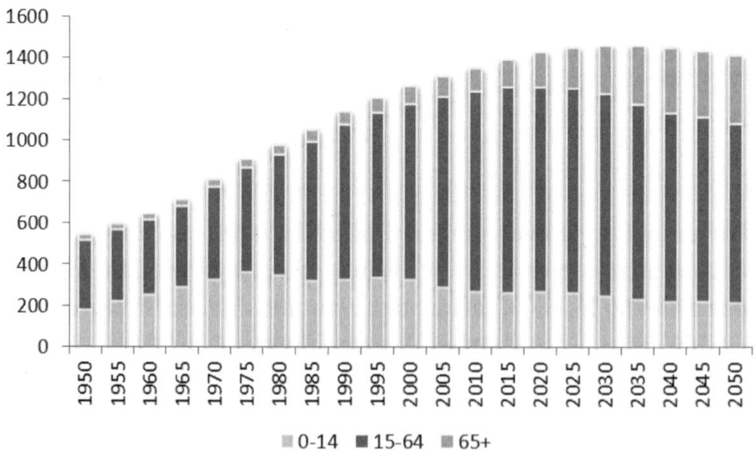

Fig. 7.4. Population structure in China (medium variant).

Source: *World Population Prospects: The 2008 Revision*, Population Division of the Department of Economic and Social Affairs of the United Nations Secretariat.

Table 7.4. Incidence of chronic disease by age groups (%).

	1993	1998	2003	2008	2008–1993
0–4	19.2	13.4	6.3	6.4	−12.7
5–14	19.2	18.6	9.6	8.7	−10.5
15–24	26.0	25.8	18.0	20.2	−5.8
25–34	66.4	72.5	58.3	51.3	−15.1
35–44	162.0	142.2	117.1	121.7	−40.3
45–54	263.4	232.0	219.5	259.5	−3.8
55–64	430.5	386.5	362.1	419.9	−10.6
65 and over	540.3	517.9	538.8	645.4	105.1

Table 7.5. Rural-urban health disparity.

	1991	2000	2005	2007
Infant mortality (%)	50.2	32.2	19	15.3
urban	17.3	11.8	9.1	7.7
rural	58	37	21.6	18.6
Under 5 mortality (%)	61	39.7	22.5	18.1
urban	20.9	13.8	10.7	9
rural	71.1	45.7	25.7	21.8
Maternal mortality (1/100 thousands)	80	53	47.7	36.6
urban	46.3	29.3	25	25.2
rural	100	69.6	53.8	41.3

Source: *China Health Statistic Yearbook.*

rates are during year 15–44 (Table 7.4). Same pattern is found in incidence of chronic diseases (Table 7.5), which implies that as population is aging, the morbidity rate and incidence of chronic diseases will be increasing.

It is worth noting that, the morbidity rate was decreasing over time in children and young age groups, but it was increasing in older age groups, especially in terms of the incidence of chronic diseases, which means, averagely speaking, that the increase in incidence of chronic diseases happens in older age group. It is understandable that with longer life expectancy, more people might have a certain kind of disease, so we observe an increasing incidence in the group of people older than 65 over time. Besides, obesity has been increasing in each age group (Wang *et al.*, 2005) and one of the results might be that the incidence of chronic disease increased in older age. However, it needs more careful work to understand the age-related change pattern of different variety of chronic disease. Incidences of some diseases have been increasing even in younger age group. For example, in a 2002 survey, the prevalence of hypertension in people aged 18 years or older increased by 30% since 1991 (Wang *et al.*, 2005).

7.2.4. *Inequality in health outcomes*

During health transition, the inequality in health outcomes has been worsening. There have been large disparities in the access to health service and health financing between rural and urban areas and between developed and under-developed regions. Liu *et al.* (1999) observe that the growing gap in health status between urban and rural residents is correlated with the increasing gaps in income and health care utilization. The number of professional health staff every 1,000 persons in uran areas is 3 times that in rural areas. In terms of rural-urban disparity, China National Maternal and Child Surveillance reports that the 2007 rates for maternal, infant and under-5 mortalities in rural areas were twice as much as those in urban areas — 0.04%, 1.9%, and 2.2% vs. 0.02%, 0.8%, and 0.9%, respectively (Table 7.5). By quoting WHO (2005), we show that the disparity is further supported by provincial-level data. Variation of life expectancy across provinces suggests that health is also generally poorer in provinces with higher share of rural population (Figure 7.5). It shows that provinces and municipalities with the lowest share of China's rural population, Shanghai, Beijing, Tianjin, and Guandong, have significantly longer life expectancy than those with more rural residents, such as Guizhou, Gansu and Yunnan.

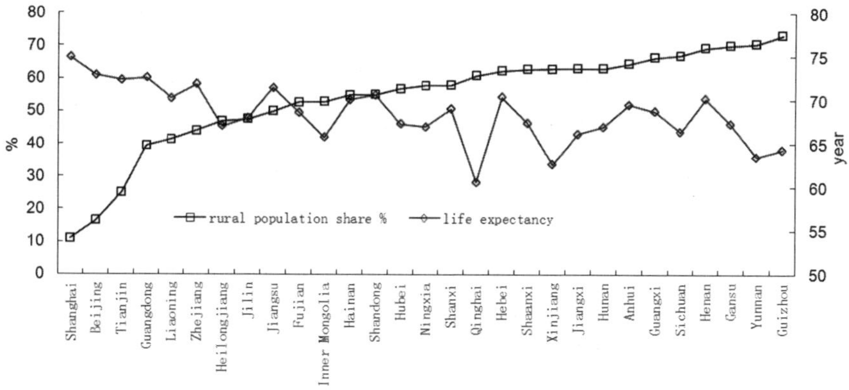

Fig. 7.5. Rural urban disparity of life expectancy.

Source: *China Statistic Yearbook*, 2006.

Note: Life expectancy is obtained by population census in year 2000. Rural population share is the information of year 2005.

As to regional disparity, there is a clear correlation between regional development and life expectancy — the higher the GDP per capita, the longer the life expectancy of this province. While infant and childhood mortality rates in coastal areas mirror those of industrialized countries, rates in most western provinces are 3–5 times higher. Yip and Mahal (2008) find an increase in interprovincial inequality in life expectancy and infant mortality between 1980 and 2000. Figure 7.6 shows the contrast of life expectancy in richest 7 provinces and poorest 6 provinces and there is an average 8 years gap in life expectancy between the richer provinces and the poorer provinces. This is consistent with rural-urban disparity, since rural-urban disparity is one of the most important sources for regional disparity. Provinces with more proportion of rural residents are more like to be under-developed regions.

7.3. Health Expenditure and Projecting for Future

The major consequences of health transition are the increasing demand for health care and the rapid rising of health care expenditure. Looking at past three decades, expenditures on health care have increased in terms of both

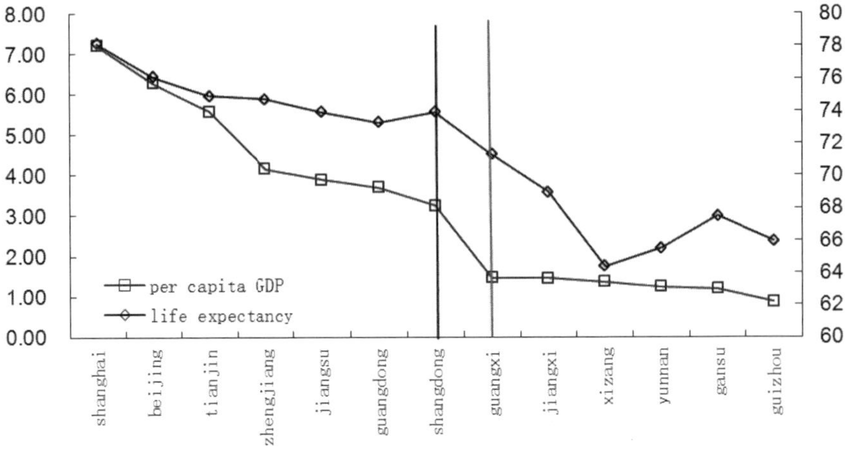

Fig. 7.6. Regional disparity of life expectancy.

Source: *China Statistic Yearbook,* 2009.
Note: Life expectancy is obtained by population census in year 2000. Per capita GDP is the data of year 2008.

of their share in GDP and per capita expenditure. Figure 7.7 shows the share in GDP is going from 3% in 1978 to 5% in 2009 and per capita expenditure from RMB 11.5 to RMB 1,289 in the same period of time.[7] The upward trend in spending is universal and appears to hold in both developed and developing countries, which is due to several fators including eonomic development, population aging and the increased diffusion of technology (Newhouse,1992; Culter, 2004).[8]

But the critical issue in China differs from many other developed countries, where cost containment is the main target. On the one hand, government investment on health care is to be increased to meet the rising demand

[7] Per capita health expenditure here is nominal price without adjustment by price index.

[8] Newhouse (1992) finds that, over 1940–1990 in the United States, income can account for an increase in health expenditure of 35–70% while health spending overall has increased by over 700%, which made him to conjecture that a large part of the increase is due to other factors such as demographic change and technology improvement. Recent Studies on US and Canada show that aging population and income explain a relatively small portion of health expenditure when the impact of time effects, which is a partial proxy for technological change, is controlled for (Di Matteo, 2005).

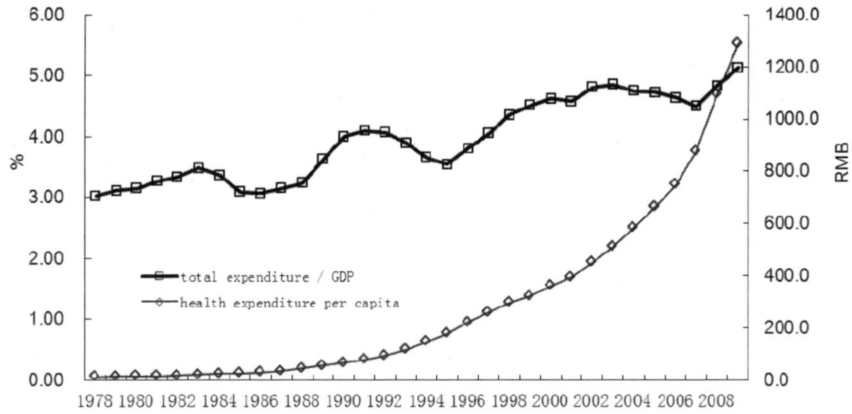

Fig. 7.7. Increasing health care expenditure in China.

Source: *China Health Statistic Yearbook*, 2010.

and narrow the rural-urban disparity and regional disparity in health care. As a developing country, health care expenditure as a percentage of GDP in China is mucher lower than developed countries, for example, Japan (8.0%), France (11.0%), German (10.4%), UK (7.0%), even lower than a lot of developing countries, for example, Brazil (8.4%), Vietnam (7.1%) (WHO, 2010).[9] On the other hand, the financial burden caused by disease has been always a problem for most of the households since economic transition and medical burden has been one of the main reasons for poverty, so health care provision and financing are needed to manage effectively to alleviate out-of-pocket health care expenditure. Important questions for a developing and aging country like China are: what are the main drivers of health care expenditure? and how will health care expenditure to be in future?

7.3.1. *Economic development, population aging and health expenditure*

Health economists have devoted considerable efforts to disentangling the drivers of health care spending by using econometric analyses and using

[9] Data are of the year 2007 for each country.

international, national and regional level data, especially for OECD countries (e.g., Parkin *et al.*,1987; Gerdtham *et al.*, 1992b). These analyses have been of two types. Some have examined variations in per capita spending across countries (e.g., O'Connell, 1996; Gerdtham *et al.*, 1992a), and others have examined cross-country differences in the growth rates in per capita health spending (e.g., Barros, 1998). Income growth is certainly the main driver of expenditure. Earlier cross-country study on the relationship between real per capita health care expenditure and real per capita GDP has argued that there is not only a strong positive correlation between the two variables in developed countries, but also the GDP explains a high percentage of the variation of health care expenditure (Newhouse, 1977). Several regession analyses based on cross-section and panel data, aiming to explain the international differences in health expenditure, get a common result that aggregate income appears to be the most important factor determining health expenditure variation between countries (Gerdtham and Jönsson, 2000). However, the vast literature on this topic is inconclusive on the income elasticity. At an aggregate level, numerous studies find a higher income elasticity, even more than one, which means that health care is a luxury good.[10] This result has been criticized because intuition suggests that health care is more of a necessity than a luxury and there might be omitted variable bias as well as the presence of unobserved country and year specific effects in estimating income elasticity (Culyer, 1988). Getzen (2000) then shows that individual income elasticity are typically close to zero while national health expenditure income elasiticies are often greater than one.

Aging or the elderly share of the population is another possible driver of national health spending. Although aging of population increases the demand and cost of health services tends to go upward naturally, it has been difficult to show empirically that population aging

[10] A cross-section study of 19 OECD countries found income elasticity between 1.12 and 1.18 (Parkin *et al.*, 1987). Gerdtham *et al.* (1992a) used a single cross-section of 19 OECD countries in 1987 and reported an income elasticity of 1.33. Hitiris *et al.* (1992) used 20 OECD of 1960–1987 and found a strong and positive correlation between per capita health spending and GDP with an income elasticity of about unity. Barros (1998) used data for 24 OECD countries of 1960–1992 to examine differences in growth rates rather than levels and also found an income elasticity close to one.

is definitively associated with net increases in aggregate health expenditure at the national level (Cherinchovsky and Markowitz, 2004). Some studies find statistically significant evidence, but some do not. Most studies are limited to OECD countries.[11] The main conclusion that one can draw from these studies is that for developed countries, the share of the population that is elderly does not have a substantially positive impact on overall health spending, nor on increases over time. The reality is that the linkages between aging and health spending are much more complex than usually thought of. Institutional change and technological change are accompnying with population aging. In absence of control of institutional and technological factors, the real effect of population aging cannot be obtained.

In health sector, technological progress have both cost press and cost saving effects. If new techniques generate a cheaper way of treating health outcomes, there could be expenditure reductions associated with technological change (Cutler *et al.*, 1998). If expensive new treatments are devised, the technological change can also be associated with rising health expenditure. A variety of technological innovations have been responsible for rising health expenditures, for example, the high-tech computer tomography (CT) scanners, magnetic resonance imaging (MRI) systems. Some studies confirm that technology is the major determinant of increased health care costs (Newhouse, 1992; Okunade and Murthy, 2002).[12]

---

[11] O'Connell (1996) examined the relationship between 1975 and 1990. In some of these aging was significant, and some models suggested that the impact of aging varied across countries. Other authors have occasionally reported similarly positive results, but in most cases, these are sensitive to the details of models used (Gerdtham *et al.*,1992b). In a later panel data analysis, Gerdtham *et al.* (1998) applied data from 22 OECD countries for the period 1970–91 to examine the effect of a number of institutional and non-institutional variables on health care expenditure. In all model specifications the elasticity of health care expenditure with respect to the proportion above 75 years was negative but close to zero. Barros (1998) used data from 24 OECD countries from 1960–90 and estimated growth rates rather absolute levels of health care expenditure. The explanatory variables included economic, demographic and institutional variables.

[12] Newhouse (1992) touted technological progress as another major factor, and conjectured it could account for as much as 75% of the 50 years increase in the US medical care expenditure. Okunade and Murthy (2002) explicitly test the role of broad-based measures

Most important Institutional change in health care is the reform of health financing system. Extensions of health insurance play an important role in determining aggregate health spending. Generally speaking, the more generous arrangements for health insurance, the greater share of income spending on health care. Studies show that the traits of health care system (such as general practitioner, public health financing) have a significant effect on health expenditure (Gerdtham and Jönsson, 2000).

The existing literature focused on developed countries due to scarcity of health expenditure data from developing countries. China has some unique backgrounds. Lower income, lower government investment, lower coverage of health insurance, higher rural-urban disparity and rapid aging differ China from OECD countries. It is believed that fiscal decentralization in health care, wrong incentives in public hospitals which will be discussed later, all contribute to expenditure increase.

7.3.2. *Main drivers of health expenditure in China*

We use aggregate provincial-level data to investigate the main drivers of health care expenditure in China.[13] In an economic transition and demographic transition context, indicators of age structure such as share of population of 65 and over, share of population of 14 and less, and per capita income are controlled. And following literature, other related variables, including human captial (share of college graduates in the province), enviornment quality (SO_2 emission), rural-urban income gap, insurance coverage rate and provincial fixed characteristics and time dummies are controlled. The effect of technological change can be proxied a number of ways in literature. Proxying health care technology by total R&D spending or R&D spending specific to health care is one way. Another

---

of the R & D expenditure, as interchangeable proxies for technical change in health care, as a major driver of increased health care costs in the US during the 1960–1997 period, and find that technological change is a statistically significant long-run driver of the rising health care expenditure.

[13] We use provincial data of 2002–2008, including 30 provinces except Xizang (Tibet). The sources of data are *China Statistic Yearbook, China Health Statistic Yearbook, China Population and Employment Statistic Yearbook, China Rural Statistic Yearbook, China Environment Statistic Yearbook* and CEIC dataset.

approach is to incorporate a time trend to serve as a simple measure of technological change. An often used way is to simply ascribe it to the residual after all other factors have been controlled for (Di Matteo, 2005). Since there is no data of R&D spending specific to health care in China and general R&D spending seems to be little correlated with technology change in health care, we do not include R&D spending in the regression. But we will control time dummies that may capture some other effects, such as institutional change, social structure change as well as other unobservable differences. However, estimating the effect of technological change is not our purpose, so through controlling time dummies and provincial dummies, the effect of other factors including technological change, policy change and some unobservable factors will be captured.

The dependent variable, real per capita health expenditure, is consisted of three parts, government expenditure, out-of-pocket expenditure and expenditure covered by health insurance. We use consumer price index to adjust it into real per capita health expenditure, excluding the effects of inflation and population growth rate. Provincial-level data of 2002–2008 show that there is a positive correlation between real per capita health expenditure (PCHE) and regional real per capita income (PCGDP), also a positive correlation between PCHE and the share of population older than 65 (PROP65) (Figures 7.8 and 7.9).

Following Di Matteo (2005), we adopt fixed effect models to estimate the determinants of real per capita health expenditures. Regression results are presented in Table 7.6. Model 1 regresses PCHE on PCGDP, PROP65, PROP14 and province-specific dummy variables. Time dummies are added in Model 2. A more complex specification was estimated in Model 3 which adds institutional variables and environmental variables. In Models 4, 5, 6, the specifications are the same as Models 1, 2, 3 respectively, but the dependent variable is Ln(PHCE). Considering the possible causality issue between health expenditure and population aging, we use one-period-lagged value of PROP65 and PROP14.

All 6 models can account for 98% of the variation of dependent variables. PCGDP and PROP65 are significantly positive in all specifications. The coefficients of income and aging are reduced after controlling year dummies and other variables. From Model 6, we obtain an income elasticity of 0.276 and an aging elasticity of 0.268. The income elasticity is rather low

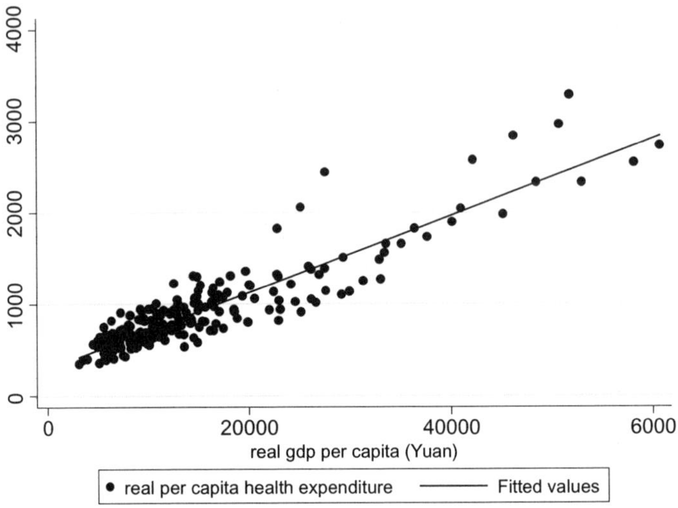

Fig. 7.8. Relationship between real per capita health expenditure and income.
Sources: China Statistic Yearbooks and *China Health Statistic Yearbooks*.

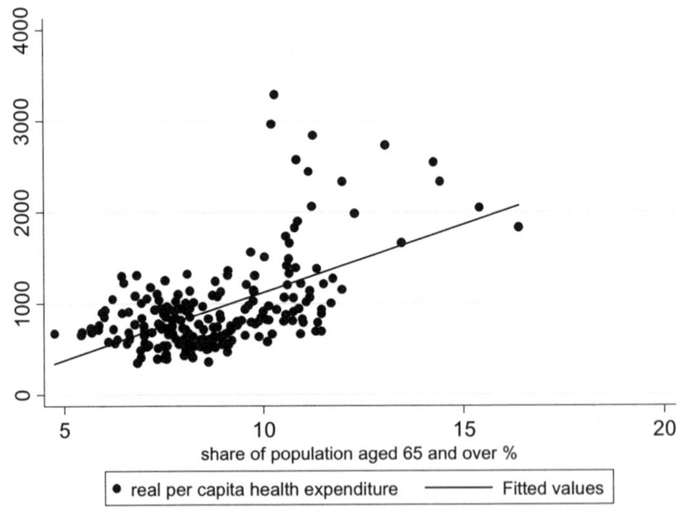

Fig. 7.9. Relationship between real health expenditure and population aging.
Sources: China Statistic Yearbooks and *China Health Statistic Yearbooks*.

Table 7.6. Determinants of per capita health expenditure.

	(1)	(2)	(3)	(4)	(5)	(6)
Variables		**PCHE**			**Ln(PCHE)**[a]	
PCGDP	0.035***	0.028***	0.020***	0.590***	0.283***	0.276***
	(0.001)	(0.002)	(0.003)	(0.034)	(0.078)	–0.091
L.PROP65	58.178***	29.244***	16.434*	0.380***	0.289***	0.268***
	(7.626)	(9.449)	(10.241)	(0.078)	(0.079)	–0.087
L.PROP14	–6.317**	2.325	2.353	–0.281***	–0.115	–0.185*
	(2.486)	(3.039)	(3.313)	(0.075)	(0.085)	–0.097
Share of college			15.597**			0.001
graduate			(6.539)			–0.005
SO_2 emission			1.806**			0.002*
			(0.878)			–0.001
Rural-urban income			–5.302			0.083
gap			(59.644)			–0.056
Insurance coverage			–0.085			0.001***
rate			(–0.521)			(0.000)
2003		44.860**			0.066***	
		(19.578)			(0.021)	
2004		60.70**	19.564		0.084***	0.008
		(24.277)	–19.462		(0.031)	–0.022
2005		117.792***	84.223**		0.177***	0.045
		(29.786)	–36.39		(0.045)	–0.042
2006		114.573***	86.530**		0.197***	0.086*
		(32.081)	–33.29		(0.053)	–0.047
2007		164.471***	158.721***		0.261***	0.127**
		(39.416)	–43.932		(0.065)	–0.061
2008		235.326***	256.895***		0.336***	0.177**
		(44.844)	(57.182)		(0.075)	–0.074
Constant	706.874***	1067.232***	1144.104***	1.479***	4.318***	4.405***
	(114.244)	(133.633)	(238.104)	(0.461)	(0.811)	(0.976)
Provincial dummies	yes	yes	yes	yes	yes	yes
Observations	210	210	180	210	210	180
R-squared	0.982	0.985	0.983	0.978	0.982	0.978

[a]*Variables PCGDP, PROP65, PROP14 are also in log forms in model 4, 5, 6. Standard errors are reported in parentheses. ***, **, and * indicate statistical significance at 1%, 5%, and 10%, respectively.*

Table 7.7. Estimating contributions to real per capita health expenditure growth.

	Change 2002 to 2008	Real per capital GDP (%)	Share of 65 and over (%)	Year dummy (%)	Others (%)
PHCE growth	RMB 591	39.98	4.47	43.44	12.10
PHCE growth rate	89%	33.81	8.62	27.11	30.46

compared to OECD countries, which is close to 1 (OECD, 2006). The result implies that during economic growth, the accessibility and affordability of health care failed to improve accordingly. Meanwhile insurance coverage was a positive determinant of health expenditure. Possibly there exists a mechanism that insurance coverage (institutional factor) contributes to the increase of health expenditures which lead to mediate the effect of PCGDP and PROP65. Year dummies are significant, especially in 2006, 2007 and 2008, which is consistent with intuition that there has been a health care inflation in recent years.

In an effort to draw a clearer picture regarding the impact of the various determinants, Table 7.7 takes the Model 3 and Model 6 regression results to access the contributions to expenditure growth of real per capita health expenditure from 2002 to 2008. The growth of real per capita health expenditure is RMB 591. Model 3 specification finds that about 40% of the increase in attributable to rising real per capita GDP and another 4.5% to growth in the proportion over age 65, while time dummy accounts for 43.4% of the growth and other factors account for the rest 12%. Contributions to the growth rate during 2002 to 2008 can be calculated from Model 6. Annual growth rate of real per capita health expenditure is 9.5%. Real per capita GDP growth rate is responsible for 34% of total growth rate during this period, population aging contributes 8.62%, time dummy accounts for 27%, and other factors account for 30.5%.

7.3.3. *Projecting health care expenditure*

Projection is useful in helping policy-makers understand key issues, and take appropriate measures to tackle the difficulties ahead such as population aging. The ideal projection approach would take into account all the factors that influence health spending and incorporate a framework that reflects the complexity of the underlying dynamics. However, fully specified models are not possible. In practice, simplification is required to ensure that we use methods that are feasible to compute, as well as practical with the data that are available. Following the suit of OECD (2006), we decompose changes in future expenditure into attributable factors (Equation 7.1).

$$\Delta \ln PHCE = \varepsilon_1 \Delta \ln PCGDP + \varepsilon_2 \Delta \ln PROP65 + \Delta \ln residuals \quad (7.1)$$

Where we put all the effects of other factors into a term "residual", including the effects of health insurance, technological change, policy change. Furthermore, in future, there are several reforms which might happen to change the effects of income, population aging and residual term. First, the extension of health insurance coverage has a positive effect on health care demand and expenditure. Second, narrowing rural urban disparity and regional disparity also will increase the accessible of health care. Third, improving the efficiency of health care sector, especially reforming public hospital, will reduce the cost. So we use coefficients estimated by Model 6 to get $\varepsilon_1 = 0.276$, $\varepsilon_2 = 0.268$ in period before 2015 and assume a linear change of effect of income and aging to an unitary income elasticity and unitary aging elasticity in 2050 which refer to OECD countries (OECD, 2006). Using data of 2002 to 2008, we obtain the growth rate of residual term is 5% annually. So we assume several alternatives for the growth of residual to simulate future expenditures (see Table 7.8).

In projecting, we use population prospects for China by United Nations to get population aging process till 2050. We also take consideration of possible economic growth rate. Four scenarios are set for future:

Figure 7.10 presents the growth rate of real per capital health care expenditure under each scenario. The results are dependent on assumptions made, but according to the resonable assumptions, health care expenditure will keep increasing in future and the growth rates are higher espcially under high population aging and high economic growth rate scenarios. The declining growth rate during 2040–2045 in each scenario is due to the lower aging process after 2040 in population projection.

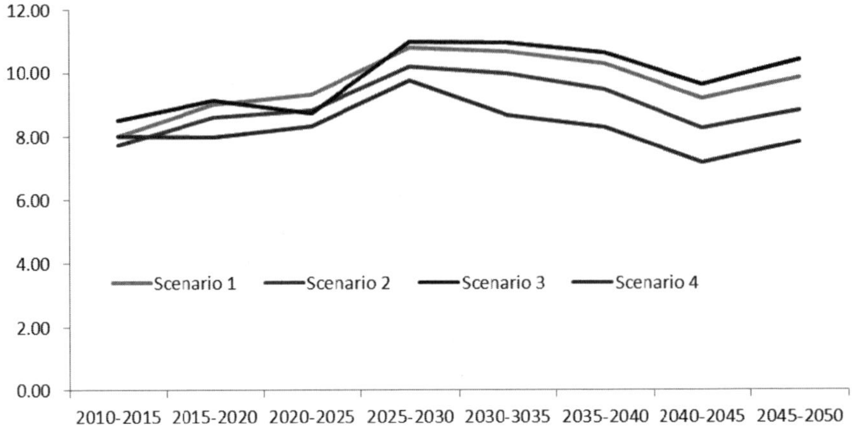

Fig. 7.10. Projecting the growth of real health care expenditure.

Table 7.8. Assumptions made under each scenarios.

	PCGDP	PROP65[a]	Residual term
Scenario 1 High economic growth	8% p.a. before 2015 6% 2015–2030 4% 2030–2050	Medium variant 15.9% (2030); 23.3% (2050)	5% p.a.
Scenario 2 Low economic growth	7% before 2015 5% 2015–2030 3% 2030–2050	Medium variant 15.9% (2030); 23.3% (2050)	5% p.a.
Scenario 3 High population aging	8% p.a. before 2015 6% 2015–2030 4% 2030–2050	Low fertility 16.8% (2030); 26.8% (2050)	5% p.a.
Scenario 4 Low medical inflation	8% before 2015 6% 2015–2030 4% 2030–2050	Medium variant 15.9% (2030); 23.3% (2050)	5% before 2015 3% 2015–2030 1% 2030–2050

[a] Share of population aged 65 and over refers to *World Population Prospects: The 2008 Revision*, Population Division of the Department of Economic and Social Affairs of the United Nations Secretariat.

7.4. Health Care Financing: Future Challenges and Reforms

Facing the situation of increasing demands in future, we have to consider how China could have efficient financing arrangements for health care. In fact, China's health care sector failed to meet the demand during the economic transition. As National Health Services Survey reveals, in 2003, 14% of those surveyed refused outpatient services when sick, and 41% of those who were referred to hospitals refused inpatient care. The non-use rates rise significantly from the first four high income groups to the three low income groups (Table 7.9). Financial non-affordability was the primary factor for these decisions and averagely 67% of those health care non-users reported due to economic difficulty and the number even higher in certain groups, for example, 76% of farmers and 77% of unemployed.

On the other hand, despite the high out-of-pocket payments, many people have to seek care to keep healthy or alive. A high incidence of catastrophic out-of-pocket spending and high rates of impoverishment are hence reflected. Van Doorslaer *et al.* (2007) find that the fraction of the population experience "catastrophic" health expenses was higher in China in 2000 than elsewhere in Asia, and higher sill among the poor.[14] Liu *et al.* (2008) find that the incidence of catastrophic payment fell in urban areas between 1998 and 2003, but increased in rural area in same period of time.

Huge amount of literature has discussed the issues and reforms of health care sector in China (e.g. Hsiao, 1995; Liu and Hsiao, 1995; Ministry of Health, 2005; Liu *et al.*, 2008; Yip and Hsiao, 2009b; Wagstaff *et al.*, 2009c; Herd *et al.*, 2010). The financial obstacles to health service and financial burden of disease in China are largely related to two factors. First, the cost and price of health services are rising at an alarming rate. Second, the majority of China's population heavily depended on out-of-pocket spending to cover the cost of health services and the health insurance coverage dropped dramatically during the period of time after economic reform (Liu, 2004; Yip and Hsiao, 2008). To meet the demand for health care and allievate financial burden of disease, there is a widespread challenge to future financing system in terms of how to control health care price, increase government investment and improve the effect of health insurance.

[14] Here catastrophic expenses are defined as more than a percentage of total non-food consumption, e.g., 25% or 40%. In most other countries, catastrophic rates were found to be lower among the poor.

Table 7.9. Non-use of care due to non-affordability (2003 survey).

2003 survey	**Total**	**Manager**	**Technical**	**Office staff**	**Worker**	**Farmer**	**Retired**	**Unemployed & home worker**
Sample (number)	111795	4522	4055	8423	3894	73644	5967	11290
Sick in two weeks prior to survey (%)	14.4	9.51	8.80	8.63	10.81	14.96	26.63	13.54
But did not seek care (%)	14.00[a]	9.53	12.32	8.53	11.88	15.39	9.31	14.52
Sick but not hospitalized (%)	41.03[b]	12.99	20.17	25.22	52.29	42.10	48.15	56.92
Due to economic difficulty (%)	67.38	36.84	33.33	32.69	34.62	76.31	55.00	77.27

Source: Minstry of Health (Chen and Standing, 2007).

Note: [a] This percentage includes the surveyed population reporting illness or injuries within the two-week period prior to the survey who did not seek any treatment.

[b] This percentage indicates the rates of people failing to be hospitalized despite being referred by a doctor among those reported illness in two weeks previous to the survey.

7.4.1. *Financing structure in health care and future change*

The most criticized problem of China's health care financing is the heavy dependence on out-of-pocket spending. Since 1986, the share of government expenditure in total expenditure kept decreasing and only accounted for 15.7% in 2002. Accordingly, out-of-pocket share was increasing. In peak year 2001, out-of-pocket spending accounted for 60% of total health spending (Figure 7.11). In rural areas, the share of out-of-pocket as a portion of total spending was as high as 90%. Fiscal decentralization is regarded as one important reason. Central government transferred most of the responsibility for health financing to provincial and local governments: in 2007 about 95% of the total government health spending came from local governments (Kaufman, 2005; Herd *et al.*, 2010). Fiscal decetralization then casued a wide variation in public spending on health across regions with different levels of economic development. In 2002, per capita public spending on health ranged from RMB 40 in Guizhou to RMB 187 in Shanghai and the gap persists in later years, with RMB 177 in Geizhou and RMB 678 in Shanghai in 2008.

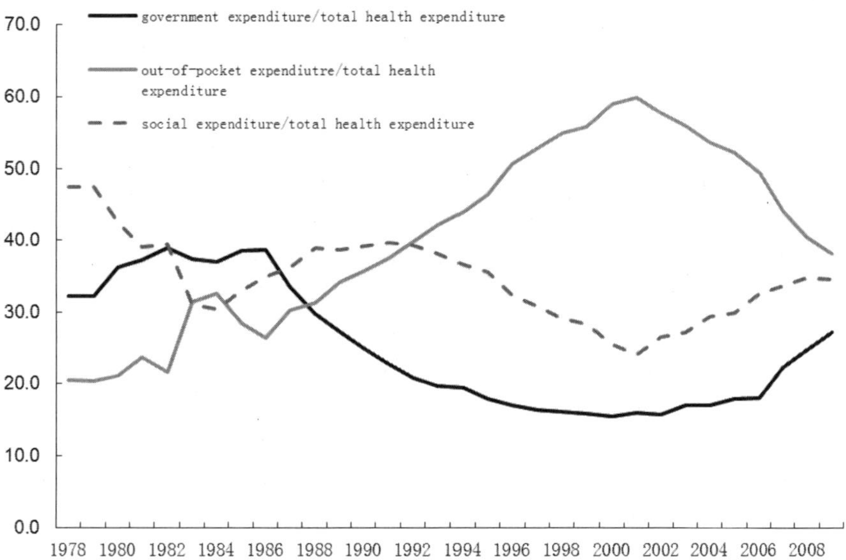

Fig. 7.11. Evolution of health care financing structure in China.

Generally speaking, local government lacks incentive to invest in health care. The policy priorities of local government are those programs which can bring economic growth in a short time. As a result, government spending on health as a share of total government spending fell from more than 6% in the early 1990 to 4.5% in 2000. Lack of government input thus changed the behavior of public hospitals. With only 10% total revenues from government subsidy, they had to increase revenue through promoting the use of high-tech services and selling expensive drugs. This change in financing greatly increased the cost to users. Between 1990 and 2008, the outpatient expenditure per visist soared twelve-fold and inpatient expenditure per patient rose ten-fold.

We notice that the turning point happened in 2003, and since then the share of government investment keeps increasing and reached 27% in 2009 (Figure 7.11). This picture suggests that central government has recognized the fundamental problem of insufficient government investment in health care sector and some measures have been introduced since then. Government running and subsidizing health insurance system in rural area (New Cooperative Medical System, NCMS) was launched at the beginning of 2003. The central and local governments each subsidized RMB 10 per farmer in western and central provinces in 2003, with the farmer paying an additional RMB 10 as annual contribution to enroll in the program. The government subsidy has increased to RMB 126 per capita in 2010, shared by central and local government. By the end of 2009, there are about 830 million participants in NCMS and the participation rate is 94%. On supply side, government has more investment in lower-level facilities to reduce the cost. The Chinese government approved guidelines for reform of the health-care system and published an action plan of targets for reform in 2009. Estimates suggest that governmental investment (both central and local) of RMB 850 billion (about USD125 billion) will be injected into the health-care system in the coming years, doubling the average annual governmental expenditure compared with 2008 (Yip and Hsiao, 2009a). The target officially declared recently is to reduce the share of out-of-pocket to no more than 30% in near future.

7.4.2. *Health insurance coverage and future improvement*

Health insurance coverage dropped dramatically since economic reforms. In rural areas, the coverage dropped from a peak of around 85% in 1975 to about 9.5% in 2003. Between 1993 and 2003, the health insurance coverage rate in urban areas dropped from 70% to 55%. The decline was especially significant for the poor, with the coverage rate for the bottom quintile income group plunging from 37% to 12% (National Health Services Survey). Public financing of health care was reformed to use insurance system rather than the budget after economic transition and the basic medical insurance scheme (BMI) started in 1998, but only for urban workers. The coverage rate of BMI is growing from 20% of the total urban employees in 1998 to 52% in 2009. A marked change of government policy started from 2003 and the rate of coverage keeps increasing (Figure 7.12). The first was NCMS as mentioned in previous paragraph, which is the main contributor for the enlarging coverage. In 2007 another health insurance program known as Urban Resident Basic Medical Insurance scheme (URBMI) covered those urban residents not covered by BMI introduced. This new scheme covers children, the elderly, the disabled and other non-working urban

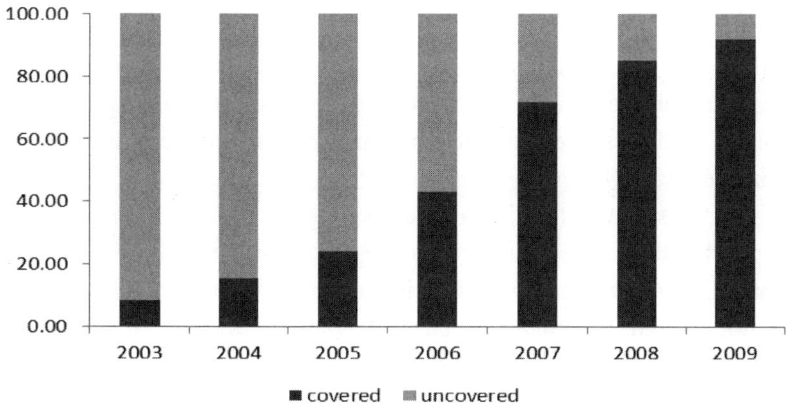

Fig. 7.12. Increasing coverage of health insurance.

Source: *China Health Statistic Yearbook.*

residents. Like NCMS, there is government subsidy for premium in URBMI. By 2009, Among the whole population of 1.3 billion, 1.2 billion have been covered by insurance, including 0.8 billion covered by NCMS, 0.2 billion by BMI, and 0.2 billion by URBMI. So the target of universal coverage of insurance is reaching soon without any uncertainty.

However, the effect of health insurance needs to be improved in future. Economic theory and international experience have found that when health insurance is expanded with no appropriate supply-side controls, health care expenditure will grow as a result of demand-side moral hazard and, more importantly, supply-side moral hazard (Yip and Hsiao, 2009a; Feldstein, 1973). This is what is happening in China. The price increase caused by introducing health insurance offsets the effect of government subsidy. In our study of the effect on price of NCMS empirically, using village- and county-level panel data and employing difference-in-difference method, we find that NCMS has no impact on village clinic price, but will cause a rise of county hospital price. Furthermore, the higher the reimbursement ratio, the higher the price, and the percentage of price increasing is almost equivalent to reimbursement ratio (Feng *et al.*, 2010). The results testify the theoretical prediction that in a health care market where the provider has market power and is profit-oriented, such as county hospital, introducing health insurance will cause health care price inflation and offset the effect of health insurance. Other studies show that the urban scheme does not seem to have reduced catastrophic medical expenditure and may have increased financial risk from a hospital stay, as hospitals tend to subject insured patients to more procedures (Wagstaff and Lindelow, 2008).

Another issue in health insurance system is that the reimbursing coverage provided by these programmes is very small (Hu *et al.*, 2008). Outpatient services are either very inadequately insured or, in some rural area, not insured. Inpatient services leave patients with significant costs to bear. Study finds that reimburse arrangement in NCMS has significant effect on the demand for health care. For farmers in China, the expenditure of outpatient care is a significant fraction of the household income, so reimbursing outpatient care can also reduce the financial burden by a large extent. The simulation of the outcomes of various arrangements shows that only reimbursing inpatient care cannot reduce the average financial burden, while reimbursing both inpatient and outpatient care is a better choice (Feng and Li, 2009). Because of the low reimbursement rate, moral hazard is not a serious issue in rural health insuarnce.

What we are discussing here could explain why most of studies find that the effect of the NCMS to improve access to care and reduce the financial burden is limited (e.g., Wagstaff *et al.*, 2009a; Lei and Lin, 2009). Expending insurance coverage is not enough and other arrangements are required. Regulating price, changing the fee for service payments, and improving competition in health delivery should always be considered. China had some successful attempts in some cities such as Hainan and Ningbo to move away from fee-for-service within the urban insurance system toward a system of perspective payments. Studies find that compared with a comparable set of hospitals to be paid via fee for service, the growth of expenditure of those hopital with prepayment reform is slower (Yip and Eggleston, 2001; Yip and Eggleston, 2004). Reform on reimbursement arrangement is also initiated. Ministry of Health recently set a target to increase the contribution of NCMS to RMB 300 during the period of the "Twelveth Five-Year Plan", which implies that the reimbursement rate will be rasied. Raising inpatient reimbursement ratio and insuring more outpatient service are being considered by the policy makers.

7.4.3. *Non-government investment in health care and future policy*

Introducing non-government investment is a complimentary source to finance health care. From the 1950s to the late 1970s, China developed large public health care institutions, which were designed to provide basic medical service to people at affordable prices. With the remarkable economic growth, China found itself faced with the challenge of a supply shortage of health facilities. In 1980, the State Council approved the Ministry of Health's request to permit private practice. In 1989, Ministry of Health and Ministry of Foreign Trade issued a document on the regulation of joint venture hospitals. In 2000, Chinese government issued regulations on nonprofit and for-profit health care organizations and categorized hospitals into three groups: government nonprofit hospitals, private nonprofit hospitals and private for-profit hospitals. Nonprofit hospitals are tax-exempted but subject to the government's price regulation; and for-profit hospitals can set up their own prices. Government gives tax-exemption to private for-profit hospitals in the first three years.

The private hospital has grown rapidly since the mid-1990s. The private sector has grown both through privatization and new entry. Many ownership reforms have taken place in the form of joint stock operations, resulting in share-holding by a mix of public agencies, private individuals, and institutional investors. The emergence and growth of the private sector in rural areas has primarily been through ownership conversions, and new entry in hospitals, including through joint ventures with foreign investors, has been more important in urban areas. However, there are certain kinds of discrimination against private hospitals in China, which make these hospitals difficult to improve the quality. It is harder for them to attract high-skilled doctors because these hospitals lack official personnel evaluation system or social security. Also, purchasing high-tech equipment has been regulated in a region and private hospitals hardly can get the license. As a result, although the number of private hospitals is increasing, the market share of these hospitals is very small and keeps declining (Figure 7.13).

The declining market share might be due to the recently increasing government investment. Also, the market share of non-government hospitals is decreasing with GDP per capita. In a more developed region, there is less demand for health care delivered by non-government hospital — such hospital usually implies a lower quality of the care. Some studies provide evidence of lower price and lower quality of private hospitals. Huang *et al.* (2006) find from a survey in Guangdong Province that the prices charged by non-governmental hospitals are generally lower than or equal to those of government hospitals. Liu *et al.* (2006) use individual survey data to show that private providers serve disproportionately low-middle income groups due to lower price.

Government and private roles in health care market remain controversial in theory and in practice of many countries, so do in China. Limited evidence of the ownership and performance in health service delivery in China is far from conclusive. There are lots of studies for other countries, but with no conclusion on the ownership differences. Reviews of literature

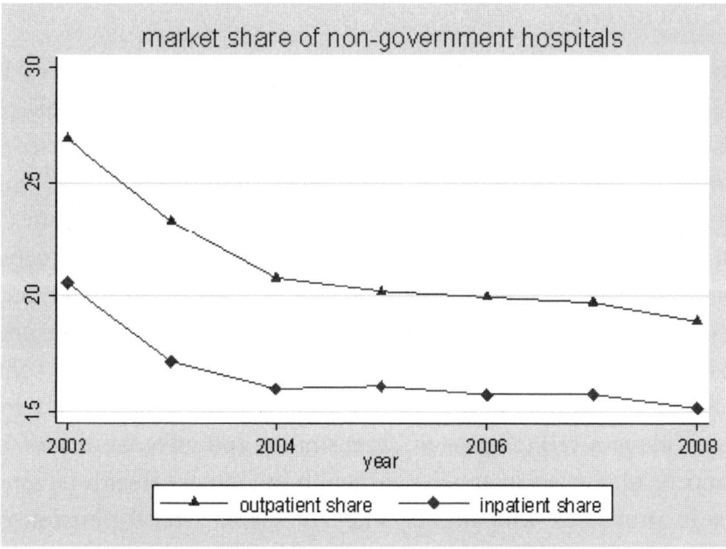

Fig. 7.13. Market shares of non-government hospitals.

Source: *China Health Statistic Yearbook.*

Notes: Hospital here includes comprehensive hospitals, Chinese hospitals and specific hospitals and does not include preventive center, community health center, village clinics, etc.

about ownership and quality or ownership and financial performance suggest that much of the variation in the results can be explained by differences in regions, methods and data quality (e.g., Eggleston *et al.*, 2008; Shen *et al.*, 2007). However, the excess and differentiated demand offer part of the explanation for the development of private sectors in health care (Hou and Coyne, 2008). In China the demand for health care will keep increasing according to our projection and public hospitals face challenge to meet the rapidly increasing demand. Public hospitals are often crowded with patients.

In 2009, health policy reforms call for expansion of private investments in health service delivery in China, transforming almost universal government ownership of hospitals into greater ownership diversification. Government investment will focus on basic health care. Policies are required to lead private hospitals to offer services of better quality and serve for the richer people.

7.5. Conclusions

Economic transition has led to a significant improvement in general health status of Chinese population. Infant mortality rate has been reduced and life expectancy has risen. But compared to many other countries, including some developing countries, the step of improvement was smaller. There is a special health transition during economic transition in China, which is characterized by a declining of infectious diseases and increasing of non-communicable hypertension, cardiovascular disease and diabetes. Income growth and population aging are changing people's consumption behavior and incidence of chronic diseases, which are the main contributors to health transition. However, in China, it is worth noting that institution also plays a critical role in accessibility and affordability of health care and results in an inequality in health outcomes. Health is generally poorer in provinces with higher share of China's rural population and there is a significant positive correlation between regional income level and life expectancy.

Rapid rising of health care expenditure has been most complained of for Chinese health care system. In future, the rising trend of real per capita expenditure will continue. According to our simulation, economic growth, population aging, technological change and institutional reform will generate a 7–10% growth rate of real per capita health care expenditure during 2010–2050. In the past 30 years, the financial obstacles to health care and financial burden of disease in China are largely related to two factors — one is the wrong incentive in public hospitals to over-prescription or over-examination, and the other is the lower coverage of health insurance.

Recent reform in health care sector has called for more government investment and central government is increasing inputs to health care system since 2003. Health insurance reform and public hospital reform have also required local government to match spending for those inputs from the central government. However, there is an incentive issue in public hospitals, which cannot be solved simply by increasing government spending. Payment arrangement and competition in health care market are necessary measures to change the profit-seeking behavior and low efficiency problem of public hospitals.

The government has successfully rolled out three health insurance programs for urban employees, urban residents and farmers. For the moment, the coverage rate of health insurance is more than 90%. In future, the main target is not only universal coverage, but also the effectiveness of health insurance in reducing financial burden of health care. More attention should be paid to the interaction between health insurance and behavior of health care supplier. Recent practice in rural China shows that health insurance will cause health care price inflation and offset the effect of health insurance. As a third-party payer, health insurance program can play a role in changing payment arrangement from fee-for-service to prospective payment. There are already some experiments in China, but more research and policy analysis need to be done in this area.

The outcome of competition in health care market is inconclusive in literature. Practices in other countries are of high diversity. In US, 60% of hospitals were private nonprofits, 25% were operated by governments, primarily local governments. In UK, the number of public hospitals accounted for 95% in 2000. In Germany, 37% of hospitals were public ones in 2003. Currently, the market share of private hospital is less than 20% in outpatient service and even lower in inpatient service. Most of private hospitals provide low quality, low price service. Ignorance still remains regarding to what the proper share of private hospital is and what the role of private hospital in China's health market will be.

References

Barros, P.P. (1998). "The Black Box of Health Care Expenditure Determinants." *Health Economics*, 7, 533–544.

Chen, L. and Standing, H. (2007). "Gender Equity in Transitional China's Health Care Policy Reforms." *Feminist Economics*, 7(13), 189–212.

Chernichovsky, D. and Markowitz, S. (2004). "Aging and Aggregate Costs of Medical Care: Conceptual and Policy Issues." *Health Economics*, 13, 543–562.

Culter, D.M. (2004). *Your Money or Your Life: Strong Medicine for America's Health Care System*. New York: Oxford University Press.

Culter, D.M., McClelaan, M., Newhouse, J.P. and Remler, D. (1998). "Are Medical Prices Declining? Evidence from Heart Attack Treatments." *Quarterly Journal of Economics*, 113(4), 991–1024.

Culyer, A.J. (1998). "Health Care Expenditures in Canada: Myth and Reality; Past and Future." Canadian Tax Paper, no. 83, Canadian Tax Foundation, Toronto.

Di Matteo, L. (2005). "The Macro Determinants of Health Expenditure in the United States and Canada: Assessing the Impact of Income, Age Distribution and Time." *Health Policy*, 71, 23–42.

Eggleston, K., Schmid, C., Lau, J. and Shen, Y. (2008). "Systematic Review of Hospital Ownership and Quality of Care: What Explains the Different Results in the Literature?" *Health Economics*, 17, 1345–1362.

Feldstein, M. (1973). "The Welfare Loss of Excess Health Insurance." *The Journal of Political Economy*, 81(2), 251–258.

Feng, J., Qin, B. and Yu, Y. (2010). "Wealth, Education, and Demand for Medical Care: Evidence from Rural China." In G. Liu and S. Zhang (eds.), *Investing in Human Capital for Economic Development in China*. Singapore: World Scientific Publishing Co. Pte. Ltd.

Feng, J. and Li, Z. (2009). "Risk Management for Health Care in Rural China" (in Chinese). *Jingji Yanjiu (Economic Research Journal)*, 4, 103–115.

Feng, J., Liu, F. and Chen, Q. (2010). "Impact of New Cooperative Medical System on Health Care Price" (in Chinese). *Economic Research Journal*, 11, 127–140.

Gerdtham, U.G. and Jönsson, B. (2000). "International Comparisons of Health Expenditure: Theory, Data and Econometric Analysis." In A.J. Culyer and J.P. Newhosuse (eds.), *Handbook of Health Economics*, vol. 1, Amsterdam: Elsevier Science.

Gerdtham, U.G., Jönsson, B., MacFarlan, M., Oxley, H. (1998). "The Determinants of Health Expenditure in the OECD Countries: A Pooled Data Analysis." In P. Zweifel (ed.), *Health, the Medical Profession and Regulation: Developments in Health Economics and Public Policy*, 6, 113–134.

Gerdtham, U.G., Sögaard, J., Jönsson, B. and Andersson, F. (1992b). "A Pooled Crossed Section Analysis of the Health Expenditure of the OECD Countries." In P. Zweifel and H. Frech (eds.), *Health Economics Worldwide*. Dordrecht: Kluwer Academic Publishers.

Gerdtham, U.G., Sögaard, J., Andersson, F. and Jönsson, B. (1992a). "Econometric Analysis of Health Expenditure: A Cross-Sectional Study of the OECD Countries." *Journal of Health Economics*, 11, 63–84.

Getzen, T.E. (1992). "Population Aging and the Growth of Health Expenditures." *Journal of Gerontology, Social Sciences*, 47, S98–S104.

Getzen, T.E. (2000). "Health Care is an Individual Necessity and a National Luxury: Applying Multilevel Decision Models to the Analysis of Health Care Expenditures." *Journal of Health Economics*, 19(2), 259–270.

Herd, R., Hu, Y.W. and Koen, V. (2010). "Improving China's Health Care System." OECD Economic Development Working Papers No. 751.

Hitiris, T. and Posnett, J. (1992). "The Determinants and Effects of Health Expenditure in Developed Countries." *Journal of Health Economics*, 11, 173–181.

Hou, X. (2008). "Urban-Rural Disparity of Overweight, Hypertension, Undiagnosed Hypertension, and Untreated Hypertension in China." *Asia-Pacific Journal of Public Health*, 20, 159–169.

Hou, X. and Coyne, J. (2008). "The Emergence of Proprietary Medical Facility in China." *Health Policy*, 88, 141–151.

Hsiao, W.C. (1995). "The Chinese Health Care System: Lessons for Other Nations." *Social Science and Medicine*, 41(8), 1047–1055.

Hu, S., Tang, S., Liu, Y., Zhao, Y., Escobar, M.L. and Ferranti, D. (2008). "Reform of How Health Care is Paid for in China: Challenges and Opportunities." *The Lancet*, 372(9652), 68–76.

Huang, C., Zhai, Z., Sun, B., Chen, S. and Liang, H. (2006). "Analysis of Problems with the Development of Non-Governmental Hospital in Guangdong Province" (in Chinese). *Chinese Health Economics*, 25(8), 31–33.

Kaufman, J. (2005). "China: the Intersections Between Poverty, Health Inequity, Reproductive Health, and HIV/AIDS." *Development*, 48(4), 113–119.

Lei, X. and Lin, S. (2009). "The New Cooperative Medical Scheme in Rural China: Does more Coverage Mean more Service and Better Health?" *Health Economics*, 18, 25–46.

Liu, X. and Hsiao, W.C. (1995). "The Cost Escalation of Social Health Insurance Plans in China: Its Implication for Public Policy." *Social Science and Medicine*, 41(8), 1095–1101.

Liu, Y, Rao, K., Wu, J. and Gakidou, E. (2008). "China's Health System Performance." *The Lancet*, 372(9653), 1914–1923.

Liu, Y, Hsiao, W.C. and Eggleston, K. (1999). "Equity in Health and Health Care: The Chinese Experience." *Social Science and Medicine*, 49, 1349–1356.

Liu, Y. (2004). "Development of the Rural Health Insurance System in China." *Health Policy and Planning*, 19(3), 159–165.

Liu, Y., Rao, K. and Fei, J. (1998). "Economic Transition and Health Transition: Comparing China and Russia." *Health Policy*, 44, 103–122.

Liu, Y., Berman, P., Yip, W., Liang, H., Meng, Q., Qu, J. and Li, Z. (2006). "Health Care in China: The Role of Non-Government Providers." *Health Policy*, 77(2), 212–220.

Ministry of Health (2005). *Report on China's Healthcare System and Reform.* Beijing.

Mocan, H.N., Erdal, T. and Jeffrey, Z.S. (2004). "The Demand for Medical Care in Urban China." *World Development*, 32(2), 289–304.

Newhouse, J.P. (1977). "Medical Care Expenditure: A Cross-National Survey." *Journal of Human Resources*, 12, 115–125.

Newhouse, J.P. (1992). "Medical Care Costs: How much Welfare Loss." *Journal of Economic Perspectives*, 6(3), 3–21.

O'Connell, J.M. (1996). "The Relationship between Health Expenditures and the Age Structure of the Population in OECD Countries." *Health Economics*, 5(6), 573–578.

OECD (2006). "Projecting OECD Health and Long-Term Care Expenditures: What are the Main Drivers." OECD Economic Development Working Papers No. 477.

Okunade, A.A., Murthy, V.N.R. (2002). "Technology as a 'Major Driver' of Health Care Costs: A Cointegration Analysis of the Newhouse Conjection." *Journal of Health Economics*, 21(1), 147–159.

Parkin, D., McGuire, A. and Yule, B. (1987). "Aggregate Health Care Expenditures and National Income: Is Health Care a Luxury Good." *Journal of Health Economics*, 6, 109–127.

Popkin, B.M. (2008). "Will China's Nutrition Transition Overwhelm its Health Care System and Slow Economic Growth?." *Health Affairs*, 27(4), 1064–1076.

Shen, Y., Eggleston, K., Lau, J. and Schmid, C. (2006). "Hospital Ownership and Financial Performance: A Quantitative Research Review." National Bureau of Economic Research, Working Paper, No. 11662.

Van Doorslaer, E., O'Donnell, O., Rannan-Eliya, RP., Somanathan, A., Adhikari, SR., Garg, C.C., Harbianto, D., Herrin, A.N., Huq, M.N., Ibragimova, S., Karan, A., Lee, T., Leung, G.M., Lu, J., Ng, C.W., Pande, B.R., Racelis, R., Tao, S., Tin, K., Tisayaticom, K., Risnantoro, T.L., Visasvid, C. and Zhao, Y. (2007). "Catastrophic Payments for Health Care in Asia." *Health Economics*, 16, 1159–1184.

Wagstaff, A. and Lindelow, M. (2008). "Can Insurance Increase Financial Risk? The Curious Case of Health Insurance in China." *Journal of Health Economics*, 27(4), 990–1005.

Wagstaff, A., Lindelow, M., Gao, J., Xu, L. and Qian, J. (2009a). "Extending Health Insurance to the Rural Population: An Impact Evaluation of China's New Cooperative Medical Scheme." *Journal of Health Economics*, 28(1), 1–19.

Wagstaff, A., Lindelow, M., Wang, S. and Zhang, S. (2009b). *Reforming China's Rural Health System*. World Bank: Washington, DC.

Wagstaff, A., Yip, W., Lindelow, M. and Hsiao, W.C. (2009c). "China's Health System and its Reform: A Review." *Health Economics*, 18, S7–S23.

Wang, L., Kong, L., Wu, F., Bai, Y. and Burton, R. (2005). "Preventing Chronic Diseases in China." *Lancet*, 366, 1821–1824.

Wang, Y., Mi, J., Shan, X.-Y., Wang, Q. J. and Ge, K.-Y. (2007). "Is China Facing an Obesity Epidemic and the Consequences? The Trends in Obesity and Chronic Disease in China." *International Journal of Obesity*, 31, 177–188.

World Health Organization (2010). *World Health Statistics 2010*. Geneva, Switzerland: WHO Press.

World Health Organization, Office of Representative in China (2005). "China: Health, Poverty and Economic Development." Report Prepared Under the WHO's Macroeconomics and Health Initiative, Beijing.

Yip, W. and Mahal, A. (2008). "The Health Care System of China and India: Performance and Future Challenges." *Health Affairs*, 27, 921–932.

Yip, W. and Eggleston, K. (2001). "Provider Payment Reform in China: The Case of Hospital Reimbursement in Hainan Province." *Health Economics*, 10(4), 325–339.

Yip, W. and Eggleston, K. (2004). "Addressing Government and Market Failures with Payment Incentives: Hospital Reimbursement Reform in Hainan, China." *Social Science & Medicine*, 58, 267–277.

Yip, W. and Hsiao, W.C. (2008). "The Chinese Health System at a Crossroads." *Health Affairs*, 27, 460–468.

Yip, W. and Hsiao, W.C. (2009a). "China's Health Care Reform: A Tentative Assessment." *China Economic Review*, 20, 613–619.

Yip, W. and Hsiao, W.C. (2009b). "Non-Evidence-Based Policy: How Effective is China's New Cooperative Medical Scheme in Reducing Medical Impoverishment?" *Social Science and Medicine*, 68(2), 201–209.

CHAPTER 8

ENHANCING THE INCOME DISTRIBUTION EFFECT OF THE SOCIAL SECURITY SYSTEM IN CHINA: EMPIRICS AND POLICY SUGGESTIONS

Lixin He

8.1. Introduction

Modern social security system originated in the Bismarck Administration of Germany in the 1880s and expanded gradually to other industrialized countries. Through its past development of more than 100 years, social security has become an important social responsibility for all governments, including those in developing countries. It has unique functions in regulating income redistribution compared with other measures. With social and economic development, social security accounts for a larger and larger proportion in national revenue and public expenditure. In many developed countries, social security expenditure makes the most important part of public expenditure, becoming one of the most influential factors in public finance operation. After the 1970s, with rapid population aging and increasing uncertainty in economy, social security has become a hot topic and stayed in the focus of policy makers, experts and even ordinary people.

In China, social security also draws the attention of all walks of life. Compared with other countries, China's expanding income gap and new poverty problems have enhanced people's wish that the social security system play a full role in the income distribution in China. Despite the

30-year development that leads to the tremendous improvement in living standards for both urban and rural residents and the substantial decrease in the population below the poverty line, the income disparity is gradually expanding at the same time. According to the World Bank (2003), China's Gini coefficient increases most of all developing countries, rising rapidly from around 0.20 in the early 1980s to 0.42 in 1993, and reaches 0.437 in 1999. What is more worrisome is that after breaking the international warning line of 0.4, China's Gini coefficient is still on the increase year by year, reaching 0.485 in 2007. Meanwhile, as Chen *et al.* (2006) pointed out, certain sub-groups have been regressively affected or have been unable to participate in the new economic opportunities due to their lack of skills, long-term illnesses or disabilities. Some of the "left behind" households started poor and some became poor, even though aggregate poverty rates have tended to fall over time. Urban areas have figured prominently in these concerns about the "new poor".[1]

The aging population is also a crucial test to China's social security. According to the United Nations' prediction on population,[22] the proportion of the population aged above 65 will account for 14% of the total population by the year 2025, increasing from 7% in 2000. And the population aged above 65 will pass 200 million between 2025 and 2030. By 2040, that population will be more than 300 million, a number greater than the total population of Japan, Britain and many other countries. Predictably, how to maintain the long-term financial balance to meet the income and medical needs of elderly people will be a real and unavoidable problem for China in the next few decades.

Social security system generally includes social insurance system, social assistance system and social welfare system. Social insurance requires the insured persons to pay certain insurance premiums or taxes in order to obtain corresponding rights, which is generally not for the purpose of income redistribution. For some social insurance plans, however, benefits actually received have little to do with contribution and the benefits may not depend completely on the amount paid. Thus social

---

[1] For studies on urban and rural poverty in China, see Chen and Ravallion (2004, 2007, 2008), Ravallion and Chen (2007), Chen *et al.* (2006), Xia *et al.* (2007), and Luo (2010).

[2] *World Population Prospect: the 2006 Revision* (Medium variant).

insurance plans also contribute to income redistribution to a certain extent. Funded by public finance, social assistance and social welfare, on the other hand, are direct income redistribution plans. Theoretically, if social security system in one country mainly targets at providing social insurance, it has less income distributive effects; if social assistance and social welfare, funded by public finance, constitute the major part of social security system, or if the returns that the insured get are weakly related to what they have paid, the system has relatively strong income distributive effects. In addition, the scopes of population covered by social security and the extent of protection provided by social security also have direct impacts on its income distributive effects. Therefore, the role which the social security system plays in income distribution depends on the composition and specific designs of the security system.

Current social security in China was established on the basis of reforming various systems in the era of planned economy. So far, China has set up the social security system including social insurance (which consists pension, medical care, and unemployment, etc.), and social assistance (e.g. minimum living standard guarantee, etc.). It is difficult to fully evaluate the system's impact on income distribution. In this chapter, after summarizing the major achievements and problems of social security in China, we will present empirics on income distributive effects of social security in China from both intra-generational and inter-generational aspects as well as policy suggestions. And we will pay special attention to the role of income transfer which comes from social security in improving the income of low-income group and decreasing the income gap, and the inter-generational redistributive effect of public pension estimated by lifetime income. The part "Development of social security in China" will describe the establishment and development of major systems and reveal some problems existing in China's social security on the basis of macro data. In Section 8.3, we will analyze income distributive effects of China's social security on different groups using annual macro statistics and micro survey data, and then estimate lifetime earnings of individual to analyze the intra-generational and inter-generational income distributive effect of public pension in China. Section 8.4 discusses issues related to enhancing income distributive effects of social security and makes policy suggestions. And Section 8.5 provides conclusions.

8.2. Development of Social Security System

Chinese social security system in the Planned Economy period dates back to the early 1950s. Under the Dual Track economic structure, to guarantee development of industries and construction of cities was the first target of all social policies. The social security system ran differently in urban and rural areas as well. While social security for farmers mainly relied on land and family protection, social security for urban workers was based on "Regulations Concerning Labour Insurance" issued in 1951. That regulation was a social security system including retirement, disability, death, sickness, maternity, work-related injuries and medical care, taking work units as the basis to implement security policies in its organization and management. The benefits, including pension, medical care, housing, and other income subsidies, were financed from enterprise or state's budget, the employees had no necessary to pay for their benefits.

As China transits itself to a market economy, however, the old social security system fell further and further behind the requirement of economic development. Since the 1980s, China started to reform the old social security system. Especially in the late 1990s, it made relatively great adjustments to insurance systems including pension and medical care covering urban areas. Up to now, China has set up the Urban Social Security System including social insurance (made up by five projects — pension, medical care, unemployment, work-related injuries and maternity) and social assistance insurance (consisting of minimum living standard guarantee and medical aid, etc.). Since the beginning of the 20th century, China has gradually introduced social security programs including medical care and pension as well as social assistance programs that target at rural residents. We could say that up to the first decade in the 21st century, the social security framework covering urban and rural residents in China has been basically established. Meanwhile, there are also some problems in this system such as limited coverage of those programs, low payment standards, and great regional differences. To understand the role of current social security system in China, we would briefly introduce the timetable of reform, content and implementation of major social security programs first.

8.2.1. *Social insurance program*

The most important pension reform was introduced in 1995 and revised in 1997. The State Council issued a new document, No 26, in July 1997 and established a new pension system for urban employees in enterprises, the so-called Basic Pension Insurance.[3] The Basic Pension Insurance was available for all employees of all urban enterprises, including state-owned enterprises, collective enterprises, foreign-owned enterprises, etc.[4] The 1997 structure has three pillars: a pooled account distributed among all recipients, compulsory individual accounts, and voluntary supplementary pensions provided via commercial insurance. The first pillar was financed by a payroll tax of 17% (paid by employers) to assure that the employees who have worked for more than 15 years have a replacement ratio of 20%. The second pillar (paid jointly by employers and employees) established an individual account for each employee. The contribution rate for this account is 11% of an employee's wage, of which the employer contributes 3%–8%. During his retirement, the employee receives from this account a monthly benefit amounting to its accumulated value divided by 120. A change in December 2005 adjusted the percentage paid to the individual account and the method for calculating and receiving payments (see Appendix). On the other hand, benefits of public sector employees[5] were still calculated and provided in the same way as they were before the reform, i.e., according to certain proportion (75% to 100%) of the individual's wages before retirement.

China began its exploration on public pension program targeting at rural residents in the late 1980s. In 1992, the Ministry of Civil Affairs promulgated the *Rural Social Old-age Insurance Program* and put forward the basic ideology and framework of establishing rural social pension insurance system. However, due to the drawbacks of the program

---

[3]The note on the pension system here is mainly based on Feng, He and Sato (2011).

[4]Some public institutions began to take part in the insurance system since 1999, but the percentage was very small. For insured staffs in public institutions, the percentage was 6.7% in 1999 and 9.8% in 2007 among all the participated employees (*The China Statistical Yearbook,* 2008).

[5]Public sector here refers to institutions and state organs that are mainly financed by fiscal spending, such as government sector, education sector, health sector, etc.

itself, such as relatively low benefits and insufficient encouragement, and the immature social and economic conditions, this system has mainly stayed in stagnation since 1999. In September 2009, the State Council issued the *Guiding Opinions on Carrying out the Pilot Projects for Establishing a New Type Old-age Insurance System for Rural Residents*, and decided to carry out pilot projects of the new rural social pension insurance in 10% of the counties (cities, districts, and banners — county-level administrative divisions in the Nei Monggol Autonomous Region) and gradually expand the pilot. As of the end of 2009, the number of rural pension social insurance program participates was 86.91 million, which accounted for 12.19% of the rural population, making it clear that the family was still the main body of rural pension system.

In 1998, the State Council selected a new model for urban workers' health insurance, called the Basic Health Insurance System (BHIS).[6] The BHIS program replaced the Labour Health Insurance System for workers and their dependents, and the Government Health Insurance System for civil servants and public workers. The implementation of the BHIS had begun in almost all of the pooling areas of the country, but was not yet complete; many of the employees that were supposed to be covered by the new medical insurance system remained under one of the old systems or no longer covered at all (Drouin and Thompson, 2006). The BHIS was designed to rely on combining individual accounts to finance out-patient care and social pooling to finance in-patient care. The contribution rate was 2% of an employee's wages in order to be insured. As for rural residents, the New Rural Co-operative Health Insurance System was put into practice in 2003. It is a medical insurance program mainly sponsored and subsidized by the government. Of all contribution, 20–30 yuan is paid by per farmer and 40–60 yuan by the central and local governments respectively, forming the amount of 100–150 yuan per capita to let the system perform the mutual assistance function of "reservoir."

In January 1999, the State Council issued the "Regulations on Unemployment Insurance", expanding the coverage from the stated-owned enterprises only to all enterprises and institutions, meanwhile

---

[6]For more information on medical insurance, see the relevant chapter by Feng Jin in this book.

adjusting the contribution rate of unemployment insurance. Individuals began to pay contributions and the common payment mechanism was established, with the 2% of the contribution from employers and 1% of gross wages from workers. Benefits of unemployment insurance are linked with the minimum living standard guarantee (below the local minimum wage and above the minimum living standard) and the monthly insurance ranges from 12 to 24 months. Since its implementation, the number of insured workers rose from 98.52 million in 1999 to 127.15 million in 2009, of which the migrant workers took up 16.43 million, 940 thousand more than the number at the end of the previous year.[7]

8.2.2. *Social assistance program*

On 1 October 1999, the State Council issued the "Regulation on the Minimum Urban Living Standard Subsidy Program of Urban Residents", which indicated the establishment of Urban Minimum Living Standard Guarantee (hereinafter referred to as U-MLSG) system nationwide. It targeted at poor urban residents whose household income per capita was below the local minimum living standard guarantee. The fund needed was listed in the fiscal budget by local governments and included in the items of expenditures by special fund for social security, while the minimum living standard was decided by departments of civil affairs in local governments together with departments of finance, statistics and price, etc. In 2007, the State Council issued the "Circular on Establishing the System of Guaranteeing Minimum Subsistence in Rural Areas throughout the Country" and established Rural Minimum Living Standard Guarantee (hereinafter referred to as R-MLSG). It targets at rural residents whose per capita annual net income of households is below the local minimum living standard, those who living in difficult mainly due to illness and deformity, age and infirmity, disability, and bad living conditions. Local governments are responsible for the implementation of R-MLSG and the fund needed is included in fiscal budget, while poor areas receive subsidies from the central government. The MLSG program is the largest transfer payment aimed at low-income population in China at the moment. By the end of

[7] *China Human Resources and Social Security Development Statistics Bulletin,* 2009.

2008, 23.35 million people were included nationwide in the U-MLSG system with an average minimum security standard of 205 yuan per month per capita, 15.61% of the per capita monthly disposable income of urban households; 43.05 million people were included nationwide in the R-MLSG system with an average minimum security standard of 82 yuan per month per capita, 5% of the per capita monthly net income of rural households.[8]

In addition to assistance in terms of income, China has also set up a medical aid system, starting medical aid for rural and urban areas in 2003 and 2006 respectively. The urban and rural medical aid systems are funded by government funds and public donations to offer medical expense assistance for rural households enjoying the five guarantees and poor peasant families suffering from serious illness, people who are covered in the urban minimum living standard guarantee program but not in the basic urban health insurance system, people who are covered by the basic urban health insurance system but still have heavy burdens, and people who have other special difficulties. By the end of 2009, the National Rural Medical Aid helped 47.89 million people, seven times the number of 7.29 million people helped in 2004 and thirteen times the number of 1.15 million people helped in 2005.[9]

In short, by 2010, China has established social insurance programs which are contributed by employers and workers and cover pension, medical care, unemployment, work-related injuries, etc., and social assistance programs which are funded by public finance and include minimum living standard guarantee and medical aid, etc. A social security system that covers urban and rural residents has formed. However, the system construction in rural areas is still in its infancy with a very low pension insurance coverage and a much lower security protection level than those enjoyed by urban residents in pension and other programs. Besides, there are various differences in coverage and eligibility among various urban social security programs.

[8]Data sources: 4th China Social Security Forum, *China Urban Life and Price Yearbook*, 2009, and *China Yearbook of Rural Household Survey*, 2009.
[9]*China Medical Statistical Yearbook*, 2010.

8.2.3. *Coverage of major social security programs*

We have already known from the introduction of the system that reforms on social security programs in China were mainly carried out in the late 1990s. Based on timetables of various reforms and macro data released by the government, we calculate the coverage of social security system after the reform (Figure 8.1).

It can be seen from Figure 8.1 that the coverage of all social insurance programs in urban employed residents has increased in the past 10 years, with the coverage of medical insurance growing the fastest, from 7% in 1998 to 52% in 2009. The coverage of pension insurance grows from 38% in 1998 to 57% in 2009 whereas the coverage of unemployment insurance remains at approximately 40%. Overall, despite the fact that more and more urban employed population is covered by new social insurance, nearly half of the working population still drifted away from various social insurance programs until 2009.

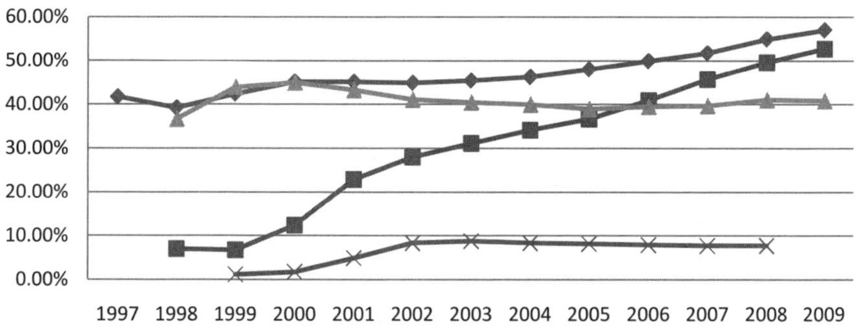

Fig. 8.1. Coverage of the social security system after the reform.

Sources: *China Statistical Yearbook*, 2010. *China Civil Affairs' Statistical Yearbook*, 2009.

Notes:

Coverage of Basic Pension Insurance = Contributors of Basic Pension Insurance/Number of Employed Persons in Urban Areas × 100.

Coverage of Basic Medical Care Insurance = Contributors of Basic Medical Care Insurance/Number of Employed Persons in Urban Areas × 100.

Coverage of Unemployment Insurance = Contributors of Unemployment Insurance/Number of Employed Persons in Urban Areas × 100.

Coverage of Minimum Living Allowance = Number of Persons Receiving Minimum Living Allowance in Urban Areas/Number of Employed Persons in Urban Areas × 100.

Here, contributors indicate the number of employees participated in the above insurance programs.

Under general circumstances, expanding social security system coverage will enhance the income distributive effect of social security and reduce the inequality in income distribution. But in the late 1990s, before the social security system reform, individuals paid little for social security and could get various subsidies from their workplace while retirees were able to get pensions at a certain percentage of their standard pre-retirement wages. Thus social security system in this period had the characteristic that made individuals with both high and low incomes benefited more than they contributed. After the reform, however, individuals pay more for social security, including contributions of pension and medical insurances, certain proportion of medical expenses, and some social security benefits that they should have received but hard to obtain because this system is still on the way of continuous improvement. Therefore, compared with the situation before the reform, it is uncertain whether individuals' benefit in social security system is greater than the contributions or not. We need empirical study to test the level of Chinese residents' income improvement achieved through the income transfer of social security system. Section 8.3 of this chapter will use macro and micro data to estimate the specific income distributive effect of social security system in China.[10]

8.3. Empirical Study on Income Distributive Effect of Social Security in China

8.3.1. *Literature and concepts*

Introducing various social security systems would cause income transfer among people and affect the original social income distribution, thus regulating income gap between different income groups and reducing poverty. Literature of studies in many countries available now has confirmed the

[10]Due to the fact that social security system in rural China (e.g., rural pension insurance) is still in its infancy, we are constrained by the system and data available. It is very hard to analyze, in a quantitative method, the income distributive effect of rural social security system in China. So our empirical study in this section will only target at urban social security system.

role of social security in poverty alleviation and income redistribution.[11] Among them, Barrientos (2007) concludes that emergent tax-financed social security in developing countries holds the promise to make an impact on global poverty and vulnerability, and the main challenge is to ensure this contributes to the development of comprehensive social security systems. Diamond (2004) discusses the role of American Social Security in providing retirement income for older adults and possibilities for reforming the current system to bring it into actuarial balance. Kaseke (2010) argues that the role of social security in South Africa is to prevent and reduce poverty and to promote reintegration. The social security system needs to be strengthened in order to enhance effectiveness.

Studies on China, however, are concentrated on poverty issue and certain social security system. Saunders (2007) compares poverty rates among the aged living by themselves (or with their spouses) in urban China with those existing in a range of other, mainly richer industrial countries. It uses data from a national survey of the aged in China conducted in 2000 and estimates derived from the Luxembourg Income Study (LIS), and the results provide a robust assessment of how well China has performed in reducing poverty among older people. He (2008b) investigated regional and occupational disparities in pension benefits. Wei and Gustafsson (2005) found inequality in medical expenses between urban and rural residents and among China's eastern, middle, and western regions. Ren *et al.* (2004) conducted a macro study on the intergenerational imbalance of the pension system using generational accounting. He (2008a) utilized one year's micro data to examine differences in the income transfer effects among several pension plans. Generally, these studies addressed only one aspect of the social security system, or used only limited data of one year. They did not examine the total redistributive effect of all social security policies or how redistribution affected income inequality.

In this section, we will measure the income redistributive effect of social security system in China using data from macro statistics and micro survey, focusing on effects of social security system on different income

---

[11] Relevant literature: Forster *et al.* (2008); Nelissen (1998, 2000); Diamond (2004); Nelson (2004); Mahler (2006); Barrientos (2007); Kim and Kim (2008); Mastrobuoni (2009); Kaseke (2010), etc.

groups, with special concentration on whether the income transfer of social security has improved income of low-income group and reduced the ratio of poverty. We will also pay attention to the redistributive effect of social security on working population and the inter-generational redistribution role of public pension.

A basic method in estimating the effect of distribution policy is to compare the inequality degree of initial income and redistributed income. Initial income refers to total income earned from personal labour and capital, etc., before redistribution, including income from wages and salaries, business income, interest revenue, commercial insurance premiums, and income in kind, etc. Redistributed income equals initial income deduced by various taxes and fees, plus the granted benefits of social assistance and social security such as pension. Social security benefits include not only cash benefits like pensions, but also paid in kind such as medical and educational services. The taxes and fees consist of income tax, property tax, and social security-related pension insurance premium and medical insurance premium, etc. By comparing the difference between initial income and redistributed income, we could examine the distribution effect of redistributive policy. Specifically, it could be measured by two indicators. The first one is the Musgrave–Sinn Index (MT),[12] a classic method that calculates the absolute change in inequality. If the Gini coefficient of initial income is greater than that of redistributed income, it means that the redistributive policy has reduced income inequality and has a positive redistributive effect; otherwise, that policy has increased income inequality and has a negative redistributive effect. The second indicator is the redistribution coefficient that measures relative changes in inequality. Due to limitations of data accessibility, people often use income data of a particular year to estimate the income distributive effect. However, the annual income data have their own limitations (Rosen, 2008, Chap.12), we should use the lifetime income instead, especially when we estimate the income distributive effect of public pension system.

[12]This method was brought up by Musgrave and Thin (1948). Coronado *et al.* (2000) once estimated EP (effective progression) by adapting this method.

Because the contributions and benefits of pension insurance spread across different life cycles of individuals, the income distributive effect of pension insurance system is reflected throughout their lives. So in addition to analyzing from the view of one specific time point, we also need to analyze the redistributive effect of pension insurance system from the perspective of costs and benefits across one's whole life. Several literature that estimates the income distributive effect of public pension system or during the process of pension reform from a micro point of view dates back to as early as the 1980s (Hurd and Shoven, 1985; Nelissen, 1987). In recent years, Feldstein and Liebman (2002) as well as Borelia (2004) estimated the income distributive effect of public pension reforms in the U.S. and in Italy respectively. Nelissen (1998) discussed in detail and from different perspectives the necessity of using annual income and lifetime income.

8.3.2. *Analysis based on annual data*

In China, transfer income originating from the social security system mainly consists of: cash transfer income, which includes pension, unemployment assistance, social assistance, etc., and in-kind transfer income, which covers medical care, compulsory education, etc. However, public data generally will only provide cash transfer income status. If we could obtain income and expenditure data of urban households over the years, we would be able to characterize the evolution of income distributive effect of social security system in China. Unfortunately, urban household expenditure data released before 2002 did not include social security expenditure such as pension insurance. The items which composed the income statistics differed from those after 2002 as well. Therefore, in this section, we will estimate the income distributive effect of social security system in China by using firstly the micro data available in 1995 and 2002, and then the urban households annual cash income and expenditure statistics of 2002–2008 published by Bureau of Statistics.

The micro data used in this chapter are from the China Households Income Project (CHIP) survey, which was conducted in 1996 and 2003 by the Institute of Economics at the Chinese Academy of Social Sciences. The samples of CHIP data were drawn from the large samples used by the

NBS in its annual household survey.[13] Statistics from CHIP's two surveys covered, respectively, 21,696 people (6931 households) in 11 provinces and cities and 20,632 people (6835 households) in 12 provinces and cities,[14] involving personal characteristics and income of household members and household assets, etc. From the data we can obtain information on individual's income and age, employment status, as well as ownership and industry of the work unit etc.

We will firstly examine the role of social security in reducing urban poverty in China. Referring to the method of Cai, Giles and Meng (2006), we calculate the proportion of families below the poverty line. The poverty line is based on the minimum living standard consumption per capita line calculated by the Ministry of Labour and Social Security for each capital city. The average annual poverty line across the twelve capital cities of CHIP provinces is 2,454 yuan/capita in 2002. In 2002, households with annual household initial income per capita lower than 2,454 yuan account for 17% of all while households with annual redistributed income per capita take up 2% only, indicating that social security contributes a lot to poverty reduction. For 1995, however, the minimum living standard guarantee system was not yet introduced, and we use the relative poverty rate instead due to the absence of minimum living standard consumption per capita line data.

In accordance with the definition in OECD's study on international comparison of income distribution, we consider the group as relatively poor if its income is less than 50% of overall median income. The median income of initial income in 1995 is 4,876 yuan. Households with income lower than 50% of that figure or 2,438 yuan account for 18.2% of all while that rate of households with redistributed income lower than 2,438 decreases to 3.2%, with a decrease rate of 82.4%. In the same way, the relative poor rate of initial income in 2002 we get is 23.6% whereas the relative poor rate based on redistributed income is 6.6%, showing a

[13] For more detailed data explanations, see Li *et al.* (2008).

[14] Survey in 1995 included Beijing, Liaoning, Jiangsu, Guangdong, Anhui, Henan, Hubei, Sichuan, Yunnan, Shanxi and Gansu. Survey in 2002 added Chongqing on the basis of the survey in 1995. For sampling, see He and Sato (2008). In addition, this section has made partial reference to He and Sato (2011).

Table 8.1. Income distributive effect of social security (Gini coefficient and its variations).

		Initial income (A)	Redistributed income 1 (B)	Redistributed income 2 (C)	Redistribution coefficient 1 (A-B)/A	Redistribution coefficient 2 (A-C)/A
1995	all age	0.35437	0.25904	0.35317	26.90%	0.34%
	working age	0.29138	0.25689	0.29052	11.84%	0.30%
	elderly	0.63855	0.26315	0.63514	58.79%	0.53%
2002	all age	0.40592	0.30102	0.40231	25.84%	0.89%
	working age	0.3508	0.3037	0.34686	13.43%	1.12%
	elderly	0.62874	0.28832	0.62626	54.14%	0.39%

Sources: CHIPS (1995, 2002).

Notes: 1. Both initial income and redistributed income are the incomes of family equivalent scale (i.e., household initial income or distributed income divided by the square root of family members).

2. Initial income[i] = salary income + net income of private business + property income + other minor sources of income.

Redistributed income 1 = initial income + social security benefits – social security payments.

Redistributed income 2 = initial income + social security benefits (pension not included) — social security payments (pension insurance excluded).

3. Working age: 16–59 for male and 16–54 for female.

4. Elderly: above 60 for male and above 55 for female according to regulations on retirement age in China.

decrease rate of 72%. Relatively poor ratios before and after redistribution in 2002 increased a little than those in 1995, indicating an increase in low-income population. Xia *et al.* (2007) also found that the relatively poor urban population in China is on the increase.

Secondly, we will examine the different income distributive effects of social security on different groups of people. Table 8.1 shows the Gini coefficient and redistributive coefficient calculated with different incomes in 1995 and 2002. We can see from Table 8.1 that: (a) redistributive coefficients of different groups are all positive, indicating that social security has narrowed inequality and has positive income distributive effect; (b) yet we also notice that the Redistributive Coefficient 2 in the rightmost column in Table 8.1 is much smaller than Redistributive Coefficient 1, implying that, if pension insurance benefits and costs are not included, social security will have little effects on reducing inequality with the maximum of 1.12%, where income distributive effect of social security is almost negligible; (c) on the other hand, we find that no matter in 1995 or in 2002, the Redistributive Coefficient 1 of elderly population is greater than 50% whereas that of working age population is a little more than 10%, indicating that the income distributive effect of social security is mainly reflected in elderly population but has little influence on working age population; and (d) compared with 1995, Gini coefficients of both initial income and distributed income are larger. For working age population especially, the inequality in initial income increased 20%, from the 0.29138 in 1995 to 0.3508 in 2002 while the inequality in distributed income increased 18%, from the 0.25689 in 1995 to 0.3037 in 2002. It shows that, as time goes on, the inequality in urban income distribution is expanding. Although the overall income inequality is reduced through income transfer of social security, such income distribution is not great enough to offset the increase of inequality in initial income, thus making the Gini coefficients of working age population and elderly population in 2002 greater than those in 1995.

The result can be explained in two aspects. The first one is that compared with the situations in 1995, various income shocks (such as being laid-off or unemployed) with which the individuals are faced in 2002 increased initial income inequality. China began its reform on labour market in 1996, creating a large number of laid-off workers. The number of laid-off workers increased from 8,916,337 in 1996 to 14,352,155 in 1997 and 19,771,986 in 1998. From 1999 to 2001, more than 2 million people lost their jobs each year and laid-off workers took up approximately 19% of the urban on-the-job workers of that year. In 2002, the number of laid-off workers fell down slightly, but was still as high as 19,594,870, accounting for 18.56% of urban on-the-job workers in that year.[15] The study by Xia *et al.* (2007) using the CHIP data also showed that in 1995, only 5.55% of all households had laid-off workers, whereas in 2002, that ratio increased almost 3 times and reached 20%. According to the regulations, laid-off workers can get a severance payment from the original work unit. Yet only 18% of households with laid-off workers got

[15] Sources: *China Labour Statistical Yearbook*, 1997–2003.

the payment in 2002. In 2002, average annual income of those laid-off or unemployed was only 29% of that of the working or employed people. Those income shocks undoubtedly increased inequality in initial income distribution.

On the other hand, although by the end of the 1990s China has established social security systems such as Basic Pension Insurance, Unemployment Insurance and Minimum Living Allowance, etc., we can see from Figure 8.1 that in 2002 the coverage of various insurance systems was still very limited. Pension insurance, which had the widest coverage, only covered less than 50% of all. And in 2002, since the government promised to bear the social security responsibility and asked the laid-off workers to end contract with the original work units, aid offered by work units reached the minimum. In fact, however, only a few families in difficulty received aid from social security system. Of all households with laid-off workers in 2002, only 11% had received unemployment benefits and 8% had got the minimum living standard guarantee (Xia *et al.*, 2007). In addition, pension arrears also happened in some areas (Cai, Giles and Meng, 2006) and the insured cannot regularly get their pensions. Thus, while inequality has been reduced through the income transfer of social security system, this improvement is limited. To better understand how the social security system in China plays its role in regulating income distribution, we will examine the payment transfer that people of different income groups get through social security system.

We put all the individual samples into five groups according to the redistributed income of family equivalent scale, from the lowest to the highest (Group 1 is the lowest income group while Group 5 is the highest income group), and then put all the samples into three groups based on the provisions of pension age in China, namely young (labour1), middle-aged (labour2) and the elderly (elderly). We then examine the distributions of social security net benefits among different income groups and among different age groups. Figure 8.2 shows that whether or not in-kind benefits such as the free medical care are included in social security benefits, net social security benefits of age groups other than the young group showed the same distribution trend. In terms of net-benefits that includes all groups of people (NB-total), all income groups get more income transfer from social security system than social security payment and all get

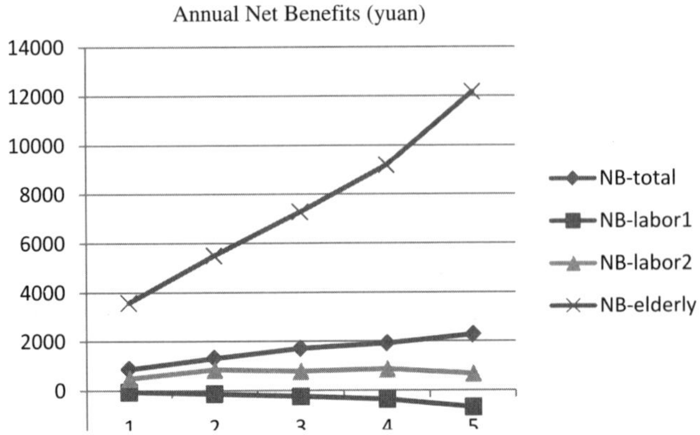

Fig. 8.2a. Net benefits of social security for redistributed income groups (2002, in-kind benefits excluded).

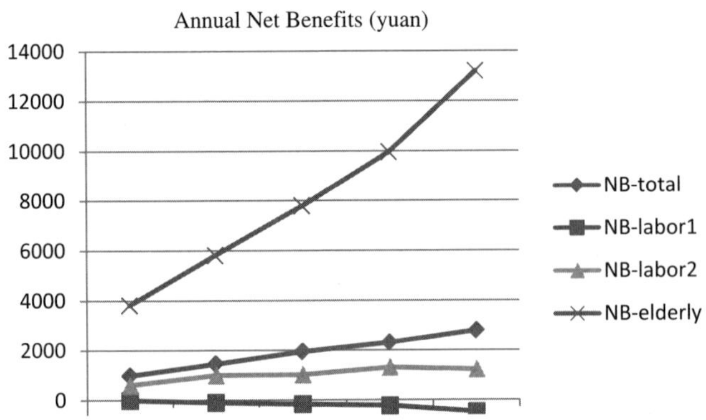

Fig. 8.2b. Net benefits of social security for redistributed income groups (2002, in-kind benefits included).

Sources: CHIPS (1995, 2002).
Notes: NB = social security benefits- social security payments.
Labour1: population aged 16–39.
Labour2: working age people aged above 40.

positive benefits which increase with income. In the elderly group, the net benefits increase most, with the net benefit of highest income group 3.4 times that of the lowest income group among the elderly.

Moreover, for the young group, the net income is negative for both high income group and low income group, which means that their social security payments exceed social security benefits, leading to negative benefits. And these negative benefits increase with income. That is to say, the one with more income will pay more for social security system, indicating that social security has vertical equality among the young population. At the same time, however, we also see that in terms of net benefits, the young and low income group also has a negative net benefit, which indicates that low-income population is also carrying the burden, though limited, of social security costs. It is worth mentioning that though belonging to middle and low income groups, the young population has negative net benefits whereas the middle-aged and elderly populations have positive net benefits. We can discern that social security redistribution in China is mainly aimed at the middle-aged and elderly populations, with few programs for young people. This can also be proved from the composition of fiscal expenditure on social security (see Figure 8.7 in Section 8.4).

People usually expect to see a positive income transfer of social security system, which is to transfer from the high-income group to the low-income group. Focusing on European countries and the U.S, several international comparative studies on income distribution conducted by OECD indicate that redistribution policies in developed countries have the redistributive function to transfer income from the high-income group to the low-income group. In China, however, analysis of both Table 8.1 and Figure 8.2 shows that the redistribution of social security system in China mainly lies in inter-generational income transfer rather than transfer between high-income population and low-income population. At the same time, although middle-aged and elderly people with low income get positive income transfer from social security system, the high-income population benefits more from it. Viewed as a whole, the net benefit of the highest income group is 2.8 times that of the lowest group. For the elderly group, the net benefit of the highest income group is 3.4 times that of the lowest group, indicating that there is an adverse transfer tendency in Chinese urban residents' income obtained from various social security systems. Our calculation based on macro data also confirms the same situation of adverse transfer.

Figure 8.3 shows that, in China, if seen from the view of income transfer in one certain year, the one that benefits most from social security

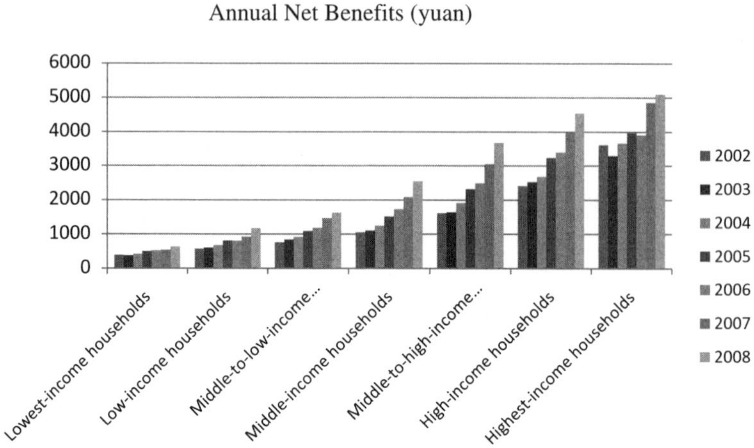

Fig. 8.3. Net benefits of social security for different urban households (2002–2008).

Sources: *Survey on China's Price and the Income and Expenditure of Urban Residents,* 2002–2003, *Yearbook of China's Cities,* 2004, 2005 and *China Urban Life and Price Yearbook,* 2006–2009.

Note: The method to group urban household income is to line all households surveyed according to disposable income per capita, from low to high. And put them into seven groups: the lowest-income households, low-income households, middle-to-low-income households, middle-income households, middle-to-high income households, high-income households and the highest-income households by the ratio of 10% 10%, 20%, 20%, 20%, 10%, and 10%.

system is high-income group instead of low-income group. For each year from 2002 to 2008, the amount of net benefits obtained by families increase with income, and for each year, income transfer that the highest-income households get is 7.4–9.3 times the transfer that the lowest-income households get. Moreover, from the trend of improvement, net benefits for the lowest-income group has slightly increased during 2002–2008, with the absolute benefits far less than that of the middle- and high-income households. Thus the situation of reverse income distribution of urban social security system in China has witnessed no improvement so far.

8.3.3. *Redistributive effects of different pension designs based on lifetime income*

As Rosen (2008) points out, annually-calculated income may not fully reflect one's real economic situation. Especially when we discuss the income distributive effects of pension insurance, annual income cannot tell the real benefits that one gets from the pension insurance system. Since pension insurance system contributions and benefits spread across the different stages of one's life cycle, if we consider his/her income at a young age only, the contributions of pension insurance will surely exceed the benefits, showing a negative net benefit. On the contrary, if we only look at his/her income at an old age, the benefits will be greater than the contributions. Yet it is uncertain that whether the net benefit one gets from pension insurance in a lifetime is positive or negative. Our previous study based on annual income shows that social security system in China has an adverse income transfer. However, if we use the lifetime income to estimate the redistributive effect, will the situation of adverse income transfer still exist? In this section, we will discuss income transfer of China's urban pension insurance system among different income groups of the same generation and between different generations, mainly based on the study by He (2008a).

He (2008a) uses the micro individual data of Liaoning, Guangdong, and Sichuan from the urban household survey in China in 2002, estimates individuals' lifetime income and the lifetime net benefits from the Basic Pension Insurance, and then estimates the income distribution income effects under the 1997 Reform Plan and the 2005 Reform Plan. He (2008a) finds that if calculated according to pension insurance reform plan in 1997, lifelong net benefit of individuals younger than 45 in 2002 decreases as their working income increases. For example, the average lifelong net benefits from pension insurance is –5,277 yuan for the lowest-income-group aged 20–29 whereas –186,866 yuan for the highest-income-group aged 20–29 (for more detailed information, see Table 8.2 in He (2008a)); for individuals aged above 45, however, their lifelong net benefits basically increase with their wage income. In other words, there is an adverse income transfer tendency in group aged above 45 whereas there is no such reverse transfer in group aged below 45 where pension insurance plays the redistribution role of income transfer from the high-income group to the low-income group. Meanwhile, He (2008a) also finds that compared with the plan in 1997, the adverse income transfer through pension insurance system under the plan in 2005 has moved to a lower age-group, from the original above 45 to the above 40 and with a greater

Table 8.2. The level of national pensions over the years (1999-2008).

Year	Benefits-1	Benefits-2	Benefits-3	Rate 1	Rate 2	Rate 3
1999	494	721	725	0.73	0.97	1.00
2000	544	947	871	0.71	1.13	1.08
2001	556	940	894	0.64	0.93	0.93
2002	618	1077	1031	0.62	0.92	0.93
2003	640	1124	1091	0.57	0.86	0.90
2004	667	1223	1154	0.51	0.82	0.84
2005	719	1257	1208	0.48	0.72	0.77
2006	835	1364	1290	0.49	0.70	0.73
2007	947	1717	1576	0.47	0.72	0.73
2008	1121	1822	1663	0.47	0.65	0.67

Sources: *China Human Resources and Social Security Yearbook,* (2009). *China Labour Statistical Yearbook,* (2000–2009).

Benefits-1: Pension Benefits for Enterpsise's Retirees.
Benefits-2: Pension Benefits for Agencies and Organizations' Retirees.
Benefits-3: Pension Benefits for Institutions' Retirees.
Rate1: Benefits-1/Average Wage of urban enterprises's employees (yuan/month).
Rate2: Benefits-2/ Average Wage of urban agencies and Organization (yuan/month)
Rate3: Benefits-3/ Average Wage of urban institution (yuan/month).

degree of reverse transfer. Figure 8.4 shows the different degrees of reverse transfer under the two different plans. We can see that similar with the trend of NB-elderly in Figure 8.3, the lifetime net benefits of different income groups in Figure 8.4 also show a curve tilt to the upper-right direction, which means that the higher income individuals receive, the more they will benefit from pension insurance. Thus the adverse income transfer existing in annual income estimation is also manifest in the lifetime-income estimation.

The above comparison is on the absolute amount of lifetime net benefits of different income groups. What would happen if we compare the lifetime net benefits that individuals get from public pension with their lifetime wage income? Figure 8.5 shows the distribution of the lifetime net income transfer ratio (the ratio of lifetime net benefits to lifetime wage income) in Guangdong under the reform plans in 1997 and in 2005

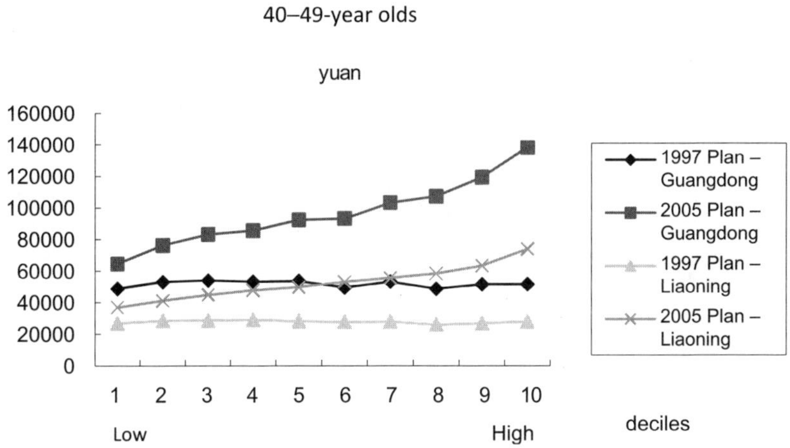

Fig. 8.4a Comparison of lifetime net benefits of annual wage income in deciles.

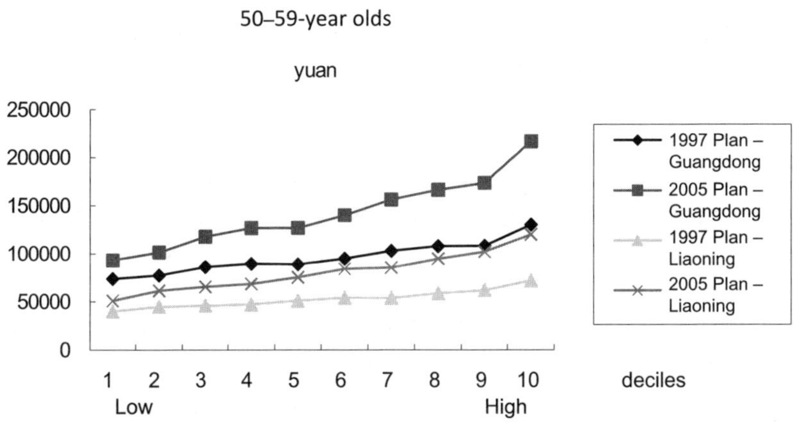

Fig. 8.4b Comparison of lifetime net benefits of annual wage income in deciles.
Source: He (2008a).

respectively,[16] with the vertical axis presenting the average lifetime net transfer ratio of the samples of all age groups and the horizontal axis showing their ages in 2002. We can see from the figure that the lifetime net transfer ratio crosses the horizontal axis at the age of 35 under the

[16]For distributions in Liaoning and Sichuan, see He (2008a).

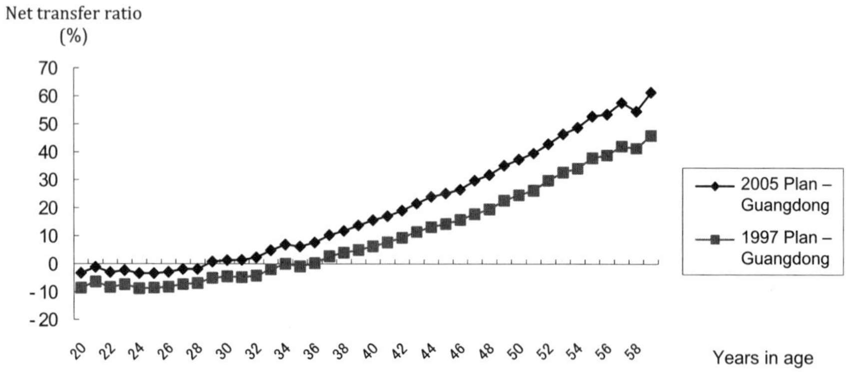

Fig. 8.5 Lifetime net transfer ratio of different age groups.

Source: He (2008a).

Notes: 1. Lifetime net transfer ratio = (Lifetime pension benefits — Lifetime pension contributions) / lifetime wage income∗ 100.

2. Lifetime pension benefits equal the discounted values in 2002; Age equals ages in 2002.

1997 Plan, indicating that individuals aged around 35 receive almost the same lifetime pension benefits as their lifetime pension insurance payments. Individuals younger than 35, however, have more pension payments than pension benefits and approximately 1–10% of their lifetime wage income is transferred to others through public pension system. Meanwhile, generation aged above 35 receives positive income transfer, with the older ones getting the more net benefits. Under the plan in 2005, the lifetime net transfer ratio of all age groups has been improved. Yet, generation aged below 30 still has negative pension net benefits, which means that the young generation suffers economic loss by participating in the public pension system. The income transfer of public pension may affect young people's enthusiasm to participate in public pension system. In addition, we also find that the less-paid employees in the private and individual enterprises and of flexible employment benefit most from participating in the public pension system. Yet they also carry the heaviest burden seen from the lifetime premium ratio, with a ratio of lifetime payments to lifetime income as high as 30–40%. It is unrealistic for them to participate in public pension system. Thus, in order to expand the coverage of public pension and stimulate the enthusiasm and activeness of employees from all kinds of urban enterprises to participate in this system, we need other supporting redistribution measures.

8.4. Problems and Suggestions

At present, Chinese economy is getting further integrated into the global economy and stepping into the period of accelerating industrialization and urbanization development. The social security system construction is faced with many challenges which are mainly reflected in: accelerated industrialization and increased uncertainties in economic life demanding for improvement of various social insurances in risk-sharing; dramatic changes in urban-rural structure highlighting social security issues like pension and medical care in rural areas; oncoming rapid aging population making social security faced with great pressure of how to maintain long-term fund balance; and a deeper impact of globalization leading social security to seeking balance between improving social security and reducing operation costs and maintaining international competitiveness. In this section, we will discuss issues related to improving the income distributive effect of social security and offer some policy suggestions against this background.

8.4.1. *Various imbalances in social security*

8.4.1.1. *Imbalances between urban and rural areas*

In Section 8.3 we have discussed the income distributive effect of urban social security system in China but did not refer to the rural social security system. This is mainly because rural social security system in China is still in its infancy and relevant data are not yet available. Yet we also know from the introduction in Section 8.2 that compared with urban areas, there are few social security programs in rural China, and that the protection level is still very low even if there are such programs. Though empirical analysis in Section 8.3 shows that China's urban social security system reduces the urban income gap to a certain degree, social security may increase the overall income gap if we consider the fact that rural residents get far less transfer income than urban residents. Li and Luo (2007) estimate that if we consider urban social security expenditure as hidden income and add it to income of urban residents, the income gap between urban and rural residents will be further expanded.

Therefore, the income distributive effect of social security will be enhanced if we establish a unified social security system for urban and rural areas. Since the early 1950s, when China established its social security system, there have always been different policies that treat urban and rural areas separately, and it is impossible to carry out, in a limited period of time, a unified social security system. However, we can at least raise social assistance input and improve the rural minimum living standard guarantee. In 2008, the average minimum living standard guarantee in urban areas is 205 yuan per month per capita, which assumes 15.61% of urban household disposable income per month per capita, whereas the average minimum living standard guarantee in rural areas is 82 yuan per month per capita, which accounts for 5% of rural household net income per month per capita. No matter considered in terms of the amount of minimum living standard guarantee or the ratio to average income of residents, the social security in rural areas is less than half of that in urban areas. By the end of 2008, 23.35 million urban residents and 43.05 million rural residents accept the minimum living standard guarantee. If we set a unified standard for urban and rural minimum living standard guarantee, this will undoubtedly reduce rural population in poverty and narrow the urban-rural income gap.

8.4.1.2. *Imbalances among different sectors and areas*

One important conclusion in the empirical analysis of Section 8.3 is that, in terms of both annual income and lifetime income, social security has adverse income transfer among the elderly population and that low-income population gets less net benefits from social security than high-income population. As Song (2010) points out, the reverse income distribution regulating in China's social security is closely related to different institution designs. The macro context is that the social security reform in China is initially designed as a supporting measure for the reform of state-owned enterprises, leading to the situation that the unified protection and treatment of other employees are ignored in urban areas and social security issues are not addressed in rural areas. Here we will look at the differences of pension in different sectors and regions.

Different from the regulations in the U.S or in Japan, public pension benefits in China are paid to the insured themselves only, excluding their dependents or survivors. Thus China's public pension benefits will not differ in different types of family. However it does differ between enterprise and public sector. Table 8.2 lists the monthly pensions of retirees in agencies & organizations, institutions, and enterprises in China. It shows that although public pension benefits for retirees in all three sectors have been improved during the past decade, the pension in agencies & organizations and institutions is obviously greater than that in enterprises — 1.45–1.83 times the latter. There are mainly two reasons for this situation: (a) the way pension benefits are calculated and paid; and (b) the wage difference. As is mentioned above in the system introduction, the methods that enterprises use to calculate and pay insurance benefits are different from those applied by the institutions, agencies and organizations. While pension of enterprise retirees consists of social pooling and personal account which offer a combined 58.5% of targeted replacement ratio, pension of government institution retirees is paid according to a certain percentage (75–100%) of their pre-retirement wage. That ratio is significantly higher than replacement in enterprises. Judged from previously wage statistics, the average wages in agencies & organizations and institutions are both higher than the average wage in enterprises. That is to say, the pension replacement ratio and wage before retirement in agencies & organizations and institutions are higher than those in enterprises. With the concertation of these two factors, the pension benefits of enterprises retirees unsurprisingly differ so much from those of agencies & organizations and institutions retirees.[17]

On the other hand, we can see from Table 8.2 that during the last decade, public pension replacement ratios in enterprises, agencies & organizations, and institutions are generally on the decline. Compared with agencies & organizations and institutions, the enterprises have a relatively less decrease in pension replacement ratio, but their pension

[17] Surely the policy-makers have already started to change this situation by issuing new policies. In 2009, the Ministry of Human Resources and Social Security of the People's Republic of China issued the *Plan for the Reform of Pension Insurance System in Institutions* and carried out pilot projects in Shanxi, Shanghai, Zhejiang, Guangdong and Chongqing. One important aspect of this reform is to reduce the old-age pension benefits of institution retirees to the same level as that of enterprise employees. Meanwhile, the pension of enterprise employee has been raised consecutively in recent years.

replacement is still lower than that in agencies & organizations and institutions. Pension benefits also vary among different regions. In terms of the amount of monthly pension, we will find that in 2008, regions with the highest amount are Tibet (1,754 yuan), Beijing (1,691 yuan) and Shanghai (1,501 yuan) while Hainan (862 yuan), Jiangxi (868 yuan) and Hunan (914 yuan) have the lowest amount of monthly pension.[18] And in terms of replacement ratio which compares pension with the average wage of on-post personnel, in 2008 retirees in most regions can get pension equivalent to 40%–60% of the national average monthly wage of on-post employees in enterprises (Figure 8.2). We can also see that pension replacement ratios of Beijing (72%), Shanghai (64%), and Tibet (74%) are far above the national average ration (47%). However, if compared with the average monthly wage in the region, the pension replacement ratios in Shanghai and Beijing become the lowest ones (33% and 37% respectively) while replacement ratios in other regions mainly remain between 40%-60%. Thus when using pension replacement ratio as an indicator to measure retirees' income, we should pay attention to the specific definition of that indicator. In Chapter 4, He (2008b) estimates various pension replacement ratios using micro data in 1995. Pension replacement ratios of different regions fall between 60–80%. The replacement ratio shown in Figure 8.6 drops 20 percentage points compared with that in 1995, declining even greater than the targeted replacement ratio set by the 1997 reform. With the increasing aging population, how to ensure the income of elderly population is an important issue. So far, pension constitutes the most important income source for urban elderly population, taking up over 85% of total income. If other income sources not are exploited, the decline in pension replacement ratio may increase new elderly poor population. Therefore, when carrying out the public pension reform, we should pay special attention to developing policies that will enhance income transfer towards the elderly population.

In addition, as far as medical insurance is concerned, the central state agencies, most local government offices and many institutions are still carrying out the medical treatment at public expenses. Even those

[18] *China Human Resource and Social Security Yearbook,* 2009.

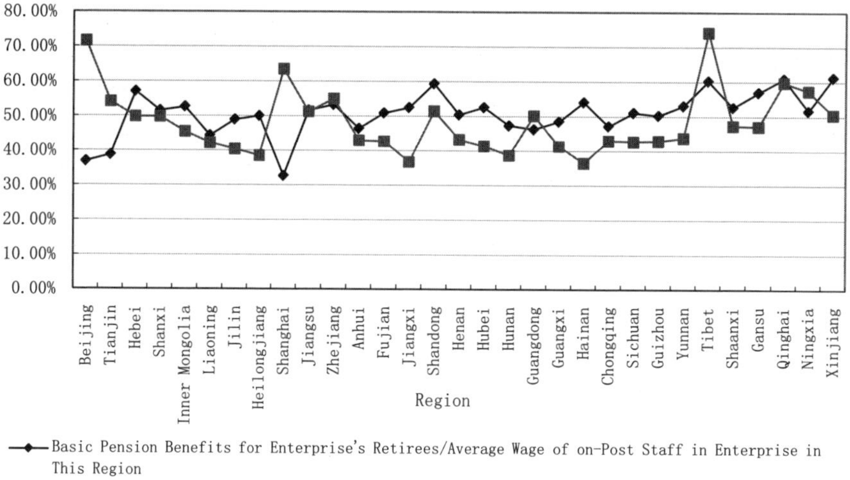

Fig. 8.6. Regional differences in pension replacement ratios measured by different indictors (2008).

Sources: *China Human Resources and Social Security Yearbook*, 2009. *China Labour Statistical Yearbook*, 2009.

government agencies & organizations and public institutions that have already participated in basic medical insurance are still offering economic compensation in forms of medical benefits, partial reimbursement of medical expenses, etc. The enterprise employees enjoying the basic medical insurance, however, can only enjoy medical insurance according to basic medical insurance system, without income compensation in any forms — creating great medical care treatment gap between enterprises and agencies & organizations and institutions (Song, 2010).

Although the limited evidence makes us unable to quantitatively analyze the influence of different social security benefits among different sectors on the role of social security in reducing income gap, we could say that the gap will further weaken the role of social security in narrowing the income gap. Therefore, to change the reverse income distribution of social security in China, one important policy is to promote the combination of different pension and medical insurance systems for different urban employees, and to establish unified basic public pension and medical insurance covering urban employees in all sectors.

With regard to the macro background of urbanization, aging and globalization, construction of social security system cannot surpass the support ability of economic development. For specific policies, we can consider adjusting the fiscal expenditure composition first and developing industries that can absorb rural surplus labour so as to render labour income improvement a primary way to narrow urban-rural divide. Meanwhile, we should set up a unified urban-rural social insurance system that can improve labour mobility between urban and rural areas. When establishing the unified system, we should pay special attention to the setting of protection level. Yuan *et al.* (2009) propose a system design which sets different insurance rates for different income groups and it should become a reference for policy-makers.

8.4.2. *Financing issues*

In our previous empirical study, we find that the redistribution of social security in China mainly targets at the elderly population, with little concentration on young people. We will now verify this situation from the perspective of fiscal expenditure composition.

Figure 8.7 presents ratios of major social security expenditures to total expenditures in several fiscal years. From 1999 to 2008, pensions on the retired of administrative institutions account for the largest proportion of fiscal expenditure and remain relatively stable, at more than 3%. Ratio of financial allowance for social insurance to total expenditure exhibits fairly large fluctuations but an overall upward trend. Beginning from 2002, fiscal expenditures on subsidy on employment, financial allowance for minimum living standard, and disaster relief have increased significantly. However, by the end of 2008, these expenditures only take up just over 0.5% of total expenditure, remaining at a very low level. On the other hand, proportion of financial allowance for social insurance in fiscal expenditure fluctuates between 1.2%–2.6% with an overall upward trend. Average proportion of pensions on the retired of administrative institutions in total expenditure has reached 3.3%, far above the proportions of subsidy on employment, financial allowance for urban minimum living standard, and disaster relief. Judging from such expenditure composition, the social insurance participants and retirees in China are major

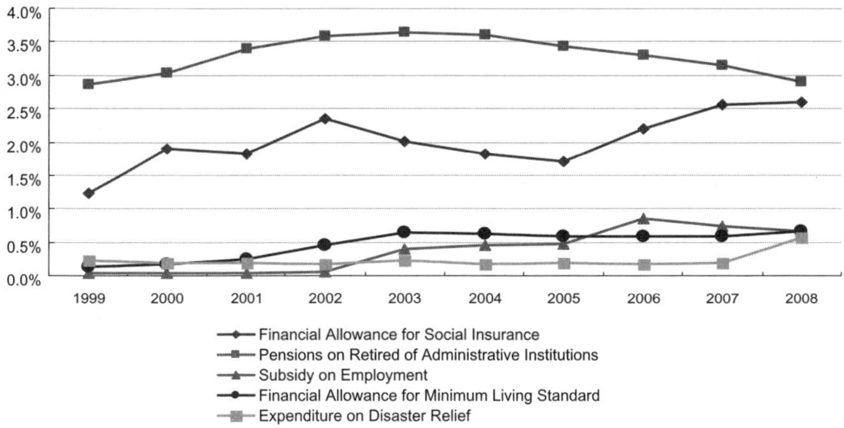

Fig. 8.7. Ratios of major social security expenditures to total expenditures (1999–2008).

Source: *Financial Yearbook of China,* 2009.

beneficiaries of transfer payment of social security system while other group members such as low-income persons and people who have difficult in employment fail to receive significant benefits. Empirical study in Section 8.3 has already verified that point. In order to enhance the income distributive effect of social security system, we need to adjust the financial composition of expenditure on social security and increase financial input for the low-income group through transfer payments such as the minimum living standard guarantee and medical aid.

In addition, our empirical study also finds that public pension in China has an imbalanced inter-generational distribution. At the time of reform, the young generations pay more for public pension than benefits they receive in their life time, which means that young people who participate in public pension system will receive negative income. The reason for this imbalance mainly lies in the flaws of system design. In the 1990s, the public pension reform tried to carry out transformation towards the partially funded pension system. But the system design neglected specific financing channels to solve the pension debts accumulated under the old system and attempted, instead, to use the high fees of new participants to cover those debts. Therefore, the premium rate of the existing public pension system is as high as 28% of individual wages. In order to change this situation, we need to further adjust the system design and require some financial input.

We know from previous introduction that various social insurance systems in China are designed to receive fund from premium instead of fiscal income transfer; however when a financial gap appears in social insurance plan, fiscal revenue will make it up. Therefore, in spite of social assistance like minimum living standard guarantee, fiscal expenditure in China also covers financial allowance for social insurance, subsidy on employment, and other expenses. From 2003 to 2008, expenditure for social safety net and employment effort[19] increases from 271.2 billion yuan to 680.4 billion yuan, with an average growth rate of 16.7% per year. In 2009, expenditure for social safety net and employment effort is 760.668 billion yuan, 11.8% more than that of 2008. In regard to the pension insurance, since the reform in 1997, the pension insurance fund has been unable to make both ends meet. Financial allowance for public pension fund has increased from more than 5 billion yuan in 1997 and over 10 billion yuan in 1998 to 132.629 billion yuan in 2009, and further to 156.1 billion yuan in 2010,[20] an increase of 30 times over the short period of more than ten years. Therefore, though China has established public pension plan based on contributions of employers and employees, the actual operation of the system is still dependent on government's financial support. With further population aging, long-term balance of public pension fund is faced with great challenge, especially under the public pension reform in 2005 that has increased public pension benefits for people of all generations and improved the imbalance in inter-generation income distribution. Under this program, however, the pressure of financing public pension will increase, thus making the financial

[19]Expenditure for social safety net and employment effort: It refers to the spending of government on social safety net and employment, including the expense on administration of social safety net and employment, civil affairs, budgetary subsidy on the social insurance funds, subsidy on National Social Security Fund, retirees of administrative units and institutions, subsidy on enterprise reform, subsidy on employment effort, pension, placement of ex-serviceman, social welfare, the handicapped undertakings, the system of cost of living allowances for urban residents, other urban social relief, rural social relief, living relief of natural disasters, affairs of Red Cross Society, etc.

[20]*The Fourth China Social Security Forum*, Chapter 3, He (2008b).

sustainability of the system problematic. According to simulation analysis of various reform plans on China's public pension by Oksanen (2010), if no further adjustments are to be made, the current system would not exhibit financial sustainability. And any adjustments to the system could not ignore the issue of inter-generational distribution. As Barr and Diamond (2009) points out, public pension system, based either on fund accumulation system or on pay-as-you-go model, must make a choice regarding inter-generational distribution. Policy that transforms towards the fund accumulation system by raising payment of the younger generation through reform or reducing benefits of pension for the elder generation at the time of reform is to distribute from current generations to future generations. We can see that China chooses to raise the payment without reducing benefits of pension. The transitional costs of public pension system are mainly shouldered by generations that have not yet entered the age for receiving pensions. In 2000, China established the National Social Security Fund and has accumulated 282.769 billion yuan. Its main sources of funding are the central budgetary appropriations and the reduction or transfer of possession of state-owned shares in listed companies. If national social security fund becomes one funding source for public pension, it will partially narrow the pension funding gap, lower the public pension contributions and relieve the public pension burden of the younger generation. Moreover, to solve the problem of funding gap by issuing government bonds could also distribute the transitional costs among the future generations and improve the imbalanced inter-generational distribution of public pension.

8.5. Conclusion

After more than half a century's development, the urban social security system in China has been rather comprehensive, with pension, medical care, unemployment, work-related injuries, and maternity social insurances to satisfy the major insurance demand of birth, old age and illness, etc. It also covers the minimum living standard guarantee targeting at the poor and social assistance for other special groups of people. In contrast, rural social security is relatively under-developed. China is at the stage of rapid industrialization and urbanization where the contradictions in distribution are high-lightened and the urban-rural income gap is expanding. In this context, establishing and improving rural social security system will help to give full play to the distribution role of social security system in narrowing income gap and to promote the balanced development of Chinese economy. Chinese government has already realized the importance of developing rural social security system in this period; and upon entering the 21st century, the government has enacted a series of social security policies for rural areas, established the R-MLSG System, the New Rural Co-operative Medical System and Rural Medical Assistance System, and has also begun the rural public pension pilot after 2009. We can say that China has made remarkable achievements in the construction of social security system. Yet is the existing social security system really playing the role of regulating income distribution that people expect and is it really narrowing the income gap? In this chapter, we carry out empirical study on income distributive effect of social security system using macro and micro data available. We find that, from the aspect of its income distribution role, many problems still exist in China's social security system development, such as the adverse income transfer of social security among the middle-aged and elderly population, too little financial investment in workforce employment security which leads to too heavy social security burden on working population, great differences in benefits between urban and rural social security systems, the imbalanced inter-generational distribution of public pension, etc. These problems not only affect people's incentives in participating the insurances and the expansion of the system, but also will greatly weaken the redistribution role of social security system in regulating income distribution and narrowing the income gap. Therefore, China's reform on social security system is far from perfect. To implement policies that eliminate the divisions of social security systems between urban and rural areas as well as among different sectors inside urban areas, reduce the social security burden of low-income population with the help of tax policy, and enhance income transfer towards the low-income group will be the direction of the reform. And how to develop and execute relevant policies to improve the income distributive effect of social security system will remain major challenges for our future study.

References

Atkinson, A.B., Rainwater, L. and Smeeding, T. (1995). *Income Distribution in OECD Countries: Evidence from the Luxembourg Income Study*. Paris: Organisation for Economic Cooperation and Development.

Barr, N. and Diamond, P. (2009). "Reforming Pensions: Principles, Analytical Errors and Policy Directions." *International Social Security Review*, 62(2), 5–29.

Barrientos, A. (2007), "The Role of Tax-Financed Social Security." *International Social Security Review*, 60(2–3), 99–117.

Borelia, M. (2004). "The Distributional Impact of Pension System Reforms: An Application to the Italian Case." *Fiscal Studies*, 25, 415–437.

Cai, F., Giles, J. and Meng, X. (2006). "How Well Do Children Insure Parents Against Low Retirement Income? An Analysis Using Survey Data from Urban China." *Journal of Public Economics*, 90(12), 2229–2255.

Chen, S. and Ravallion, M. (2004). "How Have the World's Poorest Fared Since the Early 1980s." Discussion Paper WPS3341, World Bank.

Chen, S. and Ravallion, M. (2007). "Absolute Poverty Measures for the Developing World, 1981–2004." *Proceedings of the National Academy of Science of the United States of America*, 104/43, 16757–62.

Chen, S. and Ravallion, M. (2008). "China is Poorer than We Thought, But No Less Successful in the Fight Against Poverty." Policy Research Working Paper 4621, World Bank.

Chen, S., Ravallion, M. and Y. Wang (2006). "Di Bao: A Guaranteed Minimum Income in Urban China?" Policy Research Working Paper Series 3805, World Bank.

Coronado, J.L., Fullerton, D.D. and Glass, T. (2000). "The Progressivity of Social Security." NBER Working Paper 7520.

Diamond, P. (2004). "Social Security." *AER*, 94(1), 1–24.

Drouin, A. and Thompson, L.H. (2006). "Perspectives on the Social Security System of China." Extension of Social Security Working Paper No. 25.

Feldstein, M. and Liebman, J.B. (eds) (2002). *The Distributional Aspects of Social Security and Social Security Reform*. Chicago: University of Chicago Press.

Feng, J., He, L.X. and Sato, H. (2011). "Public Pension and Household Saving: Evidence from Urban China." *Journal of Comparative Economics*, http://dx.doi.org/10.1016/j.jce.2011.01.002.

Forster, M.F. and D'Ercole, M.M. (2005). "Income Distribution and Poverty in Selected OECD Countries in the Second Half of the 1990s." OECD Social, Employment and Migration Working Papers No.22.

He, L.X. (2008a). "The Distributional Effects of Public Pension Reform in Urban China." *Frontiers of Economics in China*, 3(2), 55–278.

He, L.X. (2008b). *The Public Pension System Reform in China: An Institutional and Empirical Analysis of the Economic System Transition Period* (In Japanese). Tokyo: University of Tokyo Press.

He, L.X., and Sato, H. (2008). "Social Security and Income Redistribution in Urban China 1995–2002." Hitotsubashi University Fukino Research Project Discussion Paper Series No. 004.

He, L.X. and Sato, H. (2011). "Income Redistribution in Urban China by Social Security System — An Empirical Analysis Based on Annual and Lifetime Income." Hitotsubashi University Global COE Programs Discussion Paper.

Hurd, M.D. and Shoven, J.B. (1985). "The Distributional Impact of Social Security." In D.A. Wise (ed.), *Pensions, Labour, and Individual Choice*. University of Chicago Press.

Kaseke, E. (2010). "The Role of Social Security in South Africa." *International Social Work*, 53, 159–168.

Kim, S.K. and Kim, S.-W. (2008). "Developmentalism in Korea: A Useful Tool for Explaining the Role of Social Security in the Reduction of Poverty and Inequality." *Asian Social Work & Policy Review*, 2, 91–110.

Li, S. and Luo, C.L. (2007). "Re-Estimating the Income Gap Between Urban and Rural Households in China." (In Chinese). *Journal of Peking University (Philosophy And Social Sciences)*, 2, 111–120.

Li, S., Luo, C.L., Wei, Z. and Yue, X.M. (2008). "Appendix: The 1995 and 2002 Household Survey: Sampling Methods and Data Description." In B. Gustafsson, S. Li and T. Sicular (eds.), *Inequality and Public Policy in China*. New York: Cambridge University Press.

Luo, C.L. (2010). "Poverty Dynamics in Rural China" (in Chinese). *Economic Research Journal*, 5, 123–138.

Mahler, V. (2006). "Income Redistribution by the State: A Comparative Analysis of the Developed World." Conference Papers, American Political Science Association.

Mastrobuoni, G. (2009). "Labour Supply Effects of the Recent Social Security Benefit Cuts: Empirical Estimates Using Cohort Discontinuities." *Journal of Public Economics*, 12.

Musgrave, R.A. and Thin, T. (1948). "Income Tax Progression, 1929–48." *The Journal of Political Economy*, 56, 498–514.

Nelissen, J. (1987). "The Redistributive Impact of the General Old Age Pension Act on Lifetime Income in Netherlands." *European Economic Review*, 31, 1419–1441.

Nelissen, J.H.M. (1998). "Annual Versus Lifetime Income Redistribution by Social Security." *Journal of Public Economics*, 68, 223–249.

Nelissen, J.H.M. (2000). "Lifetime Income Redistribution by Social Security." *Journal of Population Economics*, 8, 89–105.

Nelson, K. (2004). "Mechanisms of Poverty Alleviation: Anti-Poverty Effects of Non-Means-Tested and Means-Tested Benefits in Five Welfare States." *Journal of European Social Policy*, Nov.

Oksanen, H. (2009). "The Chinese Pension System — First Results on Assessing the Reform Options." Directorate-General for Economic and Financial Affairs, European Commission. Mimeo.

Oshio, T. (2002). "Intra-Age, Inter-Age and Lifetime Income Redistribution." *Journal of Population and Social Security*, 1, S36–S49.

Oshio, T. (2005). "Social Security and Intra-Generational Redistribution of Lifetime Income in Japan." *Japanese Economic Review*, 56, 105–139.

Ravallion, M. and Chen, S. (2007). "China's (Uneven) Progress Against Poverty." *Journal of Development Economics*, 82(1), 1–42.

Ren, R., Jiang, Y., Xu, N. and Lin, L. (2004). "Generational Accounting in China and Pension Reform from the Perspective of Generational Accounting" (in Chinese). *Economic Research Journal*, 9, 118–128.

Rosen, H.S. and Gayer, T. (2007). *Public Finance*, 8th ed. Burr Ridge, Il.: McGraw-Hill/Irwin Companies, Inc.

Rosen, H.S. and Gayer, T. (2008). *Public Finance*, 8th ed. (in Chinese). Beijing: China Renmin University Press.

Saunders, P. (2007). "Comparing Poverty Among Older People in Urban China Internationally." *China Quarterly*, 190, 451–465.

Sicular, T., Yue, X.M., Gustafsson, B. and Li, S. (2007). "The Urban-Rural Income Gap and Inequality in China." *Review of Income and Wealth*, 53(1), 93–126.

Song, X. (2010). http://economy.caing.com/2010-06-13/100152366.html.

Wei, Z. and Gustafsson, B. (2005). "Inequity in Financing China's Healthcare" (in Chinese). *Economic Research Journal*, 12, 26–34.

World B and (2003). China Country Economic Memorandom: Promoting Growth with Equity." Document of the World Bank, Report No. 24169-CHA.

Xia, Q., Song, L. and Simon, A. (2007). "Trends and Patterns of Urban Poverty in China." (in Chinese). *Economic Research Journal*, 9, 96–111.

Yuan, Z., Li, Z. and Feng, J. (2009). "A Study on the Proper Level of Old-aged Social Insurance During China's Urbanization" (in Chinese). *Nankai Economic Studies*, 4, 3–14.

Appendix. Contribution and benefit structure in pension plan 1997–2005.

Item		Old participants	In-between participants	New participants
Definition		Personnel retired before 1997's reform	Personnel retired after 1997's reform bus started working before 1997's reform	Personal started working after 1997's reform
Contribution	Pension plan 1997	N/A	28% of wage (contributed jointly by employee and employer), 11% of which is reserved in individual account	Same as the in-between group
	Pension plan 2005	N/A	28% of wage (contributed jointly by employee and employer), 8% of which is reserved in individual account	Same as the in-between group
Benefit	Pension plan 1997	Same as the pre-reform terms, which is X% of the individual standard retirement wage	Basic pension (20% of last year's average monthly wage of local employees) + Individual account pension (the amount of individual account savings/120)+ Transitional pension (average indexed monthly earning × modulus × years without an individual account)	Basic pension (20% of last year's average monthly wage of local employees) + Individual account pension (the amount of individual account savings/120)
	Pension plan 2005	Same as the pre-reform terms, which is X% of the individual standard retirement wage	Basic pension (Years of contribution* 1%0.5 (average indexed monthly earnings + last year's average monthly wage of local employees))+ Individual account pension (the amount of individual account savings / months of payment scheduled (depends on average life expectancy of urban population at the time of retirement & age of retirement)+ Transitional pension (average indexed monthly earnings × years without an individual account)	Basic pension (Years of contribution*1%0.5 (average indexed monthly earnings + last year's average monthly wage of local employees)) + Individual account pension the amount of individual account savings / months of payment scheduled(depends on average life expectancy of urban population at the time of retirement & age of retirement)

CHAPTER 9

THE CHALLENGE OF HOUSING AFFORDABILITY IN URBAN CHINA

*Jie Chen**

9.1. Introduction

There are many reasons for the public to care about housing affordability (Quigley and Raphael, 2004). First, the expenditure on housing consists of the biggest single item in the budget of most households. Thus even a small variation of the financial burden of housing expenditure has substantial impacts on household welfare as well as the operation of aggregate economy. Second, access to a decent and at the same time affordable housing is the prerequisite for individuals to live and work in cities. Though the notion of "housing affordability" remains vague in the literature, it is commonly agreed that there exists a minimum socially acceptable standard of affordability for any given society at any given time (Bertaud, 2009). In most advanced countries governments are carrying a public-recognized commitment to ensure "a decent housing for every household at a cost within their means". That is, it has gradually formed a consensus that everyone is entitled the right to be accommodated with socially imposed minimum standard of living conditions.

In recent years, housing affordability has become a top acute social issue in China. Although providing affordable housing to every household is a tremendous task faced by all countries, it is especially challenging in

*Associate Professor, School of Management, Duty Director for Center for Housing Policy Studies, Fudan University; Email: jiech@fudan.edu.cn; Postal address: Guoshun Road 670, Shanghai 200433. Tel: 0086 21 25011106; Fax: 0086 21 65642411.

China. This is not only because China has the largest population in the world, but also because Chinese urban housing sector has evolved from a government-dominated welfare system to a market-driven one in little more than a decade (Zhang, 2000; Rosen and Ross, 2000; Chiu, 2001; Zhao and Bourassa, 2003). During the past 20 years, China has made impressive record in reforming its urban housing sector and has improved the housing conditions for hundreds of millions of households within such a short time (Bertaud, 2009). But the upsurge in house prices since 2001 in most major Chinese cities has spurred growing doubts about whether the market is really more appropriate than the welfare system as the primary allocation mechanism for urban housing (see Shen, 2006, for example).

This chapter aims to provide new insights into housing affordability in urban China. Commonly used point-in-time (static) measures cannot capture fully the nature of affordability in a dynamic transitional system with growing incomes, prices and an emphasis on mortgaged housing-ownership. In this chapter we attempt to improve these indicators by employing a dynamic analysis that enables us to identify patterns of affordability as housing businesses progress. Through this methodological development, the chapter also aims to contribute to the international literature on housing affordability.

The chapter is organized as follows: Section 9.2 provides an overview of housing reform in urban China and some indicators of affordability for the general population of permanent residents in China. Section 9.3 discusses the conceptual issues associated with the definition of housing affordability and alternative ways of measuring it. Empirical findings are presented in Section 9.4, together with a discussion of policy implications. The final section contains our conclusions.

9.2. Housing Reform and Housing Market Development in China

9.2.1. *Housing reform in China*

Residential housing was treated as a welfare good rather than a commodity in China during the era of the planned economy. Before 1978, most people in urban China were housed by the welfare housing system in which the government, or state-owned enterprises, produced and allocated housing almost free of charge (Zhang, 2000). However, the system could not be sustained in economic terms. Before 1978, the government on average spent RMB 25 billion yuan on new housing construction and another RMB 10 billion on maintenance but it received only RMB 1 billion from rents (Cui, 1991). Consequently, investment in welfare housing was consistently incredibly low (*ibid.*).

In the 1980s and until 1998, there was a small-scale programme of public housing sales. Since then there has been widespread housing privatization in urban China. In March 1998, partly to stimulate the economy following the 1997 Asian financial crisis, Chinese Premier Zhu Rongji introduced a series of radical reforms, which involved the rapid phasing out of the welfare housing system, with urban residents encouraged either to buy their current housing from the state-owned enterprises or purchase housing from the market. Crucially, all new residential housing units built after 1 January 1999 were to be sold on the open market and state-owned enterprises were prohibited from building any more welfare housing for their employees. This policy finally paved the way for the development of a market-oriented housing sector in urban China. Whereas in 1997, some 80% of urban housing was in the public sector, by 2002 around 80% was privately-owned (Wang, 2007).

Nonetheless, as the land in China is still nationalized according to the law, all residents and companies can only "rent" land or buy the rights of land use for a specified tenure term, but not be able to "buy" land itself. Thus, in the law, dwelling purchasers can hold the legal rights of property only up to a certain period, for example, 70 years for residential property, 30–50 years for commercial building, and 20 years for industrial building. The occupants can transfer their property, together with the rights of land use, to the third party at market prices during the tenure period. However, it is still an unsolved legal issue over which people are puzzled: what will happen when the 70-year tenure of residential land use comes to the end Should housing purchasers need to pay a new payment for the land use? Will the right of land use get renewed automatically? The government needs time to deal with this issue.

9.2.1. *Housing market in urban China*

Anyway, despite the uncertainty of property's legal rights and other institutional obstacles, Chinese housing market has been growing at a dazzling speed for more than one decade. For instance, the trading space of first-hand housing in urban China remarkably increased more than 10 times between 1997 and 2009, rising from 78.64 million square meters at the end of 1997 to 852.94 million square meters at the end of 2009. For the same period, the market value of first-hand housing market skyrocketed from RMB 140.7 billion to RMB 3,815.7 billion, achieving an amazing growth of 27 folds. If all types of housing included, the market value was RMB 43,944 billion at the end of 2009, which was 24 times that of 1997. At the same time, the housing price keeps a strong upward trend since 1991 except a slight downward adjustment in 2008 due to shocks of the global financial crisis (Figure 9.1).

By any standard, residential housing industry is currently playing a significant role in mainland China's economy. Especially for the past two years, it has contributed a very proactive function in tacking with the global financial crisis. According to the National Bureau of Statistics of

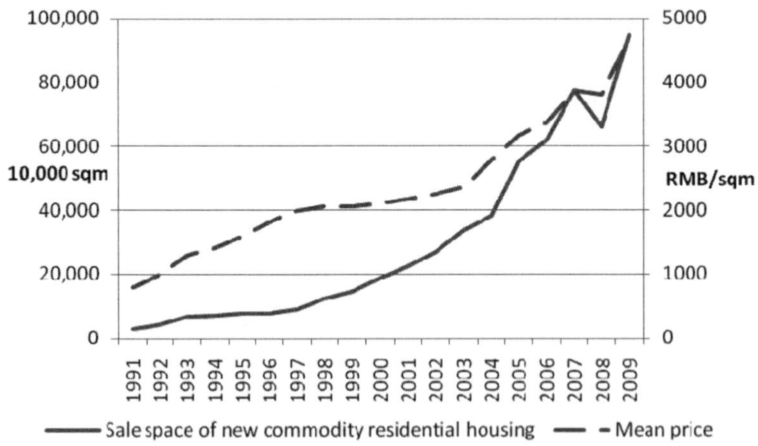

Fig. 9.1. Sale space and prices of new commodity residential housing in China, 1991–2009.

Source: *China Statistics Yearbook* (various years).

China, the investment in the Chinese housing sector was RMB 3.62 trillion in 2009 (including non-residential housing investment), contributing a share of 16.1% in total fixed investment. Moreover, the share of housing investment as percentage of GDP has been continuously increasing and it was 10.64% in 2009, which was almost 2.5 times that of 1997.

The great increase of housing supply leads to substantial additions of housing stock and significant improvements of housing conditions for average households in urban China. For example, the living space per capita in urban China averagely grows with 1 sqm annually since 1998. By the end of 2009, the average space per capita in urban China was 30 m^2, which was 4 times that of 1978.

As suggested by Table 9.1, the home ownership ratio in urban China is fairly high and does not have substantial differences over different income groups. This is largely attributable to the massive wave of privatization of public housing in the late 1990s (see discussion above). That is the first "secret" that why the majority of Chinese urban households can survive under seemingly intolerably high housing prices without producing many homeless people. Consequently, the affordability issue in urban China mainly refers to the one faced by the new generation, the generation that formed independent family after the privatization reform. However, as the share of new market entrants in the total urban population grows over

Table 9.1 Housing situations in urban China in 2005 (%).

Income category	Lowest income, 10%	Lower income, 10–20%	Lower middle, 20–40%	Middle income, 40–60%	Upper middle, 60–80%	High income, 80–90%	Highest income, top 10%
Share (%)	10	10	20	20	20	10	10
Home ownership (%)	76.3	81.9	85.0	87.2	88.3	88.7	90.0
With second housing (%)	3.4	4.6	5.3	7.0	9.9	13.7	21.0
Space size of housing (m^2)	69.5	75.0	79.6	84.4	88.5	92.6	99.5
Housing value (10,000 RMB)							

Source: *The 2005 Household Survey* by China Statistics Bureau, REICO Database.

time, the affordability issue becomes increasing acute and needs careful analysis. This chapter focuses on the housing affordability of new market entrants.

9.2.3. *Housing mortgage market in China*

The first mortgage in China was issued in 1986, but it is only since the 1998 housing reform that the market has grown significantly, with funding coming mainly from retail deposits. Since the 1998 abolishment of welfare housing system, as a key tool to mobilize households' housing purchase power, housing mortgage loans have been fervidly promoted to common urban households and quickly become the primary financing tool for Chinese citizen's housing purchase. The nominal benchmark mortgage rate of 5-and-plus-year mortgage was cut heavily from 12.4% in 1997 to 5.04% in 2000 and kept relatively stable with a fluctuation of less than 1.5% points since then.

Housing mortgage service in China is currently mainly provided by commercial banks. The flourish of this service not only injects liquidity into the housing market, but also brings massive profitable business opportunities to commercial banks. The housing mortgage loan of China has developed rapidly since 1999, and attracted more and more attention due to its diversified risk and low default rate. Commercial banks are now legally independent, though the sector is still dominated by five state-owned banks and the banking system has become an important instrument for the government to finance its policy lending targets.

The development performance of Chinese mortgage business since 1997 is truly spectacular. According to the People's Bank of China, the outstanding balance of housing mortgage has enlarged by more than 250 times between 1997 and 2009, soaring from RMB 19 billion to RMB 4,760 billion. At the end of March 2010, the housing mortgage loan consisted 12.52% of all RMB banking loan balance and its share in the long-term banking loan was 21%.

When the banking loans to developers are included, the outstanding balance of the property-related credit stood at 8,180 billion at the end of March 2010, and consisted 19% of total banking loan balance and 33% of long-term loan. The high dependence of banking loans on housing activities composes a great systematic risk for the whole Chinese financial system and is an important driving reason behind the Cabinet's recent cooling-down policy.

The terms of mortgage loans are currently regulated as follows: the maximum loan-to-value ratio is 80% (of the lower of the appraisal value or purchase price) (Deng *et al.*, 2005), and the maximum mortgage term is 30 years. Mortgage interest rates are controlled and set to track central bank rates (*ibid.*). While new products are emerging, the self-amortizing mortgage remains the most common.

Commercial banks dominate the primary housing mortgage market in China and the four state-owned banks, "the big four", are the largest market leaders. In 2004, the total amount of housing mortgage provided by the four state-owned banks was RMB 1.27 trillion, accounting for 80% of total housing mortgage loans in China. The non-performing rate of housing mortgage was 1.5% , substantially lower than the non-performing rate of other loan services (People's Bank of China, 2005).

In the literature, the mortgage depth, or the ratio of mortgage balance as percentage of GDP, is often employed to assess the risk status of housing mortgage business. At the end of 2009, the mortgage depth in China was 14.19% and almost 10 times the level ten years ago (see Figure 9.2). However, compared to those of the advanced economies where the ratio of mortgage/GDP is usually above 40%, Chinese mortgage market still has a large room to develop. In addition, taking account of the low ratio of mortgage in relative to household savings, Chinese mortgage business is fairly safe.

9.3. The Concept and Methodology of Housing Affordability

This chapter aims to assess the ability of new market entrants to access and afford owner-occupied housing in urban China. However, although "Housing affordability" has become a widely used term in public debate and policy-making, it remains an ill-defined and contested concept (Stone, 2006a). In essence, although "housing as a right" is widely recognized (Hartman, 1998), what can be termed the "housing problem" or "housing

Fig. 9.2. The mortgage depth and mortgage rates, 1997–2009.

Sources: People's Bank of China; *China Statistics Yearbook* (various years).

Note: The mortgage rate refers to the benchmark mortgage rate for mortgages with a maturity of 5 and above years.

poverty" is unclear (Linneman and Megbolugbe, 1992). With an eye-catching title "house poor or simply poor?", Thalmann (2003) asked whether the "housing problem" has any meaning that is distinct from the general problem of income poverty. The principal justification for treating housing separately lies in its distinctive and essential characteristics: house prices and rents vary greatly even within localities and these differences are likely to persist due to relatively low supply elasticity (Stone, 2006a). Moreover, it is often difficult to adjust or even select consumption levels appropriate to income due to housing's indivisibility and high transaction costs (Hancock, 1993). Despite on-going attempts to reach a consensus on the meaning of affordability (Field, 1997), there remains a tension between, for example, the "cannot pay" economic principle (Hancock, 1993) and the "needs" principle (Whitehead, 1991). Many economists prefer to define housing affordability as a household's ability to meet housing costs without imposing excessive constraints on non-housing consumption, hence any definition of housing affordability should reflect the opportunity cost between housing and non-housing consumption (Hancock, 1993).

9.3.1. *Price or expenditure to income ratio approach*

The price or expenditure-to-income ratio indicator is the most widely used measure of housing affordability (Hulchanski, 1995). Typically, this indicator employs the ratio of median/mean market price of a standardized housing unit to median/mean (either before-tax or disposable) household/family income. The expenditure-to-income indicator is intuitively straightforward and technically simple. It has been applied widely to compare geographically different housing markets (Bogdon and Can, 1997) and is frequently used in international comparisons (Thalmann, 1999).

We can distinguish between the house-price-to-income indicator, which can be used as an indicator of access to housing, and the expenditure-to-income ratio, which is used as an indicator of affordability once access has been attained.

The house-price-to-income measure can be seen as a pre-condition for affordability in a housing system such as China's where mortgaged housing-ownership is becoming more important for new households. Its utility lies in the ability to relate it to the general terms of mortgage availability, i.e. the multiple of earnings that can be borrowed within a given maximum loan-to-value ratio. As such it can perform a useful role as an indicator of the ability of households to access finance with which to purchase owner-occupied housing. When allied to lender underwriting conventions the price-to-income measure attains a status of quasi-externalized validity. Nonetheless, even when used in this way, the price-to-income ratio performs the role of surrogate affordability indicator, since it arises from the lender's assessment of the borrower's likelihood of default.

The expenditure-to-income ratio follows naturally from the price-to-income ratio, once access to housing-ownership has been achieved. Beyond its enduring intuitive appeal to policy makers this measure has some clear deficiencies. Of these Stone's (2006a) claim that it implies that either the (absolute) income required to finance non-housing needs diminishes as income falls with no minimum, or that the ratio must decrease to zero as incomes fall is the most powerful (for further discussions see Hancock, 1993; Hulchanski, 1995; Thalmann, 2003).

Yet, while some critics of the (single) ratio approach have suggested that it is inequitable because it allows a greater disposable income for better-off households (Whitehead, 1991), the residual income approach (discussed below) may well engender a rather parsimonious attitude to housing affordability (which may be reflected in Stone's label of *shelter*-induced poverty).

9.3.2. *Residual income approach*

An increasing number of scholars are advocating the "residual income" approach to assess the extent of housing affordability (Stone, 2006b). The residual income approach assumes that housing costs become a problem only when income after housing expenditure falls below the amount required to support a socially acceptable or desirable level of non-housing consumption. This level of poverty, which develops from the concept of shelter poverty (Nunez, 1994; Bratt, 1995; Armenoff, 1998; Stone, 2006a), has been identified alternatively as housing-induced poverty (Kutty, 2005).

The residual income approach clearly has a number of merits. First, it relates to both the individual housing decision and the socially desirable level of consumption. Some rich households may spend 80% of their income on luxury housing, but still maintain high living standards. This could not be regarded as a social problem. In contrast, some extremely poor families may struggle to maintain a basic level of subsistence even if they spend a relatively low proportion of their income on housing. In the middle, some households' under-consumption of housing services (compared to a socially-desirable level) may simply relate to personal utility preferences rather than budget constraints. Hancock (1993) refers to such individuals as "can pay, won't pay". These individuals certainly should be distinguished from those who "can't pay". Second, the residual income approach is useful in guiding policymakers to identify the target level of "maximum affordable" housing expenditure. And third, the residual income approach helps policymakers to set the appropriate level of housing assistance for poor households.

The key challenges with the residual concept lie in its implementation. As with the ratio approach it depends first on the (normative) identification of a socially acceptable level of housing consumption (in terms of size and quality) and an assessment of the likelihood of its attainment.

9.3.3. *Dynamic approach*

A limitation of the way in which affordability is measured (rather than conceived) is that it occurs at a particular point in time. This may be called a static approach, and is adequate for identifying the possibility of access to mortgaged housing-ownership for new households in any given year.

But it is evidently inadequate for identifying on-going affordability given that incomes and housing costs change over time. In a housing market like China where mortgaged housing-ownership is becoming more important, where there has been (until very recently) strong house price growth, and where incomes are rising rapidly, although unevenly, point-in-time measures of affordability are liable to disguise more than they reveal. The well-known tendency for mortgaged housing-ownership costs to be front-end loaded (Hills, 1991) exacerbates the problem.

We therefore propose a methodological development by introducing a dynamic element into the measurement of affordability: A *"point-of-entry" trend* can be employed to identify the initial affordability of housing when households enter the market in any one year. A *"cohort" trend* can be used to identify the way in which affordability evolves for each cohort of entrants. These can be used to enhance both the indicators of "burden" and "housing-induced poverty".

9.3.4. *Setting up and data source*

Our analysis and simulations are based on actual income levels and distributions applied to the purchase of housing at the mean price for a standard size. Income data are obtained from the *China Statistics Yearbook* (1991–2010), and are drawn from an annual sample household survey conducted by the Survey Office of the National Bureau of Statistics of China (NBSC). During the period under review China experienced rapid economic growth. Between 1991 and 2009 average disposable income per capita in urban China grew by 184% (adjusted for CPI), although its growth was uneven (see Figure 9.3).

The annual levels of house price are based on official figures from the *China Statistics Year Book* (1997–2009). We assume a standard unit of housing is a new apartment with the size of 90m^2. This choice could be questionable. The definition of a standardized housing unit is a key

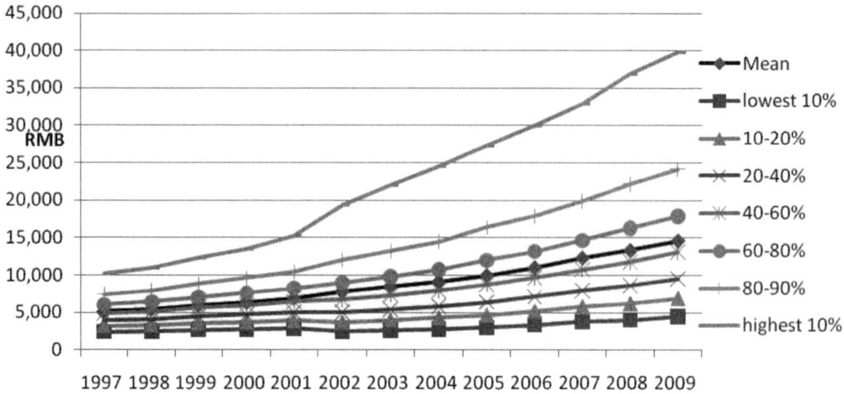

Fig. 9.3. Household disposable income per capita trend of Chinese urban residents, 1997–2009.

Sources: *China Statistics Yearbook* (various years).
Note: Values are in RMB yuan and adjusted for CPI (in 1997 price).

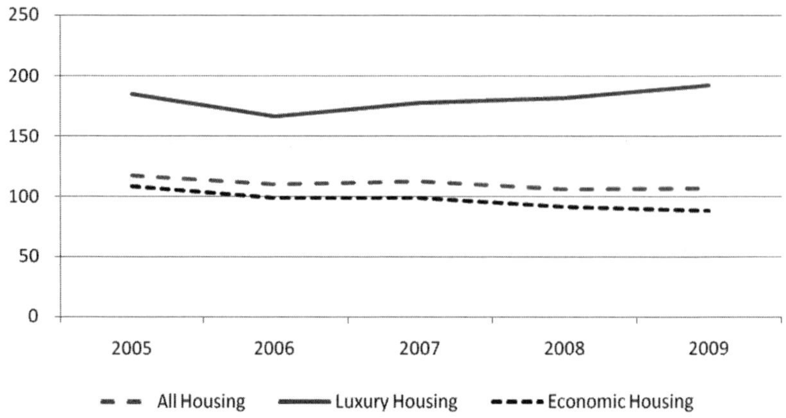

Fig. 9.4. Space size of new housing sold in China, 2005–2009 (construction space, m^2).
Source: Author's calculation based on data from *China Statistics Yearbook* (various years).

difficulty in housing affordability studies (Field, 1997), but it should take account of both social norms and practical feasibility. However, the problem is that, in urban China, the market supplies only a very limited number of small units (see Figure 9.4). For example, in 2009 the average size of new housing units sold was 107 m^2. A higher proportion of dwellings in the second-market are smaller than this, but they are mostly located in the expensive downtown area. Hence, 90 m^2 seems to be a suitable size that we can realistically assume for a standardized house in urban China

The size of mortgage payments required to purchase a standard unit is based on an 80% loan-to-value (LTV) self-amortizing mortgage with 25-year maturity, so it includes both interest and capital with the interest rate set according to the year in which it would have been taken out and updated each year.

9.4. Empirical Findings

9.4.1. *Accessibility to housing via mortgage*

We are taking access to mean the ability of new market entrants to secure sufficient mortgage finance to purchase a standard unit of housing. At the beginning of the analysis, following standard practice we calculated the price-to-income ratio (PIR) by dividing the purchase price of a standardized housing unit by annual household disposable income. We have broken it down for each income category and for each year (see Figure 9.5). A standardized housing unit is defined as being 90 m^2 priced at the mean value for such properties (see discussion above).

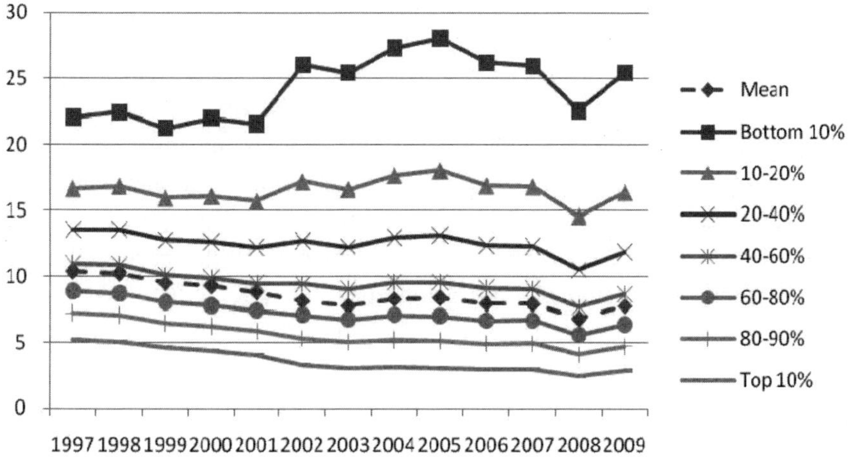

Fig. 9.5. Price-to-income ratios in China, 1995–2009, by income category.
Source: Author's calculation based on data from *China Statistics Yearbook* (various years).

Interestingly, it shows that the PIR is fairly stable before and after the 1998 reform. This suggests the speed of housing price growth does not exceed much of income growth during the period 1997–2009. But compared to international standards of affordability, most new market entrants in urban China have much more serious difficulties to access housing. More than 60% households experienced PIR higher than 6 throughout the period and only households with incomes in the top 20% experienced PIR lower or close to 5 after the year 2003. According to the 6th Annual Demographia International Housing Affordability Survey, a widely cited international survey of housing affordability and employing the "Median Multiple"-based PIR (median house price divided by gross annual median household income) to rate housing affordability, a housing market with PIR larger than 5.1 should be regarded as "severely unaffordable". Over 272 cities surveyed by Demographia in nine countries in 2009, only 62 were rated as "severely unaffordable".

Since we have adopted the PIR as a measure of access to housing we have adopted the maximum loan-to-income ratio that would be permitted by banks, which is in effect 8.5 incomes, combined with the ceiling on the LTV, which is 80%. Our figures require a caveat, which is that a deposit would also be required to cover the 20% of the property value that is above the LTV ceiling. Moreover, as noted above, this is not intended to be a sufficient criterion for the attainment of on-going affordability.

The following figure shows the proportion of monthly disposable income that would be taken by mortgage payments by income category. We use a threshold ratio of mortgage payments of 50% of disposable income (MIR) as the affordability indicator, as this ratio is the maximum level allowed by commercial banks in China. This threshold is higher than what is normally adopted in most western countries. For example, the European Commission (EC) has adopted a threshold of 40% in its recently agreed housing indicators (EC, 2009). Eligibility for key federal assistance programmes in the US is triggered by payment-to-income ratios of 30%, which is also the usual underwriting criterion for mortgages, although much higher ratios have been used in affordable lending programmes and a 50% threshold as an indicator of "worst case housing needs" (Kutty, 2005).

Using the threshold criterion of 50% MIR, it is not surprising that very few people could afford to own housing through mortgage financing before 1999, since open market housing was considered to be a luxury good for only top rich people and the mortgage financing has not been librated (Zhao and Bourassa, 2003). However, with large cut of mortgage rates since 2000, those households with incomes in the top 40% of the income distribution fell within the access criteria, although those in the 60–80% income quintile usually faced MIR exceeding 40%. An important insight which we can draw is that, even when the price-to-income ratio had not improved significantly, a sharp reduction in the mortgage interest rate alone could significantly improve the accessibility of housing (see Figure 9.6). This finding well illustrates the importance of mortgage instrument in supporting affordability. Nonetheless, such observation should be interpreted with great caution since we here ignore the likely stimulus effect of low mortgage interest on price growth. On the other hand, the figure also suggests that, throughout the period of 1997–2009, households with incomes in the bottom 60% would never have been able to access sufficient mortgage financing for housing.

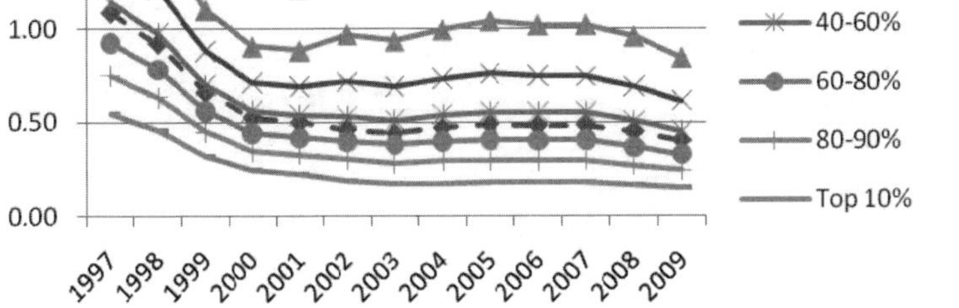

Fig. 9.6. M/I, monthly mortgage payments for a standardized housing unit as share of monthly disposable income, China, 1995–2009, by income category.

Source: Author's calculation based on data from *China Statistics Yearbook* (various years).
Note: The monthly mortgage repayment is computed for average-priced 90 m^2 housing with mortgage terms specified as: LTV = 80%, maturity = 25 years, and mortgage interest rates at the beginning of each year.

Thus, almost a decade after the government ended its obligation to provide housing and claimed that "it is now the market that supplies all housing" (Quan, 2006), market housing remains inaccessible for the overwhelming majority of residents.

9.4.2. *The time-varying "burden" of housing expenditure*

We have argued that the point-in-time static measures of affordability are inadequate for identifying on-going affordability given that incomes of homeowners change over time. Our dynamic expenditure-to-income ratio aims to reveal the evolution of housing affordability for each cohort of market entrants once access has been achieved (the "cohort" trend). The following figure simulates the "cohort" trend affordability for households entering the market in 1999 (see Figure 9.7).

We can see that a household belonging to the middle (40–60%) income quintile would have found house purchase to have been unaffordable in the sense that housing costs would have absorbed much more than 50% of income if they had purchased a standard house in 1999. However, if they

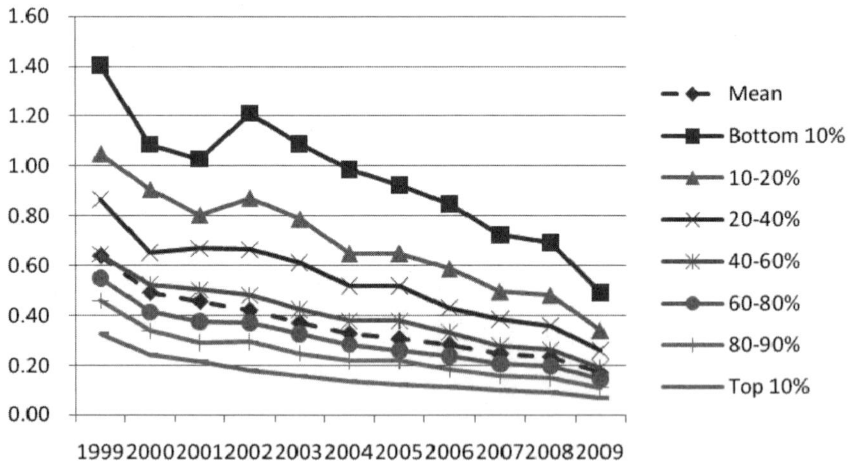

Fig. 9.7. Monthly mortgage payment as share of monthly disposable income for households that bought housings in 1999, by income category.

Source: Author's calculation based on data from *China Statistics Yearbook* (various years).
Note: Applying the same mortgage terms as specified in Figure 9.6.

had managed to obtain a mortgage in 1999 and their incomes grew in line with the average for that income group, their house would have become affordable four years later (i.e. the M/I would have fallen below 0.5) and in turn become relatively easily afforded six years later (M/I less than 0.36).

The following figure depicts how the "point of entry" trend of affordability for each new cohort of market entrants varies over time and how the "cohort trend" of affordability evolves within each cohort once access to housing is obtained (see Figure 9.8). Results are shown for the mean-income group only but the patterns are very similar for other income groups. The figure illustrates the generally opposing direction of these trends based on mean incomes: the "point of entry" trend is generally upward, suggesting that the effects of rising house prices outweighed those of rising incomes and falling interest rates. In contrast, the trend of affordability within each cohort (the "cohort" trend) is sharply downward in each income group, but there are important differences over time. The steepest drop of burden within a cohort occurred in 2009, which witnesses the largest mortgage interest cut in the period (from 6.66% to 4.16%). In addition, as we would expect, it takes much longer for a purchaser in the second lowest income quintile to reach the 50% affordability threshold (six or seven years) compared to the middle quintile (between two and four years).

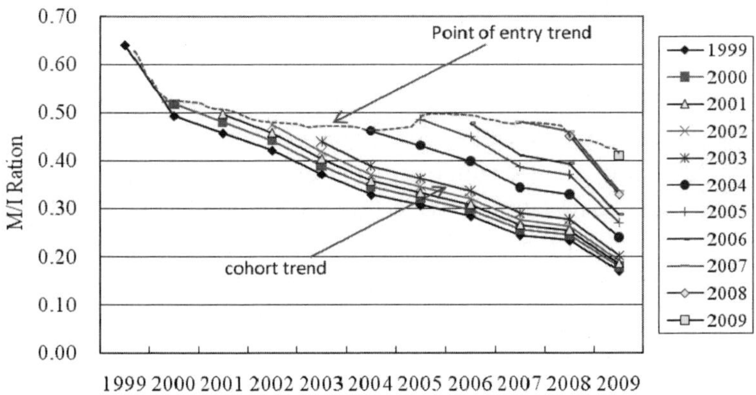

Fig. 9.8. Point of entry and cohort trends in housing affordability (MIR) 1999–2009 (mean income group).

Source: Author's calculation based on data from *China Statistics Yearbook* (various years).
Note: Applying the same mortgage terms as specified in Figure 9.6.

9.4.3. *Housing-induced poverty*

Even if a mortgage can be obtained to attain access, we need to assess whether interest and capital payments are reasonably affordable in the sense that they do not take too great a proportion of a household's disposable income. As we have noted that the housing "burden" measure provides an indication of the balance between housing and non-housing costs. By itself the attainment of a given ratio does not guarantee that sufficient "residual" income exists after housing expenditures are met to finance a minimum level of non-housing consumption.

Using the residual income approach, this section provides an assessment of housing affordability in urban China. When income after the expenditure required to meet the costs of a standardised unit of housing falls below the prescribed level of the minimum acceptable non-housing budget, this is defined as housing-induced poverty (Kutty, 2005), or, alternatively, shelter poverty (Stone, 2006a).

We have called our housing-induced poverty line the "minimum non-housing budget" (MNHB). In searching for a poverty line to reflect a socially acceptable minimum we did consider using the qualifying income for the Urban Living Standard Guarantee System (*dibao* in Chinese) which may be taken as a proxy for an urban poverty line to determine the MNHB. But there exist two important problems. First, it is always set at an unreasonably low level. For example, even in Shanghai, the richest city in China, this line was only RMB 350/month per person, which is much lower than the actual expenditures of low income households. And second, it is only updated every few years. The unsuitability of this line is confirmed by the State Council's recent decision to review the poverty line with a view to updating it. We do not wish to replicate the deficiencies in Stone's use of an official budget line that is based on an outdated basket of goods and which has been updated only in line with prices (when general standards of living rise more quickly than this). These considerations become even more important in a fast-growing economy such as China. Hence we decide to derive our MNHB from the monthly non-shelter expenditure of the bottom 20% income group in each year.

The following figure simulates the incidence of housing-induced poverty on "point of entry" basis for each cohort of market entrants from 1997–2009 by calculating the differences between post-housing incomes and the

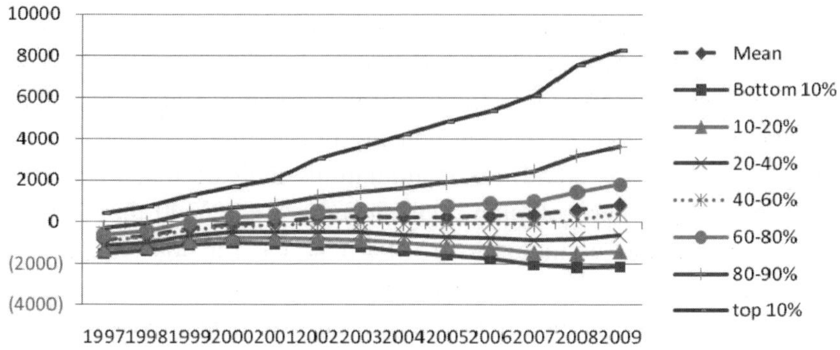

Fig. 9.9. Housing-induced poverty incidence in urban China, 1997–2009 (RMB per month).

Source: Author's calculations based on data from *China Statistics Yearbook* (1998-2010).
Note: The figures show the differences between post-housing expenditures and the minimum non-housing budget (MNHB) for each group. The housing expenditures include both standardized mortgage payments and maintain/utilities costs of housing (including electricity, fuel, and water) for each group. The negative values identify the relevant groups are trapped in housing-induced poverty.

minimum non-housing budget (MNHB). The negative values identify the households in each group that are simulated as being in housing-induced poverty (see Figure 9.9). The housing costs implied by the purchase of a standard unit of housing from the market would cause the majority of Chinese new market entrants to fall into housing-induced poverty. Only households in the top 10% of the income spectrum would avoid housing-induced poverty throughout the period and top 40% income group becomes to have such chance only after 2000. The residual incomes (the difference between post-housing incomes and MNHB) deteriorated in almost every year for those groups in the bottom 20% income spectrum. In contrast the residual incomes of those in the top 20% have improved significantly.

The number of the difference between post-housing incomes and the minimum non-housing budget also illustrates the poverty "gap", i.e. the amount by which residual income falls below the MNHB. This could constitute a useful basis for the government to calculate how much housing subsidy should be allotted to each income group in order to maintain for them both a decent living standard and minimum socially acceptable housing consumption.

We also apply our dynamic approach in combination with residual income concept to identify the improvements in after-shelter incomes that we would anticipate from rising incomes once entry into owner-occupation has been attained (the "cohort" trend). For the sake of brevity we only provide a figure of subsequent evolution of shelter affordability assumed for buying housing in 2000 for different income groups (the "cohort" trend). Our simulations indicate that for households entering owner-occupied housing in the year 2000 they experience improvements as incomes rise. Particularly, for households with mean incomes and beyond, housing-induced poverty persists for only one or two years, if at all. However, the situation is markedly different between different income groups. For example, households in the second lowest income quintile entering the market in 2000 rise out of housing-induced poverty only in 2008. For households in the bottom 20% income quintile, their housing-induced poverty persisted for more than ten years.

Using the concept of housing-induced poverty, we can infer what maximum affordable shelter costs for each income group are in each year. The following figure presents our computation results and it suggests that even for the top 20% rich households, they could not afford housing with monthly costs higher than RMB 5,600 in 2009 (see Figure 9.10).

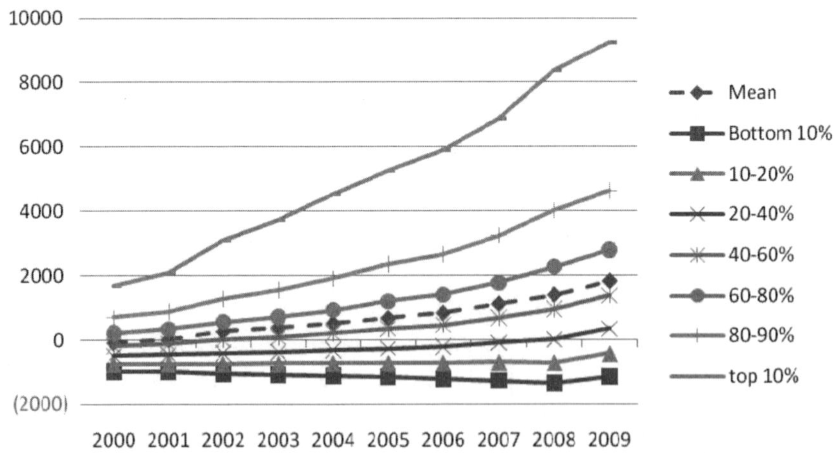

Fig. 9.10. Evolution of housing-induced poverty incidence for households that bought housings in 2000, 2000–2009 (RMB per month).

Source: Author's calculations based on data from *China Statistics Yearbook* (1998–2010).

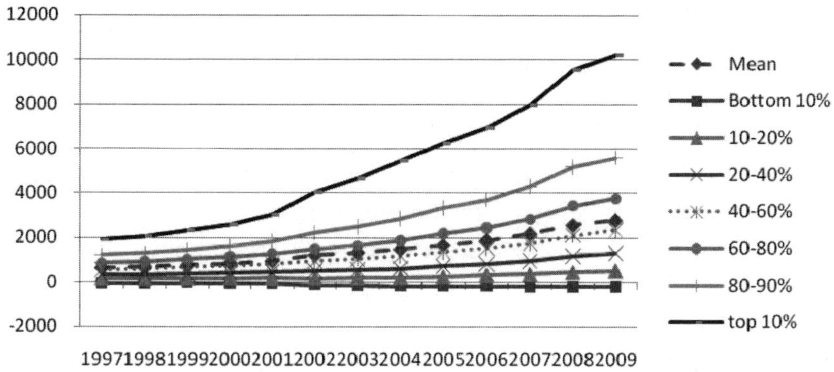

Fig. 9.11. Maximum affordable shelter costs (monthly) = family disposable income minus MNSB (minimum non-shelter costs), 1997–2009

We can also correspondingly calculate the maximum affordable housing prices for each income group (see Figure 9.11). For example, to avoid the top 20% income group to be trapped in housing-induced poverty in the year 2009, the housing price in that year should not exceed RMB 13,000/m^2 (assumed mortgage on the basis of 80 LTV, 25-year maturity and 5.5% mortgage rate). With same terms of mortgage, the maximum affordable housing price for mean-income households is RMB 5,500/m^2, while the bottom 40% income group could not afford housing prices higher than RMB 3,100/m^2. These analyses provide a guiding principle for the government to assess whether the housing price is too *unaffordable* and what is the desirable target level of housing price for certain groups.

9.4.4. *Policy implications*

In the analysis we have examined the individual components of a broader concept of affordability that encapsulated access, balance of housing and non-housing expenditure ("burden") and housing-induced poverty. All are necessary but none is fully sufficient to attain affordability. In this section we present a "rounded" picture of affordability according to different income groups. (We omit households in the lowest income quintile for whom mortgaged housing-ownership seems unrealistic, and the top income quintile for whom affordability appears unproblematic.) This approach enables us to make some more nuanced observations concerning policy interventions designed to improve affordability.

In general, the study suggests that without housing policy interventions the housing market will serve to replicate and over time exacerbate income inequalities. However, the findings also suggest that policy interventions need to be carefully designed for different income groups. The findings suggest that for all of these income groups discussed above access is a problem, at least for some period of the time, and that this might be improved by encouraging the construction of smaller units and developing policies to facilitate down-payments. Since the summer of 2006, the Chinese Ministry of Construction has instructed that at least 70% of new housing should be smaller than 90 m^2 (State Official Document No. 2006-37). Although some cities have put this policy into full effect, many governments, including Shanghai and Beijing, have not yet done so.

The analysis also suggests that demand-side subsidy instruments should be targeted not simply on lower income households, but especially in the early years of ownership. In principle the Housing Provident Fund aims to do the latter, but several evaluations suggest that it benefits most the high-income households (Duda *et al.*, 2005; World Bank, 2006). In practice any significant development of demand-side subsidies should take into account their potentially inflationary (and hence counter-productive) impact on house prices.

Perpetual subsidies (implied by supply-side subsidies) may not be a very efficient way of enhancing affordability for *most* income groups except in so far that the approach may be less inflationary than a rapid expansion in demand-side subsidies. A significant role of new "economic and affordable" housing seems improbable since very little has been built after 1999; but it is difficult to envisage mortgaged housing-ownership ever being a viable option for the lowest income households. Since affordability problems are likely to persist, the case for supply-side subsidy, including the provision of housing leased out at below market rents, is thus strengthened.

9.5. Chinese Government's Efforts to Solve Affordability Issue

Apart from the privatization in the 1990s, two principal policy instruments have been developed to enhance housing affordability.

First, the Housing Provident Fund (HPF), based on the Singaporean model, was introduced in Shanghai in 1991 and across the whole of urban China after 1994. The fund is supported by tax-free payroll contributions from employees matched by those of employers. Contribution rates vary between cities, but under a typical scheme the contribution rate is 7% from either side (Duda *et al.*, 2005). In return the fund provides various forms of assistance including subsidized mortgages.

Nonetheless, the HPF loan that one can borrow is based on a multiple of the savings in his/her HPF account, for example, 40 times in Shanghai. In addition, there is a cap on the maximum of HPF loan that one household can apply, which varies substantially across cities. In the year of 2009, the cap of HPF loan was typically RMB 600,000 in advanced large cities and RMB 400,000 in less-advanced cities. Given the soaring housing prices in major cities, the credit from HPF loans is often insufficient for the whole financial need of one's housing purchase. Therefore, many households apply for HPF loans and commercial mortgage loans simultaneously to finance their first housing purchase.

Although HPF's mortgage rate is usually one percentage point less than that of commercial mortgage, it has been overshadowed by commercial banks in its role as lender and savings vehicle since 1999. Compared to commercial mortgage, the lending activity of HPF achieves only modest expansion and is currently about 22% of mortgage lending by banks. A major problem of HPF system lies in the fact that few low-income households have chance to utilize HPF loan. It is reported that only 15% contributors have ever borrowed HPF loans (World Bank, 2006). Soaring house prices in recent years make things worse. It seems that lower-income savers cross-subsidize a smaller number of better-off borrowers (World Bank, 2006). Therefore HPF system does not contribute much in improving the housing affordability for common households in China.

Second, supply-side subsidies are provided through the "economic and comfortable" housing programme. The instruments employed include the allocation of land at zero cost combined with profit caps on developers. Prices fall within agreed thresholds to prevent developers from capturing the subsidy. Originally, the programme was aimed at the bulk of the urban population, but since 2003 its target has been narrowed to the low-to-middle income groups (Chen and Hao, 2007).

The "economic and comfortable" housing programme is deemed to have two major limitations. First, its size is too small in relation to commercial housing. Throughout the period of 1978–2009, the total supply of "economic and comfortable" housing was 354 million square meters and accounted only 7.8% of total new urban housing sold. Thus this programme could hardly be expected to have major impacts on solving housing affordability in urban China.

The second one is more serious. Its price was usually set too high and often much higher beyond the reach of low-income households. The following figure suggests that, although economic housing is affordable for mean-income households, it is definitely unaffordable for the low-income households, especially for the lowest households (see Figure 9.12). There are many reports suggesting that the majority of buyers of economic housing were actually middle-class households and even high-income households. Therefore this programme does not help the targeted low-income group as claimed.

There are some signs of reform of both in recent months and the Chinese central government has now placed a greater priority on housing affordability (a central government guideline for housing market development was issued on April 13. 2010, State Official Document No. 2010-10). Further,

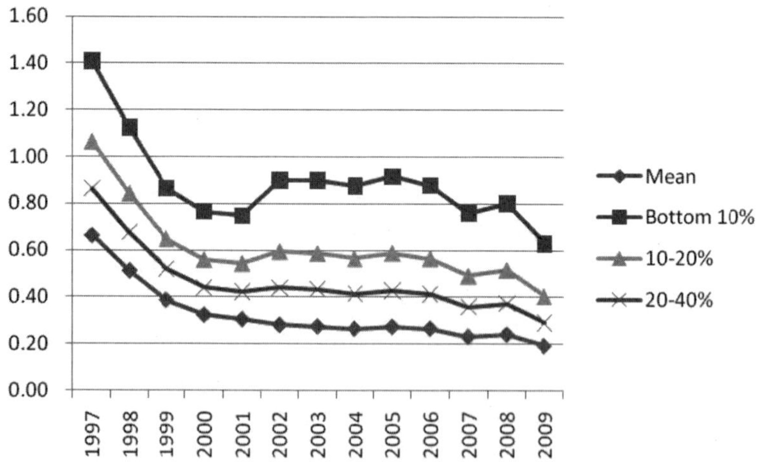

Fig. 9.12. MIR for "economic and comfortable" housing, 1997–2009.

Source: Author's calculations based on data from *China Statistics Yearbook* (1998–2010).
Note: Applying the same mortgage terms as specified in Figure 9.6.

Chinese government has realized the problems of HPF system and economic housing. It has tried to reform the HPF system as well as shifted the emphasis of affordable housing construction from economic housing to public rental housing and cheap rental housing, believing that the latter two are more accessible to low-income households. The effects of these initiatives and changes, however, will have to be assessed by future studies.

9.6. Conclusions

During the last 20 years, China has made impressive record in reforming its urban housing sector and has improved the housing conditions for hundreds of millions of households within a short period of time. However, the affordability of housing still imposes a severe challenge in urban China.

This chapter examines the development trend of housing affordability in urban China before and after the 1998 housing reform. As there is a large bulk of Chinese urban households owned their home at low cost through the privatization of public housing in the reform, this chapter focuses on the housing affordability for new market entrants since the reform. For these households, three dimensions of housing affordability (namely access, the burden of housing costs and housing-induced poverty) are estimated. Further, beyond conventional static indicators of affordability, two dynamic indicators are developed to simulate the affordability experience between and within successive cohorts of new market entrants. It is found that, while there is a general declining trend in affordability for each successive cohort of market entrants, the evolution of affordability within each cohort after entry improved quickly within a short period of time. Nonetheless, there are substantial differences of affordability experiences across income groups.

The findings have important policy implications concerning the nature, extent and duration of public housing policies for different income groups in urban China. For example, our analysis could help to provide a useful basis for the government to calculate how much housing subsidy should be allotted to each income group in order to maintain for them both a decent living standard and minimum socially acceptable housing consumption. Based on our analysis, one can also straightforwardly calculate the maximum affordable housing prices for each income group. The analysis also provides a guiding principle for the government to assess whether the housing price is too *unaffordable* and what is the desirable target level of housing price for certain groups.

We also put forward a preliminary analysis on the major policy instruments that Chinese government have adopted to alleviate housing affordability issue — HPF and economic housing. But we find that they both have significant deficiencies and need substantial improvements in the future.

References

Armenoff, K. (1998). "Shelter Poverty: New Ideas on Housing Affordability." *Journal of Urban Affairs*, 20(3), 359–362.

Bertaud, A. (2009). "Housing Affordability in China: A Stock-Flow Approach." Paper presented at Peking University at the Symposium on Low-Income Housing in China, Beijing, July 10–11, 2009.

Bogdon, A.S. and Can, A. (1997). "Indicators of Local Housing Affordability: Comparative and Spatial Approaches." *Housing Economics*, 25(1), 43–80.

Bratt, R.G. (1995). "Review of 'Shelter Poverty — New Ideas on Housing Affordability' by ME Stone." *Journal of the American Planning Association*, 61(2), 285–286.

Chen, J. and Hao, Q.J. (2007). "Housing Market Development and Housing Affordability in Shanghai." The International Conference on China Urban Land and Housing in the 21st Century, Hong Kong Baptist University, 13–15 December.

Chinese Statistics Yearbook. (1995 to 2010). Beijing: China Statistics Office.

Chiu, R. (2001). "Housing Policy and Practice in China." *Urban Studies*, 38(1), 221–223.

Cui, D. R. (1991). "*Research on China Urban Housing System Reform* (in Chinese), Beijing:" Finance and Economics Press.

Deng,Y., Zheng, D. and Ling, C. (2005). "An Early Assessment of Residential Mortgage Performance in China." *Journal of Housing Finance and Economics*, 31(2), 117–136.

Duda, M., Zhang, X. and Dong, M. (2005). "China's Housing Ownership-Orientated Housing Policy: and Examination of Two Programs Using Survey

Data from Beijing, W05-7." Cambridge, MA: Joint Center for Housing Studies, Harvard University.

European Commission (2009). "Set of Indicators Approved on 30 June 2009: Definitions and Tables."

Field, C.G. (1997). "Building Consensus for Affordable Housing." *Housing Policy Debate*, 8(4), 801–832.

Hancock, K. (1993). "Can Pay — Won't Pay — or Economic Principles of Affordability." *Urban Studies*, 30(1), 127–145.

Hartman, C. (1998). "The Case for a Right to Housing." *Housing Policy Debate*, 9(2), 223–246.

Hills, J. (1991). "Unravelling Housing Finance: Subsidies, Benefits and Taxation." Oxford: Oxford University Press.

Hulchanski, J. (1995). "The Concept of Housing Affordability — Six Contemporary Uses of the Housing Expenditure-to-Income Ratio." *Housing Studies*, 10(4), 471–491.

Kutty, N. (2005). "A New Measure of Housing Affordability: Estimates and Analytical Results." *Housing Policy Debate*, 16(1), 113–142.

Linneman, P. and Megbolugbe, I. (1992). "Housing Affordability — Myth or Reality." *Urban Studies*, 29(3–4), 369–392.

Nunez, R. (1994). "Review of "Shelter Poverty — New Ideas on Housing Affordability" — Stone, ME." *Political Science Quarterly*, 109(2), 379–381.

People's Bank of China (2005). "*China Real Estate Finance Report 2004*. Beijing" China Financial Press.

Quan, Z.X. (2006). "Institutional Transformation and Marketization: The Changing Patterns of Housing Investment in Urban China." *Habitat International*, 30(2), 327–341.

Quigley, J.M. and Raphael, S. (2004). "Is Housing Unaffordable? Why Isn't it More Affordable?" *Journal of Economic Perspectives*, 18(1), 191–214.

Rosen, K. and Ross, M. (2000). "Increasing Housing Ownership in Urban China: Notes on the Problem of Affordability." *Housing Studies*, 15(1), 77–88.

Shen, X. (2006). "The Black Humour of 8-year Housing Reform" (in Chinese). *Liaowang Orient Weekly*, October 31.

Stone, M.E. (2006a). "What is Housing Affordability? The Case for the Residual Income Approach." *Housing Policy Debate*, 17(1), 151–184.

Stone, M.E. (2006b). "A Housing Affordability Standard for the UK." *Housing Studies*, 21(4), 453–476.

Thalmann, P. (1999). "Identifying Households Which Need Housing Assistance." *Urban Studies*, 36(11): 1933–1947.

Thalmann, P. (2003). "'House Poor' or Simply "Poor'?" *Journal of Housing Economics*, 12(4), 291–317.

Wang, Y.P. (2007). "From Socialist Welfare Support to Housing-Ownership: The Experience of China." In R. Groves, Murie, A. and Watson, C. (eds.), *Housing and the New Welfare State: Perspectives from East Asia and Europe*, Aldershot: Ashgate, pp. 127–154.

Whitehead, C.M.E. (1991). "From Need to Affordability — An Analysis of UK Housing Objectives." *Urban Studies*, 28(6), 871–887.

World Bank (2006). *China Economic Outlook 2006 Quarter 3*, Washington: World Bank.

Zhang, X.Q. (2000). "The Restructuring of the Housing Finance System in Urban China." *Cities*, 17(5), 339–348.

Zhao, Y. and Bourassa, S. (2003). "China's Urban Housing Reform: Recent Achievements and New Inequities." *Housing Studies*, 18(5), 721–744.

CHAPTER 10

INTERGOVERNMENTAL TRANSFER AND REGIONAL BALANCED DEVELOPMENT: NEW REFORM AGENDA

Ziying Fan

10.1. Introduction

China is a large country in terms of both territory and population and also a country with distinct regional disparity. For example, 94% of Chinese population is scattered on less than 43% of the territory to the southeast of the Aihui-Tengchong line while the population density of 57% of the west area is only one fourth of the average level of the world. This disparity in initial endowments determines the varied development potentials of different regions. At the primary stage of Chinese economic development where export-oriented economy predominates, the east area, with the advantages of sea transportation, took the initiative to step into international market at a low transportation cost. At this stage, the government's preferential policies have also been concentrated on these areas. For example, the earliest special economic zones were built within the Zhujiang River Delta, then coastal cities were allowed to open and finally the major inland cities followed up. The geographic variance among different regions, coupled with government policies, has contributed to the great changes in Chinese original economic structure. From 1994 to 1998, export volume of the three provinces in the Zhujiang River Delta constituted 46% of the national export volume while seven provinces and cities in the northeast and north coastal regions fell behind, with their export volume decreasing to 23% between 1994 and 1998 from the 39% in 1978, and the industrial ratio to 8.6% in 2002 from the 16.1% in 1980 (Naughton, 2007). Affected by incremental reform and international trade, economic gaps between different regions are becoming more and more significant. GDP share of the east area increased to 59.68% in 2006 from the 50.15% in 1980 while that of the central area and the west area during the same period kept decreasing. GDP share of the west area decreased to 17.14% in 2006 from the 20.24% in 1980. The central area had the sharpest decrease, from 29.62% in 1980 to 23.19% in 2006. The concern over "collapsing central region" has turned into reality.

The development policies during the 1980s completely followed the principle of "Two General Situations" proposed by Mr. Xiaoping Deng. According to this principle, the limited resources in a country with weak economic foundation and enormous internal diversity should be allocated to the most efficient regions and sectors at first. Only after these regions have been developed to a certain extent and the signs of industrial upgrading begin to emerge can other inland regions get benefit from the industrial transfer and therefore develop themselves. Thereupon, an apparent "fly geese" developing pattern will be formed from coastal regions to inland areas. The balanced development among different areas is usually hard to achieve, mainly due to two reasons. First, the inland areas always lack adequate infrastructures, which hinder the spreading of technologies and industries (Abramowitz, 1985). Second, the theory of new economic geography holds that economy takes an overt clustering tendency, which means that after a region has achieved some preliminary development advantages, the clustering effect will be initiated and reinforced, resulting in the formation of a growth pole with single center in these regions (Fujita *et al.*, 1999). Therefore, how to implement the second general situation has become the major problem for the policy makers. In the early 1990s, the overall rationing system in original fiscal system has weakened the fiscal power of the central government to such a serious extent that the central government had no more resources to carry out macroeconomic management and balance regional economic differences after finishing the expenditure assignment at the central level. The tax sharing reform launched in 1994 again centralized to some extent the fiscal power to the central government. Two ratios, the ratio of the revenues to GDP and the ratio of the central government's revenues to the total revenues, have significantly increased, rising from 11.2% and 22% in 1993 to 20.4% and 53.3% in 2008, respectively. With a surplus of fiscal revenue, the central government began to implement regional strategies with specified objectives. In 1999, China launched the "Western Development" strategy which covered twelve provinces, cities and municipalities in the west and provided support in terms of investment for infrastructure, policy and fiscal transfer, etc. In 2003 and 2004, China launched the plans of "revitalization of the old industrial base of the northeast" and "rise of the central China", with detailed policies similar to those provided for "Western Development".

Of all the policies, fiscal policies were taken as an important means in regional development strategy. Since 1994, the central government implemented a series of fiscal reforms to raise the revenues of central government and a large proportion of these revenues was transferred to less developed regions through fiscal transfers. In this way, the central government drew resources from the east area by raising shares and invested them to less developed regions. The ratio of the transfers obtained by the inland provinces in the national total correspondingly increased from 68.1% in 1995 to 82.8% in 2007. The transfers were gradually becoming the major part of the fiscal expenditure of the central government. Taking the year of 2004 for example, the central government spent 54% of its total expenditure in subsidizing local governments at all levels.

The success of these strategies is obvious. The enormous investments and expenditures by the government in short tem have provided the inland provinces with a vigorous economic momentum. For example, among top five rapidly developing provinces in 2008, all but Tianjin were inland provinces and three of them were located in the west. The side effect brought by these policies, however, cannot be ignored. For example, although fiscal transfers have boosted market integration in China, they indirectly caused the expansion of inland governments, induced local corruption, and reduced the administrative efficiency of the governments. Moreover, the transfer of some industries from one place to another led by the government, coupled with local government's strong motivation to develop economy, has deteriorated local environment and increased the potential cost of improving environment in the future.

Based on the above knowledge, this chapter will systematically review the transitions, influence and reform direction of Chinese fiscal transfer system. The outline of this chapter is as follows: Section 10.2 is a review of the institutional background of previous adjustments that have been made to fiscal transfer system and the policy dilemma expected to be solved by adjusted transfers; Section 10.3 mainly discusses the relationship between transfers and economic growth; Section 10.4 evaluates the effect of transfers on local economy and the behaviors of local governments; Section 10.5 elaborates corresponding reform agenda; and Section 10.6 presents the major conclusions.

10.2. The Fiscal Transfer System in China

There are five levels of governments in China — the central government, the province (municipality), the city, the county and the town. Each level of government will provide transfers to the lower level of governments, and transfers between governments of the same level are rare. Thereupon, the transfers in China are mainly vertical and most of them are from the central government to the provincial governments. Before 1994, the absolute amount of the transfers of the central government was trivial. At that time, the transfers were limited to some fiscal subsidies given by the central government to make up the gap of several regions. For example, the transfers in 1991 valued only 6.45 billion yuan, accounting for less than 4% of the total expenditure of the central government in the same year, with little impact on local governments. When it comes to 2008, the transfers provided by the central government to the local governments have exceeded 200 billion yuan, taking up 63% of the total expenditure of the central government in the same year.

From 1980 to 1993, China carried out the fiscal contract responsibility system. This system fully stimulated the local governments to develop economy. However, the credibility of the central government was poor. The local government intentionally hid its fiscal revenues, or turned the budgetary revenues into the extra-budgetary revenues. During this period, the central government often failed to make both ends meet. In several years, the central government was even forced to ask the local governments "to make contributions" (i.e., turning over their revenues to the central government). For example, due to fiscal problems, the central government borrowed from the local governments 7 billion yuan in 1980 and 4 billion in 1982, which were never paid back. In 1983, the central government took a severer measure, namely, transferring debts of this kind into the amount of reducing expenditure contract base of the local governments, and adjusting the sharing proportion and subsidy amount correspondingly, in order to narrow the fiscal gap of the central government (Jia and Zhao, 2008). Transfers in 1993 even reached –5.57 billion yuan. The amount contributed by the local governments largely exceeded the transfers of the central government, whereupon the central government had no surplus resources for transfers. In order to reverse the declining trend of the fiscal power of the central government, the tax sharing system established in 1994 legislatively stipulated the part shared by the central government. The initial revenue sharing system was changed into a tax sharing system. Namely, all the taxes were classified into three types: the national taxes, the local taxes, and taxes shared by the central government and the local governments. This tax sharing system changed the relationship between the central government and the local governments from three perspectives. First, the uniformity of tax rates and the tax sharing system guaranteed the credibility of the central government. As the tax sharing ratios were the same for all provinces, the developed regions did not need to worry that the central government would take more shares. Next, separating the national taxes from the local taxes lessened the motivation of the local governments to hide revenues. The national taxing sectors collected not only the national taxes, e.g., customs duties, but also taxes shared by the central government and the local governments, e.g., VAT. Therefore, the local government was unable to decrease the tax revenues of the central government by hiding tax base. Moreover, since the largest tax, VAT, was shared, raising the tax base was also beneficial for the fiscal revenues of the local governments. Finally, large-scale vertical transfers enabled the central government to carry out microeconomic management and intentionally balance regional economic gaps (Ma, 1997).

The tax sharing system established in 1994 greatly enhanced the centralization and fiscal position of the central government, raising both the ratio of fiscal revenues to GDP and the ratio of the fiscal revenues of the central government to the fiscal revenues of the whole country. The ratio of the fiscal revenues to GDP increased from 10.8% in 1994 to 20.6% in 2007. The ratio of the fiscal revenues of the central government to the fiscal revenues of the whole country jumped from 22% to 55.7% in 1994, and basically remained at the level of 50% from then on. Strictly speaking, real transfers did not emerge until 1994. The net transfers offered by the government increased from 181.9 billion yuan in 1994 to 1,271.4 billion yuan in 2006, with an average annual growth rate of 17.6%, which exceeded the increase of the fiscal revenue of the central government in the same year. The ratio of the transfers to the expenditures of the central government in the same year increased from 43.9% to 54.4% (see Figure 10.1). It can be seen from the development process in previous years that there were two jump points. The first one is the year of 1994 when the transfers increased by 200 billion yuan. But the transfers were mainly the tax rebates, which was a compromise of the central government on advancing tax sharing system. The second jump point is the year of 1999. Increasing trend remained after that point. It was related to the economic policy of western development (Wang, 2004).

From the perspective of the resources of the fiscal revenues, apart from the fact that the tax sharing system changed the original distribution pattern, after 2000, the central government made large adjustments to tax sharing and items of taxation. These adjustments further enhanced fiscal centralization of the central government and decreased the resources of the local governments. These adjustments were accompanied by the alteration of the transfer system. In particular, if the rebates of the 'two taxes', the consumption tax and VAT, are also considered as a kind of transfer,[1] then it is a match, for the first time, between fiscal reform and transfer reform. In addition, it should be noted that redistribution of the revenues of the central government and the local governments in the original system remained, and that the subsidy offered by the central government before 1994 was distributed according to the original pattern,

[1]Strictly speaking, tax rebate is similar to the factor method transfer, because the shared taxes are collected by central government and then distributed accord the tax revenue of 1993 and 30 per cent of the tax growth, so the process is the same as lump-sum fiscal transfer.

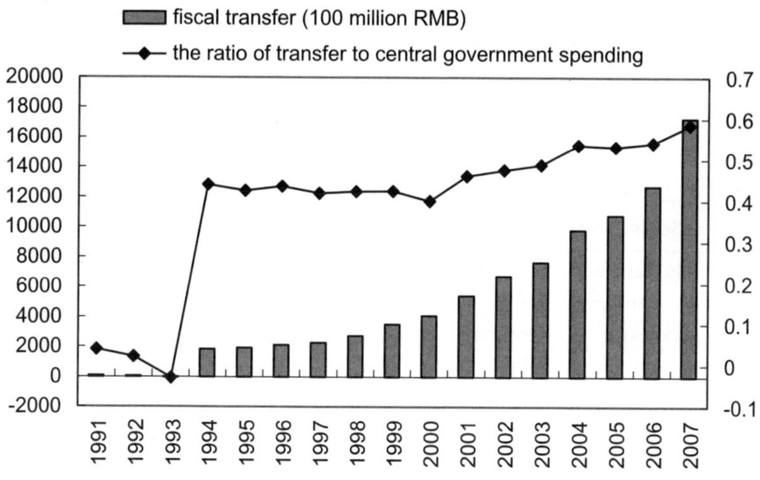

Fig. 10.1. The fiscal transfer and its ratio to central government spending.

while the provinces which were required to contribute to the central government according to the fiscal contract system continued to fulfill their duties. This subsidy and contribution rule in the original system remains to this day. The implementation of tax sharing system enhanced the fiscal power of the central government. As a result, central government then formally introduced the general transfer to adjust the regional differences in 1995 (see Table 10.1). This type of transfers not only granted preferences to the minority regions, but also subsidized the regions with considerable fiscal gap. As this transfer mode was on trial, such general transfers were also called transitional transfers. Though they were not sufficient to reverse the enlarging trend of the financial power differences due to the limited amount of these transfers, the increase of their ratio to the revenues of the central government from 0.64% in 1995 to 1.61% in 2001 could indicated indirectly that fiscal balance gradually became the major objective of the central government in providing transfers. The reform beginning at 2000 substituted regular taxes for administrative charges, integrated the extra-budgetary revenues into budgetary revenues, and decreased the rates of taxes on special agricultural products and cancelled the slaughter tax meanwhile. These measures sharply reduced the tax resources of the basic level of government, with a resultant decrease

Table 10.1. The reform of revenue sharing and transfer after 1990.

Year	1994			2001	2002	2004
Reform of revenues	Tax sharing system			Tax and charges reform	Income tax sharing	Agricultural tax relief
Year	**Before 1994**	**1994**	**1995**	**2000**	**2001**	**2005**
New transfer items	1) Targeted transfers 2) Quota subsidies	(Subsidies of the old system) 1) Tax rebates 2) Subsidies from the treasury bonds 3) Increase in wage transfer	1) General transfer	1) Transfer to minority areas	1) Transfer from the rural tax and charges reform	1) Transfer to counties for administration reform

of financial investments in basic public services, e.g., education. Therefore transfers based on local needs seemed to be under great pressure. For example, since 2001, a transfer for rural taxes and charges reform had been set up by the central government. Provinces except Beijing, Tianjin, Shanghai, Jiangsu, Zhejiang, and Guangdong were subsidized (Tsui, 2005; Yin *et al.*, 2007). From 2004, the central government began to advance agricultural tax reduction and exemption in some provinces. From 2006, agricultural tax was cancelled nation-wide. In view of the decrease of the fiscal power of the lower level of government, the central government correspondingly offered subsidy for the cancellation of taxes on special agricultural products and the reduction of agricultural tax rate in 2004 and further offered subsidy to relieve the financial difficulties of counties and townships in 2005. These financial subsidies maintained the regular operation of the basic level of governments. On the other hand, different from the reform of reducing the resources of the lower level of governments, the central government carried out the reform of sharing income tax revenues in 2002, enabling the central government to take 60% of the income tax revenues which were initially all collected by the local governments. This reform once elevated the proportion of the financial revenues of the central government by 3 percentage points. The newly increased revenues of the central government were also used to offer the general transfer to the local governments. From 2002, reducing the financial gaps between different regions has gradually become one of the major objectives of the central governments in making transfers to the local governments.

Basically, transfers can be classified into two types, i.e., transfers without specified purposes and those with specified purposes. For example, tax rebates and fiscal transfers belong to transfers without specified purposes while targeted transfers belong to transfers with specified purposes. The current tax rebates include rebate of VAT and consumption tax and rebate of income tax. Rebates of the two former taxes will be calculated based on the taxes of 1993 and returned to the local governments according to the ratio of 1 to 0.3. Namely, taking the year of 1993 as the base year, for every 1 percentage point increase in the revenues of the two taxes in 1994, the central government will return 0.3 percentage point of the increased amount to the local governments. Fiscal transfers were generally used to fill the financial gap of the local governments. Firstly a certain "formula" will be used to calculate the needs of different regions. Then the transfers will be allocated according to a certain proportion. This method is comparatively objective and fair. For example, the general transfers introduced in 1995 to balance regional financial differences were allocated using the following formula:

The amount of general transfer to a region = (standard fiscal expenditure of that region – standard fiscal revenues of that region) × coefficient of transfer for that region

Where, the standard fiscal revenues are the sum of the local tax revenues and other subsidies from the central government; the standard expenditures are the sum of the expenditures of each relevant sectors; and the transfer coefficient is determined according to the fiscal surplus of the central government in that year. Along the growth of the fiscal revenues of the central government, the transfer coefficient has been raised from

4.2% in 1995 to 47.3% in 2005 (Li, 2006) and the subsidy began to increase sharply from 2002.

The other type of transfers is targeted transfers which are distributed according to projects. Compared to fiscal transfers, the targeted transfers have three exclusive characteristics. The first one is that the local governments are required to share some responsibilities. For example, as to the "two exemptions and one allowance" policy for compulsory education carried out in 2005, the central government undertook 80% of the expenditure at most and the local governments were required to take some money from their budgets to pay for the rest part. The second one is that the targeted transfers are for specified purposes. Strictly speaking, it is forbidden to use them against the specified purposes. Moreover, most of such transfers is invested in the fields in which the local governments are reluctant to get involved, e.g., agriculture, social security, compulsory education, etc (see Table 10.2). Lastly, targeted transfer projects belong to different sectors. There is considerable overlap in the establishment of projects, without explicit transfer rules. For example, in 2005, the central

Table 10.2. Transfer in 2007.

	Category	100 million	Share(%)
Fiscal transfer	General transfer	2 505	35.5
	Transfer to minority areas	173	2.4
	Transfer from the rural Tax Reform	759	10.7
	Wage transfer	2 234	31.5
	Transfer to counties for administration reform	339	4.8
	Others	1 083	15.3
Targeted transfers	Education	391	5.7
	R & D	75	1.1
	Social Security	1 961	28.4
	Medical and Health	630	9.1
	Environment	748	10.8
	Agriculture and Water	961	13.9
	Others	2 133	30.9

Source: Ministry of Finance http://www.mof.gov.cn.

Note: Other fiscal transfers include transfer for rural and urban compulsory education, transfer for resource-exhausted cities, transfer from the old system, etc. Other targeted transfers include transfers to public service, defense, public safety, culture, sports, media, transportation, etc.

government allocated 239 targeted transfer projects, among which 41 projects were overlapping and 65 projects without any (explicit) administrative rules (The Audit Bureau, 2006).

The transfers between the central and different provinces are comparatively much more transparent and standardized while the fiscal arrangement and transfers between governments under the provincial level are much vaguer. Because it is not expressly stipulated that uniform rules should be applied to governments under the provincial level, there is more space for the provincial and urban governments to operate in their own way. Taking the increasing rebate for VAT and consumption tax as an example, the central government offers the provincial governments an increasing rebate rate of 1 to 0.3, i.e., the rebate will increase by 0.3% point every time the "two taxes" revenues increase by 1 percentage point, while Qinghai government offers the local governments an increasing rebate rate of 1 to 0.21, i.e., the provincial government takes away 30% of the rebate which the central government offers to the governments of counties and township. When the counties are divided into county-level cities and standard counties, the standard counties will get more support in many types of transfers except targeted transfers, environment transfer and tax rebate, because the economic development level of county-level cities are twice better than that of the standard counties whereupon they are more likely to provide satisfactory matching conditions for targeted transfers. More fiscal transfers, however, flow to counties with poor economic performance. But even among the standard counties, there is a great disparity. For the counties with poorer economic performance, the amount of transfers they obtain is inversely proportional to their fiscal revenues while for the standard counties with developed economy no distinct relationship exists between these two elements. For the economically well developed county-level cities, however, the fiscal transfers are directly proportional to the revenues of the local governments. This phenomenon shows that the standard counties are more likely to get fiscal transfers while the count-level cities have higher possibilities to get targeted transfers, and that those rich standard counties and comparatively poorer count-level cities will be systematically neglected by the central and the provincial governments (Yao, 2007).

10.3. Fiscal Transfer and Economic Growth

Fiscal transfers are equivalent to increasing revenues of the local governments, which allows the local governments to reduce the real tax rates and provide more public services (Scott, 1952; Wilde, 1971). Consequently, the fiscal transfers will change the expenditure structures of the local governments.

Herein, based on the method applied by Jia and Guo (2008), the government expenditures are divided into economic expenditures, social expenditures and maintenance expenditures, expressed respectively by the ratios of infrastructure expenditures, scientific and education expenditures and administrative expenditures to the total expenditures of the local governments. There exists a U-shape relationship between the economic expenditures and the transfers. As shown in the scatter diagram in Figure 10.2, most provinces lie to the left of the U-line, indicating that for most provinces the economic expenditures decreased as the transfers increased. The provinces with more economic expenditures were located at the two ends of the U-line. Namely, provinces getting less fiscal transfers, e.g. coastal regions, and provinces getting substantial fiscal transfers, e.g., the west areas, had a

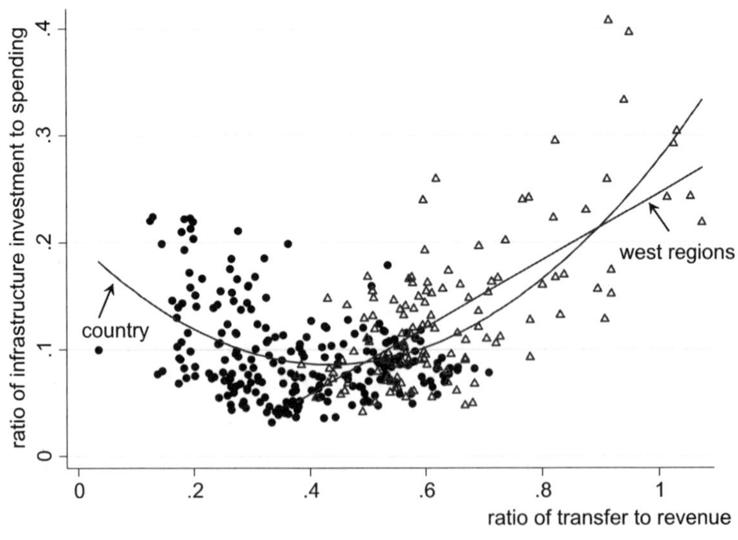

Fig. 10.2. The relationship between infrastructure investment and transfer.

high ratio of economic expenditures. Taking the west area for an example, the transfers will drive these regions to improve infrastructure. As can be seen from the above analysis, the west areas get considerable transfers from the treasury bonds which have been targeted for specific purposes. Most of funds must be invested into infrastructure and related fields.

From the perspective of economic growth in the long term, such social expenditures as education and medical are more important because they can elevate the human capital and bring a resultant endogenous economic growth (Romer, 1986; Lucas, 1988). As shown in Figure 10.3, however, there was no proof that the transfers were beneficial to relieving the problem of insufficiency of social expenditures. The ratio of the social expenditures represented by education and medical spending decreased as the transfers increased. This inverse correlation was more obvious in the west areas, indicating that the implementation of the "Western Development" and other economic strategies stimulated the fiscal expenditures in these regions while the social expenditures did not increase simultaneously. According to the figure at the bottom, there existed an obvious positive correlation between the maintenance expenditures represented by the ratio of administrative expenditures and the fiscal transfers. Although the fitting line for the west areas is smooth, the positive correlation relationship is obvious. It indicates that the transfers increased by every one percentage point, the maintenance expenditures of the government would increase more than one percentage point accordingly.

In the framework proposed by Barro (1990), there exists a inverse correlation between the maintenance spending and the economic growth while a positive relationship between the social and economic spending and the economic growth. Since 1994, the economic expenditures have not significantly promoted the economic growth as China's infrastructure has reached a comparatively high level, imposing no constraints on economic growth. The social spending, however, has been increasingly important. The maintenance spending has a significant inverse correlation with economic growth (Jia and Guo, 2008). Therefore, the relationship between the transfers and the economic growth in the long term is vague. The relationship between these two variables is to be determined according to statistics and the mechanism is to be interpreted in the following sections.

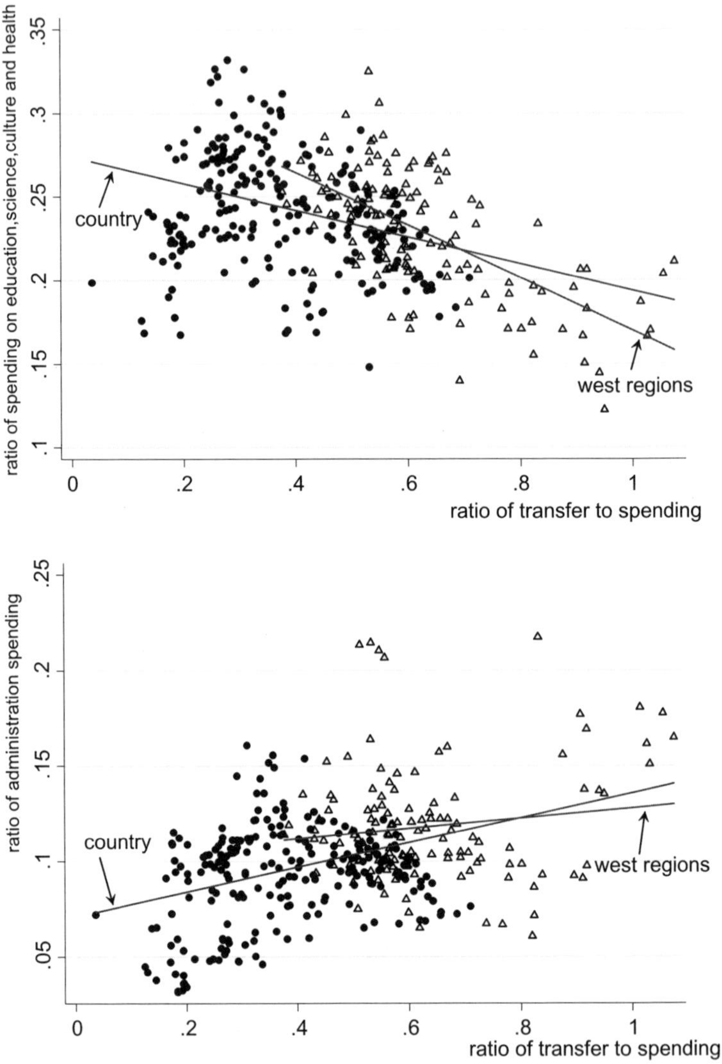

Fig. 10.3. The social expenditure, administrative expenditure and transfer.

Either the fiscal transfers aimed at equalizing public services, or the targeted transfers with more direct relationships with the economic growth, the original intention of these transfers going along with regional development strategies is to enhance the growth of inland economic development.

Thus it is appropriate to measure the effect of transfers from the perspective of economic growth. Moreover, the "West Development" strategy has been advanced for a decade, which is long enough to produce long-term economic growth. Related literature is the relationship between international aid and growth. Theoretically, international assistance can not only alleviate the problem of insufficient capital in backward countries, but also stimulate poor countries to improve governance, which enables the international assistance to promote the economic growth. The conclusions based on empirical studies are ambiguous. Even taking into account the diverse characteristics of different countries and the endogeneity of international aid, a significant positive correlation between aid and growth cannot be guaranteed (Clemens *et al.*, 2004; Rajan and Subramanian, 2007).

Since our focus is rather on the economic growth than on the balance among local financial resources, thus it is more appropriate to use a growth model here. For this reason, the following model is built:

$$Y_{it} = \alpha + \sum_{j=1}^{n} \beta_j Tran_{i,t-j} + \gamma X_{i,t-1} + \eta_i + e_{it} \tag{10.1}$$

Where, Y is real GDP growth rate of a region. *Tran* is the transfer intensity, i.e., the central subsidy received by each province minus the local contribution (to the central government) and then divided by the local government expenditure. Here the traditional method of identifying the gap between the fiscal expenditures and fiscal revenues with the transfers is discarded out of the reason that these transfers contain too many noises, for example, the revenues from local government bonds and foundations basically have nothing to do with the central fiscal transfers. η is a regional fixed effect, to reflect the geographical influence on economic growth. X includes other variables to be controlled. In this chapter, the following factors are to be considered:

Labour: Although the labour does not constitute a constraint to local economic growth, it is still treated as a control variable. Here the ratio of the employed population to the total population is applied.

Human capital (edu): According to the new growth theory proposed by Romer and Lucas, human capital is a key factor in technological innovation, which is also supported by other studies (Romer, 1986; Lucas, 1988;

Acemoglu and Zilibotti, 1999). Here this variable is measured by the ratio of students in the schools of secondary and higher education to the total population, to reflect the contribution of the human capital investment to economic growth.

Investment (invest): Investment clearly constitutes the restriction of element in local economic growth. Here the ratio of the fixed asset investment to GDP is applied.

Inflation (cpi); When the expected inflation rate rises, rational person will exchange money into assets, whereupon the investment increases and the economic growth accelerates, resulting in the so-called "Tobin-Mundell" effect. If the inflation rate is too high, however, economic activities will be suppressed, with a resultant decrease of economic growth (Stockman, 1981). Here the consumer price index is used to reflect the actual inflation rate.

The level of urbanization (urban): A higher urbanization rate represents more human capital. In addition, the aggregation effect of the city will produce a higher return of the capital. But the higher the urbanization rate is, the higher the public spending is. Consequently, the effect of transfers may be partially offset. Here the level of urbanization is represented by the proportion of the urban population in the total.

Openness (open): Economic opening can reduce government intervention in the economy and restrict the government to spending more for productive investment. Thus openness can speed up economic growth. Here the ratio of import and export amount to GDP is used to represent the opening level.

Tax burden (tax): Distortion of taxation would be detrimental to economic growth, so there is an inverse correlation between tax rates and economic growth. Here the ratio of local government revenues to GDP is used to represent the tax burden in general.

Fix effects are used to do the calculation based on model (10.1). Taking into account the finiteness of samples, excessive loss of freedom degree will inevitably cause some variables insignificant. Therefore, lag items are gradually added. All the independent variables would automatically lag one period to ease the endogeneity problem. With only lagged one transfer included (the 2nd column in Table 10.3), it is shown that the transfer has

Table 10.3. Estimation of model (10.1).

var	(1)	(2)	(3)	(4)	(5)	(6)	(7)
tran	3.891***	2.757*	3.179**	4.988***	3.867**	3.925**	3.539**
	(1.388)	(1.447)	(1.392)	(1.535)	(1.548)	(1.568)	(1.596)
L1.tran	−3.653	3.750**	4.260***	4.663***	4.668***	4.169***	4.181***
	(3.264)	(1.489)	(1.458)	(1.475)	(1.476)	(1.504)	(1.536)
L2.tran	7.706***	−0.181	1.884	2.420	3.653**	4.080***	4.856***
	(1.259)	(3.242)	(1.466)	(1.528)	(1.472)	(1.481)	(1.503)
L3.tran	0.162***	8.794***	1.602	0.439	2.554*	2.693*	4.015***
	(0.020)	(1.338)	(3.187)	(1.487)	(1.496)	(1.507)	(1.479)
L4.tran	6.173***	0.132***	9.331***	2.599	−2.926**	−0.831	1.238
	(2.165)	(0.032)	(1.424)	(3.296)	(1.460)	(1.545)	(1.557)
L5.tran	−1.252	4.594**	0.010	10.663***	3.197	−4.435***	1.337
	(6.603)	(2.184)	(0.050)	(1.606)	(3.233)	(1.617)	(1.798)
L6.tran	45.802***	18.643**	3.073	−0.088	12.247***	2.319	−6.461***
	(12.735)	(7.756)	(2.194)	(0.064)	(1.701)	(3.261)	(2.341)
labour	46.889***	23.667*	30.384***	3.038	−0.142**	12.985***	0.989
	(10.388)	(13.808)	(7.870)	(2.368)	(0.064)	(1.831)	(3.201)
invest		39.094***	7.926	32.790***	3.130	−0.176**	10.442***
		(10.568)	(13.829)	(8.487)	(2.492)	(0.068)	(1.909)
cpi			41.705***	3.064	27.857***	3.245	−0.203***
			(10.582)	(15.131)	(8.194)	(2.817)	(0.073)
urban				40.073***	−5.481	17.558*	−0.306
				(11.041)	(15.439)	(9.935)	(3.163)
open					32.382***	−1.735	19.739*
					(10.930)	(16.144)	(10.923)
tax						31.064***	−10.684
						(11.209)	(18.038)
edu							23.816**
							(11.387)
R-sq	0.557	0.618	0.677	0.685	0.670	0.639	0.571
obs	360	330	300	270	240	210	180
AIC	3.792	3.686	3.571	3.565	3.447	3.392	3.260
SC	4.202	4.135	4.065	4.111	4.057	4.077	4.041

Note: Data in parentheses are standard errors, and *, ** and *** indicate 10%, 5% and 1% significant levels respectively.

significantly promoted local economic growth. With each percentage point of increase of the transfer intensity, the economic growth rate in the next year would increase 0.039 percentage point, indicating that short-term economic growth effects exist. As we continue to add lagged items of transfers (the 3rd column in Table 10.3), it can be found that two lagged items are significantly positive, and that the effect of current period begins to decrease while the effect of the lagged period is stronger, indicating that the short-term effects of transfers on economic growth mainly occur in the following year. This result is supported by most calculations later. Each percentage point of increase of transfer intensity would cause 0.028 percentage point of increase in GDP in the same year and 0.038 in the next year. When transfers lagged for two periods are added to the third estimation, the results show that the effects of these two items lagging for two periods are not significant while items in the same period and items lagging for one period are still significant.

Another interesting finding is that when we continue to add lagged transfer items in a fixed effects model (the 6th column in Table 10.3), the first three periods of transfers have positive effects on economic growth, and the fourth lagged item is only significant at 10% level, whereas the fifth lagged transfers and economic growth are negatively correlated, indicating that in the medium term, transfers may be detrimental to local economic growth. Lagged items are added again according to AIC criteria and finally to sixth lag. It is found that as new lagged items are added, the negative coefficient of the last lag keeps increasing from –2.926 to –6.461. It indicates that even the transfer could speed up economic growth in short term, and it would cause negative effect in the long term and the negative effect would increase as time goes by. With one percentage of the transfer increased, the local economic growth would change according to the following rules: GDP increases with 0.035 percentage point in the next year, and 0.042, 0.049 and 0.04 percentage point from the third year to the fifth year, respectively; the positive effects are offset by the negative effects in the sixth year and seventh year; and the negative effects become significant in the eighth year, causing the GDP growth to decrease by 0.065% point.

Seven regressions are listed in Table 10.3. Labour in these regressions is not significant, suggesting that labour does not, whereas the scanty capital does, constitute a constraint to local economic development. The investment ratios in all regressions are significantly positive. As the investment ratio increases one percentage point, the economic growth would rise 0.077–0.122 percentage point accordingly. The higher the degree of openness is, the more the government behavior would be constrained to form an effective market economy. Therefore, it is positively correlated with economic growth in the regressions. The coefficient of inflation is positive in some regressions, but it is negative in the fifth regression. The price factor does not significantly affect local economic development. The urbanization is not significant, as the human capital and the excessive public spending caused by urbanization offset the effects in a mutual way. The relationship between tax burden and economic growth is not obvious.

In the above regressions, however, the effect of the lagged items is actually supposed to be linear, which probably makes our calculations biased. As more and more lagged items are added, the loss of degree of freedom prevents us from obtaining the estimation after the seventh lag. Therefore, it is difficult to calculate the accurate long-term effects and accumulative effects. In view of these problems, the framework proposed by Mitchell and Speaker in 1986 is used in this study because of its two advantages. First, both the linear and nonlinear lagged effects are allowed in this method. In addition, indefinite delay similar to the Almon (1965) method is used to avoid artificial identification problem. And second, estimation can be done using OLS. The benchmark model is:

$$Y_{it} = a + \sum_{j=0}^{\infty} w_j Tran_{i,t-j} + \gamma X_{i,t-1} + \lambda_t + \eta_i + e_{it} \tag{10.2}$$

The difference between model (10.2) and model (10.1) lies in the weight w, which is expressed by:

$$w_j = \sum_{\tau=2}^{n} \frac{b_\tau}{(j+1)^\tau} \qquad j = 0, 1, \ldots, \infty \tag{10.3}$$

b in formula (10.3) is the coefficient to be computed, and j is the rank of lag. Substituting formula (10.3) into formula (10.2), we get:

$$Y_{it} = a + \sum_{\tau=2}^{\infty} b_\tau \sum_{j=0}^{t-1} \frac{Trans_{i,t-j}}{(j+1)^\tau} + \sum_{\tau=2}^{n} \sum_{j=t}^{\infty} \frac{b_\tau Tran_{t-j}}{(j+1)^\tau} + \gamma X_{i,t-1} + \lambda_t + \eta_i + e_{it} \quad (10.4)$$

When t > 8, the third item in the right side of formula (10.4) will approach 0, so it can be ignored. Thus the formula (10.4) can be expanded as:

$$\begin{aligned} Y_t = a + b_2(Tran_{it} + \frac{1}{2^2} Tran_{i,t\text{-}1} + \frac{1}{3^2} Tran_{i,t\text{-}2} + \ldots + \\ \frac{1}{m^2} Tran_{i,t\text{-}m+1}) + b_3(Tran_{it} + \frac{1}{2^3} Tran_{i,t\text{-}1} + \frac{1}{3^3} Tran_{i,\,t\text{-}2} \ldots + \\ \frac{1}{m^3} Tran_{i,t\text{-}m+1}) + \ldots + b_n(Tran_{it} + \frac{1}{2^n} Tran_{i,t\text{-}1} + \\ \frac{1}{3^n} Tran_{i,t\text{-}2} + \ldots + \frac{1}{m^n} Tran_{i,t\text{-}m+1}) + \gamma X_{i,t-1} + \lambda_t + \eta_i + e_{it} = \\ a + b_2 PIL_2 + b_3 PIL_3 + \ldots + b_n PIL_n + \gamma X_{i,t-1} + \lambda_t + \eta_i + e_{it} \end{aligned} \quad (10.5)$$

The various coefficients will be computed using formula (10.5) and then be substituted into the formula (10.3) to obtain the value of *w*. Then w_0, i.e., the effect of transfers in the same period, and w_i ($i = 1,\ldots\infty$), i.e., the lag effect of transfer in the following periods, and the accumulative effects $\sum_{i=0}^{\infty} w_i$ can be obtained. Finally the model can be used to compute how much the local economy will be affected in the short term and in the long term when the central transfers are increased by every one unit.

Prior to the computation, there are two parameters to be set. The first one is the value of *n*, i.e., the number of polynomials. As the true model form is unknown, the method to select *n* depends on the fitting capacity of the model. According to the formula (10.4), the collinearity between adjacent items will get increasingly serious as the value of *n* increases. Therefore, the method employed by Mitchell and Speaker (1986) is used in this study, starting from the highest rank of *n* ($n = 7$), and gradually removing insignificant polynomials. The other one is the value of parameter *m*. Referring to the approach applied by Wan *et al.* (2006), assume $m = 9$. Namely, it is assumed that the effects after the

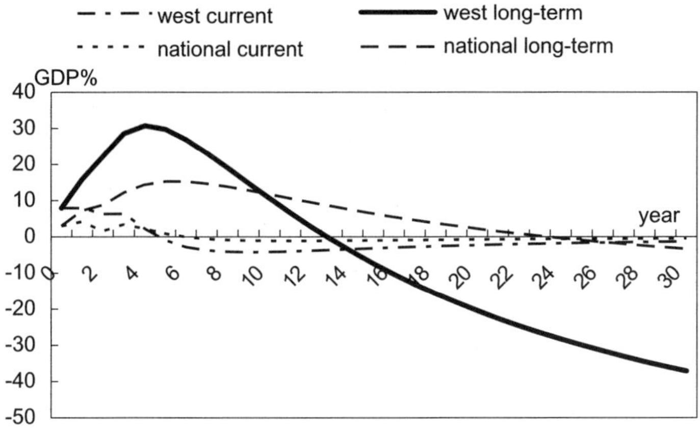

Fig. 10.4. The short-term and long-term effects of transfer on growth.

eighth periods will be so small that it would not make the estimated value of b biased.

In order to obtain robust results, one-way fixed effects, two-way fixed effects, and the lagged dependent variables are employed. Growth effects of the east areas, the central areas, and the west areas are computed, respectively. The estimated values of parameters of each polynomial are computed by the regression of formula (10.5). Effects in each period and the accumulative effects are computed by formula (10.3). Growth effects in each year are presented in Figure 10.4 where effects in each period and the accumulative effects are showed by the dotted lines and the solid line, respectively. As the ratio of transfers to the local fiscal revenues increases by one percentage point, GDP growth of the current year increases by 0.03 percentage point, and that of the next year increases by 0.04 percentage point which is the highest. The effects of the transfers begin to decrease continuously from the third year. Transfers begin to have negative effects from the seventh year and the negative effect reaches the highest level in the twelfth year. From then on, transfer effects begin to converge to zero. If the positive and negative effects are evaluated comprehensively, the accumulative effects on economic growth begin to be negative from the 25th year. If the observation period is extended to 30 years, the transfer increasing by one percentage point would make the long-term local economic growth decrease by 0.03 percentage point. The cumulative effect of the western region is the largest. The economic growth in the west region would decrease by 0.37 percentage point within 30 years with every percentage point of increase in the intensity of transfers. The coefficient values of polynomials in equation (10.5) differ when the year dummy is controlled, but the effect of transfer is identical with Figure 10.4. All the cumulative effects of transfer are negative, the difference being that when the negative effects first appear.

The comparison of the previous two methods shows that our estimation is consistent. Correlation coefficient between the results in Figure 10.4 and in the eighth column in Table 10.3 reaches 0.744 and passes the test at the significant level of 5%. If only the effects in the west region calculated by the two methods are analyzed, the correlation coefficient of the effects lagged for five periods reaches 0.956 and passes the test at the level of 1%. It indicates that the framework proposed by Mitchell and Speaker can not only calculate long-term cumulative effects, but also produce the same results of short-term effects with those calculated by traditional methods. This method can be understood in a simple way that lagged effect of model (10.1) is simulated using polynomials to obtain values of each period.

There are some basic conclusions. The short-term effects of transfers are positive, because from the short-term perspective, more transfers imply more government spending and investments, which directly constitute economic growth of the year. From the long-term perspective, however, effects of transfers on economic growth begin to be negative from the seventh period and remains so from then on. The accumulative effect would also change from positive to negative. Therefore, on average, any transfers will be detrimental to efficiency. Furthermore, providing less developed regions with more transfers will further reduce the efficiency.

10.4. The Structural Changes Generated by Fiscal Transfer

The relationship between fiscal transfer and economic growth might imply the difference of fiscal transfer from revenues. While fiscal transfer may increase capital in less developed provinces and improve the quality of infrastructure, the structural changes incurred by such transfer cannot be ignored. The areas with more fiscal transfers might experience worse market institution and government governance, which will be deteriorated by nontransparent transfer allocation from the central government.

10.4.1. *Transfer has not narrowed the regional fiscal disparities*

The tax sharing system established in 1994 has vertically improved the fiscal power of the central government, while the horizontal disparities still exist. The system protects the vested interest of local governments and ensures that the revenue in coastal areas would not decline through tax rebate. Meanwhile, the fiscal disparities between different areas are expected to be balanced through the transfer from the old system, namely the transfer from the old system and the contribution (to the central government) before tax sharing system, which is actually far from enough to bridge the fiscal disparities, with some provinces even canceling the transfer from the old system to local governments. In 1995, transitional transfer, i.e., increased transfer to impoverished provinces, was introduced to stop the enlarging fiscal disparities. As is shown in Figure 10.5, transitional transfer does not effectively ease the fiscal disparities. On the contrary, the disparity in spending per capita in 2000 is larger than that in 1994. The Lorenz Curve of spending per capita also shows that, in 2000, the spending in some counties is remarkably higher than the average spending of the whole nation.

As for fiscal balance, with the data from over 2000 counties in China and the decomposition method proposed by Shorrocks, Tsui (2005) has found that, among all the fiscal transfers, the transfer from the old system is the only way that can help bridge the fiscal disparity. In 2000, more than 21% of the fiscal disparities were caused by tax rebate. Furthermore, the transfer system in the transitional period, which offered subsidy to areas with fiscal gap according to a fixed formula so as to achieve fiscal equalization, in effect expanded the fiscal disparities and 3% of the disparities were caused by transitional transfer. In western development, a large number of fiscal resources are transferred to the west. As a result, the

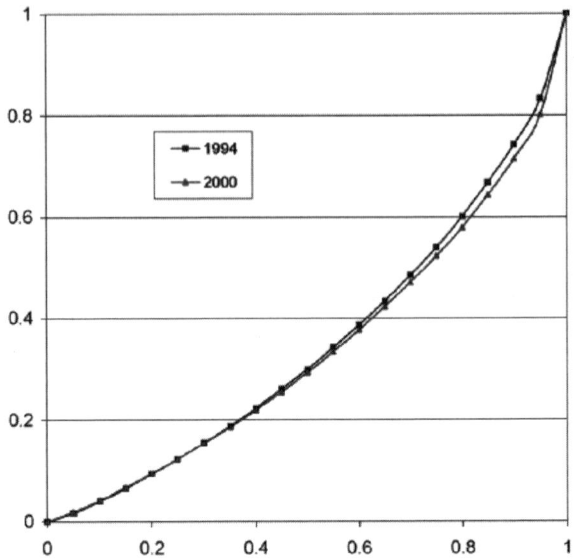

Fig. 10.5. The Lorenz Curve of county-level government spending per capita.

eastern and central provinces are unable to acquire those resources due to their geological locations. In fact, the fiscal disparities within a region are larger than those between different regions, which implies that problems still exist in the approach of allocating transfer by dividing the nation into eastern, central and western regions.

Among all the categories of the fiscal transfer, targeted transfers and tax rebates are the most unequal since these two are not aimed at narrowing the fiscal disparities (Shih and Zhang, 2007). In 2003, the fiscal resources per capita in the richest province were 37.4 times as large as those in the poorest province, with targeted transfers accounting for 17.7% of the disparity (Yin *et al.*, 2007). Targeted transfers require matching funds from local governments, which makes it impossible for the impoverished areas to get the transfers and thus expands the fiscal disparities (Ahmad, 1998; Park *et al.*, 1996). Meanwhile, the allocation of fiscal transfer depends on both economic and political factors. The economic factors include income and urbanization. The province with the lowest income acquires more fiscal transfer, while urbanization rate is positively correlated with fiscal transfer since urbanization level represents necessary amount of public expenditure. Though the economic factors help address the expanding disparities, in the allocation formula of fiscal transfer, even the transfer aimed at narrowing the fiscal disparities is based on fiscal gap of the local governments rather than on the development level of the economy. This makes the local governments, especially those at county-level, increase the standard fiscal spending by recruiting more staff and as a result enlarge the financial gap to get more resources from the central government. The central government, consequently, has to increase the transfer to cover the financial gap of the local governments so as to maintain political stability (Shih and Zhang, 2007). On the other hand, the importance of political factors in the allocation of fiscal transfer outweighs that of economic factors. For instance, the federal government of the United States offers more fiscal transfers to the states which are responsible for the re-election of the president. This, however, more often than not, leads to the contradiction of economic factors and political factors, for the states with great political importance always have higher level of income. As a result, the states with higher income get more fiscal transfers (Wallis, 1996). For another instance, each year after the integration of East Germany and West Germany in 1990, the federal government transfers 5% of the output of West Germany to narrow the disparity between the east and west of Germany. As is true in China, the central government offers more transfers to minority areas (Wang, 2004). Also, in the allocation of transfer types, it is found that the provinces where more members in the CPC (Communist Party of China) Central Committee have ever worked get more targeted transfers (Fan and Zhang, 2010a), which is similar to the conclusion of Knight (2002).

10.4.2. *Transfer has enlarged the size of government*

Targeted transfer requires changes in local government behaviors, while fiscal transfer requires no such changes. However, fiscal transfer will also bring changes to local government behaviors and thus have an impact on the economic development and administrative efficiency if the transfer is not entirely in accordance with the revenue of the local governments. The early public finance and Wagner's Law hold that the main factor affecting the size of a local government is the income constraint, while the income components make little difference. In other words, local governments regard both fiscal transfer and local tax as their income, so they will lower the tax rate if they get more transfer and correspondingly raise the tax rate if they get less transfer. The transfer from higher levels of government will only bring income effect and extend the budget constraint of the local governments. Therefore, the size of government will not change according to the change of income structure (Bradford and Oates, 1971). In effect, this also implies that the fiscal policy made by the central government would not affect the size of local governments. Nevertheless, empirical studies show that the expansion of government size is far beyond Wagner's Law and the public finance. The increase of one dollar in local revenues only leads to an increase of spending by 0.02–0.05 dollar, while the same increase in transfer will result in the increase of spending by almost one dollar or even more than one dollar. This indicates that, with the same income, the size of government will be larger in province with more transfers. This "Anomaly" phenomenon is called "Flypaper Effect" (Hines and Thaler, 1995; Brennan and Pincus, 1996). There are two factors accounting for this effect. One factor has much to do with the features of the transfer recipient, such as the special institution, uncertainties and fiscal illusion of the local governments (Bailey and Connolly, 1998). The other factor is concerned with the transfer appropriator, the central government, which may prohibit local governments from using the transfer to cover other spending. The flypaper effect will become more remarkable if the use of transfer is supervised (Chubb, 1985). It is found that the flypaper effect in China ranges from 0.6 to 1.3, which means that each unit of transfer will lead to the increase of 0.6 to 1.3 units in government spending. This is similar to most countries (Fan and Zhang, 2010a).

However, the impact of transfer on the size of government is far beyond this, and transfer is closely related to the staff redundancy in government. In China, this redundancy in government has always been the focus of administration reform due to the unique political system of "being responsible for higher authorities". For instance, the policy of "three incentives and one subsidy" was implemented by the central government in 2005 to encourage local governments to lay off employees. China has experienced six large-scale reforms ever since 1982 without palpable successes.

Among the six reforms, the one in 1998 was the most vigorous, with the ministries in State Council reduced from 40 to 29, departments and bureaus reduced by 1/4, and government staff reduced from 33,000 to 16,000. The reform was extended to local governments in 1999 and was accomplished in 2002, stipulating that the staff in provincial governments be halved and the staff in governments in cities, counties and towns be reduced by 20%. As a result, the staff in administrative authorities at various levels decreased from 7.39 million to 6.24 million, with the largest number of staff being reduced among the six reforms. Though governments had been scaling down since 1995 and reached their lowest level in 2002–2003, they were bouncing back after that and in 2007 reached the same level as they were before the reform. It can be seen in Figure 10.6 that redundancy is more likely to appear in inland areas, with no remarkable influence from the administration reform. Currently the size of government staff per 10,000 in inland areas is twice the size in eastern areas.

Based on the data at county level from 1994 to 2003, Yuan *et al.* (2007) find that the more dependent on transfer the local government is, the more government staff there will be. They also explain that the redundancy in less developed areas is caused by the fact that, due to their economic disadvantages, the governments are more likely to increase staff to establish the local political support network and maintain the stability of the areas when they get fiscal transfer. Nevertheless, it is found in our research that,

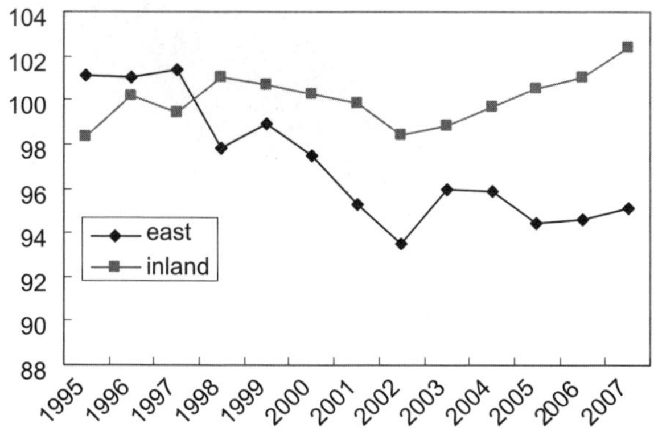

Fig. 10.6. The size of government staff per 10,000.

compared with fiscal subsidies, targeted transfers are more likely to cause redundancy in local governments, for the increase of 10,000 yuan in targeted transfers per capita will lead to the increase of 98.6 government staff per 10,000, which doubles the current size. Central government has to be tolerant towards such situation on the grounds that targeted transfers are supposed to provide public goods though they will bring about the expansion of spending and government staff (Fan and Zhang, 2010b). The reason why targeted transfers will lead to the expansion of government staff is that specialized staff members are needed by local governments to operate the transfers, which results in the growth of government size (Shih and Zhang, 2007). Provincial and municipal governments even encourage and induce county governments to recruit more staff to get more transfer from central government, and intercept part of the transfer. Under the frame of decentralized governance, it is difficult for central government to get across provincial governments and directly adjust the size of county governments (Shih *et al.*, 2010). Statistically, with the data at county level in 2005, Figure 10.7 reveals that fiscal transfer is positively correlated with fiscal dependents.

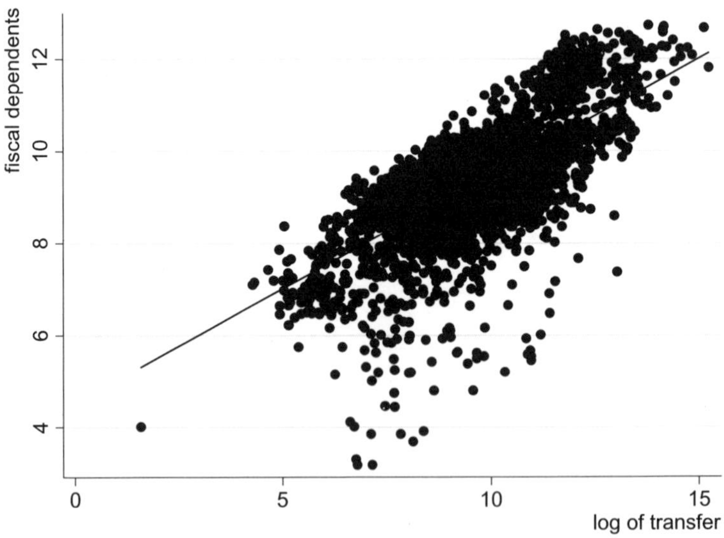

Fig. 10.7. The fiscal dependents and transfer in 2005.

10.4.3. *Transfer induces the local corruption*

Since corruption is illegal, government officials will make every effort to avoid being detected when they search for rents and accept bribes. Therefore, corruption tends to exist in areas where effective supervision is impossible. Meanwhile, officials will look for potential bribes by changing government spending. As a result, corruption will lead to distortion effect, which includes two parts: one is less individual effort and the other is influenced government spending. Government may have inadequate spending in some fields but excessive supply in other fields. A cross-country research made by Mauro (1998) shows that the countries with more corruption will spend more on large-scale infrastructure and intricate national defense equipment but less on education.

Similar is the case of China. For instance, from 1997 to 2002, three directors of Traffic Office of Henan Province were dismissed for corruption, which implies that corruption is common in fields of infrastructure in China. Figure 10.8 shows the relationship between infrastructure investment and corruption. It can be seen from the figure that infrastructure and corruption manifest the same trend in time sequence. Both infrastructure

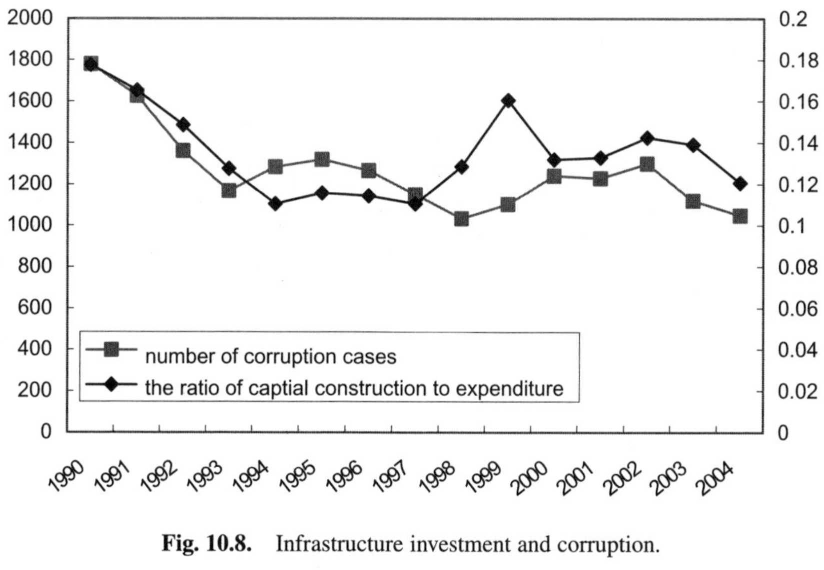

Fig. 10.8. Infrastructure investment and corruption.

investment and corruption were declining from 1990 to 1994 and then remained stable until 1997. Since 1998, expansive fiscal policy was adopted to stimulate economic growth, and infrastructure investment was increased substantially backed by fiscal deficit and debt. Consequently, the ratio of capital infrastructure to expenditure increased from 11% in 1997 to 16% in 1999, and remained at a relatively high level thereafter. At the same time, the number of corruption cases also increased from 1,032 in 1998 to 1 240 in 2000, an increase of more than 20%.

Transfer causes corruption in two ways. On one hand, the areas with more transfer will invest more on infrastructure (Figure 10.2), so the transfer will lead to corruption directly. On the other hand, transfer will influence the efficiency of infrastructure investment and thus causes indirect corruption. This indirect influence refers to the weakened supervision of local governments on corruption. Most studies on corruption suggest that governmental supervision can effectively prevent corruption (Skidmore, 1996). Intuitively, the appropriate measurement of the effort of governmental supervision should be the persons and resources that are devoted by local anti-corruption authorities, however no such spending is specified in China. Therefore, juridical spending is used as a dummy. To put it simply, the more a local government spends on the legal system, the more it will spend on anti-corruption. Meanwhile, anti-corruption is an essential element of the legal system. Figure 10.9 shows the relationship between ratio of juridical spending to expenditure and ratio of transfer to expenditure. The scatter diagram indicates that these two factors are negatively correlated, which suggests that the local governments with more transfer will loosen the supervision on funds for the reason that, compared with the local fiscal revenues, the cost of transfer is lower. Even if corruption will lead to lower utilization efficiency of funds, local governments will be more tolerant if the funds are from the central government. Consequently, less effort will be devoted to anti-corruption.

10.5. The Fiscal Reform Agenda

The fiscal policy in China is one of the most critical bridges connecting the higher levels of governments and lower levels of governments. Fiscal

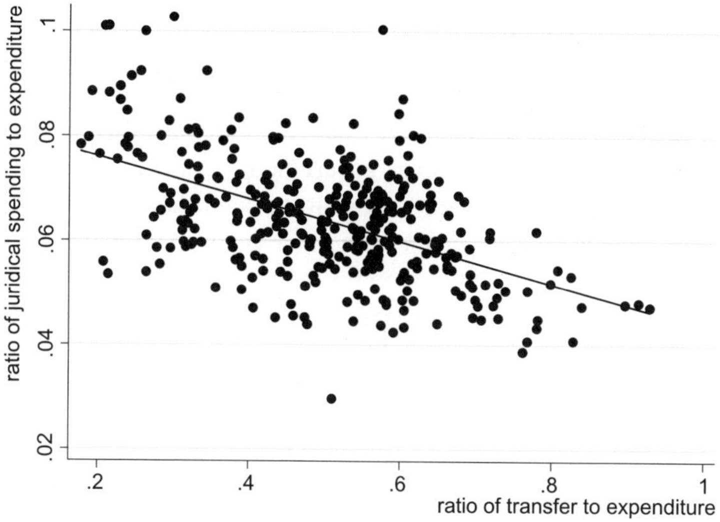

Fig. 10.9. Anti-corruption and transfer.

relation is used by the central government to coordinate the behaviors of local governments. Thus, fiscal system is closely related to the political system of a nation. In a nation with a policy of being responsible for higher authorities, fiscal system should match the centralization of politics. Otherwise, there will be a disconnection between economic powers and political powers. Therefore, this section mainly discusses how to improve the Chinese fiscal policy to make it function more positively and at the same time avoid the above-mentioned side effects against the current background.

10.5.1. *Reform of fiscal revenues*

As for the sharing of fiscal revenues, there are impulses and incentives for the central government to share more revenues of local governments, with the reform of income tax sharing in 2002 as a typical example. Therefore, to lower the share of the central government is implausible and is contradictory to the centralization of politics. Nevertheless, many reforms concerned with fiscal revenues are worth promoting. First of all, for the management of land lease rent, the central government extracts 75% of value-added tax, the largest tax and controls such good tax types as tariff, with a comparatively small part of the tax left to local governments. Meanwhile, the transfer from the central government is more likely to be offered to the less developed areas and the responsibility of spending increases the burden of the local government. In developed provinces, local governments cannot get much from tax and therefore turn to non-budgetary revenues so as to increase their income with the economic growth. Nevertheless, traditional extra-budgetary revenues cannot meet their demand and have been squeezed by previous reforms of the budget system. Therefore, land lease rent has become a good alternative for local governments. Land lease rent, which is highly fluctuating, belongs neither to budgetary revenues, nor to non-budgetary revenues, but to government fund revenues. An economically developed city will attract more labour force, which will raise the house prices. Accordingly, land lease rent increases, which indicates that land lease rent rises with the growth of economy. Besides, according to the land system in China, more of the land lease rent belongs to county governments, which is in accordance with the current division of responsibilities to lower authorities. The booming land sales can even be attributed to the match of revenues and the division of responsibilities to lower authorities.

However, the drawbacks in land lease rent are obvious. It raises house prices and the savings ratio of residents, causing lower ratio of consumption to GDP. In some coastal cities, such as Hangzhou, land lease rent is even larger than budgetary revenues. The local government is resistant to the central regulating policies in real estate market nation-wide, and the pro-cyclical behavior of local governments aggravates the fluctuation of macro-economy. Land lease rent is generally spent on urban construction, which improves the infrastructure and traffic condition of the city, but inevitably enhances investment level and lowers investment efficiency. Moreover, non-standardized management of land lease rent also causes corruption.

As for the reform of land lease rent, the rent should be turned over to the state treasury and gradually managed as extra-budget revenue, with its receipt and expenditure managed separately. As for the use of land lease rent, a major share of it should be spent on livelihood projects so as to enlarge the input on public service. However, it is difficult to standardize the policy for land lease rent. One plausible approach is to impose house property tax to partly replace of the land lease rent, which is also the international practice. This can avoid the impact of local governments' behavior on macro-economy and make the local revenue sustainable.

Another reform related to fiscal revenue is the reform of value-added tax. Currently, the value-added tax in China is a kind of investment tax, which is detrimental to the development of enterprises. The VAT reform was tried out in the three northeast provinces (Jilin, Liaoning and Heilongjiang) in 2004. Though it was planned to be publicized in the whole country in 2005, it did not happen as planned. Therefore, it is necessary to implement consumption-type VAT for the development of private economy. Another characteristic of VAT is its collection by the total amount, and this is harmful for the specialized production of intermediate goods which is a crucial element for industrial agglomeration. Hence, there should be different VAT rates for different products, and in particular, favorable tax policies should be made for intermediate goods. The third characteristic of VAT is its collection by affiliated areas. In other words, VAT is collected by the area to which the headquarters is affiliated, which will aggravate the segmentation by local governments. Thus, the reaction of local governments needs to be re-evaluated for the collection of VAT.

10.5.2. *Reform of fiscal expenditures*

The provision of China's current public services is the primary responsibility of local governments, and corresponding subsidy is provided by the central government, which constitutes the reason why China has such a huge fiscal transfer payment. The institutional reform implemented by the Zhu Rongji Administration significantly compressed the central ministries, and a large number of expenditure responsibilities were further delegated to lower governments. Considering that a series of fiscal reforms has reduced the financial sources of local governments, subsidies are given by the central government in the form of fiscal transfers. For example, subsidies for social security increased from 10 billion yuan in 2000 to 111.8 billion yuan in 2003, and subsidies for the salary of civil servants increased to 100 billion yuan in 2003. However, a series of studies has found that this system is not very effective. When the central government delegates the responsibilities to local governments, the first response of local governments is to expand their staff payroll. Some less-developed areas even have to compress the spending on education and agriculture due to the rapid expansion of staff, which means that the increase in transfer payments is not used in public services, but is absorbed by the local governments instead. In addition, the provision of public services is based on economies of scale, and the policies made by the central government are decentralized, which is detrimental to the efficiency in both the quantity and quality.

If the degree of decentralization in China is measured by expenditure, it is the huge fiscal transfer that makes local spending account for more than 55%, and China is a country with very thorough decentralization. As a horizontal contrast, available data in 100 countries reveal that this proportion is only 13% in developing countries, and only 35% in developed countries, far below the level of China. The reason for this situation in China is the excessive delegation of responsibilities to lower governments.

Based on the above arguments, it is necessary for Chinese central government to withdraw some of the expenditure responsibilities. The benefit is two-fold. On the one hand, the standard of public services can be enhanced, because the increase of state revenues can avoid the embezzlement of funds and assist the equalization of public services. On the other hand, the increase of state revenues can avoid problems arising from huge transfer payments and reduce the size of local governments. All expenditures for social security should be provided by the central government, because social security, especially the social safety net, is the bottom line of residents in a society, and the provision of expenditures by the central government safeguards the basic rights of residents. Moreover, expenditures for public safety should also be provided by state revenues, for the regional differences in such expenditures are relatively small, and there is less informational asymmetry. Finally, the expenditures on education and health can be jointly provided by the central and local governments, but the expenditures from the central government should be able to maintain the basic expenditures in these areas, and more investment can be added to these areas based on local economic conditions.

10.5.3. *Reform of fiscal transfers*

Reform is imperative to reduce the negative effects brought by the transfer and improve the transfer system. As is mentioned above, China's current fiscal transfer has given rise to some negative effects. For example, the distribution of transfer payments does not play the role of fiscal capacity equalization, the transfer induces the local governments to expand staff members, and it also causes corruption of local governments, and so on. The difficulty related to the reform of fiscal transfer is that it is necessary for the transfer not only to reach the goal of the central government such as promoting the livelihood projects, but also to play a role in maintaining the centralization of powers and coordinating the behaviors of local governments — however, these two goals sometimes conflict with each other.

First, for targeted transfers, although it is necessary to adopt some matching requirements to encourage the investment from local governments, the ratio of local tax can be added in order to avoid the negative impacts of targeted transfers on the incentives of collecting local taxes. Meanwhile, it is necessary to change the current "multiple policies from different departments" for targeted transfers, and integrate the same or similar projects into the same department, or to centralize the powers for the grant so as to create a relatively uniform and transparent disbursement formula to avoid rent-seeking activities.

Second, for the fiscal transfer, the role of factor method should be strengthened, but in the mechanism design more objective indicators should be used to avoid the indicators which can be operated by local governments, such as the standard fiscal expenditures based on total population instead of fiscal dependents. In addition, the current policy of distributing the transfer by eastern, central and western areas should be changed, and the transfer should be directly linked to fiscal equalization.

10.5.4. *Other reforms related to balanced regional development*

Balanced regional development is crucially important, but its objective should be based on the economic output per capita, and thus the reforms should focus on promoting the convergence of output per capita. In addition, the overall investment in public services is relatively low, which is detrimental to future economic growth. Meanwhile the government's spending behavior is affected by the current political system, and therefore it is necessary to reform the administrative system to stimulate the function of government public finance.

In the short term, the central government needs to reform the existing system to ease the embarrassing situation at the present stage. First, in the near future, reform the evaluation system to avoid the "non-cooperative game" by the less-developed areas, and to encourage local governments to focus on economic development rather than on the next-stage central subsidy. Therefore, one focus of reform is to enhance the evaluation on livelihood projects, and encourage local governments to pay closer attention to the provision of public services. On the other hand, different GDP evaluation indices should be implemented in different regions to avoid the non-cooperation of local governments, such as GDP scale for eastern regions and GDP per capita for less developed regions. Secondly, the current structure of government and administrative boundaries must be reformed. As can be seen from the above analysis, provincial governments, especially municipal governments, play a negative role in fiscal transfers, and therefore, based on the current trial of "reinforcing county government for its prosperity", the government structure of "county directly governed by the province" should be implemented gradually to weaken the administrative power of municipal governments.

The current factor market is still very imperfect, and there are explicit or implicit barriers in capital, land, and trans-regional mobility of labour. It is the inadequate factor marketization that makes the central government to try to use administrative power to promote the balanced regional development. To a certain extent, the mobility of factors and government transfer payments can replace each other, and more transfer means less local revenues and more local public goods, so the marginal utility acquired by local residents in public goods is in line with that in private goods, thus reducing the mobility of factors (Breton, 1965). Conversely, if the factor mobility between regions is limited because of the system or the cost, the Pareto optimal can be gained by fiscal transfers from the central government. The analysis in this chapter shows that China's transfer at this stage plays a limited role in regional balance. Even if it functions positively in the provision of public goods, the structural changes brought by it cannot be ignored. In the case of free movement of factors, the residents can increase the supply level of public goods through the mechanism of "voting with their feet", which can avoid the negative effects brought by the transfer. Meanwhile, because of the existence of economies of scale, free movement of factors can help make a bigger "cake" and, at the same time, allocate the "cake" more rationally. Therefore, future reform should be based on enhancing the mobility of factors among different regions. On the one hand, the political barriers impeding the mobility of factors should be eliminated, such as the abolition of the residential permit system (*hukou* in Chinese) and the establishment of cross-region urban and rural social security system. On the other hand, the cost of factor mobility should be reduced as much as possible by providing basic skills training, establishing regional labour markets, etc.

10.6. Conclusion

As is indicated in *World Development Report 2009*, it is unprecedented to promote balanced development by administrative power of the government, and China is no exception. The ratio of GDP in western and central areas to domestic GDP declined respectively from 20.24% and 29.62% in 1980 to 17.14% and 23.19% in 2006. Since the beginning of the second decade of Western Development, the central government continued to offer more support to inland areas through administrative support in order to narrow the disparities between different areas. However, our research shows that this policy proves to be dissatisfactory in promoting economic growth. The areas with more transfers may exhibit substantial short-term economic growth, but the long-term growth might be worse. The reasons for this negative effect are complex. On the one hand, many drawbacks exist in the distribution of the transfers. The current transfer system comprises multiple political, economic and social objectives that conflict with each other. For example, minority areas get more transfers, but the economic conditions in those regions are not the worst. However, for the stability of the central government, the distribution plans for targeted transfers are subject to changes, keeping the investment efficiency of many projects at a low level. On the other hand, the transfer received by inland provinces also fails to effectively promote economic growth, not only because of the low efficiency of resource utilization, such as over-investment in infrastructure and under-investment in education and health care, but also because of the structural changes brought by the transfer, which makes it more difficult for those less developed areas to form a competitive market system and effective governance. Finally, transfer will expand the size of the local governments and cause corruption of local governments.

In addition, the reforms of the fiscal system since the 1990s are limited to the revisions of the original system, and lack an in-depth reform of the whole system. Under the existing administrative system, the central government wants to have absolute authority, and also hopes to reach its objectives through local governments, such as the provision of public goods and economic balance. Thus, it can only adjust the form of the transfer to stimulate local governments, and reallocate, by its fiscal power, the resources to different regions and governments at all levels. We hope that the reform of the fiscal system and other corresponding systems can achieve the following three objectives. First, the public financial function will be promoted to withdraw governments from economic activities and to improve the market economic system. Governments will only play the public financial function in economic activities and be mainly responsible for the provision of public services. Next, factors will move freely, and the inter-regional GDP per capita will converge continuously so as to reach the goal of balanced regional development in terms of economic output per capita. And finally, the relationship between central and local governments will be stable and explicit, the rights of governments at all levels in revenues and expenditures will match their corresponding responsibilities, and the public services in different regions will be equalized.

References

Abramowitz, M. (1985). "Catching Up, Forging Ahead, and Falling Behind." *Journal of Economic History*, 66, 385–406.

Acemoglu, D. and Zilibotti, F. (1999). "Productivity Differences." NBER Working Paper 6879.

Ahmad, E. (1998). "The Reform of the Fiscal Transfer System." In D. Brean (ed.), *Taxation in Modern China*. London: Routledge.

Almon, S. (1965). "The Distributed Lag Between Capital Appropriations and Net Expenditures." *Econometrica*, 33, 178–196.

Bailey, S.J. and Connolly, S. (1988). "The Flypaper Effect: Identifying Areas for Further Research." *Public Choice*, 95, 335–361.

Barro, R.J. (1990). "Government Spending in a Simple Model of Endogenous Growth." *Journal of Political Economy*, 98, 103–125.

Bradford, D.F. and Oates, W.E. (1971). "The Analysis of Revenue Sharing in a New Approach to Collective Fiscal Decisions." *Quarterly Journal of Economics*, 85(3), 416–439.

Brennan, G. and Pincus, J.J. (1996). "A Minimalist Model of Federal Grants and Flypaper Effects." *Journal of Public Economics*, 61, 229–246.

Chubb, J.E. (1985). "The Political Economy of Federalism." *American Political Science Review*, 79, 994–1015.

Clemens, M.A., Radelet, S. and Bhavnani, R. (2004). "Counting Chickens when they Hatch: The Short Term Effect of Aid on Growth." Working Paper No. 44, Center for Global Development.

Fan, Z. and Zhang, J. (2010a). "Flypaper Effect: An Explanation to the Expansion of Government Size" (in Chinese). *China Industrial Economics*, 12, 5–15.

Fan, Z. and Zhang, J. (2010b). "Intergovernmental Transfer, Provision of Public Goods and the Expansion of Government Size" (in Chinese). Working paper.

Fujita, M., Krugman, P.R. and Venables, A.J. (1999). *The Spatial Economy: Cities, Regions and International Trade*. Cambridge, Mass.: MIT Press.

Hines, J.R. and Thaler, R.H. (1995). "Anomalies: The Flypaper Effect." *Journal of Economic Perspectives*, 9(4), 217–226.

Jia, J. and Guo Q. (2008). "The Effects of Intergovernmental Assignments of Public Revenue and Expenditure Responsibility on the Regional Economic Growth" (in Chinese). *The Economic Research Journal*, 6, 37–49.

Jia, K. and Zhao, Q. (2008). *Thirty-Year Reform of China: The Fiscal and Tax System* (in Chinese). Chongqing: Chongqing University Press.

Knight, B. (2002). "Endogenous Federal Grants And Crowd-out of State Government Spending: Theory and Evidence from the Federal Highway Aid Program." *American Economic Review*, 92(1), 71–92.

Li, P. (2006). *The Figure Interpretations of Chinese Inter-Governments* (in Chinese). Beijing: Chinese Fiscal and Economic Press.

Lucas, R.E. (1988). "On the Mechanism of Economic Development." *Journal of Monetary Economics*, 22(1), 3–42.

Ma, J. (1997). *Intergovernmental Relations and Economic Management in China.* England: Macmillan Press.

Mauro, P. (1998). "Corruption and the Composition of Government Expenditure." *Journal of Public Economics*, 69, 263–279.

Mitchell, D.W. and Speaker, P.J. (1986). "A Simple, Flexible Distributed Lag Technique." *Journal of Econometrics*, 31, 329–340.

Naughton, B. (2007). *The Chinese Economy: Transitions and Growth.* Cambridge, Mass.: The MIT Press.

Park, A., Rozelle, S. Wong, C. and Ren, C. (1996). "Distributional Consequences of Reforming Local Public Finance in China." *China Quarterly*, 147(9), 751–778.

Rajan, R.G. and Subramanian, A. (2008). "Aid and Growth: What does the Cross-Country Evidence." *Review of Economics and Statistics*, 90(4), 643–665.

Romer, P. (1986). "Increasing Returns and Long-Run Growth." *Journal of Political Economy*, 94(5), 1002–1037.

Scott, A.D. (1952). "The Evaluation of Federal Grants." *Econometric*, 19, 377–394.

Shih, V. and Zhang, Q. (2007). "Who Receives Subsidies: A Look at the County Level in Two Time Periods." In V. Shue and C. Wong (eds), *Paying for Progress in China.* London: Routledge.

Shih, V., Zhang, Q. and Liu, M. (2010). "When the Autocrat Gives: Determinants of Fiscal Transfers in Authoritarian China." Submitted to *World Politics.*

Skidmore, M.J. (1996). "Promise and Peril in Combating Corruption: Hong Kong's ICAC." *Annals of the American Academy of Political and Social Science*, 547, 118–130.

Stockman, A.C. (1981). "Anticipated Inflation and the Capital Stock in a Cash-in-Advance Economy." *Journal of Monetary Economics*, 8, 378–393.

The Audit Bureau (2006). *The Audit Report of Central Government's Budget in 2005.*

Tsui, K. (2005). "Local Tax System, Intergovernmental Transfers and China's Local Fiscal Disparities." *Journal of Comparative Economics*, 33, 173–196.

Wallis, J.J. (1996). "What Determines the Allocation of National Government Grants to the States?" NBER Working Papers Series on Historical Factors in Long Run Growth.

Wan, G., Lu, M. and Chen, Z. (2006). "The Inequality-Growth Nexus in the Short and Long Runs: Empirical Evidence from China." *Journal of Comparative Economics*, 34(4), 654–667.

Wang, S. (2004). "The Change to the People" (in Chinese). *Strategy and Management*, 2, 51–60.

Wilde, J.A. (1971). "Grants-In-Aid: The Analytics of Design and Response." *National Tax Journal*, 24, 143–156.

Yao, Y. (2007). "Investigating the Equalization and Incentive Effect of Intergovernmental Grants in China." Working paper, Cornell University.

Yin, H., Kang, L. and Wang, L. (2007). "The Equalization Effects of Fiscal Transfer" (in Chinese). *Management World*, 1, 48–55.

Yuan, F., Tao, R., Xu, Z. and Liu, M. (2008). "Fiscal Transfers and Expansion of Fiscal Dependents in China's Fiscal Recentralization" (in Chinese). *The Economic Research Journal*, 5, 70–80.

CHAPTER 11

REDESIGNING CHINA'S TRADE POLICY IN THE POST-CRISIS ERA

*Changyuan Luo and Lin Chen**

11.1. Introduction

More than three decades have passed since China implemented the opening-up policy. From 1978 to 2009, the average annual growth rate of GDP and per capita GDP reaches 10% and 8.8% in comparable price (previous year price = 100).[1] Calculated in the price of 1978, GDP and per capita GDP in 2009 were 18.6 times and 13.4 times those in 1978. Such achievements could hardly be achieved without China's active participation in the global division of labour. In 1978, the total trade volume was 35.5 billion yuan, a 9.74 percentage of GDP; while in 2009, it reached 15.06 billion yuan, accounting for 44% of GDP. Especially, the past four years have witnessed several historical records in China's foreign trade. In 2008, the total trade volume hit its peak of 17.99 trillion yuan since 1978. In 2006 and 2007, the proportion of trade in GDP reached its maximum of 67%. Trade balance surplus climbed to its peak of 2.09 trillion yuan in 2008,

*The authors thank Yiwei Chen and Yan Jin for their research assistance. Financial supports from National Social Science Foundation of China (11CJL039) and 985 Project for Social Science Research of Fudan University are greatly appreciated. Changyuan Luo is the corresponding author, Email: chyluo@fudan.edu.cn. Lin Chen, Email: lchen@jjx.ecnu.edu.cn.

[1] Statistics are quoted from *China Statistical Yearbook* of relevant years unless otherwise stated.

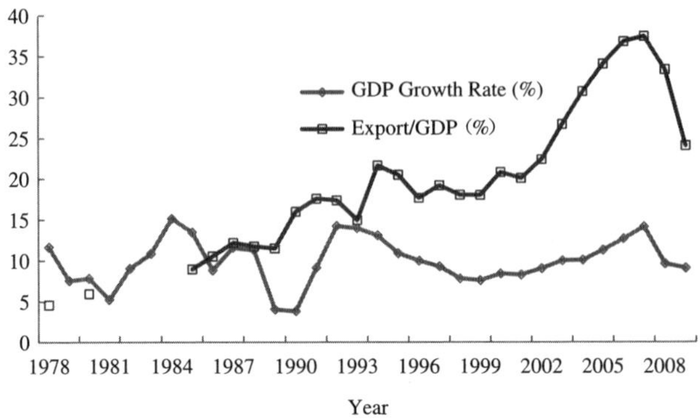

Fig. 11.1. China's export and GDP growth rate in the last three decades.
Source: *China Statistical Yearbook* of relevant years.

and its ratio to GDP arrived at the highest 8% in 2007. Regarding the fact that China could make so rapid progress in economic growth, the existing literature has already achieved some consensus, among which export expansion is deemed as an important factor. Figure 11.1 shows the GDP growth rate and the proportion of export in GDP.[2] Taking logarithm and plotting the scatter diagram, we will find that these two variables are strongly positively related.

In empirical studies with respect to trade's effects on economic growth, in order to obtain robust results, the endogeneity of trade should be taken into account; otherwise the estimation will be biased. One effective way to address endogeneity is to find suitable instrumental variables for the endogenous variable. A qualified instrumental variable should satisfy two conditions (Woodridge, 2006): first, it should bear no relationship with the explained variable; and second, it should be strongly correlated with the endogenous variable. These criteria qualify *trade policy* a feasible instrumental variable of *trade*, because firstly it is related to trade, and secondly it has relatively strong exogeneity. We know that export orientation is an important development policy in East Asia. China, as a member in this

[2] Wong (2010) investigates the relations among export, domestic demand and economic growth in China. The empirical results show bidirectional Granger causality among these variables.

area, is not an exception.[3] As a catching-up economy, China can copy the trade policy of its industrialized neighbors, which is so-called "backward advantage". Therefore, we can say that China's trade policy is exogenous because it simply follows its neighboring countries. Based on these discussions, we find a nexus between trade policy and economic growth, namely, trade policy affects economic growth via its influence on trade, which actually reveals the necessity of our discussion in this chapter. However, the questions in which we are more interested are as follows: What changes of the trade policies have been made in the past thirty years and how to evaluate these changes? What challenges the global economy has to face currently? And what they mean for China's future trade policies?

We have to mention that RMB exchange rate would not be included in our discussion. Most agree that RMB should appreciate, and the disagreement only lies on how fast and how much RMB should appreciate. More importantly, it is no longer a pure economic issue, more political concerns are also involved (Lafrance, 2008; Goldstein and Lardy, 2008). The remaining part of this chapter is as follows. Section 11.2 reviews the changes of China's trade polices over the past three decades. Section 11.3 discusses the FTAs (free trade agreements) China joins in. Section 11.4 explores the challenges of the global economy and the implication for China's future trade policies. And Section 11.5 is the conclusion.

11.2. Trade Policy Change

China's trade policy has undergone profound changes since the reform and opening-up, deserving efforts to review and remark. Our previous work (Luo and Zhang, 2008; Luo and Zhang, 2010) shows that these changes can be roughly divided into three phases. The first phase extended from 1978 to 2001, during which period, in particular the 15 years after

[3] Krugman (1994) mentioned East Asian economies especially Singapore with the Former Soviet Union in the same breath, which aroused great controversies. Even his teacher Bhagwati (1996) disagreed with him. It is quite unexpected that Krugman, as an international economist, neglected a fundamental difference between East Asian economies and the Former Soviet Union. Namely, the former valued export-oriented policy as crucial development strategy without exception while the latter was basically a closed economy.

1987, China was dedicated to regaining its founding membership in GATT and joining WTO. In line with these motivations, inside the country, China set market economy as the objective of economic system reform, and to the outside world, China conformed to the rules of world trade system and further opened its market. The second phase, spanning from 2002 to 2006, was a time period when China completely fulfilled its commitments in WTO entry. Especially, those previously protected industries like automobile, banking and telecommunications are under free entry and competition. The third phase, from 2007 till now, has witnessed drastic changes in domestic and global economic environment. These changes will reshape China's trade policy in the coming decades.

11.2.1. *1978–2001: The long march to global trade*[4]

11.2.1.1. *Tariff*

In 1951, China promulgated its first *Customs Import and Export Tariff*. In order to meet the needs of reform and opening up, the second *Customs Import and Export Tariff* was released in 1985. In this new tariff schedule, import tariff rates of 1,152 tariff items were reduced, accounting for 55% of the total tariff items. At the same time, the tariff structure was also changed: for exports, the tariff had six rates, ranging from 10% to 60%; for imports, except some duty-free goods, the lowest tariff had seventeen rates, ranging from 3% to 15% and the general tariff had sixteen rates from 8% to 180%. From year 1986 to 1991, the government lowered and raised the tariff for 83 and 140 imported products respectively. Before the large-scale tariff reduction in 1992, China's average tariff rate was about 47%.

To speed up the negotiation on resuming the seat in the GATT, and to fulfill the promise at APEC leaders' summit, China voluntarily lowered its tariff between 1992 and 2001 (see Table 11.1). The average tariff level was reduced from 42.9% in 1992 to 23.9% in 1996. On 1 October 1997,

[4] In terms of the division of trade policies in the past thirty years, we are enlightened by two treatises. One is *China and the Long March to Global Trade: The Accession of China to World Trade Organization* written by Alenxandroff *et al.* (2003) and another is *China's WTO Accession: The Road to Implementation* written by Abnett and Cassidy (2002).

Table 11.1. Tariff reduction between 1992 and 2001.

Year	Tariff items	Adjusted items	Arithmetic average tariff rate (%)	Weighted average tariff rate (%)
1992	6525	225	42.9	40.6
1993	6321	3371	39.9	38.4
1994	6350	2944	36.3	35.5
1995	6350	23	35.6	25.0
1996	6549	4998	23.9	25.4
1997	6633	4874	17.6	18.2
1999	6490	1014	17.5	10.8
2001	7111	3462	15.3	10.5

Source: *World Development Indicators*.

Table 11.2. Nominal tariff rate and real tariff rate in China.

Year	Nominal tariff rate (%)	Real tariff rate (%)
1992	40.6	4.8
1993	38.4	4.3
1994	35.5	2.7
1995	25.0	2.6
1996	25.4	2.6
1997	18.2	2.7
1999	10.8	4.1
2001	10.5	4.2

Notes: 1. Nominal tariff rate is just the weighted average tariff rate in Table 11.1. 2. Real tariff rate = tariff revenue/total imports. Related information is from *China Statistical Yearbook*, 2002.

the tariff was further reduced to 17.6%. By 2001, the arithmetic average tariff rate was 15.3%.

One issue regarding China's tariff is the discrepancy between the real tariff rate (the tariff revenue divided by the total import value) and the nominal tariff rate (see Table 11.2). There might be two reasons about this. First, China's tariff system includes numerous tax cuts and exemptions. Processing trade is an example, which takes up almost one half of China's export and is always targeted by these policies. Second, China's tariff system is far from perfect. There exist numerous illegal activities under no effective control such as tax evasion, tax avoidance and smuggling.

11.2.1.2. *Export tax rebate*

Export tax rebate, a trade policy allowed by WTO rules, is widely used in the world. In China, tax rebate also plays a crucial role in expanding the exports. In 1980, the Ministry of Finance reduced industrial and commercial tax on exported goods. In 1985, the industrial and commercial tax was divided into product tax, value-added tax, commercial tax and salt tax. On 1 April 1985, the State Council decided to launch tax rebate on exports. VAT tax rates and export tax rebate rates were set as follows: coal and agricultural products levied 5% to 7% and 3% rebated; industrial goods levied 13%, 10% rebated; others levied 17%, 14% rebated. However, the coexistence of product tax and value-added tax often resulted in deficiency or duplication of taxation. These problems were not resolved until the tax reform in 1994. Since then, VAT tax would be collected on all goods and consumption tax would be levied on selected goods. The State Administration of Taxation issued in February 1994 the *Regulation Methods on Exemption and Refund of Taxes of Exported Goods* which stipulated that export goods should be zero rated.

Export tax rebate has greatly stimulated exports. In 1994 and 1995, China's export growth rate reached 32% and 23%, respectively. The rapid expansion of export and export tax rebates sharply increased the government's fiscal pressure. This situation together with the inflation in 1993–1994 triggered a series of restrictive policies. In 1995 and 1996, the Chinese government twice reduced the export tax rebate rate. The average tax rebated rate was lowered to 8.2%. However, one year later, the Asian financial crisis broke out. To alleviate the negative impact on exports, the Chinese government had to raise export tax rebate rate three times in 1998 and 1999. As a result, the average export tax rebate rate was increased to 13.6% in 1999.

11.2.1.3. *Processing trade*

Processing trade is a trade pattern under which enterprises import raw materials and components, and assemble them into finished products for export. In China, due to preferential policies, low-cost labour forces and global industrial shifts, processing trade boomed quickly. Since 1993, processing trade has overweighed general trade, becoming the main form of China's exports (see Figure 11.2).

When China embarked on opening up in the early 1980s, the "Four Asian Tigers" were about to transfer their labour-intensive industries to other countries. This rendered China an opportunity to develop processing trade. Guangdong, adjacent to Hong Kong, quickly became a prominent example in this respect. In the 1990s, the opening-up in China was deepened and broadened. Shanghai, Dalian and Tianjin bonded areas have been established. With business environment being improved, processing trade has expanded rapidly. In 1999, exports in processing trade reached 110.88 billion U.S. dollars, 4 times those in 1989. At the same time, foreign direct investment (FDI) quickly entered the manufacturing industry and soon became a major contributor in processing trade. In 1999, foreign-invested enterprises exported 74.54 billion U.S. dollars in processing trade, accounting for 67.2% in China's exports in processing trade and 86.8% of foreign-invested companies' total exports. In the late 1990s, in

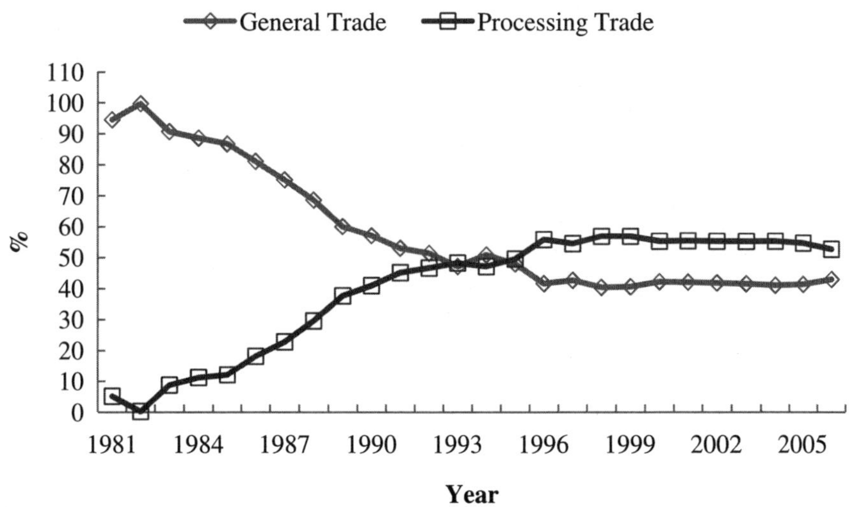

Fig. 11.2. China's general trade and processing trade.

Source: *China Statistical Yearbook*, 2009.

response to the changes in domestic and foreign economic environments, upgrading the product structure of processing trade was put on the agenda. For instance, in May 1999, the State Economic and Trade Commission (the predecessor of the Ministry of Commerce) grouped processing trade into three categories, prohibited, restricted and permitted ones.

11.2.1.4. *Foreign direct investment*

In July 1979, the *Law of the People's Republic of China on Chinese-foreign Equity Joint Ventures* was issued, symbolizing that China was determined to attract and utilize FDI. Stable investment environment, abundant labour resources and huge market potential provide incentives for FDI inflow. Since 1993, China has become the largest developing country in utilizing FDI. In 2002, China was once the world's largest country in attracting foreign investment.

At the beginning of reform and opening-up, FDI inflow was quite limited. Deng Xiaoping's Southern Tour Speech in 1992 signaled a turning point (see Figure 11.3). Since then, foreign investment has increased tremendously. In 1998 and 1999, negatively affected by the Asian financial crisis, China's foreign capital inflows slightly declined. This situation turned better after the year of 2000. The entry of foreign investment was in tandem with the process of China's opening-up. In 1980, the Chinese government approved two provinces, Guangdong and Fujian, to adopt

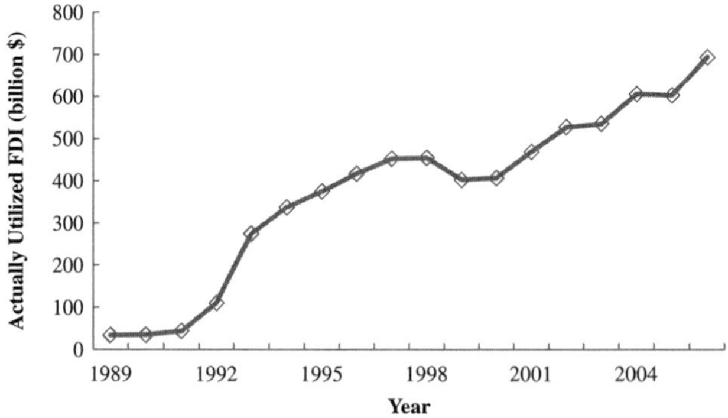

Fig. 11.3. China's FDI inflow.

Source: *China Statistical Yearbook*, 2007.

flexible economic policies. Four Special Economic Zones, Shenzhen, Zhuhai, Shantou and Xiamen, were set up. After 1984, 14 port cities were opened and 13 coastal economic development regions were established. All of these indicated that China was devoted to changing its attitudes towards foreign capital. However, in this period, foreign investment in China was still in the exploratory stage and the scale of investment was fairly small. The majority of investors came from Hong Kong and mainly invested in labour-intensive industries.

In March and October 1986, the Chinese Government released the *Law of the People's Republic of China on Foreign Capital Enterprises and Provisions for the Encouragement of Foreign Investment* consecutively. In 1988 and 1990, the *Law of the People's Republic of China on Chinese-foreign Contractual Joint Ventures, Regulations on Encouraging Taiwanese Investment and Provisions on Encouraging Investment from Overseas Chinese and Compatriots from Hong Kong and Macao* were issued. With the legal and policy framework on FDI in place, more regions and industries were opened. In 1988, the Liaodong Peninsula, Shandong Peninsula and other coastal areas were opened to foreign investors. In the same year, Hainan Special Economic Zone was set up. In 1990, Shanghai Pudong New Area was founded. During this period of time, foreign investment gradually shifted from tourism, commerce and service industries to manufacturing industry. More and more investments from Europe, North America, Japan and Singapore flowed in.

Deng Xiaoping's Southern Tour Speech in 1992 quickened China's steps in reforming and opening up. The reform oriented towards market economy provided confidence for foreign capital. Meanwhile, the all-round opening-up pattern has been in shape. Multinational companies speeded up their paces to enter the Chinese market. By the end of 1995, more than 200 of the world's top 500 companies had investment in China. The foreign investment in capital- and technology-intensive industries, such as communications, instruments, pharmacy and chemistry, grew significantly.

However, controversies have also been aroused with the boom of foreign investment. Especially, some industries are monopolized by foreign-invested companies. Some domestic enterprises, in particular those state-owned enterprises, are facing merger and acquisition by multinational corporations. Foreign investors have been accused of enjoying super-national treatment. As a response, the government introduced some corrective measures. In June 1995, the State Council promulgated the *Provisional Regulations on Direction Guide to Foreign Investment* and the *Catalogue for the Guidance of Foreign Investment Industries*, in which foreign-invested projects were divided into encouraged, permitted, restricted and prohibited ones. The foreign investment policy was shifted from welcoming investment in all industries to focusing on specific industries. After the outbreak of the Asian financial crisis, in order to avoid the sharp decline of foreign investment, the Chinese government took some new measures. In December 1997, the revised *Catalogue for the Guidance of Foreign Investment Industries* expanded the areas for foreign investment. In comparison with the *Catalogue* of 1995, the number of encouraged items reached 186, a net increase of 15 items.

11.2.2. *2002–2006: The road to implementation*

On 11 December 2001, China was approved the WTO membership. After that, to fulfill the commitments, China further reduced tariffs, eliminated some non-tariff barriers and abolished some export subsidies contradictory to the WTO principles. Meanwhile, China adjusted its trade policy according to the "non-discrimination principle", reduced government intervention on trade and increased the transparency of trade policy.

According to the agreement: in 2005, the tariff on industrial products should be reduced to 10%; in 2010, the overall tariff rate should be lowered to 10%; in 2020, the tariff should be further reduced to 5% and all the non-tariff measures conflicting with WTO agreement should be eliminated. To achieve these, China reduced import tariffs gradually since 2002. The general tariff level was lowered from 15.3% in 2001 to 9.8% in 2010: for agricultural products, the average tax rate was reduced from 18.8% to 15.2%; and for industrial products, from 14.7% to 8.9% in 2010. In 2002, the tariff rates of more than 5,300 imported goods were reduced and the general tariff level decreased from 15.3% in 2001 to 12%. In 2005, tariffs on 900 products were reduced and the general tariff level decreased from 10.4% in 2004 to 9.9%.

China's service sector also became more open to foreign investors. In December 2001, China's video market was opened to foreign investment. In April 2002, China widened the openness in five areas of commodity trade, service trade, intellectual property, investment and transparency. Since then, foreign investors have had greater access to service industries such as banking, insurance, telecommunications, logistics and transportation. In 2006, the service sector was the fastest growing area in utilizing foreign investment. The increase of foreign investment was more than 30% in some sectors, such as public administration and social organizations, residential services and other services, transportation, logistic and postal industry, wholesale and retail industries, renting and business services. The foreign investments in technical services and geological mining, information technology and software industry grew by more than 10%.

After joining WTO, China was facing a greater fiscal pressure because of the rapid increase in export and export tax rebates. Furthermore, in 2003, there was a partial overheating of the economy. In light of this, the Chinese government adopted a series of restrictive measures. In October 2003, the average level of export tax rebate was reduced from 15.1% to 12.1%. According to product types, the export tax rebate rate was adjusted to 17%, 13%, 11%, 8% and 5% respectively. For high-tech machineries and electronic products, the export tax rebate rate remained at 17%. The rebate rate for ordinary products was cut down from 17% to 13%. The rebate for some resource products was canceled, while the rebate rate for other resource products fell from 8% to 5%. Agricultural products still maintained rebate rates of 5% and 13%. In 2003, under the circumstance of a partly overheated economy, the processing trade policy was also tightened. In November 2004, the *Catalogue of Prohibited Commodities in Processing Trade* first listed the commodities in detail. In November 2006, the *Catalogue of Prohibited Commodities in Processing Trade* included a total of 804 prohibited trade goods. Although China's processing trade policy started adjustment after the year of 2000, this did not keep the processing trade surplus from soaring up.

11.2.3. *2007 till now: A shock therapy*[5]

For trade policy, the year of 2007 is a watershed. Earlier and later this year, a series of important events took place both within and without

[5] We partly refer to Luo and Zhang (2010) regarding trade policy adjustments in this period.

Table 11.3. Important events within and without China 2006–2008.

Type	Time	Events
Domestic	2006.10	The Sixth Plenum of the 16th CPC Central Committee approved the "*Resolution on Major Issues Regarding Building of Harmonious Socialist Society*", emphasizing the concept of "Harmonious Socialist Society".
	2007.07	A sudden rise in the inflation rate marked the end of China's decade-long situation of high economic growth and low inflation.
	2007.10	The 17th National Congress of the CPC officially included "the Scientific Outlook on Development" in the Party Constitution.
	2008.08	The impact of the subprime mortgage crisis on China's economy gradually showed up; trade policy began to change.
Global	2007.07–08	U.S. subprime mortgage crisis quickly spread to the world and triggered the "financial tsunami".
	2008.11–2010.11	G-20 held five summits in search of ways to cope with the global financial crisis.

Source: The authors' compilation according to related materials.

China. They are the underlying factors inducing subsequent changes of the trade policy in China (see Table 11.3). Regarding politics in China: the Communist Party of China (CPC) passed a resolution on "Harmonious Society" in October 2006, and "Scientific Outlook on Development" was included in the Party Constitution on the 17th National Congress of the CPC the next year — these two concepts serve as the general principles of policy adjustments hereafter. With respect to the Chinese economy: July 2007 saw the highest inflation rate since the past decade, and the shock of the subprime mortgage crisis on China gradually showed up: these two factors directly influenced China's subsequent trade policies. In international society, the subprime mortgage crisis emerging in the U.S. quickly spread to other countries and triggered the "financial tsunami" in July and August 2007 — the G-20, a new international organization, was established to cope with this crisis, and it held five summits by December 2010.

11.2.3.1. *July 2007 till July 2008: Hello, shock therapy*

In China, the political resolutions of the CPC usually set the keynote of the policy changes. On 11 October 2006, the Sixth Plenum of the 16th CPC Central Committee approved the "*Resolution on Major Issues Regarding the Building of a Harmonious Socialist Society*". The emphasis on harmonious society laid down the guidelines for the following economic policies. *The 2007 Catalogue of Prohibited Commodities in Processing Trade* issued by the Ministry of Commerce on 5 April 2007 included 184 new items, making a total of 1,138 items of prohibited commodities. The high inflation rate starting in July 2007 not only ended China's 10-year-long economic development of high growth and low inflation, but also prompted the following constraining policies. On 1 July 2007, the Ministry of Commerce and the State Administration of Taxation adjusted the export tax rebate of 2,831 commodities, accounting for 37% of all the tariff-applied commodities. The export rebate rate was lowered for 2,268 commodities which tended to cause trade frictions, and the rebate was canceled for 553 commodities which were "energy-consuming, highly polluting and resource-intensive". *The 2007 Catalogue of Restricted Commodities in Processing Trade* issued by the Ministry of Commerce on 23 July 2007 newly added 1,853 items, totaling 2,247 items. On 15 October 2007, the 17th National Congress of the Communist Party of China was held, which officially included "Scientific Outlook on Development" in the Party Constitution. "Harmonious Society" reflects the pursuit of decision-makers regarding China's society, while "Scientific Outlook on Development" is supposed to point out the way to realize that goal. Shortly after, the National Development and Reform Commission (NDRC) and the Ministry of Commerce issued *the Catalogue for the Guidance of Foreign Investment Industries (Amended in 2007)* on 1 December 2007. It encouraged foreign capital to enter the high-tech and service sectors, while setting limitations on sectors like rare and non-renewable resources. On 21 December, the Ministry of Commerce released *The 2007 Second Batch of Prohibited Commodities Catalogue* which included another 589 items. *The 2008 Catalogue of Restricted Commodities in Processing Trade* taking effect on 5 April 2008 added 39 more items and the total number amounted to 1,816 items.

In response to the government's measures, the legislative body also took actions. The Standing Committee of the National People's Congress (NPC) approved three laws in 2007: *Enterprise Income Tax Law* on 13 March, *Labour Contract Law* on 29 June, and *Anti-Monopoly Law* on 30 August. The first two laws took effect on 1 January 2008 and the third one on 1 August. In principle, these laws apply to all the legal entities within China. However, for foreign-invested companies which have long enjoyed favorable treatments, these laws might imply a backward step in China's policy. The core clause of the *Enterprise Income Tax Law* is to unify the income tax rate for domestic and foreign-invested companies. The super national tax policies for foreign-invested enterprises were removed; instead an identical income tax rate applies to domestic firms and foreign-invested firms. The core clause of the *Labour Contract Law* stressing non-fixed-term labour contract causes panic in the foreign-invested enterprises. It entitles an employee the right to ask for a non-fixed-term employment contract with the employer in which he/she has been working for ten years, or with which he/she has already signed two successive fixed-term contracts. The *Anti-Monopoly Law* requests M & A of foreign-invested firms in China should undergo review of concentration of business operators and national security review.

In a word, trade policies from mid-2007 to mid-2008 were "a shock therapy", which was distinctly marked by "tightness": raising the threshold of processing trade, lowering the export rebate rate, narrowing the product scope of export rebate, improving the requirement of FDI inflows, and removing the preferential policies for foreign-invested enterprises. Guangdong Province, known as the pioneer of China's reform and opening-up, serves as an example in this aspect. Wang Yang, then the Secretary of Chongqing Municipal Committee of the CPC, was elected as a member of the Political Bureau on the 17th National Congress of the CPC in October 2007. Soon after, he was nominated as the Party Chief of Guangdong Province. On taking office, Wang kicked off structural reforms immediately. A series of slogans were proposed, like "empty the cage for new birds" and "eliminating the obsolete is exactly equal to keeping ahead". Wang is not only a well-recognized regional official but also a member of the CPC Political Bureau. His special position makes

Guangdong an ideal test field to implement the top leaders' will.[6] However, transformation and upgrading of Guangdong's economy soon confront difficulties when the global economic environment quickly worsens.

11.2.3.2. *August 2008 till now: Goodbye, shock therapy*

In July and August 2007, the financial crisis incurred by subprime mortgage dealt a heavy blow to the United States, the European Union and Japan. It is of no doubt that, China, as a country highly relying on these markets (so-called G3), would therefore suffer greatly. In order to reduce the negative effects of the crisis, all these countries relaxed their monetary policy, injecting vast amount of liquidity into the market to avoid great depression like that in the 1930s. Ironically, while deflation was other economies' major concern, China was then fighting against an unprecedented inflation. All economic policies during that period of time were aimed at cooling down the economy. Quite obviously, China's decision-makers have underprepared for the crisis and underestimated its possible effects. Otherwise the measures taken preciously would have not displayed features of "a shock therapy". Take Guangdong as an example. Under the double shock of tightened domestic policies and severe shrinking of export market, Zhujiang River Delta went into trouble very soon. The top leaders were astonished by this situation and many of them had to go there to see what actually happened. Premier Jiabao Wen visited Guangdong three times (2008/7/19–20, 2008/11/14–15 and 2009/4/19–21). And every time upon his returned to Beijing, the trade policies were adjusted accordingly.[7]

On 1 August 2008, the Ministry of Finance and the State Administration of Taxation raised the export rebate rate of products such as textiles and

---

[6] His position as a member of the Political Bureau ensures that reform at the local level is consistent with the idea of the top leaders (Bai *et al.*, 2008).

[7] Besides Premier Jiabao Wen, Jinping Xi went on two inspection tours to Guangdong for 2008/7/4–5 and 2008/12/3–5. Guoqiang He visited Guangdong for 2008/11/14–18. Keqiang Li left for Guangdong on 2009/2/9. Qishan Wang inspected Guangdong for 2009/2/20–21.

clothing. The rebate rate was further raised six times thereafter (2008/11/1, 2008/12/1, 2009/1/1, 2009/2/1, 2009/4/1, and 2009/6/1), covering all the major export commodities like textiles, clothing, mechanical, electrical products, etc.[8] Take the adjustment in 1 November 2008 as an example, at that time, export rebate rate was raised for 3,486 commodities, accounting for 25.8% of all tariff-applied commodities. The Ministry of Commerce and the General Administration of Customs eliminated 1,747 items from the *Catalogue of Prohibited Commodities in Processing Trade* issued on 31 December 2008, and only 500 items remained. *The 2009 Catalogue of Prohibited Commodities in Processing Trade* issued on 3 June 2009 included 1,759 items, a sharp reduction compared to the 2008 Catalogue. In order to attract foreign capital to the inland provinces, the NDRC and the Ministry of Commerce released *Catalogue of Priority Industries for Foreign Investment in Central & Western Regions (Amended in 2008)* on 23 December 2008. The *Reply of the General Office of the State Council to Issues concerning Facilitation of Service Outsourcing Industry* forwarded by the Ministry of Commerce on 22 January 2009 emphasized that foreign capital should be utilized further in service sector, especially in service outsourcing area. Since the second half of 2009, China's trade policies remain stable in general, except for some minor adjustments made to promote exports. For instance, the Customs Tariff Commission canceled and lowered the export tariff rate of some agriculture products and agriculture-used goods on 1 July 2009. The Ministry of Commerce and the State Administration of Taxation also eliminated the export tariff of some steel and nonferrous metal.

Over this three-year period, trade policies experienced a V-shaped reversal. China radically tightened the trade policies from 2007 till mid-2008, reflecting the pursuit of "Harmonious Society" and "Scientific Outlook on Development" of top leaders. The sudden increase of the inflation in mid-2007 further promoted the tightened trade policies. Until mid-2008, the decision-makers began to be aware of the severe impacts of the subprime mortgage crisis on China. After that, China's trade policies

[8] An interesting fact is that the adjustments of export tax rebate made by the Ministry of Finance and the State Administration of Taxation were started promptly after Premier Jiabao Wen's inspections.

were on the whole loosened. Luo and Zhang (2010) provided an explanation to the trade policies in this period based on a political economy approach. They point out that, under the current political system, China's trade policies are "top down" and "outside in", that is, trade policies are often determined by the decision-makers' views on economic development as well as international pressures. Nevertheless, trade policies formed in this way may lag behind since decision-makers do not have timely and first-hand information about the market. As a result, China, an economy highly dependent on export, was not fully prepared for the impact of the financial crisis, leaving the coastal areas in trouble.

11.2.4. *The effects of China's participation in the global labour division*

From 1987 to 2001, China made great endeavors to adapt to the rules of global trade system and become a membership of WTO. This is a precondition for China to have chance to fairly compete with other countries in the world market. The fifteen-year efforts to resume its GATT membership and to join WTO can be roughly divided into two phases: prior to 1992, China was trapped in choosing planned economy or market economy; and after 1992, China speeded up its negotiations with partners over bilateral market access. The year of 1992 is a turning point due to Deng Xiaoping's Southern Tour Speech in China. Since then, China has embarked on establishing market economy, in which market plays the key role in resource allocation.

China's comparative advantage has been brought into play since its WTO entry on 11 December 2001. The export of labour-intensive products enabled China's abundant labour forces allocated on a global basis. First, the vast export market greatly stimulates China's production potential and resolves the problem of shortage economy once for all. Second, the global market consumes China's capability in production that would otherwise cause surplus in the limited domestic market. And third, resources and intermediate products sourced from other countries free China from the frequently occurred bottleneck problems. Being admitted into the WTO stimulates the production potential, while globalization is an "express way" to realize and consume this potential. The economic

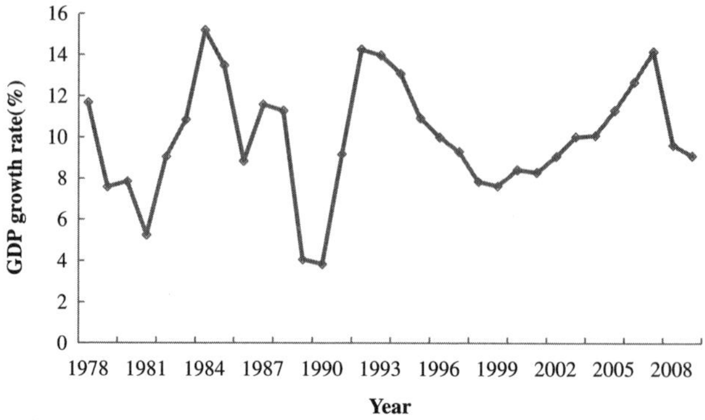

Fig. 11.4. GDP growth rate in China since 1978.

Source: *China Statistical Yearbook* of relevant years.

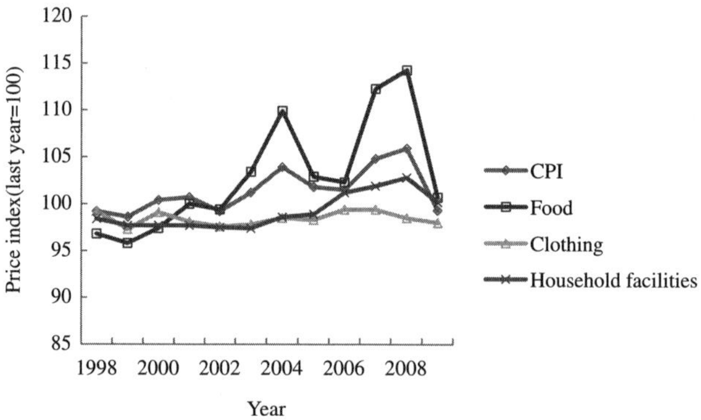

Fig. 11.5. Inflation rate in China since 1998.

Source: *China Statistical Yearbook* of relevant years.

cycle of China has also been "smoothened" thanks to being involved in globalization. The pattern of "stop and go" in the 1980s and 1990s has gone forever. Instead, China steps on the way of decade-long steady and fast growth (see Figure 11.4).[9] Figure 11.5 shows CPI and the prices of

[9] Brandt and Zhu (2000) gave a very insightful explanation towards the economic cycle of "boom-bust" and "stop-go" in China since 1978 till the mid 1990s. The argument that they proposed is still instructive for us to understand the feature of "high growth rate but low inflation rate" after the mid 1990s. However, they did not take into account the role played by the export-oriented strategy.

major consumer products during this period. CPI is quite stable, and a few consumer products even display a deflating trend.

Now let's turn to China's major trading partners to see what has happened to them in the first seven years since China's entry into the WTO. Figure 11.6 shows the growth rates of these economies since 2001, most having a relatively steady growth, though far less than that of China. Prices of these economies are shown in Figure 11.7, most of which are fairly stable. The correlation coefficients of the CPI series of China and its trading

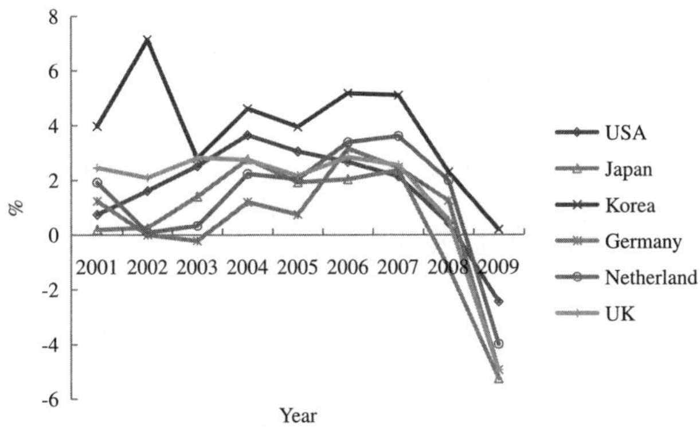

Fig. 11.6. GDP growth rate in China's major export markets.

Source: WDI.

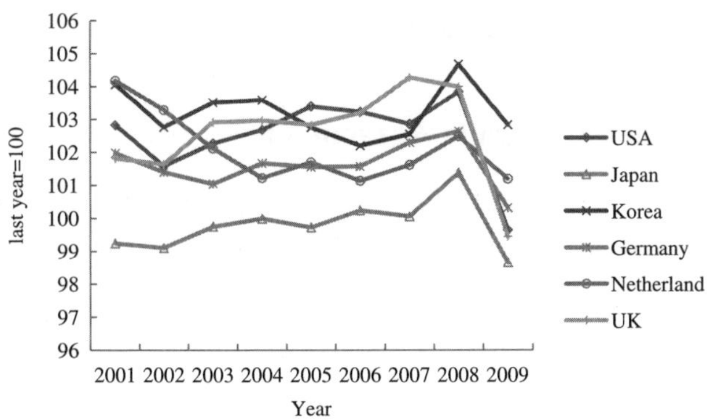

Fig. 11.7. Inflation rate in China's major export markets.

Source: WDI.

partners are positive, most over 0.6, except for Netherlands. As stated above, China's CPI is quite stable in this period of time and the prices of clothing and household equipments even deflate to some extent. Therefore, it is quietly likely that China has exerted a downward pressure on prices of its trading partners, partly supporting the argument of "China exports deflation" (Kamin *et al.*, 2004; Weinstein and Broda, 2008; Fu *et al.*, 2009).

However, the optimistic viewpoint that both China itself and the world can benefit from the former's participation in the global labour division is finally disillusioned by the global financial crisis. The crisis is a self-correcting process of the market to address the disequilibrium of the world economy. However, we want to know what kind of role that China plays in the disequilibrium. To answer this question, we shall firstly understand the significance of "export boom" for China. Most trade surplus of China is created by private sectors (Luo and Zhang, 2010). Under *the compulsory foreign exchange surrender*, foreign currencies earned by private firms should be exchanged into RMB. These foreign currencies are handed to the central bank and become China's newly added foreign reserves.[10] The price of dollar-denominated assets soars up when these reserves are reinvested in the U.S. market. In addition, as a country in lack of natural resources, China's energy-consuming exports (Weber *et al.*, 2008) also push up the global prices of energy and resources. The inflation in mid-2007 is an example. Figure 11.6 shows that most of the inflation can be attributed to food's price rise. This reflects the fact that many agricultural products are used in the production of alternative energy. The upsurge of energy price and asset price is unsustainable and a crisis is unavoidable.

11.3. Bilateral Free Trade Agreement

As a major trading nation, China has actively participated in the process of multilateral trade liberalization since its entry into WTO, and has also greatly promoted bilateral free trade with other countries. By October 2010, China has signed free trade agreements with the ASEAN, Pakistan, Chile, New Zealand, Singapore, Peru and Costa Rica, and the *Asia-Pacific*

[10] The compulsory foreign exchange surrender had been in effect for 13 years since 1994. On 13 August 2007, it has been replaced by voluntary foreign exchange surrender.

Free Trade Agreement with Bangladesh, India, Laos, South Korea and Sri Lanka. Besides, the mainland China also signed the Closer Economic Partnership Agreement (CEPA) with the two special administrative regions (SARs), Hong Kong and Macau. Furthermore, China is currently engaged in free trade talks with Australia, Iceland, Norway, the Gulf Cooperation Council (GCC) and the Southern Africa Customs Union (SACU). The feasibility study of FTA with Korea, India and Switzerland has been launched and feasibility study of FTA between China, Korea and Japan has been jointly carried out by government departments, enterprises and academic institutions since May 2010. China is the largest trading partner of Chile, the second largest partner of New Zealand, Peru and Costa Rica, the third largest partner of Singapore, and the fourth largest partner of the ASEAN and Pakistan. For Hong Kong and Macau, CEPA offers an opportunity for these two SARs to better utilize the vast market of the mainland China. Pakistan has a special diplomatic relation with China, so the FTA between them may have more political concerns. Though political factor is also a driving force in China's trade relations with the ASEAN, the FTA is actually a natural response to the fact that the economic integration of China and the ASEAN has been deepened since the Asian financial crisis in 1997. Ko (2010) carries out an empirical research about China's trade partnership with ASEAN countries, and finds that the trade cooperation between them is more of economic concern rather than politic concern. New Zealand is the first developed country which has signed FTA with China. This is an important step for China to win the recognition of full market economy status from developed countries (Luo and Zhang, 2010).[11] Countries that have launched negotiations over FTA like Australia, Iceland and Norway, as well as Switzerland which has started the feasibility study, have all acknowledged China's full market economy status. China's FTA with Chile and Peru is intended to enhance the trading relation with Latin America, and to meet the huge

[11] New Zealand has always been a forerunner of developed countries in terms of developing relationship with China. It is the first developed country to reach a bilateral agreement on China's entry into the WTO, to acknowledge China's full economy market status, to launch bilateral FTA negotiations, and to sign the FTA with China and Hong Kong SAR of China.

needs in resource supply, as these two countries have abundant mineral reserves. The negotiation with the GCC is also related to the fact that the Gulf region has the world's richest oil-gas resources. China's FTA with Costa Rica indicates the former's efforts to strengthen the economic and trading associations with Central America countries. Most countries with so-called "diplomatic relations" with Taiwan are in this region. To China's disappointment, however, its major trade partners, especially EU and U.S. have neither started talks on FTA with China nor acknowledged its full market economy status.

11.4. Global Challenges Ahead and China's Trade Policy in Future

China has made great achievements in economic and social development since the reform and opening-up. During this period, China has been frequently adjusting its trade policies in order to utilize resources and expand markets both within and without the country. We give a review above. This part will focus on the global economy at present and in the coming decades, and analyze the implication on China's future trade policies.

11.4.1. *Global disequilibrium*

Large economies play crucial roles in the global economy. Besides, they also affect other countries via economic and trade linkages. We shall go through some basic facts about the large economies and their trade patterns so as to understand the global economic disequilibrium.

11.4.1.1. *GDP of large economies*

In terms of GDP, EU-27, the U.S. and China rank the top three in the global economy. According to IMF's estimation, their GDPs in 2010 would reach, respectively, \$16.1 trillion, \$14.6 trillion and \$5.7 trillion, accounting for 26%, 23.6% and 9.3% of the world's total GDP. Their GDPs total more than a half of the world's GDP. The estimation also predicts that by 2015, their GDPs will reach \$19.0 trillion, \$18.0 trillion and \$10.0 trillion, accounting for 23.2%, 22.0% and 12.2% of the total GDP of the world. Though their overall share in the world's GDP is still over 50%, only China's share is still increasing. The shares of the other three countries of "Golden Bric" in the world's GDP, namely Brazil, Russia and India, will rise from 3.3%, 2.4% and 2.3% to 3.4%, 3.1% and 2.9% respectively.

11.4.1.2. *Trade of large economies*

Ranked by the total trade volume in 2009, EU, the United States and China were also the three largest economies. Among all the sovereign states, U.S., China, Germany and Japan had the largest trade volume of respective \$2.4 trillion, \$2.2 trillion, \$2.1 trillion and \$1.0 trillion (source: *CIA World Factbook*). In terms of current account balance, China ranked first in 2009 with \$296.2 billion surplus. Japan ranked second and Germany the third, with surplus of \$131.2 billion and \$109.7 billion respectively, while United States ranked the last running a deficit of \$380.1 billion. With regard to the ratio of current account balance in GDP, we have 5.97% for Germany, 3.43% for Japan, 3.37% for China and −5.33% for the United States. For the other three countries of "Golden Bric", this ratio was 2.31% for Russia indicating a surplus while −1.21% for Brazil and −0.71% for India indicating a deficit (source: *CIA World Factbook*, November 2010). EU-27 had a ratio of the current account deficit in GDP of −1.1% in 2009, comparing to −1.9% a year before (source: *Eurostat*).

11.4.1.3. *Trade between the U.S. and other large economies*

Let's take a look at merchandise trade of the U.S. with other large economies (Table 11.4). China, Japan and Germany are the second, fourth and fifth largest trading partners, accounting for 15%, 5.6% and 4.4% respectively. In terms of trade deficit of the U.S., China ranks the first, Japan the third and Germany the fifth. The trade deficit with China accounted for nearly 44% of the \$517 billion merchandise trade deficit of the U.S. in 2009, while Japan accounted for 9% and Germany 5%. Obviously, in contrast to the trade share, China, Japan and Germany — China in particular — account for too much in the U.S.'s trade deficit.

Table 11.4. The U.S. major trading partners in 2009 (billion dollars).

Five Countries with the Largest Merchandise Trade Volume	**Canada**	**China**	**Mexico**	**Japan**	**Germany**
	429.64	365.98	305.53	147.13	114.55
Five Countries with the Largest Merchandise Trade Deficit	**China**	**Mexico**	**Japan**	**Canada**	**Germany**
	−226.83	−47.54	−44.77	−20.18	−27.95

Source: U.S. Census Bureau.

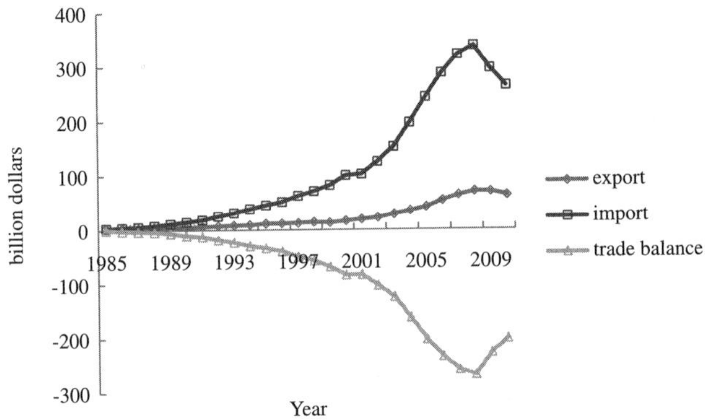

Fig. 11.8. Trade between the U.S. and China.

Source: U.S. Census Bureau.

11.4.1.4. *Trade between the U.S. and China*

In nominal terms, the U.S.'s merchandise trade deficit with China has increased by almost 100 times from \$2.8 billion in 1987 to \$268 billion in 2008 (Figure 11.8). Figure 11.9 shows the U.S.'s international trade as a whole. The total trade deficit has nominally increased by 4.4 times from \$152.1 billion in 1987 to \$816.2 billion in 2008. The correlation coefficient is over 0.95 between the U.S.–China trade deficit series and the U.S. total trade deficit series. If we take the former series as the x-axis and the later as the y-axis to plot the scatter diagram, we could get a linear function with coefficient equal to 2.75 ($R^2 = 0.89$). Therefore, it seems that the U.S.–China trade imbalance is an overwhelming factor in the overall trade

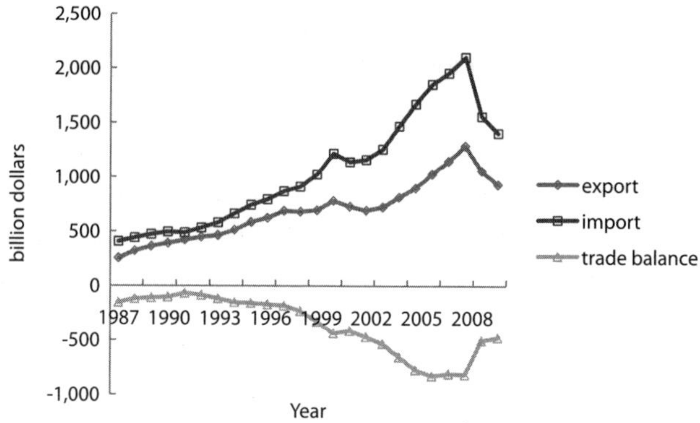

Fig. 11.9. The U.S. foreign trade.

Source: U.S. Census Bureau.

Table 11.5. Leading foreign owners of US treasury securities (July 2010).

Nation/territory	Billions of dollars	%
China	846.7	20.8
Japan	821.0	20.2
UK	374.3	9.2
Oil exporters	223.8	5.5
Caribbean Banking Centers[2]	150.7	3.7
Brazil	162.2	4.0
HK	135.2	3.3
Russia	130.9	3.2
Taiwan	130.5	3.2

Source: U.S. Treasury.

Note: Oil exporters: Saudi Arabia, Venezuela, Libya, Iran, Iraq, the United Arab Emirates, Bahrain, Kuwait, Oman, Qatar, Ecuador, Indonesia, Algeria, Gabon, and Nigeria. Caribbean Banking Centers: Bahamas, Bermuda, Cayman Islands, Netherlands Antilles, British Virgin Islands and Panama.

imbalance of the U.S. (Bown *et al.*, 2005).[12] In comparison with U.S.–China relations in the real economy, the monetary side of their relations shows that China is holding increasing amount of U.S.–dollar assets. Table 11.5 shows

[12] Elwell (2008) gave a thorough analysis on the causes, consequences and cures of the U.S. trade deficit.

that China is the largest holder of U.S treasury securities, accounting for 20.8%. Countries running trade surplus with the United States like China and oil exporters have chased dollar assets, pushing the assets' prices up and causing the asset bubbles, which finally leads to the subprime mortgage crisis.[13] The global economy is currently in disequilibrium. Both China and the U.S., the two largest sovereign states in GDP, one with the most trade surplus and the other the most deficits, should adjust their development strategies and trade policies.

11.4.2. *Global financial and economic crisis*

The global financial crisis is an inevitable result of global economic disequilibrium. It also provides a chance for the global economy to restore the equilibrium. Nevertheless, structural reforms are unlikely to be finished in the short run. Therefore, at present the crisis implies trouble rather than opportunities for most countries. This is particularly true for China, a country highly depending on external markets. The financial crisis triggered by subprime mortgage has exerted severe impacts on China's major exporting markets. The depression of these economies produces negative impact on China via three channels. First, a direct effect is the reduction of these economies' imports from China. Second, the depression of these countries also spills over to other economies, especially the emerging economies, which also imposes negative effects on China's exports. And third, protectionism resurfaces in the context of global recession, threatening all countries especially China. According to *China Statistical Yearbook,* from 2008 to 2009, China's merchandise export decreased by 16%, among which exports to its largest market, EU, dropped by 19%, exports to other major trading partners, the United States, Japan, Korea and Germany, dropped by 13%, 16%, 27% and 16% respectively, and exports to G-20 dropped by 15%. With global economy going worse, China is confronting more and more trade protection. According to *Foreign Market Access Report 2010* released by the Ministry of Commerce, in 2009, China's exporting products encountered 116 trade

[13] However, Fernando (2010) pointed out, oil, not China, is the real destroyer of American's trade balance.

Table 11.6. Top 10 targets and users of antidumping investigations 1995–2008.

Antidumping targets		Antidumping users	
China	677	India	564
Korea	252	USA	418
USA	189	EC	391
Taiwan	187	Argentina	241
Indonesia	145	South Africa	206
Japan	144	Australia	197
Thailand	142	Brazil	170
India	137	China	151
Russia	109	Canada	145
Brazil	97	Turkey	136

Source: http://www.antidumpingpublishing.com.

remedy investigations, the value involved amounting to $12.7 billion. Among them there were 76 antidumping cases, 13 anti-subsidy cases, 20 cases of safeguard measures and 7 cases of special safeguard measures. Among the initiators, the United States launched 12 antidumping investigations, 10 anti-subsidy investigations and 1 special safeguard measure investigation. EU launched 7 antidumping investigations. In fact, China was the target of 677 antidumping cases from 1995 to 2008, far more than Korea which ranked the second with 252 cases (Table 11.6). On the one hand, reduction in exports is the result of the depression of the global market, as well as related to the increasing trade protectionism. On the other hand, the reduction is also a correction to the export boom in previous years. China needs to make adjustments in its trade policies to address these new problems.

11.4.3. *Climate change and global warming*

Climate change and global warming have become global concerns. Among large economies, China is facing ever increasing pressure in reducing carbon dioxide emission. According to the data from *International Energy Outlook 2010* by the U.S. Energy Information Administration, in the period of 2007 to 2035 (see Figure 11.10), China will have the highest

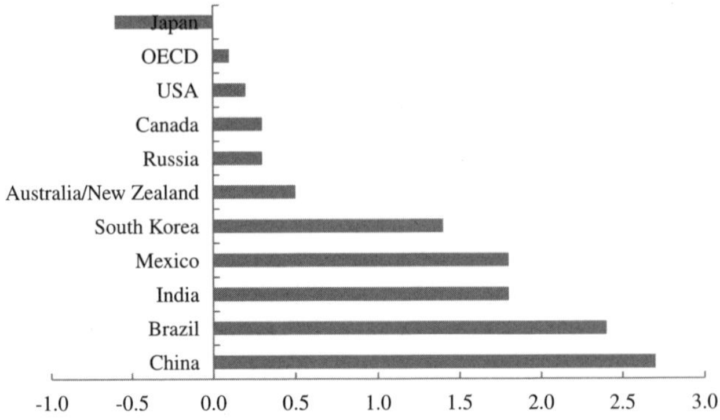

Fig. 11.10. Average annual growth in energy-related carbon dioxide emissions (%, 2007–2035).

Source: U.S. Energy Information Administration, *International Energy Outlook,* 2010.

growth rate in carbon dioxide emission of 2.7%. The other three "Golden Bric" countries, Brazil, India and Russia, will be ranked the second, the third and the sixth respectively, with rates of 2.4%, 1.8% and 0.3%. The United States will rank the seventh with 0.2%. Japan, the third largest economy in the world and the second largest country running trade surplus with the U.S., will have a growth rate of –0.6%. The report also shows that, till 2035, China's per capita carbon dioxide emission will still be less than the United States and Russia. However, the growth rate of per capita emission will be the highest and per capita emission will approach Japan's level in 2035. India, Brazil and Russia will also be on the rise, but at a lower pace. Per capita emission of India and Brazil will remain at a relatively low level in 2035, with India even less than China's level in 1990 (see Figure 11.11). In addition, in terms of total energy consumption, China, only after the U.S., ranked the second with $85*10^{15}$ BTU in 2008. Russia, India and Brazil ranked the third, fifth and ninth, and their energy consumption was, respectively, only 35%, 22% and 12% of China's (source: U.S. Energy Information Administration, *International Energy Statistics*). Finally, in terms of energy consumption per unit of GDP, China ranked second only to Russia among G-20 countries in 2008. In this respect, India and Brazil was only 70% and 38% of that in China, and only 27% for the United States. (source: U.S. Energy Information Administration, *International Energy Statistics*). Taking into account

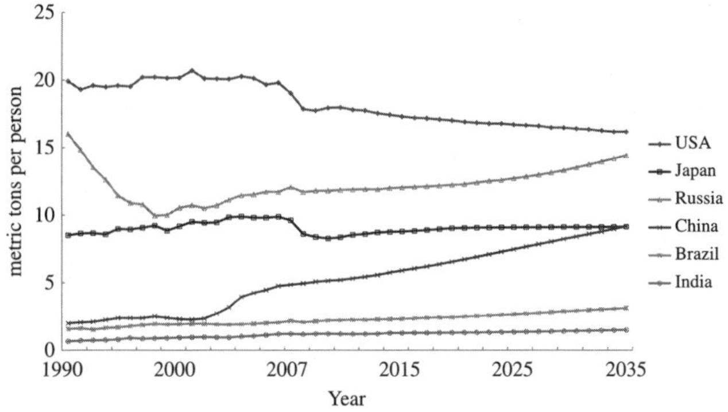

Fig. 11.11. Non-OECD carbon dioxide emissions per capita (metric tons per person).
Source: U.S. Energy Information Administration, *International Energy Outlook*, 2010.

China's high dependency on external market, such high level of energy consumption implies that China's further development will certainly push up world's basic commodities' prices. In order to play a responsible role in combating climate change and global warming, China also has to make adjustments in its trade policies.

11.4.4. *China's trade policy in future*

According to the discussions above, both internal and international pressures suggest that China's trade policy should undergo drastic changes. In line with the proposal for the *Twelfth Five-Year Plan*,[14] we suppose that the adjustments of trade policy will involve four aspects.

First, we will improve the structure of foreign trade. In the total trade, we should further boost imports rather than exports; relative to processing trade, we should further stress general trade rather than processing trade; and we should further promote the intra-industry trade rather than inter-industry trade. In terms of export, we should promote the export of products with high added value and high technology content rather than the low-end products; we should further enhance the competitiveness of domestic exporting enterprises, especially private enterprises, rather than

[14] CPC Central Committee's proposal for the Twelfth Five-Year Plan has been unveiled on 28 October 2010.

the foreign-owned enterprises, and change the competition mode from "low cost" to "high quality"; as the major export regions, coastal areas, especially the Changjiang River and Zhujiang River Delta as well Bohai Bay Rim should build up their own comparative advantages, and avoid overlapping in industrial structure; while maintaining our competitiveness in the European Union, the United States and Japan, we should promote the diversification of exporting markets, especially enlarge our market share in the emerging economies. In terms of import, we should increase imports of equipments and resource products with long-term strategic value rather than ordinary resource products; we should increase the imports of consumer goods, especially middle- and high-grade consumer goods, rather than manufacturing equipments; we should increase the import of tradable services rather than the merchandises; and, we should appropriately increase agricultural imports rather than the industrial products.

Second, we will better employ foreign investment. In China, foreign capital has always preferred investing in labour-intensive industries. This is related to the fact that foreign capital is attracted by the cheap labour forces and preferential policies. With preferential policies gradually being phased out, the management of foreign capital in China is gradually geared to the usual international practices. We should broaden the fields of foreign capital inflow. To be specific, we should speed up introducing foreign capital to modern manufacturing industries and high-tech industries rather than the traditional manufacturing industry; we should further encourage foreign capital to enter productive service industries rather than manufacturing industry; and we should encourage foreign capital to enter the service outsourcing areas rather than the processing trade. We also need to optimize the spatial location of foreign capital in China, allocating research and development, manufacturing and services in coastal and inland areas accordingly.

Third, we will encourage China's enterprises to invest abroad. We should take advantage of the opportunity, when other countries are undergoing structural reforms, to transfer the production without comparative advantages any longer to other countries. In the past five or six years, China's overseas investment has experienced a fast growth but has concentrated in neighboring countries and in resource sectors (Luo and Zhang, 2010). In the future, Chinese enterprises should expand their investment to developed countries and emerging markets, avoiding blindly focusing on resource industries. They should also grasp the opportunity to merge and acquire assets with long-term strategic values. Specifically, in addition to resource seeking, we should aim our motivation at seeking efficiency, market and strategic asset; and in addition to green-field investment, we should develop various market entry modes like merge and acquisition and brown-field investment.

And fourth, we will actively participate in the multilateral and bilateral free trade negotiations. At present, the collapse of Doha Round Talks and the resurfacing of protectionism are detrimental to China. Hufbauer and Lawrence (2010) point out that China and the United States should shoulder the major responsibility to restart the Doha Round. They suggest that China should dedicate itself in following aspects: China should agree to join the WTO's Government Procurement Agreement; China should join sector liberalization agreements in chemicals, information technology hardware, and environmental goods; and China should be at the front of talks to liberalize services. In return, developed countries including the United States should admit China's full market economy status. The concession of China and the United States will instill new energy into the global free trade process. Furthermore, there are still many opportunities to expand bilateral free trade: in Asia, in addition to deepening and implementing the free trade agreement with ASEAN, we should strive for breakthrough in free trade talks between China, Japan and Korea, given the reality that close trade connection among the three countries already exists; and in international community, we should give priority to the FTAs with the "Gloden Bric" countries — Brazil, Russia and India. This is because China has different comparative advantages with these countries.

11.4.5. *But only trade policy change can't work!*

Through the trade policy adjustments mentioned above, we expect to achieve the following three objectives. First, achieve more balance between import and export of commodities and services, and a more appropriate trade surplus. Second, realize the coordination between inflow and outflow of capital, and a more diversified usage of private and official foreign exchange reserves. And third, sign more free trade agreements to guarantee the orderly flow of goods and capital between China and other countries. To achieve these goals, two external conditions need to be satisfied: internationally, in structural reform and policy design, trading partners should coordinate to avoid the game of "prisoners' dilemma"; and domestically, trade policy should coordinate with other economic policies, avoiding conflicts and internal friction. Because of space limitation, we shall briefly discuss the second condition. Among the eleven tasks listed in the proposal for the *Twelfth Five-Year Plan*, opening-up is placed at the end of a long list.[15] If the prior ten tasks can be implemented fully, trade policy adjustments will achieve better effects. At present, the reform has entered the deep water. Among numerous reforms, it is very important to resolve the incompatibility between the outputs of real sectors and the fund allocation of financial sectors. In particular, it is still difficult for the private sectors to obtain financial support while there is fund abuse in state-owned sectors. An efficient financial system, backbone of innovation in real sectors, does not exist in China. Without innovation, Chinese enterprises, especially private enterprises, are to be locked in low-end products. With price competition stiffening and trade condition deteriorating, private capital needs to be transferred to other sectors and industries. However, it is not so easy to accomplish this task because of institutional constraints and financial constraints. Under this situation, private capital flows to speculative fields, especially real estate. We have already stated that private firms are the main contributors of China's trade surplus. In the absence of formal financial support, making small profits

---

[15] The CPC Central Committee proposal for the Twelfth Five-Year Plan outlines the following eleven tasks: to accelerate economic transformation, boost domestic demand, advance rural modernization, nurture new strategic industries, promote more balanced regional development, emphasize the importance of scientific research and education, strengthen social security network, enhance cultural soft power, break through new areas of reform, and deepen opening to the outside world.

through processing trade becomes a primary channel for private sectors' capital accumulation. Great efforts should be made to reform China's financial sectors — such reform not only reduces the dependence of private enterprises on exports, thus preventing blind expansion of export, but also promotes the entry of private capital into manufacturing and service areas with high added value.

11.5. Conclusion

China's economic development has made remarkable progress in the past three decades, to which foreign trade especially export has been a significant contributor. In this process, trade policy also plays an important role. As a catching-up economy in East Asia, China has a backward advantage in trade policy design, which implies that it can learn from its industrialized neighbors, particularly Japan, Korea and Taiwan Territory. A well-designed trade policy greatly expands export, thus promoting sustainable economic growth. The abundant labour forces of China participate in the global division of labour through utilizing foreign capital and developing processing trade. Globalization and industrialization, mutually supportive of each other, go hand in hand.

For the first 24 years since 1978, in particular the 15 years after 1987, China was dedicated to regaining its founding membership in GATT and joining the WTO. During this period, domestically, China set market economy as the objective of economic system reform; and internationally, China conformed to the rules of world trade system and opened its market further. During the first five years after its entry into WTO, China fully fulfilled its WTO commitments and deepened the opening-up. It was during this period of time that China's comparative advantage was brought into full play. Export and trade surplus increased much faster than expected. China's trade policy has taken on a new look since 2007. From July 2007 to July 2008, under the guidelines of "Harmonious Society" and "Scientific Outlook on Development", along with the sudden increase of the inflation in July 2007, China's trade policies were sharply tightened. However, under the severe impacts of global financial crisis triggered by the subprime mortgage, trade policies have to be loosened again since August 2008.

The past three decades have witnessed a dramatic development in China's real economy, especially the manufacture industry, as a result of the export-oriented policy. Foreign consumers have also been able to share the demographic dividend of China via importing low price but high quality of Chinese products. However, in the last decade, real sectors in the United States have seen little technological innovation, while the competition posed by emerging economies' manufacturing industries has become fiercer than before. Large amount of capital flows into the financial sector of the United States, facilitating overspreading of financial derivatives and enabling marketization of "toxic assets". Via trade connections, the US dollars issued by the Federal Reserves become the dollar reserves of countries that either have a trade surplus (e.g., China) or export oil. These reserves flow back to America by purchasing dollar assets, further boost the "toxic assets" and plant the seeds of the financial crisis.

The world is currently in disequilibrium. The United States and China are the two largest economies in the world — one with the largest trade deficits and the other with the biggest trade surplus. Meanwhile, China accounts for nearly 40% of the U.S. trade deficits. Therefore, adjustments must be made to China's trade policies in the long run. While in the short term, in order to relieve the impacts on economic growth, export shrinkage due to the financial crisis has to be taken into account when China redesigns its trade policies. The financial crisis is a result and also a self-correction of the world economic disequilibrium. However, since fundamental reforms cannot be finished overnight, the crisis implies more trouble than opportunities for most countries, including China. Another emergent issue posed to the international community is climate change and global warming. China is in an unfavorable position in terms of growth rate of per capita emission, level of per capita emission, total amount of emission and per unit GDP emission. Under these conditions, in order to reconcile long-term and short-term goals, as well as to balance domestic and international pressures, the proposal for the *Twelfth Five-Year Plan* points out four aspects of trade policy adjustments: first, improve the structure of foreign trade; second, better utilize foreign investment; third, encourage China's enterprises to go abroad; and fourth, deepen and broaden multilateral and bilateral free trade talks.

References

Abnett, W. B. and Cassidy, R. B. (2002). *China's WTO Accession: The Road to Implementation.* Seattle: The National Bureau of Asian Research.

Alexandroff, A. S., Ostry, S. and Gomez, R. (2003). *China and the Long March to Global Trade: The Accession of China to the World Trade Organization.* Routledge.

Bai, C., Tao, Z. and Tong, Y. (2008). "Bureaucratic Integration and Regional Specialization in China." *China Economic Review*, 19(2), 308–319.

Bhagwati, J. (1994). "The Miracle that did Happen, Understanding East Asia in Comparative Perspective." Keynote Speech delivered on May 3, 1996 at Cornell University on the occasion of the Conference on 'Government and Market: The Relevance of the Taiwanese Performance to Development Theory and Policy' in honor of Professors Liu and Tsiang.

Bown, C. P., Crowley, M. A. McCulloch, R. and Nakajima, D. J. (2005). "The U.S. Trade Deficit: Made in China?." *Economic Perspectives*, 4, 2–18.

Brandt, L. and Zhu, X. (2000). "Redistribution in a Decentralized Economy: Growth and Inflation In China Under Reform." *Journal of Political Economy*, 108(2), 422–439.

Elwell, C. K. (2008). "The U.S. Trade Deficit: Causes, Consequences and Cures." CRS Report for Congress, January 25.

Fernando, V. (2010). "Oil, not China, is the Real Destroyer of American's Trade Balance." www.businessinsider.com, accessed 11 April 2010.

Fu, Xiaolan, Kaplinsky, R. and Zhang, J. (2009). "The Impact of China's Exports on Global Manufactures Prices." SLPTMD Working Chapter Series, No. 032.

Goldstein, M. and Lardy, N. R. (2008). *Debating China's Exchange Rate Policy.* Peterson Institute for International Economics.

Hufbauer, G. and Lawrence, R. (2010). "Let's make a Deal: How to Bring the Doha Trade Talks to A Close." *Foreign Affairs*, August 17.

Kamin, S. B., Marrazi, M. and Schnidler, J. W. (2004). "Is China 'Exporting Deflation.'" International Finance Discussion Chapters No. 791, Board of Governors of the Federal Reserve System.

Ko, A.l H.-M. (2010). "Not for Political Domination: China's Foreign Economic Policy Towards Vietnam, Singapore, and Malaysia in the Open Era." Ph.D. Dissertation, Department of Politics, University of Glasgow.

Krugman, P. (1994). "The Myth of Asia's Miracle." *Foreign Affairs*, November/December.

Lafrance, R. (2008). "China's Exchange Rate Policy: A Survey of the Literature." Bank of Canada Discussion Paper 2008–5.

Luo, C. and Zhang, J. (2010). "China Trade Policy Review: A Political Economy Approach." *The World Economy*, 33(11), 1390–1413.

Weber, C. L., Peters, G. P. Guan, D. and Hubacek, K. (2008). "The Contribution of Chinese Exports to Climate Change." IIOMME08, July 9–11, Seville, Spain.

Weinstein, D. and Broda, C. (2008). "Exporting Deflation? Chinese Exports and Japanese Prices." Working Paper 2008–29, Federal Reserve Bank of San Francisco.

Wong, H. T. (2010). "Exports, Domestic Demand, and Economic Growth in China: Granger Causality Analysis." *Review of Development Economics*, 14(3), 625–639.

Wooldridge, J. (2008). *Introductory Econometrics: A Modern Approach*. South-Western College Publishing.

CHAPTER 12

ENERGY-SAVING AND EMISSION-ABATING: CHINA'S NEW DEVELOPMENT STRATEGY IN 2009–2049

Shiyi Chen

12.1. Introduction

To achieve an agreement among countries to promissorily abate carbon dioxide after the expiration of Kyoto Protocol in 2012, all countries began to launch a new round of negotiations. The negotiation is extremely difficult due to the dispute of abatement obligations and the worry of slowdown of economic growth, especially during the period of financial crisis. There was no substantial progress on how to extend the Kyoto Protocol in Copenhagen and the Cancun climate conference in the past two years. Compared with the avoidance of global responsibility, however, many countries regard that the low-carbon economy will lay the foundation of future growth and invest much in green dimension in the stimulus packages to challenge the financial crisis. For example, the important component of the American Recovery and Reinvestment Act proposed by President Barack Obama is to develop renewable energy. The House of Representatives also passed the landmark American Clean Energy and Security Act in 2009 in order to make renewable energy and low-carbon technique as the new economic drive. In 2009, the UK also released the white papers of national strategy, *Low Carbon Transition Plan to 2020*, for becoming a low carbon country: cutting emissions, maintaining secure energy supply and maximizing economic opportunities.

According to HSBC's report (Robins *et al.*, 2009), with sizeable financial reserves and a tradition of long-term planning, in November 2008, China launched its RMB 4,000 billion (USD 584 billion) package, almost 40% of which was allocated to green themes, most notably rail, grids and water infrastructure, along with dedicated spending on environmental improvement. Elsewhere in Asia, South Korea introduced a dedicated Green New Deal, with more than 80% allocated to environmental themes. The new American Recovery and Reinvestment Plan committed USD 787 billion to kick-start the economy, with USD 94 billion for renewables, building efficiency, low-carbon vehicles, mass transit, grids and water. Although the green component was smaller than China's, it was more broadly based, and the only plan with a real boost to renewables. The existence of substantial automatic fiscal stabilizers in Europe meant that the EU stimulus was far smaller in size. However, the climate change dimension was greater than the USA, due to a focus on low-carbon investment in France, Germany and at the EU level.

So why do countries have totally distinct attitudes towards the same matter domestically and internationally? In fact, all countries are clear about the inevitability of energy saving and environment protection in the long run since it is crucial for the economic transformation and future competition in novel technology. Whereas in the short run, especially under the circumstance of financial crisis, energy-saving and emission-abating will use up limited resources which may be put into other fields of production, slowing the pace of economy resuscitation. That is the reason why all the countries hesitate on the promise of emission reduction in international climate negotiations. As a matter of fact, there are also two opposite arguments on how energy saving and emission reduction may influence the economy in the academic field. On one side, Porter Hypothesis argues that energy saving and emission reduction can bring opportunities for win-win development, i.e. simultaneous improvements in both environmental quality and productivity, meeting both social and economic goals. On the other side, some scholars raise doubts on the existence of this win-win development because if it does exist it will be unnecessary for the government to impose extra environmental protective costs on the firms. Many researches focus on the empirical study of the existence of this win-win development possibility, which will be surveyed in Section 12.2 of this chapter.

China is the 2nd largest energy consumer in the world, next to the US. More specifically, the US and China are respectively the 1st and 2nd largest coal consumers, which correspondingly makes the two countries the top 2 greenhouse gases emitters in the world. And in 2007, China's carbon dioxide emission exceeded the US, which brought China much burden from the outside world. With the proposal of scientific outlook on development, energy saving and emission abating have also become the propeller of China's economic structural adjustment and transformation of the development model (Cai, 2008). Hence, an in-depth analysis is needed on both the positive and negative effects of energy saving and emission reduction on China's economy, especially the output growth and productivity of the real economy after the financial crisis. Searching for an optimal energy-saving and emission-abating path which can induce a win-win development for China in the following decades, a strategically critical period, is also a practical and edging issue, prompting the motivation for this research. As is known to all, industry as a major part of China's real economy is the primary origin of China's carbon dioxide emission. It counts for over 80% of the total amount of emission, which makes it the primal target of energy saving and emission abating. China has been in the mid-industrialization process which is characterized by a booming heavy industry with large energy consumption and pollutant emission. Energy and emission intensive industries such as iron and steel, cement and chemistry industries will continue to play pivotal roles in future economic growth. Thus, we can foresee that there will be more negative impact brought by energy-saving and emission-abating activities on China's industry, especially the heavy industry. All in all, a correct understanding of the relationship between energy and environment, and industrial output and productivity is tremendously meaningful for China's industrial economy and public decisions. This chapter focuses on 38 sub-industries and proposes a dynamic version of activity analysis model (AAM) modified from the directional distance function (DDF) to examine the existence of the Porter Hypothesis in China. Based on the proposed model, we also attempt to search for an optimal energy-saving and emission-abating path which could lead to the win-win development possibility for China's industry from now till the 100th anniversary of the People's Republic of China.

This rest of this chapter is organized as below: Section 12.2 surveys the empirical studies to examine the existence of Porter Hypothesis; Section 12.3 designs the different energy-saving and emission-abating paths, which will be added into the direction vector of DDF so as to extend the AAM into a dynamic version; Section 12.4 measures the magnitude of these win-win opportunities among a set of sub-industries corresponding to different paths designed in the former section to pin down an optimal path for China's industrial win-win development during 2009 to 2049; and Section 12.5 conclude this chapter.

12.2. Literature Review

In the last 20 years, the relationship among energy, environment and economy (3E) has always been a focal topic of scholars and policy makers. The traditional established notion on environmental protection is that the extra costs which the government imposes on the firms can jeopardize their international competitiveness. Porter, however, first challenged this argument in his one-page paper published in 1991 (Porter, 1991). He regarded large energy consumption and pollutant emission as a form of economic waste and a sign of incompletion and inefficiency of resources using. In his opinion, the amelioration of this inefficiency will provide firms with the win-win opportunity of improving both the productivity and environment. And the efforts of environmental protection can help firms to identify and eliminate the production inefficiency and regulatory disincentives that prevent the simultaneous improvements in both productivity and environmental quality. Thus, whether these types of environmental policy initiatives are successful depends on the extent to which such inefficiencies are widespread in the sub-industries, particularly in the energy/pollution intensive industries. However, due to deficient management systems, firms are not aware of certain opportunities that could easily be seized by these firms once they are equipped with rational environmental policies. Porter and van der Linde (1995) further emphasized that properly designed environmental protection policy in the form of economic incentives can trigger innovation that may partially or more than fully offset the costs of complying with relevant policies. Such innovation offsets occur mainly because pollution regulation is often coincident with improved efficiency of resource usage and the inference is that stiffer environmental regulation results in greater productivity and competence. These arguments are entitled as the Porter Hypothesis (Ambec and Barla, 2002). Admittedly, many scholars criticize the Porter Hypothesis, arguing that it is a fundamental challenge to efficient market hypothesis and neoclassical theory. They question that why firms do not see these win-win opportunities by themselves, which at least implies that the argument does not have a general validity (Palmer *et al.*, 1995; Jaffe *et al.*, 1995; Faucheux and Nicolaï, 1998).

There are many empirical researches related to the Porter Hypothesis. Combining the idea of ecological economics on capital substitution and the Porter Hypothesis, Karvonen (2001) works on the development of Finland's capital-intensive paper industry in the past 20 years, and reveals how the use of new technologies help the industry achieve a win-win situation and how human-made capital investments influence the quality of natural capital. Mohr (2002) derives results consistent with the Porter Hypothesis by employing a general equilibrium framework with a large number of agents, external economies of scale in production and discrete changes in technology. The model shows that endogenous technical change makes the Porter Hypothesis feasible. However, a policy that produces results consistent with the Porter Hypothesis is not necessarily optimal. Murty and Kumar (2003) estimate the output distance function of India's manufacturing industry using the stochastic parametric approach and come to the conclusion that the technical efficiency of firms increases with the intensity of environmental regulation and the water conservation efforts, which supports the Porter Hypothesis about environmental regulation. Beaumont and Tinch (2004) find that the abatement cost curve methodology proves to be a valuable management tool in identifying barriers to achieving the win–win state, or at least win–draw scenario for industry and the environment, and also in providing future direction for the waste management strategy. Greaker (2006) provides some support for the Porter Hypothesis. The result clearly has a general appeal that policy should be more stringent when a well-developed market for new abatement equipment does not exist. The simulations show that environmental policy has very little effect on export market share as long as the price of pollution abatement equipment is decreasing in the stringency of environmental policy; thus, governments should *a priori* be less afraid of introducing a sufficiently stringent environmental policy. Kuosmanen *et al.* (2009) propose a new approach to environmental cost-benefit analysis (ECBA) which does not require prior valuation of the environmental impacts and is based on shadow prices, and conducts efficiency analysis of ten alternative GHG abatement timing strategies, taking into account the ancillary benefits. There are also a few papers whose conclusion is neutral or against the Porter Hypothesis. Boyd and McClelland (1999) construct efficiency measures based on Shephard's distance function and view it as a test of the Porter Hypothesis. The findings support aspects of both sides of the Porter debate; that is, there is evidence of a win–win potential to increase production and reduce pollution as well as evidence of losses to potential output due to environmental constraints. Thus, comparing the estimates with other studies must be approached with caution, since there can be substantial differences in methodologies. By allowing for nonlinearities, Feichtinger *et al.* (2005) focus more explicitly on learning and technological progress, and maintain that in the presence of learning, implementing a stricter environmental policy with the aim to reach a certain target of emissions reduction has a stronger negative effect on industry profits, which implies quite the opposite as to what is described by the Porter Hypothesis.

As stated previously, theoretical and empirical researches have provided arguments for both positions and have not been conclusive so far, which may be due to different data sets used, the regulatory regime in a country, the cultural setting, customer behaviour, the type of industries or size of companies analysed, the time span, etc. However, the main reason for the conflicting results of the various empirical studies may lie in the lack of a reasonable theoretical framework within which one can investigate the links between environmental regulation and economic performance (Schaltegger and Synnestvedt, 2002). For example, the commonly used CGE model well fits static analysis but its dynamic extension in empirical study is still rather scarce and too simple; parametric macroeconometric model is restricted to its a *priori* functional form and distribution assumption; environmental cost and benefit analysis firstly needs the economic evaluation on environmental effects, which constitutes a technical challenge itself; the analysis based on the theories of property rights, externality and transaction cost cannot soundly quantify the economic influence of environmental regulation; traditional Shepherd distance function cannot distinguish the different characteristics between two outputs of both GDP and pollution, and so on. Not until the presence of directional distance function do we find a reasonable framework to capture the difference between GDP and environmental pollution. DDF allows for the type of inefficiency that is typified by the Porter Hypothesis that increases desirable output while simultaneously decreases undesirable output, which means that DDF provides the most appropriate tool to examine the Porter Hypothesis. By employing two kinds of DDF based on the strong and weak disposability of pollution, respectively, proposed by Boyd *et al.* (2002), this chapter attempts to measure the potential revenues and output loss, corresponding change of production efficiency, technical progress and total factor productivity (TFP) resulted from energy-saving and emission-abating regulation. In order to forecast the win–win development possibility from now on till the year 2049 and find the optimal environmental regulatory path, in particular with different energy-saving and emission-abating paths with the time lag operator introduced into direction vector of DDF to form a dynamic version of AAM. Such a methodology is described in Section 12.3.

12.3. Methodology

12.3.1. *Design the energy-saving and emission-abating paths*

Different energy-saving and emission-abating paths will have obviously different impacts on economy. This section designs five energy-saving scenarios and nine emission-reducing scenarios, totaling forty-five policy paths combinations, and simulates their effects on the potential output and productivity in the future so as to look for the best regulatory path leading to a win–win development possibility for the Chinese industry.

The design of energy saving scheme is based on the promissory targets to save energy stipulated in China's Eleventh Five-Year Plan in 2006, i.e. decreasing the energy consumption per unit of GDP (energy intensity) by 20% during 2006 and 2010 (4% per year). In view of the possibility of easier realization, in fact, this section just chooses a lower value of 3% as the reduction rate annually for energy intensity. Based on this, if we assume that the average growth of China's gross industrial output value is likely to be one of the five possibilities (4%, 6%, 8%, 10%, and 12%) in the future, we can then calculate that the corresponding average annual growth rate of energy consumption is 0.9%, 2.8%, 4.8%, 6.7% and 8.6%, respectively. Compared with average annual 11.2% and 6% growth rate of industrial output and energy consumption, respectively, between 1981 and 2006 provided by Chen (2009a and 2009b), five growth possibilities for output and energy consumption set previously are moderate and very likely to be realized.

This section designs the scheme of emission reduction based on the principle from gradual reduction to sharp one, the former caters to the state condition that China is a developing country whose major task is to develop. The design is also attributable to the generalized understanding of emission abatement concept that emission reduction does not necessarily refer to the absolute decline in aggregate emission level and a declining emission growth rate or declining relative to BaU is also a type of emission abatement corresponding to the gradual or moderate principle. Therefore, as shown in Figure 12.1, the nine kinds of emission reduction paths from the most moderate to the strongest abating intensity designed in this section are listed as follows: 1) the growth of dioxide carbon for different sub-industries evenly decreases from the respective growth rate

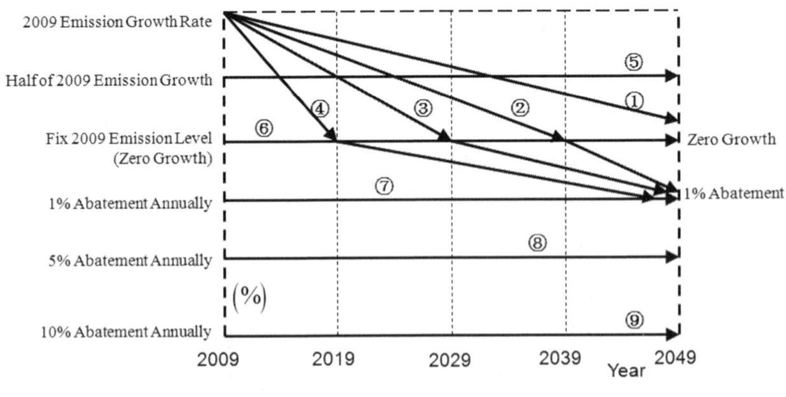

Fig. 12.1. Design of carbon dioxide abatement paths (1–9) for Chinese industry (2009–2049).

of emission in the year of 2009 to zero growth in 2049, that is, the emission peak will appear in the mid-21st century; 2) the emission growth of all sub-industries reduces from 2009 growth level to zero growth in 2039 and after the emission peak, continuously and steadily decreases to −1% growth rate in 2049 (i.e., the annual abating rate is 1% in 2049); 3, 4) the 3rd and 4th paths are similar to the 2nd path but the emission peak is shifted to 2029 and 2019, respectively; 5) the emission growth of all sub-industries maintains half of their growth rate of emission in 2009 till 2049; 6) the dioxide carbon emission for each sub-industry remains the same as in 2009, i.e. the emission growth is to be zero ever since 2009; 7, 8, 9) as for path 7, 8 and 9, a respective annually emission abating rate is 1%, 5% and 10% during the entire forecasting horizon.

The forty-five energy-saving and emission-abating policy paths designed above will be introduced into the dynamic activity analytical model through direction vector as we will discuss in the following sections.

12.3.2. *Dynamic activity analysis model*

In this subsection, a novel dynamic activity analysis model (DAAM for short), not addressed so far, is proposed to simulate the effect of energy-saving and emission-abating regulation on economy in the long run, which is extended from the standard DDF and AAM provided by Chambers *et al.* (1996) and Chung *et al.* (1997). In this study, the decision-making units (DMU) are 38 two-digit sub-industries ($i = 1, 2, \ldots, 38$). The forecasting time span is from 2009 to 2049 ($t = 2009, 2010, \ldots, 2049$). For each sub-industry, there are three types of input ($j = 1, 2, 3$, corresponding to capital, labour and energy), one type of desirable output (gross industrial output value, GIOV), and one type of undesirable output (carbon dioxide emission, CO_2). The sample data sets between 1980 and 2008 used for simulation are based on Chen (2011b) and Chen *et al.* (2011). The panel data for nearly 40 sub-industries, rather than aggregate data, significantly enhance the information that could be obtained to analyze microeconomic performance, particularly when examining the efficiency of each unit.

The principle of DDF is illustrated in Figure 12.2. The technology is represented by the output set $P(\mathrm{x})$ to which the output vector of A point

$(\mathbf{y}, \mathbf{b})$ belongs. Shaephard's output distance function radially scales the original vector from point A proportionally to point D to describe the simultaneous increase of desirable and undesirable output. In contrast to this, more general DDF starts at A and scales in the direction along ABC to capture simultaneously the increase of desirable outputs (or goods) and decrease of undesirable outputs (or bads) which make it possible to investigate the Porter Hypothesis that allows for the possibility of crediting units for the reduction of pollutions. Formally, DDF is defined as

$$\bar{D}_o(\mathbf{x}^i, \mathbf{y}^i, \mathbf{b}^i; \mathbf{g}^i) = \sup\{\beta : (\mathbf{y}^i, \mathbf{b}^i) + \beta\mathbf{g}^i \in P(\mathbf{x}^i)\} \quad (12.1)$$

where $\mathbf{g}$ is the direction vector in which outputs are scaled. In standard case, $\mathbf{g} = (\mathbf{y}, -\mathbf{b})$, as shown in Figure 12.2; in dynamic version proposed by this study, $\mathbf{g}^t = (\mathbf{y}^t, -\mathbf{b}^t) = [(1+u)]\mathbf{y}^{t-1}, -(1+v)\mathbf{b}^{t-1}]$, where u and v respectively represent the varying rate of current goods and bads relative to previous time point which does amount to the growth rate of gross industrial output value and the growth or abating rate of carbon dioxide emission from 2009 to 2049 designed in section 12.3.1 of this chapter. β is the maximum feasible expansion of the desirable outputs and contraction of the undesirable outputs when the expansion and contraction are identical proportions for a given level of inputs, which amounts to the value of DDF to be measured.

As shown in Figure 12.2, because the point A remains within the efficient production frontier, the inefficiencies resulted from such factors as high energy consumption and heavy emission give the producer the potential room to increase the output, given the inputs and current output, by saving energy and abating emission.[1] But whether the observation vector projects from the point A to point B or C depends on the weak or free disposal assumption of undesirable output. Given that the undesirable output is strongly or freely disposal, that is, the disposability costs nothing, the producers will voluntarily get rid of the unwanted by-products, then potential output growth based on current desirable output is maximized which amounts to the distance function value β_s, i.e., the ratio of

[1] In this case, the value of β is greater than zero which tells us the sizes of inefficiencies for the unit.

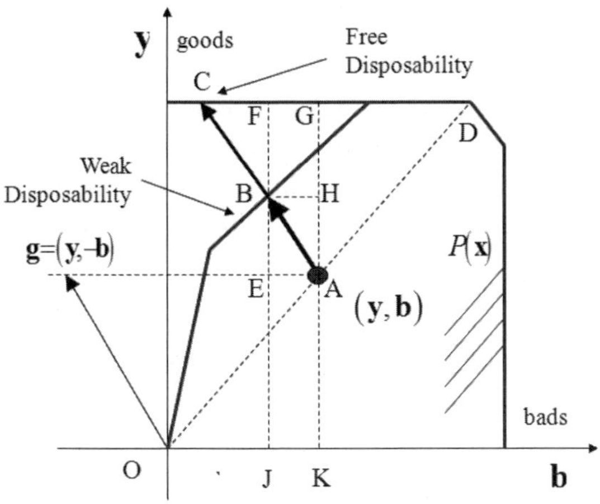

Fig. 12.2. Principle of directional output distance function.

AC/Og. In this case, energy and environment impose no restriction on output, and then the production in point C is the most efficient. However, it is impossible to shoulder no cost to reduce undesirable output in reality. The producers therefore are not willing to reduce the bads because the cost makes use of the important inputs and then translates into lost goods given inputs. The bads reduction only can be achieved by environmental regulation; corresponding to this, the more appropriate assumption is weak disposability of undesirable output, the point A projecting into B on the frontier, which is the standard DDF, or referred to as environment regulatory AAM, the value being β_w (equal to AB/Og). In this case, the potential goods growth is a tradeoff between more goods and less bads, bound to less than the maximized β_s corresponding to highest level of inefficiency under the strong disposability of bads.

The difference between β_w and β_s reflects the potential output loss caused by the observable lack of free disposability (more vividly, due to enforced regulation), i.e., $l = \beta_w - \beta_s < 0$ (Boyd *et al.*, 2002). The value of l is analogous to the hyperbolic output loss measure introduced by Färe *et al.* (1989). The potential output loss l and potential output growth β_w reveal the extent of the win–win potential for each sub-industry, given current output at some time point. If potential β_w exceeds or equals the absolute value of l, $|l|$, from the perspective of output, the win–win opportunity due to energy-saving and emission-abating regulation, described in the Porter Hypothesis, happens, to some extent suggesting that improved production efficiency can make up for the losses imposed by regulations; otherwise, environmental regulation does not lead to win–win development. This chapter will make use of this method to find the best energy-saving and emission-abating path that leads to the win–win development potentials.

The DAAM of DDF with the weak disposal assumption of undesirable output models the energy-saving and emission-abating activity under environmental regulation; therefore, it can be used to measure the change of TFP and its decomposition, allowing for the energy and environment restriction, by calculating the Malmquist–Luenberger Productivity Index (MLPI). The Malmquist–Luenberger index is the most widely used productivity index and is particularly attractive since it does not rely on prices, specifically the price of CO_2 which appeared in this study, in order to construct it. The MLPI can be decomposed as the product of two terms: the change of production efficiency (MLECH) and the change of technical progress (MLTCH). If MLPI > 1, it means that TFP grows over the adjacent period; while MLPI < 1 indicates that TFP declines.

12.4. Forecasting Analysis

12.4.1. *Simulate the win–win prospect under different energy-saving and emission-abating paths*

Table 12.1 reports the potential industrial output growth β_w, loss l and corresponding net value of loss averaged over the entire forecasting period under the total forty-five environmental regulatory paths combined by five energy-saving scenarios and nine emission-reducing scenarios.[2]

In Table 12.1, the potential output growth, output loss and net value of loss caused by energy-saving and emission-reducing exhibit a quite regular pattern in distribution of their values. With the increase of GIOV

[2] For the convenience of report, Table 12.1 does not report the result of the group with 12% of GIOV growth, in which the trend is same as the rest of Table 12.1. Particularly, the potential net values of loss in this group are greater than the former four GIOV groups; thus, there exists no optimal energy-saving and emission-abating path in this group.

Table 12.1. Win–win development forecasts corresponding to different energy-saving and emission-abating paths (%).

Carbon Dioxide Abatement Paths			GIOV Growth, 4%			GIOV Growth, 6%		
			βw	$l=\beta w-\beta s$	Net Value	βw	$l=\beta w-\beta s$	Net Value
Gradual Abatement	Path 1	Emission Peak in 2049	73.43	−91.55	−18.12	69.46	−92.42	−22.96
	Path 2	Emission Peak in 2039	73.52	−91.46	−17.94	69.47	−92.43	**−22.95**
	Path 3	Emission Peak in 2029	73.52	−91.45	**−17.93**	69.46	−92.50	−23.04
	Path 4	Emission Peak in 2019	73.41	−91.59	−18.18	69.46	−92.48	−23.02
Sharp Abatement	Path 5	Half of 2009 Emission Growth	74.41	−106.58	−32.17	70.30	−101.82	−31.53
	Path 6	Keeping 2009 Emission Level	74.55	−155.68	−81.14	70.17	−152.12	−81.95
	Path 7	Abating 1% Annually	74.71	−174.94	−100.23	69.92	−176.01	−106.09
	Path 8	Abating 5% Annually	74.81	−201.17	−126.37	69.96	−203.87	−133.91
	Path 9	Abating 10% Annually	73.93	−244.64	−170.71	70.11	−248.87	−178.77

Carbon Dioxide Abatement Paths			GIOV Growth, 8%			GIOV Growth, 10%		
			βw	$l=\beta w-\beta s$	Net Value	βw	$l=\beta w-\beta s$	Net Value
Gradual Abatement	Path 1	Emission Peak in 2049	63.51	−92.95	−29.44	60.68	−97.09	**−36.41**
	Path 2	Emission Peak in 2039	63.62	−92.71	**−29.09**	60.67	−97.10	−36.43
	Path 3	Emission Peak in 2029	63.52	−92.81	−29.29	60.66	−97.35	−36.69
	Path 4	Emission Peak in 2019	63.48	−92.90	−29.42	60.68	−97.24	−36.56
Sharp Abatement	Path 5	Half of 2009 Emission Growth	67.46	−105.09	−37.63	64.38	−111.17	−46.80
	Path 6	Keeping 2009 Emission Level	65.20	−158.39	−93.19	62.49	−158.51	−96.02
	Path 7	Abating 1% Annually	65.59	−178.36	−112.77	62.72	−174.66	−111.94
	Path 8	Abating 5% Annually	65.72	−203.70	−137.98	63.19	−202.69	−139.50
	Path 9	Abating 10% Annually	65.53	−245.96	−180.43	63.17	−248.40	−185.23

growth, the magnitude of potential output growth decreases gradually from about 73% in the group with 4% of GIOV growth to a bit more than 60% with 10% of GIOV growth. Therefore, the more rapid growth of industry will reduce the widespread extent of production inefficiencies, leading to the shrinking of improving space for potential output growth. However, the potential output loss brought by energy saving and emission reduction keeps a roughly rising trend (though some values cross among the groups). Thus, the comparison between the potential output growth and loss enables us to see that the net value of output loss increases in fact from the range of [−18.12%, −170.71%] in the group with 4% of GIOV growth to [−36.41%, −185.23%] in the group of 10% GIOV growth. Such evidence implies that the optimal path of energy saving and emission reduction must be in the group with lower growth rate of gross industrial output value.

Table 12.1 classifies the former four moderate abating paths as the gradually abating group and the latter five strong abating paths as the sharp abating group. Obviously, as the abating strength enhances from 1st path to 9th path, the potential output growth varies not much but the output loss increases sharply from [−91.55%, −97.09%] for path 1 to [−244.64%, 248.87%] for path 9. The corresponding increase of net loss indicates that the optimal energy-saving and emission-abating path must be in the gradual abating group. The lowest value of net loss in each GIOV group is marked in a bold style in Table 12.1. It is easy to pin down that the lowest value among all groups is −17.93% in the group with 4% of GIOV growth which corresponds to path 3. Considering that economic development is the prior task and then the growth rate of gross industrial output cannot be too slow in China, we finally choose the 2nd path in the group with 6% of GIOV growth, corresponding to the lowest net loss −22.95%, as the best energy-saving and emission-abating path for Chinese industry in the next 40 years, in which the matching growth of energy consumption consistent with the target of annual 3% reduction in energy intensity is 2.8%. As stated previously, fully allowing for China's state condition, the chosen best path for sub-industries belongs to gradual abating group that evenly abates the carbon dioxide emission from their respective emission growing rate in the year of 2009 to zero growth in 2039 (i.e., the peak of emission for all sub-industries) and then evenly to abating rate of 1% in 2049, the end of our forecasting period. Since all the potential net losses shown in Table 12.1 are negative, it seems that all paths cannot lead to the win–win development suggested by the Porter Hypothesis, even though the best energy-saving and emission-abating path has been chosen above.

The findings in Table 12.1 are consistent with most other researches. Kuosmanen *et al.* (2009) suggest that if one is only interested in greenhouse gases (GHG) abatement at the lowest economic cost, then equal reduction of GHGs over time is preferred. These researches all support the gradual or moderate emission abatement. Similar to the idea of our study that there is a close relationship between emission reduction and development, Reddy and Assenza (2009) also suggest that the integration of climate policies with those of development priorities is vitally important for developing countries and stress the need for using sustainable development as a framework for climate change policies. Of course, the optimal path chosen here means that the combination of a relatively high growth of output and energy consumption may have a relation with the traditional industry development model that is hazardous to the win–win development of China's industry. An adjustment on the speed of output growth and a moderate reduction of energy consumption may be more beneficial to the structural reconstruction, development model transformation and sustainable development for China's industry in the future.

12.4.2. *The impact of best energy-saving and emission-abating path on future potential output*

Murty and Kumar (2003) pointed out that the win–win opportunities from the environmental regulation could be found more in some industries and less in others, and the studies for specific industries could help us to identify the industries with no such opportunities so that the monitoring and enforcement could be directed to those industries in which incentives are absent. As a matter of fact, it is also the reason why we focus on the analysis of China's 38 two-digit sub-industries instead of merely the aggregated industry. Therefore, proceeding along the optimal path of energy save and emission reduction chosen in the previous section, this section further simulates the potential output growth and loss for all

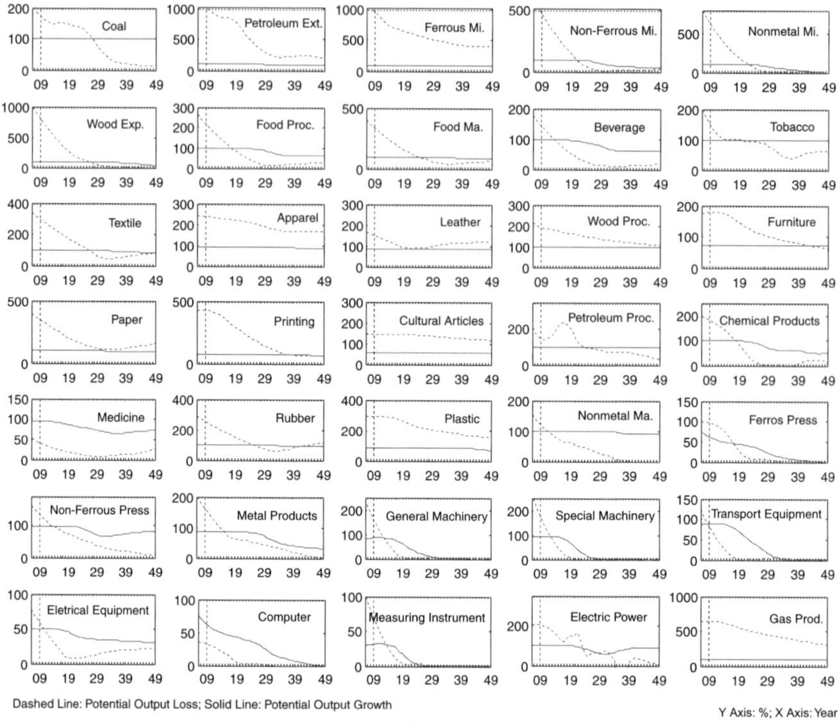

Fig. 12.3. Sub-industrial win–win development forecasts under the best energy-saving and emission-abating path (2009–2049).

sub-industries in the following 40 years. Figure 12.3 illustrates the forecasting prospects for each sub-industry.[3]

Table 12.1 shows that the average net losses brought by different regulatory paths are all negative, even if by the best energy-saving and emission-abating path. However, if we analyze the individual sub-industry at different time point rather the aggregated industry, the situation will be a totally different story. The dashed line in Figure 12.3 represents absolute value of potential output loss caused by energy saving and emission

[3] For convenience's sake, only 35 sub-industries are included in this figure, excluding production and supply of water (heavy industry), manufacturers of chemical fibers (light industry) and other industries. The win-win forecasting prospect of the three sub-industries is also in accord with the conclusion of this paper.

reduction and the real line represents potential output growth. In this figure, the potential output loss exhibits a declining trend for all sub-industries and the potential output growth of most sub-industries does not change much. Except for six sub-industries such as ferrous ores mining, apparel manufacturing, leather manufacturing, cultural articles manufacturing, plastic manufacturing and gas production and supply, the potential loss for all the other sub-industries decreases continuously and then appears to be smaller than potential output growth at some time point before 2049. This indicates that for most sub-industries, the energy-saving and emission-abating activity can bring the win–win development opportunity via which the potential output growth exceeds the potential output loss. Even for the above exceptional six sub-industries, their potential output losses tend to decline, too, and are bound to be lower than the potential growth at certain time after the year of 2049, leading to expected win–win development.

The reason why the average net values of potential loss for all paths, even the best one, are minus is that all the sub-industries (except medicine manufacturing, and communication equipment and computer manufacturing) have large potential losses in the near future. It is thus clear that the aggregation analysis is undependable and even leads to the opposite conclusion. Specifically, the potential output losses of those energy and emission intensive sub-industries such as petroleum extraction, ferrous ores mining, wood exploiting, and gas production and supply are particularly large, which should be one of the causes of the negative weighted potential loss for aggregated industry. Moreover, what we care about the energy saving and emission reduction is its final influential level instead of accumulative effect; hence, the high potential loss in the nearer future is just meaningful for that period and useless for the analysis on the future opportunity of win-win development. As mentioned above, the medicine manufacturing and communication equipment and computer manufacturing are the only two sub-industries maintaining the win-win development over the whole prediction time span. As for general machinery manufacturing, special machinery manufacturing, transport equipment manufacturing and measuring instrument and machinery, they realize efficient production around the year of 2029, which means they are on the production frontier and have no space to improve the potential output growth no matter if there is energy saving and emission reduction or not. All in all, the sub-industrial simulation results shown in Figure 12.3 manifest that, from the perspective of potential output, energy-saving and emission-abating can bring costs on output, which means that the Porter Hypothesis will not be satisfied in the very near future, but as time goes by, it will lead to the win-win development possibility for China's industry, finally supporting the Porter Hypothesis.

According to the theory in Chenery *et al.* (1986) and current empirical work in Chen *et al.* (2011), the standard perception of industrialization is a general shift in relative importance from light to heavy industry. Light industry is of great importance normally at the early stage of industrialization and labour-intensive in nature with relatively low ratios of capital to labour; while heavy industry is at the middle or late stage and capital-intensive with relatively high ratios of capital to labour. Therefore, we divide all sub-industries into light and heavy industrial groups according to the ranking of capital to labour ratio (K/L) in 2008. That is, the light industrial group corresponds to the top half of sub-industries with the lower K/L ratio, and the heavy industry to the last half of sub-industries with the larger K/L ratio. We refer to them as light industry and heavy industry in brief from now on in this chapter. This is because 38 sub-industrial patterns of potential output growth and loss are too complicated to see clearly all at once, and sometimes we want to observe the difference just between the light and heavy industries instead. Figure 12.4 depicts the weighted average potential output loss (bar with light color) and output growth (deep color) for light and heavy industries (panel a and b) and aggregated industry (panel c) corresponding to the best environmental regulatory path, in which the sub-industrial weight is its respective share of gross industrial output value.

As Figure 12.4 shows, in light industry, the average potential loss declines prominently from −173.95% in 2009 to −46.85% in 2049 while the potential output growth decreases less evidently from 80.51% in 2009 to 46.86% in 2049; in heavy industry, the corresponding varying range of average potential output loss, [−67.95%, −16.32%], and growth, [50.62%, 27.75%], is much less than that in light industry. Apparently, both the potential output loss and growth for light industry are high whereas for heavy industries they are the opposite. The light industry does not reach a

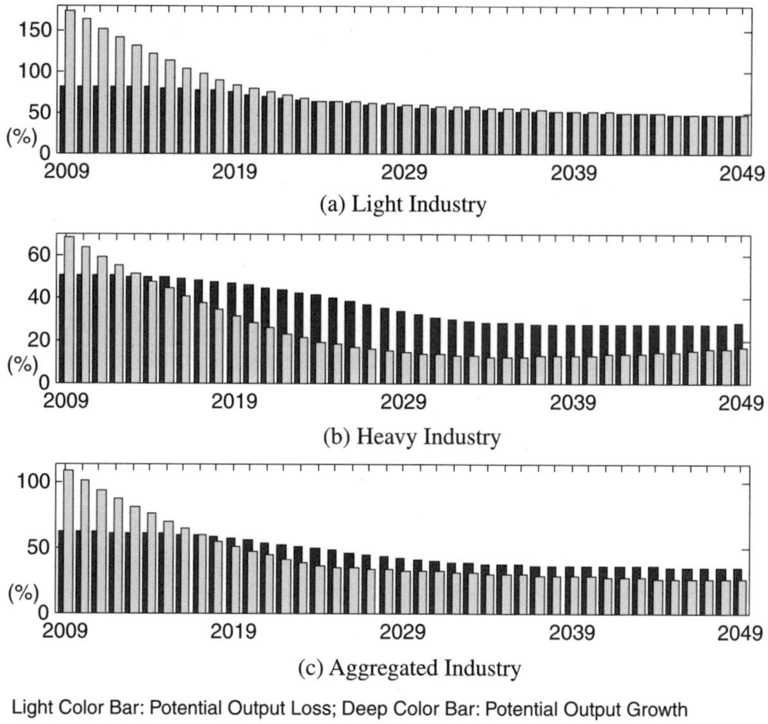

Fig. 12.4. Average industrial win–win development forecasts under the best energy-saving and emission-abating path (2009–2049).

comparable level for potential output loss and growth until 2024 and keeps the similar situation to 2049, just about meeting the win–win development condition. But for the heavy industry, the win–win situation is reached ever since the earlier year of 2014 and the potential output growth holds a large advantage over the loss. Therefore, heavy sub-industries are the beneficiaries of energy saving and emission reduction, but light sub-industries are not the losers. For the aggregated industry, the potential output loss declines from −108.72% in 2009 to −25.55% in 2049, the potential output growth decreases from 62.11% in 2009 to 34.97% at the end of the forecasting period — being between those of light and heavy industries. Since heavy sub-industries have the greater weights, the varying pattern of the potential output for aggregated industry is dominated by and more similar to that of heavy industry — realizing the win–win development in the year of 2018 with a distinguished advantage.

12.4.3. *The effect of best energy-saving and emission-abating path on future industrial productivity*

Following the same group classification and weights as in Figure 12.4, Figure 12.5 exhibits the average changing trends of TFP (i.e. the Malmquist–Luenberger Productivity Index, MLPI) and its decompositions, MLECH and MLTCH, under the best path of energy saving and emission reduction for light and heavy industries (panel a and b) and aggregated industry, respectively. Three subfigures show a similar pattern.

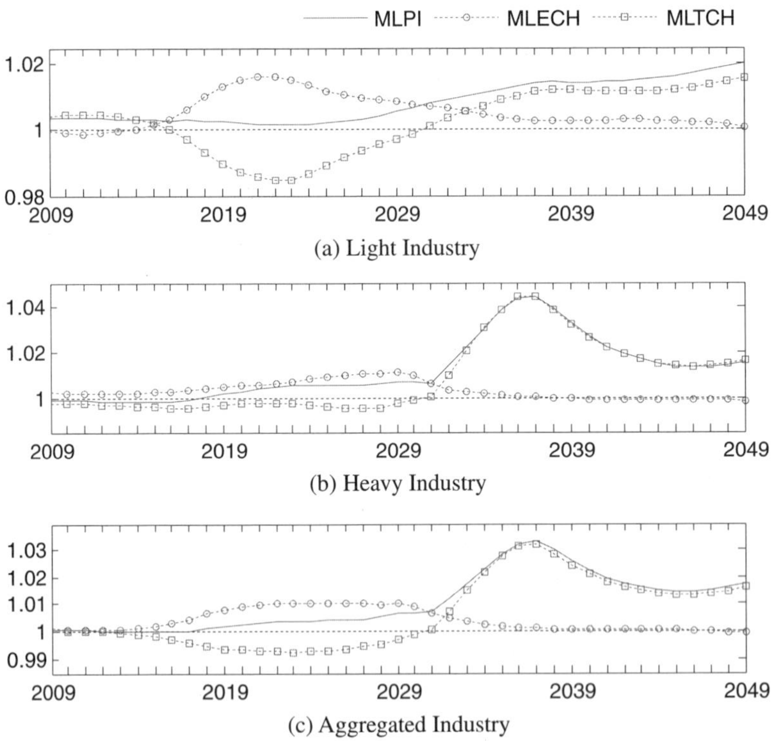

Fig. 12.5. Average productivity forecasts and its decomposition under the best energy-saving and emission-abating path.

That is, China's industrial TFP before the year of 2032 or 2033 is mainly influenced by production efficiency in which the catching-up effect of adoption of the frontier technologies due to the environmental regulation is very obvious. When the production efficiency reaches its utmost limits and the catching-up energy is almost released, the technical progress begins to serve as the major propelling force through gradual accumulation, i.e., the change of TFP after the year of 2033 will be mainly affected by the technical progress. Therefore, as illustrated in Figure 12.5, the behavior of the overall TFP index shows that the industrial development has generally shifted in a win–win fashion.

More specifically, at the early stage, energy-saving and emission-abating policy mainly negatively affects the industrial technical progress, and such impact will be exerted more on light industry than on heavy industry. For instance, for light industry, the level of technical progress in 2023 is just 98.48% of 2022, reaching the largest backward magnitude of production frontier, –1.52%, over the whole forecasting period; the largest backward extent of technical progress for heavy industry is –0.5% in 2026 and the largest one for the aggregated industry is –0.74% in 2024. However, due to the obvious catching-up effect and improved production efficiency (at the peak of efficiency improvement, the index of MLECH of light industry in 2022 is 1.016 times that of the previous year; that of heavy industry in 2029 is 1.011 times that of 2028; that of the aggregated industry in 2023 is 1.01 times that of the previous year), the TFP growth will keep an increasing trend at the earlier forecasting phase. After 2031, the negative effect of environmental regulation on technical progress fades gradually and turns to be positive. Three or four years latter, the catching-up effect disappears, especially in heavy industry; in around 2037, the technical progress reaches its peak due to the long-term introduction, absorption, adoption and innovation of the advanced technologies — particularly in energy and emission intensive heavy industries whose technical progress in 2036 reaches 1.044 times that of 2035. After that, the technical progress and productivity for light industry keep stable with slight increase, and those for heavy industry and the aggregated industry, dominated by heavy industry, will drop at first and then rise more steadily due to the enhancement of abating strength after the peak of carbon dioxide emission in 2039. In a word, from the perspective of productivity, energy-saving and emission-abating activity has a negative impact on industrial technical progress at the earlier stage, but positive on production efficiency and combined TFP. During the entire forecasting period from 2009 to 2049, the TFP grows steadily with the annual average growth rate of 0.81% for light industry, 1.11% for heavy industry and 1% for the aggregated industry. As we forecast, in 2049, the growth rate for light, heavy and aggregated industry will reach 2.02%, 1.54% and 1.72%, respectively. This is a win–win development prospect since productivity is grown and the targets of energy saving and emission reduction are also achieved.

12.5. Conclusion

To challenge global warming and boost the development model transformation, energy-saving and emission-abating and developing a low-carbon economy have become necessary approaches for all countries to achieve a sustainable economic development (Chen, 2011a). However, the energy saving and environment protection will take up important materials originally planned for normal production, causing the decline of the desirable output and competitiveness, especially in the recovery period from the financial crisis. The conflicting views are also reflected in academic area, either in favor or against the Porter Hypothesis. This chapter makes use of the directional distance function that precisely embodies the spirit of the Porter Hypothesis that the goods increase and bads decrease simultaneously, and proposes a novel dynamic activity analysis model (DAAM) to forecast the win–win development possibilities for Chinese sub-industries between 2009 and 2049, thus probing the existence of the Porter Hypothesis in China.

From the perspective of potential output, the empirical results show that energy saving and emission reduction can cause bigger potential output loss at an early stage; but in the long run, the loss will decline gradually and become lower than potential output growth, finally achieving the win–win development prospect stated in the Porter Hypothesis. Of course, compared with light industry, there exists a bigger win–win opportunity resulting from the environmental regulation in heavy industry and the aggregated industry. For example, the potential output loss and growth for the aggregated industry in 2049 attain −25.55% and 34.97%, respectively, finally reaching 9.42% of net growth of potential output. From the viewpoint of productivity, the prediction analysis manifests that energy-saving and emission-reducing policy will have a larger negative impact on industrial technical progress at an early stage, especially for light industry. However, due to the obvious catching-up effect and increasing production efficiency in the first half of the forecasting period and the rising technical progress dominated in the second half period, the industrial TFP is not negatively influenced and always maintains a steadily but gradually increasing trend. During the whole forecasting period from 2009 to 2049, the annual average growth rate of productivity is 0.81% for light industry, 1.11% for heavy industry and 1% for the aggregated industry. Overall, although energy-saving and emission-abating regulation will cause certain loss at an early stage, in the long run, it will not only realize the target of improving environment quality but also increase the output and productivity, finally leading to the win–win development in the next 40 years. Our forecasting analysis in this chapter favors the Porter Hypothesis.

References

Ambec, S. and Barla, P. (2002). "A Theoretical Foundation of the Porter Hypothesis." *Economics Letters*, 75(3), 355–360.

Beaumont, N.J. and Tinch, R. (2004). "Abatement Cost Curves: A Viable Management Tool for Enabling the Achievement of Win–Win Waste Reduction Strategies?" *Journal of Environmental Management*, 71(3), 207–215.

Boyd, G.A. and McClelland, J.D (1999). "The Impact of Environmental Constraints on Productivity Improvement in Integrated Paper Plants." *Journal of Environmental Economics and Management*, 38, 121–142.

Boyd, G.A., Tolley, G. and Pang, J. (2002). "Plant Level Productivity, Efficiency, and Environmental Performance of the Container Glass Industry." *Environmental and Resource Economics*, 23, 29–43.

Cai, F. Du, Y. and Wang, M. (2008). "The Political Economy of Emission in China: will a Low Carbon Growth be Incentive Compatible in Next Decade and Beyond?" (in Chinese). *Economic Research Journal*, 6, 4–11.

Chambers, R., Chung, Y.H. and Färe, R. (1996). "Benefit and Distance Function." *Journal of Economic Theory*, 70, 407–419.

Chen, S. (2009a). "Energy Consumption, CO_2 Emission and Sustainable Development in Chinese Industry." *Economic Research Journal*, 4, 41–55.

Chen, S. (2009b). "Engine or Drag: Can High Energy Consumption and CO_2 Emission Drive the Sustainable Development of Chinese Industry?" *Frontier of Economics in China*, 4, 548–571.

Chen, S. (2011a). "The Abatement of Carbon Intensity in China: Factor Decomposition and Policy Implications." *The World Economy*, to be published.

Chen, S. (2011b). "Estimates of Sub-Industrial Statistical Data in China (1980–2008)" (in Chinese). *China Economic Quarterly*, to be published.

Chen, S. Jefferson, G.H. and Zhang, J. (2011). "Structural Change, Productivity Growth and Industrial Transformation in China." *China Economic Review*, to be published.

Chenery, H.B., Robinson, S. and Syrquin, M. (1986). *Industrialization and Growth: A Comparative Study*. New York: Oxford University Press.

Chung, Y. H., Färe, R. and Grosskopf, S. (1997). "Productivity and Undesirable Outputs: a Directional Distance Function Approach." *Journal of Environmental Management*, 51, 229–240.

Faucheux, S. and Nicolaï, I. (1998). "Environmental Technological Change and Governance in Sustainable Development Policy." *Ecological Economics*, 27, 243–256.

Feichtinger, G., Hartl, R. F., Kort, P. M. and Veliov, V. M. (2005). "Environmental Policy, the Porter Hypothesis and the Composition of Capital: Effects of Learning and Technological Progress." *Journal of Environmental Economics and Management*, 50(2), 434–446.

Greaker, M. (2006). "Spillovers in the Development of New Pollution Abatement Technology: a New Look at the Porter-Hypothesis." *Journal of Environmental Economics and Management*, 52(1), 411–420.

Jaffe, A., Peterson, S., Portney, P. and Stavins, R. (1995). "Environmental Regulation and the Competitiveness of U.S. Manufacturing: What Does the Evidence Tell Us?" *Journal of Economic Literature*, 33(1), 132–163.

Karvonen, M.-M. (2001). "Natural Versus Manufactured Capital: Win–Lose or Win–Win? A Case Study of the Finnish Pulp and Paper Industry." *Ecological Economics*, 37(1), 71–85.

Kuosmanen, T. Bijsterbosch, N. and Dellink, R. (2009). "Environmental Cost–Benefit Analysis of Alternative Timing Strategies in Greenhouse Gas Abatement: a Data Envelopment Analysis Approach." *Ecological Economics*, 68(6), 1633–1642.

Lee C.F., Lin, S.J., Lewis, C. and Chang, Y.F. (2007). "Effects of Carbon Taxes on Different Industries By Fuzzy Goal Programming: A Case Study of the Petrochemical-Related Industries." *Taiwan, Energy Policy*, 35(8), 4051–4058.

Lin, J.Y. (2004). "Is China's Growth Real and Sustainable?" *Asian Perspective*, 28, 5–29.

Mohr, R.D. (2002). "Technical Change, External Economies, and the Porter Hypothesis." *Journal of Environmental Economics and Management*, 43(1), 158–168 .

Murty, M.N. and Kumar, S. (2003). "Win–Win Opportunities and Environmental Regulation: Testing of Porter Hypothesis for Indian Manufacturing Industries." *Journal of Environmental Management*, 67(2), 139–144.

Palmer, K., Oates, W.E. and Portney, P.R. (1995). "Tightening Environmental Standards: The Benefit-Cost or the No-Cost Paradigm." *Journal of Economic Perspectives*, 9(4), 97–118.

Porter, M. E. (1991). "America's Green Strategy." *Scientific American*, 264(4), 168.

Porter, M.E. and Van Der Linde, C. (1995). "Toward a New Conception of the Environment — Competitiveness Relationship." *Journal of Economic Perspectives*, 9(4), 97–118.

Reddy, B.S. and Assenza, G.B. (2009). "The Great Climate Debate." *Energy Policy*, 37(8), 2997–3008.

Robins, N, Clover, R. and Singh, C. (2009). "A Climate for Recovery: The Colour of Stimulus Goes Green." *HSBC Global Research*, 25 February issue, 1–45.

Schaltegger, S. and Synnestvedt, T. (2002). "The Link Between Green and Economic Success: Environmental Management as the Crucial Trigger Between Environmental and Economic Performance." *Journal of Environmental Management*, 65(4), 339–346.

CHAPTER 13

THE COSTS AND BENEFITS OF RELATIONAL GOVERNANCE AND CHINA'S ROAD TO MODERNITY

*Yongqin Wang**

13.1. Introduction

The last 30 years have witnessed great changes in China's economy and society. This chapter is an attempt to explore the social foundations of China's market-oriented transition and to further unravel the "China Paradox": sustained economic growth without a formal institutional infrastructure, which includes a sound legal system, well-defined property rights, and an efficient financial system since reform and opening-up in the late 1970s. Naturally this leads us to search for the alternative informal mechanisms underlying the transition.

In this chapter, we will show that the transition from a planned economy to a market-oriented economy requires market completion and perfection, which has important implications for economic governance. In particular, during China's transition thus far, informal institutions based

*Yongqin Wang, China Center for Economic Studies and School of Economics, Fudan University, Shanghai, China. Email: yongqinwang@fudan.edu.cn. We thank Matthew Hummer for valuable comments. Wang thanks Project 985 of Fudan University, China Social Science Foundation Project (05CJL014), the MOE Project of Key Research Institute of Humanities and Social Sciences at Universities (07JJD790130 and Shanghai Leading Academic Discipline Project (B101) for financial support. The usual disclaimers apply.

on relational contracting[1] have made up for the missing or imperfect markets and formal institutions.

With the further development of China's economy, the cost of relational contracting has grown increasingly high due to the diseconomies of scale, which arises from small-scale transactions that are completed using relational contracts. Inequality is a consequence of relational contracting, which encourages social segregation, specifically the division between "insiders" and "outsiders". Most importantly, if personal connections are embedded in the network of sociopolitical power, China's income gap will be further widened, leading to more resource misallocation and increased social inequality.

This chapter shows how the early stages of China's economic transition have caused relational contracts and interlinked arrangements to become effective substitutes for missing and imperfect markets. It will also show that transactions based on relational contracts may distort the emerging market mechanism, which in turn undermines further transition to a modern society. Specifically, relational contracting prevents the development of arm-length transactions and formal institutions, which is conducive to scale economy. To facilitate the emergence of formal institutions, China's market economy must be decoupled from its sociopolitical powers. In this regard, there are two possible future scenarios of China's economic transition. One scenario is that China's markets are so developed that they are dis-embedded from sociopolitical powers. The other scenario is that China's markets are less developed and embedded in sociopolitical powers, a trend that is characterized by many developing countries.

This chapter is organized as follows. Section 13.2 is a historical account of the relation-based society of China. Section 13.3 contextualizes relational contracts within China's economic transition. Section 13.4 goes on to provide a theoretical account of relational contracting in China's economic transition. Section 13.5 analyzes how economic development will unravel the relation-based governance. Section 13.6 presents a taxonomy of governance and development models in historical and

[1] "Relational contracting" and "relational governance" are used interchangeably in this chapter.

international perspectives. Section 13.7 draws some important lessons from the world development history. In light of this, Section 13.8 discusses some pitfalls of China's reform and Section 13.9 looks ahead to China's unfinished reforms and her road to modernity.

13.2. Relational Society in China: A Historical Account

There are historical rationales for the relation-based governance in China. As we will see, relational transaction is a natural response to China's specific economic structure and political structure. Economically, China has been an agricultural society with low level of labour mobility and division of labour, which has caused people living in the same communities to form long-term relationships.

In particular, when markets are incomplete, as is the case in many developing economies, contractual relationships between agents are at once relational and multiplex. A typical case of this type of contractual relationship exists between a landlord and his tenant in an agrarian society. The tenant usually pays his rent in kind as agreed upon in the contractual relationship. In addition, the landlord and tenant may share exposure to agriculture risks through a sharecropping arrangement, and in some cases the landlord will offer credit to the tenant. Thus, the same pair of parties interacts in multiple personalized markets (land, credit, insurance, labour and product), making their relationship both relational and multiplex. By contrast, in economies with more complete markets, people will transact with other agents in separate specialized markets. For instance, in these economies, farmers share risk with insurance companies.

Interlinked transactions are commonly observed in rural China. For example, Family A may ask Family B to lend a hand in building houses without financial payment. When harvesting time arrives, Family B may collect on this favor by asking Family A for assistance in harvesting crops. This type of interlinked transactions effectively addresses the issue of a missing labour market for rural construction and harvesting.

One advantage of interlinked contracts is that they mitigate the problem of moral hazard and adverse selection that may exist in a single market by offsetting losses in one market with gains in another. In other words, unviable transactions in a single market may become viable with interlinked contracts since people care more about the net surplus in the bundled transactions. Therefore, interlinked contracts can enlarge the feasible set of relational contracts (Wang, 2007). In societies with missing markets, interlinked contracts can make up for specialized markets and achieve Pareto improvements. Historically, there are a least three particular foundations for China's relation-based governance.

13.2.1. *Social networks based on extended family*

Families have played an essential role in traditional Chinese agricultural society. As recent as 1953, 90% of the Chinese populations lived in rural area (Chao, 2006). In such a society, families and extended families were the basic organizations around which production, consumption and other economic activities were centered. Economic exchanges mainly took place mostly at the local level of villages and townships, a trend that arose from missing specialized markets and ultimately encouraged transactions between the agents to be relational and interlinked. This governance was in line with the limited scale economy of agricultural society and enforceable due to the repeated interactions of the agents. Except for a short unsuccessful period during the Mao era when the agricultural sector was divided into communes, families and extended families have been the basic agricultural production unit.

13.2.2. *Centralized hierarchy in polity*

China's political system has long been based on a centralized hierarchy system since the Qin Dynasty and during its agrarian era, dual governance has been the norm. The state has a strong control over higher-level jurisdiction, while at the local-level, landed gentry have an informal authority within their localities through community-wide networks.

Since 1949 and the beginning of Communist China, a centralized hierarchy system has been used to allocate resources based on planning and rationing. This system was used instead of a well-functioning market system and over time has caused personal connections to play a critical role in obtaining scarce resources.

13.2.3. *Low level of labour mobility*

In 1958 the Chinese government adopted the *hukou* system, a residential permit system that places restrictions on mobility, particularly between the rural and urban sectors. Many suspect that the *hukou* system is largely responsible for the rural-urban divide that exists in China today. In the rural sector, the grass-root organizations are village governments. In the urban sector, *danwei* (work unit(s)) is a basic organization. Due to the repression of markets, *danwei* became an encompassing state-sponsored organization that provided housing, medical care, and other life-long services to people belonging to work units. In effect, *danwei* provided further disincentives for mobility within both the urban and rural sectors during the planning era.

Low mobility and absence of markets make relational contract a feasible and rational choice for people both in rural and urban sectors. While in the rural sector, village community-based interlocking relationships act as an effective substitute for missing markets, the work unit in the urban sector system is essentially an interlinked relational contract between the state and the urban workers. In what follows we will elaborate more on these points.

13.3. The Role of Relational Governance in China's Transition

Transition from a centrally planned economy to a market economy is a process of market completion. In the process, interlinked relational governance as transitional governance has played an important role.

13.3.1. *The role of families*

In rural areas, families, as basic economic and social units, contributed much to the success of Household Responsibility System (HRS), a family-based farming system under collective land ownership. In strong contrast with People's Commune System, under HRS, family members have little incentive to shirk or free ride on other members. Thus, at early stages of reform and the opening-up of China's economy, this new system fostered the development of rural sectors. Under the HRS, land and other means of production are used by families. Family members share the consumption of the family's output. In a social context, an individual is not completely independent and family members take responsibility for each other's behavior. It is now clear to us that this system not only improved productivity, but also constituted an effective risk sharing mechanism. In urban sectors, family also plays an important role in transition. Take laid-off workers as an example. Without transfer and support from other family members, these workers could hardly with stand risks of unemployment and other hazards that they are exposed to during such a transition.

One important form of risk-sharing and consumption smoothing within families is transfers between generations and across family members of the same generation. Primary education in rural sectors is a good example of inter-generational transfers. During 1994–1999 much of the financial burden of primary education in rural areas fell on families. Before the rural tax and fee reform, township governments were responsible for most of the compulsory education financing. As a result, families also contributed to precautionary savings. Table 13.1 illustrates household savings before the transition and a couple of years immediately after the transition. Comparison between urban sectors and rural sectors is also shown in Table 13.1. It can be inferred that the savings rate has been increasing since China's economic transition, particularly in rural areas.

Table 13.1. Household savings in China.

Sector	Ratio to national saving
1957	5.3%
Urban	5.7%
Rural	4.9%
1982	20%
Urban	4.8%
Rural	26.8%
1984	24.7%
Urban	7.9%
Rural	32%

Source: Qian (1988).

In China, a family's role in risk-sharing is also demonstrated in old-age support. Children usually provide certain income and health care to their parents at old age. Both in the urban and rural sectors, a substantial proportion of daily care for aged people is given by their children. The ratio is 60.8% in rural areas and 53.3% in urban areas. On average children pay 43.8% of their parents' costs in rural areas and 33.5% in urban areas. The lower urban ratio is partly due to the fact that urban residents usually have higher security pensions (Zimmer and Kwong, 2003) (see Table 13.2). Obviously children play an important role in providing income smoothing for aged parents.

13.3.2. *Community-level networks*

A family's ability to deal with problems of missing or imperfect markets is rather limited. When the whole family is subject to certain risk or shock, the limitation of a single family to withstand such risk or shock will surface. Furthermore, a family can hardly meet demands for a large amount of money and solve other problems. Social interaction on community level can mitigate these problems. It enables families and individuals to allocate resources in a broader scope, which fosters production, consumption and other social interactions on a larger scale. The following two tables, which show two-level mutual insurance (within and without the village) in Zouping County, Shandong Province, indicate that cooperation at the community level can improve welfare.

Table 13.2. Percentage receiving instrumental and financial support by source and rural/urban residence.

	Instrumental support		**Financial support**	
Source	**Rural area**	**Urban area**	**Rural area**	**Urban area**
From Children	60.8	53.3	43.8	33.5
From Other Source	2.8	4.4	9.7	5.4
From Both Sources	6.0	3.8	29.1	13.0
From Neither Sources	30.4	38.5	17.4	48.1
Total	100	100	100	100

Source: Zimmer and Kwong (2003).

Table 13.3. Potential for risk sharing.

Types	Coefficient of variation
Autarky (consumption = income)	29.5
Village-level Risk Sharing	14.0
County-level Risk Sharing	5.4

Source: Morduch and Sicular (2001, p. 224).

Table 13.3 depicts mutual insurance in the form of consumption smoothing among community members. For insurance, provided among family members, the coefficient of variation of consumption, as a measure of consumption risk, is as high as 29.5. The coefficient of variation of consumption can be reduced by 15.5 if a mutual insurance arrangement can be achieved at the level of village community. If the mutual insurance is further extended to the county level, the coefficient can be reduced to only 5.4.[2] Table 13.3 differentiates two levels of mutual insurance: within and across villages. Data in Table 13.3 are measured in currency unit. The table shows that 23.6% of families sampled received transfers from within the village community, with each family getting 150.3 yuan. It also shows that 9.8% of families sampled received transfers from outside the village, with each family getting 307.5 yuan.

Investigation of different forms of transfers in Table 13.4 is enlightening. Morduch and Sicular (2001) examined transfers in kind such as meat and food as well as pure cash among villagers, but not labour transfer. They also showed that labour transfer is an important form of mutual help. About 19.2% of the families surveyed experienced labour transfers.

Aside from informal insurance mechanism, informal finance based on relationship played an important role when it is very difficult for a person or private enterprise to obtain a loan from the banking sector. Informal finance is a form of borrowing from relatives, friends and acquaintances. Tsai (2002) examined informal finance by collecting data from southern and northern cities in China. Tsai's findings, included in Table 13.5, show that many people (above 50% in northern China) are satisfied with borrowing via informal finance channels. During the period in question,

[2]Note the risk sharing in village community was among 16 villages.

Table 13.4. Transfers received inside versus outside the village.

	Households receiving transfers from households within the village	Households receiving all transfers from outside the village
Percentage of observations 100%	23.6%	9.8%
Average value of within-village transfers 35.5	150.3	79
Average value of outside village transfers 30.1	66.4	307.5
Average household income 1277	1499.2	1352.8

Source: Morduch and Sicular (2001, p. 226).

Table 13.5. Informal finance in China.

Area Average interest rate	Ratio of people who borrowed	Average amount (yuan)	Average duration (month)
North China 0.32%	59.0	18,863	10.5
South China 1.14%	43.6	43,003	6.1

Source: Tsai (2002, p. 57).

informal financing met 75% of the demand for loans in private sector. Thus, there is evidence that informal finance played a pivotal role in the development of China's private sector.

Partly because businesses tend to resort to family support for financing, labour employment, etc, China's private businesses usually take the form of family firms. As a result, China boasts a large number of family firms which in essence are a form of business organization associated with family partly due to missing or imperfect markets.

13.3.3. *Social interaction between families, communities and local governments*

In fact, during China's economic transition, aside from these voluntary relational transactions, there are also interactions between family, community and government, which are not necessarily based on explicit rules or laws. Township and village enterprises (TVEs) are a typical case of such interaction.

At the early stages of transition, factor market such as the credit market and the land market were either missing or far from perfect. In this context, TVEs arose as "an interlinked contract" between entrepreneurs and local governments across multiple markets. On the one hand, in the case of imperfect factor market, entrepreneurs focused on establishing cooperative relationships with local governments who controlled resources and also granted property right protection. On the other hand, local governments need to address issues of revenue and employment through local economic development.

Due to the lack of financial markets, TVEs cannot easily get financing. Therefore, it is necessary for families, communities, and governments to form long-term relationships. In all, the investment to set up a new business consists of: fund pooling of original village teams, which accounted for 28.17% of the investment; bank loans backed by village property, which accounted for 17% of investment; bank loans guaranteed by village officials, which accounted for 11% of investment; and loans guaranteed by governments, which accounted for 20.5% of investment. During the 7th "Five-Year Plan" period, a report was issued that showed private firms (TVEs) receiving 15% of financing from their relatives and friends, and 1.9% of funding provided by employees themselves (Chen, 1995). Similarly, land is owned collectively and there is no sound land market at the early stage of transition, entrepreneurs needed to develop a cooperative relationship with local governments — such relationship is usually aimed at the favourable treatment of land use.

TVEs help local governments solve employment problem. In TVEs labour recruitment usually is done through collaboration between firm owners and local governments. After implementation of HRS a large amount of surplus labour emerged in rural areas. Local governments were faced with unemployment problem, which became an important drive for establishing TVEs. In fact, about 40.5% of the TVE workers were placed by local officials. Moreover, about 75% of TVE managers were assigned by leaders of township and village governments (Chen, 1995).

Because TVEs are "an interlinked relational contract" between entrepreneurs and local governments, it is natural that the allocation of control right of and residual claims in a township and village enterprise are different from those of a standard business — these rights are divided between firms and governments.[3] Take rights of management as an example. In thirteen important rights of management decision making of TVEs, 33% of decisions are made solely by township governments, another 33% are jointly made by the government and the firm, and the remaining 34% are made independently by the firm (Chen, 1995). In profit allocation, the government has received much more than it could by taxation and fee. Part of the profit share of government was returned to the society through public goods and service provision. TVEs themselves also took corresponding social responsibility in supporting primary education and public health. The remaining profit is usually equally allocated among workers.

Apart from TVEs, a form of organization started with cooperation between entrepreneurs, communities and local governments. Some private firms managed to seek an identity of a state-owned or collectively owned enterprise through various means (for example, affiliated with a government organization or a state-owned company). These private businesses in the form of a state-owned or collectively owned company (the so-called "red-capped" enterprises) can have access to resources (financial resources, right to export, etc.) otherwise unavailable to private firms, and enjoy more property right protection from the government. Local governments and related organizations can receive a lump sum of administrative charges and alleviate the unemployment problem by transferring some workers from state-owned companies to those affiliated private firms.

Like TVEs, "red-capped" enterprises were a kind of transitional institutional organizations in line with imperfect factor markets and insufficient private property protection during China's early transition. By the end of 1990s, factor markets developed quickly and private property was better protected by constitution and other statutes, which speeded up the

---

[3]For alternative explanation, see Weitzman and Xu (1993). They argue that the community-level cooperative culture played an important role.

transformation of TVEs into private firms and disappearance of "red-capped" phenomena.[4]

13.3.4. *Interlinked arrangements in urban state sector*

The market-oriented reform of state sectors is in essence a process of dismantling the planning system in general and Work Unit System in particular. Take the reform of state-owned enterprise (SOEs) for example. This reform concerns changes in multiple markets such as labour, education, medical care, insurance and housing. Historically employees got low pay with government's provision of benefit package and life employment. SOEs maintain interlinked relationship with their employees for a long time since the reform kicked off. In particular, there was an arrangement called *xiagang* (layoff). In that case, even if an employee got laid off, he was still entitled to a certain level of allowance, and other welfare programs. As evidenced in a survey (Development Research Center of State Council, 2004), which elaborated on costs of SOEs restructuring, per capita payments of central government-controlled SOEs amounted to 14,000 yuan while per capita payments of local government controlled SOEs amounted to 40,500 yuan (State Council, 2005).

In conclusion, at the early stage of transition, due to incomplete markets of credit, insurance, land and labour and weak protection for private property, there appeared a series of substitute cooperative relationship and institutional arrangement in rural sector, which has fostered economic development while reducing cost of transition.

13.4. The Role of Relational Governance in Transition: A Theoretical Summary

During economic transition, due to missing markets and formal institutions, relational transaction provided a substitute for those missing institutions in social economy. In this part we present a brief theoretical summary of the roles of relational governance in China's transition.

[4]For further analysis on TVEs, see Wang and Li (2008).

13.4.1. *Relational governance as an effective substitute for missing and imperfect markets*

Transition is a process of dismantling the old institutions in the planned economy. Some alternative mechanism is the key to the performance of transition before market system is in place. And sequence of liberalization also matters. Since rural residents have more solid traditional network than urban citizens, starting reform from rural areas was a better choice. Had the reform started with urban sectors, it could have brought more risk to the reform because the social network is weaker for urban residents and it could have been the case that formal and informal institutions were both missing. In rural areas, the market-oriented reform progressed without breaking social networks as we discussed above.

The success of rural reform made urban reform relatively easy. The development of rural areas not only expanded market for industrial products of cities, but also supplied raw materials needed by cities and released cheap surplus labour force for urban development. As we discussed above, urban reform beginning in 1984 did not immediately break the social relationship based on "work unit system". In the absence of a well-functioning labour market, credit and social security system, arrangement of labour, housing, medical care and financing, those work units (mostly SOEs) still kept close interlinked relationship in labour, housing, medical care and the like with their employees until the mid-1990s when many specialized markets came into being.

13.4.2. *Relational governance as a self-enforcing substitute mechanism for formal institutions*

Under "cold turkey" transition in Russia and other transition economies, old regime was dismantled almost overnight and there was a long period of "institutional vacuum". To fill these vacua, other forms of governance, like mafia governance, has appeared. In contrast, one feature of China's gradualism is that the market-oriented reform advanced without major changes of original political and social structures.

Considering rather limited function of formal legal system during economic transition, China's economic transition was based on informal institutions. The underlying rationale is that interlinked relational transactions involve long-run multiplex interests that are hard to verify and enforce in courts and the agents may rationally not resort to court. A survey of 2002 shows that even in the Changjiang (Yangtze) River Delta where market economy is more developed many firms chose to settle their disputes by direct negotiation, through intervening of local governments or in a private way (by local business partners) (See Table 13.6).

13.4.3. *Relational governance is cost-effective when market extent is limited*

Relational contracts are self-enforcing through long-term relationship between fixed agents. It only requires that local information is common knowledge to both parties and they have shared expectations. Transactions based on formal institutions require that relevant information be verifiable by the third party (for example, the court). In addition, high fixed cost for institutional infrastructure has to be invested.[5] Therefore, informal institutions through self-enforcing relational contracts and formal institutions enforced through courts have their comparative advantages.

Table 13.6. Perceived most efficient conflict resolutions in Changjiang River Delta (%).

Resolutions	Foreign firms	SOEs	Private firms	Collective firms
Negotiation	46.6	52.5	56.4	54.9
Court	37.5	36.0	35.6	33.3
Local Government Intervention	17.8	15.8	8.6	9.8
Private Means	8.7	5.0	11.8	5.9
No way	5.5	6.5	5.7	5.9
Otherwise	4.0	2.2	4.9	3.9
Total	120.2	118.0	123.0	113.7

Source: Wang *et al*., (2007, p. 154).
Note: Due to multiple choices, the totals are more than 100%.

[5]Interestingly, Shleifer and Mulligan (2005) also show this empirically. Using state-level data in US, they show that states with larger populations have more regulation.

At the early stages of development and transition when market extent is limited, relational governance is a more appropriate institution in that it has lower requirement on information structure (no third party verification needed) and it incurs no fixed cost for establishment of legal system, which greatly reduces transaction cost (Li, 2003). Because agents in a long-term relationship tend to have transactions in multiple "interlinked" markets, average transaction cost is further lowered (namely, there is scope economy with interlinked contract). Interlinked contracts expand the feasible set of transactions. If transactions are not interlinked and one party suffers a loss in a single transaction, then he may simply quit; but if transactions are interlinked, loss in a single transaction can be well offset by gains from other transactions, which makes quitting an undesirable option.

The above discussion can shed some light on the institutional foundations for different performances of transition economies.[6] Radical reform of Russia destroyed the basis of traditional system almost overnight without establishing effective formal institutions within a short period of time. The institutional void caused social anomie. China's gradualism to a large extent maintained interlinked contracts of traditional social and political systems, which partly accounted for the Chinese economic miracle upon transition.

13.5. Economic Development and the Gradual Unraveling of Relational Governance

Ironically, though the relational governance has been fostering economic development and marketization, it also has been unraveling the governance gradually. Specialized markets took over most of the functions originally performed by social networks like families and communities. And higher level of labour mobility shortens the time horizon of interaction among agents. As we will elaborate below, in many dimensions, a traditional relational society has been gradually dismantled.

---

[6] Stiglitz (2000) also underlines the importance of social capital in transition economies.

13.5.1. *Marketization and traditional social networks*

With advancement of marketization and some social policies (like one-child policy), the interlinked relationship at the level of family, community and local government has been weakened.

China's family structure is undergoing substantial changes and there is an obvious trend of the weakening of familial network. Nuclear families composed of parents and children are the major family structure in cities, towns and villages. The ratio of nuclear families to all families is the highest in cities and then in towns and the least in villages. Historically, nuclear families had constituted less than half of all families in the 1960s and now they are more than half and the number of composite families has been decreasing (Wang, 2006a). Also, among nuclear families, the ratio of "DINK" families has been increasing during transition. Families were made still smaller due to higher college admission rate. The average number of members of families has been dropped from 4.41 in 1982 to 3.96 in 1990 and 3.44 in 2000 (Wang, 2006b).

However, social network on the level of family was significantly weakened, though it will take quite a long time for profound influence of smaller families on economic life to play out. Even within a nuclear family, mutual insurance capability was weakened due to less family members than before. Minimized families will be less capable of providing for and taking care of aged people (Wang, 2006b). The weakening of family network will expose individuals to more risks in the absence of specialized insurance market, credit market and social security system.

As previously mentioned, at the level of community and government, the success of TVEs depends on good relationship between entrepreneur, community and government who have interlinked transactions in multiple markets in the context that specialized markets such as financial market and land market are missing. Government also provides political protection and favorable policies, or other public services, and in return government shares gains from development of TVEs and achieves higher level of employment. However, the development of specialized markets impaired the advantage of TVEs and entrepreneurs did not have to keep close relationship with community and government as before. In addition, with more developed labour market in place and hence higher labour mobility, people tend to work without their own communities. All this led to dismantling of many TVEs in the mid-1990s (Wang and Li, 2008). And since the mid-1990s privatization of state sectors and marketization of medical care, education and housing in cities have been advanced by government. As a result, traditional work unit system was gone, and with it the social relationship centered around those work units. Cities have changed from a community of people with long-term relationship into an anonymous world.

13.5.2. *Labour mobility and traditional networks*

Previously we briefly discussed the dismantling of close relationship associated with families, communities and governments in transition. We now highlight the effects of enhanced labour mobility has on the tradition social networks. To serve this purpose, we first review the history of China's labour mobility. Table 13.7 illustrates labour mobility in China according to the destinations in recent 20 years. At the early stages of transition, destinations of labour force were mostly villages and rural towns, which corresponded to the booming of TVEs. But after the mid-1980s, an increasing number of migrants moved to cities and the ratio of migrants into villages and towns to all migrants was decreasing, although the trend experienced a temporary turnaround during 1995–2000.

Migration within villages and towns is related to the development of TVEs. The wave of privatization of TVEs occurred during 1990–1995. In fact, labour force employed by TVEs accounted for 9.4% of rural labours in 1980 and the ratio was increased to around 26% in 1995 and kept at that level ever since (Brooks and Tao, 2003). In cities, on the other hand, the average annual employment rate was growing at 3% since 1990 even when there were large numbers of laid-off workers from

Table 13.7. Labour mobility in China.

Destination	1982–87	1985–90	1990–95	1995–2000
Cities	36.6	61.7	61.4	59.4
Towns	39.8	20.1	10.0	19.16
Rural Area	23.6	18.2	28.6	21.43

Source: Shi (2006).

SOEs (Shi, 2006). Therefore, China's labour force experienced large-scale migration with destinations changing from villages and towns to cities. This massive labour mobility during transition weakens traditional social network of the relational society and exposes the people to more risks.

13.5.3. *Development as a process of unraveling interlinked and relational institutions*

Dismantling of relational governance during China's economic transition and development can shed some light on relationship between economic development and institutional change in general. In particular, economic development has the following two effects on traditional institutions.

One is *specialization effect.* When markets become more specialized and complete, personal transaction under interlinked contract gave way to arm-length transactions on the markets. For example, in rural areas, some services that used to be delivered in the form of mutual help are now replaced by those on specialized markets. Development is a process to unravel the interlinked contracts (Wang, 2007).

The other is *market thickness effect.* With the expansion of market and deepening of division of labour, the frequency and number of transactions on specialized markets keep increasing, i.e. markets become "thicker"; this will in turn attract more buyers and sellers to join market transactions due to lower search cost. Arm-length markets will dominate reciprocal exchange when the markets are thick enough (Kranton, 1996).

For the match between development stage and governance, at the stage when market extent is limited and the specialization level is low, relational governance is cost-effective in that it is self-enforcing and requires no set-up cost for formal institutional infrastructure. With economic development and market expansion, the cost of relational governance grows and formal institutions will become more attractive. In other words, due to large fixed cost associated with formal institutions, transactions based on formal institutions enjoy economy of scale, i.e., the more transactions, the lower average transaction cost. Therefore, optimal institutional arrangement depends on the stage of economic development.

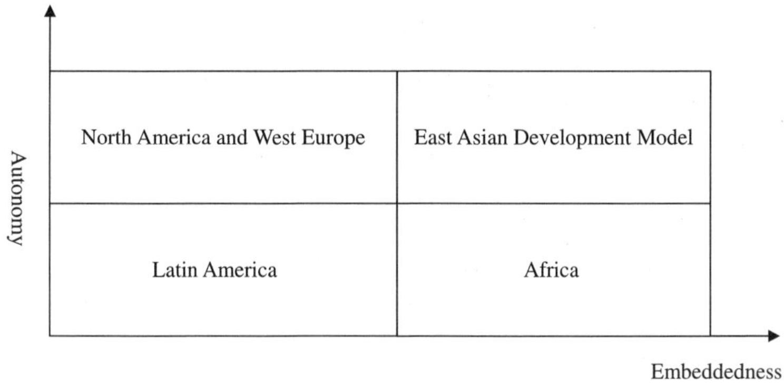

Fig. 13.1. Taxonomy of development models.

Generally speaking, economic development will transform a relational society to a society based on formal institutions through specialization effect and market thickness effect. This transformation will trigger further economic development, as indicated in Figure 13.1. In the words of Polanyi, this is the great transformation from the equilibrium where economic relationship is embedded in social relationship to a equilibrium where social relationship is embedded in economic relationship (1957).

The final realization of the great transformation depends on whether effects of specialization and market thickness work well. There are some forces against these two effects in China's current political and social structures, which we will discuss below.

13.6. Governance and Development Models in International and Historical Perspectives

To predict the future of China's development trajectory, it is useful to put China in an international and historical perspective. The theoretical framework that we have developed can naturally lead us to the taxonomy of development models. With the possible danger of oversimplification, we can have four "ideal types", to borrow the term of Max Webber, of development models. We can characterize a development model along two dimensions, embeddedness and autonomy. As we have seen, embeddedness mirrors the fact that the markets are missing. Therefore, degree of

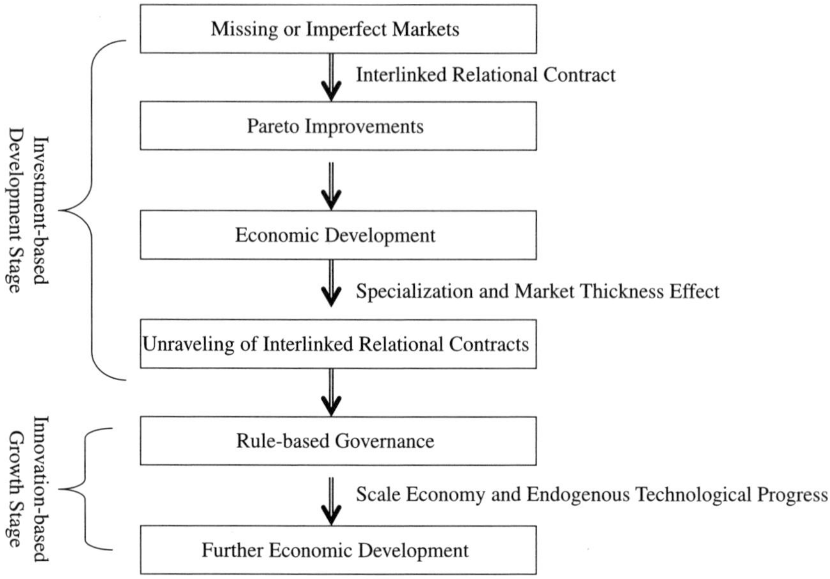

Fig. 13.2. Relationship between governance and development.

marketization can be approximated as that of embeddedness. Autonomy refers to the independence of the state from the capture of special interest group in the process of policy making, which is highly related with social and economic inequality. With this in mind, broadly we have the taxonomy as shown in Figure 13.2.

East Asian Model constitutes a useful benchmark for our exposition. After World War II only four Asian Newly Industrial Economies (NIEs) — Hong Kong, Taiwan, Singapore and Korea — stand out as new members of developed economies.[7] This has drawn much interest in the East Asian Development Model (EADM) and its implication for development of economic theories and public policy. Despite subtle institutional differences among these economies, from the perspective of development patterns and institutions, these economies at least share the following six characteristics: (1) during economic takeoff after World War II, authoritarian governments

[7] In what follows, we will mainly take Japan, Korea and Taiwan as examples, since they are more representative given their size, while Hong Kong and Singapore are basically city economies.

played a pivotal role in economic development by adopting extensive industrial policies to intervene the economy; (2) the role of legal system was not that pervasive as in the West, while social norms based on long-term relation played an important role in socioeconomic life; (3) the economic structure was centralized and there were a few big firms and banks as major players in economic arena. There is a long-term relationship between banks and firms, and banks are dominant financing sources for large corporations; (4) due to the "tiller to land" egalitarian land reforms in the 1950s and other social norms (like life employment), these economies have achieved inclusive growth; (5) from the perspective of political transformation, economic development was followed by political transition in these economies after 30 years of rapid growth; and (6) economic success at preliminary stages, once dubbed as Asia's miracle, was followed by economic crises in many economies by the end of 1990s.

A key feature of EADM is that the governance structure is stage-dependent. In the early stage of their development, their economic institutions were embedded in the political system through the so-called "industrial policies". As we has emphasized elsewhere (Wang, forthcoming), industrial policies are basically a sort of "interlinked relational contract" between the state and firms, which can improve economic allocation when markets are missing. State, analogous to the landlord in our example mentioned above, interacts with the firms in several "markets" (credit market, labour market, insurance market and so on). Features (2) and (3) of EADM are consistent with the relational governance. Feature (4) shows that equal endowments are crucial for the trickle-down effects to happen in the process of economic development. Feature (5) shows that "appropriate institutions" are stage contingent, while Feature (6) shows there may be some kind of "governance failure" during the transition from relational governance to rule-based governance. And now they fall into the same category of North American and West European countries with high autonomy and low embeddedness.

With EADM in mind, we are now in a position to characterize other development models in the highly stylized matrix in Figure 13.1. The most ideal one is West European and North American countries, characterized by low embeddedness and high autonomy, since they have complete markets and liberal democracy thanks to the equal endowments at the early stage of development (Engerman and Sokoloff, 2000). The other extreme is African economies. Despite their sociopolitical and economic diversity, taking as a whole, their markets are highly incomplete and imperfect, their economic relations are highly embedded in sociopolitical relations, and their political systems are divided and captured by conflicting ethnic groups, rendering the state both weak and lacking autonomy. With the same caveat of diversities of country characteristics, Latin American countries are the flip side of EADM in terms of liberalization and governance and its distributional consequences. Highly unequal endowments from the very start of their development have made the state lack autonomy and captured by various special interest groups. In strong contrast with EADM and African economies, economic liberalization in these economies is much quicker and it makes the economic relations less embedded in social relations. The lacking of autonomy and the instability of politics in both African and Latin American economies make state unable to implement Pareto-improving industrial policies, which aim at long-run social goals.

The match between development stage and governance echoes an old theme in economic development. Economic historian Gerschenkron (1962) pointed out long ago, "In a number of important historical instances, industrialization processes, when launched at length in a backward country, showed considerable differences with more advanced countries, not only with regard to the speed of development (the rate of industrial growth) but also with regards to the productive and organizational structures of industry . . . these differences in the speed and character of industrial development were to a considerable extent the result of application of institutional instruments for which there was little or no counterpart in an established industrial country."

Theoretically, there are two salient features unique to developing economies. First, compared with the complete market system in developed countries, markets are either missing or imperfect in developing countries. And second, developing countries are far from the world technological possibility frontier.

Understanding the above two differences is essential for understanding economic development and government's role in economic development. Missing markets imply that there is room for Pareto-improving interventions; being far from the world technology possibility frontier implies that developing countries can learn or simply mimic existing technologies without undertaking their own research and development. Therefore, appropriate intervention of government can improve resource allocation by facilitating technology adoption. In particular, in the absence of well-functioning markets, government can make Pareto-improving interventions through interlinked institutional arrangements like industrial policies. Such interventions can help exploit the existing technologies, mobilize resources and investment, and ensure a stable relationship among major economic players. In terms of Acemoglu *et al.* (2006), this stage of development is investment-based growth, in contrast to the innovation-based stage where the technology is on the world frontier and hence innovation is the key to growth, as has happened in the most advanced economies. Industrial policies are more likely to succeed in equal societies since social consensuses are more likely.

13.7. Important Lessons from World Development History

A general idea that we can draw from the above discussion is that the role of government is a function of an economic development stage: at the early stage of development, government may adopt a series of policies to make up for the missing markets and support market development; at the stages with high level of economic output and sound market system, government should withdraw from areas once intervened with direct approaches and set up a level playing field for market competition. At certain point in the development process, political transition is needed for institutionalization with democracy and rule of law. Specifically, the following lessons can be drawn from the case of EADM.

13.7.1. *The importance of equal initial endowments*

Egalitarian land reform started before economic take-offs in big East Asia economies. The reforms created equal economic conditions for people and the fruit of economic growth thus can be enjoyed by the public, which makes it easier for government to implement pro-growth policies. Moreover, large groups of middle class formed at the certain stage of economic development may assure smooth and consolidated democratization.

A glance at developing countries in Africa and Latin America shows that the equality of initial endowments led to divergent development trajectories. In Africa and Latin America, initial economic inequality rendered social policies benefiting all the people (Pareto improvement) impossible. For instance, agricultural policies in many African countries seem to foster economic development by government intervention, but they are actually used to gain support from elite groups of urban and rural areas and increase private benefit of government officials, which helps unite these interest groups to keep the regime (Bates, 1981). This is also the case with Latin America where inequality in initial endowments led to a large income gap which made it difficult for government to maintain its autonomy and adopt long-term policies conducive to inclusive growth. And the democratization is also not consolidated. Left-wing government tends to use redistribution policy with high tax rate, which will cause dissatisfaction from social elites (rich people) who will then try to organize to overthrow the government. When they succeed in reining the government, representatives of elites tend to adopt low tax rates favoring the elites themselves. Now the poor people get dissatisfied and left wing will attempt to regain the power; and so on so forth. There is thus a vicious political cycle as we have observed in these countries.[8]

13.7.2. *Stage-dependent roles of state and the nature of modernity*

EADM shows that authoritarian governments can contribute to economic success at the early stage of development. In particular, due to limited market extent or missing markets at this stage, interlinked institutional arrangements (e.g., industrial policies) between government and entrepreneurs (or/and other social groups) can work as transitional substitutes for markets. At the stage of investment-based economic development, institutional arrangements of interlinked relational contract can help effectively

[8]Acemoglu and Robinson (2005) offer perfect theoretical studies on income inequality and consolidation of democracy.

mobilize and organize resources and foster development. The basic mechanism of interlinked relational contract is long-term games along multiple dimensions. Transactions between agents tend to be multiplex and interlinked. Effective policies can internalize externalities and make up for missing markets. In addition, this type of games must have multiple equilibria and thus coordination is very important. The more important coordination is, the greater government's role (in choosing effective equilibria) will be. But with economic development and completeness of market, the multiplex relationship will unravel.

From the perspective of transaction cost, self-enforcing relational contract is an economizing device since it involves no set-up cost for a formal institutional infrastructure. Thus, for the early stages of economic development, this relational governance is an "appropriate institution". However, with further economic development and completion of markets, the diseconomy of the relational contract will set in, while then formal institutions can enjoy economy of scale and foster endogenous technological progress. Rule-based governance (formal institution) now becomes the "appropriate institution". In this regard, the transition from interlinked relational governance to impersonal rule-based governance, driven by market completion is the institutional nature of modernization. As Bailey puts it, "The watershed between a traditional society and a modern society is exactly the distinction between single interest and multiplex relationships. The hallmark of a modern society is the specialized role and the whole apparatus of its productive prosperity rests upon the division of labour between specialized roles" (Bailey, 1971).

13.7.3. *Timing and sequencing for economic liberalization*

The proposition that the role of government is a function of economic development stages implies that government should withdraw from substantial economic intervention at a certain point of time during the development process. Therefore, the timing and sequencing for economic liberalization and opening-up, either domestic or international, weigh heavily for sustainable growth.

There is an apparent difference between EADM and practice of Latin American countries as far as economic liberalization is concerned. In East

Asian countries or regions, economic opening up and liberalization started when market system and economic organizations at home were fairly developed. While in Latin America, most countries were engulfed in the capitalist world system before domestic market system grew strong enough (Evans,1987). Large amounts of foreign investment surged in Latin American countries and formed powerful interest groups dominating domestic economies in these countries. As a result, relatively weak domestic organizations and capital were overwhelmed by strong foreign groups and government's autonomy and state capacity were weak (Pang, 1997). Therefore, the timing of economic liberalization should be contingent on the development of domestic market system.

13.7.4. *Timing for political transition*

At certain stage of economic development, the role of government needs to change, and this always happens with political democratization. Political democratization is a natural result of inclusive economic growth under EADM. A case in point is Taiwan. The Democratic Progressive Party (DPP) was founded in Taiwan in 1986. The Nationalist Government leader Chiang Ching-kuo recognized its legal status in the same year and lifted the ban on political parties, and a general election was held in the next year. Korea followed the same pattern. Military government let by President Park Chung-Hee in the 1960s and 1970s was basically an authoritarian government. However the inauguration of President Roh Tae-woo in 1987 witnessed the beginning of political democratization in Korea.

Part of the reason why timely political transition matters is that timely political democratization helps prevent the coalition formation between economic powers, political powers and interest groups which would obstruct economic development by exacerbating social injustice. The logic is simple: favorable industrial policies adopted by government at the early stages fostered development of some sectors and industries, creating rents for these groups. Democratization before interest groups become powerful enough is necessary for sustainable growth. Therefore democratization usually goes hand in hand with economic liberalization (breaking monopoly and deregulation). In particular, at the early stage of economic development in East Asia, centralized economic system and barriers to entry are conducive to long-term investments. But when it comes to the innovation-based growth stage, monopolized market structures restrict free entry and undermine technological innovation and future economic development.[9]

At the early stages of economic development, self-enforced interlinked relational contract (either between government and firms or between firms) sustained socioeconomic life. With the limited extent of market at the early stages, the relationship-based contract is a more cost-effective governance structure than the formal contract (democratization and rule of law). But with the deepening of labour division and market expansion, the relationship-based contract with apparent limitations will gradually give way to the formal institutions enforced by the third party.

The relationship between economic development and institutional change can be summarized in Figure 13.2.

13.8. Some Pitfalls of China's Reform

Relational governance has played an important role in addressing missing market problem in China's transition. With increasing market completeness, the governance should be transformed into a rule-based one. There are some pitfalls in the current system and some pitfalls may arise during the "great transformation."

13.8.1. *Chinese-style federalism and market segmentation*

In the last 30 years Chinese-style federalism has promoted economic growth through yardstick competition among jurisdictions under a powerful central government. However, it also led to a beggar-your-neighbor competition, in the form of segmentation of markets and public services, which undermines economy of scale and the expansion of markets. Therefore it constitutes an impediment to the great transformation. The key lies in the incompatibility of provincialism of local governments with the call for a more integrated and specialized domestic market system.

---

[9]Acemoglu *et al.* (2006) analyze the political economy of the relationship capitalism and technological innovation.

13.8.2. *Marketization embedded in sociopolitical powers*

There are two possible future trajectories of China's market-oriented reform. One possibility is that the markets are so developed that they are decoupled from sociopolitical powers. The other possibility is that the markets are less developed and embedded in sociopolitical powers, characterized by Latin American countries. Under gradual transition, traditional power structure remains and the market value of powers has been "capitalized" during marketization. Therefore the markets are embedded in sociopolitical powers.

Some empirical studies on the effect of powers on income demonstrate that favorable political identity and social networks did improve one's income.[10] Because the markets are embedded in sociopolitical powers, there is a separation of "insiders" and "outsiders" in the process of policy making with insiders enjoying more power of resource allocation. From the dynamic perspective, people with more power can amass a fortune more quickly and then they invest money in gaining more power, which exacerbates social polarization. What's even worse is that the trend of polarization can go on across generations.

Markets embedded in sociopolitical powers may hinder transformation of a relational society into a society based on formal institutions through market thickness effect. If relational contracting prevails in the socioeconomic transactions, the specialized market will become thinner due to the higher search costs. Reciprocal exchange will be a self-sustaining equilibrium (Kranton, 1996). A typical example is labour market. If people get their jobs through social relations, labour market will become thin.

Let us turn to the relations between firms and governments. In theory, in jurisdictions with higher ratio of private enterprises, private enterprises may gain more by keeping good relations with government officials. A World Bank survey on investment environment of 23 cities in China shows that it is indeed the case. In this survey, the ratio of the cost of bribing government officials and regulators to sales were measured. What

---

[10] For instance, employing China's urban data, Knight and Yueh (2002) find that, Communist Party membership substantially increased personal income in private firms.

merits our attention is that Shenzhen and Wenzhou, two cities with high ratio of private firms, also have high abnormal payments (World Bank, 2003).

Markets embedded in sociopolitical powers and social relations are perilous. The quandary of economic development in many less developing countries is related to distorted resource allocation due to the fact interest groups abused powers in the process of resource allocation. The distortion not only jeopardizes social justice and economic efficiency, but also thwarts efforts in effective social reform. To avoid crony capitalism, China should prevent markets from being embedded in sociopolitical powers and social relationship.

13.8.3. *The possibility of institutional vacuum*

Previously we explored the case that marketization may dismantle a relational society. And we also analyzed some hindrances to transformation of a traditional society into a modern one. Ideally, when economy develops to the extent that markets are relatively complete and extensive, formal institutions are adopted. But in reality, market maturity and formal institution may not go hand in hand. The critical point where a traditional society turns into a modern society based on formal institutions is risky because it is the time when institutional vacuum may occur since both traditional governance and modern governance may be absent. And economic crisis and political crisis may ensue at this point.[11] Interestingly, China's development since reform and opening-up shares four of six characteristics of EADM except the fourth and the sixth ones. Since China is similar to East Asian economies in social structure and culture, to study EADM is of great significance to China's transition. We will turn back to the similarities between China and EADM later on. Therefore when economic development comes to a certain point, the timing for introducing formal institutions is both essential and caution-demanding.

---

[11] For instance, Li (2003) argues that the East Asian financial crises in the late 1990s were due to the institutional vacuum between the two systems.

13.9. Concluding Remarks: China's Road to Modernity

Economies of EADM, most of which were still undeveloped agricultural economies (Korea and Taiwan, for example) in the 1940s, achieved rapid inclusive economic development and political democratization after World War II. EADM created a miracle in human development history. Since reform and opening up in 1978, China has been working another economic wonder with a staggering growth rate. There are some similarities between China's miracle and that of EADM. In particular, in the absence of a sound market system, interlinking institutional arrangements between government, economic organizations and economic agents achieved Pareto improvement (Wang and Li, 2008). There are also differences between Development Model of China and EADM. The following key differences may shed some light on China's future trajectory.

13.9.1. *Factor market reform*

One characteristic of EADM is egalitarian reform of factor markets, especially land market, before their economic take-offs. Equal endowments resulting from factor market reform is the key to inclusive economic growth and consolidated democratization. In a widened perspective, we find the differences in development paths of North and South Americas can also be attributed to differences in endowment distribution. Initial distribution of factors (especially land) is relatively even among people in North America who have greater incentives to invest in human capital. In contrast, initial endowments were highly unequal in South America and people with little land had low bargaining power in society and low share of fruit from economic growth, which lessened their incentive to invest in human capital. This has contributed to the big divergence between the developments in North and South Americas (Engerman and Sokoloff, 2000).

Different from North America's experience and EADM, China's reform occurs without egalitarian ownership of land and other factors. Although goods markets have been liberalized in China, liberalization of factor markets is yet to come. For example, in urban areas, land, nominally state-owned, is actually monopolized by local governments. Due to *hukou* system, labour flow between rural and urban areas is strictly limited, which resulted in an undeveloped labour market. Considering the fact that private firms have negligible profit margin in the labour-intensive industries which are highly competitive, high prices of factors due to state monopoly have negative impact on the development of the firms and widen income gaps between different industries.

All these lag-behind reforms in factor markets have created special interest groups including urban elites and government agencies, which constitute barriers to further economic liberalization. In theory, there are two possible scenarios. One is that the relational contract unravels when some specialized markets are well developed. The other is that the economy is trapped in relational contracting and arm-length markets cannot be well developed. Either of the two systems, namely, reciprocal contracting and arm-length contracting, is self-sustaining. Which one finally prevails depends on the interaction between market dynamics and the interlinked relational arrangements. In particular, as long as the *total* surplus from the interlinked relational arrangements is less than the total surplus from specialized markets, both the politicians and entrepreneurs have no incentive to deviate from the relationship. In that case, the factor markets cannot be liberalized. This will in turn undermine the growth of the economy and increase the income gap, creating barriers to political democratization in the future. In the long run, as the interlinked arrangements unravel, profound socioeconomic and political changes may occur. In this sense, China still has a long way to go towards a full modernization.

Aside from factor market reform lagging behind, there is asymmetry between reforms in rural areas and in urban areas. Although urban residents do not have land ownership, they own the property established on the land. Since the value of land can be "capitalized" into the price of real estate, land ownership actually belongs to urban property owners and is transferable. While in rural areas residents do not have land ownership, either *de jure or de facto*. This widens income gap between people of cities and those of villages. The development of labour market and credit market is also asymmetric between cities and villages. Cities enjoy higher labour mobility and more credit resources than villages. This also contributes to income gap between urban and rural areas. Another source of income gap is that imperfect factor market reform leaves room for corruption of government officials who have real control of the factors. China's Gini coefficient is close to 0.5, while under EADM, Gini coefficient is much less. In Korea and Taiwan, the number has been around 0.3 and in Japan it has been a little more than 0.2. If no action is taken, income inequality will have negative influence on China's sustainability of economic growth and smooth political transition in the future. It follows that a key element in further reform is to reduce income gap through factor market reform and other reforms.

13.9.2. *Domestic economic liberalization and deregulation*

Under EADM, opening up occurs when there was a well-functioning domestic market system. Historically, other developed countries (European or American countries) followed the same pattern (Chang, 2002). In contrast, economic liberalization happens without a sound market system at home in China. In this respect, China is more like Latin American countries. Moreover, in many economic sectors of China, foreign investment is more welcomed than private capital at home. While this kind of discrimination may have created some positive effects on GDP growth, it caused certain domestic distortions, among which the entry barriers to many industries for Chinese private sector are prominent. In the next decade or so, China should create a level playing field, in terms of entry, regulation and taxation, for all firms in China.

As under EADM, Chinese government has a certain number of giant SOEs, monopolizing financial institutions, energy, natural resources, telecommunications and other so-called "key" industries. These industries not only have created inefficiencies, but also have contributed substantially to income inequality in China (Chen *et al.*, 2010). Therefore, deregulation is critical to both efficiency and equity.

13.9.3. *Timing for rule of law and democratization*

Interlinked relational contract is an appropriate institution for the early stage of economic development with limited market extent. However, further economic development involves greater market extent and more complete market system, which calls for formal institutions enforced by the third party. Good timing of this great transformation is needed for a sustainable economic growth and human development. As we have shown previously in the case of EADM, equality is very important for a consolidated democratization. It is also imperative for China to bring down the high income inequality before and during its political transition. It may also be more feasible and practical to phase in an independent judicial system before the establishment of a full-fledged voting-based democracy.

References

Acemoglu, D. and Robinson, J. (2005). *Economic Origins of Democracy and Dictatorship*. Cambridge: Cambridge University Press.

Acemoglu, D., Aghion, P. and Zilibotti, F. (2006). "Distance to Frontier, Selection, and Economic Growth." *Journal of the European Economic Association*, 4(1), 37–74.

Bates, R. (1981). *Markets and States in Tropical Africa*. Berkeley: University of California Press.

Brooks, R. and Ran, T. (2003). "China's Labour Market Performance and Challenges." IMF Working Chapter, November.

Chang, H. (2002). *Kicking Away the Ladder: Development Strategy in Historical Perspective*. Anthem Press.

Chao, K. (2006). *Essays on the Development of Chinese Cities* (in Chinese). Beijing: Xinxing Publishing House.

Chen, J. (1995). "The Property Rights Structure and Its Effects on Resource Allocation." *Economic Research Journal*, 9, 24–32.

Chen, Z., Wan, G. and Lu, M. (2010). "Inter-Industry Income Inequality: An Increasingly Important Cause of the Income Disparity in Urban China — Regression-Based Decomposition." *China Social Sciences*, 3, 65–76.

Engerman, S. and Sokoloff, K. (2000). "History Lessons: Institutions, Factors Endowments, and Paths of Development in the New World." *Journal of Economic Perspectives*, 14(3), 217–232.

Evans, P. (1987). "Class, State and Dependence in East Asian: Lessons From Latin Americanists." In F. C. Deyo (ed.), *The New Asian Industrialism*. Ithaca and London: Cornell University Press.

Gerschenkron, A. (1962). *Economic Backwardness in Historical Perspective*. Cambridge: Harvard University Press.

Knight, J. and Yueh, L. (2002). "The Role of Social Capital in the Labour Market in China." Working Chapter, Oxford University.

Kranton, R. (1996). "Reciprocal Exchange: A Self-Sustaining System." *American Economic Review*, 86(4), 830–851.

Li, S. (2003). "Relation-Based Versus Rule-Based Governance: An Explanation of the East Asian Miracle and Asian Crisis." *Review of International Economics*, 11(4), 651–6731.

Morduch, J. and Sicular, T. (2001). "Risk and Insurance in Transition: Perspectives From Zouping County, China." In M. Aoki and Y. Hayami (eds.), *Communities and Markets in Economic Development.* Oxford: Oxford University Press.

Pang, J. (1997). "The Role of State in East Asian Economic Transformation." In J. Luo and Z. Wang (eds.), *Behind the Miracle: Understanding East Asian Modernization* (in Chinese). Oxford: Oxford University Press.

Polanyi, C. (1957). *The Great Transformation: The Political and Economic Origins of Our Time*. Boston: Beacon Press.

Qian, Y. (1988). "Urban and Rural Household Saving in China." Staff Chapters, International Monetary Fund.

Shi, A. (2006). "Migration in Towns in China, a Tale of Three Provinces: Evidence From Preliminary Tabulations of the 2000 Census." World Bank Policy Research Working Chapter 3890, April.

Shleifer, A. and Mulligan, C. (2005). "The Extent of the Market and the Supply of Regulation." *Quarterly Journal of Economics,* 120(4), 1445–1473.

State Council (2005). *A Survey Report of Restructuring of SOEs in China.*

Stiglitz, J. (2000). "Formal and Informal Institutions." In P. Dasgupta (ed.), *Social Capital: A Multifaceted Perspective*. The World Bank.

Tsai, K. (2002). *Back-Alley Banking: Private Entrepreneurs in China.* Ithaca: Cornell University Press.

Wang, Y. (2007). "Interlinking Markets, Relational Contract and Economic Transition." *The Studies of Regional Development*, 39(1), 161–187.

Wang, Y. (2010). "Understanding Economic Development and Institutional Change: East Asian Model Reconsidered With Implications for China." *Journal of Chinese Political Science*, forthcoming.

Wang, Y. and Li, M. (2008). "Unraveling the Chinese Miracle: A Perspective of Interlinked Relational Contract." *Journal of Chinese Political Science*, 13(3), 269–285.

Wang, Y. (2006a). "Changes of Family Structure in Contemporary China." (in Chinese). *The Society,* 3, 118–136.

Wang, Y. (2006b). "An Analysis of the Changes of Family Structure in Contemporary China." (in Chinese). *China Social Sciences,* 1, 96–108.

Weitzman, M. and Xu, C. (1993). "Chinese Township and Village Enterprises as Vaguely Defined Cooperatives." *Journal of Comparative Economics*, 18, 121–145.

World Bank (2003). *Improving City Competitiveness Through the Investment Climate: Ranking 23 Chinese Cities.*

Zimmer, Z. and Kwong, J. (2003). "Family Size and Support of Older Adults in Urban and Rural China: Current Effects and Future Implications." *Demography*, 40(1), 23–44.

CHAPTER 14

THE FUTURE TRAJECTORY OF CHINA'S POLITICAL REFORM: A PROPERTY RIGHTS INTERPRETATION

*Gary H. Jefferson and Jun Zhang**

14.1. Introduction

In recent years, a vibrant debate has emerged in the economics literature whether institutional reform causes growth or growth leads to institutional reform. In particular, the debate focuses on whether democratic institutions that constrain the power of government, cause growth or whether growth, through the active exercise of government that achieves economic development and the accumulation of human capital, induces change in a nation's political institutions. In this chapter, we argue that China's reform experience exemplifies the latter case; that is, rising incomes and human capital accumulation are driving China's political reform. More importantly, we go beyond the general argument that economic development motivates political reform to examine the specific forces that are slowly reshaping China's political transition from an authoritarian regime to a multi-polar political system in which the authority of the central leadership is being increasingly contested.

Since China inaugurated its economic reform program in 1978, it has delivered the highest sustained rates of growth of GDP and living

*Gary H. Jefferson, Department of Economics, Brandeis University, Waltham, MA 02454 jefferson@brandeis.edu. Jun Zhang, China Center for Economic Studies, Fudan University, Shanghai, China, junzh_2000@fudan.edu.cn.

standards on record. That growth was largely achieved by a reform process that sanctioned the reassignment of a wide range of property rights from the state to individuals. Among the rights received by individuals are those regarding the use of agricultural land, the right of labour mobility, control over managerial decisions and corporate assets, and home ownership. As this property dispersed to Chinese citizens living standards for most, China's reform process could be broadly characterized as "reform without losers".

Beginning in the early to the mid-1990s, however, as China's reform process accelerated and it prepared for accession to the World Trade Organization, the dual track system, which had guaranteed certain entitlements, was essentially phased out, and tens of millions of workers were laid off as China's publicly-owned enterprises were increasingly privatized. At the same time, the expanding reach of rapid growth created negative spillovers including environmental degradation, corruption, the displacement of farmers home owners, and labour migration that highlighted the costs of China's frayed social safety net. As China's economy increasingly took on the features of a nascent capitalist economy, it has exhibited the growing social conflict and tension associated with the stratification of economic class. Increasingly, reform is creating both winners and losers. The Party's emphasis on policies intended to nurture a "harmonious society" illustrates both the extent of these divisions and the concern that they carry for China's political elite.

The central argument of this chapter is that in the absence of a competitive, multi party political system, and the procedural legitimacy that results from the electoral process, the Chinese Communist Party (CCP) has established and maintained performance legitimacy through the provision of widespread economic prosperity. By reassigning property rights that have incentivized much of China's population, the CCP has enjoyed a sustained period of growth and prosperity that has reinforced its performance legitimacy. However, while the political system has effectively managed China's economic reform process, the privatization created the conditions for the emergence of economic class, as well as economic and political risk. As a result, the economic function of the political system is being transformed from that of economic reformer and manager to that of mediator. Having to contend with the conflict associated with clarifying the broad swath of property rights that remain ambiguous and which generate unequal returns, the political system is having to develop the institutional arrangements needed to mediate these conflicts. This chapter discusses these arrangements.

The argument of this chapter rests on a particular perspective on the role of political systems within advanced capitalist economies. Within the OECD economies, the political system largely cedes to the private sector the task of managing the economy, that is, an economic system in which households and firms set economic goals and hold sway over the majority of the resources deployed by these units for the purpose of achieving their goals. While the government invests in public infrastructure, its task is largely one of creating the institutions that mediate the conflicts among firms, households, and other non-governmental groups that arise from the exercise of property rights within the private sector. These mediating institutions include the legal system and regulatory structure that establish and enforce the "rules of the game". They include also legislative bodies through which diverse constituencies that hold contending interests can contest these differences through the electoral process. A civic culture in which individuals and private groups can utilize the media, public protest, and non-governmental organizations to advocate on behalf of their rights is also essential to the capacity of political systems to provide the mediation services needed to resolve conflict inherent in the decentralization of economic rights. This chapter argues that, albeit in its formative stage, China's political system is increasingly having to tolerate, and in some measure nurture, the emergence of institutional arrangements that enable it to deliver the mediation services needed to maintain the efficient functioning of China's economic system.

The chapter is organized as follows. Section 14.2 reviews relevant literature on the association between economic growth and development and the function of political systems. Section 14.3 reviews the evolving functions of China's political system over the past three decades. Section 14.4 outlines four stages involving the interaction of China's economic and political reform. Section 14.5 identifies the emerging channels of contestability and accountability within China's political system. Section 14.6 argues that the CCP has effectively become a contestably monopoly, so that in meaningful ways it is having to behave as a representative government. Finally Section 14.7 concludes and discusses certain implications of the argument of the chapter.

14.2. Review of the Literature

An unresolved debate within economic research relates to the relationship between institutions and growth. The first approach emphasizes the need for democracy and other institutional checks on government as the mechanisms needed for securing property rights. With such economic and political institutions in place, investment and economic growth can be expected to follow. The second approach emphasizes the need for human capital and rising living standards to start the process. It holds that even without institutional constraints pro-market dictators can secure property rights as a matter of policy choice. From the vantage point of poor countries, this latter perspective sees democracy and other institutional improvements as the consequence of rising levels of education and income, not as their cause.

Both approaches have their advocates. The importance of constraining government has its origins in the renaissance literature of the 19th century, e.g., Smith (1776), as well as the New Institutional Economics Literature (e.g. North (1990), Coase (1992). Empirical support for this view has been established by Delong and Shleifer (1993), Knack and Keefer (1995), and Easterly and Levine (2003).

And yet, the reverse idea that growth and human capital cause institutional improvement also has its own robust intellectual roots. Lipset (1960) believed that educated people are more likely to resolve their differences through negotiation and voting than through violent disputes. Education and literacy also spread knowledge about the government's malfeasance and empowers people to engage with government institutions. From this perspective, the key spillover of human capital may not be technological diffusion; rather it may be the demand for popular participation and political accountability associated with higher income and better educated societies.

In support of the schooling-and-growth-first perspective, Glaeser *et al.* (2004) invoke the experiences of North and South Korea. We reproduce their Figure 1, which shows a kind of natural experiment resulting from their separation following the Korean War. Prior to the division of the North and

South, they shared a similar history; at the end of the War in 1950, both were poor. In Figure 14.1, Glaeser *et al.* measure as the polity's "constraints on the executive." Using this measure, executive constraint, measured over the interval 0 to 7, averaged 1.71 for North Korea and 2.16 for South Korea between 1950 and 1980. Over this period, South Korean dictators chose capitalism and secure property rights; the country grew rapidly, reaching a per capita income level of US $1,589 in 1980. The North Korean dictator, in contrast, chose socialism; the country reached a level of per capita income in 1980 that was less that one half that of the South. Figure 14.1 shows that, starting in 1981, the quality of South Korea's political institutions rose markedly as measured by constraints on the executive. From this sequence, Glaeser *et al.* conclude that the rise in institutional quality was the outcome of economic growth after 1950 rather than its cause.

One important theme in the New Political Economics literature is the notion that dictatorship provides political stability, which in turn secures an environment within which nations can nurture a civic culture or that is

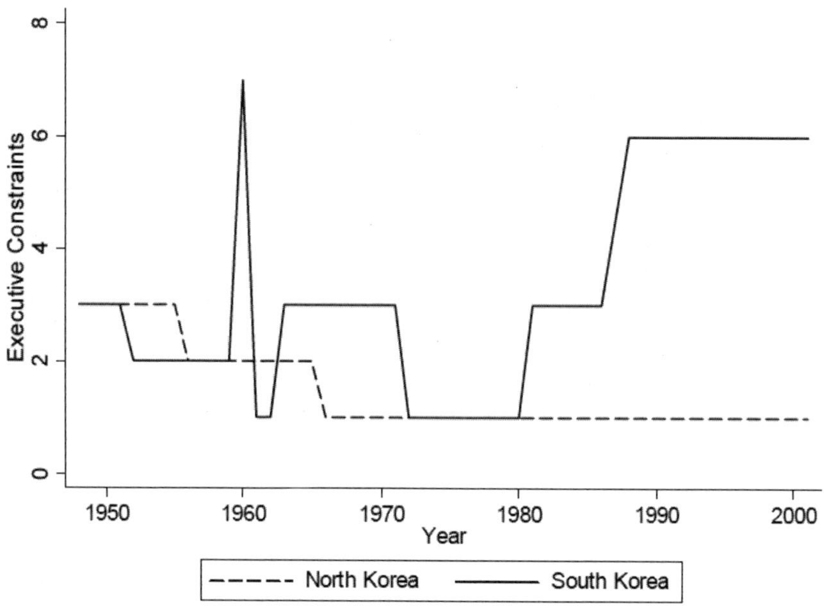

Fig. 14.1. Executive constrains 1948–2001 North versus South Korea.
Source: Glaeser *et al.* (2004).

amenable to the development of well-functioning market and democratic institutions. Popov (2007) emphasizes the critical role of state institutions: "The ability of state institutions (can be) understood as the ability of the state to enforce its own rules and regulations...." According to Popov, "... the data seem to suggest that both authoritarian and democratic regimes can have strong rule of law and can deliver efficient institutions, whereas under the weak rule of law, authoritarian regimes do a better job in maintaining efficient institutions than democracies." (p. 28). Popov concludes that "It is precisely this strong institutional framework that should be held responsible for both (China's and Vietnam's success), where strong authoritarian regimes were preserved and CPE institutions were not dismantled before new market institutions were created..." (p. 3). This perspective is clearly consistent with the argument of Glaeser *et al.* (2004), who conclude that schooling and growth, spawned in a stable political environment, are essential preconditions for political change.

In a similar vein, Djankov *et al.* (2003) analyze the tension between disorder and dictatorship, which is the tradeoff between social losses due to private expropriation and social losses due to state expropriation. They represent this tradeoff in the form of the Institutional Possibilities Frontier (IPF), i.e., the locus of points, such that disorder (dictatorship) cannot be reduced without increasing dictatorship (disorder). In their formulation, dictatorship compensates for the absence of an established, well-functioning rule of law. The view of Glaeser *et al.* (2004) is therefore consistent with Popov's argument that under a weak rule of law, authoritarian regimes perform better in nurturing efficient institutions than democracies. However, if there are diminishing returns to dictatorship over time, Djankov–Popov model may be increasingly unsuited for China.

Enjoying the economic fruits of a stable political regime, China's leadership and much of its intelligentsia and prospering middle class remain leery of the risks associated with moving too quickly along the IPF so long as dictatorship is able to orchestrate the reassignment of property rights and maintain a stable political environment in which these rights can be broken in, exercised, and mediated. However, the reassignment of property rights, originally motivated by the imperative felt by China's party leadership to incentivize the economy and re-legitimate the Party following the Cultural Revolution, has itself created a growing circle of individuals and organizations that are intent on both securing these newly acquired rights and extracting from them the maximum returns. As the owners of corporate assets, homeowners, landowners, and owners of intellectual property exercise their newly acquired rights, ambiguity concerning the definition and legitimate exercise rights is increasingly likely to engender conflict that requires effective avenues of mediation. It falls to the political system to develop these institutional channels through which it can deliver the requisite mediation services, both directly through governmental agencies, such as courts and regulatory agencies, and indirectly through non-governmental channels, including law firms and NGOs.

14.3. The Evolving Function of China's Political System

The starting point of our analysis is that China's leadership is driven by a powerful motivation to sustain China's rapid economic growth and its global geo-political-economic realignment. As underscored by Solow (1956), the only means of sustaining the growth of living standards over long periods is to maintain a continuous increase in productivity, which in practice accrues from continuous technological advance, institutional change, and their interaction. This motive to sustain rising living standards and the leadership's political legitimacy has led to the generally sustained, if fitful, reassignment of property rights associated with physical, financial, and human capital from the state to the individual. Among the specific rights that have been reassigned from the state to individuals and private groups are:

- Household agricultural production — the assignment of rights to farmers to use land for agricultural purposes, to choose the mix of crops under cultivation, to pay rent to the government in the form of a crop production quotas, and to retain production in excess of the quota.
- Labour and human capital — abolition of the labour allocation system with the grant to workers of labour mobility; liberalization of the household registration (*hukou*) system and reduction of restrictions on migration.
- Corporate ownership — liberalization allowing for the expansion and entry of non-SOEs, including collectives (dominated by TVEs),

foreign-invested enterprises, and individual owned enterprises. Passage of the company law allowing for individual ownership of enterprises and enterprises shares.

- Homeownership — the sale at subsidized prices of housing owned by work units (*danwei*) to their employees and the right to buy and sell housing on a housing market.
- Intellectual property rights — the right to apply for and receive grants of patents, trademarks, and copyrights to secure control over intellectual property and to secure remedies for the improper infringement on such property.
- Social insurance — the right to be insured, in some measure, against unemployment, poor health, and penury in old age and to receive support for unemployment, medical, and pension assistance.

With the exception of an extensive system of social insurance, these rights had not existed prior to the commencement of reforms in 1978.

This reallocation of property rights from the state to individuals has, in turn, incentivized China's population to invest and accumulate assets, which is resulting in the emergence of a burgeoning middle and entrepreneurial class with varied property interests. A further consequence of this reallocation of property rights is that as property rights and the resulting incomes and wealth have expanded and become more unevenly distributed, the political system has increasingly had to mediate among the diverse interests arising from these uneven distributions. While early in the reform period, it was possible to characterize the reform process as "reform without losers" (Lau *et al.*, 2000), China's economic restructuring now generates extensive negative spillovers, include a maldistribution of income, land seizures, a fragmented social insurance system, and environmental degradation, that all fall disproportionately on an increasingly identifiable lower class.

So long as the principal function of China's leadership was to advance the reform that enabled the vast majority of China's population to be measurably better off, the government could use the robust economic performance of the economy to legitimate its rule.[1] The political system

[1] In addition to economic prosperity, the other cornerstones of the CCP's performance legitimacy are social stability and national sovereignty.

enjoyed performance legitimacy. However, as the function of the political system has increasingly shifted to mediating tradeoffs and conflicts associated with the reassignment of property rights and from which emerge winners and losers, the population, particularly those whose relative position has eroded, is questioning the government's legitimacy to function as society's adjudicator. The initiative of former President and Party Chief Hu Jintao and the CCP to promote a "harmonious society" may be viewed as an attempt to extend and legitimate the government's role as mediator. However, if the functioning of capitalism in the OECD economies is a guide, their experience suggests that eventually the contending parties will require the leadership to be legitimated by a contest, i.e. through a competitive electoral procedure. That is, the political leadership will need to acquire procedural legitimacy to effectively exercise the functions of government in a modern pluralistic society. Without a political system that can effectively perform this mediation function, the legitimacy of the rights assignments are likely to be eroded thereby reducing the value and effective exercise of property rights. Unresolved conflicts over the assignment and exercise of property rights increase transaction costs associated with the use and exchange of rights. Rising transaction costs, in turn, are likely to increase the social and economic cost of development and substantially slow economic growth.

14.4. Four Stages of Political Reform

We can broadly identify several stages of China's political reform process. These start with the diffusion of property rights required to motivate economic incentives and accumulation described in Section 3. The diffusion of property rights, in turn, results in the unequal distributions of property, income, and economic interests. The unequal distribution of economic resources and interests gives rise to factions that cannot be reconciled through performance alone, since the fruits of performance are necessarily distributed unevenly and the efforts by government to address the interests of one group are likely to compromise those of other groups. Governments can no longer rely on performance legitimacy alone; they must establish procedural legitimacy, such as that established through electoral procedures.

Below, we summarize the logic of each of these four stages.

1. **The early diffusion of property rights; reform without losers enables the CCP to establish performance legitimacy.** Following the political instability and relatively weak economic performance during the Cultural Revolution, the CCP sought to spur economic growth through the limited introduction of markets. The decollectivization of China's countryside and restoration of family farming through the adoption of the Household Responsibility System (HRS) was far more extensive and rapid than had been intended by China's central leadership. However, the incentive effects of the HRS were dramatic as agricultural productivity surged and rising household demand spurred the rapid growth of rural industrialization. In the space of a decade, hundreds of millions of rural residents were lifted from poverty.

   Decollectivization was but the first of an array of rights later extended to labour mobility and the ownership of corporate assets, housing, and intellectual property that were devolved from the state to individuals and private groups. As the reassignment of property rights incentivized China's population leading to high growth, rising incomes, and expanded economic mobility for most residents, the performance legitimacy of the CCP markedly improved. This phase of China's economic transition has been characterized as "reform without losers."
2. **Unequal assignments of property rights lead to winners and losers.** Increasingly, the deepening of China's economic reform has resulted in an unequal distribution of rights and an increasingly unequal distribution of income and wealth acquired through these rights. These implications of reform for income distribution are reflected in the model of Aghion *et al.* (2004). In that model, if no reform is implemented, all individuals obtain the same income. With positive amounts of reform, "as a reform materializes through the effort of a leader…the population at large 'matures' (and acquires) definitive preferences about the reform, for instance, as they learn more precisely who will be a winner or loser from the reform." (p. 569). The greater the reform, typically the more skewed the distribution of its impact, so that while more may gain than lose in an absolute sense, the relative differences in the distribution of benefits grows. Nearly

three decades of reform in China has resulted in an increasingly skewed distribution of property rights, wealth, and income.

With the reassignment of rights to individuals, within China, a propertied class has emerged that derives the majority of its livelihood from its ownership of physical, financial, and human capital. In contrast, China's working class depends primarily on the application of its less skilled labour to the capital of others. An implication of a high rate of growth is the generation of negative spillovers that may fall disproportionately on the working class and residents of poorer regions of the country. Negative and unequal spillovers associated with high growth — income inequality, a fragmented social insurance system, abuses of partially guaranteed land rights, the impacts of environmental degradation — all create winners and losers that result in groups with identifiably different economic interests. In China, the emergence of these disparate economic groups tracks with steadily rising Gini Index as shown in Figure 14.2.

3. **Unequal assignment and accumulation leads to social and political tensions, which alter the function of the political system.** In addition to the growing unequal distribution of property rights and the

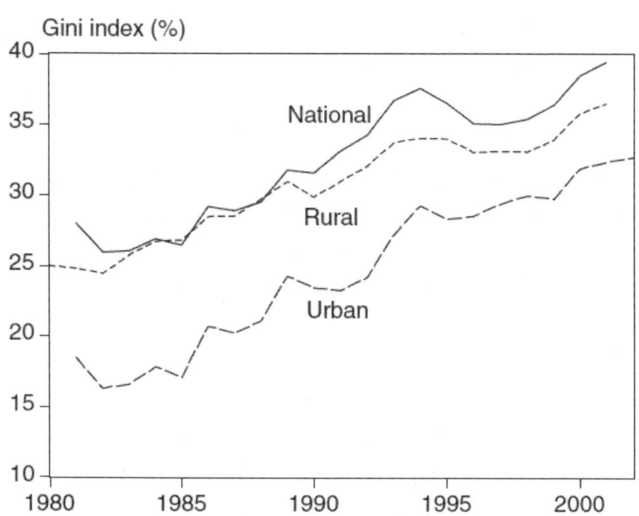

Fig. 14.2. Evolving Gini Index in China's economy.

Source: Ravallion and Chen (2007).

returns they generate, the exercise of the ownership of property rights may be ambiguous. In the case of the household responsibility system and housing reform, for example, the fact that the government retains ownership of the land renders ambiguous the control of the farmer his non-land assets and the homeowner over the structure, particularly in the face of pressures for redevelopment of the area in which the farming or housing is located.

Ambiguities and conflict associated with recently reassigned property rights may lead to corruption and wasteful litigation, thus increasing the transaction costs associated with the use and exchange of rights. Both haves and have-nots seek clarification — or redefinition — of rights. The property class demands institutionalized guarantees for private property, such as those in the Property Rights Law enacted by the National People's Congress during the spring of 2007. Simultaneously, those with limited incomes and accumulations of property rights demand relief from the government. Up to a threshold, a single party can expand and diversify its political agenda to embrace and coop the various interests. The mantra of "harmonious society" is an effort by Hu Jintao and the Party to sustain a consensus society. However, as classes emerge, the variety of claims become too heterogeneous and contentious to be managed effectively by a single political entity. Most fundament, a single political party, the CCP in China's case, may not have the legitimacy to choose among competing priorities, especially when the disaffected elements have the right to protest claims on the system that go against them.

4. **The political system begins to establish procedures that enable it to deliver mediation services.** A political economy comprised by heterogeneous, conflicting, irreconcilable interests, the contending factions requires the political system to make choices that favor one factor over another. At this stage, when consensus government is no longer attainable, the government and prevailing political party need not be accepted by all key factions, but the institutional means by which the agent came to acquire the authority to adjudicate does has to be viewed by the stakeholders as legitimate. In order for its choices to be viewed as legitimate, the contending factions may require that the adjudicating agent acquire its authority through a transparent, competitive process, involving argument, debate, protest, and possibly a vote.

> The requirement for procedural legitimacy may come late in the process, after the initial assignment of property rights has been completed. However, circumstances may exist that require the early establishment of procedural legitimacy. That is, rights over land and corporate assets may be assigned through a process that is viewed as corrupt, in which assignments have been made as a result of side payments to well-placed officials. Under these circumstances, the need to broaden the authority's legitimacy through a competitive selection process is required not only for establishing the legitimacy required to mediate control over rights, but for legitimizing the initial assignment of rights. From this perspective, the objections to the property rights law that was recently enacted by the NPC may not have arisen so much from objections to private property rights in principle as much as objections to the means by which they were initially assigned. That is, either the particular political authorities or the decision process through which assignments were made was believed not to be legitimate.

Naughton (2006) summarizes the challenge and response of the Chinese Communist Party as it has nurtured reform during the past quarter of a century:

> China is in no way a democracy, the Chinese Communist Party has learned that newly emerging economic forces present long-run challenges to Party power while also offering the only possible route to prosperity. In order to forestall challenges, the Party has developed the capability to listen to its people and its critics, and build a rough consensus from time to time about what desperately needs to be done. And when it achieves that consensus, it acts on it. (p. 7)

The question raised by this passage is whether given the increasingly unequal distribution of property rights and income, for how long can the Party successfully sustain consensus around the key issues that drive China's economic development and social stability. The critical stage in the political reform process is the tipping point at which China's political leadership is no longer able to establish a consensus through political managed within the Party. The central question is how the political system evolves to create the institutional infrastructure that is able to open the monopoly party to challenges that can be resolved in procedural ways that sufficiently satisfy the relevant contending factions.

Both Popov and Djankov *et al.* view dictatorship as a means of achieving political stability and order. Political stability and order, in turn, provide an environment within which institutions can evolve. This characterization aptly describes China's institutional evolution over the past three decades. The evolution has fundamentally altered the functional requirements of China's political system in managing its economy.

14.5. China's Current Political Condition: The Emerging Channels of Contestability and Accountability

While performance that yields benefits for some factions enable China's political system to maintain its legitimacy with these groups, other groups are encountering outcomes that are widely viewed as unequal and inequitable. Among these groups, performance legitimacy for the political system may be unattainable. This fragmenting of economic interest and attitudes toward political legitimacy are becoming increasingly pronounced. High growth is forming a middle class and entrepreneurial class that generally accept the government's legitimacy. At the same time, rural farmers and in cities, unemployed workers, the elderly, and recent migrants, perceive their property endowments as modest, tenuous, and yielding relatively low or stagnant living standards.

Increasingly, this segment of the population has begun to resort to legal claims and organized protest to acquire relief and redress. Under these circumstances, establishing performance legitimacy with one portion of the population is likely to erode legitimacy with other portions of the population. One solution to the breakdown of the consensus government, or harmonious society, is the establishment of a competitive contest from which a democratically constituted authority emerges with the legitimacy to mediate public choices.

In advancing the principle of a "harmonious society", the Party is focused on creating the political and administrative capacity to manage the conflict created by the unequal distribution and exercise of property rights through an emphasis on inclusiveness and consultation. The 6th

Plenum of the 16th Central Committee of the Communist Party of China (CPC) concluded on October 11, 2006 with the passage of a resolution to establish a harmonious society by 2020. The harmonious socialist society proposed by the 6th Plenum would encompass the following four conditions: (i) a democratic society under the rule of law; (ii) a society based on equality and justice; (iii) an honest and caring society; and (iv) a stable, vigorous and orderly society. In this emphasis, the Party can be seen as attempting to expand the basis for its performance legitimacy while, as indicated by the first condition, seeking to complement its performance legitimacy through procedural means.

Over the past decade, in particular, a number of emergent procedural channels that either provide or promise the potential for political legitimacy have come into view. We examine these below.[2]

1. **The Party leadership: selection procedures and tenure limits**: The Communist Party has developed an elaborate system to ensure that the nation's top Party leaders are accountable to the Party and its members. This system starts with term limits in which the key Party leaders are limited to two-terms of five years. The General Secretary of the Party is chosen by the Plenary Session of the Central Committee of the Communist Party of China (CPC), which meets every five years. The CPC Central Committee's 198 full members and 158 alternate members attended the First Plenum in 2003, which elected the current generation of members and alternates of the Political Bureau of the CPC Central Committee, members of the Standing Committee of the Political Bureau of the CPC Central Committee and the General Secretary of the CPC Central Committee. Based on the nomination of the Standing Committee of the Political Bureau of the CPC Central committee, it approved the members of Secretariat of the CPC Central Committee, members of the Central Military Commission, and the secretary, deputy secretaries and the Standing Committee members of the Central Commission for Discipline Inspection (CCDI), elected at the First Plenum of the CCDI. While leadership changes in the

[2] For a comprehensive description of the elements of China's political structure, see: C:\Documents and Settings\erjgdsgsdhg\Desktop\China's political system.htm

President of the PRC is elected by National People's Congress in the May following the fall selection of the CPC General Secretary. Under this set of checks, balances, and term limits has been installed since the rule of Chairman Zedong Mao, the head(s) of the party and government are subject to a higher degree of accountability than that in force during either the Mao or Deng eras.

2. **Factional interests/smaller parties within the Party.** In recent years, intra-party factions and debate have become more visible. In particular, the conservatives or leftists have become active in their advocacy for a slowing of the reform process to protect workers who have been laid off or otherwise vulnerable to economic insecurity as a result of the dismantling of the state-owned enterprise sector. What is notable about the advocates representing this political faction have had their views widely published in outlets, such as the *People's Daily*, *Huaxia Forum*, and *Mainstream* magazine.[3]
3. **An increasingly independent and deliberative legislative branch.** The National People's Congress (NPC) is composed of deputies elected from the provinces, autonomous regions and municipalities directly under the Central Government and deputies elected by the armed forces. Members of the NPC are elected for terms of five years. The NPC meets in session once a year and is convened by its Standing Committee. While observers correctly note that when legislation is brought to a vote in the NPC it is generally met with little opposition or debate, in fact this legislation is sometimes subject to intense debate and amendment behind the scenes.

   One such legislative example is that of China's Bankruptcy Law. Prior to its passage in 2007, the bankruptcy legislation was subject during the preceding 12 years to extensive deliberation and drafting. Substantial compromises were made in the final law by retaining for a limited number of SOEs provisions of the previous law that gave preference to workers over creditors in the distribution of liquidated assets. Active debate and disagreement were clearly also in play leading up to the passage of the property law. The legislation, first published in 2002, was subsequently deferred, failed again in its reading at the 2006

[3] Lam (2001). Also see Hook (2007).

National People's Congress because of a dispute over its contents. Then in its eighth reading it was passed in 2007.

4. **Local elections.** The 1998 Organic Law on Villager Committees (VC Law) requires villager committees, the lowest level of civil administration in China, to implement democratic administration with the intent of subjecting local fiscal accountability. The Law provides for (i) open, direct nominations by individuals rather than groups; (ii) multiple candidates; (iii) secret ballots; (iv) the use of secret voting booths; (v) a public count of the votes and an immediate announcement of the results; and (vi) recall procedures. While the VC Law is weak on explicit enforcement provisions and charges of election irregularities are widespread, villagers have demonstrated a grasp of their rights and have been quick to file administrative complaints. According to one account, "the themes the government articulated in justifying the introduction of village democracy — including the complementary nature of political and economic reforms and the intimate relationship between democracy and rule of law — are not being repeated in a national context."[4]
5. **An increasingly independent judiciary branch**. The promulgation of the Administration Litigation Law (ALL) in 1989 made it possible for individuals to bring a case against the administration and has also laid down the relevant criteria and procedures for administrative litigation. Lu (2008) describes several high profile cases of public interest litigation (PIL) in China and the growing incidence of administrative litigation in China and the growth of PIL activists. Figure 14.3 shows a dramatic growth in the incidence of administrative litigation from approximately 25,000 filed suits in 1991 to nearly 93,000 suits in 2004. Available data indicates that the probability of losing a lawsuit in 2004 was approximately 67% (see Figure 14.3).
6. **Non-governmental organizations.** In recent years, the Party and Government are "facing growing pressure from a population that is awakening to the power of independent organization. Uncounted millions of Chinese, from the rich cities of the east to the impoverished countryside, are pushing an inflexible political system for redress over

[4] Horsley (2001).

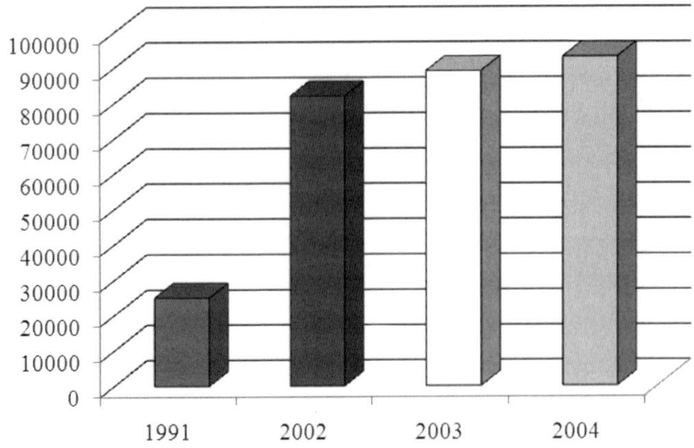

Fig. 14.3. Administrative Litigation Act (# of lawsuits).

The Probability of Losing the Lawsuit in 2004: 67%.
Source: Chinese newspaper "Workers' Daily" at:
http://www.grrb.com.cn/new/news detail.asp?news id=234400&type id=108

> issues from shoddy health care and illegal land seizures to dire pollution and rampant official corruption." (French, 2006)
>
> Those non-governmental organizations have become critical players in driving social change and reform. Officially, there are more than 300,000 NGOs registered in China, an extraordinary number considering there were virtually none as recently as the early 1990s. Some experts estimate the actual number as high as two million, many of them very small and most of them simply ignoring government registration requirements.[5]
>
> This explosion has begun to change the relationship between citizens and the government. Many activists say it has gradually pushed the authoritarian system in the direction of greater openness and accountability. The proliferation of NGOs has also aroused strong concerns within the government, with some officials warning that nongovernmental organizations could become vehicles for Western-style democratization.

Taken together, these institutional arrangements provide the emerging outline of a functionally competitive political system. We address this claim below.

[5] French (2006).

14.6. The Current Situation: Contestable Monopoly?

The key conclusion to be drawn from the description above is that key elements of the political institutional infrastructure needed for a pluralistic, competitive political system currently exists in China. The institutions are sufficiently differentiated to accommodate the growing pluralism of Chinese society. The absence of tension among these institutional parts is largely the result of a consensus regarding the key components of China's economic policy. However, as factions evolve and social policy becomes increasingly important relative to economic policy, tension is likely to emerge within and among these multi-faceted institutional arenas.

During the reform period, the emerging institutional differentiation and specialization is contributing to the pluralism of China's political institutional landscape. A better educated and more sophisticated population is increasingly seeking to establish and utilize channels of influence to challenge and influence the government's decisions. These include NGOs, a more diversified media, and factions within the established political system, i.e. within the party, the government, legislative bodies, and the electoral process.

The political system is developing in ways that increasingly enable a wide variety of interests to articulate their demands within the political system. Disputes over land use, pollution and corruption are rife in much of the countryside. The Public Security Ministry reported 87,000 public protests in 2005, up from 10,000 in 1994. According to Tanner "[Many] police see a new social logic taking hold, with disgruntled citizens increasingly convinced that peaceful protests is significantly less dangerous and not only effective but often unavoidable as a means to win concessions. Police sources now routinely quote a popular expression: 'Making a great disturbance produces a great solution. Small disturbances produce small solutions. Without a disturbance, there will be no solution." (Tanner, 2004, pp. 137–156).

At the same time, the proliferation of non-governmental organizations has begun to change the relationship between citizens and the government. China's leaders seem to be of two minds in confronting the trend. Predictably enough, many warn of the dangers an independent civil society poses to the authority of the state. But there are others who now recognize, however, tentatively, that the government cannot deal with every issue without contributions from advocates, civic organizations and intellectuals.

Contestability also comes from the diversification of channels of mobility. In the Maoist era, the CCP was the only viable channel of upward mobility. This included not only explicit political mobility, but also acceptance as an intellectual, an enterprise manager, and even an ordinary worker. However, as Manion (2007) points out, in recent decades, new paths of upward mobility have emerged. These include higher education in the West, the accumulation of personal wealth, which can be paths for political careers. In recent years, CCP recruitment has favored intellectuals and private entrepreneurs.

Indeed performance legitimacy requires the continuation of a harmonious society. However, as a result of the division of interests, it is not possible for China to achieve a harmonious society through performance alone. It is more likely to return to a condition of "class struggle" — not that imposed from the top down in the Maoist era, but one that operates through democratic channels similar to the advanced democratic states... According to Naughton (2006):

> ...the growth of independent economic powers, the increasing education and sophistication of the population, and the expanding demands for property rights and personal security will challenge the Party. Powerful interest groups currently grouped within the Communist Party will fragment, struggle over distribution of spoils and protection from losses. At some point, interest groups will stare at each (other) over a chasm of social chaos, and decide that a real rule of law and political democracy are better than a fight to the death. A truce in the struggle for wealth and power is more likely to lead to political democracy than is a carefully constructed harmonious society.... (p. 10)

In this passage, Naughton share the argument of this chapter that (i) increasingly levels of education and incomes are driving demands for political reform; (ii) specifically conflicting demands for property rights and contending interest groups are challenging the authority of the Party; and (ii) the resolution of these tensions will require further innovations in the realm of political democracy to avert the social chaos that would ensue from an unreformed political system.

14.7. Conclusions and Discussion

China's political system is evolving from a consensus elite with performance legitimacy to a contested government in search of procedural legitimacy. While full-scale national elections are likely eventually to be required to satisfy China's contending factions, in the meantime a substantial range of channels are opening up that accommodate claims and advocacy made by these disparate groups. We argue that the CCP is becoming a contestable monopoly. Its "Harmonious Society" agenda that frames its economic, social, and political program is an attempt to address the range of fractious groups that have emerged from China's economic reform process. However, having been promulgated by the elite rather than through institutional avenues that are able to channel a wide range of disparate needs and disputatious views into a consensus program, the Harmonious Society is likely to have limited or temporary effect.

Two features stand out that highlight the similarity of China's political reform with its economic reform program. The first is that it is gradual and experimental. As with its economic reform, China's leadership is moving in a largely cautious, conservative manner testing alternative institutional arrangements before embracing these as general policy or practice or Party doctrine. Local elections are one such example. The other similarity is that much of China's political reform process, like aspects of the economic reforms, is being driven from outside the initiative of the central authorities. China's vastness and institutional complexity, as well as shifting underlying forces, particularly in the economic realm, are making claims and forcing choices on China's authorities that require the leadership, directly or indirectly, explicitly or implicitly, to accept certain institutional innovations that it may not have welcomed. The household responsibility system is the key example in the economic realm; in the political realm, the proliferation of non-governmental organizations has met with ambivalence.

The future remains uncertain. Two questions loom: Will China's leadership be able to take a proactive role in facilitating and directing the evolution of China political system toward a modern, open, competitive political system? Or, alternatively, will it fall into a reactive role in which it responds, sometimes with violent resistance, to the underlying changes in its political economy associated with the reassignment of property rights as described in this chapter? The second question is: Whether the party takes a proactive or reactive role, will its initiative be largely pragmatic or doctrinaire? Xiaoping Deng famously expressed his pragmatic vision with the words: "It does not matter whether the cat is white or black, so long as it can catch the mouse." When the conditions that have created performance legitimacy — i.e. rising economic prosperity, social stability, and national sovereignty — become threatened by economic divisions and the fraying of political consensus, will the Party undertake the measures that are needed to establish procedural legitimacy for China's political system? This paper argues that from the economic reforms involving the reassignment of property rights, the institutional infrastructure is evolving for the purpose of mediating the conflicts typically associated with a robust capitalist economy. These institutional channels that have been created to mediate the exercise of property rights provide promise that China's political system will continue to envolve so as to provide China's political leadership with the procedural legitimacy needed to function effectively as overseer of its economy system.

References

Aghion, P., Alesina, A. and Trebbi, F. (2004). "Endogenous Political Institutions." *Quarterly Journal of Economics*, 119(2), 565–611.

Coase, R. H. (1992). "The Institutional Structure of Production." *American Economic Review*, 82(4), 713–719.

Delong, J. B. and Shleifer, A. (1993). "Princes and Merchants: City Growth Before the Industrial Revolution." *Journal of Law and Economics*, 36(2), 671–702.

Djankov, S., Glaeser, E., La Porta, R., Lopez-de-Silanes, F. and Shliefer, A. (2003). "The New Comparative Economics." *Journal of Comparative Economics*, 31(4), 595–619.

Easterly, W. and Levine, R. (2003). "Tropics, Germs, and Crops: How Endowments Influence Economic Development." *Journal of Monetary Economics*, 50(1), 3–39.

French, H. W. (2006). "Chinese Turn to Civic Power as a New Tool." *New York Times*, April 11. http://www.nytimes.com/2006/04/11/world/asia/11china.html.

Glaeser, E.L., Rafael La Porta, Florencio Lopez-de-Silanes and Andrei Shleifer (2004). "Do Institutions Cause Growth?" NBER Working Paper No. 10568.

Hook, L. (2007). "China's Rising New Left." *Far Eastern Economic Review*, 170(3), 24–28.

Horsley, J. P. (2001). "Village Elections: Training Ground for Democratization." *The China Business Review*. http://www.chinabusinessreview.com/public/0103/horsley.html

Knack, S. and Keefer, P. (1995). "Institutions and Economic Performance: Cross-Country Tests Using Alternative Measures." *Economics and Politics*, 7(3), 207–27.

Lam, W. W.-L. (2001). "Hoisting the Red Flag to Counter the Red Flag." http://edition.cnn.com/2001/WORLD/asiapcf/east/05/08/willy.column/index.html

Lau, L. J., Qian, Y. and Roland, G. (2000). "Reform Without Losers: An Interpretation of China's Dual-Track Approach to Transition." *Journal of Political Economy*, 108(1), 120–143.

Lipset, S. (1960). *Political Man: The Social Basis of Modern Politics*. New York: Double day.

Lu, Y. (2008). "Public Interest Litigation and Political Activism in China." Droits et Democratic (Rights & Democracy). http://www.dd-rd.ca/site/_PDF/publications/demDev/Litigations%20China%204.pdf

Manion, M. (2007). "From Mao to Deng and Beyond: the Fate of Policy Oscillations in the Quest for a 'Harmonious Society'." http://www.fpri.org/footnotes/122.200702.manion.maodengharmonioussociety.html.

Naughton, B. (2006). "Reframing China Policy: the Carnegie Debates, Debate 2: China's Economy." (arguing against the motion). The Carnegie Endowment for International Peace.

Naughton, B. (2007). *The Chinese Economy: Transitions and Growth*, Cambridge, MA.: MIT Press.

North, D. C. (1990). *Institutions, Institutional Change, and Economic Performance*, Cambridge: Cambridge University Press.

Popov, V. (2007). "Shock Therapy Versus Gradualism Reconsidered: Lessons from Transition Economies After 15 Years of Reforms." *Comparative Economic Studies*, 49(1), 1–32.

Smith, A. (1776). *An Inquiry into the Nature and Causes of the Wealth of Nations*, edited by Edwin Canaan. Chicago, Illinois: University of Chicago Press.

Solow, R. (1956). “A Contribution to the Theory of Economic Growth.” *Quarterly Journal of Economics*, 70(1), 65–94.

Ravallion, M. and Chen, S. (2007). “China’s Uneven Progress Against Poverty.” *Journal of Development Economics*, 82(1), 1–42.

Tanner, M. Scott (2004). “China Rethinks Unrest.” *The Washington Quarterly*, 27(3), 137–156.

INDEX